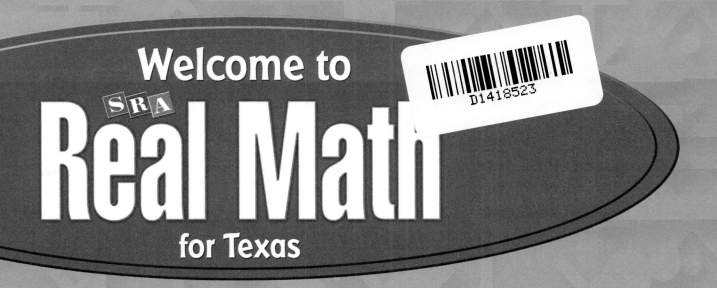

Welcome to
SRA Real Math
for Texas

Discover the Difference
of Real Math

- A complete curriculum designed to fully align with the Texas Essential Knowledge and Skills (TEKS)

- A balanced curriculum of concept and skill development, problem solving applications, algebra readiness, math games, technology, and assessment

- Offers assessment tools to prepare students for Texas Assessment of Knowledge and Skills (TAKS)

Real Math
for Texas

Comprehensive support for Texas teachers

With guided instruction, hands-on-activities, math games, technology and more, *Real Math* offers clear, explicit instruction that meets the Texas Essential Knowledge and Skills (TEKS).

Texas Student Edition contains research-based lessons, developmental activities, practice exercises, and math games to help develop understanding of core concepts and higher-order thinking.

SRA Real Math's Texas Teacher Edition offers systematic, thorough instruction designed to meet Texas guidelines, with page-by-page references to the TEKS objectives.

Texas Practice Workbook provides a practice page for every lesson. It includes the core TEKS for the lesson and provides additional practice on the skills needed for mastery.

TAKS Preparation Book contains four quarterly benchmark tests and two comprehensive practice TAKS tests to help ensure students' preparation.

TEKS/TAKS Practice Workbook features two to four pages of TAKS-formatted practice problems for each of the TEKS objectives.

Texas Assessment Book provides assessments and rubrics based on *Real Math* lessons. Each Chapter Test lists the TEKS objectives that it covers.

Enrichment Support Guide allows proficient students to explore concepts in greater depth and rigor.

English Learner Support Guide contains methods for English as a Second Language students to preview and review lessons and develop vocabulary.

Intervention Support Guide works as a part of **Real Math's** Differentiated Instruction, providing alternative approaches, more intense instruction, and additional practice of prerequisite skills to help struggling students get back on track.

Reteach Support Guide offers suggestions and recommendations for presenting ideas in different ways so all students learn the concepts.

Across the Curriculum Math Connections show how math fits into our lives, using engaging cross-curricular projects in language arts, science, social studies, art, and technology.

Home Connection Blackline Masters help keep parents and family members involved in student learning. It includes newsletters, surveys, and activities to encourage school-to-home communications.

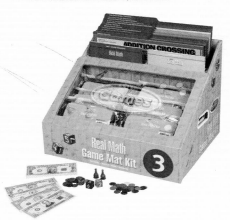

Game Mat Kits are correlated to Texas standards. Game Mats offer a variety of mathematical challenges so students learn critical thinking while practicing their math skills and preparing for the state test.

Manipulatives give students a feel for how math works every day. Number cubes, money, fraction tiles, rulers, and much more let students work through problems in a concrete way.

Go to
review.realmath.com
for a free preview

Integrated online technology supports and enhances math instruction

Real Math offers these integrated, interactive software programs:

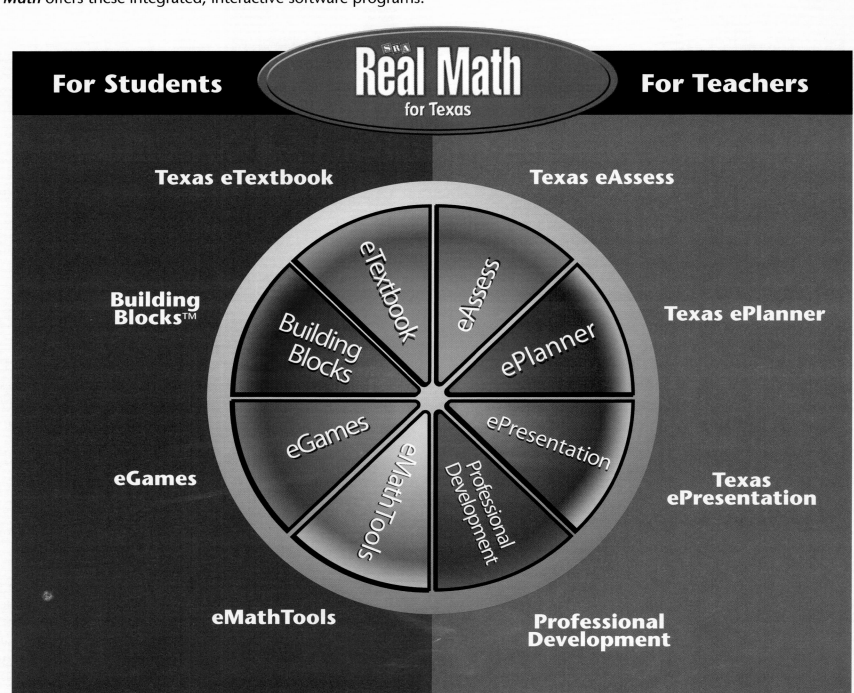

Real Math for Texas

For Students

Texas eTextbook

Building Blocks™

eGames

eMathTools

For Teachers

Texas eAssess

Texas ePlanner

Texas ePresentation

Professional Development

eTextbook · eAssess · ePlanner · Building Blocks · eGames · eMathTools · Professional Development · ePresentation

For Students

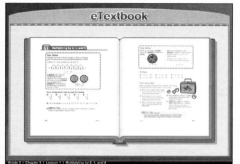

Texas eTextbook
An electronic version of the *Real Math Texas Student Edition*, *eTextbook* gives students the ability to continue learning on their own.

Building Blocks™
The result of National Science Foundation-funded research, *Building Blocks* allows students to explore math concepts through interactive games and activities.

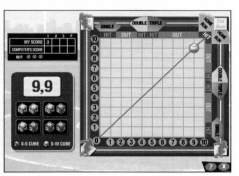

eGames
Students have fun while they learn with electronic games that motivate, challenge, and develop skills like addition, multiplication, fractions, and many others.

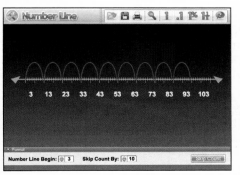

eMathTools
Student participation is enhanced through these electronic manipulatives. *eMathTools* offer a fresh approach to presenting math concepts that students will enjoy.

For Teachers

Texas eAssess
eAssess is an electronic testing, recording, and reporting tool for all *Real Math* assessments. TEKS tests can be created for practice and review.

Texas ePlanner
The *ePlanner* provides yearly, monthly, and daily lesson plans that are correlated to the TEKS objectives. The *ePlanner* previews all electronic and print lesson resources, making planning faster and easier.

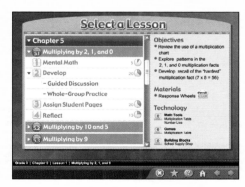

Texas ePresentation
This teacher presentation tool enables you to present every *Real Math* lesson in an engaging, interactive, electronic format. This helps you keep the entire class engaged in the learning process.

Professional Development
Real Math offers the resources and support to build your knowledge and expertise in teaching the curriculum.

All components available online and on CD-ROM.

4

SRA Real Math for Texas

Lessons matched to TEKS and TAKS boost student achievement

TEKS provides defined expectations for what students should know at every grade level. *Real Math* aligns its lessons to these guidelines, to help you meet Texas standards.

Key Ideas introduce the new concept in the lesson and explain strategies for solving problems.

TEKS sections in every lesson spell out which objectives are being addressed.

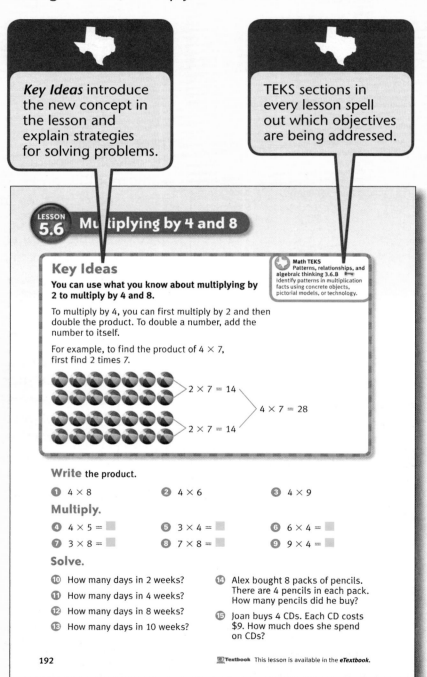

LESSON 5.6 Multiplying by 4 and 8

Key Ideas

You can use what you know about multiplying by 2 to multiply by 4 and 8.

To multiply by 4, you can first multiply by 2 and then double the product. To double a number, add the number to itself.

For example, to find the product of 4×7, first find 2 times 7.

$2 \times 7 = 14$
$2 \times 7 = 14$
$4 \times 7 = 28$

Math TEKS Patterns, relationships, and algebraic thinking 3.6.B Identify patterns in multiplication facts using concrete objects, pictorial models, or technology.

Write the product.

1. 4×8
2. 4×6
3. 4×9

Multiply.

4. $4 \times 5 = $ ■
5. $3 \times 4 = $ ■
6. $6 \times 4 = $ ■
7. $3 \times 8 = $ ■
8. $7 \times 8 = $ ■
9. $9 \times 4 = $ ■

Solve.

10. How many days in 2 weeks?
11. How many days in 4 weeks?
12. How many days in 8 weeks?
13. How many days in 10 weeks?

14. Alex bought 8 packs of pencils. There are 4 pencils in each pack. How many pencils did he buy?
15. Joan buys 4 CDs. Each CD costs $9. How much does she spend on CDs?

192 **eTextbook** This lesson is available in the *eTextbook*.

Student Edition, Grade 3

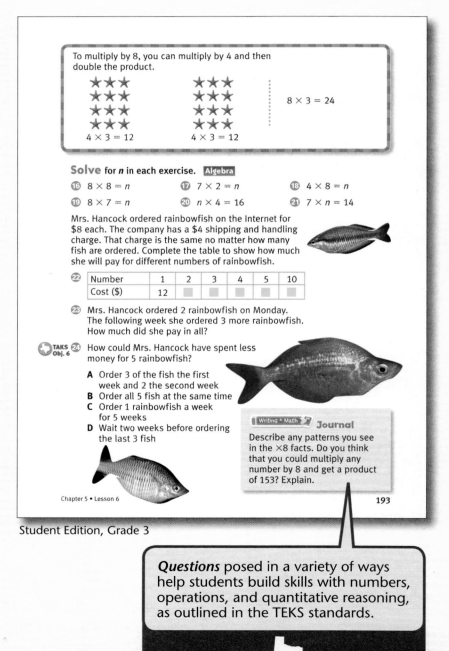

To multiply by 8, you can multiply by 4 and then double the product.

★★★ ★★★
★★★ ★★★
★★★ ★★★
★★★ ★★★
$4 \times 3 = 12$ $4 \times 3 = 12$

$8 \times 3 = 24$

Solve for *n* in each exercise. **Algebra**

16. $8 \times 8 = n$
17. $7 \times 2 = n$
18. $4 \times 8 = n$
19. $8 \times 7 = n$
20. $n \times 4 = 16$
21. $7 \times n = 14$

Mrs. Hancock ordered rainbowfish on the Internet for $8 each. The company has a $4 shipping and handling charge. That charge is the same no matter how many fish are ordered. Complete the table to show how much she will pay for different numbers of rainbowfish.

22.

Number	1	2	3	4	5	10
Cost ($)	12	■	■	■	■	■

23. Mrs. Hancock ordered 2 rainbowfish on Monday. The following week she ordered 3 more rainbowfish. How much did she pay in all?

TAKS Obj. 6 24. How could Mrs. Hancock have spent less money for 5 rainbowfish?

A Order 3 of the fish the first week and 2 the second week
B Order all 5 fish at the same time
C Order 1 rainbowfish a week for 5 weeks
D Wait two weeks before ordering the last 3 fish

Writing + Math Journal
Describe any patterns you see in the ×8 facts. Do you think that you could multiply any number by 8 and get a product of 153? Explain.

Chapter 5 • Lesson 6   193

Student Edition, Grade 3

Questions posed in a variety of ways help students build skills with numbers, operations, and quantitative reasoning, as outlined in the TEKS standards.

Student Edition, Grade 3

Spiral review for TEKS and TAKS

TEKS objectives are continually reviewed and reinforced to ensure mastery, along with review of TAKS Test Items

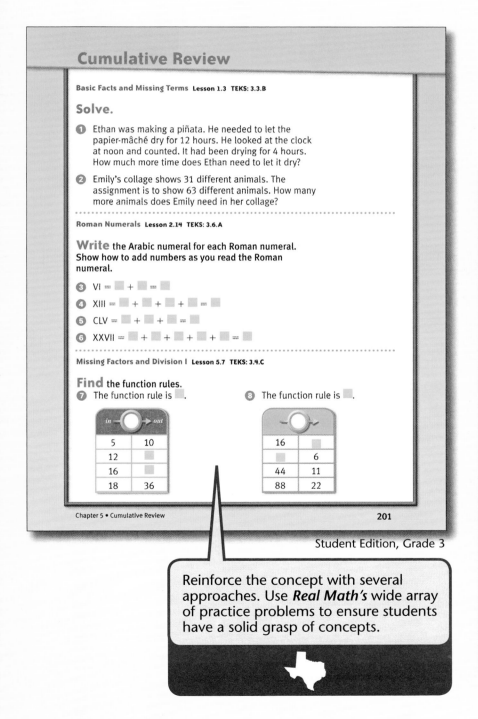

> There is variety built into the entire program. *Real Math* gives you a choice of ways to review, from straightforward math problems to more complex story problems.

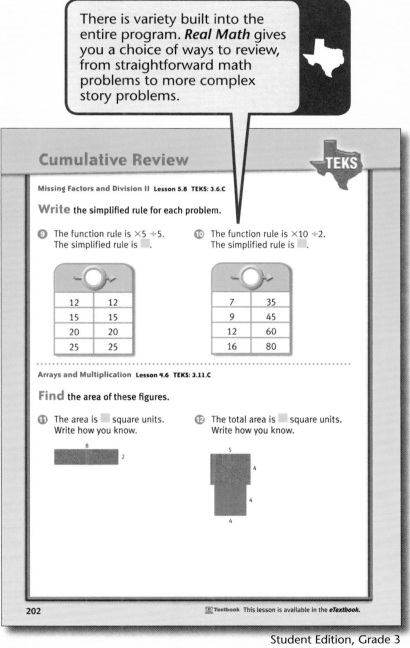

Student Edition, Grade 3

> Reinforce the concept with several approaches. Use *Real Math's* wide array of practice problems to ensure students have a solid grasp of concepts.

Student Edition, Grade 3

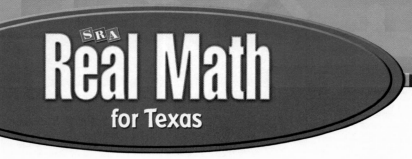

See what they've learned with the Texas Practice Workbook and TEKS/TAKS Practice Workbook

The TAKS provides benchmarks that schools must follow to determine students' comprehension and mastery of skills. *Real Math* helps you meet those benchmarks, with practice pages that provide a clear picture of student progress.

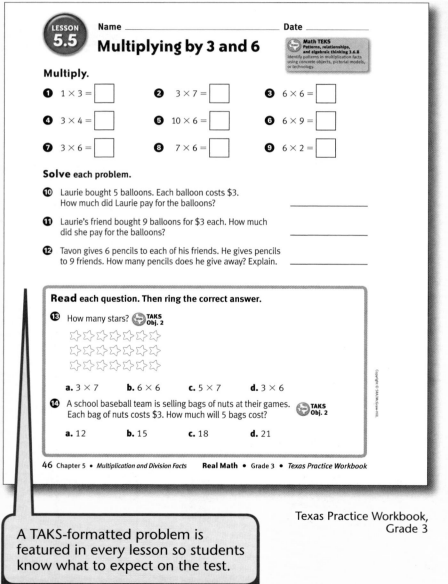

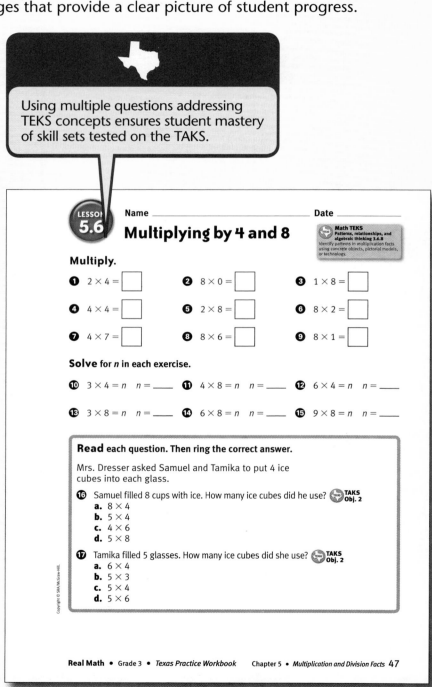

LESSON 5.5

Name _____ Date _____

Multiplying by 3 and 6

Math TEKS
Patterns, relationships,
and algebraic thinking 3.6.B
Identify patterns in multiplication facts
using concrete objects, pictorial models,
or technology.

Multiply.

❶ $1 \times 3 =$ ☐   ❷ $3 \times 7 =$ ☐   ❸ $6 \times 6 =$ ☐

❹ $3 \times 4 =$ ☐   ❺ $10 \times 6 =$ ☐   ❻ $6 \times 9 =$ ☐

❼ $3 \times 6 =$ ☐   ❽ $7 \times 6 =$ ☐   ❾ $6 \times 2 =$ ☐

Solve each problem.

❿ Laurie bought 5 balloons. Each balloon costs $3. How much did Laurie pay for the balloons? _____

⓫ Laurie's friend bought 9 balloons for $3 each. How much did she pay for the balloons? _____

⓬ Tavon gives 6 pencils to each of his friends. He gives pencils to 9 friends. How many pencils does he give away? Explain. _____

Read each question. Then ring the correct answer.

⓭ How many stars? **TAKS Obj. 2**

a. 3×7 **b.** 6×6 **c.** 5×7 **d.** 3×6

⓮ A school baseball team is selling bags of nuts at their games. Each bag of nuts costs $3. How much will 5 bags cost? **TAKS Obj. 2**

a. 12   **b.** 15   **c.** 18   **d.** 21

46 Chapter 5 • *Multiplication and Division Facts*   **Real Math** • *Grade 3* • *Texas Practice Workbook*

A TAKS-formatted problem is featured in every lesson so students know what to expect on the test.

Using multiple questions addressing TEKS concepts ensures student mastery of skill sets tested on the TAKS.

LESSON 5.6

Name _____ Date _____

Multiplying by 4 and 8

Math TEKS
Patterns, relationships, and
algebraic thinking 3.6.B
Identify patterns in multiplication facts
using concrete objects, pictorial models,
or technology.

Multiply.

❶ $2 \times 4 =$ ☐   ❷ $8 \times 0 =$ ☐   ❸ $1 \times 8 =$ ☐

❹ $4 \times 4 =$ ☐   ❺ $2 \times 8 =$ ☐   ❻ $8 \times 2 =$ ☐

❼ $4 \times 7 =$ ☐   ❽ $8 \times 6 =$ ☐   ❾ $8 \times 1 =$ ☐

Solve for *n* in each exercise.

❿ $3 \times 4 = n$ $n =$ ____   ⓫ $4 \times 8 = n$ $n =$ ____   ⓬ $6 \times 4 = n$ $n =$ ____

⓭ $3 \times 8 = n$ $n =$ ____   ⓮ $6 \times 8 = n$ $n =$ ____   ⓯ $9 \times 8 = n$ $n =$ ____

Read each question. Then ring the correct answer.

Mrs. Dresser asked Samuel and Tamika to put 4 ice cubes into each glass.

⓰ Samuel filled 8 cups with ice. How many ice cubes did he use? **TAKS Obj. 2**
   a. 8×4
   b. 5×4
   c. 4×6
   d. 5×8

⓱ Tamika filled 5 glasses. How many ice cubes did she use? **TAKS Obj. 2**
   a. 6×4
   b. 5×3
   c. 5×4
   d. 5×6

Real Math • *Grade 3* • *Texas Practice Workbook*   Chapter 5 • *Multiplication and Division Facts* 47

Texas Practice Workbook, Grade 3

Texas Practice Workbook, Grade 3

Problem-solving strategies with real-world applications to science, social studies, careers, and technology

Real Math ties math to other subjects, so students see math's use throughout their lives. *Real Math* helps you show how concepts are used in other disciplines, making math come alive.

Problem-Solving Strategies

Draw a picture	Make a graph
Guess, check, and revise	Make a list
Look for a pattern	Work backwards
Make a table	Make a physical model
Make a diagram	Make a plan

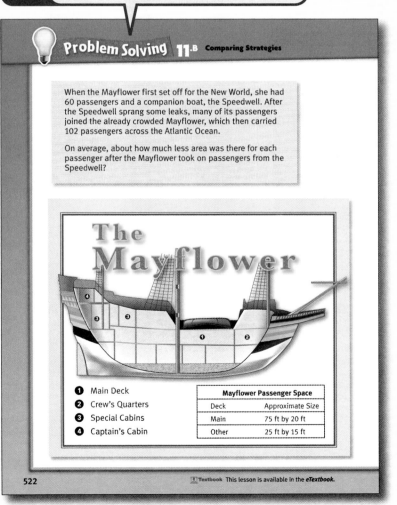

Problem Solving 11.B Comparing Strategies

When the Mayflower first set off for the New World, she had 60 passengers and a companion boat, the Speedwell. After the Speedwell sprang some leaks, many of its passengers joined the already crowded Mayflower, which then carried 102 passengers across the Atlantic Ocean.

On average, about how much less area was there for each passenger after the Mayflower took on passengers from the Speedwell?

The Mayflower

❶ Main Deck
❷ Crew's Quarters
❸ Special Cabins
❹ Captain's Cabin

Mayflower Passenger Space	
Deck	Approximate Size
Main	75 ft by 20 ft
Other	25 ft by 15 ft

📖 Textbook This lesson is available in the *eTextbook*.

Student Edition, Grade 4

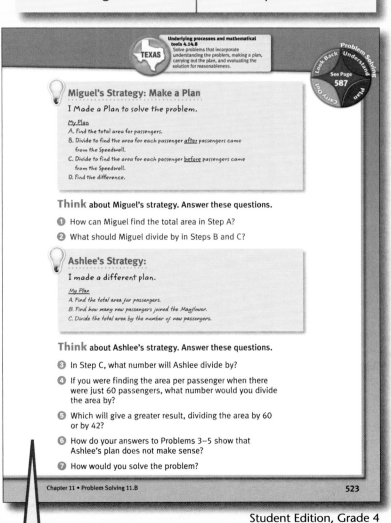

TEXAS

Underlying processes and mathematical tools 4.14.B
Solve problems that incorporate understanding the problem, making a plan, carrying out the plan, and evaluating the solution for reasonableness.

See Page 587

Miguel's Strategy: Make a Plan

I Made a Plan to solve the problem.

My Plan
A. Find the total area for passengers.
B. Divide to find the area for each passenger *after* passengers came from the Speedwell.
C. Divide to find the area for each passenger *before* passengers came from the Speedwell.
D. Find the difference.

Think about Miguel's strategy. Answer these questions.

❶ How can Miguel find the total area in Step A?

❷ What should Miguel divide by in Steps B and C?

Ashlee's Strategy:

I made a different plan.

My Plan
A. Find the total area for passengers.
B. Find how many new passengers joined the Mayflower.
C. Divide the total area by the number of new passengers.

Think about Ashlee's strategy. Answer these questions.

❸ In Step C, what number will Ashlee divide by?

❹ If you were finding the area per passenger when there were just 60 passengers, what number would you divide the area by?

❺ Which will give a greater result, dividing the area by 60 or by 42?

❻ How do your answers to Problems 3–5 show that Ashlee's plan does not make sense?

❼ How would you solve the problem?

Student Edition, Grade 4

When used to solve real-life problems, math becomes accessible. *Real Math* introduces and reinforces problem-solving steps so that problem solving becomes routine.

Teacher support throughout

Real Math is packed with support materials to help you make the best use of your time. The all-inclusive program gives everything needed to address the day's lesson. With teaching tips, activity ideas, practice sessions, and more—all aligned to TEKS—everything is right at your fingertips.

In the *Lesson Planner*, you get a quick snapshot of the day's lesson, including the TEKS objectives to be covered. Materials needed and technology available are always listed, so your planning is quick and efficient.

Differentiated Instruction provides tools to reach students learning at different speeds and in different ways.

Intervention strategies are provided for every lesson. When students have difficulty understanding a concept, *Real Math* guides you on what materials to use to address the problem.

Language skills grow with math skills. Every lesson offers tips on explaining concepts to students who don't have a firm grasp of the English language.

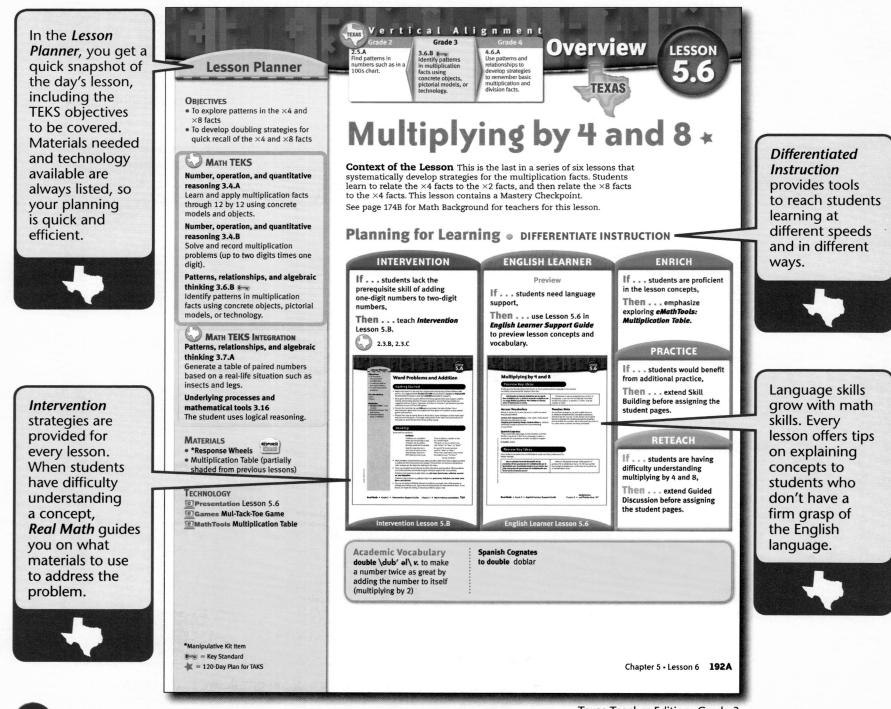

Lesson plans that work for Texas teachers

Lessons use a four-step approach: develop, use student pages, reflect, assess and differentiate. This makes learning math understandable for students and systematic for teachers.

These daily exercises provide review of previously taught concepts and give you a quick assessment of student understanding.

Guided Discussion gives students the chance to verbalize their understanding using these discussion guides. They offer discussion points and stimulating exercises, as well as suggestions for how to present materials.

Real Math offers a full array of stimulating Games that instruct through engaging activities and are correlated to the TEKS.

Use Student Pages gives students an opportunity to practice the objectives that have been taught throughout the lesson.

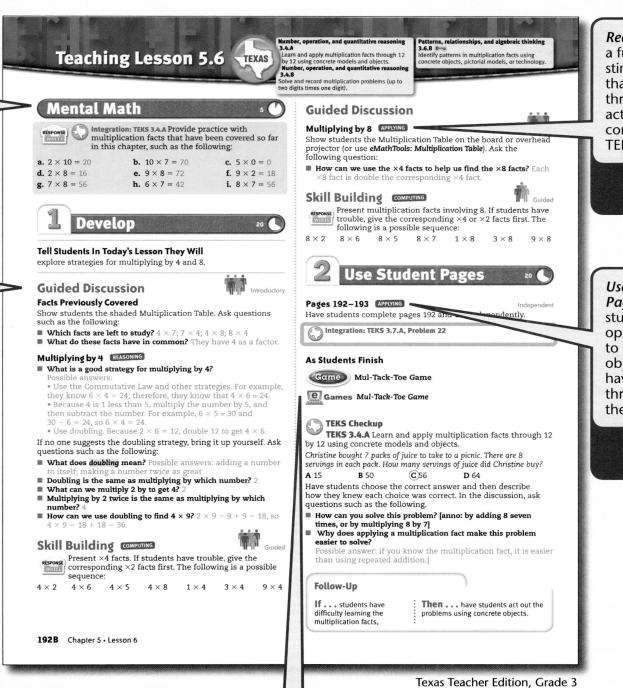

Teaching Lesson 5.6 [TEXAS]

Number, operation, and quantitative reasoning
3.4.A Learn and apply multiplication facts through 12 by 12 using concrete models and objects.
Number, operation, and quantitative reasoning
3.4.B Solve and record multiplication problems (up to two digits times one digit).

Patterns, relationships, and algebraic thinking
3.6.B Identify patterns in multiplication facts using concrete objects, pictorial models, or technology.

Mental Math   5

RESPONSE WHEEL **Integration: TEKS 3.4.A** Provide practice with multiplication facts that have been covered so far in this chapter, such as the following:

a. $2 \times 10 = 20$ b. $10 \times 7 = 70$ c. $5 \times 0 = 0$
d. $2 \times 8 = 16$ e. $9 \times 8 = 72$ f. $9 \times 2 = 18$
g. $7 \times 8 = 56$ h. $6 \times 7 = 42$ i. $8 \times 7 = 56$

1 Develop   20

Tell Students In Today's Lesson They Will
explore strategies for multiplying by 4 and 8.

Guided Discussion   Introductory
Facts Previously Covered
Show students the shaded Multiplication Table. Ask questions such as the following:
■ **Which facts are left to study?** 4×7; 7×4; 4×8; 8×4
■ **What do these facts have in common?** They have 4 as a factor.

Multiplying by 4 [REASONING]
■ **What is a good strategy for multiplying by 4?**
Possible answers:
• Use the Commutative Law and other strategies. For example, they know $6 \times 4 = 24$; therefore, they know that $4 \times 6 = 24$.
• Because 4 is 1 less than 5, multiply the number by 5, and then subtract the number. For example, $6 \times 5 = 30$ and $30 - 6 = 24$, so $6 \times 4 = 24$.
• Use doubling. Because $2 \times 6 = 12$, double 12 to get 4×6.
If no one suggests the doubling strategy, bring it up yourself. Ask questions such as the following:
■ **What does doubling mean?** Possible answers: adding a number to itself; making a number twice as great
■ **Doubling is the same as multiplying by which number?** 2
■ **What can we multiply 2 by to get 4?** 2
■ **Multiplying by 2 twice is the same as multiplying by which number?** 4
■ **How can we use doubling to find 4×9?** $2 \times 9 = 9 + 9 = 18$, so $4 \times 9 = 18 + 18 = 36$.

Skill Building [COMPUTING]   Guided
RESPONSE WHEEL Present $\times 4$ facts. If students have trouble, give the corresponding $\times 2$ facts first. The following is a possible sequence:
4×2 4×6 4×5 4×8 1×4 3×4 9×4

192B Chapter 5 • Lesson 6

Guided Discussion

Multiplying by 8 [APPLYING]
Show students the Multiplication Table on the board or overhead projector (or use *eMathTools: Multiplication Table*). Ask the following question:
■ **How can we use the $\times 4$ facts to help us find the $\times 8$ facts?** Each $\times 8$ fact is double the corresponding $\times 4$ fact.

Skill Building [COMPUTING]   Guided
RESPONSE WHEEL Present multiplication facts involving 8. If students have trouble, give the corresponding $\times 4$ or $\times 2$ facts first. The following is a possible sequence:
8×2 8×6 8×5 8×7 1×8 3×8 9×8

2 Use Student Pages   20

Pages 192–193 [APPLYING]   Independent
Have students complete pages 192 and 193 independently.

🔹 **Integration: TEKS 3.7.A, Problem 22**

As Students Finish

Game Mul-Tack-Toe Game

e Games Mul-Tack-Toe Game

🔹 **TEKS Checkup**
TEKS 3.4.A Learn and apply multiplication facts through 12 by 12 using concrete models and objects.
Christine bought 7 packs of juice to take to a picnic. There are 8 servings in each pack. How many servings of juice did Christine buy?
A 15   **B** 50   **C** 56   **D** 64
Have students choose the correct answer and then describe how they knew each choice was correct. In the discussion, ask questions such as the following.
■ **How can you solve this problem?** [anno: by adding 8 seven times, or by multiplying 8 by 7]
■ **Why does applying a multiplication fact make this problem easier to solve?**
Possible answer: if you know the multiplication fact, it is easier than using repeated addition.]

Follow-Up

If . . . students have difficulty learning the multiplication facts,

Then . . . have students act out the problems using concrete objects.

Texas Teacher Edition, Grade 3

eGames are part of the software component in *Real Math*. Texas students can have fun while strengthening their mathematical understanding.

Ensure Texas students are successful in mathematics

In using *Real Math*, Texas teachers present all the math concepts students need to learn to be successful in school and in life. Ideas are divided, so learning is easier while incorporating a variety of activities that also make learning fun.

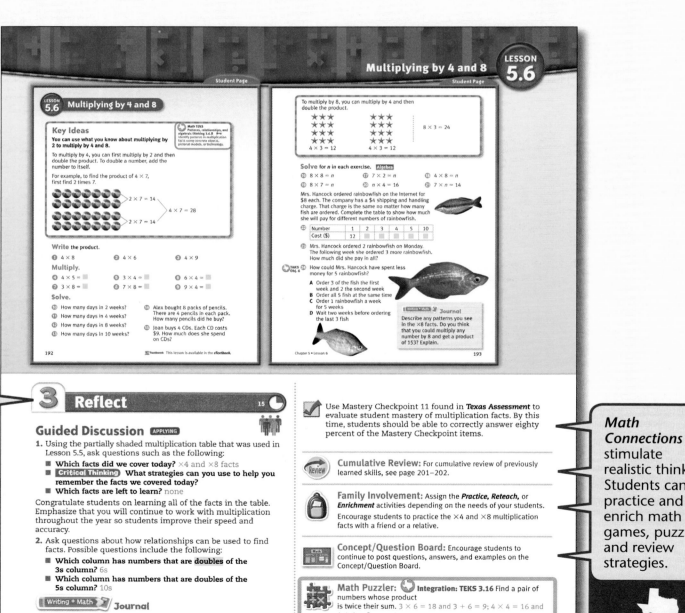

Reflect provides an excellent aid for the lesson to ensure that students are mastering the TEKS objectives.

Math Connections stimulate realistic thinking. Students can practice and enrich math with games, puzzles, and review strategies.

Lesson assessment and follow-up

Assess and Differentiate uses *Informal Daily Assessments* to observe how students are progressing on a daily basis. You can also evaluate students' progress over longer periods of time with *Pretests, Practice Tests, Chapter Tests*, and other formal assessments.

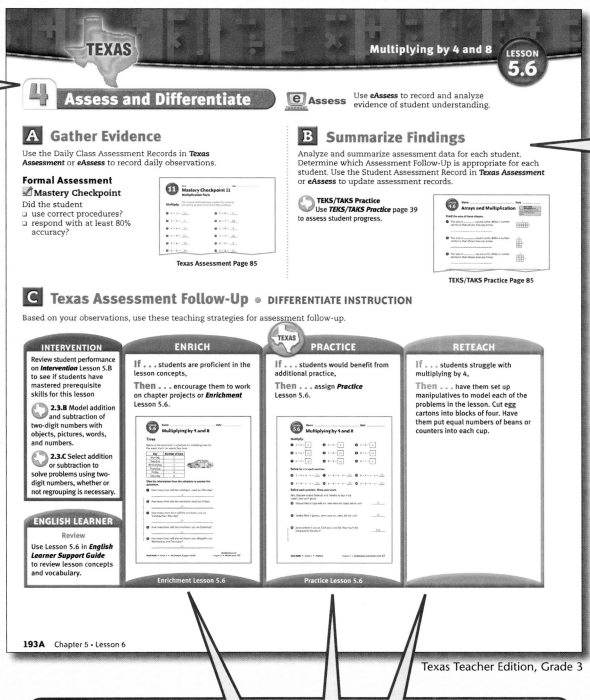

Using *Texas eAssess*, you analyze and summarize student proficiency on a regular basis. These findings can be compared to TEKS standards to see how well students are performing.

Texas Teacher Edition, Grade 3

Students learn at different paces. That's why *Real Math* incorporates strategies in every lesson for students with different levels of proficiency.

Assessments to address TEKS and TAKS

Aligning itself with Texas assessment requirements is an integral part of the **Real Math** program. Using formal and informal assessments, via print and technology, the program allows you to analyze student understanding.

Name _____ Date _____

TEKS/TAKS Practice

TAKS Obj. 1: Number, operation, and quantitative reasoning

TEXAS

TEKS 3.4.A: Learn and apply multiplication facts through 12 by 12 using concrete models and objects.

Read each question and choose the best answer.

1 Use the picture to help you find the product.

$2 \times 6 =$ ___
- 8
- 11
- 12
- 14

2 Use the picture to help you find the product.

$10 \times 5 =$ ___
- 50
- 45
- 55
- 60

3 Use the picture to help you find the product.

$8 \times 3 =$ ___
- 26
- 24
- 18
- 32

4 Use the picture to help you find the product.

$4 \times 10 =$ ___
- 14
- 50
- 30
- 40

Lesson Follow-Up
If... students need practice with basic multiplication facts
Then... have them play the **Multiplication Table Game.**

Real Math • Grade 3 • *TEKS/TAKS Practice*

27

Texas Assessment, Grade 3

> Provides **assessments and rubrics** based on *Real Math* lessons.

Name _____ Date _____

Obj. 1: Number, operation, and quantitative reasoning
TEKS 3.4.A, continued

5 Use the picture to help you find the product.

$11 \times 7 =$ ___
- 70
- 18
- 77
- 84

6 Use the picture to help you find the product.

$1 \times 8 =$ ___
- 9
- 8
- 7
- 16

7 Use the picture to help you find the product.

$6 \times 6 =$ ___
- 12
- 36
- 30
- 24

8 Use the picture to help you find the product.

$3 \times 4 =$ ___
- 13
- 7
- 10
- 12

28

Real Math • Grade 3 • *TEKS/TAKS Practice*

Includes **benchmark** tests and **comprehensive** tests so students can practice before taking the actual TAKS test.

Texas Assessment, Grade 3

CD-ROM Assessments

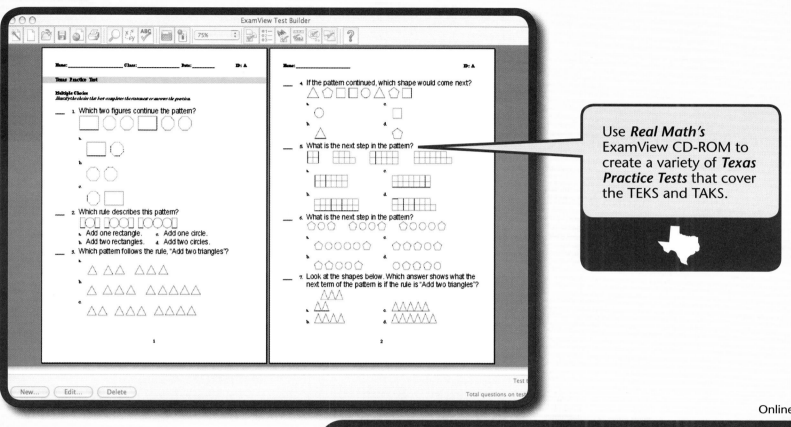

Use *Real Math's* ExamView CD-ROM to create a variety of *Texas Practice Tests* that cover the TEKS and TAKS.

Online Assessments

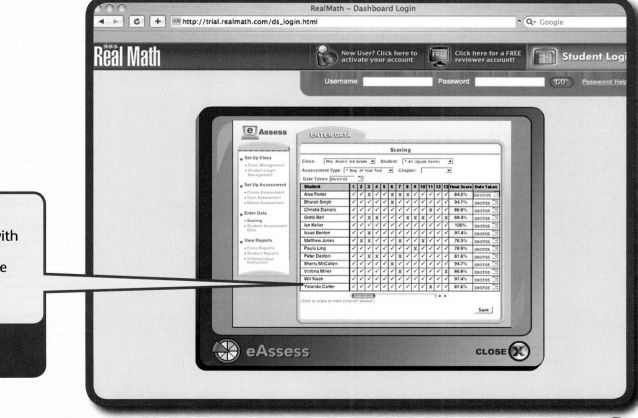

Real Math's unique assessment system with detailed student and class reports to gauge student mastery of TEKS/TAKS.

Discover how Real Math is right for Texas

- Fully aligned to Texas Essential Knowledge and Skills (TEKS)

- Develops enduring understanding of concepts by using concrete, pictorial, and abstract models

- Balances concepts, skills, and applications

- Emphasizes problem-solving as a process skill

- Unique integrated technology reinforces skills and prepares students for TEKS/TAKS

- Math Games help students learn new skills and further their math knowledge

- Provides Differentiated Instruction to ensure success for all learners

- Offers formative assessments to drive instruction and summative assessments to show how students are progressing

- Easy to teach and manage

SRA

Real Math

Teacher's Edition

Grade 2 • Volume 2

Stephen S. Willoughby

•

Carl Bereiter

•

Peter Hilton

•

Joseph H. Rubinstein

•

Joan Moss

•

Jean Pedersen

•

Edward Manfre

•

Hortensia Soto-Johnson

•

Erica Walker

Columbus, OH

Authors

Stephen S. Willoughby is Professor Emeritus at both New York University and the University of Arizona. He has taught all grades from first through twelfth and has been a professor of both education and of mathematics at the University of Wisconsin and at New York University, and a Professor of Mathematics at the University of Arizona. Dr. Willoughby served as President of NCTM from 1982-1984. He has published more than 200 books and articles on mathematics and mathematics education and is the principal author of Real Math. In 1995, he received the Lifetime Achievement Medal for Leadership in Mathematics Education from the Mathematics Education Trust.

Carl Bereiter is a Professor Emeritus of Educational Psychology and Special Advisor on Learning Technology at the Ontario Institute for Studies of the University of Toronto. He has published widely on a variety of topic in instruction, cognitive psychology, and educational policy. Honors include a Guggenheim Fellowship, fellowships at the Center for Advanced Study in the Behavioral Science, and election to the U.S. National Academy of Education.

Peter Hilton is Distinguished Professor of Mathematics Emeritus of the State University of New York, Binghamton, and Distinguished Professor of Mathematics at the University of Central Florida, Orlando. He is the author of eighteen books and over 500 research articles. His areas of special interest are algebraic topology, homological algebra, and group theory. Professor Hilton has served as Chairman of the United States Commission of Mathematical Instruction and Secretary/Treasurer of the International Commission on Mathematical Instruction. He was the Alan Turing Memorial Lecturer at Bletchley Park in July of 2006.

Joseph H. Rubinstein is Professor of Education at Coker College in Hartsville, South Carolina, where he prepares prospective mathematics and science teachers. He holds A.B., M.S. and PhD degrees from New York University and did basic research in biology before becoming interested in curriculum development. That interest was sparked by his participation in the development of the Conceptually Oriented Program in Elementary Science (COPES). During that time he worked in the New York City public schools helping teachers implement science programs while, at the same time, completing a post-doctoral fellowship in teacher education. Dr. Rubinstein served as the Director of Open Court Publishing Company's Mathematics and Science Curriculum Development Center during the early development and field-testing of Real Math. He joined the Coker College faculty in 1984 and was chair of the education department for 15 years.

Joan Moss is an Associate Professor of Mathematics Education at University of Toronto. Her extensive research has included studies of the development of children's understanding of rational numbers and the development of early algebraic reasoning. Dr. Moss has been widely published with research articles and chapters for the National Council of Teachers of Mathematics as well as the National Academy of Science. She is a member of the National Council of Teachers of Mathematics, American Educational Research Association, the North American Chapter of the Psychology of Mathematics Education, and the Canadian Mathematics Education Study Group.

Jean Pedersen is Professor of Mathematics and Computer Science at Santa Clara University, California. She is the author of eight books and over 200 articles in mathematics (many co-authored with Peter Hilton). Her research interests include polyhedral geometry, combinatorics, and the teaching of mathematics, especially geometry, to pre-college students. Professor Pedersen was the 1997 recipient of a Distinguished University Teaching Award from the Northern California Section of the Mathematical Association of America; and in 2002 she received, from Santa Clara University, the Joseph Bayma, S.J. award for life-time scholarly and creative work.

PreKindergarten and Building Blocks Authors

Douglas H. Clements, Professor of Early Childhood, Mathematics, and Computer Education at the University at Buffalo, State University of New York, has conducted research and published widely on the learning and teaching of geometry, computer applications in mathematics education, the early development of mathematical ideas, and the effects of social interactions on learning. Along with Julie Sarama, Dr. Clements has directed several research projects funded by the National Science Foundation and the U.S. Department of Education's Institute of Educational Sciences, one of which resulted in the mathematics software and activities included in Real Math.

Julie Sarama is an Associate Professor of Mathematics Education at the University at Buffalo, State University of New York. She conducts research on the implementation and effects of software and curricula in mathematics classrooms, young children's development of mathematical concepts and competencies, implementation and scale-up of educational reform, and professional development. Dr. Sarama has taught secondary mathematics and computer science, gifted math at the middle school level, preschool and kindergarten mathematics enrichment classes, and mathematics methods and content courses for elementary to secondary teachers.

Contributing Authors

Edward Manfre is an educational consultant, instructional designer and former teacher who helps students use mathematics to make sense of the world and think independently. He has authored or co-authored textbook series, workbook programs, software packages, diagnostic tests and other curriculum materials that are both research-based and classroom friendly.

Hortensia Soto-Johnson is Assistant Professor of Mathematics, University of Northern Colorado. B.S. Chadron State College (Mathematics); MS in Mathematics, University of Arizona; Ph.D. in Educational Mathematics, University of Northern Colorado. Her research area is mathematics education; she is primarily interested in preservice teachers' understanding of undergraduate mathematics.

Erica Walker is Assistant Professor of Mathematics and Education, Teachers College, Columbia University. B.S. cum laude, Birmingham-Southern College (Mathematics, Spanish minor); M.Ed., Wake Forest University (Mathematics Education); Ed.M., Ed.D., Harvard University (Administration, Planning, and Social Policy).

Texas Advisory Board

Amber Barbarow, Math Specialist, T.L. Pink Elementary, Richmond, Texas
Kerri Blevins, Elementary Math Coordinator, Lake Dallas ISD, Lake Dallas, TX
Janet M. Groff, Local Campus Coach, Rayburn Elementary School, San Antonio, Texas
Penny M. Jones, Teacher, Sienna Crossing Elementary, Missouri City, TX
Stacey Payton, 5th Grade Math Teacher, Giddens-Steadham Elementary School, Rowlett, Texas, Garland ISD

Elvia O. Perez, South San Antonio ISD, San Antonio, TX
Donnelle Smith, Kindergarten Teacher, Giddens-Steadham Elementary, Rowlett, TX
Michele Warren, 1st grade teacher, Steadham Elementary, Rowlett, Texas
Jennifer Weis, Math Coordinator, 5-8, Lake Dallas ISD

SRAonline.com

Send all inquiries to this address:
SRA/McGraw-Hill
4400 Easton Commons
Columbus, OH 43219

ISBN: 978-0-07-611122-0
MHID: 0-07-611122-9

2 3 4 5 6 7 8 9 WEB 12 11 10 09 08

The **McGraw·Hill** Companies

Problem Solving Theme: Teamwork—Library

Addition Facts

Problem Solving **Theme: Pets**

Subtraction Facts

CHAPTER 3

CHAPTER 4

Measurement, Graphing, and Probability

 **Problem Solving** Theme: Toy Factory

Two-Digit Addition

💡 **Problem Solving** Theme: Parks and Picnics

💡 **Problem Solving** Theme: Zoo

Fractions CHAPTER 7

Problem Solving Theme: Museums

Problem Solving · Theme: Dinosaurs

Three-Digit Addition and Subtraction

CHAPTER 9

💡 **Problem Solving** Theme: Mail Delivery and The Pony Express

Measurement

 Problem Solving **Theme: Growing Plants**

Introducing Multiplication and Division

CHAPTER
11

Problem Solving Theme: Ethnic Food

CHAPTER 12 Patterns and Algebra

 Problem Solving Theme: Frontier and Native American Homes

Additional Resources

Getting Started with *Real Math*

Real Math is a standards-based, comprehensive math curriculum for the state of Texas. To most effectively use the program, it is important to understand what resources are available, how the program is organized, how it will help schools meet the Texas Mathematics Standards, and how to use its distinctive elements to their best advantage.

Real Math is a math curriculum that had its beginnings in the 1970s. Over the years it has been upgraded to address the new research and changing emphases in the field of mathematics. The core goals of the program, however, have remained unchanged.

Real Math Core Goals
Teach basic skills with understanding so students can use them fluently to solve real problems and help understand the real world.
Teach students to think mathematically so they can reason, understand, and apply mathematics meaningfully in order to identify, solve, and communicate about real problems.
Teach students to reason so they have sufficient confidence and understanding to reconstruct or even construct mathematical methods that have been forgotten or never learned.
Engage students in mathematics so they enjoy math, see it as understandable and useful, and willingly use it to help them understand their environment.

Real Math is Distinctive

- **Research Base**—Based on four types of research:
  - o Foundational Research—based on the best educational research available
  - o Field Test Qualitative Research
  - o Efficacy Studies
  - o Long-Term Effectiveness
- **Concept Development**—Concepts developed with understanding and reviewed and refreshed throughout the program.
- **Learning Trajectories**—Based on research that identifies how children learn mathematics.
- **Balance of Skills, Procedures, Conceptual Understanding, and Problem Solving**—Skills and procedures taught explicitly with meaning so that they can be used effectively in solving real problems.
- **Communication**—Emphasizes communicating mathematically in every lesson to build understanding.
- **Teacher Support**—Background information and clear, step-by-step instructional plans for delivering an effective mathematics curriculum.
- **Student Engagement**—Proven strategies and activities to get students excited about math.
- **Differentiated Instruction**—Comprehensive strategies and resources to address the needs of every learner.
- **Technology**—State-of-the-art technology applications for both teachers and students. The entire curriculum can be delivered electronically.

Program Resources

Program Materials

Print Components

The *Real Math* print components provide a complete, comprehensive math curriculum for students in grades PreK–5.

Component	Grades	Description
Core Components		
Texas Teacher's Edition	PreK–5	Comprehensive, specific, research-based background and strategies to provide quality instruction; aligned to TEKS
Texas Student Edition	K–5	Development and practice for all concepts; aligned to TEKS
Essential Materials Module	K–5	Response devices, **Number Cubes**, and other manipulatives needed for almost every lesson
Support Components		
Texas Practice Workbook	K–5	Workbook version of extra practice aligned to TEKS
Texas Practice Blackline Master	K–5	Extra practice for every lesson in blackline form with answers in the back aligned to TEKS
Texas Assessment	K–5	Variety of assessment options evaluate student proficiency and inform instruction
TEKS/TAKS Practice Workbook	K–5	Provides diagnostic evaluation of each of the grade-level Texas TEKS in a student workbook
TEKS/TAKS Practice Blackline Master	K–5	Provides diagnostic evaluation of each of the grade-level Texas TEKS in blackline master form
TAKS Preparation	1–5	Includes benchmark tests and practice tests for the TAKS
Enrichment Support Guide	K–5	Activities for every lesson designed to expand lesson concepts for advanced students
Reteach Support Guide	K–5	Alternative strategies for presenting lesson concepts for students who are struggling with a particular lesson
Intervention Support Guide	K–5	Instruction and practice for prerequisite skills for every chapter for students who lack the prerequisite skills to complete a chapter
Across the Curriculum Math Connections	K–5	Cross-curricular projects and WebQuests to apply mathematics in real-world activities
Big Books	PreK	Counting trade books specifically chosen for preschoolers
English Learner Support Guide	K–5	Strategies for previewing and reviewing lesson concepts and vocabulary for English learners
Game Mat Kit	K–5	Math board games and manipulatives for classroom use
Home Connection	PreK–5	Newsletters, surveys, and activities to encourage home and school communications
Home Connection Game Kit	K–5	Math Games Kit that includes all of the game mats from a grade level for home use
Manipulative Kits • Individual Manipulative Kit • Essential Materials Module • Manipulative Topic Modules • Teacher Manipulative Kit	PreK–5	Complete manipulative kit to support concept development, available in convenient packaging options. Includes **Number Cubes** and **Response Wheels** used in almost every lesson Manipulative Topic Modules include: Base Ten Counting Fractions Geometry I Geometry II Measurement I Measurement II Money Probability Time

Technology Components

The *Real Math eSuite* is a state-of-the-art suite of math applications for teachers and students to deliver more exciting, effective, efficient, and engaging instruction. It includes nine different integrated applications that work together. The proven effective strategies from the print components are the same in the *eSuite* applications, but are enhanced through the use of technology.

All *eSuite* applications come in both individual CD and online formats. The online version of each application has all of the features of the CD plus seamless integration with other *eSuite* software applications. Additional online features include online management and tracking systems. The CD formats are available for schools or classrooms lacking reliable online access.

The online Dashboard is the launching pad for all of the *eSuite* applications.

For Teachers		For Students	
e Planner	**Grades K–5** A paperless planner that allows teachers to make yearly, monthly, and daily lesson plans, and to preview all electronic and print lesson resources. Aligned to TEKS.	**Building Blocks**	**Grades PreK–5** More than 150 multilevel, online math activities that engage students in developing fundamental math skills and concepts along mathematical learning trajectories
e Presentation	**Grades K–5** A teacher presentation tool that enables teachers to present every *Real Math* lesson in an engaging, interactive, electronic format. Includes step-by-step visual, animated, and interactive demonstrations of every part of every lesson. Aligned to TEKS.	**e Textbook**	**Grades K–5** An electronic version of the student edition that students can access from home. Includes key resources such as: ▪ *eMathTools* ▪ Electronic **glossary** of math terms ▪ Electronic **index** hyperlinked to *eTextbook* pages ▪ Zoom feature to highlight specific exercises or parts of a specific page ▪ Every lesson aligned to TEKS
e Assess	**Grades K–5** An electronic test generator, recording, and reporting tool for all *Real Math* assessments. Aligned to TEKS. Provides immediate feedback for each answer as well as prescriptions based on student performance.	**e Games**	**Grades K–5** More than 30 multilevel, electronic versions of a variety of the *Real Math* games that motivate students to: ▪ deepen math understanding. ▪ build math strategies. ▪ practice math skills.
	Professional Development Six comprehensive electronic courses include video interviews with math experts and educators and readings from research, and provide professional development in teaching the five math proficiencies: ▪ Teaching Computational Fluency ▪ Teaching for Understanding ▪ Teaching Applications of Mathematics ▪ Teaching Mathematical Reasoning and Problem Solving ▪ Engaging Children in Mathematics ▪ Mathematics Classroom Management	**e MathTools**	**Grades K–5** Twenty-eight multilevel, interactive electronic manipulatives and tools that enable teachers to demonstrate and students to explore key concepts in mathematics. Includes: ▪ Calculation and Counting Tools ▪ Measurement and Conversion Tools ▪ Geometric Exploration Tools ▪ Data Organization and Display Tools

Chapter Organization

All chapters in *Real Math* are organized in the same way.

Chapter Overview

The first few pages of each chapter explain the chapter focus and overview how concepts are developed.

- **Teaching for Understanding** provides the big ideas of the chapter.

- **Prerequisite Skills** help determine if students are ready for the chapter.

- **Skills Trace** shows where concepts were previously introduced and how they will be followed up.

- **Big Ideas** provides an overview of the Big Ideas to develop in the chapter.

- **Math Background** provides a refresher of the mathematics principles relevant to the chapter.

- **Academic Vocabulary** lists key math terms used in the chapter.

- **Cognates** gives common Spanish cognates to build vocabulary.

- **Access Vocabulary** provides an overview of terms in the chapter that may not be familiar to English learners.

- **What Research Says** offers insights into how children learn and research-based teaching strategies.

- **Chapter Planner** lists objectives that explain how the key concepts are developed lesson-by-lesson and which resources can be used in each lesson.

- **Technology Resources** lists what resources are available to help with planning or support instruction.

Chapter Introduction

This section introduces concepts and provides ways to assess prior knowledge.

- **Pretest** helps you evaluate what students know and don't know about the chapter concepts.

- **Access Prior Knowledge** offers preliminary discussion about chapter concepts to determine what students know.

- **Problem Solving** introduces chapter theme and concepts by encouraging students to think of ways to solve real-world problems.

- **Concept/Question Board** establishes connections and applications of the chapter concepts to students' thinking and lives outside the classroom.

- **Assess and Differentiate** helps you use assessments to summarize and analyze evidence of student understanding and plan for differentiating instruction.

- **Math Across the Curriculum** outlines two projects per chapter that students can work on to apply that chapter's math concepts across the curriculum.

Lessons

Multiple lessons in each chapter provide overview, ideas for differentiating instruction, complete lesson plans, teaching strategies, and assessments that inform instruction. (More about how lessons are organized on page T36.)

Problem Solving **Problem Solving** is the focus of every lesson and activity in *Real Math*. There are three lessons—one located at the beginning, middle, and end of each chapter—that focus on a rich problem to develop problem-solving strategies and provide models of alternative ways of solving problems.

Individual Oral Assessment

This feature appears in the middle of each chapter and affords an opportunity to individually evaluate student understanding.

- **TEKS Checkups** are diagnostic and prescriptive mini assessments within the lessons that provide keys to student progress toward meeting standards.

Chapter Wrap-Up

Provides ways to review chapter concepts and assess student understanding.

- **Cumulative Review** in the middle and end of the chapter provides practice using open-answer and standardized-test formats, and allows you to evaluate whether students are retaining previously developed concepts and skills.

- **Thinking Story** **Thinking Stories** and **Problem Solving** activities at the end of each chapter offer applications of lesson concepts and development of students' mathematical thinking and problem-solving abilities.

- **Key Ideas Review** refreshes student knowledge of the key concepts.

- **Error Analysis** includes math problems and flawed solutions for teachers and students to discuss as they summarize chapter concepts and skills in order to develop understanding of common errors.

- **TEKS/TAKS Practice and Benchmark Tests** give insight into progress toward meeting standards.

- **Chapter Review** provides a review of chapter concepts.

- **Practice Tests** in the same format as the Chapter Test give students an opportunity for self-assessment before taking the Chapter Test.

Lesson Organization

Every lesson in *Real Math* is organized in the same way.

Lesson Planner

The first page of each lesson helps teachers prepare to teach.

- **Objectives**—clear objectives focus the instruction.

- **Math TEKS**—identify the content and reasoning standards developed in the lesson. Key standards are identified with a key icon.

- **Math TEKS Integration**—are Content Standards that are integrated into the lesson.

- **Vertical Alignment**—identifies how the main lesson standard builds on previous grade-level standards and lays the foundation for subsequent grade standards.

- **Context of the Lesson**—explains the lesson in the context of the program Scope and Sequence of learning.

- **Planning for Learning**—prepares teachers with strategies for addressing different types of learners *during* the lesson.

- **Academic Vocabulary** and **Access Vocabulary**— include specific words and phrases with definitions to alert teachers to vocabulary students may not know.

Mental Math

Each lesson begins with Mental Math, which provides cumulative review and maintenance of skills. Teachers can use Mental Math as a daily informal assessment of computational fluency.

Develop

The Develop part of each lesson is the core of the lesson instruction. Research-based strategies built on field-tested results provide teachers with effective, engaging instructional strategies to give students a firm foundation in the concept, and multiple opportunities to understand the mathematics in the lesson. Strategies involve **developing concrete, pictorial, and abstract representations** of the lesson concepts.

In most cases students do not have student books open during Develop instruction. Instead of teaching from the student pages, Develop provides instructional models, hands-on activities, discussion, and strategy-building exercises that offer a variety of ways for students to understand lesson concepts. The following strategies are included:

- **Tell Students In Today's Lesson They Will**—sets the lesson objective for students.

- **Guided Discussion**—includes interactive discussion, modeling, and critical thinking questions to instruct and activate prior knowledge to develop understanding.

- **Skill Building**—allows teachers to assess students' understanding and remediate if necessary before assigning the student pages.

- **Skill and Strategy Building**—provides interactive activities that build student proficiency and provide teachers with informal assessment opportunities to check for understanding.

Use Student Pages

After concepts have been introduced and practiced, students begin work on the student book pages. The student pages are a review of the instruction in the Develop section, rather than the core instruction of the lesson.

- **Progress Monitoring**—offers suggestions for progress monitoring and remediation as students work through the lesson.

- **As Students Finish**—provides activities for students who finish early. These include engaging math activities such as Games, *Building Blocks* activities, or *eMathTools* explorations.

- **Student Pages**—provide independent practice of the lesson concepts presented in the Develop section. Student pages include:

  o **Key Ideas** that summarize the lesson Big Idea and provide examples and models

  o **Exercise Sets** that often include patterns to encourage students to strategize and think mathematically, instead of learning through rote practice

  o **Multistep Problems** are identified for the teacher.

  o **Extended Response** problems are included to develop critical thinking skills

  o **Review** problems are identified for teachers to check on skill maintenance.

- **Journal** These suggestions are included to develop applications, reasoning, and understanding, and provide teachers with portfolio-assessment opportunities.

- **UNDERSTANDING** Understanding, Engaging, Applying, Computing, and Reasoning activities are identified to show how all five math proficiencies are developed in every lesson.

Reflect

The Reflect section, a critical part of every *Real Math* lesson, provides opportunities for students to summarize and apply lesson concepts and for teachers to informally assess student understanding. **Additional Activities**—are included to extend and further develop lesson concepts:

- **Real World Curriculum Connection** suggestions apply lesson concepts to real-world experience:

- **Cumulative Review** offers suggestions for continual review to maintain skills.

- **Family Involvement** offers ideas for homework.

- **Concept/Question Board** includes reminders to keep the Concept/Question Board introduced in the Chapter Opener current.

- **Math Puzzler** provides opportunities for a "problem of the day" to challenge and engage students.

Instructional Model

Real Math presents a three-phase instructional model identified in every lesson.

Phase 1
Develop   Introductory

In this phase the teacher demonstrates, explains, questions, and conducts discussions about the lesson topic. Students are actively involved in answering questions and discussing topics.

Phase 2
Develop   Guided

In this phase activities are specifically designed so that teachers or peers can provide students with substantial help. Students receive feedback on their performance.

Phase 3
Use Student Pages   Independent

In this phase teachers assess a student's individual abilities through informal and formal assessments and Progress Monitoring suggestions. Students demonstrate their ability to work independently, generalize, and transfer their knowledge.

Real Math Routines

Real Math is a program that includes a lot of variety in the activities presented, but maintains certain routines that will make classroom management more effective and efficient.

Routines for Mental Math

Step 1 Present a problem orally, by writing it on the board or by using *ePresentation*.

Step 2 Students find the answer and display it with their *Response Wheels*, *Number Cubes*, or other response device.

Step 3 Students hide the answer while you provide enough time for the rest of the class to find the answer.

Step 4 Students show the answer to you, while you show and tell the answer to the class.

Routines for Guided Discussion

1. **Pay attention** to others. Give your full attention to the person who is speaking. This includes looking at the speaker and nodding to show that you understand.

2. **Wait** for speakers to answer and complete their thoughts. Sometimes teachers and other students get impatient and move on and ask someone else or give the answer before someone has a chance to think and speak. Giving students time to answer is a vital part of teaching for understanding.

3. **Listen.** Let yourself finish listening before you begin to speak. You can't listen if you are busy thinking about what you want to say next.

4. **Respect** speakers by taking turns and making sure that everyone gets a chance to speak, and that no one dominates the conversation.

5. **Build** on others' ideas by making connections, drawing analogies, or expanding on the idea.

6. **Ask questions.** Asking questions of another speaker shows that you were listening. Ask, if you are not sure you understand what the speaker has said, or ask for clarification or explanation. It is a good idea to repeat in your own words what the speaker said so you can be sure your understanding is correct.

Routines for  Games

1. Familiarize yourself with the rules of each game by playing it before showing students how to play it.

2. Show, don't just tell, how a game is played. Usually two students should play the game in front of the class. Overhead versions of the *Game Mats* are provided for demonstrating games in front of the class. The *ePresentation* or *eGames* can be displayed for the class to see how to play those games.

3. Let students who already know the game rules (perhaps from a previous grade) help students who are new to the games.

4. Encourage students to develop game-playing strategies, and discuss their strategies in small groups or as a class.

Routines for  Thinking Story

1. Read each story aloud.

2. Stop for each question and discuss possible answers for each question after you ask it. Some questions have brief answers and should be handled quickly. Others call for deeper thinking or have a range of possible answers and will require several minutes of discussion. Encourage and discuss answers. Wait for students to respond. A minute or two of silence while students think is a good thing.

3. If your students enjoy a particular story, consider reading it again another day.

Routines for Use Student Pages

1. Make sure students know what pages to work on and any special requirements of those pages.

2. Tell students whether they should work independently or in small groups as they complete the pages.

3. Tell students how long they have to work on the student pages before you plan to begin the Reflect part of the lesson.

4. Tell students what their options are if they finish early. Suggested options are listed under the Assign Student Pages heading in each lesson. These include

   a. *eMathTools*

   b. *Game Mats*, Cube Games, *eGames*, and *Building Blocks* activities

   c. Writing+Math Journal activities

5. As students work on the student pages, circulate around the room to monitor their progress. Use the Progress Monitoring suggestions for ideas on what to look for. Comment positively on student work and stop to ask exploring, synthesizing, clarifying, or refocusing questions.

6. You may also use this time to work with English learners or students who need intervention.

7. Complete the Informal Assessment Checklists on the last page of each lesson.

8. Because games are an important and integral part of the program and provide necessary practice in traditional basic skills as well as higher-order thinking skills, when games are included in a lesson be sure to stop work on student pages early enough to leave enough time to play the game. Students may complete student pages outside of school in that case.

Routines for Reflect

1. At the designated time, have students stop their activity and direct their attention to reflecting on the lesson.

2. Use the suggested questions in Reflect or ask students to consider these ideas:

   a. Think about related matters that go beyond the scope of the lesson

   b. Summarize student's ideas about the lesson concepts

   c. Compare how the lesson concept or skill is like or different from other skills

   d. Ask how students have seen or can apply the lesson in other curricular areas, other strands of mathematics, or in the world outside of school

   e. Discuss student solutions to Extended Response questions

Routines for [Assess and Differentiate]

Based on your informal assessments and observations, choose from the following to differentiate for homework.

- Complete the student pages
- Family involvement suggestions
- Enrichment ideas
- Practice
- Reteach

Routines for DIFFERENTIATING INSTRUCTION

1. **Plan for differentiation**

   - As you prepare for a lesson, scan the suggestions in Planning for All Learners for differentiating instruction on the first page of each lesson. Be prepared to differentiate the content or process depending on your estimation of student understanding.

   - English Learner strategies **differentiate the process** for introducing the lesson by previewing key concepts and vocabulary.

   - Intervention lessons **differentiate content** for those students who have not yet mastered prerequisite skills.

   - Enrichment strategies **differentiate the process** if students already understand the content.

   - Practice strategies **differentiate the process** if students need practice.

   - Reteach strategies **differentiate the process** if students are not understanding lesson material.

   - Projects in the *Across the Curriculum* resource **differentiate the product** students produce.

2. **Monitor student progress** As students participate in Mental Math, Guided Discussion, Skill Building, Strategy Building, Games and other lesson activities, be alert to signs of understanding and misunderstanding. The Informal Assessment Checklists include rubrics to help gather evidence about students' math proficiency.

3. **Follow-Up** Summarize your formal assessments and informal observations and consider how to differentiate student progress in the lesson follow-up assignments. Program resources include

   - **Enrichment** activities for students who have a secure understanding

   - **Practice** activities for students who have adequate understanding

   - **Reteach** activities for students who have an emerging understanding

4. **Adjust tomorrow's lesson** Based on student understanding and performance, consider how the next lesson should be adjusted for different learners.

Routines for Using e Technology

1. Determine rules for computer use and communicate them to students. Rules should include
   a. **Sharing Available Computers.** Some teachers have a computer sign-up chart for each computer. Some teachers have the students track their computer usage themselves.
   b. **Computer Time.** You might limit the amount of time students can be at the computer or allow students to work in pairs. Some teachers have students work until they complete an activity. Others allow students to continue with additional activities.

2. Train students on your rules for proper use of computers, including how to turn computers on, load programs, and shut down the computer. Some teachers manage computers themselves; others have an aide or student in charge of computer management.

3. Using the suggestions for As Students Finish under **2 Use Student Pages** in each lesson, make sure the computers are on and the programs are loaded, and that students know how to access the software.

4. Make sure students know what to do when they complete the computer activity.

Pacing and the 120-Day Plan

The 120-Day Plan provides a way to ensure that all TEKS are addressed before spring testing. Instructional lessons on the 120-Day Plan are indicated by a red star. These lessons should be emphasized.

The lessons that are not highlighted may be taught after spring testing. These lessons will provide review or application of key concepts or lay the foundation for the following year's math class. The lessons not on the 120-Day Plan fall into the following categories:

1. Review Lessons that review previous grade-level content

2. Application Lessons that provide additional applications of grade-level content

3. Foundation Lessons that lay a foundation for subsequent grade-level instruction

   Based on student performance, teachers may wish to differentiate the curriculum by adding Review Lessons, Application, or Foundation Lessons to the 120-Day Plan.

Problem Solving and *Real Math*

 **Problem Solving** Lessons in every chapter provide specific opportunities to develop problem-solving strategies in meaningful contexts using the skills and procedures students have learned. Problems in these lessons are carefully written so they can be solved in a variety of ways.

- **Introducing Strategies** in each chapter opener provides students an opportunity to preview the chapter concepts in problem-solving applications.
- **Comparing Strategies** in the middle of the chapter involves the comparison of two different ways to solve a problem related to chapter concepts. After students compare, they use their own strategy to solve the problem.
- **Using Strategies** at the end of the chapter involves students using the problem-solving steps and strategies to solve an interesting real-world problem related to the chapter concepts.

Introduce Problem-Solving Steps and Strategies

Near the beginning of the year, introduce the concept of problem-solving steps and strategies with students of any grade level. Discuss each step and strategy, and emphasize the nature of problem solving as a thoughtful and often creative process, not as a rote set of steps or procedures to follow. Problem solving is facilitated when students have solid math skills, including fluency with facts and algorithms, so they can focus on the problem and not the skills.

These steps and strategies will be used again and again as students use mathematics to solve problems in and out of school. For more information about problem solving, see Appendix A, page A24.

Problem-Solving Stages

There are four stages of problem solving that can occur in any order and that can occur again and again in attempting to solve a problem.

- **Understand** the problem. This is of paramount importance and is often the cause of errors. When students attempt to apply rules in unthinking ways or look only for key words, they frequently make mistakes. Students must concentrate on the details of the problem.
- **Plan.** Planning is a matter of thinking about what needs to be done to solve the problem. Planning may be informal or formal.
- **Carry Out.** In carrying out the plan, students often find that they need more information or that their answers are not reasonable. At this point, going back to understand the problem or adjust the plan is in order.
- **Look Back.** This is the most important stage of problem solving and one that students often skip. Reflecting on a problem and considering the appropriateness of the solution and how the problem was solved is a key to truly understanding real-world use of mathematics.

Problem-Solving Strategies

There is an unlimited number of strategies that people use to solve mathematics problems. Modeling different types of strategies in problem solving is useful in helping students see that there are different ways that the same problem could be solved. The Comparing Strategies lessons in the middle of each chapter provide models for these and other strategies:

- Draw a Picture
- Look for a Pattern
- Guess, Check, and Revise
- Make a Table or Graph
- Work Backward
- Work on an Easier Problem
- Detect Absurdities
- Ask the Right Questions
- Approximate

Routines for Problem-Solving Lessons

1. Read the lessons with students.
2. Discuss the problems and any sample solutions so that everyone understands what the problem is asking.
3. Allow students to solve problems on their own or in small groups. Showing students how to do a problem robs them of the opportunity to develop valuable thinking skills and their investment and confidence in their own solutions.
4. Facilitate a discussion of alternative problem solutions and have students discuss advantages, limitations, unique features, and generalizable features of different solutions.

Fractions

Teaching for Understanding

This chapter has students explore common fractions in a variety of contexts. In this chapter students learn how to write and create fractions. Students also learn how to find fractions of a number, of a set of objects, and of plane figures. The chapter covers all common fractions up to twelfths. It also discusses creating other fractions, such as sevenths and ninths. Students learn about equivalent fractions and fractions that are greater than one, such as $\frac{11}{5}$. Later in the chapter, students learn about common fraction expressions in relation to time, such as half past and quarter to.

Prerequisite Skills and Concepts

• Recognizing Equal Parts • Telling Time to the Nearest Hour • Estimating Fractional Parts

Fractions Skills Trace

Before Grade 2	Grade 2	After Grade 2
Grades K–1 Informally and formally introduced fractions, focusing on halves and fourths	**This chapter** develops fluency with fractional notations and the properties of fractions.	Review and mastery of fractions and introduction to the relationship between fractions and percentages is developed. Later grades include formal introduction and mastery of more complex fractions.

Lessons

= 120-Day Plan for TAKS

BIG Ideas! in Chapter 7

This chapter develops the following ideas running throughout elementary mathematics:

• Numerical quantities can be compared in a variety of ways, such as using fractions to compare a part to a whole.

In Lesson 7.1, students are reintroduced to the fractions, halves and fourths, using linear and measurement models. Students learn how to represent fractions in Lesson 7.2 using the correct vocabulary terms, *numerator* and *denominator*.

In Lessons 7.3 and 7.4, students explore fractions of a whole further using thirds, sixths, and eighths. Numerators greater than one is also introduced in these lessons.

• A comparison of a part or parts to a set can be represented using a fraction.

The concept of fractions is applied to parts of set models in Lessons 7.5 and 7.6, where students learn about fifths as a fraction. The *Fraction Game* is used to provide practice in recognizing fractional areas up to fifths.

• Every fraction can be represented by an infinite set of equivalent fractions.

In Lesson 7.7, students are formally introduced to the concept of equivalent fractions using various models to represent fractions such as 1/2, which is equal to 2/4, which is equal to 4/8, and so on. In Lesson 7.8, students learn about fractions of numbers using manipulatives such as money and bundles of craft sticks.

Fractions are used to reinforce how to tell time to the hour, the half hour and quarter hour in Lessons 7.9 and 7.10. Lesson 7.11 further develops fraction skills when fractions greater than one are introduced and explored.

TEXAS

Math TEKS addressed in each lesson can be found in the Chapter Planner on page 243E.

Math TEKS addressed in Problem Solving, Review, and Assessment lessons are on page 243G.

Complete text of the standards appears on the Lesson Overview page and first Teaching page of each lesson.

Math Background
Fractions

What Are Fractions?

- At this level a fraction is understood by students as an operator used to indicate a part of a whole or set. In later grades of **Real Math,** students will learn more about fractions, ratios, decimals, and percentages as names of rational numbers.

- A *rational number* is the result of dividing two integers (with the divisor, or denominator, greater than 0) and can be placed on the number line.

- Two fractions are *equivalent* if they describe the same proportion or number. For example, two parts out of four equal parts is the same portion as one part out of two equal parts, so the fractions $\frac{2}{4}$ and $\frac{1}{2}$ are equivalent.

- *Improper fractions* represent quantities greater than one whole. For example, if a number of oranges are cut into four equal slices, then seven slices represent $\frac{7}{4}$ of an orange, or $1\frac{3}{4}$ oranges. Of course, there is nothing improper about using improper fractions. The term comes from the idea that a "proper" part of the whole is less than or equal to the whole.

Key Ideas about Fractions

There are several key ideas about fractions that students must understand to avoid common errors.

- A fraction is expressed using two numbers, although it represents a single quantity. The bottom number (denominator) names the total number of equal parts, and the top number (numerator) names the number of parts being considered.

- It is important to reinforce the idea that when dividing things into thirds (or any other fraction), the group is divided into three equal parts called thirds (as represented by the denominator). For sets divided into fractional parts, the number of objects in each third depends on the size of the set. This understanding will develop slowly over time.

- It is also important to foster an understanding of fractional parts as objects that can be counted. If you know the kind of part you are counting, then you know how many parts are needed for one whole and how many parts are more than one whole. This is a crucial understanding to make sense of improper fractions.

Models for Fractions

Several different models for fractions are used in this chapter to help students build a strong understanding of the meaning of fractions.

- Linear measurement

This model was introduced in Grade 1 of **Real Math.** Fractions can represent the distance along a path. For example, $\frac{1}{4}$ of a length is the length of one part when the length is divided into four equal parts.

- Area

An area model uses fractions to describe equal parts of a geometric figure. In this model, $\frac{1}{4}$ is the size of one part when the whole is separated into four identical parts. A key concept with fractions of area is that the figure may be divided in any way, as long as all parts are equal. For example, a square can be divided in halves with a horizontal line, a vertical line, or a diagonal.

- Sets

A fraction of a set is a more concrete concept than a fraction of a continuous length or area. However, this model may be more confusing to students because numbers of objects are involved. Students may run into difficulty when considering fractions in terms of dividing up sets because the answer to "What fraction of the set?" may be confused with "How many objects?" in the subset. For example, when thinking about dividing a set of six objects into thirds, students may divide the set into two groups of three instead of three groups of two.

- Time

Using time is a way to connect the area model and the fractions of a number model. In $\frac{1}{2}$ of an hour, the minute hand travels through half the area of the circle. Because an hour is 60 minutes long and 30 + 30 = 60, we can say that $\frac{1}{2}$ of an hour is 30 minutes.

What Research Says
About Fractional Parts of a Whole

"Students' informal notions of partitioning, sharing, and measuring provide a starting point for building the concept of rational number. Young children appreciate the idea of 'fair shares,' and they can use that understanding to partition quantities into equal parts. In some ways, sharing can play the role for rational numbers that counting does for whole numbers."

Kilpatrick, J., J. Swafford, and B. Findell, eds. *Adding It Up: Helping Children Learn Mathematics.* Washington, D.C.: National Research Council/National Academy Press, 2001, p. 7.

Over time, the child develops counting strategies and greater understanding of part/whole relationships as part of their deepening number sense. The child recognizes that the whole is bigger than parts, but has an inexact grasp of the relative size of parts and wholes. The child develops recognition that larger numbers can be decomposed or broken into smaller parts, while also developing the understanding that when an amount of something are shared with more people, each person will receive a smaller amount of what is being shared.

While engaging in measurement activities, the child becomes aware of the ability to use one object to measure another. By counting the number of times the one object fits alongside the other object, the child gains the foundational understanding of units as fractions or multiples of what is being measured. This can be applied to such measures as length, time, capacity and other areas of measurement.

From such experiences, the child learns to partition units and develops a sense of the relationships that exist between different units of measure. This understanding also assists the child in making sense of fractional parts of the whole.

Clements, D. H., J. Sarama, & A.-M. DiBiase, eds. *Engaging Young Children in Mathematics: Standards for Early Childhood Mathematics Education.* Mahwah, NJ: Lawrence Erlbaum Associates, 2004.

"As children work with numbers, they gradually develop flexibility in thinking about numbers, which is a hallmark of number sense . . . Number sense develops as students understand the size of numbers, develop multiple ways of thinking about and representing numbers, use numbers as referents, and develop accurate perceptions about the effects of operations on numbers."

National Council of Teachers of Mathematics. *Principles and Standards for School Mathematics.* Reston, VA: NCTM, 2000, pp. 78–80.

The highly complex and abstract nature of mathematics requires the use of representations, especially as our youngest mathematicians are still developing their number sense. Representations to support the ability to use numbers for ordering or comparing objects or collections might include the use of counters, coins, symbols, words, actions or pictures. These physical representations of what is occurring abstractly in the child's thoughts support meaningful mathematical conversations, calculations and thoughts. The meaningful use of interpretation and representation of mathematical ideas is evident at all levels of mathematics.

Kilpatrick, J., J. Swafford, and B. Findell, eds. *Adding It Up: Helping Children Learn Mathematics.* Washington, D.C.: National Research Council/National Academy Press, 2001, pp. 94–95.

RESEARCH IN ACTION

Fractions Chapter 7 develops concepts to support an understanding of part-whole number concepts and an understanding of what fractional parts of a whole represent.

Combining and Separating Collections Throughout Chapter 7 students will develop language, concepts, contexts, and procedures for understanding part-whole number concepts.

Academic Vocabulary

denominator (Lesson 7.2) the number below the line in a fraction, indicating the number of equal parts which make up the whole

eighth (Lesson 7.4) one of eight equal parts into which something is or can be divided

fifth (Lesson 7.6) one of five equal parts into which something is or can be divided

fourth (Lesson 7.1) one of four equal parts into which something is or can be divided

half (Lesson 7.1) one of two equal parts into which something is or can be divided

numerator (Lesson 7.2) the number above the line in a fraction, indicating the number of equal parts being considered

quarter (Lesson 7.8) one-fourth of something; a coin of the United States equal to twenty-five cents, or one-fourth of a dollar

sixth (Lesson 7.4) one of six equal parts into which something is or can be divided

third (Lesson 7.3) one of three equal parts into which something is or can be divided

English Learner

Cognates

For English learners, a quick way to acquire new English vocabulary is to build on what is known in the primary language.

English	Spanish
equal parts	partes iguales
denominator	denominador
color	colorear
decorate	decorar
parts	partes
represents	representa
equality	igualdad
fractions	fracciones
hour	hora
quarter	cuarto

Access Vocabulary

English learners may understand words in different contexts or not understand idioms. Review chapter vocabulary for this concern. For example:

hiking trail	a path people follow when walking in the woods or wilderness
shaded	lightly colored to distinguish one section from others
figure	shape
zigzags	continuous diagonal lines in the shape of the letter z
a full set	A set is a group of objects or numbers that go together.
match the fractions that are equal	compare fractions to determine which are equal and then pair them
farther	a comparison of distance; we don't say *more far* or *farrer*.
bundle	a bunch or group tied together
clock face	a flat surface where the numbers are placed on a clock
quarter to	fifteen minutes before the hour
slice of pie	a small wedge section cut from a pie

Texas Chapter Planner

Lessons	Objectives	NCTM Standards	TEXAS Math TEKS
7.1 Halves and Fourths pages 245A–246A 45–60 minutes	To review the fractions *halves* and *fourths* using linear models	Number and Operations, Measurement, Problem Solving, Representation	2.2.A 2.1.3.A
7.2 Writing Fractions pages 247A–248A 45–60 minutes	To review fractions $\frac{1}{2}$ and $\frac{1}{4}$ using linear models, to introduce fraction symbols, and to introduce the terms *numerator* and *denominator*	Number and Operations, Problem Solving, Representation	2.2.A 2.13.A 2.2.C
7.3 Halves, Fourths, and Thirds pages 249A–250A 45–60 minutes	To review the fractions $\frac{1}{2}$, $\frac{1}{4}$, and $\frac{1}{3}$ using area models and to practice using numerators greater than 1	Number and Operations, Algebra, Problem Solving, Representation	2.2.A 2.14
7.4 Sixths and Eighths pages 251A–252A 45–60 minutes	To introduce the concept of sixths and eighths	Number and Operations, Algebra, Problem Solving, Representation	2.2.A
7.5 Fractions of a Set pages 253A–254A 45–60 minutes	To reintroduce fractions of a set	Number and Operations, Algebra, Problem Solving, Representation	2.2.B
7.6 Fifths pages 255A–256A 45–60 minutes	To reintroduce the concept of fifths, to introduce the **Fraction Game**, and to informally introduce the addition of common fractions that sum to more than $\frac{1}{2}$	Number and Operations, Algebra, Problem Solving, Representation	2.2.A 2.2.C
7.7 Equivalent Fractions pages 261A–262A 45–60 minutes	To introduce the concept of equivalent fractions	Number and Operations, Algebra, Problem Solving, Representation	2.2.B
7.8 Fractions of Numbers pages 263A–264A 45–60 minutes	To relate fractions to numbers using money	Number and Operations, Connections, Representation	2.2.B
7.9 Telling Time—Hour and Half Hour pages 265A–266A 45–60 minutes	To relate telling time to an understanding of fractions and geometric models	Number and Operations, Measurement, Connections, Representation	2.10.B 2.14
7.10 Telling Time—Quarter Hour pages 267A–268A 45–60 minutes	To relate telling time to an understanding of fractions and geometric models	Number and Operations, Measurement, Connections, Representation	2.10.B 2.2.A 2.12.A 2.14
7.11 Fractions Greater than One pages 269A–270A 45–60 minutes	To introduce the concept of naming fractional parts that are greater than one	Number and Operations, Geometry, Representation	2.2 2.2.C

★ = 120-Day Plan for TAKS

🔑 = Key standard

Academic Vocabulary	Manipulatives and Materials	Games to reinforce skills and concepts
fourth half	• *Number Cubes* • Strings of equal length and scissors • 6 clear, equal-sized jars with straight sides • Colored water	
denominator numerator	• *Number Cubes* • Set of paper strips for each student • Rulers • SRA Math vocabulary cards	
third	• *Number Cubes* • 2 sheets of $8\frac{1}{2}$ by 11 inch paper per student	
eighth sixth	• *Number Cubes* • Set of paper strips for each student • Strings of equal length and scissors • Construction paper	
	• *Number Cubes* • Cutouts of 8 objects (such as circles), 6 green and 2 red • Masking tape • Counters • Egg carton cut in half	
fifth	• *Number Cubes* • **Fraction Game Mat** • Colored pencils	Fraction Game
	• *Number Cubes* • Set of paper strips for each student • **Fraction Game Mat** • Colored pencils	Fraction Game
quarter	• *Number Cubes* • Overhead coins and bills • Craft sticks • Clear overhead transparency • **Fraction Game Mat** • Colored pencils	Fraction Game
	• *Number Cubes* • Demonstration clock • Clock faces • **Fraction Game Mat** • Colored pencils	Fraction Game
	• Demonstration clock • Clock faces	
	None	

Additional Resources

Differentiated Instruction

Intervention Support Guide Provides instruction for the following prerequisite skills:

- Lesson 7.A Parts and Hours–1
- Lesson 7.B Parts and Hours–2
- Lesson 7.C Parts and Hours–3

Enrichment Support Guide Extends lesson concepts

Practice Reinforces lesson skills and concepts

Reteach Support Guide Provides alternate instruction for lesson concepts

English Learner Support Guide Previews and reviews lesson concepts and vocabulary for English learners

Technology

The following electronic resources are available:

🖥 **Planner** Lessons 7.1–7.11

🖥 **Presentation** Lessons 7.1–7.11

🖥 **Textbook** Lessons 7.1–7.11

🖥 **Assess** Lessons 7.1–7.11

🖥 **MathTools** *Fractions* Lessons 7.1–7.8, 7.11

🖥 **Games** *Fraction Game* Lessons 7.6–7.9

Assessment
Informal Assessment rubrics at the end of each lesson provide daily evaluation of student math proficiency.

Problem Solving

Problem Solving	When to Use	Objectives	NCTM Standards	Math TEKS
Problem Solving 7.A (pp. 243I–244C) 15–30 minutes	Use before beginning Chapter 7.	To introduce chapter concepts in a problem-solving setting	Problem Solving, Communication	2.2.A, 2.14
Problem Solving 7.B (pp. 257–258, 258A) 30–45 minutes	Use anytime during the chapter.	To explore methods of solving nonroutine problems	Problem Solving, Communication	2.2.A, 2.12.C
Problem Solving 7.C (pp. 271–272, 272A) 45–60 minutes	Use anytime during the chapter.	To explore methods of solving nonroutine problems	Problem Solving, Communication	2.2.A, 2.12.C
Thinking Story—Half a Job (pp. 283A–283E, 283–284) 20–30 minutes	Use anytime during the chapter.	To develop logical reasoning while integrating reading skills with mathematics	Number and Operations, Problem Solving	2.2.A, 2.12.A

Review

Review	When to Use	Objectives	NCTM Standards	Math TEKS
Cumulative Review (p. 259–260) 15–30 minutes	Use anytime after Lesson 7.6.	To review concepts and skills taught earlier in the year	Number and Operations	2.2.A, 2.3.A, 2.3.B, 2.5.C
Cumulative Review (p. 273–274) 15–30 minutes	Use anytime after Lesson 7.11.	To review concepts and skills taught earlier in the year	Number and Operations	2.13.A, 2.2.B, 2.2.A
Chapter 7 Review (pp. 277A, 277–278) 30–45 minutes	Use after Lesson 7.11.	To review concepts and skills taught in the chapter	Number and Operations	NS 4.2, NS 4.1, MG 1.4

Assessment

Assessment	When to Use	Objectives	NCTM Standards	Math TEKS
Pretest (*Assessment* pp. 122–123) 15–30 minutes	Entry Use prior to Chapter 7.	To provide assessment of prerequisite and chapter topics	Number and Operations, Problem Solving	2.2.A, 2.2.B, 2.2.C, 2.10.B, 2.13.A, 2.14
Informal Assessment Rubrics (pp. 246A–270A) 15 minutes	Progress Monitoring Use at the end of each lesson.	To provide daily evaluation of math proficiency	Number and Operations, Communication	2.2.A, 2.2.B, 2.2.C, 2.10.B, 2.13.A, 2.14
Individual Oral Assessment (p. 260A) 5 minutes per student	Progress Monitoring Begin use after Lesson 7.6.	To provide alternate means of assessing students' progress	Number and Operations	2.2.A, 2.2.C, 2.4.B
Mastery Checkpoint (*Assessment* pp. 88–90) 5 minutes per student	Use in or after Lessons 7.8 and 7.10.	To provide assessment of mastery of key skills	Number and Operations	2.2.A, 2.10.B
Chapter 7 Practice Test (pp. 279–280, 281–282) 30–45 minutes	Progress Monitoring Use after or in place of the Chapter 7 Review.	To provide assessment of the chapter concepts	Data Analysis and Probability, Number and Operations	2.2.A, 2.2.B, 2.2.C, 2.10.B, 2.13.A, 2.14
Chapter 7 Test (*Assessment* pp. 236–239) 30–45 minutes	Summative Use after or in place of the Chapter 7 Review.	To provide assessment of the chapter concepts	Data Analysis and Probability, Number and Operations	2.2.A, 2.2.B, 2.2.C, 2.10.B, 2.13.A, 2.14

Texas Technology Resources

Visit SRAonline.com for online versions of the *Real Math* eSuite.

TEXAS Technology for Teachers

e Presentation	**Lessons 7.1–7.11** Use the *ePresentation* to interactively present chapter content.
e Planner	Use the Chapter and Lesson Planners to outline activities and time frames for Chapter 7.
e Assess	Students can take the following assessments in *eAssess:* • Chapter Pretest • Mastery Checkpoints **Lessons 7.8, 7.10** • Chapter Test Teachers can record results and print reports for all assessments in this chapter.
e MathTools	**Fractions Lessons 7.1–7.8, 7.11**

TEXAS Technology for Students

e Textbook	An electronic, interactive version of the **Student Edition** is available for all lessons in Chapter 7.
e MathTools	**Fractions Lessons 7.1–7.8, 7.11**
e Games	**Fraction Game Lessons 7.6–7.9**
TECH KNOWLEDGE	**TechKnowledge** Level 2 provides lessons that specifically teach the Unit 10 Internet applications that students can use in this chapter's project.

Fractions

Introduce Chapter 7   10

Chapter Objectives

Explain to students that in this chapter they will build on what they already know about fractions. They will

- identify fractions.
- create and use fractions.

Pretest ✓ COMPUTING

Administer the Chapter 7 Pretest, which has similar exercises to the Chapter 7 Test.

- If most students do *not* demonstrate mastery on the Pretest, proceed at a normal pace through the chapter. Use the differentiated instruction suggestions at the beginning and end of each lesson to adapt instruction to and follow up on the needs of each student.

- If most students show mastery of some or all of the concepts and skills in the Chapter 7 Pretest, move quickly through the chapter, de-emphasizing lessons linked to items which most students answered correctly. Use the Individual Oral Assessments to monitor progress, and, if necessary, modify your pacing. These assessments are especially useful because they can help you distinguish among different levels of understanding. For example, a student who has mastered a particular skill but does not show a deep understanding of the relevant concepts still needs thorough coverage of the lesson material.

- If you do move quickly through the chapter, be sure not to skip games, Problem- Solving lessons, and Thinking Stories. These provide practice in skills and nonroutine thinking that will be useful even to students who already understand the chapter content. Also, be alert to application problems embedded within lessons that may show students how math topics are used in daily life.

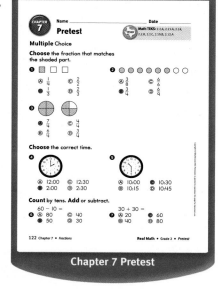

Chapter 7 Pretest

Access Prior Knowledge ✓ UNDERSTANDING

As students look at the illustration on page 243, ask questions such as the following:

- ■ **Have you ever been to a science museum?**
- ■ **What were some things you did while you were there?**
- ■ **What were some of the displays you saw?**
- ■ **Have you ever made an impression of a seashell or leaf on clay?**

Problem Solving 💡 7.A Introducing Strategies

Tell Students In Today's Lesson They Will

- separate a ball of clay into three equal portions.
- show how they solved the problem and prove that the portions are equal.

Materials

- Clay
- Balance scale, rulers, number strips, measuring cups, and so on
- Sticks, string, or plastic implements for cutting clay
- Assortment of small containers, at least three of the same size
  See Appendix A page A24 for instruction and a rubric for problem solving.

Guided Discussion

Using Student Pages APPLYING

Have students share what they know about fossils. You might explain to them that fossils are the remains of plants or animals such as dinosaurs from long ago. Fossils are not only the actual parts (bones, teeth, and so on) of once-living things but also their imprints such as footprints, tracks, and burrows. Explain that scientists often make casts and molds of fossils, using special rubbery materials.

As students look at the illustration on page 244, present this problem:

Imagine that you and two friends are working together on a display of three casts for a fossil display at the science museum. Your group has one large ball of clay to share for making the casts. How can you divide the clay so that each person has the same amount?

Guided Discussion UNDERSTANDING

To make sure students understand the problem, ask questions such as the following:

- ■ **What are you supposed to do with the clay?** divide it into three pieces
- ■ **What must be true about the three pieces you make?** Each piece must have the same amount of clay.
- ■ **Why would you want the three pieces to be equal?** to be fair; so each person has the same amount of clay to make a fossil impression for the display
- ■ **What are some ways you can use to divide the clay?** Cut the ball; roll out the ball, and then cut it; make it into three smaller balls; pinch off pieces, and so on.
- ■ **What are some ways you can make sure your three pieces have the same amount of clay?** Weigh them; stack them on top of each other, and see if they match; put them in containers that are the same size; measure them with a ruler, and so on.
- ■ **If you have three equal pieces and then you form them into three different shapes, would each of them still have the same amount of clay?** Yes; changing a shape doesn't change how much clay is in it as long as you don't add or take away any clay.

TEXAS

Number, operation, and quantitative reasoning 2.2.A
Use concrete models to represent and name fractional parts of a whole object (with denominators of 12 or less).

Underlying processes and mathematical tools 2.14
The student is expected to justify his or her thinking using objects, words, pictures, numbers, and technology.

Give each student a softball-sized ball of clay. Place balance scales, containers, and cutting and measurement tools where students can access them easily. Have students recall what they have already learned about measurement (Chapter 4). Remind students that they will be required to prove they have divided the clay ball into three equal pieces. Encourage students to work together, use measurement tools, and discuss their strategies with each other.

When students are convinced they have divided their balls into three equal pieces, have them show their method and proof on page 244. As students work on the page, remind them to use pictures, words, symbols, or a combination of these to show how they divided the clay into three pieces and to explain how they know the three pieces are equal.

If students finish early, encourage them to try a different way to divide their clay and/or a different way to prove the pieces are equal.

Concept/Question Board   APPLYING

Questions
Have students think of and write three questions they have about fractions and how they can be used. Then have them select one question to post on the Question side of the Board.

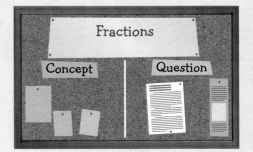

Concepts
As students work through the chapter, have them collect examples of how fractions are used in everyday situations. For each example, have them write a problem that relates to the item(s). Have them display their examples on the Concept side of the Board. Suggest the following:

- gardening
- telling time

Answers
Throughout the chapter, have students post answers to the questions and solutions to the problems on the Board.

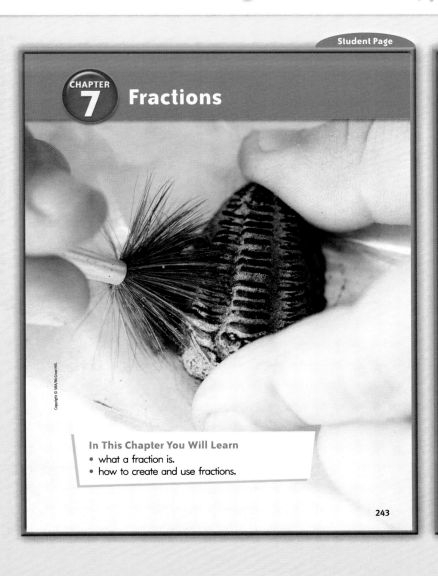

CHAPTER **7** **Fractions**

In This Chapter You Will Learn
- what a fraction is.
- how to create and use fractions.

243

Problem Solving **7.A** Introducing Strategies

Math TEKS
Underlying processes and mathematical tools 2.14 The student is expected to justify his or her thinking using objects, words, pictures, numbers, and technology.

Name _____ Date _____

Listen to the problem.

Show how you made three equal portions.

How do you know the three portions are equal?

_____

_____

See Teacher's Edition.

Reflect 20

Effective Communication Have students display their clay pieces, demonstrate how they divided the large ball, and explain or demonstrate how they know their pieces are equal.

- ■ **How did you divide your ball into three equal pieces?** See Sample Solutions Strategies below.
- ■ **What does it mean for pieces to be equal?** They have the same amount of clay; they weigh the same; they look exactly the same; and so on.
- ■ **What did you do to make the pieces equal?** We weighed them; we used them to fill up containers of the same size; we measured them with a ruler; we stacked them on top of each other; and so on.
- ■ **How can you convince the class that your three pieces are equal?** We can show how we made sure they were the same; we can weigh them for the class; we can ask someone else to check, using a different method from the one we used; and so on.

In discussion, also bring out the following points:

- There are different ways to check that amounts are equal.
- Pieces can look different and still have the same amount of material.
- When you divide a whole into equal pieces, each of those equal pieces is the same *fraction* of the whole.

Extension

Have students use their clay to make impressions of seashells, twigs, leaves, or other items from nature. Then have them make a class display of the impressions.

Sample Solutions Strategies

Students might use one or more of the following strategies to help them divide the clay ball into three equal pieces.

Use Spatial Sense

Students might form the clay into a symmetrical solid that is easy for them to cut into three pieces of the same size and shape. They might roll the clay into a cylinder or use a symmetrical container to shape the clay. They might form a large round or rectangular pancake of uniform thickness.

Use Measurement/Guess, Check, and Adjust

- After making three portions, students might compare two of them on the balance scale and keep moving pieces from the heavier portion onto the lighter portion until the two portions balance. Then they could compare the third portion with one of the two equal portions. Students could continue comparing and adjusting until all three portions are of equal weight.
- Students might roll their three pieces into flat, round pancakes of the same thickness. Then they could use a ruler to measure across each one or simply compare them directly and then move clay from one to another until all three pancakes are the same.
- Students could find three containers of the same size and shape and put some clay in each, adjusting until the clay in each container reaches the same level.

Use Number Sense

Students might form many small equal pieces by using a small container as a mold. Then they could make three equal portions by distributing the pieces into three batches with the same number of pieces in each batch.

Home Connection

At this time, you may want to send home the letter on pages 26–29 of *Home Connection.* This letter describes what students will be learning and what activities they can do at home to support their work in school.

Home Connection
Page 26

Assess and Differentiate

 Assess   Use *eAssess* to record and analyze evidence of student understanding.

A   Gather Evidence

Use the Daily Class Assessment Records in *Texas Assessment* or *eAssess* to record Informal and Formal Assessments.

Informal Assessment	**Informal Assessment**	**Formal Assessment**
✔ **Access Prior Knowledge**	✔ **Concept/Question Board**	✔ **Pretest** COMPUTING
Did the student UNDERSTANDING	Did the student APPLYING	Review student answers on the Chapter 6 Pretest.
❏ make important observations?	❏ apply learning in new situations?	❏ If most students do not demonstrate mastery, move at a normal pace through the chapter.
❏ extend or generalize learning?	❏ contribute concepts?	❏ If most students answer most questions correctly, move quickly through the chapter, emphasizing those lessons for which students did not answer correctly, as well as games, Problem-Solving lessons, and Thinking Stories.
❏ provide insightful answers?	❏ contribute answers?	
❏ pose insightful questions?	❏ connect mathematics to real-world situations?	

B   Summarize Findings

Analyze and summarize assessment data for each student. Determine which Assessment Follow-Up is appropriate for each student. Use the Student Assessment Record in *Texas Assessment* or *eAssess* to update assessment records.

C   Texas Assessment Follow-Up ● DIFFERENTIATE INSTRUCTION

Based on your observations of each student, use these teaching strategies for a general approach to the chapter. Look for specific Differentiate Instruction and Monitoring Student Progress Strategies in each lesson that relate specifically to the lesson content.

ENRICH	 PRACTICE	RETEACH	INTERVENTION	ENGLISH LEARNER
If . . . students demonstrate a **secure understanding** of chapter concepts, **Then . . .** move quickly through the chapter or use *Enrichment* Lessons 7.1–7.11 as assessment follow-up to extend and apply understanding.	**If . . .** students grasp chapter concepts with **competent understanding**, **Then . . .** use *Practice* Lessons 7.1–7.11 as lesson follow-up to develop fluency.	**If . . .** students have prerequisite understanding but demonstrate **emerging understanding** of chapter concepts, **Then . . .** use *Reteach* Lessons 7.7 and 7.11 to reteach lesson concepts.	**If . . .** students are not competent with prerequisite skills, **Then . . .** use *Intervention* Lessons 7.A–7.C before each lesson to develop fluency with prerequisite skills.	Use *English Learner Support Guide* Lessons 7.1–7.11 for strategies to preteach lesson vocabulary and concepts.

Math Across the Curriculum

Preview the chapter projects with students. Assign projects or have students choose from the projects to extend and enrich concepts in this chapter.

Go on a Scavenger Hunt 1–5 days

 SCIENCE WebQuest

 TEKS

MATH: Measurement 2.10.B Read and write times shown on analog and digital clocks using five-minute increments.
SCIENCE: Science concepts 2.8 The student distinguishes between living organisms and nonliving objects.
TECHNOLOGY: Information acquisition 04 The student uses a variety of strategies to acquire information from electronic resources, with appropriate supervision.

Have students use technology to

- practice telling time.
- collect different information about fossils.
- print Web pages.

For this project, students use the Internet to investigate the following information:

- how to tell time in hours and minutes
- what fossils are, where they are found, how to look for them, and how to identify them
- how to use coordinates to identify locations on a map

Go on a Scavenger Hunt

Activity 1

History of Math
The measurement systems that we use today are based on five ancient systems. The ancient Hindu system used fractional units based on halves, fourths, and eighths. The ancient Chinese and Egyptian systems used a system of measurement based on decimals, or units of ten. The Roman measurement system was based on units of twelve, while the Babylonian system was based on units of sixty.

73

For specific step-by-step instructions for this project, see *Across the Curriculum Math Connections* pages 72–77.

 **Knowledge Age Skills**

Problem Formulation, Planning, and Strategizing Students strategize where and how to unearth fossils.

Self-Monitoring and Self- and Group Assessment Students monitor their progress through interactive responses.

TECH KNOWLEDGE *TechKnowledge* Level 2 provides lessons that specifically teach the Unit 10 Internet applications that students can use in this project.

Create a Board Game about Fossils 1–2 weeks

LANGUAGE ARTS

 TEKS

MATH: Number, operation, and quantitative reasoning 2.2.A Use concrete models to represent and name fractional parts of a whole object (with denominators of 12 or less).
LANGUAGE ARTS: Writing purposes 2.14 The student writes for a variety of audiences and purposes, and in various forms.
TECHNOLOGY: Foundations 02.D Produce documents at the keyboard, proofread, and correct errors.

Have students use mathematics to design a game board and make game cards. To broaden the language arts concept, have students design their games around works you are currently studying.

As part of the project, students should consider the following issues:

- facts about fossils
- board game design
- how to write fractions
- proper keyboarding technique

Create a Board Game about Fossils

Activity 2

Profiles in Math
Willard Libby (1908–1980) was an American chemist who developed carbon-14 dating to find the age of biological artifacts. Because the amount of carbon-14 in a living thing decays at a specific rate after death, Libby used the amount of carbon-14 left in plant or animal remains to calculate the time since death. Carbon-14 dating has been used to date fossils, mummies, dwellings, and other artifacts.

79

For specific step-by-step instructions for this project, see *Across the Curriculum Math Connections* pages 78–81.

 **Knowledge Age Skills**

Teamwork Students work in groups to create game boards and write questions and answers.

Problem Formulation, Planning, and Strategizing Students figure out which fractions will work for their game boards.

Grade 1
Number, operation, and quantitative reasoning 1.2.A Separate a whole into two, three, or four equal parts and use appropriate language to describe the parts such as three out of four equal parts

Grade 2
Number, operation, and quantitative reasoning 2.2.A Use concrete models to represent and name fractional parts of a whole object (with denominators of 12 or less).

Grade 3
Number, operation, and quantitative reasoning 3.2.C Use fraction names and symbols to describe fractional parts of whole objects or sets of objects.

Lesson Planner

OBJECTIVES
To review the fractions *halves* and *fourths* using linear models

MATH TEKS
Number, operation, and quantitative reasoning 2.2.A 🔑
Use concrete models to represent and name fractional parts of a whole object (with denominators of 12 or less).
Underlying processes and mathematical tools 2.13.A
Explain and record observations using objects, words, pictures, numbers, and technology.

MATH TEKS INTEGRATION
Number, operation, and quantitative reasoning 2.3.B
Model addition and subtraction of two-digit numbers with objects, pictures, words, and numbers.
Underlying processes and mathematical tools 2.14
The student is expected to justify his or her thinking using objects, words, pictures, numbers, and technology.

MATERIALS
- *Number Cubes (0–5 and 5–10)
- String cut at equal lengths and scissors
- 6 clear equal-sized jars with straight sides
- Colored water

TECHNOLOGY
🅔 **Presentation** Lesson 7.1
🅔 **MathTools** Fractions

Halves and Fourths ⭐

Context of the Lesson "This is the first of an eleven-lesson sequence that develops concepts of fractions using a variety of models. Students were introduced to fractions in Grade 1. In Chapter 1 of Grade 2, students learned about halves informally in the context of odd and even numbers. This lesson reintroduces the concepts of halves and fourths using linear and measurement models."

See page 243B for Math Background for teachers for this lesson.

Planning for Learning • DIFFERENTIATE INSTRUCTION

INTERVENTION
If . . . students lack the prerequisite skill of recognizing equal parts,

Then . . . teach *Intervention* Lesson 7.A.

🔲 1.2.A, 1.8

Intervention Lesson 7.A

ENGLISH LEARNER
Preview
If . . . students need language support,

Then . . . use Lesson 7.1 in *English Learner Support Guide* to preview lesson concepts and vocabulary.

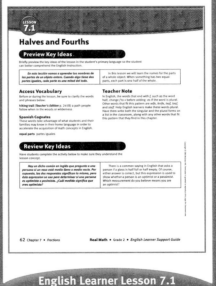

English Learner Lesson 7.1

ENRICH
If . . . students are proficient in the lesson concepts,

Then . . . emphasize chapter projects.

PRACTICE
If . . . students would benefit from additional practice,

Then . . . extend Skill Building before assigning the student pages.

RETEACH
If . . . students are having difficulty understanding halves and fourths,

Then . . . extend Guided Discussion before assigning the student pages.

Academic Vocabulary
fourth \fôrth\ *n.* one of four equal parts into which something is or can be divided

half \haf\ *n.* one of two equal parts into which something is or can be divided

Access Vocabulary
hiking trail a path people follow when walking in the woods or wilderness

Spanish Cognates
equal parts partes iguales

Math TEKS
Number, operation, and quantitative reasoning 2.2.A
Use concrete models to represent and name fractional parts of a whole object (with denominators of 12 or less).
Underlying processes and mathematical tools 2.13.A
Explain and record observations using objects, words, pictures, numbers, and technology.

Mental Math 5

INTEGRATION: 2.3.B Provide two-digit addition and subtraction practice. Students should respond with **Number Cubes,** using the find, hide, and show routine. Possible examples include the following:

a. 70 + 30 = 100	**b.** 100 − 50 = 50	**c.** 40 + 40 = 80
d. 51 + 49 = 100	**e.** 10 + 92 = 102	**f.** 10 + 67 = 77
g. 70 − 49 = 21	**h.** 12 − 3 = 9	**i.** 12 − 6 = 6

1 Develop 30

Tell Students In Today's Lesson They Will

learn about the fractions *half* and *fourth*.

Guided Discussion UNDERSTANDING Introductory

Halves

Begin by asking students to tell you what they know about halves.

■ **What is one-half of something?** Emphasize that dividing something in halves means dividing it into two equal pieces or fair shares.

Hold up a piece of string.

■ **How would you cut the string into halves?**
■ **Critical Thinking** **How could you be sure that both halves are exactly the same length?** Possible answer: Hold the pieces beside each other to make sure they are the same length.

Distribute a length of string to each student, and tell them to cut it into halves. Remind students that the halves must be equal.

■ **How many pieces of string did you end up with?** two

Explain that these two pieces are called halves, and two halves make one whole piece of string. Write $\frac{1}{2}$ on the board, and tell students that this is how you write one-half.

Fourths

Hold up another piece of string.

■ **What is one-fourth of something?** one of four equal pieces
■ **Critical Thinking** **How would you divide the whole string into fourths?** If no one volunteers, suggest to students that cutting each half in halves would result in four equal pieces.

Cut the string into fourths.

■ **How many parts are there?** four
■ **Are the parts equal?** yes
■ **What do we call each part?** one-fourth

Explain that when something has been divided into four equal parts, the parts are called fourths or quarters. Write $\frac{1}{4}$ on the board, and tell students that this is how you write one-fourth or one-quarter.

Strategy Building ENGAGING Guided

Use this activity to provide further practice with halves and quarters.

Present two equal-sized cylindrical jars to students. Pour colored water into the first jar until it is full. Then begin pouring water from the first jar into the second jar. Tell students to say "stop" when they think that you have poured the water to the halfway mark on the second jar.

■ **Critical Thinking** **How can you find out if the estimate is correct?** Possible answers: by setting the jars side by side and adjusting if the water is not the same height.

 Integration: TEKS 2.2.C Place an empty jar next to the jar that is half full. Pour a quantity of water into the jar. Tell students to call the empty jar 0 and the full jar 1. Ask whether the amount of water in the jar is closest to 0, $\frac{1}{2}$, or 1. Repeat with different amounts of water.

Show five empty jars. Fill one jar, then begin filling the second jar. Tell the class to say "stop" when you have filled the jar one-fourth full. Fill the remaining three jars to the same level.

■ **Critical Thinking** **How can you check this estimate?** If students suggest comparing heights, allow them to try. If they continue to think this is a solution, have them combine the one-fourth-filled jars into one jar.

Skill Building APPLYING Guided

Have students work in pairs. Tell students to take turns drawing lines of different lengths and having the other student estimate and draw lines that are one-half or one-fourth as long. To check their estimations, ask students to cut string to the same length as the line drawn and to fold it in half to check the estimated one-half line or to fold it in fourths (half and then half again) to check the estimated one-fourth line. Demonstrate how to do this.

2 Use Student Pages 10

Pages 245–246 UNDERSTANDING 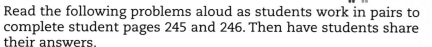 Independent

Read the following problems aloud as students work in pairs to complete student pages 245 and 246. Then have students share their answers.

1. Ferdie and Manolita were hiking along this trail. Halfway along the trail Manolita stopped to look at wildflowers. Draw an M where she stopped. Ferdie stopped to look at butterflies one-fourth of the way along the trail. Draw an F where he stopped.

2. If you want to walk $\frac{1}{2}$ of the hall, mark where you would stop.

3. Mark where one-fourth of the rope is.

 Integration: TEKS 2.14, Problem 5

Student Page

Name _____ Date _____

LESSON 7.1 | **Halves and Fourths**

Key Ideas

Math TEKS
Number, operation, and quantitative reasoning 2.2.A
Use concrete models to represent and name fractional parts of a whole object (with denominators of 12 or less).

When something has two equal parts, each part is one-half of the whole.

When something has four equal parts, each part is one-fourth of the whole.

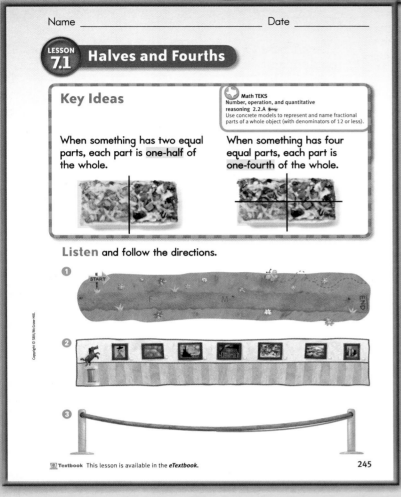

Listen and follow the directions.

Textbook This lesson is available in the *eTextbook*.

245

LESSON 7.1 · Halves and Fourths

④ Draw lines to show one-half of each ribbon.

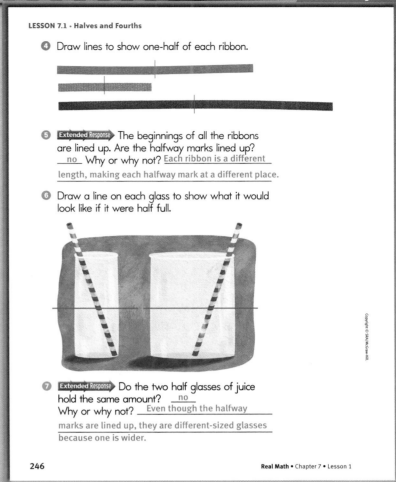

⑤ **Extended Response** The beginnings of all the ribbons are lined up. Are the halfway marks lined up? __no__ Why or why not? Each ribbon is a different length, making each halfway mark at a different place.

⑥ Draw a line on each glass to show what it would look like if it were half full.

⑦ **Extended Response** Do the two half glasses of juice hold the same amount? __no__ Why or why not? Even though the halfway marks are lined up, they are different-sized glasses because one is wider.

246

Real Math · Chapter 7 · Lesson 1

---

3 Reflect   10

Guided Discussion REASONING

Have students examine the pieces of string that have been cut into fourths and halves.

■ **How many halves make one whole?** 2
■ **How many fourths make one whole?** 4
■ **How many fourths make one half?** 2

Now line up three pieces of string—one that is whole, one that is one-half of the whole, and one that is one-fourth of the whole.

■ **Critical Thinking** **What do you notice?** Each string is half the length of the previous one.

Now hold up a piece of string of random size.

■ **Is this string closer in size to the $\frac{1}{4}$ string, the $\frac{1}{2}$ string, or the whole string?** Confirm the answer by holding the piece of string up to the fourth-, half-, and whole-size strings

Cumulative Review: For cumulative review of previously learned skills, see page 259–260.

Family Involvement: Assign the *Practice, Reteach,* or *Enrichment* activities depending on the needs of your students. Have students practice dividing things in halves and quarters with family members.

Concept/Question Board: Have students look for additional examples using fractions and post them on the Concept/Question Board.

Math Puzzler: Ferdie and Portia each had one banana. They wanted to share the two bananas equally with Willy, so each of them gave him one-half of a banana. Were the bananas shared equally? no **Why not?** Willy had two halves; Ferdie and Portia each had one-half.

Chapter 7 · Lesson 1 **245–246**

4 Assess and Differentiate

 Assess Use *eAssess* to record and analyze evidence of student understanding.

A Gather Evidence

Use the Daily Class Assessment Records in *Texas Assessment* or *eAssess* to record daily observations.

Informal Assessment
☑ **Mental Math**

Did the student **COMPUTING**
- ❏ respond accurately?
- ❏ respond quickly?
- ❏ respond with confidence?
- ❏ self-correct?

Informal Assessment
☑ **Guided Discussion**

Did the student **UNDERSTANDING**
- ❏ make important observations?
- ❏ extend or generalize learning?
- ❏ provide insightful answers?
- ❏ pose insightful questions?

 TEKS/TAKS Practice

Use *TEKS/TAKS Practice* page 13 to assess student progress.

B Summarize Findings

Analyze and summarize assessment data for each student. Determine which Assessment Follow-Up is appropriate for each student. Use the Student Assessment Record in *Texas Assessment* or *eAssess* to update assessment records.

C Texas Assessment Follow-Up • DIFFERENTIATE INSTRUCTION

Based on your observations, use these teaching strategies for assessment follow-up.

INTERVENTION

Review student performance on *Intervention* Lesson 7.A to see if students have mastered prerequisite skills for this lesson.

1.2.A Separate a whole into two, three, or four equal parts and use appropriate language to describe the parts such as three out of four equal parts.
1.8 The student understands that time can be measured. The student uses time to describe and compare situations.

ENGLISH LEARNER

Review

Use Lesson 7.1 in *English Learner Support Guide* to review lesson concepts and vocabulary.

ENRICH

If . . . students are proficient in the lesson concepts,

Then . . . encourage them to work on the chapter projects or *Enrichment* Lesson 7.1.

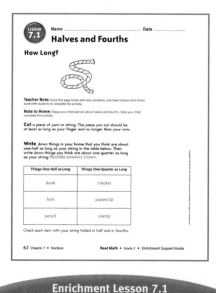

Enrichment Lesson 7.1

 PRACTICE

If . . . students would benefit from additional practice,

Then . . . assign *Practice* Lesson 7.1.

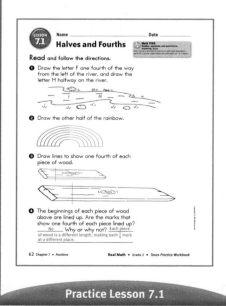

Practice Lesson 7.1

RETEACH

If . . . students are having difficulty understanding measuring halves and fourths of lengths,

Then . . . remind them that *half* means two equal pieces and *fourth* means four equal pieces.

TEXAS Vertical Alignment

Grade 1
Number, operation, and quantitative reasoning 1.2.A Separate a whole into two, three, or four equal parts and use appropriate language to describe the parts such as three out of four equal parts

Grade 2
Number, operation, and quantitative reasoning 2.2.A Use concrete models to represent and name fractional parts of a whole object (with denominators of 12 or less).

Grade 3
Number, operation, and quantitative reasoning 3.2.C Use fraction names and symbols to describe fractional parts of whole objects or sets of objects.

Overview — LESSON 7.2

TEXAS

Lesson Planner

OBJECTIVES
- To review fractions $\frac{1}{2}$ and $\frac{1}{4}$ using linear models
- To introduce the mathematical symbols of $\frac{1}{2}$ and $\frac{1}{4}$
- To introduce terminology such as *numerator* and *denominator*

🔑 MATH TEKS
Number, operation, and quantitative reasoning 2.2.A
Use concrete models to represent and name fractional parts of a whole object (with denominators of 12 or less).

Number, operation, and quantitative reasoning 2.2.C
Use concrete models to determine if a fractional part of a whole is closer to 0, $\frac{1}{2}$, or 1

Underlying processes and mathematical tools 2.13.A
Explain and record observations using objects, words, pictures, numbers, and technology.

🔑 MATH TEKS INTEGRATION
Number, operation, and quantitative reasoning 2.3.B
Model addition and subtraction of two-digit numbers with objects, pictures, words, and numbers.

Underlying processes and mathematical tools 2.14
The student is expected to justify his or her thinking using objects, words, pictures, numbers, and technology.

MATERIALS
- *Number Cubes (0–5 and 5–10)
- Set of 4 paper strips (8 in. by about $1\frac{1}{4}$ in.) per student
- *Rulers
- SRA Math Vocabulary Cards ✏

TECHNOLOGY
- 🄴 **Presentation** Lesson 7.2
- 🄴 **MathTools** Fractions

Looking Ahead
The paper strips used in this lesson will be needed again in Lesson 7.4. Students should keep their strips in a safe place.

---

*Manipulative Kit Item 🔑 = Key standard

Writing Fractions ⭐

Context of the Lesson This is the second of an eleven-lesson sequence that develops concepts of fractions using a variety of models. This lesson reviews written fraction notation, which was introduced in Grade 1. In this lesson students learn what the parts of a fraction represent. Students will continue to practice writing fractions by using the proper notation throughout Chapter 7.

Planning for Learning • DIFFERENTIATE INSTRUCTION

INTERVENTION
If . . . students lack the prerequisite skill of estimating fractional parts,

Then . . . teach *Intervention* Lesson 7.A.

 1.2.A, 1.8

Intervention Lesson 7.A

ENGLISH LEARNER
Preview

If . . . students need language support,

Then . . . use Lesson 7.2 in *English Learner Support Guide* to preview lesson concepts and vocabulary.

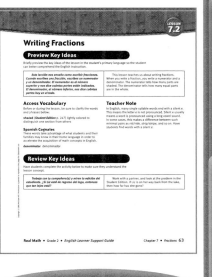

English Learner Lesson 7.2

ENRICH
If . . . students are proficient in the lesson concepts,

Then . . . emphasize Guided Discussion in Reflect.

PRACTICE
If . . . students would benefit from additional practice,

Then . . . extend Skill Building before assigning the student pages.

RETEACH
If . . . students are having difficulty understanding writing fractions,

Then . . . extend Guided Discussion before assigning the student pages.

Academic Vocabulary
✏ **denominator** \di nä´ mə nā´ tər\ *n.* the number below the line in a fraction, indicating the number of equal parts into which the whole is divided

✏ **numerator** \nü´ mə rā´ tər\ *n.* the number above the line in a fraction, indicating the number of equal parts being considered

Access Vocabulary
shaded lightly colored to distinguish one section from others

Spanish Cognates
denominator denominador

⭐ = 120-Day Plan for TAKS

Teaching Lesson 7.2

 TEXAS

Math TEKS
Number, operation, and quantitative reasoning 2.2.A Use concrete models to represent and name fractional parts of a whole object (with denominators of 12 or less).
Number, operation, and quantitative reasoning 2.2.C Use concrete models to determine if a fractional part of a whole is closer to 0, $\frac{1}{2}$, or 1.

Underlying processes and mathematical tools Explain and record observations using objects, pictures, numbers, and technology.

Mental Math   5

 INTEGRATION: 2.3.B Provide two-digit addition and subtraction practice. Write problems on the board. Students should respond with their **Number Cubes,** using the find, hide and show routine. Possible examples include the following:

a. $100 - 30 = 70$ **b.** $100 - 40 = 60$ **c.** $100 - 50 = 50$

d. $40 + 20 = 60$ **e.** $40 + 30 = 70$ **f.** $40 + 40 = 80$

1 Develop   30

Tell Students In Today's Lesson They Will

learn to how to write fractions.

Guided Discussion   UNDERSTANDING

 Introductory

Halves

Distribute sets of paper strips to each student. A copy of these strips can be found on page 126 of **Practice.** Hold up one strip, and ask students the following:

■ **How can you divide this into halves?** Fold the strip so the ends line up.

Have students fold one of their strips into halves as you do the same to the strip you are holding.

■ **How many parts is the strip divided into?** two

Write the number 2 on the board to represent that there are two halves. Next fold the strip so only one of the halves is showing.

■ **How many halves of the strip am I showing?** one

Write the number 1 above the 2, and draw a fraction line between the numbers. Explain what the fraction tells us—the bottom number tells the kind of parts you are counting (in this case, halves), and the top number tells how many parts you are currently looking at.

Have students label each half of their strip.

Fourths

Hold up another strip.

■ **Critical Thinking** **How can you divide this into fourths?** Discuss different ideas, with an emphasis on folding the strip into halves and folding those halves into halves.

Have students fold one of their strips into fourths as you do the same to the strip you are holding.

■ **How many parts is the strip divided into?** four

Write the number 4 to represent fourths. Then fold the strip so only one section is showing, and ask the following:

■ **How many fourths of the strip am I showing?** one

Write a 1 above the 4, and draw a fraction line between the numbers. Point out that you are showing them one section of a strip divided into fourths.

Have students label each fourth of their strip.

Thirds

For the next strip, allow students to practice folding into thirds. After they have folded their strips into thirds, have them label each section by writing $\frac{1}{3}$. Have students save their strips because they will be used again in Lesson 7.4.

After all strips have been folded and labeled, draw a horizontal line on the board, and label it 12 centimeters (this line does not have to be to scale; it just needs to be big enough so everyone can see it). Tell students that all their strips are 12 centimeters long.

Draw a mark halfway through the horizontal line.

■ **Critical Thinking** **How long are each of the $\frac{1}{2}$ sections?** 6 centimeters

■ **How do you know?** $6 + 6 = 12$ or half of 12 is 6

Draw a mark halfway between the end of the line and the halfway mark.

■ **How long are the $\frac{1}{4}$ sections?** 3 centimeters

■ **Critical Thinking** **How do you know?** Half of 6 is 3, or $3 + 3 + 3 + 3 = 12$

Skill Building   APPLYING

 Guided

Have students work in pairs and use rulers to measure their strips and the length of each fractional section. See if their measurements correspond to the class answers. Discuss any discrepancies. For each fractional part, have students identify whether it is closer to 0, $\frac{1}{2}$, or 1. Students should notice that $\frac{1}{4}$ is exactly halfway between 0 and $\frac{1}{2}$ and that $\frac{3}{4}$ is exactly halfway between $\frac{1}{2}$ and 1.

2 Use Student Pages   10

Pages 247–248 UNDERSTANDING

 Independent

Have students complete pages 247 and 248 independently.

 **Integration: TEKS 2.14, Journal**

As Students Finish

 Game   Allow students to play any previously introduced game, or assign a game based on needed skill practice.

e MathTools Have students use **Fractions** to explore fractions.

Student Page

Name _____ Date _____

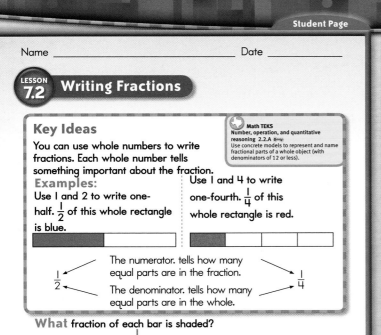

LESSON 7.2 Writing Fractions

Key Ideas

You can use whole numbers to write fractions. Each whole number tells something important about the fraction.

Math TEKS
Number, operation, and quantitative reasoning 2.2.A
Use concrete models to represent and name fractional parts of a whole object (with denominators of 12 or less).

Examples:

Use 1 and 2 to write one-half. $\frac{1}{2}$ of this whole rectangle is blue.

Use 1 and 4 to write one-fourth. $\frac{1}{4}$ of this whole rectangle is red.

$\frac{1}{2}$
The numerator. tells how many equal parts are in the fraction.

$\frac{1}{4}$
The denominator. tells how many equal parts are in the whole.

What fraction of each bar is shaded?

❶ ___ $\frac{1}{2}$

❷ $\frac{1}{4}$

❸ The red figure shows $\frac{1}{2}$ of a rectangular garden. Draw the rest of the garden.

247

📱 Textbook This lesson is available in the *eTextbook*.

LESSON 7.2 · Writing Fractions

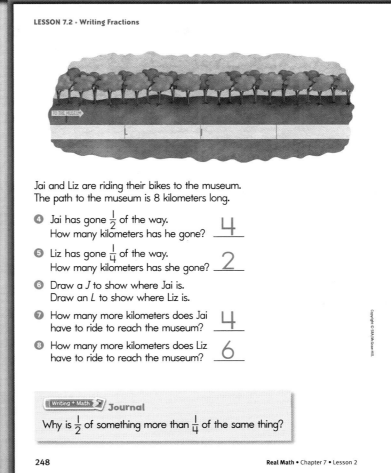

Jai and Liz are riding their bikes to the museum. The path to the museum is 8 kilometers long.

❹ Jai has gone $\frac{1}{2}$ of the way. How many kilometers has he gone? ___ 4

❺ Liz has gone $\frac{1}{4}$ of the way. How many kilometers has she gone? ___ 2

❻ Draw a *J* to show where Jai is. Draw an *L* to show where Liz is.

❼ How many more kilometers does Jai have to ride to reach the museum? ___ 4

❽ How many more kilometers does Liz have to ride to reach the museum? ___ 6

Writing + Math ✏️ **Journal**
Why is $\frac{1}{2}$ of something more than $\frac{1}{4}$ of the same thing?

248   **Real Math** • Chapter 7 • Lesson 2

---

③ Reflect   10

Guided Discussion ✓ REASONING

Discuss the following question with students:

■ **Looking at the fraction strips, what do you notice about the relationship between the number in the denominator and the size of the parts?** If students need guidance, ask whether making the bottom number greater makes the parts bigger or smaller.

■ **Critical Thinking Why is this?** Because the strips are all the same length, as the number of parts increases, there is less room for each one. For example, in the fraction $\frac{3}{4}$, there are 4 parts needed to make a whole. In the fraction $\frac{1}{5}$, there are 5 parts needed to make a whole. The greater the denominator becomes, the more parts are needed.

Writing + Math ✏️ **Journal**

Discuss student answers. One-half is greater because you are dividing the object into larger pieces. In other words, you are splitting it fewer times.

Review **Cumulative Review:** For cumulative review of previously learned skills, see page 259–260.

🎒 **Family Involvement:** Assign the *Practice, Reteach,* or *Enrichment* activities depending on the needs of your students. Have students practice writing fractions with family members.

Concept/Question Board: Have students look for additional examples using fractions and post them on the Concept/Question Board.

🧩 **Math Puzzler:** How many sections would you have if you folded a square in half three times and then unfolded it? 8

Assess and Differentiate

 Assess Use *eAssess* to record and analyze evidence of student understanding.

A Gather Evidence

Use the Daily Class Assessment Records in *Texas Assessment* or *eAssess* to record daily observations.

Informal Assessment
☑ **Student Pages**
Did the student UNDERSTANDING
- ❑ make important observations?
- ❑ extend or generalize learning?
- ❑ provide insightful answers?
- ❑ pose insightful questions?

Informal Assessment
☑ **Guided Discussion**
Did the student REASONING
- ❑ provide a clear explanation?
- ❑ communicate reasons and strategies?
- ❑ choose appropriate strategies?
- ❑ argue logically?

 TEKS/TAKS Practice
Use *TEKS/TAKS Practice* page 13 to assess student progress.

B Summarize Findings

Analyze and summarize assessment data for each student. Determine which Assessment Follow-Up is appropriate for each student. Use the Student Assessment Record in *Texas Assessment* or *eAssess* to update assessment records.

C Texas Assessment Follow-Up • DIFFERENTIATE INSTRUCTION

Based on your observations, use these teaching strategies for assessment follow-up.

INTERVENTION

Review student performance on *Intervention* Lesson 7.A to see if students have mastered prerequisite skills for this lesson.

1.2.A Separate a whole into two, three, or four equal parts and use appropriate language to describe the parts such as three out of four equal parts.
1.8 The student understands that time can be measured. The student uses time to describe and compare situations.

ENGLISH LEARNER
Review
Use Lesson 7.2 in *English Learner Support Guide* to review lesson concepts and vocabulary.

ENRICH

If . . . students are proficient in the lesson concepts,

Then . . . encourage them to work on the chapter projects or *Enrichment* Lesson 7.2.

Enrichment Lesson 7.2

PRACTICE

If . . . students would benefit from additional practice,

Then . . . assign *Practice* Lesson 7.2.

Practice Lesson 7.2

RETEACH

If . . . students are having difficulty understanding $\frac{1}{2}$ or $\frac{1}{4}$,

Then . . . have them use fraction tiles to review the portions.

Grade 1	Grade 2	Grade 3
Number, operation, and quantitative reasoning 1.2.A Separate a whole into two, three, or four equal parts and use appropriate language to describe the parts such as three out of four equal parts	Number, operation, and quantitative reasoning 2.2.A Use concrete models to represent and name fractional parts of a whole object (with denominators of 12 or less).	Number, operation, and quantitative reasoning 3.2.C Use fraction names and symbols to describe fractional parts of whole objects or sets of objects.

Overview

LESSON 7.3

TEXAS

Lesson Planner

OBJECTIVES
• To review the fractions of $\frac{1}{2}$, $\frac{1}{4}$, and $\frac{1}{3}$ using area models
• To provide practice with numerators greater than 1

MATH TEKS
Number, operation, and quantitative reasoning 2.2.A
Use concrete models to represent and name fractional parts of a whole object (with denominators of 12 or less).
Underlying processes and mathematical tools 2.14
The student is expected to justify his or her thinking using objects, words, pictures, numbers, and technology.

MATH TEKS INTEGRATION
Number, operation, and quantitative reasoning 2.3.B
Model addition and subtraction of two-digit numbers with objects, pictures, words, and numbers.

MATERIALS
• *Number Cubes (0–5 and 5–10)
• 2 sheets of $8\frac{1}{2} \times 11$-inch paper per student

TECHNOLOGY
Presentation Lesson 7.3
MathTools Fractions

Looking Ahead
You will need an empty egg carton cut in half in Lesson 7.5. You will also need eight cut out objects (such as circles), six green and two red, for Lesson 7.5.

Halves, Fourths, and Thirds ⭐

Context of the Lesson This is the third of an eleven-lesson sequence that develops concepts of fractions using a variety of models. This lesson builds on Lesson 7.2. In this lesson, students explore halves, fourths, and thirds, now by using area models (dividing geometric shapes into halves, fourths, and thirds). Students also use numerators greater than one.

Planning for Learning ● DIFFERENTIATE INSTRUCTION

INTERVENTION
If . . . students lack the prerequisite skill of telling time to the nearest hour,

Then . . . teach *Intervention* Lesson 7.A.

1.2.A, 1.8

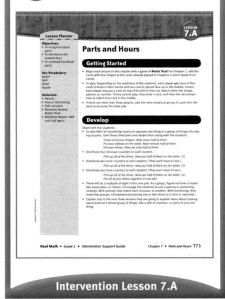

Intervention Lesson 7.A

ENGLISH LEARNER
Preview

If . . . students need language support,

Then . . . use Lesson 7.3 in *English Learner Support Guide* to preview lesson concepts and vocabulary.

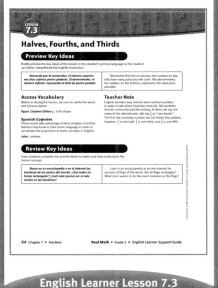

English Learner Lesson 7.3

ENRICH
If . . . students are proficient in the lesson concepts,

Then . . . emphasize Guided Discussion in Reflect.

PRACTICE
If . . . students would benefit from additional practice,

Then . . . extend Skill Building before assigning the student pages.

RETEACH
If . . . students are having difficulty understanding halves, fourths, and thirds,

Then . . . extend Guided Discussion before assigning the student pages.

Academic Vocabulary	**Access Vocabulary**	**Spanish Cognates**
third \thûrd\ *n.* one of three equal parts into which something is or can be divided	figure shape	color colorear

Teaching Lesson 7.3

Math TEKS
Number, operation, and quantitative reasoning 2.2.A
Use concrete models to represent and name fractional pa█
of a whole object (with denominators of 12 or less).
Underlying processes and mathematical tools 2.14
The student is expected to justify his or her thinking usin█
objects, words, pictures, numbers, and technology.

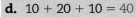

Mental Math 5

 INTEGRATION: 2.3.B Provide students with three-addend addition practice. Students should respond with their *Number Cubes,* using the find, hide and show routine. Possible examples include the following:

a. $10 + 10 + 10 = 30$ **b.** $30 + 30 + 30 = 90$ **c.** $20 + 20 + 20 = 60$
d. $10 + 20 + 10 = 40$ **e.** $20 + 30 + 20 = 70$ **f.** $40 + 40 + 10 = 90$

1 Develop 25

Tell Students In Today's Lesson They Will

learn about thirds and show fractions by using parts of figures.

Guided Discussion UNDERSTANDING Introductory

 Folding Fractions
Distribute to each student a sheet of paper, and ask students to fold their sheets of paper into halves (students can fold end to end or side to side).

■ **How many halves are in one whole sheet of paper?** two
■ **Are the two halves equal to each other?** yes

Write $\frac{1}{2}$ on the board.

Now have students fold their halved papers in half again and then unfold.

■ **How many parts are there now?** four
■ **Are the parts equal?** yes
■ **What do we call these parts?** fourths

Write $\frac{1}{4}$ on the board.

■ **Critical Thinking** **How many fourths are in one-half?** two **How many fourths are in the whole sheet of paper?** four

Now distribute another sheet of paper to each student. Have students try to fold the paper into three equal sections. Then have students compare their results.

■ **Critical Thinking** **How close were you to making equal folds?** Thirds are difficult to fold precisely because it is more difficult to estimate thirds and fifths. One reason is because you can't line up edges of the paper when folding thirds.

■ **What are these parts called?** thirds

Shading Fractions

● Draw a rectangle on the board, and have a student divide it into halves. Have another student shade one-half. Write $\frac{1}{2}$ on the board.
● Draw another rectangle on the board, and ask a student to divide it into fourths. Have another student shade one-fourth. Write $\frac{1}{4}$ on the board.
● Draw a third rectangle on the board, and ask a student to divide it into thirds. Have another student shade one-third. Write $\frac{1}{3}$ on the board.

Using the rectangle divided into thirds, shade another third.

■ **How many thirds are now shaded?** two

Write $\frac{2}{3}$ on the board, and explain that two-thirds of the rectangle has been shaded. Review what the numerator and denominator stand for.

● Draw a circle on the board, and divide it into fourths. Shade three sections, and write the fraction $\frac{3}{4}$. Explain that the circle is divided into fourths, and three of those fourths are shaded. Three-fourths of the circle is shaded. For added challenge, come up with different ways to shade the circle.

Skill Building APPLYING Guided

Have students work in pairs, testing each other to shade different-sized areas of rectangles. Students can ask each other to shade $\frac{1}{2}, \frac{1}{4}, \frac{2}{4}, \frac{3}{4}, \frac{1}{3}, \frac{2}{3}, \frac{2}{4}, \frac{4}{4}$, and so on. Write these fractions on the board for students to use as a reference.

2 Use Student Pages 20

Pages 249–250 UNDERSTANDING Independent

Have students work in pairs to complete pages 249 and 250. Have them share their answers when finished. For added challenge in exercises one through six, have students copy the figures and show different ways to color in the given fraction. Students may find it interesting that there are an equal number of different ways to show $\frac{1}{4}$ as there are to show $\frac{3}{4}$.

As Students Finish

 Game Allow students to play any previously introduced game, or assign a game based on needed skill practice.

 MathTools Have students use *Fractions* to explore halves, fourths, and thirds.

 RESEARCH IN ACTION

"Students' informal notions of partitioning, sharing, and measuring provide a starting point for building the concept of rational numbers. Young children appreciate the idea of "fair shares," and they can use that understanding to partition quantities into equal parts. In some ways, sharing can play the role for rational numbers that counting does for whole numbers."

Kilpatrick, J., J. Swafford, and B. Findell, eds. *Adding It Up: Helping Children Learn Mathematics.* Washington, D.C.: National Research Council/National Academy Press, 2001, p. 7.

Name _____ Date _____

LESSON 7.3 Halves, Fourths, and Thirds

Key Ideas

Math TEKS
Number, operation, and quantitative reasoning 2.2.A
Use concrete models to represent and name fractional parts of a whole object (with denominators of 12 or less).

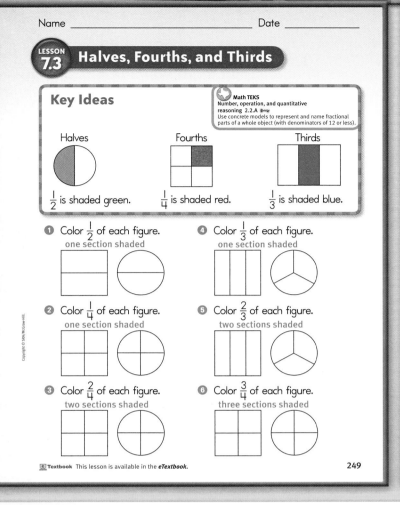

Halves

$\frac{1}{2}$ is shaded green.

Fourths

$\frac{1}{4}$ is shaded red.

Thirds

$\frac{1}{3}$ is shaded blue.

❶ Color $\frac{1}{2}$ of each figure.
one section shaded

❷ Color $\frac{1}{4}$ of each figure.
one section shaded

❸ Color $\frac{2}{4}$ of each figure.
two sections shaded

❹ Color $\frac{1}{3}$ of each figure.
one section shaded

❺ Color $\frac{2}{3}$ of each figure.
two sections shaded

❻ Color $\frac{3}{4}$ of each figure.
three sections shaded

Textbook This lesson is available in the *eTextbook*.

249

Student Page

LESSON 7.3 · Halves, Fourths, and Thirds

Laura's class studied flags of the world.
This is the flag of Ireland:

$\frac{1}{3}$ of the flag is green. $\frac{1}{3}$ of the flag is white.

$\frac{1}{3}$ of the flag is orange.

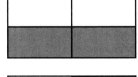

Students in Laura's class designed their own flags.
Color the rectangles to show what each flag might look like. Possible answers are shown.

❼ Jeff colored $\frac{1}{2}$ of his flag purple.

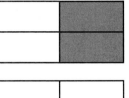

purple

❽ Consuela drew a symbol on $\frac{1}{4}$ of her flag.

X

❾ Emmy made a flag that was $\frac{3}{4}$ blue and $\frac{1}{4}$ green.

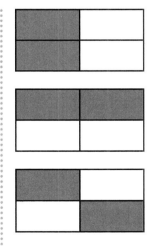

blue | green

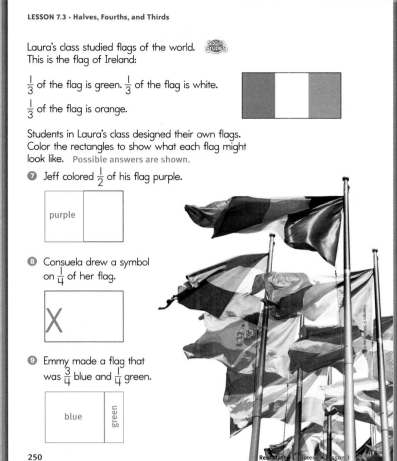

250

Real Math · Chapter 7 · Lesson 3

---

3 Reflect

10

Guided Discussion REASONING

Draw six rectangles on the board, each divided into four equal sections.

Now ask a volunteer to come to the board and shade $\frac{1}{2}$ of the first rectangle. Ask a second volunteer to shade $\frac{1}{2}$ of a second rectangle in a different way from the first student. Continue until each rectangle has $\frac{1}{2}$ shaded a different way.

Critical Thinking How many different ways can you shade $\frac{1}{2}$ of the rectangle? 6

Family Involvement: Assign the *Practice, Reteach,* or *Enrichment* activities depending on the needs of your students. Have students make flash cards that show fractions and corresponding shaded figures with family members.

Math Puzzler: Ms. Eng wanted to give Marcus some books. "I have 6 books. If I give you 2 of them, the other children can each have 2." How many other children are there? 2

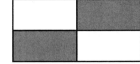

4 Assess and Differentiate

 Assess Use *eAssess* to record and analyze evidence of student understanding.

A Gather Evidence

Use the Daily Class Assessment Records in *Texas Assessment* or *eAssess* to record daily observations.

Informal Assessment
✓ **Guided Discussion**

Did the student **UNDERSTANDING**
- ❑ make important observations?
- ❑ extend or generalize learning?
- ❑ provide insightful answers?
- ❑ pose insightful questions?

Informal Assessment
✓ **Student Pages**

Did the student **UNDERSTANDING**
- ❑ make important observations?
- ❑ extend or generalize learning?
- ❑ provide insightful answers?
- ❑ pose insightful questions?

TEKS/TAKS Practice

Use *TEKS/TAKS Practice* page 13 to assess student progress.

B Summarize Findings

Analyze and summarize assessment data for each student. Determine which Assessment Follow-Up is appropriate for each student. Use the Student Assessment Record in *Texas Assessment* or *eAssess* to update assessment records.

C Texas Assessment Follow-Up ● DIFFERENTIATE INSTRUCTION

Based on your observations, use these teaching strategies for assessment follow-up.

INTERVENTION

Review student performance on *Intervention* Lesson 7.A to see if students have mastered prerequisite skills for this lesson.

1.2.A Separate a whole into two, three, or four equal parts and use appropriate language to describe the parts such as three out of four equal parts. **1.8** The student understands that time can be measured. The student uses time to describe and compare situations.

ENGLISH LEARNER

Review

Use Lesson 7.3 in *English Learner Support Guide* to review lesson concepts and vocabulary.

ENRICH

If . . . students are proficient in the lesson concepts,

Then . . . encourage them to work on the chapter projects or *Enrichment* Lesson 7.3.

Enrichment Lesson 7.3

TEXAS PRACTICE

If . . . students would benefit from additional practice,

Then . . . assign *Practice* Lesson 7.3.

Practice Lesson 7.3

RETEACH

If . . . students are having difficulty understanding fractions with numbers greater than 1 in the numerator,

Then . . . have them practice modeling these fractions by using their fraction tiles.

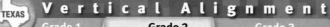
Grade 1	Grade 2	Grade 3
Number, operation, and quantitative reasoning 1.2.A Separate a whole into two, three, or four equal parts and use appropriate language to describe the parts such as three out of four equal parts	Number, operation, and quantitative reasoning 2.2.A Use concrete models to represent and name fractional parts of a whole object (with denominators of 12 or less).	Number, operation, and quantitative reasoning 3.2.C Use fraction names and symbols to describe fractional parts of whole objects or sets of objects.

Overview **LESSON 7.4**

TEXAS

Lesson Planner

OBJECTIVES
To introduce the concept of sixths and eighths

MATH TEKS
Number, operation, and quantitative reasoning 2.2.A 🔑
Use concrete models to represent and name fractional parts of a whole object (with denominators of 12 or less).

MATH TEKS INTEGRATION
Number, operation, and quantitative reasoning 2.3.B
Model addition and subtraction of two-digit numbers with objects, pictures, words, and numbers.

TECHNOLOGY
🖥 **Presentation** Lesson 7.4
🖥 **MathTools** Fractions

Sixths and Eighths

Context of the Lesson This is the fourth of an eleven-lesson sequence that develops concepts of fractions using a variety of models. In this lesson, students extend their understanding of halves, fourths, and thirds to sixths and eighths.

Planning for Learning ● DIFFERENTIATE INSTRUCTION

INTERVENTION

If . . . students lack the prerequisite skill of recognizing equal parts,

Then . . . teach *Intervention* Lesson 7.B.

🔲 1.2.A, 1.8

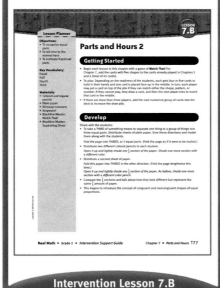

Intervention Lesson 7.B

ENGLISH LEARNER

Preview

If . . . students need language support,

Then . . . use Lesson 7.4 in *English Learner Support Guide* to preview lesson concepts and vocabulary.

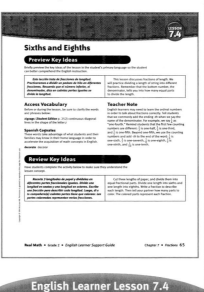

English Learner Lesson 7.4

ENRICH

If . . . students are proficient in the lesson concepts,

Then . . . emphasize Guided Discussion in Reflect.

PRACTICE

If . . . students would benefit from additional practice,

Then . . . extend Skill Building before assigning the student pages.

RETEACH

If . . . students are having difficulty understanding sixths and eighths,

Then . . . extend Guided Discussion before assigning the student pages.

Academic Vocabulary
eighth \ātth\ *n.* one of eight equal parts into which something is or can be divided

sixth \siksth\ *n.* one of six equal parts into which something is or can be divided

Access Vocabulary
zigzags continuous diagonal lines in the shape of the letter *z*

Spanish Cognates
decorate decorar

---

*Manipulative Kit Item 🔑= Key standard

⭐ = 120-Day Plan for TAKS

Teaching Lesson 7.4

Math TEKS
Number, operation, and quantitative reasoning 2.2.A
Use concrete models to represent and name fractional parts of a whole object (with denominators of 12 or less)

Mental Math 5

 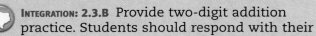

INTEGRATION: 2.3.B Provide two-digit addition practice. Students should respond with their **Number Cubes,** using the find, hide, and show routine. Possible examples include the following:

a. 41 + 41 = 82   **b.** 61 + 29 = 90   **c.** 82 + 8 = 90
d. 59 + 21 = 80   **e.** 25 + 25 = 50   **f.** 73 + 17 = 90
g. 19 + 29 = 48   **h.** 20 + 30 = 50   **i.** 13 + 57 = 70

1 Develop 25

Tell Students In Today's Lesson They Will
learn about sixths and eighths.

Guided Discussion UNDERSTANDING Introductory

 Sixths
Have students get the paper strips ($\frac{1}{2}$, $\frac{1}{4}$, and $\frac{1}{3}$) they folded and labeled in Lesson 7.2. Students can refer to the folds in their strips to help guide them in today's discussion of sixths.

On the board, draw a two-column table. Label one column *fraction* and the other column *number of pieces.*

Start by writing $\frac{1}{2}$ in the first column.

■ **How many halves can a whole piece of string be divided into?** two

Fill in the answer in the appropriate column.

Next write $\frac{1}{4}$.

■ **How many quarters or fourths can a whole piece of string be divided into?** four

Fill in the answer in the appropriate column.

Then write $\frac{1}{3}$.

■ **How many thirds can a whole piece of string be divided into?** three

Continue filling in the table appropriately.

Next write $\frac{1}{6}$. Explain that this is read as *one-sixth.*

■ **Critical Thinking How many sixths do you think a whole piece of string can be divided into?** six

Have students look for relationships or patterns in the numbers on the table and share their observations. Students should see that the denominators in one column match the number of pieces in the other column.

Distribute a new paper strip (equal in size to the previous strips).

■ **Critical Thinking Does anyone have an idea how to divide the strip into sixths?**

If students are unsure, remind them how they divided halves into fourths.

Have a student demonstrate folding thirds into halves to become sixths.

Then have another student fold halves into thirds. Have students compare their strips side by side so the whole class can see.

After all students have divided their strips into sixths, have them label each part $\frac{1}{6}$.

■ **Are the strips the same?** yes

Allow students to decide how to fold their strips.

Eighths
Return to the table and write $\frac{1}{8}$ under $\frac{1}{4}$. Explain that this fraction is read as *one-eighth.*

■ **How many eighths are in a whole piece of string?** eight

Distribute another paper strip to each student.

■ **Can you divide it into eighths?**

Have a student demonstrate dividing the strip into eighths by folding it into halves three times. After all students have divided their strips into eighths, have them label each part $\frac{1}{8}$.

Skill Building APPLYING Guided

 Have students work in pairs to cut five strings into halves, quarters, eighths, thirds, and sixths. After they have finished cutting, have them glue one fractional piece from each string onto a piece of construction paper. Have them order and label the fractional pieces from longest to shortest and label each piece with the appropriate fraction. Then have students compare these pieces to a whole piece of string.

2 Use Student Pages 20

Pages 251–252 UNDERSTANDING Independent

Have students complete pages 251 and 252 independently. To do exercises one through six, students can cut a paper strip as long as the red string and then fold it to find $\frac{1}{2}$, $\frac{1}{4}$, and $\frac{1}{8}$. Then they can match the paper strip with the pieces of string shown on the page.

Encourage students to use any method that makes sense to them, especially for $\frac{1}{3}$ and $\frac{1}{6}$, which are not as easy to find by folding. For example, to find what fraction the green piece is, students might cut strips or make markings on paper to see how many of those lengths it takes to equal the length of the red string.

Afterward, have students share and discuss their methods.

As Students Finish

Game Allow students to play any previously introduced game, or assign a game based on needed skill practice.

e MathTools Have students use **Fractions** to explore sixths and eighths.

Student Page

Sixths and Eighths

LESSON 7.4

Name _____ **Date** _____

Key Ideas

Math TEKS
Number, operation, and quantitative reasoning 2.2.A
Use concrete models to represent and name fractional parts of a whole object (with denominators of 12 or less).

The green section is one-sixth of the whole.

The orange section is one-eighth of the whole.

Each string is a fraction of the length of the red string.
Match each string with the correct fraction.

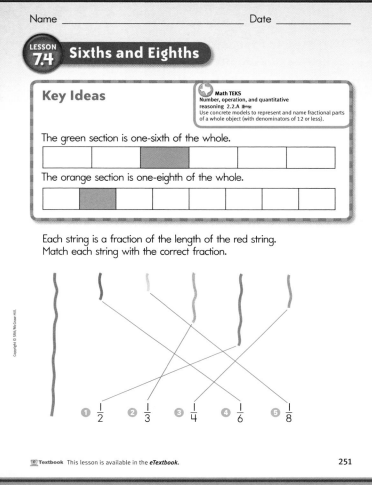

① $\frac{1}{2}$ ② $\frac{1}{3}$ ③ $\frac{1}{4}$ ④ $\frac{1}{6}$ ⑤ $\frac{1}{8}$

Textbook This lesson is available in the *eTextbook*. 251

Student Page

⑥ Manolita wants to share this sandwich with 7 friends. Draw lines to show where the sandwich should be cut to make 8 pieces of equal length.

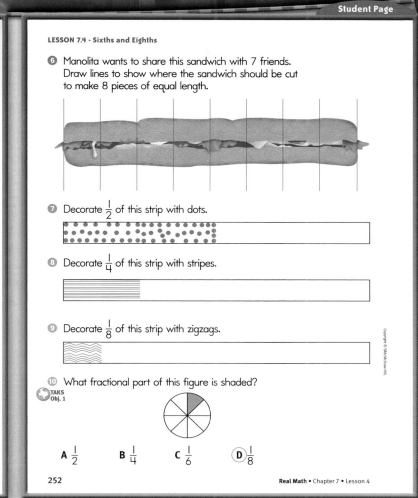

⑦ Decorate $\frac{1}{2}$ of this strip with dots.

⑧ Decorate $\frac{1}{4}$ of this strip with stripes.

⑨ Decorate $\frac{1}{8}$ of this strip with zigzags.

⑩ What fractional part of this figure is shaded?

TAKS Obj. 1

A $\frac{1}{2}$ **B** $\frac{1}{4}$ **C** $\frac{1}{6}$ **D** $\frac{1}{8}$

252   **Real Math** • Chapter 7 • Lesson 4

---

3 Reflect   10

Guided Discussion REASONING

Draw a rectangle on the board that has been divided into eight equal parts.

Have a volunteer come to the board and shade $\frac{1}{8}$ of the rectangle.

Have a second volunteer change the shading so $\frac{1}{4}$ of the rectangle is shaded.

■ **How many eighths are shaded now?** two

Have a third volunteer change the shading so $\frac{1}{2}$ of the rectangle is shaded.

■ **How many eighths are shaded now?** four

Finally have a fourth volunteer change the shading so the entire rectangle is shaded.

■ **How many eighths are shaded now?** eight

Discuss how students now know that $\frac{8}{8} = 1$. If time permits, follow the same pattern for a rectangle divided into sixths.

The concept of equivalent fractions is studied formally in Lesson 7 of this chapter.

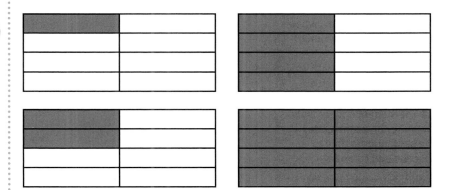

Cumulative Review: For cumulative review of previously learned skills, see page 259–260.

Family Involvement: Assign the *Practice, Reteach,* or *Enrichment* activities depending on the needs of your students. Have students look for things that are divided into sixths or eighths at home.

Chapter 7 • Lesson 4   **251–252**

Assess and Differentiate

 Assess Use *eAssess* to record and analyze evidence of student understanding.

A Gather Evidence

Use the Daily Class Assessment Records in *Texas Assessment* or *eAssess* to record daily observations.

Informal Assessment
☑ **Mental Math**
Did the student `COMPUTING`
- ❏ respond accurately?
- ❏ respond quickly?
- ❏ respond with confidence?
- ❏ self-correct?

Informal Assessment
☑ **Guided Discussion**
Did the student `UNDERSTANDING`
- ❏ make important observations?
- ❏ extend or generalize learning?
- ❏ provide insightful answers?
- ❏ pose insightful questions?

 TEKS/TAKS Practice
Use *TEKS/TAKS Practice* page 13 to assess student progress.

B Summarize Findings

Analyze and summarize assessment data for each student. Determine which Assessment Follow-Up is appropriate for each student. Use the Student Assessment Record in *Texas Assessment* or *eAssess* to update assessment records.

C Texas Assessment Follow-Up ● DIFFERENTIATE INSTRUCTION

Based on your observations, use these teaching strategies for assessment follow-up.

INTERVENTION	**ENRICH**	**PRACTICE**	**RETEACH**
Review student performance on *Intervention* Lesson 7.B to see if students have mastered prerequisite skills for this lesson. **1.2.A** Separate a whole into two, three, or four equal parts and use appropriate language to describe the parts such as three out of four equal parts. **1.8** The student understands that time can be measured. The student uses time to describe and compare situations.	**If . . .** students are proficient in the lesson concepts, **Then . . .** encourage them to work on the chapter projects or *Enrichment* Lesson 7.4.	**If . . .** students would benefit from additional practice, **Then . . .** assign *Practice* Lesson 7.4.	**If . . .** students are having difficulty with sixths and eighths, **Then . . .** have them find common items that are normally divided into sixths or eighths.

ENGLISH LEARNER
Review
Use Lesson 7.4 in *English Learner Support Guide* to review lesson concepts and vocabulary.

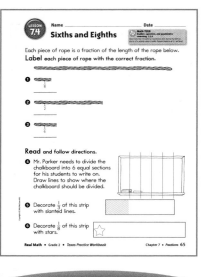

Enrichment Lesson 7.4

Practice Lesson 7.4

Grade 1	Grade 2	Grade 3
Number, operation, and quantitative reasoning 1.2.A Use appropriate language to describe part of a set such as three out of the eight crayons are red.	Number, operation, and quantitative reasoning 2.2.B Use concrete models to represent and name fractional parts of a set of objects (with denominators of 12 or less).	Number, operation, and quantitative reasoning 3.2.C Use fraction names and symbols to describe fractional parts of whole objects or sets of objects.

Overview LESSON **7.5**

TEXAS

Lesson Planner

OBJECTIVES
To reintroduce fractions of a set

MATH TEKS
Number, operation, and quantitative reasoning 2.2.B
Use concrete models to represent and name fractional parts of a whole object (with denominators of 12 or less).

MATH TEKS INTEGRATION
Number, operation, and quantitative reasoning 2.3.B
Model addition and subtraction of two-digit numbers with objects, pictures, words, and numbers.

MATERIALS
- *Number Cubes
- Cutouts of eight objects (such as apples or circles), six green and two red
- Masking tape
- *Counters
- Egg carton cut in half

TECHNOLOGY
- Presentation Lesson 7.5
- MathTools Fractions

Fractions of a Set

Context of the Lesson This is the fifth of an eleven-lesson sequence that develops concepts of fractions using a variety of models. This lesson reviews concepts of fractions as applied to parts of set models.

Planning for Learning ● DIFFERENTIATE INSTRUCTION

INTERVENTION
If . . . students lack the prerequisite skill of estimating fractional parts,

Then . . . teach *Intervention* Lesson 7.B.

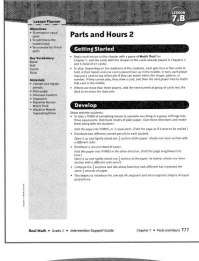

1.2.A, 1.8

Intervention Lesson 7.B

ENGLISH LEARNER
Preview

If . . . students need language support,

Then . . . use Lesson 7.5 in *English Learner Support Guide* to preview lesson concepts and vocabulary.

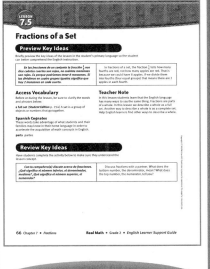

English Learner Lesson 7.5

ENRICH
If . . . students are proficient in the lesson concepts,

Then . . . emphasize Guided Discussion in Reflect.

PRACTICE
If . . . students would benefit from additional practice,

Then . . . extend Skill Building before assigning the student pages.

RETEACH
If . . . students are having difficulty understanding fractions of a set,

Then . . . extend Guided Discussion before assigning the student pages.

Access Vocabulary
a full set A set is a group of objects or numbers that go together.

Spanish Cognates
parts partes

Teaching Lesson 7.5

TEXAS

Math TEKS
Number, operation, and quantitative reasoning 2.2.B
Use concrete models to represent and name fractional
parts of a set of objects (with denominators of 12 or less

Mental Math 5

 INTEGRATION: 2.3.B Provide students with practice in finding missing addends. Students should respond with their **Number Cubes,** using the find, hide, and show routine. Possible examples include the following:

a. 30 + __30__ = 60   b. 20 + __40__ = 60   c. 50 + __10__ = 60
d. 10 + __50__ = 60   e. 40 + __20__ = 60   f. 55 + __5__ = 60

1 Develop 25

Tell Students In Today's Lesson They Will
learn about fractions of a set of objects.

Guided Discussion UNDERSTANDING Introductory

Begin by showing students a group of four cutout apples (or whatever cutout object you used)—one red and three green—arranged on the board in a 2 × 2 array. Stick the apples to the board with masking tape.

Remind students that the fractions they are studying refer to a part of a whole, explaining that when you divide a shape, the shape is the whole. When you divide a group of objects, the group is the whole.

Tell students that you want to divide this whole group of apples into fourths. Write 4 on the board to represent fourths, and write a fraction line above it.

■ **How many fourths of this whole group of apples are red?** 1

Write 1 on the board above the fraction line to make $\frac{1}{4}$.

■ **What fraction of the apples is red?** $\frac{1}{4}$
■ **What fraction is not red?** $\frac{3}{4}$

Next add four more apples to the group—three green apples and another red apple. Tell students that you are going to divide this group of apples into fourths, and write 4 on the board to represent fourths.

■ **Critical Thinking** **How many fourths of this whole group of apples are red?** 1; however, at this point, many of the students will probably answer 2.

Draw a vertical line and a horizontal line to divide the apples visually into fourths. Make sure both red apples are in the same fourth. Tell students that if the whole group of apples is divided into fourths, that means it is divided into four equal groups. For this whole group, we want to know about how many fourths are red, not how many apples are red.

■ **How many fourths are red?** 1

■ **How many apples are red?** 2

Write a 1 above the 4 with a fraction line, and ask students the following:

■ **What fraction of this whole group of apples is red?** $\frac{1}{4}$
■ **What fraction of this whole group of apples is green?** $\frac{3}{4}$

Write $\frac{3}{4}$ on the board.

Next draw six circles on the board. Tell students that these circles represent half a carton of eggs, or show students half of an egg carton.

■ **How many eggs are in the half a carton?** 6
■ **How many eggs would be in a full carton?** 12

Draw the remaining six circles on the board. If students are unsure or seem confused, ask the following:

■ **How many eggs would be in the other half?** 6
■ **Then how many eggs are there in all?** 12
■ **Does the whole carton have twelve eggs?** yes
■ **How many eggs would be in half a carton?** 6
■ **How could you divide the carton into thirds?** Divide the carton into 3 equal parts.
■ **How many eggs would be in each third of the carton?** 4 Note: Students may be confused because the one in the numerator may be confused with the number of apples in the set.

Skill Building APPLYING   Guided

 Have students work in pairs or small groups to make sets with counters. One student should make a set of 2, 4, 6, 8, 10, or 12 with counters of all the same color. Then have another student substitute some of the counters with a different color counter to illustrate either $\frac{1}{2}$, $\frac{1}{4}$, $\frac{1}{3}$, $\frac{1}{6}$, or $\frac{1}{8}$ of the set. The first student then says what fraction of the set is now a different color and what fraction of the set is the original color. To expand the activity, encourage students to start with a larger set, such as 18 or 24, or create fractions that do not have a numerator of 1, such as $\frac{2}{3}$ or $\frac{3}{4}$.

2 Use Student Pages 20

Pages 253–254 UNDERSTANDING Independent

Have students complete pages 253 and 254 independently.

As Students Finish

Game Allow students to play any previously introduced game, or assign a game based on needed skill practice.

 MathTools Have students use **Fractions** to explore fractions.

RESEARCH IN ACTION

"Equal portioning of both discrete and continuous quantities to solve fair-sharing problems can provide a key informal basis for understanding fractions. For instance, trying to share three cookies between two children can give rise to dividing each of the cookies into two equal-size pieces."

Baroody, Arthur J. "The Developmental Bases for Early Childhood Number and Operations Standards" in Clements, Douglas and J. Sarama, eds. *Engaging Young Children in Mathematics: Standards for Early Childhood Mathematics Education.* Mahwah, New Jersey: Lawrence Erlbaum Associates, Publishers, 2004, p. 210.

Student Page

Name _____ Date _____

LESSON 7.5 Fractions of a Set

Key Ideas

Math TEKS
Number, operation, and quantitative reasoning 2.2.B
Use concrete models to represent and name fractional parts of a set of objects (with denominators of 12 or less).

$\frac{1}{4}$ of this group of apples is red.

$\frac{1}{4}$ of this group of apples is red.

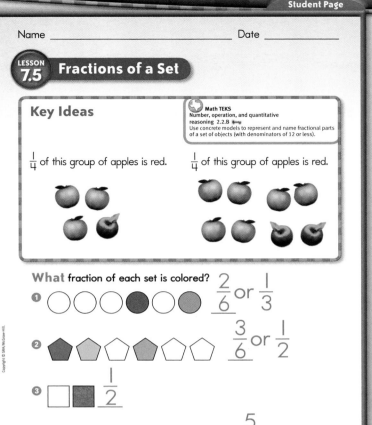

What fraction of each set is colored?

① $\frac{2}{6}$ or $\frac{1}{3}$

② $\frac{3}{6}$ or $\frac{1}{2}$

③ $\frac{1}{2}$

④  $\frac{5}{6}$

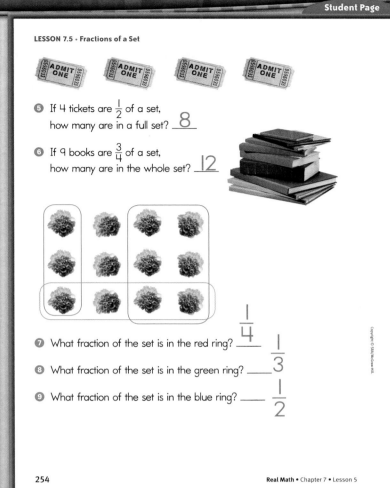

⑤ If 4 tickets are $\frac{1}{2}$ of a set, how many are in a full set? __8__

⑥ If 9 books are $\frac{3}{4}$ of a set, how many are in the whole set? _12_

⑦ What fraction of the set is in the red ring? $\frac{1}{4}$

⑧ What fraction of the set is in the green ring? $\frac{1}{3}$

⑨ What fraction of the set is in the blue ring? $\frac{1}{2}$

---

③ Reflect 5

Guided Discussion REASONING

Select four students to come to the front of the room. Give one student a book to hold.

■ **What fraction of the students is holding a book?** $\frac{1}{4}$

Now have the student give the book to one of the other students.

■ **Critical Thinking Now what fraction of students is holding a book?** $\frac{1}{4}$

Repeat once more so students see that no matter who holds the book, the fraction of students holding the book does not change.

Now add a second book to the group.

■ **What fraction of students is holding a book?** $\frac{2}{4}$ or $\frac{1}{2}$
■ **What fraction is not holding a book?** $\frac{2}{4}$ or $\frac{1}{2}$

Redistribute the books to different students in the group.

■ **Now what fraction of students is holding a book?** $\frac{2}{4}$ or $\frac{1}{2}$

Repeat with three books and then four books. Through discussion, emphasize that the fraction of students holding a book does not change if the books are in different places. Also emphasize that the combined fraction of students holding books and students not holding books should always be $\frac{4}{4}$.

TEXAS TEKS Checkup

Number, operation, and quantitative reasoning 2.2.B Use concrete models to represent and name fractional parts of a set of objects (with denominators of 12 or less).

Use this problem to assess students' progress towards standards mastery:

Which shows $\frac{1}{3}$ of this set of triangles?

Have students choose the correct answer, then describe how they knew which choice was correct.

■ **How would you represent thirds?** each set of 2 triangles is $\frac{1}{3}$ of the set

■ **Why can you eliminate Choices A and B?** one row of 3 triangles is $\frac{1}{2}$ of the set

Follow-Up
If...students have difficulty recognizing fractions of a whole,

Then...have students explore fractions use the *eMathTools: Fraction* to explore fractions.

 Assess and Differentiate

 Assess Use *eAssess* to record and analyze evidence of student understanding.

A Gather Evidence

Use the Daily Class Assessment Records in *Texas Assessment* or *eAssess* to record daily observations.

Informal Assessment
☑ **Guided Discussion**

Did the student **UNDERSTANDING**
- ❏ make important observations?
- ❏ extend or generalize learning?
- ❏ provide insightful answers?
- ❏ pose insightful questions?

Informal Assessment
☑ **Skill Building**

Did the student **APPLYING**
- ❏ apply learning in new situations?
- ❏ contribute concepts?
- ❏ contribute answers?
- ❏ connect mathematics to real-world situations?

 TEKS/TAKS Practice

Use *TEKS/TAKS Practice* page 13 to assess student progress.

B Summarize Findings

Analyze and summarize assessment data for each student. Determine which Assessment Follow-Up is appropriate for each student. Use the Student Assessment Record in *Texas Assessment* or *eAssess* to update assessment records.

C Texas Assessment Follow-Up • DIFFERENTIATE INSTRUCTION

Based on your observations, use these teaching strategies for assessment follow-up.

INTERVENTION	ENRICH	PRACTICE	RETEACH
Review student performance on *Intervention* Lesson 7.B to see if students have mastered prerequisite skills for this lesson.	**If . . .** students are proficient in the lesson concepts,	**If . . .** students would benefit from additional practice,	**If . . .** students struggle finding fractional parts,
1.2.A Separate a whole into two, three, or four equal parts and use appropriate language to describe the parts such as three out of four equal parts. **1.8** The student understands that time can be measured. The student uses time to describe and compare situations.	**Then . . .** encourage them to work on the chapter projects or *Enrichment* Lesson 7.5.	**Then . . .** assign *Practice* Lesson 7.5.	**Then . . .** have them review fraction recognition of $\frac{1}{2}$, $\frac{1}{3}$, $\frac{1}{4}$, $\frac{1}{6}$, and $\frac{1}{8}$ by using flash cards. Then use 48 counters, and divide into halves, thirds, fourths, sixths, or eighths.

ENGLISH LEARNER

Review

Use Lesson 7.5 in *English Learner Support Guide* to review lesson concepts and vocabulary.

Enrichment Lesson 7.5

Practice Lesson 7.5

Grade 1	Grade 2	Grade 3
Number, operation, and quantitative reasoning 1.2.A Separate a whole into two, three, or four equal parts and use appropriate language to describe the parts such as three out of four equal parts	Number, operation, and quantitative reasoning 2.2.A Use concrete models to represent and name fractional parts of a whole object (with denominators of 12 or less).	Number, operation, and quantitative reasoning 3.2.C Use fraction names and symbols to describe fractional parts of whole objects or sets of objects.

Overview — LESSON 7.6

TEXAS

Lesson Planner

OBJECTIVES
- To introduce the concept of fifths
- To introduce the **Fraction Game,** which helps develop mathematical reasoning with fractions
- To informally introduce the addition of common fractions with an emphasis on those that sum to more than $\frac{1}{2}$, less than $\frac{1}{2}$, or $\frac{1}{2}$

MATH TEKS
Number, operation, and quantitative reasoning 2.2.A
Use concrete models to represent and name fractional parts of a whole object (with denominators of 12 or less).
Number, operation, and quantitative reasoning 2.2.C
Use concrete models to determine if a fractional part of a whole is closer to 0, $\frac{1}{2}$, or 1.

MATH TEKS INTEGRATION
Number, operation, and quantitative reasoning 2.3.B
Model addition and subtraction of two-digit numbers with objects, pictures, words, and numbers.

MATERIALS
- *Number Cubes
- *Fraction Game Mat
- Colored pencils

TECHNOLOGY
- **Presentation** Lesson 7.6
- **Games** Fraction Game
- **MathTools** Fractions

Looking Ahead
In Lesson 7.7 students will need blank paper fraction strips like those used in Lessons 7.2 and 7.4.

Fifths ★

Context of the Lesson This is the sixth of an eleven-lesson sequence that develops concepts of fractions using a variety of models. In this lesson, students are introduced to fifths by using area, linear, and set models. Students also use fifths when playing the **Fraction Game.** The **Fraction Game** informally introduces equivalent fractions, which will be covered in Lesson 7.7.

Planning for Learning • DIFFERENTIATE INSTRUCTION

INTERVENTION
If . . . students lack the prerequisite skill of telling time to the nearest hour,

Then . . . teach **Intervention** Lesson 7.B.

1.2.A, 1.8

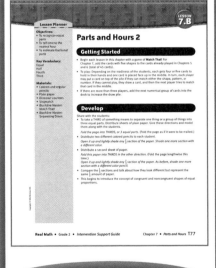

Intervention Lesson 7.B

ENGLISH LEARNER
Preview

If . . . students need language support,

Then . . . use Lesson 7.6 in **English Learner Support Guide** to preview lesson concepts and vocabulary.

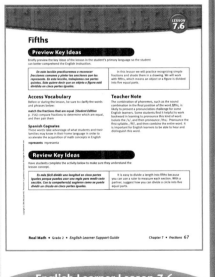

English Learner Lesson 7.6

ENRICH
If . . . students are proficient in the lesson concepts,

Then . . . emphasize additional game time.

PRACTICE
If . . . students would benefit from additional practice,

Then . . . extend Skill and Strategy Building before assigning the student pages.

RETEACH
If . . . students are having difficulty understanding fifths,

Then . . . extend Guided Discussion before assigning the student pages.

Academic Vocabulary
fifth \fifth\ n. one of five equal parts into which something is or can be divided

Access Vocabulary
match the fractions that are equal compare fractions to determine which are equal, and then pair them

Spanish Cognates
represents representa

---

*Manipulative Kit Item — = Key standard

★ = 120-Day Plan for TAKS

Teaching Lesson 7.6

Math TEKS
Number, operation, and quantitative reasoning 2.2.A
Use concrete models to represent and name fractional parts of a whole object (with denominators of 12 or less).
Number, operation, and quantitative reasoning 2.2.C
Use concrete models to determine if a fractional part of a whole is closer to 0, $\frac{1}{2}$, or 1.

Mental Math 5

INTEGRATION: 2.3.B Provide students with practice finding missing addends. Students should respond with their **Number Cubes,** using the find, hide, and show routine. Possible examples include the following:

a. 59 + <u>1</u> = 60   **b.** 1 + <u>59</u> = 60   **c.** 50 + <u>10</u> = 60
d. 59 + <u>11</u> = 70   **e.** 57 + <u>3</u> = 60   **f.** 58 + <u>20</u> = 78

1 Develop 25

Tell Students In Today's Lesson They Will
learn about fifths.

Guided Discussion REASONING

  Introductory

Ask students questions such as the following:

■ **How many equal shares will you have if you divide something into halves?** two
■ **How many equal shares will you have if you divide something into fourths?** four
■ **How many equal shares will you have if you divide something into thirds?** three **Sixths?** six **Eighths?** eight
■ **Critical Thinking** **What would it mean to divide something into fifths?** to make five equal parts

Draw a large rectangle on the board. Ask a student to divide the rectangle into fifths. Estimating fifths is difficult, so allow time for class discussion and corrections. Next ask a student to shade $\frac{1}{5}$. Write $\frac{1}{5}$ on the board. Ask another student to shade $\frac{1}{5}$. Erase the shading, and ask someone to come up and shade $\frac{2}{5}$. Write $\frac{2}{5}$ on the board. Now ask someone to come up and shade $\frac{5}{5}$. Write $\frac{5}{5}$ on the board.

Draw another rectangle on the board, and divide it into fifths. Point out that $\frac{2}{5}$ can be shown many different ways. Shade in two nonadjacent fifths.

Skill and Strategy Building ENGAGING

  Guided

 Fraction Game

Introduce the **Fraction Game** to provide practice in recognizing fractional areas up to fifths. Demonstrate the game by playing a round in front of the class with a student. Students will play as they finish the student pages.

Because students play this game in pairs, they can use the game page in their books for two games. An extra version of this game is also on page 125 of **Practice** if you wish to make copies.

Principal Skills: recognizing fractional areas of a circle, recognizing which fractional areas are more than half the area of a circle when combined

Players: two

Materials: student page 256, two different colored pencils, two 0–5 **Number Cubes**

How to Play:

1. Player One rolls both cubes. If either cube shows 0, the player loses that turn.
2. The larger number on the two cubes is the denominator, and the smaller number is the numerator. For example, a player who rolls a 4 and a 5 may color four sections of a circle that is divided into fifths. If the player chooses, the four-fifths may be divided among 2, 3, or 4 different circles.
3. Players take turns rolling, and each uses a different color to shade their sections.
4. A circle is won when a player has shaded more than half of it. That player puts his or her initials next to the circle to denote a win.
5. If a circle is divided equally by both players, the circle is a tie, and neither player wins it.
6. Play continues until all circles have been won or declared ties. The player with more circles is the winner.

Note: As students play this game, they may want to use equivalent fractions, for example, counting $\frac{2}{4}$ as $\frac{1}{2}$. Do not push equivalent fractions, but if students ask, allow the class to discuss changing the rules to allow them and let the class take a vote on how the game should be played.

2 Use Student Pages 20

Pages 255–256 UNDERSTANDING

 Independent

Have students complete page 255 independently.

As Students Finish

   Have students play the **Fraction Game** on page 256 in pairs.

 **Games** *Fraction Game*

MathTools Have students use **Fractions** to explore fifths.

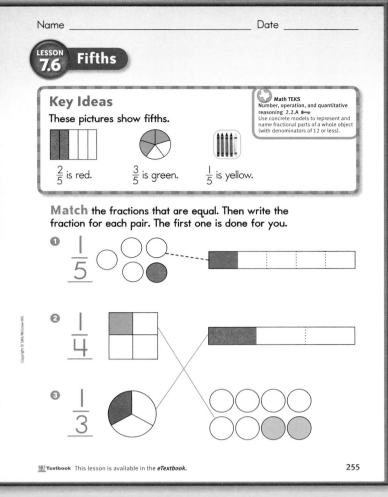

Student Page

LESSON 7.6 Fifths

Name _____ Date _____

Key Ideas

These pictures show fifths.

Math TEKS
Number, operation, and quantitative reasoning 2.2.A
Use concrete models to represent and name fractional parts of a whole object (with denominators of 12 or less).

$\frac{2}{5}$ is red. $\frac{3}{5}$ is green. $\frac{1}{5}$ is yellow.

Match the fractions that are equal. Then write the fraction for each pair. The first one is done for you.

1. $\frac{1}{5}$

2. $\frac{1}{4}$

3. $\frac{1}{3}$

Textbook This lesson is available in the *eTextbook*.   255

Fifths — LESSON 7.6

Student Page

Game

Math TEKS
Number, operation, and quantitative reasoning 2.2.C
Use concrete models to determine if a fractional part of a whole is closer to 0, $\frac{1}{2}$, or 1.

Fraction Game

Game Use these circles to play the **Fraction Game**.

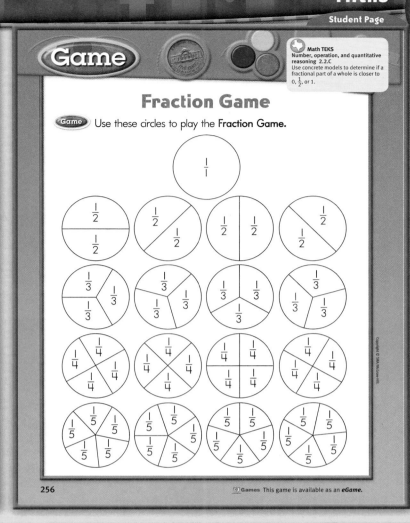

256   *Games* This game is available as an *eGame*.

---

3 Reflect   10

Guided Discussion REASONING

Based on their experience playing the **Fraction Game**, have students identify fractions that have a sum of more than $\frac{1}{2}$. For example, how many fifths would students need to have more than $\frac{1}{2}$? 3

Identify fractions that have a sum of less than $\frac{1}{2}$. For example, how many fifths can you have and still have less than $\frac{1}{2}$? 2 or 1

Then have students identify fractions that have a sum of exactly $\frac{1}{2}$. For example, how many fourths equal $\frac{1}{2}$? 2

Do not expect students to mix different denominators when adding the fractions.

TEXAS — TEKS Checkup

Number, operation, and quantitative reasoning 2.2.A Use concrete models to represent and name fractional parts of a whole object (with denominators of 12 or less).

Use this problem to assess students' progress towards standards mastery:

Which shows $\frac{3}{5}$?

 A   B

C   D

Have students choose the correct answer, then describe how they knew which choice was correct.

- **Which two choices do not show the circle in fifths?** Choice C is in fourths, Choice D is in eighths
- **To show $\frac{3}{5}$ are there 3 parts shaded or 3 parts unshaded?** shaded

Follow-Up
If... students have difficulty recognizing fractions of a whole,

Then... have students play the **Fraction Game** found on page 256 of the student edition.

Math Puzzler: Marcus folded a sheet of paper in half. Then he folded it in half again. Then he opened the paper, took a pair of scissors, and cut along all the creases he had made by folding the paper. How many pieces of paper did Marcus end up with? 4

Chapter 7 • Lesson 6   **255–256**

Assess and Differentiate

 Assess Use *eAssess* to record and analyze evidence of student understanding.

A Gather Evidence

Use the Daily Class Assessment Records in *Texas Assessment* or *eAssess* to record daily observations.

Performance Assessment	**Informal Assessment**
☑ **Game**	☑ **Guided Discussion**
Did the student **ENGAGING**	Did the student **REASONING**
❑ pay attention to others' contributions?	❑ provide a clear explanation?
❑ contribute information and ideas?	❑ communicate reasons and strategies?
❑ improve on a strategy?	❑ choose appropriate strategies?
❑ reflect on and check the accuracy of his or her work?	❑ argue logically?

 **TEKS/TAKS Practice**

Use *TEKS/TAKS Practice* page 13 to assess student progress.

B Summarize Findings

Analyze and summarize assessment data for each student. Determine which Assessment Follow-Up is appropriate for each student. Use the Student Assessment Record in *Texas Assessment* or *eAssess* to update assessment records.

C Texas Assessment Follow-Up • DIFFERENTIATE INSTRUCTION

Based on your observations, use these teaching strategies for assessment follow-up.

INTERVENTION

Review student performance on *Intervention* Lesson 7.B to see if students have mastered prerequisite skills for this lesson.

1.2.A Separate a whole into two, three, or four equal parts and use appropriate language to describe the parts such as three out of four equal parts. **1.8** The student understands that time can be measured. The student uses time to describe and compare situations.

ENGLISH LEARNER

Review

Use Lesson 7.6 in *English Learner Support Guide* to review lesson concepts and vocabulary.

ENRICH

If . . . students are proficient in the lesson concepts,

Then . . . encourage them to work on the chapter projects or *Enrichment* Lesson 7.6.

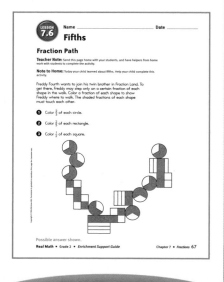

Enrichment Lesson 7.6

TEXAS PRACTICE

If . . . students would benefit from additional practice,

Then . . . assign *Practice* Lesson 7.6.

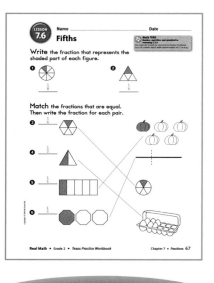

Practice Lesson 7.6

RETEACH

If . . . students have confused fifths with all the other fractions they have learned,

Then . . . have them use string or *Number Strips* to compare fifths with halves, thirds, fourths, sixths, and eighths.

Problem Solving 7.B Comparing Strategies

Objectives
- To explore the Make a Physical Model and Draw a Picture strategies
- To provide practice solving an open-ended, nonroutine problem involving fractions

Materials
- White paper, 2 or 3 sheets per student
- Scissors
- Graph paper, 2 or 3 sheets per student
- Colored markers, crayons, or watercolors—green, blue, red, and yellow for each student
- Tiles or cubes, about 40 of each color per group
- See Appendix A page A24 a rubric for problem solving.

Context of the Lesson Reasoning and problem solving are prevalent in every *Real Math* lesson. This lesson and other special problem-solving lessons allow more time for students to share and compare their strategies. While continuing the museum theme from the Chapter Introduction, this lesson also provides opportunities for students to apply what they've learned about fractions and to explore uses of fractions.

1 Develop 5

Tell Students In Today's Lesson They Will
use fractions to create a design for an art museum.

Guided Discussion

Have students look at the graph and the illustration at the top of page 257. Ask students to recall surveys they have taken and graphs they have made that display the results of those surveys. Explain that the graph shows which color people said was their favorite. Ask students to describe the results displayed in the graph.

Present this problem to students:

The Rainbow Art Museum conducted a survey to find out the favorite colors of people who visited the museum. It turned out that $\frac{1}{2}$ of the visitors chose green, $\frac{1}{4}$ of the visitors chose blue, $\frac{1}{8}$ chose red, and $\frac{1}{8}$ chose yellow. The museum is having a contest to design a painting that shows the results of the survey. The painting must be $\frac{1}{2}$ green, $\frac{1}{4}$ blue, $\frac{1}{8}$ red, and $\frac{1}{8}$ yellow. What design will you create? How will you be sure it has the correct fraction of each color?

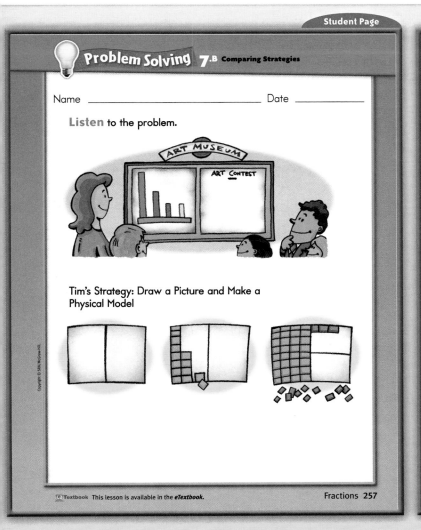

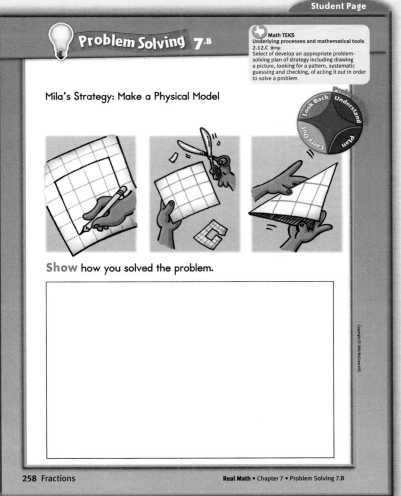

Number, operation, and quantitative reasoning 2.2.A
Model, create, and describe multiplication situations in which equivalent sets of concrete objects are joined.

Underlying processes and mathematical tools 2.12.C
Select or develop an appropriate problem-solving plan or strategy including drawing a picture, looking for a pattern, systematic guessing and checking, or acting it out in order to solve a problem.

---

2 Use Student Pages   25

Guided Discussion

Analyzing Sample Solution 1

Have students look at the picture on page 257 of Tim solving the problem. Ask questions about his strategy, such as the following:

- **In the first picture, why did Tim draw a line down the middle of the paper?** to divide the paper in half
- **Why is Tim filling in the half with green tiles?** to make half of his design green
- **In the third picture, why did Tim draw a line across the square?** to divide the square into four equal parts, or fourths
- **How will dividing the square into four equal parts help him?** He can fill one of the fourths with blue tiles to make sure that $\frac{1}{4}$ of his design is blue.
- **What might Tim do next?** Allow students to offer ideas. For example, he could draw a line to divide the remaining uncolored fourth in half and then fill one of those parts with red tiles and another with yellow tiles.
- **What might Tim do after he knows how many tiles of each color he will use?** Allow students to offer ideas; for example, he could make a design with the tiles and then draw the design on paper.

Analyzing Sample Solution 2

Tell students that Mila is using a different strategy to try to solve the problem. Have students look at the picture on page 258 of Mila's approach. Ask questions such as the following:

- **What do you think Mila is doing in the first picture?** drawing a square; drawing a 4-by-4 grid on graph paper
- **What is Mila doing in the second picture?** cutting out the 4-by-4 square
- **What is Mila doing in the third picture?** folding the square in half diagonally
- **Are there any other ways to fold the grid in half?** Yes; it could be folded vertically or horizontally.
- **What will Mila do after she folds the paper in half?** Allow students to offer ideas. She could color one of the sections green. Then she could fold it in half again to get fourths and color one of the fourths blue. Then she could fold it again to get eighths and color one of the eighths red and another yellow.
- **How will you try to solve this problem?** Allow students to share what they like about Mila's and Tim's strategies and what they would do differently.

Skill Building

Have students work on the problem individually or in pairs. They may use Mila's strategy, Tim's strategy, or one of their own. Provide support as needed, remembering to suggest approaches rather than showing them the answer. Remind students that they will need to be able to prove their picture has the correct fractions.

After students finish, have them use pictures, words, symbols, or a combination on the bottom of page 258 to show how they created their designs with the correct fractions.

---

3 Reflect   10

In discussion, bring out these points:
- Sometimes it helps to think of how one fractional part is related to another fractional part. For example, in making the design, you can use the facts that $\frac{1}{4}$ is half of $\frac{1}{2}$ and that $\frac{1}{8}$ is half of $\frac{1}{4}$.
- Some problems have many solutions.
- In this problem, the designs do not need to be the same size as long as each color is the correct part of the whole.

Sample Solutions Strategies

Students might use one or more of the following strategies instead of or in conjunction with the strategies presented on student pages 257 and 258.

Use Spatial Sense

Students might use the bar graph to help them see the relationships among the colors. By looking at the graph they might see that $\frac{1}{4}$ is half of $\frac{1}{2}$ and that $\frac{1}{8}$ is half of $\frac{1}{4}$, and they could use those relationships to help them create their designs.

Make a Diagram

Students might use Tim's strategy but without the tiles.

Work Backward/Make a Physical Model

Students might begin with the parts instead of the whole. They might use a pattern block or draw and cut out a figure to represent one-eighth of the design. Next they could make a design using eight of those pieces. Then they could color the sections with the appropriate colors.

---

4 Assess   10

When evaluating student work, focus not only on the correctness of the answer but also on whether the student thought rationally about the problem. Questions to consider include the following:
- Did the student understand the problem?
- Did the student understand the sample solution strategies?
- Was the student able to explain and illustrate his or her strategy?
- Did the student understand the relationships among $\frac{1}{2}$, $\frac{1}{4}$, and $\frac{1}{8}$?
- Did the student understand the relationship between the bar graph and the design?

Also note which students use particularly sophisticated or creative strategies.

CHAPTER 7

Cumulative Review

Use Pages 259–260

Use the Cumulative Review as a review of concepts and skills that students have previously learned.

Here are different ways that you can assign these problems to your students as they work through the chapter:

- With some of the lessons in the chapter, assign a set of cumulative review problems to be completed as practice or for homework.
  Lesson 7.1—Problems 1–3
  Lesson 7.2—Problem 4
  Lesson 7.3—Problems 5–8
  Lesson 7.4—Problems 9–10
  Lesson 7.5—Problem 11
  Lesson 7.6—Problems 12–17

- At any point during the chapter, assign part or all of the cumulative review problems to be completed as practice or for homework.

Cumulative Review

Problems 1–3 review near doubles in addition, Lesson 2.5. 2.5C

Problem 4 reviews subtracting tens, Lesson 6.2. 2.3B

Problems 5–8 review chain calculations in addition, Lesson 3.7. 2.3.A

Problems 9–10 review halves and fourths, Lesson 7.1. 2.2.A

Problem 11 reviews sixths and eighths, Lesson 7.4. 2.2.A

Problems 12–17 review two-digit addition, Lesson 5.5. 2.3.B

Progress Monitoring

If . . . students miss more than one problem in a section,   **Then . . .** refer to the indicated lesson for remediation suggestions.

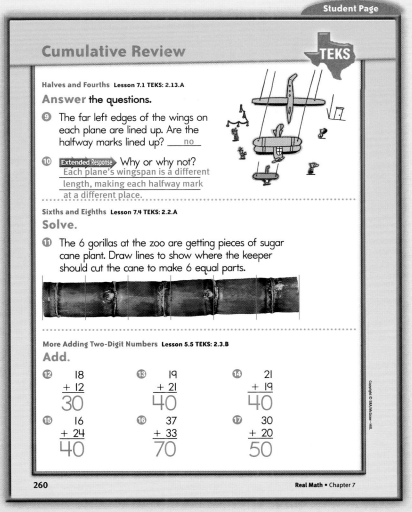

Individual Oral Assessment

Purpose of the Test

The Individual Oral Assessment is designed to measure students' growing knowledge of chapter concepts. It is administered individually to each student, and it requires oral responses from each student. The test takes about five minutes to complete. See *Texas Assessment* for detailed instructions for administering and interpreting the test, and record students' answers on the Student Assessment Recording Sheet.

Texas Assessment page 141

Directions

Read each question to the student, and record his or her oral response. If the student answers correctly, go to the next question. Stop when the student misses two questions at the same level. Students should not use scrap paper.

Materials

14 counters, 4 paper strips, fraction circles (2 sets)

Questions

Level 1: Prerequisite 2.4.B

1. (Give student counters.) Count 8 objects. Make 2 equal groups. 4 in each group

2. (Give student counters.) Count 14 objects. Make 2 equal groups. 7 in each group

3. (Give student counters.) Count 12 objects. Make 3 equal groups. 4 in each group

4. (Give student counters.) Count 12 objects. Make 4 equal groups. 3 in each group

Level 2: Basic 2.2.A

5. (Give student 1 paper strip.) Fold a paper strip to show halves. Fold to make 2 equal sections.

6. (Give student 1 paper strip.) Fold a paper strip to show fourths. Fold to make 4 equal sections.

7. (Give student 1 paper strip.) Fold a paper strip to show thirds. Fold to make 3 equal sections.

8. (Give student 1 paper strip.) Fold a paper strip to show sixths. Fold to make 6 equal sections.

Level 3: At Level 2.2.C

9. (Give student 1 set of fraction circles.) Use a fraction circle to show $\frac{5}{5}$. Point to $\frac{1}{5}$. fifths, $\frac{1}{5}$

10. (Give student 1 set of fraction circles.) Use a fraction circle to show $\frac{2}{2}$. Point to $\frac{1}{2}$. halves, $\frac{1}{2}$

11. (Give student 1 set of fraction circles.) Use a fraction circle to show $\frac{4}{4}$. Point to $\frac{1}{4}$. fourths, $\frac{1}{4}$

12. (Give student 1 set of fraction circles.) Use a fraction circle to show $\frac{3}{3}$. Point to $\frac{1}{3}$. thirds, $\frac{1}{3}$

Level 4: Challenge Application 2.2.A

13. What number is $\frac{1}{2}$ of 8? 4

14. What number is $\frac{1}{2}$ of 12? 6

15. What number is $\frac{1}{3}$ of 6? 2

16. What number is $\frac{1}{4}$ of 8? 2

Level 5: Content Beyond Mid-Chapter 2.2.A

17. (Give student 2 sets of fraction circles.) Use fraction circles to show $1\frac{1}{3}$. $1\frac{1}{3}$ or $\frac{4}{3}$

18. (Give student 2 sets of fraction circles.) Use fraction circles to show $1\frac{1}{4}$. $1\frac{1}{4}$ or $\frac{5}{4}$

19. (Give student 2 sets of fraction circles.) Use fraction circles to show $1\frac{2}{3}$. $1\frac{2}{3}$ or $\frac{5}{3}$

20. (Give student 2 sets of fraction circles.) Use fraction circles to show $1\frac{2}{6}$. $1\frac{2}{6}$ or $\frac{8}{6}$

TEXAS

Vertical Alignment

Grade 1
Number, operation, and quantitative reasoning 1.2.B Use appropriate language to describe part of a set such as three out of the eight crayons are red.

Grade 2
Number, operation, and quantitative reasoning 2.2.B Use concrete models to represent and name fractional parts of a set of objects (with denominators of 12 or less).

Grade 3
Number, operation, and quantitative reasoning 3.2.C Use fraction names and symbols to describe fractional parts of whole objects or sets of objects.

Overview

LESSON 7.7

TEXAS

Lesson Planner

OBJECTIVES
To introduce the concept of equivalent fractions

MATH TEKS
Number, operation, and quantitative reasoning 2.2.B
Use concrete models to represent and name fractional parts of a whole object (with denominators of 12 or less).

MATH TEKS INTEGRATION
Number, operation, and quantitative reasoning 2.3.B
Model addition and subtraction of two-digit numbers with objects, pictures, words, and numbers.

MATERIALS
- *Number Cubes
- Paper strips
- *Fraction Game Mat
- Colored pencils

TECHNOLOGY
- e Presentation Lesson 7.7
- e Games Fraction Game
- e MathTools Fractions

Equivalent Fractions ★

Context of the Lesson This is the seventh of an eleven-lesson sequence that develops concepts of fractions using a variety of models. Students were informally introduced to equivalent fractions in Lesson 7.6 when playing the **Fraction Game**. However, many students might not yet fully understand that concept. In this lesson, students gain an understanding of equivalent fractions by using a variety of models to generate different names for fractions. For example, $\frac{1}{2}$, $\frac{2}{4}$, or $\frac{4}{8}$; or $\frac{1}{3}$, $\frac{2}{6}$, or $\frac{4}{12}$.

Planning for Learning ● DIFFERENTIATE INSTRUCTION

INTERVENTION
If . . . students lack the prerequisite skill of recognizing equal parts,

Then . . . teach *Intervention* Lesson 7.B.

 1.2.A, 1.8

Intervention Lesson 7.B

ENGLISH LEARNER
Preview

If . . . students need language support,

Then . . . use Lesson 7.7 in *English Learner Support Guide* to preview lesson concepts and vocabulary.

English Learner Lesson 7.7

ENRICH
If . . . students are proficient in the lesson concepts,

Then . . . emphasize additional game time.

PRACTICE
If . . . students would benefit from additional practice,

Then . . . extend Skill Practice before assigning the student pages.

RETEACH
If . . . students are having difficulty understanding equivalent fractions,

Then . . . extend Guided Discussion before assigning student pages.

Access Vocabulary
farther a comparison of distance; we don't say *more far* or *farrer*.

Spanish Cognates
equality igualdad

---

*Manipulative Kit Item ⚷ = Key standard

★ = 120-Day Plan for TAKS

Teaching Lesson 7.7

TEXAS

Math TEKS
Number, operation and quantitative reasoning 2.2.B
Use concrete models to represent and name fractional parts of a set of objects (with denominators of 12 or less).

Mental Math 5

 INTEGRATION: 2.3.B Provide students with practice finding missing addends. Students should respond with their **Number Cubes,** using the find, hide, and show routine. Possible examples include the following:

a. $23 + \underline{77} = 100$ **b.** $12 + \underline{18} = 30$ **c.** $55 + \underline{45} = 100$
d. $60 + \underline{14} = 74$ **e.** $19 + \underline{11} = 30$ **f.** $21 + \underline{19} = 40$

1 Develop 25

Tell Students In Today's Lesson They Will
use different fraction names to describe the same part.

Guided Discussion UNDERSTANDING 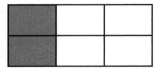 Introductory

Equality of Fractions

 Distribute one paper strip to each student. Have students fold it into halves. Write $\frac{1}{2}$ on the board. Have students unfold the strips and color half the paper strips.

Next have students fold their strips into fourths. Before they unfold, ask questions such as the following:

■ **How many sections will the strip now be divided into?** four
■ **How many will be colored?** two

Write their answers on the board. Have them unfold the strip and count how many fourths are colored.

■ **What other fractional name can be given to the part of the strip that is colored?** $\frac{2}{4}$

Write $\frac{2}{4}$.

Have students fold their strips into eighths. Again, before they unfold, ask the following:

■ **How many sections will the strip be folded into?** 8
■ **How many will be colored?** four **Critical Thinking How do you know?** because $\frac{4}{8}$ equals $\frac{1}{2}$
■ **What fractional name can now be given to the shaded part?** $\frac{4}{8}$ Write $\frac{4}{8}$.
■ **Is the part you originally colored still the same?** yes **Critical Thinking Why?** Emphasize that even though the colored part did not change, it now has three fractional names referring to it.

Area Models

 Draw a rectangle on the board, and divide it into thirds by drawing two vertical lines. Shade one-third.

■ **What fraction of the rectangle is shaded?** $\frac{1}{3}$

Write $\frac{1}{3}$. Next divide the rectangle into sixths by drawing one horizontal line.

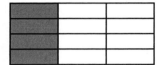

■ **What fractional name could now be given to the shaded part?** $\frac{2}{6}$

Write $\frac{2}{6}$ on the board. Now divide the rectangle into twelfths by drawing two more horizontal lines.

■ **What fractional name could now be given to the shaded part?** $\frac{4}{12}$

Now write $\frac{4}{12}$ on the board.

■ **Did the shaded part remain the same?** yes

Fractions of a Set

Draw a 2 × 3 array of figures on the board. Ask a student to circle $\frac{1}{2}$ the shapes (3 out of 6). Ask another student to come up and circle $\frac{3}{6}$ of the shapes (again, 3 out of 6).

■ **How many shapes did each person circle?** 3

Skill Practice REASONING Guided

Have students work in pairs or small groups. Have one student write a fraction. Then have another student write an equivalent fraction. Have the first student then try to write a second equivalent fraction. Then switch roles, and repeat.

2 Use Student Pages 20

Pages 261–262 UNDERSTANDING   Independent

Have students work with a partner while using their paper strips to complete pages 261 and 262.

As Students Finish

Game Have students play the **Fraction Game** in pairs.

e Games *Fraction Game*

e MathTools Have students use *Fractions* to explore equivalent fractions.

Name _____ Date _____

Equivalent Fractions

Key Ideas

A whole figure can be divided into fractions in many ways.

Math TEKS
Number, operation, and quantitative reasoning 2.2.B
Use concrete models to represent and name fractional parts of a set of objects (with denominators of 12 or less).

$\frac{1}{2}$	$\frac{1}{2}$

$\frac{1}{4}$	$\frac{1}{4}$	$\frac{1}{2}$

All the fraction strips below are the same length but are divided into different parts.

Write a fraction on each part of the fraction strips.

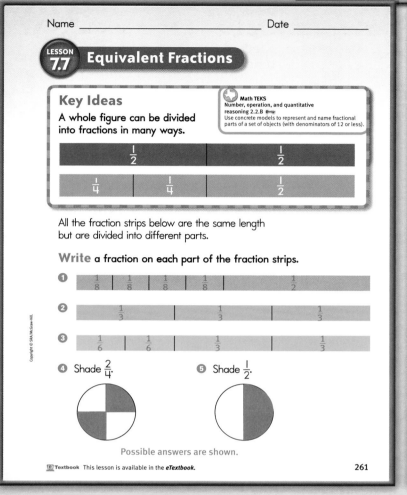

① $\frac{1}{8}$ $\frac{1}{8}$ $\frac{1}{8}$ $\frac{1}{8}$ $\frac{1}{2}$

② $\frac{1}{3}$ $\frac{1}{3}$ $\frac{1}{3}$

③ $\frac{1}{6}$ $\frac{1}{6}$ $\frac{1}{3}$ $\frac{1}{3}$

④ Shade $\frac{2}{4}$.

⑤ Shade $\frac{1}{2}$.

Possible answers are shown.

Textbook This lesson is available in the *eTextbook*.

261

Answer using pictures and words.

⑥ Which is bigger: $\frac{1}{2}$ of a pie or $\frac{5}{8}$ of a pie? $\frac{5}{8}$

⑦ Which is farther: $\frac{1}{3}$ of a mile or $\frac{2}{6}$ of a mile? _____They are the same._____

⑧ Juanita and Jorge each had six blobs of paint. Draw them.

⑨ Juanita used $\frac{4}{6}$ of hers. Ring how many she used.

⑩ Jorge used $\frac{2}{3}$ of his. Ring how many he used.

⑪ Who used more blobs of paint? _____They used the same number of blobs._____

262

Real Math • Chapter 7 • Lesson 7

---

3 Reflect   10 ⏱

Guided Discussion ☑ REASONING

Discuss the fractional names introduced today for $\frac{1}{2}$. If students have a difficult time answering this question, give them a clue.

- **How many parts did we divide the fraction strips into?** fourths, eighths, thirds, sixths
- **Are these all the fractional names that could be used to describe $\frac{1}{2}$?** no
- **How many twelfths would make up $\frac{1}{2}$ of the whole?** six
- **How about tenths? How many parts would there be?** five
- **Critical Thinking How many different fractional names are there that are equivalent to $\frac{1}{2}$?** You can divide a whole object into many small parts—there is no limit.

Cumulative Review: For cumulative review of previously learned skills, see page 273–274.

Family Involvement: Assign the *Practice, Reteach,* or *Enrichment* activities depending on the needs of your students. Have students create equivalent fractions with a family member.

Concept/Question Board: Encourage students to continue to post questions, answers, and examples on the Concept/Question Board. ☑

Math Puzzler: Carlos drew a circle. He drew lines to make 4 equal parts on the circle. He colored 3 of the 4 parts. Did he color more than half the circle? How do you know? Yes; 2 out of 4 is half, so 3 out of 4 is more than half.

4 Assess and Differentiate

 Assess Use *eAssess* to record and analyze evidence of student understanding.

A Gather Evidence

Use the Daily Class Assessment Records in *Texas Assessment* or *eAssess* to record daily observations.

Informal Assessment
☑ **Guided Discussion**

Did the student REASONING
- ❏ provide a clear explanation?
- ❏ communicate reasons and strategies?
- ❏ choose appropriate strategies?
- ❏ argue logically?

Informal Assessment
☑ **Concept/Question Board**

Did the student APPLYING
- ❏ apply learning in new situations?
- ❏ contribute concepts?
- ❏ contribute answers?
- ❏ connect mathematics to real-world situations?

🗺 TEKS/TAKS Practice

Use *TEKS/TAKS Practice* page 13 to assess student progress.

B Summarize Findings

Analyze and summarize assessment data for each student. Determine which Assessment Follow-Up is appropriate for each student. Use the Student Assessment Record in *Texas Assessment* or *eAssess* to update assessment records.

C Texas Assessment Follow-Up • DIFFERENTIATE INSTRUCTION

Based on your observations, use these teaching strategies for assessment follow-up.

INTERVENTION

Review student performance on *Intervention* Lesson 7.B to see if students have mastered prerequisite skills for this lesson.

🗺 **1.2.A** Separate a whole into two, three, or four equal parts and use appropriate language to describe the parts such as three out of four equal parts.

1.8 The student understands that time can be measured. The student uses time to describe and compare situations.

ENGLISH LEARNER

Review

Use Lesson 7.7 in *English Learner Support Guide* to review lesson concepts and vocabulary.

ENRICH

If . . . students are proficient in the lesson concepts,

Then . . . encourage them to work on the chapter projects or *Enrichment* Lesson 7.7.

Enrichment Lesson 7.7

TEXAS PRACTICE

If . . . students would benefit from additional practice,

Then . . . assign *Practice* Lesson 7.7.

Practice Lesson 7.7

RETEACH

If . . . students are having difficulty understanding equivalent fractions,

Then . . . reteach the concept using *Reteach* Lesson 7.7.

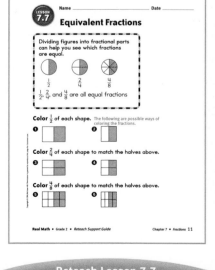

Reteach Lesson 7.7

Grade 1	Grade 2	Grade 3
Number, operation, and quantitative reasoning 1.2.B Use appropriate language to describe part of a set such as three out of the eight crayons are red.	Number, operation, and quantitative reasoning 2.2.B Use concrete models to represent and name fractional parts of a set of objects (with denominators of 12 or less).	Number, operation, and quantitative reasoning 3.2.C Use fraction names and symbols to describe fractional parts of whole objects or sets of objects.

Overview

LESSON 7.8

TEXAS

Fractions of Numbers

Context of the Lesson This is the eighth of an eleven-lesson sequence that develops concepts of fractions using a variety of models. In previous lessons students have discussed fractions in terms of parts of a shape and parts of a set. In this lesson, students begin learning about fractions of numbers. Students use money and bundles of craft sticks to find what a fraction of a number is.

Planning for Learning ● DIFFERENTIATE INSTRUCTION

INTERVENTION

If . . . students lack the prerequisite skill of estimating fractional parts,

Then . . . teach *Intervention* Lesson 7.C.

 1.2.A, 1.8

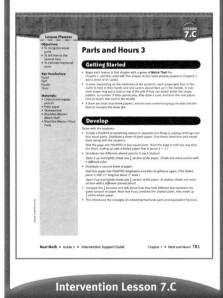

Intervention Lesson 7.C

ENGLISH LEARNER

Preview

If . . . students need language support,

Then . . . use Lesson 7.8 in *English Learner Support Guide* to preview lesson concepts and vocabulary.

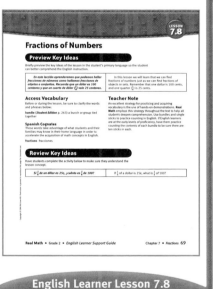

English Learner Lesson 7.8

ENRICH

If . . . students are proficient in the lesson concepts,

Then . . . emphasize Guided Discussion in Reflect.

PRACTICE

If . . . students would benefit from additional practice,

Then . . . extend Skill Building before assigning the student pages.

RETEACH

If . . . students are having difficulty understanding fractions of numbers,

Then . . . extend Guided Discussion before assigning the student pages.

OBJECTIVES

To explicitly relate fractions to numbers using money and manipulatives

MATH TEKS

Number, operation, and quantitative reasoning 2.2.B 🔑
Use concrete models to represent and name fractional parts of a set of objects (with denominators of 12 or less).

MATH TEKS INTEGRATION

Number, operation, and quantitative reasoning 2.3.B
Model addition and subtraction of two-digit numbers with objects, pictures, words, and numbers.

MATERIALS

- *Number Cubes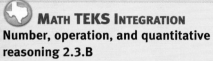
- *Overhead coins and bills
- *Craft sticks
- Clear overhead transparency
- *Fraction Game Mat
- Colored pencils

TECHNOLOGY

ⓔ **Presentation** Lesson 7.8
ⓔ **Games** Fraction Game

Academic Vocabulary

quarter \kwo(r)´ tər\ *n.* one-fourth of something; a coin of the United States equal to twenty-five cents, or one-fourth of a dollar

Access Vocabulary

bundle a bunch or group tied together

Spanish Cognates

fractions fracciones

Teaching Lesson 7.8

Math TEKS
Number, operation and quantitative reasoning 2.2.B
Use concrete models to represent and name fractional
parts of a set of objects (with denominators of 12 or less).

TEXAS

Mental Math   5

 Integration: 2.3 B Give students practice with chain
calculations. Students should respond with their *Number
Cubes,* using the find, hide, and show routine. Possible examples
include the following:

a. $2 + 7 + 8 = 17$ **b.** $6 + 8 + 4 = 18$ **c.** $5 + 7 + 3 = 15$
d. $4 + 3 + 6 = 13$ **e.** $2 + 5 + 4 + 6 = 17$ **f.** $7 + 3 + 4 + 9 + 1 = 24$

1 Develop   25

Tell Students In Today's Lesson They Will
learn about fractions of a number.

Guided Discussion UNDERSTANDING Introductory

■ **Critical Thinking** **What does it mean to divide something into
fourths?** to divide a whole object into four equal parts

Display a dollar on the overhead projector, and ask the following:

■ **How many cents is one dollar worth?** 100

Display a quarter, and ask the following:

■ **How many cents is one quarter worth?** 25

Place an overhead dollar bill on the overhead projector.

Now place the clear transparency on top of the dollar, and
draw two lines dividing the dollar into fourths. Place one of the
overhead projector quarters over each section of the dollar.

■ **How many quarters make up one dollar?** 4

Explain that if one hundred cents (one dollar) is divided into four
equal parts, each one of those parts is twenty-five cents. Write $\frac{1}{4}$
on the board.

■ **What is $\frac{1}{4}$ of 100?** 25
■ **Critical Thinking** **How much is two quarters?** Using the
overhead projector, demonstrate that two quarters is the
same as half a dollar, which is fifty cents.
■ **What is $\frac{1}{2}$ of 100?** 50

Skill Building APPLYING Guided

Organize students into small groups, and have each
group gather sixty craft sticks bundled in tens at their
desks. Have groups model the first two problems on
page 263 with you.

■ **How many equal groups must we divide the sticks into for the
first question?** four
■ **How do you know?** The denominator is four, so we are going to
divide the group into fourths, or four equal shares.

Have students work together until they discover how to divide
the sticks into four equal groups. If the sticks are bundled in tens,
then students will have to unbundle two of them.

Monitoring Student Progress

| **If . . .** students have attempted but are not successful in dividing the craft sticks, | **Then . . .** work individually in small groups, helping students divide smaller quantities, and gradually work toward greater quantities in which bundles of craft sticks must be unbundled. |

2 Use Student Pages   20

Pages 263–264 UNDERSTANDING   Independent

Have students continue to work in groups on pages 263 and 264.

As Students Finish

 Game Have students play the **Fraction Game** in pairs.

 Games *Fraction Game*

 TEXAS **TEKS Checkup**

**Number, operation, and quantitative
reasoning 2.2.C** Use concrete models
to determine if a fractional part of a
whole is closer to 0, $\frac{1}{2}$, or 1.
**Use this problem to assess students'
progress towards standards mastery:**
Which is the closest to $\frac{5}{8}$?

A
B
C
D

Have students choose the correct
answer, then describe how they knew
which choice was correct. In the
discussion, ask questions such as the
following.

■ **Which choice shows 0?** Choice A
shows 0 shaded

■ **Which choice shows 1?** Choice C
shows 8 shaded

Follow-Up
If...students have difficulty
recognizing fractions of a whole,

Then...have students play the
Fraction Game found on page 256 of
the student edition.

Student Page

Name _____ Date _____

LESSON 7.8 Fractions of Numbers

Key Ideas

Math TEKS
Number, operation, and quantitative reasoning 2.2.B
Use concrete models to represent and name fractional parts of a set of objects (with denominators of 12 or less).

You can find fractions of numbers just as you can find fractions of objects or sets.

There are 10 craft sticks in a bundle. There are 6 bundles, so there are 60 craft sticks.

$\frac{2}{6}$ of the bundles are red.

20 sticks are red.

$\frac{2}{6}$ of 60 is 20.

$\frac{4}{6}$ of the bundles are blue.

40 sticks are blue.

$\frac{4}{6}$ of 60 is 40.

 **Find** the answers. You may use craft sticks or other objects to help.

1 $\frac{1}{4}$ of 60 = __15__

5 $\frac{1}{2}$ of 60 = __30__

2 $\frac{2}{4}$ of 60 = __30__

6 $\frac{2}{2}$ of 60 = __60__

3 $\frac{3}{4}$ of 60 = __45__

7 $\frac{1}{2}$ of 100 = __50__

4 $\frac{4}{4}$ of 60 = __60__

8 $\frac{2}{2}$ of 100 = __100__

Textbook This lesson is available in the *eTextbook*.

263

LESSON 7.8 · Fractions of Numbers

I whole dollar is worth 100 cents.

$\frac{1}{4}$ of a dollar is worth 25 cents.

$\frac{2}{4}$ of a dollar is worth 50 cents.

Fill in the missing number. Think about money to help you.

9 $\frac{1}{2}$ of 100 = __50__   **10** $\frac{1}{4}$ of 100 = __25__   **11** $\frac{2}{4}$ of 100 = __50__

12 $\frac{3}{4}$ of 100 = __75__   **13** $\frac{4}{4}$ of 100 = __100__   **14** $\frac{1}{2}$ of 50 = __25__

$\frac{1}{10}$ of a dollar is worth 10 cents.

$\frac{2}{10}$ of a dollar is worth 20 cents.

Fill in the missing number. Think about money to help you.

15 $\frac{1}{10}$ of 100 = __10__   **16** $\frac{4}{10}$ of 100 = __40__

17 $\frac{9}{10}$ of 100 = __90__   **18** $\frac{5}{10}$ of 100 is the same as $\frac{1}{2}$ of __100__

264   **Real Math** • Chapter 7 • Lesson 8

---

3 Reflect

10

Guided Discussion REASONING

Use play money (or draw circles on the board) to show 2 quarters and a half dollar. Demonstrate the story below as you read it to the class.

(25¢)   (25¢)   (50¢)

Wilbec had these 3 coins that were worth one dollar altogether. She took one of the quarters and said, "This is one of my three coins, so it's one-third of my money. It's worth 25 cents. So, $\frac{1}{3}$ of 100 is 25."

■ **Do you agree with Wilbec that $\frac{1}{3}$ of 100 is 25?** Students should recall from the lesson that 25 is $\frac{1}{4}$ of 100.

■ **What mistake do you think Wilbec made?** She thinks that one of the coins is $\frac{1}{3}$ of the total amount just because there are 3 coins. But the coins are not equal parts of a dollar.

■ **Critical Thinking** **How would you explain to Wilbec why the quarter is one-fourth of a dollar and not one-third of a dollar?** Students might suggest trading the half-dollar for 2 quarters, or trading the coins for pennies. They might suggest making a diagram like this one:

25 ¢	50 ¢
25 ¢	

☑ Use Mastery Checkpoint 11 found in **Texas Assessment** to evaluate student mastery of simple fractions. By this time, students should be able to correctly answer eighty percent of the Mastery Checkpoint items.

Cumulative Review: For cumulative review of previously learned skills, see page 273–274.

Family Involvement: Assign the **Practice, Reteach,** or **Enrichment** activities depending on the needs of your students.

Concept/Question Board: Have students attempt to answer any unanswered questions on the Concept/Question Board.

Math Puzzler: "I know all about fractions," said Ferdie. "You asked me what one-third of 30 is. That's easy. It's 27." What is $\frac{1}{3}$ of 30? 10 What did Ferdie do wrong? He subtracted 3 from 30.

4 Assess and Differentiate

 Assess Use *eAssess* to record and analyze evidence of student understanding.

A Gather Evidence

Use the Daily Class Assessment Records in *Texas Assessment* or *eAssess* to record daily observations.

Formal Assessment

☑ **Mastery Checkpoint**

Did the student
- ☐ use correct procedures?
- ☐ respond with at least 80% accuracy?

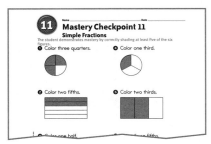

11 Mastery Checkpoint 11
Simple Fractions
The student demonstrates mastery by correctly shading at least five of the six figures.
❶ Color three quarters. ❹ Color one third.
❷ Color two fifths. ❺ Color two thirds.

Texas Assessment page 88

 TEKS/TAKS Practice

Use *TEKS/TAKS Practice* page 13 to assess student progress.

B Summarize Findings

Analyze and summarize assessment data for each student. Determine which Assessment Follow-Up is appropriate for each student. Use the Student Assessment Record in *Texas Assessment* or *eAssess* to update assessment records.

C Texas Assessment Follow-Up • DIFFERENTIATE INSTRUCTION

Based on your observations, use these teaching strategies for assessment follow-up.

INTERVENTION

Review student performance on *Intervention* Lesson 7 .C to see if students have mastered prerequisite skills for this lesson.

1.2.A Separate a whole into two, three, or four equal parts and use appropriate language to describe the parts such as three out of four equal parts.

1.8 The student understands that time can be measured. The student uses time to describe and compare situations.

ENGLISH LEARNER

Review

Use Lesson 7.8 in *English Learner Support Guide* to review lesson concepts and vocabulary.

ENRICH

If . . . students are proficient in the lesson concepts,

Then . . . encourage them to work on the chapter projects or *Enrichment* Lesson 7.8.

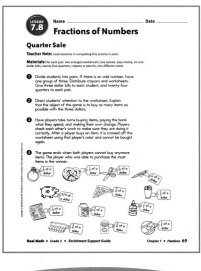

Enrichment Lesson 7.8

TEXAS PRACTICE

If . . . students would benefit from additional practice,

Then . . . assign *Practice* Lesson 7.8.

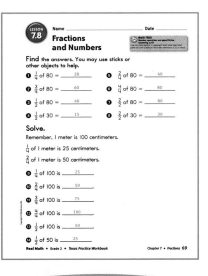

Practice Lesson 7.8

RETEACH

If . . . students have difficulty with parts of a dollar,

Then . . . have them use play money to visualize that $\frac{1}{4}$ of a dollar is 25 cents and $\frac{1}{2}$ of a dollar is 50 cents by counting with the coins.

TEXAS **Vertical Alignment**

Grade 1	Grade 2	Grade 3
Measurement 1.8.B Read time to the hour and half-hour using analog and digital clocks.	Measurement 2.10.B Read and write times shown on analog and digital clocks using five-minute increments.	Measurement 3.12.B Tell and write time shown on analog and digital clocks.

Overview **LESSON 7.9**

TEXAS

Lesson Planner

OBJECTIVES
- To relate the study of fractions to telling time to the hour and half hour
- To relate understanding of fractions using geometric and numeric models

MATH TEKS

Measurement 2.10.B 🔑
Read and write times shown on analog and digital clocks using five-minute increments.

Underlying processes and mathematical tools 2.14
The student is expected to justify his or her thinking using objects, words, pictures, numbers, and technology.

MATH TEKS INTEGRATION

Number, operation, and quantitative reasoning 2.3.A
Recall and apply basic addition and subtraction facts (to 18).

MATERIALS
- *Number Cubes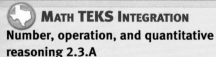
- *Demonstration Clock
- *Clock faces
- *Fraction Game Mat
- Colored pencils

TECHNOLOGY
- 🄴 **Presentation** Lesson 7.9
- 🄴 **Games** Fraction Game

Telling Time— Hour and Half Hour

Context of the Lesson This is the ninth of an eleven-lesson sequence that develops concepts of fractions using a variety of models. Telling time to the hour and half hour was introduced in Grade 1. Although this is the first lesson to formally introduce telling time in Grade 2, most students will be familiar with how to read a clock. Telling time to the quarter hour is taught in the next lesson. Telling time to the minute is taught in Chapter 10. This lesson builds on students' work with area models to introduce telling time, with a focus on the hour and half hour.

Planning for Learning ● DIFFERENTIATE INSTRUCTION

INTERVENTION

If . . . students lack the prerequisite skill of telling time to the nearest hour,

Then . . . teach *Intervention* Lesson 7.C.

 1.2.A, 1.8

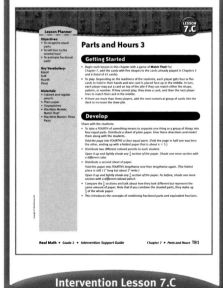

Intervention Lesson 7.C

ENGLISH LEARNER

Preview

If . . . students need language support,

Then . . . use Lesson 7.9 in *English Learner Support Guide* to preview lesson concepts and vocabulary.

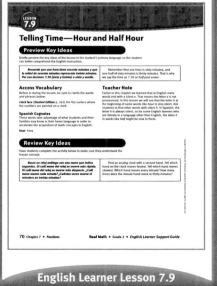

English Learner Lesson 7.9

ENRICH

If . . . students are proficient in the lesson concepts,

Then . . . emphasize chapter projects.

PRACTICE

If . . . students would benefit from additional practice,

Then . . . extend Skill Practice before assigning the student pages.

RETEACH

If . . . students are having difficulty understanding telling time to the hour and half hour,

Then . . . extend Guided Discussion before assigning the student pages.

Access Vocabulary
clock face the flat surface where the numbers are placed on a clock

Spanish Cognates
hour hora

Measurement 2.10.B
Read and write times shown on analog and digital clocks using five-minute increments.
Underlying processes and mathematical tools 2.14
The student is expected to justify his or her thinking using objects, words, pictures, numbers, and technology.

TEXAS

Mental Math 5

   INTEGRATION: 2.3.A Orally present students with chain calculations. Students should respond with their **Number Cubes,** using the find, hide, and show routine. Possible examples include the following:

a. 7 + 3 + 4 = 14   **b.** 2 + 2 + 3 = 7   **c.** 16 + 9 + 1 = 26
d. 9 + 0 + 7 = 16   **e.** 5 + 5 + 1 + 19 = 30   **f.** 3 + 2 + 6 + 4 = 15

1 Develop 25

Tell Students In Today's Lesson They Will
use fractions to tell time.

Guided Discussion UNDERSTANDING Introductory

Display the analog clock like the clocks on student page 265 set to a time on the hour, such as 7:00.

■ **Can anyone tell what the time is?** 7:00

Write 7:00 on the board. Discuss what the clock shows and where the hour and minute hands are. The minute hand is pointing straight up, and the hour hand is pointing to the 7.

Do the same for another time on the hour, making sure to write the time on the board with each example.

Then draw a circle on the board. Explain that each whole hour is divided into 60 minutes. Write 60 in the circle.

Explain that each number (on a clock numbered from 1–12) represents five minutes. Have students practice counting by fives as you move the minute hand around the demonstration clock.

Ask for a volunteer to come to the board and to divide the circle into halves.

Shade half the clock.

■ **Critical Thinking** **If a whole hour is 60 minutes, how much is half an hour?** (Remind them of dividing the sixty craft sticks into halves in the previous lesson.) 30 minutes

Write 30 on each half of the circle.

Now move the minute hand halfway around the clock from the 12 to the 6, and move the hour hand to halfway between 7 and 8. Explain that when the minute hand has traveled halfway around the clock, it is 30 minutes after the hour.

■ **What time is it?** 7:30

Write 7:30 on the board.

Explain that there are different ways to read this time—half past 7, because the minute hand has traveled halfway around the clock; 30 minutes after 7, or 7:30, because half the hour (30 minutes) has passed.

Skill Practice COMPUTING

  Guided

  Distribute clocks to each student, and have them show given times (as on student page 266). Possible examples include the following:

a. 7:30   **b.** 10:00   **c.** 11:30
d. 4:30   **e.** 9:00   **f.** 2:00

2 Use Student Pages 20

Pages 265–266 APPLYING Independent

Have students complete pages 265 and 266 independently.

Progress Monitoring

| **If . . .** students are having trouble telling time, | **Then . . .** use the classroom clock to refer to times of the day when different activities occur. |

As Students Finish

Game Have students play the **Fraction Game** in pairs.

e Games *Fraction Game*

Student Page

LESSON 7.9
Telling Time—Hour and Half Hour

Key Ideas

Math TEKS
Measurement 2.10.B
Read and write times shown on analog and digital clocks using five-minute increments.

7:00   7:30 or half past 7

What time is it? Write your answers.

1. 8:30
2. 11:00
3. 2:30
4. 12:30
5. 5:00
6. 4:30
7. 6:30
8. 9:00

Textbook This lesson is available in the *eTextbook*.   265

Show the time.

9. 4:00
12. six o'clock — 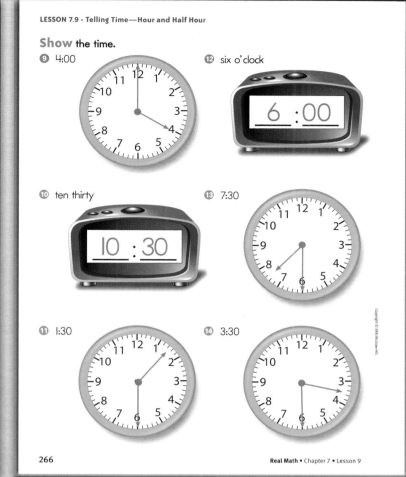 6:00
10. ten thirty — 10:30
13. 7:30
11. 1:30
14. 3:30

266   **Real Math** • Chapter 7 • Lesson 9

---

3 Reflect   10

Guided Discussion REASONING

 Lead a discussion about telling time while using the demonstration clock.

- **Critical Thinking** **What do you think *quarter after* means?** Allow students to discuss. Students may be able to infer that it means the minute hand has moved a quarter of the way around the clock.
- **Where would the minute hand be?** on the 3
- **Where would the hour hand be?** a quarter of the way between the two hours

Curriculum Connection: Students may be interested in researching how sundials can be used to tell time.

Cumulative Review: For cumulative review of previously learned skills, see page 273–274.

Family Involvement: Assign the *Practice, Reteach,* or *Enrichment* activities depending on the needs of your students.

Concept/Question Board: Have students attempt to answer any unanswered questions on the Concept/Question Board.

Math Puzzler: Jen ate one-half of a pizza. Her brother ate three-quarters of a pizza. Who ate more? How can you tell? Her brother; $\frac{2}{4}$ is half, so $\frac{3}{4}$ is more than $\frac{1}{2}$.

Assess and Differentiate

 Assess Use *eAssess* to record and analyze evidence of student understanding.

A Gather Evidence

Use the Daily Class Assessment Records in *Texas Assessment* or *eAssess* to record daily observations.

Informal Assessment
☑ **Mental Math**

Did the student COMPUTING
- ❑ respond accurately?
- ❑ respond quickly?
- ❑ respond with confidence?
- ❑ self-correct?

Informal Assessment
☑ **Guided Discussion**

Did the student UNDERSTANDING
- ❑ make important observations?
- ❑ extend or generalize learning?
- ❑ provide insightful answers?
- ❑ pose insightful questions?

TEKS/TAKS Practice

Use *TEKS/TAKS Practice* page 81 to assess student progress.

B Summarize Findings

Analyze and summarize assessment data for each student. Determine which Assessment Follow-Up is appropriate for each student. Use the Student Assessment Record in *Texas Assessment* or *eAssess* to update assessment records.

C Texas Assessment Follow-Up ● DIFFERENTIATE INSTRUCTION

Based on your observations, use these teaching strategies for assessment follow-up.

INTERVENTION	ENRICH	TEXAS PRACTICE	RETEACH
Review student performance on *Intervention* Lesson 7.C to see if students have mastered prerequisite skills for this lesson. **1.2.A** Separate a whole into two, three, or four equal parts and use appropriate language to describe the parts such as three out of four equal parts. **1.8** The student understands that time can be measured. The student uses time to describe and compare situations.	**If . . .** students are proficient in the lesson concepts, **Then . . .** encourage them to work on the chapter projects or *Enrichment* Lesson 7.9.	**If . . .** students would benefit from additional practice, **Then . . .** assign *Practice* Lesson 7.9.	**If . . .** students struggle with hours and half hours, **Then . . .** keep a clock on display during the school day. Call attention to it when it is on the hour and half hour. Have students determine what time it is.

ENGLISH LEARNER
Review

Use Lesson 7.9 in *English Learner Support Guide* to review lesson concepts and vocabulary.

Enrichment Lesson 7.9

Practice Lesson 7.9

TEXAS Vertical Alignment

Grade 1	Grade 2	Grade 3
Measurement 1.8.B Read time to the hour and half hour using analog and digital clocks.	**2.10.B** Read and write times shown on analog and digital clocks using five-minute increments.	**3.12.B** Tell and write time shown on analog and digital clocks.

Overview **LESSON 7.10**

TEXAS

Lesson Planner

OBJECTIVES
- To relate telling time to the hour, half hour, and quarter hour
- To relate understanding of fractions using geometric and numeric models

MATH TEKS
Measurement 2.10.B
Read and write times shown on analog and digital clocks using five-minute increments.
Number, operation, and quantitative reasoning 2.2.A
Use concrete models to represent and name fractional parts of a whole object (with denominators of 12 or less).
Underlying processes and mathematical tools 2.12.A
Identify the mathematics in everyday situations.
Underlying processes and mathematical tools 2.14
The student is expected to justify his or her thinking using objects, words, pictures, numbers, and technology.

MATH TEKS INTEGRATION
Number, operation, and quantitative reasoning 2.1.C
Use place value to compare and order whole numbers to 999 and record the comparisons using numbers and symbols (<, =, >).

MATERIALS
- *Demonstration Clock
- *Clock faces

TECHNOLOGY
Presentation Lesson 7.10

Telling Time— Quarter Hour

Context of the Lesson This is the tenth of an eleven-lesson sequence that develops concepts of fractions using a variety of models. This lesson builds on the students' developing understanding of fractions by using area models to introduce the concept of quarter hours. This lesson continues the formal instruction in reading a clock from the previous lesson. Telling time to the minute is taught in Chapter 10.

Planning for Learning ● DIFFERENTIATE INSTRUCTION

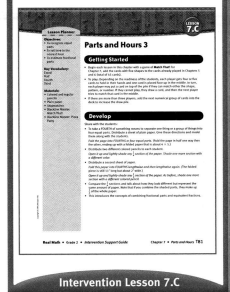

INTERVENTION
If . . . students lack the prerequisite skill of recognizing equal parts,

Then . . . teach *Intervention* Lesson 7.C.

1.2.A, 1.8

Intervention Lesson 7.C

ENGLISH LEARNER
Preview
If . . . students need language support,

Then . . . use Lesson 7.10 in *English Learner Support Guide* to preview lesson concepts and vocabulary.

English Learner Lesson 7.10

ENRICH
If . . . students are proficient in the lesson concepts,

Then . . . emphasize chapter projects.

PRACTICE
If . . . students would benefit from additional practice,

Then . . . extend Skill Practice before assigning the student pages.

RETEACH
If . . . students are having difficulty understanding telling time to the quarter hour,

Then . . . extend Guided Discussion before assigning the student pages.

Access Vocabulary
quarter to fifteen minutes before the hour

Spanish Cognates
quarter cuarto

Math TEKS
Measurement 2.10.B
Read and write times shown on analog and digital clocks using five-minute increments.
Number, operation, and quantitative reasoning 2.2.A
Use concrete models to represent and name fractional parts of a whole object (with denominators of 12 or less).
Underlying processes and mathematical tools 2.12.A
Identify the mathematics in everyday situations.
Underlying processes and mathematical tools 2.14
The student is expected to justify his or her thinking using objects, words, pictures, numbers, and technology.

Mental Math   5

 Integration: 2.1.C Provide students with greater-than, less-than, and equal-to exercises. Have students show thumbs-up for greater than, thumbs-down for less than, and an open hand for equal to. Possible examples include the following:

a. 10 + 50 ___ 20 + 45 down   **b.** 82 − 40 ___ 38 up

c. 57 − 32 ___ 56 − 31 open hand   **d.** 45 + 25 ___ 51 + 20 down

e. 17 − 7 ___ 10 − 1 up   **f.** 23 + 50 ___ 22 + 50 up

1 Develop   25

Tell Students In Today's Lesson They Will
learn to tell time with quarter hours.

Guided Discussion  UNDERSTANDING   Introductory

Using the demonstration clock, review several hour and half-hour settings. For each setting, ask students what time it is, and write the correct time on the board, emphasizing the position of the hour and minute hands for hours and half hours.

Draw a circle on the board.

■ **Do you remember how many minutes are in one hour?** sixty

Write 60 in the circle.

Now draw another circle, and ask a student to divide it into halves. Shade half of the circle.

■ **Do you remember how many minutes are in each half hour?** thirty

Write 30 in each half of the circle.

Draw a third circle, and ask a student to divide it into fourths.

■ **What does it mean to divide a whole into fourths?** four equal parts

Refer to the circles already on the board.

■ **Critical Thinking** **If one hour has sixty minutes, and half an hour has thirty minutes, how many minutes would be in quarter of an hour?** fifteen

Write 15 in each of the quarters of the circle. Explain that one-fourth is sometimes called a *quarter* and that when talking about one-fourth of an hour it is usually called a *quarter of an hour* or a *quarter hour*.

Using the analog clock, show students a time on the hour, such as 5:00.

■ **What time is it?** 5:00

Show that the hour hand points to the 5 and that the minute hand points straight up. Write 5:00 on the board.

Next show 5:15. Explain that the minute hand has gone one-fourth of the way around the clock and the hour hand has moved a quarter of the way from the 5 to the 6, so this time can be called a quarter past 5 or 5:15 because 15 minutes have passed since 5:00. Write 5:15 on the board.

Next show 5:30. Point out that the minute hand has traveled halfway around the clock, the hour hand has moved halfway from 5 to 6 too, and the time can be called half past 5 or 5:30 because 30 minutes have passed since 5:00. Write 5:30 on the board.

Finally show 5:45, and point out that the minute hand has one-fourth of the way to go to the top, and the hour hand has one-fourth of the way to go from 5 to 6, so this time can be called a quarter to 6 or 5:45 because 45 minutes have passed since 5:00. Write 5:45 on the board.

Skill Practice COMPUTING   Guided

Distribute individual clocks, and have students show given times as on the student pages. Possible examples include the following:

a. 7:45   **b.** 6:15   **c.** 11:30

d. quarter to 12   **e.** quarter after 3   **f.** 1:45

2 Use Student Pages   20

Pages 267–268 UNDERSTANDING    Independent

Have students complete pages 267 and 268 independently.

Complete the first question on each page together, and make sure students understand how to fill in the answers.

As Students Finish

 Game Allow students to play any previously introduced game, or assign a game based on needed skill practice.

Name _____ Date _____

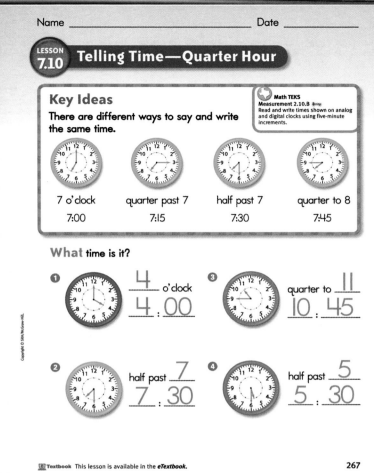

LESSON 7.10 Telling Time—Quarter Hour

Key Ideas
There are different ways to say and write the same time.

Math TEKS
Measurement 2.10.B
Read and write times shown on analog and digital clocks using five-minute increments.

7 o'clock — 7:00
quarter past 7 — 7:15
half past 7 — 7:30
quarter to 8 — 7:45

What time is it?

1. __4__ o'clock 4 : 00
2. half past __7__ 7 : 30
3. quarter to __11__ 10 : 45
4. half past __5__ 5 : 30

267

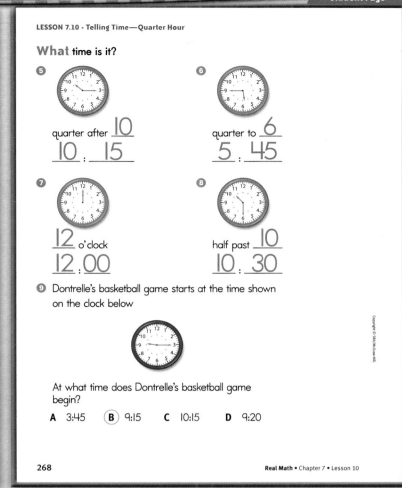

LESSON 7.10 · Telling Time—Quarter Hour

What time is it?

5. quarter after __10__ 10 : 15
6. quarter to __6__ 5 : 45
7. __12__ o'clock 12 : 00
8. half past __10__ 10 : 30

9. Dontrelle's basketball game starts at the time shown on the clock below

At what time does Dontrelle's basketball game begin?
A 3:45 **B 9:15** C 10:15 D 9:20

268 Real Math · Chapter 7 · Lesson 10

---

3 Reflect
10

Guided Discussion REASONING

 Use a clock face to extend students' understanding of fractions to twelfths.

On a clock face, show the hour hand moving halfway around. Then draw and shade to show $\frac{1}{2}$ of the clockface.

■ **What fraction of the way around has the hour hand moved?** $\frac{1}{2}$
■ **How many hours is it all the way around for the hour hand?** 12
■ **How many hours is it $\frac{1}{2}$ of the way around for the hour hand?** 6

Repeat the shading and three questions for $\frac{1}{4}$ of the way around. Repeat for $\frac{1}{12}$ of the way around.

■ **How many hours has the hour hand moved?** 1
■ **How many hours is it all the way around for the hour hand?** 12
■ **What fraction of the way around has the hour hand moved?** $\frac{1}{12}$

Repeat for other numbers of hours to show fractions such as $\frac{5}{12}, \frac{7}{12}, \frac{10}{12}, \frac{11}{12},$ and $\frac{12}{12}$.

If students are catching on, you might also use the clockface to show that fractions that are said and written differently can represent the same amount. For example, $\frac{3}{12}$ around is the same as $\frac{1}{4}$ around. Also show $\frac{4}{12} = \frac{1}{3}$ and $\frac{6}{12} = \frac{1}{2}$.

 Use Mastery Checkpoint 12 found in **Texas Assessment** to evaluate student mastery of telling time after and before the hour. By this time, students should be able to correctly answer eighty percent of the Mastery Checkpoint items.

Math Puzzler: Kenya studied spelling for 15 minutes every night from Monday through Thursday. What is the total amount of time she studied spelling? 60 minutes or 1 hour

Chapter 7 · Lesson 10 **267–268**

Assess and Differentiate

 Assess Use *eAssess* to record and analyze evidence of student understanding.

A Gather Evidence

Use the Daily Class Assessment Records in *Texas Assessment* or *eAssess* to record daily observations.

Formal Assessment

☑ Mastery Checkpoint

Did the student

☐ use correct procedures?

☐ respond with at least 80% accuracy?

Texas Assessment page 89

🦴 TEKS/TAKS Practice

Use *TEKS/TAKS Practice* page 81 to assess student progress.

B Summarize Findings

Analyze and summarize assessment data for each student. Determine which Assessment Follow-Up is appropriate for each student. Use the Student Assessment Record in *Texas Assessment* or *eAssess* to update assessment records.

C Texas Assessment Follow-Up ● DIFFERENTIATE INSTRUCTION

Based on your observations, use these teaching strategies for assessment follow-up.

INTERVENTION	ENRICH	TEXAS PRACTICE	RETEACH
Review student performance on *Intervention* Lesson 7.C to see if students have mastered prerequisite skills for this lesson. 🦴 **1.2.A** Separate a whole into two, three, or four equal parts and use appropriate language to describe the parts such as three out of four equal parts. **1.8** The student understands that time can be measured. The student uses time to describe and compare situations.	**If . . .** students are proficient in the lesson concepts, **Then . . .** encourage them to work on the chapter projects or *Enrichment* Lesson 7.10.	**If . . .** students would benefit from additional practice, **Then . . .** assign *Practice* Lesson 7.10.	**If . . .** students struggle with telling time to the quarter hour, **Then . . .** have twelve students form a circle, each holding consecutive numbers from 1 to 12. Use two dowels as hands for the clock. Stand in the center of the circle, and use the dowels to show half hours and quarter hours. Have remaining students determine what time it is.

ENGLISH LEARNER

Review

Use Lesson 7.10 in *English Learner Support Guide* to review lesson concepts and vocabulary.

Enrichment Lesson 7.10

Practice Lesson 7.10

Grade 1	Grade 2	Grade 3
1.2.A Separate a whole into two, three, or four equal parts and use appropriate language to describe the parts such as three out of four equal parts.	**2.2.C** Use concrete models to determine if a fractional part of a whole is closer to 0, $\frac{1}{2}$, or 1.	**3.2.C** Use fraction names and symbols to describe fractional parts of whole objects or sets of objects.

TEXAS

Lesson Planner

OBJECTIVES
To introduce the concept of naming fractional parts that are greater than one

MATH TEKS
Number, operation, and quantitative reasoning 2.2.C
Use concrete models to determine if a fractional part of a whole is closer to 0, $\frac{1}{2}$, or 1.

MATH TEKS INTEGRATION
Number, operation, and quantitative reasoning 2.1.C
Use place value to compare and order whole numbers to 999 and record the comparisons using numbers and symbols ($\langle$, $=$, $\rangle$).

MATERIALS
None

TECHNOLOGY
e Presentation Lesson 7.11

Fractions Greater than One

Context of the Lesson This is the last of an eleven-lesson sequence that develops concepts of fractions using a variety of models. Previously in this chapter, students have worked with fractions that are less than 1. This lesson builds on the idea that if you know the kind of part you are counting, then you know how many parts are needed for one whole and how many are more than one whole

Planning for Learning • DIFFERENTIATE INSTRUCTION

INTERVENTION
If . . . students lack the prerequisite skill of telling time to the nearest hour,

Then . . . teach *Intervention* Lesson 7.C.

1.2.A, 1.8

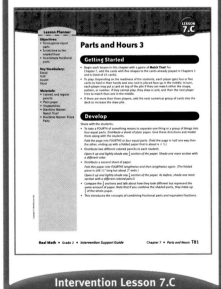

Intervention Lesson 7.C

ENGLISH LEARNER
Preview

If . . . students need language support,

Then . . . use Lesson 7.11 in *English Learner Support Guide* to preview lesson concepts and vocabulary.

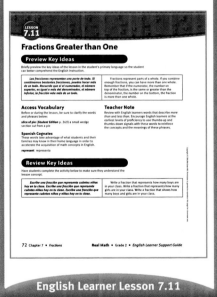

English Learner Lesson 7.11

ENRICH
If . . . students are proficient in the lesson concepts,

Then . . . emphasize additional game time.

PRACTICE
If . . . students would benefit from additional practice,

Then . . . extend Skill Practice before assigning the student pages.

RETEACH
If . . . students are having difficulty understanding fractions greater than one,

Then . . . extend Guided Discussion before assigning the student pages.

Access Vocabulary
slice of pie a small wedge section cut from a pie

Spanish Cognates
represent representa

---

*Manipulative Kit Item 🔑 = Key standard

Teaching Lesson 7.11

Math TEKS
Number, operation, and quantitative reasoning 2.2.C
Use concrete models to determine if a fractional part of a whole is closer to 0, $\frac{1}{2}$, or 1.

TEXAS

Mental Math   5

THUMBS UP

Integration: 2.1.C Provide students with greater-than, less-than, and equal-to exercises. Have students show thumbs-up if greater than, thumbs-down if less than, and an open hand if equal to. Possible examples include the following:

a. 2 ___ 100 − 98 open hand
b. 9 ___ 100 − 99 up
c. 40 ___ 50 − 9 down
d. 13 ___ 10 + 3 open hand
e. 30 ___ 51 − 22 up
f. 22 ___ 20 + 2 open hand

1 Develop   25

Tell Students In Today's Lesson They Will

learn about fractions that are greater than one.

Guided Discussion UNDERSTANDING

 Introductory

■ **What does it mean to divide a figure into fourths?** to divide it into four equal pieces or equal parts

On the board or overhead projector, show $\frac{4}{4}$ of a pizza.

■ **How many fourths are there?** four

Write $\frac{4}{4}$.

■ **How many pizzas are there?** one whole pizza

Next draw one more fourth of a pizza on the board or overhead projector.

■ **How many fourths are there now?** five
■ **How many whole pizzas are there?** one whole pizza
■ **Critical Thinking** **Do these fourths add up to more than one whole or less than one whole pizza?** more than one whole pizza
■ **How many fourths make up one whole pizza?** four
■ **If we had $\frac{3}{4}$, could we make one whole pizza?** no
■ **How many more fourths would we need to get to make one whole pizza?** one

Now draw $\frac{10}{4}$ of a pizza on the board or overhead projector.

■ **How many fourths do you see?** ten

Have students work with a partner to figure out how many whole pizzas they could make from $\frac{10}{4}$. two

Tell students this could be written as $2\frac{2}{4}$ (two whole pizzas and $\frac{2}{4}$ of a pizza) or $2\frac{1}{2}$, so $\frac{10}{4} = 2\frac{2}{4} = 2\frac{1}{2}$.

Then write $\frac{12}{4}$ on the board, and have students continue working in pairs to figure out how many whole pizzas $\frac{12}{4}$ could make. three

Skill Practice COMPUTING

 Guided

THUMBS UP

Present fractions orally, and have students show thumbs-up if it is greater than one, thumbs-down if it is less than one, and an open hand if it is equal to one. Possible examples include the following:

a. $\frac{3}{4}$ down
b. $\frac{8}{4}$ up
c. $\frac{12}{12}$ open hand
d. $\frac{4}{3}$ up
e. $\frac{7}{8}$ down
f. $\frac{6}{5}$ up

2 Use Student Pages   20

Pages 269–270 UNDERSTANDING   Independent

Have students complete pages 269 and 270 independently.

As Students Finish

Game

Allow students to play any previously introduced game, or assign a game based on needed skill practice.

Student Page

Name _____ Date _____

LESSON 7.11 Fractions Greater than One

Key Ideas

Fractions represent parts of a whole. If you put together enough fractions, you can have more than 1 whole.

Math TEKS
Number, operation, and quantitative reasoning 2.2.C
Use concrete models to determine if a fractional part of a whole is closer to 0, $\frac{1}{2}$, or 1.

The Museum Café sells pie by the slice. The afternoon tour group bought 9 slices.

When they put them together, they can see they bought more than 1 whole pie. They bought $1\frac{1}{2}$ pies. One slice of pie is $\frac{1}{6}$ of the whole pie.

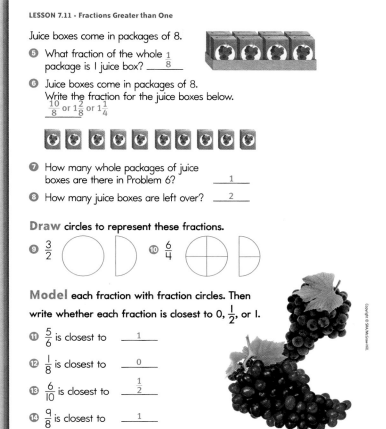

Look at the fraction. If it is more than 1 whole, rewrite it in a different form. The first one is done for you.

1. $\frac{6}{4}$ (More) or Less $1\frac{2}{4}$ or $1\frac{1}{2}$
2. $\frac{3}{2}$ (More) or Less $1\frac{1}{2}$
3. $\frac{5}{8}$ More or (Less)   _____
4. $\frac{15}{12}$ (More) or Less $1\frac{3}{12}$ or $1\frac{1}{4}$

269

LESSON 7.11 • Fractions Greater than One

Juice boxes come in packages of 8.

5. What fraction of the whole package is 1 juice box? $\frac{1}{8}$

6. Juice boxes come in packages of 8. Write the fraction for the juice boxes below. $\frac{10}{8}$ or $1\frac{2}{8}$ or $1\frac{1}{4}$

7. How many whole packages of juice boxes are there in Problem 6?   1

8. How many juice boxes are left over?   2

Draw circles to represent these fractions.

9. $\frac{3}{2}$ 10. $\frac{6}{4}$

Model each fraction with fraction circles. Then write whether each fraction is closest to 0, $\frac{1}{2}$, or 1.

11. $\frac{5}{6}$ is closest to   1

12. $\frac{1}{8}$ is closest to   0

13. $\frac{6}{10}$ is closest to $\frac{1}{2}$

14. $\frac{9}{8}$ is closest to   1

270   **Real Math • Chapter 7 • Lesson 11**

---

3 Reflect   10

Guided Discussion   REASONING

Write $\frac{1}{9}$ on the board.

- **What do you think this fraction is called?** one-ninth
- **Critical Thinking** **What do you think it means?** something has been divided into nine equal parts

Repeat for $\frac{1}{7}$, $\frac{1}{10}$, $\frac{1}{11}$, and $\frac{1}{12}$. Then have students create illustrations with shaded circles to illustrate these fractions. Then repeat the process for these denominators with numerators greater than one.

- **Critical Thinking** **What do you think $\frac{1}{376}$ means?** something has been divided into 376 parts (This is seldom useful except in highly specialized situations.)

Discuss whether fractions like this are useful in everyday situations.

Cumulative Review: For cumulative review of previously learned skills, see page 273–274.

Family Involvement: Assign the *Practice, Reteach,* or *Enrichment* activities depending on the needs of your students.

Concept/Question Board: Have students attempt to answer any unanswered questions on the Concept/Question Board.

Math Puzzler: You plan to study for half an hour. So far you have studied for 12 minutes. How much longer will you study? 18 more minutes

4 Assess and Differentiate

 Assess Use **eAssess** to record and analyze evidence of student understanding.

A Gather Evidence

Use the Daily Class Assessment Records in *Texas Assessment* or *eAssess* to record daily observations.

Performance Assessment
☑ **Game**

Did the student **ENGAGING**
- ❏ pay attention to others' contributions?
- ❏ contribute information and ideas?
- ❏ improve on a strategy?
- ❏ reflect on and check the accuracy of his or her work?

Informal Assessment
☑ **Guided Discussion**

Did the student **REASONING**
- ❏ provide a clear explanation?
- ❏ communicate reasons and strategies?
- ❏ choose appropriate strategies?
- ❏ argue logically?

 TEKS/TAKS Practice

Use *TEKS/TAKS Practice* page 17 to assess student progress.

B Summarize Findings

Analyze and summarize assessment data for each student. Determine which Assessment Follow-Up is appropriate for each student. Use the Student Assessment Record in *Texas Assessment* or *eAssess* to update assessment records.

C Texas Assessment Follow-Up ● DIFFERENTIATE INSTRUCTION

Based on your observations, use these teaching strategies for assessment follow-up.

INTERVENTION

Review student performance on *Intervention* Lesson 7.C to see if students have mastered prerequisite skills for this lesson.

 1.2.A Separate a whole into two, three, or four equal parts and use appropriate language to describe the parts such as three out of four equal parts. **1.8** The student understands that time can be measured. The student uses time to describe and compare situations.

ENGLISH LEARNER
Review

Use Lesson 7.11 in *English Learner Support Guide* to review lesson concepts and vocabulary.

ENRICH

If . . . students are proficient in the lesson concepts,

Then . . . encourage them to work on the chapter projects or *Enrichment* Lesson 7.11.

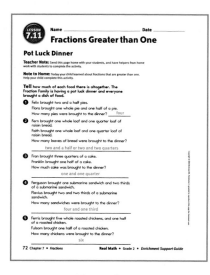

Enrichment Lesson 7.11

PRACTICE

If . . . students would benefit from additional practice,

Then . . . assign *Practice* Lesson 7.11.

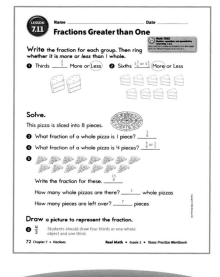

Practice Lesson 7.11

RETEACH

If . . . students are having difficulty understanding fractions greater than one,

Then . . . reteach the concept using *Reteach* Lesson 7.11.

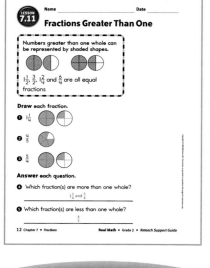

Reteach Lesson 7.11

Objectives

- To provide practice using fractions to solve a real-world, nonroutine problem
- To provide practice working with fractions of an hour
- To develop an understanding that problems can have more than one answer

Materials

See Appendix A page A24 for a rubric for problem solving.

Context of the Lesson While providing a large block of time for students to work on a single problem, this lesson provides an opportunity for students to apply what they have been learning about fractions. The lesson also continues the museum theme introduced on pages 243 and 244 and continued on pages 257 and 258.

1 Develop 5

Tell Students In Today's Lesson They Will
plan a visit to a science museum.

Guided Discussion

Remind students about an earlier activity in which they planned a visit to a zoo (pages 230 and 231). Tell them that today they will get to plan their time at a science museum.

As students look at the map on page 271, explain that the map shows the different stations in a hands-on activity room at a science museum. Have volunteers take turns reading aloud a title and speculating on what they think happens at that station.

Help students understand the map by asking and discussing questions such as the following:

- **How long does the Fossil Cave activity last?** 1 hour
- **How long does the Mystery Rocks activity last?** $\frac{1}{4}$ hour
- **Why would someone want to use a map like this?** You would use it when you visit the museum to know which activities to visit, where they are, and how long they last.

Read this problem to students as they follow along on the student page:

You are going to spend the morning at the Children's Activity Area of the science museum. At each station, the activity sessions begin at 9:00 and continue all day. You will be there from 9:00 to 11:30. Each group can decide which stations they want to go to and when. Fill in the table on the bottom of the page to show how your group will spend its time. You don't have to include time to get from one station to another because they are so close and because all activities end a little early to allow for passing time.

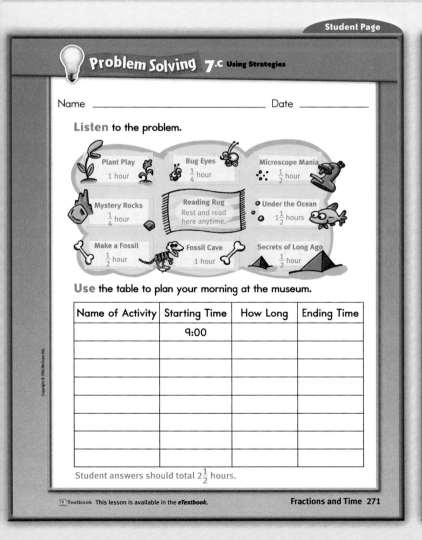

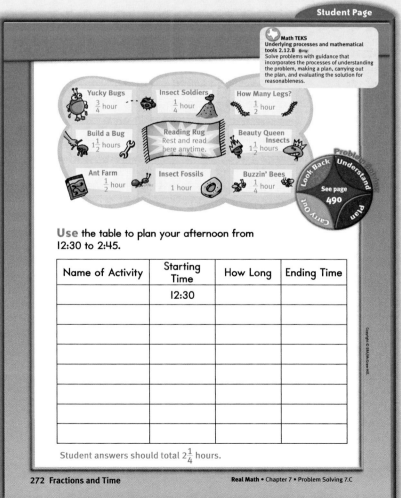

TEXAS

Math TEKS
Number, operation, and quantitative reasoning 2.2.A
Use concrete models to represent and name fractional parts of a whole object (with denominators of 12 or less).

Underlying processes and mathematical tools 2.12.C
Select or develop an appropriate problem-solving plan or strategy including drawing a picture, looking for a pattern, systematic guessing and checking, or acting it out in order to solve a problem.

 2 Use Student Pages 25

Guided Discussion

Have students work in pairs or small groups to plan their morning visit. Provide support as needed. If students seem to be having difficulty, encourage them to struggle with the problem for a while. When needed, ask guiding questions such as the following:

- **What is the first activity you would like to do?**
- **How long will it take you to do that activity?**
- **What time will it be when that activity ends?**
- **Do you have time for another activity?**

Students who finish early may use the map on page 272 to plan their afternoon visit, or you may assign page 272 as homework. The two problems are the same but contain different activities and times.

 3 Reflect 10

Knowledge Age Skills

Effective Communication Have each group present its plan, the strategies used to make the plan, and how the group knows they will get back by 11:30. Ask questions such as the following:

- **How is this problem like the one about planning a visit to the zoo?**
- **How is it different?**

Help students understand the following points:

- There are many different plans that people can make and still be finished at 11:30.
- The Reading Rug provides a convenient way to fill any leftover time or to wait for an activity to start.
- When solving problems with many steps, it is important to organize your work so you can keep track of the steps. A table is one way to organize your work.
- Problems can be about different things and still be similar enough that you can solve them in the same way. Although the problem in this lesson takes place in a science museum and the times are given with fractions, students can use similar methods to keep track of how much time they have used and how much time is left.

Sample Solutions Strategies

Students may use one or more of the following strategies to figure out and keep track of time in the problem.

Draw a Picture

Students might draw a picture of a clock face and divide it into four equal parts for $\frac{1}{4}$ hour and then figure out how many minutes would be in each section. They can do the same for $\frac{1}{2}$ hour and $1\frac{1}{2}$ hours.

Use Operations

Students might combine the fractions of time without translating them into minutes. For example, they might see that $\frac{1}{4}$ of an hour plus $\frac{1}{4}$ of an hour equals $\frac{1}{2}$ of an hour.

Use a Physical Model

Students might move the hands or change the numbers on a watch or clock to keep track of time in their plans.

Students might use fractional pieces (wholes, halves, and fourths) to represent fractions of an hour.

Add to a Picture

Students might write on the map what time they expect to begin each activity.

 4 Assess 15

When evaluating student work, focus on whether students thought rationally about the problem. Questions to consider include the following:

- Did the student understand the problem?
- Was the student able to understand and use fractions of an hour to keep track of time?
- Did the student have some organized way of planning his or her visit?
- Was the student able to record accurately in the table?
- Was the student able to explain his or her thinking?

Cumulative Review

 Review

Use Pages 273–274

Use the Cumulative Review as a review of concepts and skills that students have previously learned.

Here are different ways that you can assign these problems to your students as they work through the chapter:

- With some of the lessons in the chapter, assign a set of cumulative review problems to be completed as practice or for homework.
  Lesson 7.7—Problem 1
  Lesson 7.8—Problems 2–5
  Lesson 7.9—Problems 6–8
  Lesson 7.10—Problems 9–11
  Lesson 7.11—Problems 12–15

- At any point during the chapter, assign part or all of the cumulative review problems to be completed as practice or for homework.

Cumulative Review

Problem 1 reviews collecting and recording data, Lesson 4.6. 2.13.A

Problems 2–5 review collecting and recording data, Lesson 4.6. 2.13.A

Problems 6–8 review fractions of numbers, Lesson 7.8. 2.2.B

Problems 9–11 review fractions of a set, Lesson 7.5. 2.2.B

Problems 12–15 review telling time, including quarter-hour times, Lesson 7.10. 2.2.A

> **Progress Monitoring**
>
> **If . . .** students miss more than one problem in a section, **Then . . .** refer to the indicated lesson for remediation suggestions.

Student Page

Cumulative Review

Name _____ Date _____

Collecting and Recording Data Lesson 4.6 TEKS: 2.13.A

Write how many tally marks.

① Sierra made a survey of the 70 kids at summer camp. She asked each camper which activity he or she enjoyed. Write the count of each set of tally marks.

Activity	How Many	Number
Exploring wetlands	𝍌𝍌𝍌𝍌 I	16
Hiking	𝍌 III	8
Nature stories	𝍌𝍌	10
Safety skills	𝍌𝍌 I	11

Collecting and Recording Data Lesson 4.6 TEKS: 2.13.A

Use the table above to answer these questions.

② How many campers enjoyed hiking? __8__

③ How many campers liked safety skills? __11__

④ Which activity was enjoyed by 16 campers? __exploring wetlands__

⑤ What doesn't the table tell you? Possible answer: The table doesn't tell you if students enjoyed camp. The table doesn't tell how many students enjoyed all the activities.

Fractions of Numbers Lesson 7.8 TEKS: 2.2.A

Find the answers.

⑥ $\frac{2}{4}$ of 100 is __50__   ⑦ $\frac{1}{2}$ of 50 is __25__   ⑧ $\frac{3}{4}$ of 100 is __75__

⒠Textbook This lesson is available in the *eTextbook*.

273

Student Page

Cumulative Review

 TEKS

Fractions of a Set Lesson 7.5 TEKS: 2.2.B

Ring the correct number of sculptures.

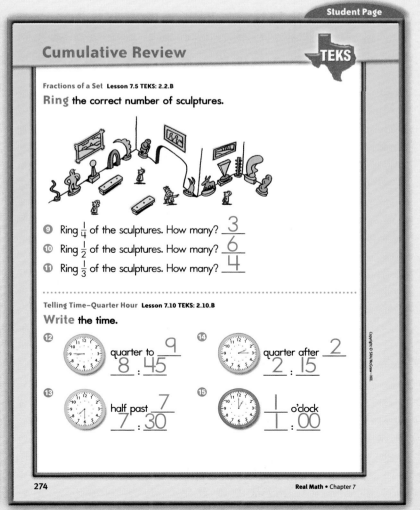

⑨ Ring $\frac{1}{4}$ of the sculptures. How many? __3__

⑩ Ring $\frac{1}{2}$ of the sculptures. How many? __6__

⑪ Ring $\frac{1}{3}$ of the sculptures. How many? __4__

Telling Time–Quarter Hour Lesson 7.10 TEKS: 2.10.B

Write the time.

⑫ quarter to __9__ __8__ : __45__

⑭ quarter after __2__ __2__ : __15__

⑬ half past __7__ __7__ : __30__

⑮ __1__ o'clock __1__ : __00__

274

Real Math • Chapter 7

Wrap-Up

1 Discuss 5

Concept/Question Board

Review the Concept/Question Board with students.

- Discuss students' contributions to the Concept side of the Board.
- Have students repose their questions, and lead a discussion to find satisfactory answers.

Chapter Projects APPLYING

Provide an opportunity for students who have worked on one or more of the projects outlined on page 244C to share their work with the class. Allow each student or student group five minutes to present or discuss their projects. For formal assessment, use the rubrics found in *Across the Curriculum Math Connections;* the rubric for **Go on a Scavenger Hunt** is on page 77, and the rubric for **Create a Board Game about Fossils** is on page 81. For informal assessment, use the following rubric and questions.

	Exceeds Expectations	Meets Expectations	Minimally Meets Expectations
Applies mathematics in real-world situations:	❏	❏	❏
Demonstrates strong engagement in the activity:	❏	❏	❏

Go on a Scavenger Hunt

- How many fossils did you find?
- What different kinds of fossils did you find?
- At what times did you find the fossils? About how long did it take to find each fossil?
- What else did you include in your book?
- What did you learn about how scientists search for fossils?
- Would you like to go on a real dig for fossils? Why or why not?

🤠 TEKS:

MATH: Measurement 2.10.B Read and write times shown on analog and digital clocks using five-minute increments.

SCIENCE: Science concepts 2.8 The student distinguishes between living organisms and nonliving objects.

TECHNOLOGY: Information acquisition 04 The student uses a variety of strategies to acquire information from electronic resources, with appropriate supervision.

Create a Board Game about Fossils

- What does your game board look like?
- What fractions did you use in your game? How could you tell they would work?
- What information about fossils did you include in your game?
- What else did you include in your game?
- Did you enjoy playing your game? Why or why not?
- Was there another group's game that you enjoyed playing? Why? What was different about that game?

🤠 TEKS:

MATH: Number, operation, and quantitative reasoning 2.2.A Use concrete models to represent and name fractional parts of a whole object (with denominators of 12 or less).

LANGUAGE ARTS: Writing purposes 2.14 The student writes for a variety of audiences and purposes, and in various forms.

TEHNOLOGY: Foundations 02.D Produce documents at the keyboard, proofread, and correct errors.

Key Ideas Review ✓ UNDERSTANDING

Review the Key Ideas concepts on pages 275-276 with the class. The Key Ideas pages should be used by students and parents as a reference when reviewing the important concepts covered in this chapter. Ask students the following discussion questions to extend their knowledge of the Key Ideas and check their understanding of the ideas.

Discussion Questions

❶ Discuss fractions and creating fractions with the students. What if you had 200 people that wanted to share something equally? How much would each person get? Each person would get $\frac{1}{200}$. You can make a fraction out of any number, however some fractions are more common than others.

❷ Can you think of situations where you would want to know the fraction of a set? Try and make up a situation that you would encounter in real life where you would have to split up a group of objects. Allow students to share ideas with the class. As they describe their situations, write the fractions they would create on the board.

❸ Why is it important to know how to tell time on different kinds of clocks? Digital clocks are very common today, but knowing how to use an analog clock (clock with hands) is important. You may be in a situation where there is no digital clock available.

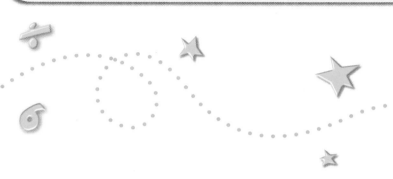

CHAPTER 7 Key Ideas Review

Name _____ Date _____

In this chapter we discussed . . .
- fractions
- numerators and denominators
- fractions of a whole
- fractions of a set
- fractions greater than one
- telling time

We used these concepts to help solve problems and answer everyday questions.

❶ In this chapter you learned about fractions. You learned that fractions are written this way:

$$\frac{2}{4}, \frac{3}{8}, \frac{1}{4}$$

The number below the line is called the denominator. It tells how many equal parts there are. The number above the line is called the numerator. It tells how many equal parts are being considered.

❷ You learned about fractions of a whole. You learned that if 3 people want to share a pizza equally, each person gets $\frac{1}{3}$ of the pizza.

❸ You learned about fractions of sets. You learned that if 4 people share 12 oranges equally, each person gets $\frac{1}{4}$ of 12 or 3 oranges.

Textbook This lesson is available in the *eTextbook*. 275

CHAPTER 7 Key Ideas Review

❹ You learned about fractions of a dollar. You learned that 4 quarters are equal to 100 cents or 1 dollar. So if you take 1 of those quarters you have taken $\frac{1}{4}$ of a dollar or 25 cents. If you take 2 of those quarters you have taken $\frac{1}{2}$ of a dollar or 50 cents.

❺ You learned that a fraction can have a numerator that is greater than its denominator. If you eat $\frac{5}{4}$ of a veggie burger, you will eat one whole veggie burger and $\frac{1}{4}$ of another veggie burger. We can write this as $1\frac{1}{4}$ veggie burgers or $\frac{5}{4}$ of a veggie burger.

❻ You have not yet learned rules for adding and subtracting fractions. But when you played the Fraction Game, you may have noticed that if you captured $\frac{1}{5}$ of a circle and then captured another $\frac{2}{5}$ of the same circle, you captured more than $\frac{1}{2}$ of that circle. So $\frac{1}{5} + \frac{2}{5}$ must be equal to more than $\frac{1}{2}$. Thinking this way will help prepare you for learning how to add and subtract fractions in third grade.

❼ You learned about equivalent fractions. For example, if you divide a cake into 6 equal parts and take 3 of those parts, you are taking $\frac{3}{6}$ of the cake. But you are also taking $\frac{1}{2}$ of the cake. That's why we say that $\frac{3}{6}$ and $\frac{1}{2}$ are equivalent fractions. Knowing about equivalent fractions will be important when you learn how to add and subtract fractions.

❽ We finished the chapter by reviewing how to tell time to the half hour and learning to tell time to the quarter hour. We learned that two quarter hours is equivalent to one half hour. Being able to tell time is useful. It will help you to be on time when you come to school. It will also help you know when a ball game or concert will begin.

276 **Real Math** • Chapter 7

Chapter 7 Error Analysis

Errors Writing Fractions

Write the following problems on the board and allow students to analyze this student's work. Discuss error patterns students find and how to help the student.

Pose this analysis as a challenging problem. When a student thinks he or she might have detected the error pattern, rather than have them tell the answer to the class, write a new exercise on the board and have the student tell you the answer that is consistent with the pattern he or she found. By using this procedure, all students will have a chance to think through the problem – not just the first student to find it.

This student completed some fraction exercises and got the following answers.

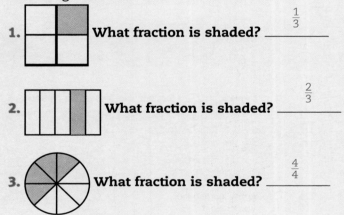

1. What fraction is shaded? $\frac{1}{3}$

2. What fraction is shaded? $\frac{2}{3}$

3. What fraction is shaded? $\frac{4}{4}$

What error is this student making?

This student consistently writes the number of shaded parts as the numerator and the number of unshaded parts as the denominator.

This student needs tutoring on the meaning of fractional parts. He or she should be helped to understand that the denominator tells how many parts there are altogether and the numerator tells how many parts are shaded. For example, in Problem 1 ask: How many equal parts are in this square? 4. How many of the parts are shaded? 1 What fraction of the square is shaded? $\frac{1}{4}$

If the student is still not sure, redraw the square with no parts shaded and ask the student to shade $\frac{1}{4}$ of the circle.

Another technique is to draw 2 identical figures side by side, one divided into 4 equal parts with 1 part shaded and the other divided into 3 equal parts with 1 part shaded. Then establish that the figure with 1 of three parts shaded is $\frac{1}{3}$ shaded. Point out that if that figure is $\frac{1}{3}$ shaded, the other figure cannot have the same answer.

At this time, you may use the **TEKS/TAKS Practice** to provide practice for standards covered in this chapter.

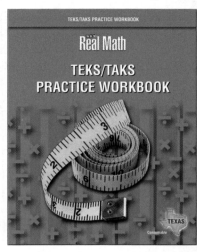

TEKS/TAKS Practice, pp. 15–16, Standard 2.2.B

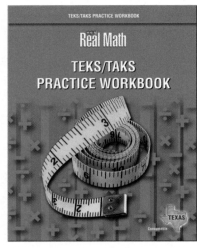

TEKS/TAKS Practice, pp. 13–14, Standard 2.2.A

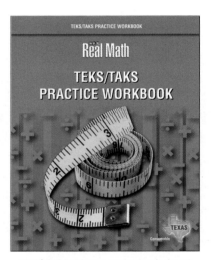

TEKS/TAKS Practice, pp. 17–18, Standard 2.2.C

Chapter Review

Use the Chapter 7 Review to indicate areas in which each student is having difficulty or in which the class may need help. If students do well on the Chapter 7 Review, you may wish to skip directly to the Chapter Test; if not, you may spend a day or so helping students overcome their individual difficulties before taking the Practice Test.

Next to each set of problems is a list of the lessons in the chapter that covered those concepts. If they need help, students can refer to a specific lesson for additional instruction. You can also use this information to make additional assignments based on the previous lesson concepts.

Have students complete pages 277–278 on their own.

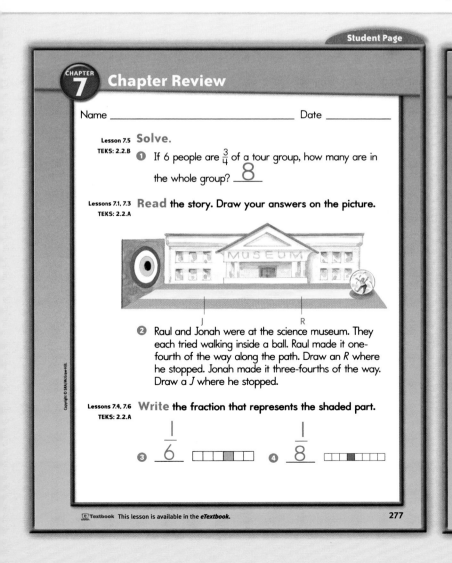

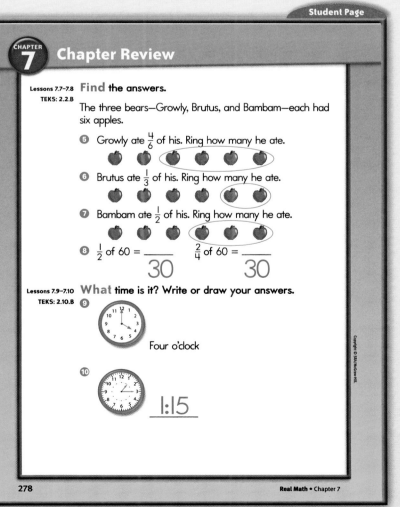

3 Chapter Tests 40

Practice Test

Student Pages 279–282

- The Chapter 7 Practice Test on *Student Edition* pages 279–282 provides an opportunity to formally evaluate students' proficiency with concepts developed in this chapter.
- The content is similar to the Chapter 7 Review, in standardized format.

Practice-Test Remediation

Multiple Choice Questions 1–2 and **Short Answer Questions 1–5** all involve fractions. If students are having difficulty with these problems, first establish if they understand what the concept of a fraction is. Explain that a fraction is a part of a whole. Give students fraction tiles or other fraction manipulatives and have them use those as a guide as they solve the problems. If students are having difficulty understanding the different fractions, such as fourths or sixths, explain to them that that is the number of pieces there are, such as four pieces or six pieces.

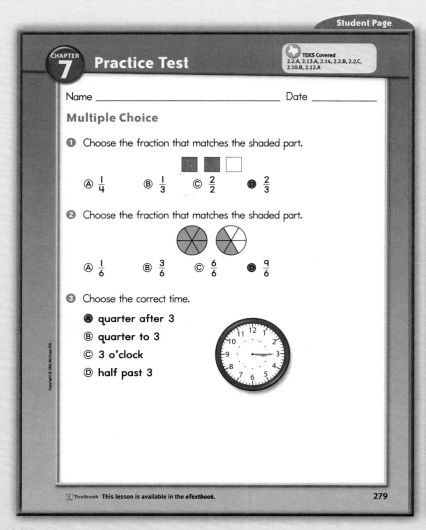

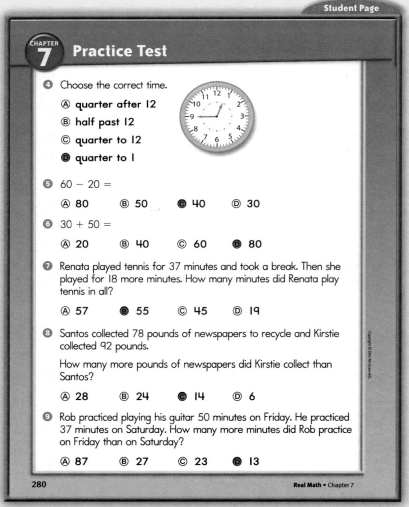

If students are having difficulty with **Multiple Choice Questions 3–4,** check to see if the difficulty occurs with students naming times, or reading the time on a clock. Either way, be sure to review the concept of telling time on a clock.

For **Extended Response Questions 6–8,** if students are having difficulty, help guide the students through the problem, using appropriate fraction materials. If it helps, provide a piece of paper, and have the students fold the paper. Then have them shade the appropriate amount of parts on the paper to represent the fraction.

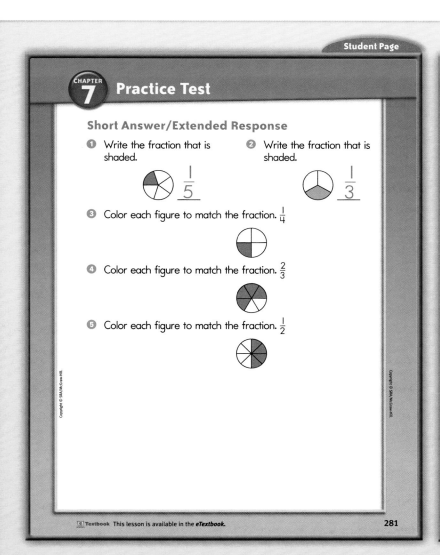

Short Answer/Extended Response

1. Write the fraction that is shaded. $\frac{1}{5}$

2. Write the fraction that is shaded. $\frac{1}{3}$

3. Color each figure to match the fraction. $\frac{1}{4}$

4. Color each figure to match the fraction. $\frac{2}{3}$

5. Color each figure to match the fraction. $\frac{1}{2}$

E Textbook This lesson is available in the *eTextbook*.

281

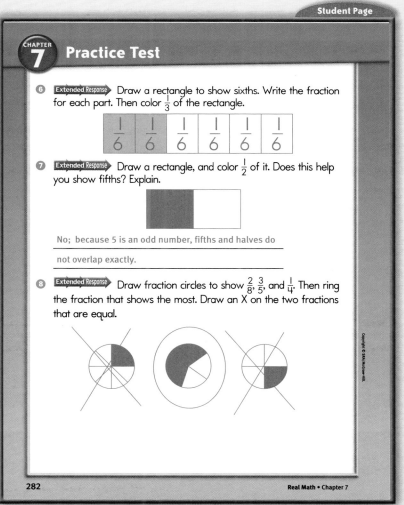

6. **Extended Response** Draw a rectangle to show sixths. Write the fraction for each part. Then color $\frac{1}{3}$ of the rectangle.

| $\frac{1}{6}$ | $\frac{1}{6}$ | $\frac{1}{6}$ | $\frac{1}{6}$ | $\frac{1}{6}$ | $\frac{1}{6}$ |

7. **Extended Response** Draw a rectangle, and color $\frac{1}{2}$ of it. Does this help you show fifths? Explain.

No; because 5 is an odd number, fifths and halves do not overlap exactly.

8. **Extended Response** Draw fraction circles to show $\frac{2}{8}$, $\frac{3}{5}$, and $\frac{1}{4}$. Then ring the fraction that shows the most. Draw an X on the two fractions that are equal.

282

Real Math • Chapter 7

4 Assess and Differentiate

 Assess Use **eAssess** to record and analyze evidence of student understanding.

A Gather Evidence

Use the Daily Class Assessment Records in *Texas Assessment* or *eAssess* to record Informal and Formal Assessments.

Informal Assessment
☑ **Key Ideas Review** UNDERSTANDING

Did the student
☐ make important observations?
☐ extend or generalize learning?
☐ provide insightful answers?
☐ pose insightful questions?

Informal Assessment
☑ **Project** APPLYING

Did the student
☐ meet the project objectives?
☐ communicate clearly?
☐ complete the project accurately?
☐ connect mathematics to real-world situations?

Formal Assessment
☑ **Chapter Test** COMPUTING

Score the test, and record the results.

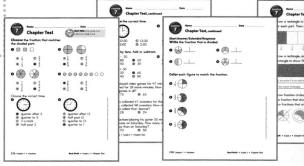

Assessment Pages 236–237   Assessment Pages 238–239

B Summarize Findings

Analyze and summarize assessment data for each student. Determine which Chapter Follow-Up is appropriate for each student. Use the Student Assessment Record in *Texas Assessment* or *eAssess* to update assessment records.

C Chapter Follow-Up ● DIFFERENTIATE INSTRUCTION

Based on your observations, use these teaching strategies for chapter follow-up.

ENRICH	PRACTICE	RETEACH	INTERVENTION
If . . . students demonstrate a **secure understanding** of chapter concepts,	**If . . .** students demonstrate **competent understanding** of chapter concepts,	**If . . .** students demonstrate **emerging understanding** of chapter concepts,	**If . . .** students demonstrate **minimal understanding** of chapter concepts,
Then . . . move on to the next chapter.	**Then . . .** move on to the next chapter.	**Then . . .** move on to the next chapter, but continue to provide cumulative review.	**Then . . .** intensive intervention is still needed before they start the next chapter.

Half a Job

Context of the Thinking Story Mr. Muddle tries to complete the job of painting a room in his museum by doing half of the job each day.

Lesson Planner

OBJECTIVES
To develop logical thinking while integrating reading skills with mathematics

MATH TEKS
NUMBER, OPERATION, AND QUANTITATIVE REASONING 2.2.A
Use concrete models to represent and name fractional parts of a whole object (with denominators of 12 or less).
Underlying processes and mathematical tools 2.12.A
Identify the mathematics in everyday situations.

ENGLISH LANGUAGE ARTS AND READING TEKS
READING/COMPREHENSION 2.9.E
Make and explain inferences from texts such as determining important ideas and causes and effects, making predictions, and drawing conclusions.
Reading/comprehension 2.9.G
Identify similarities and differences across texts such as in topics, characters, and problems.
Reading/literary response 2.10.D
Connect ideas and themes across texts.

Using the Thinking Story

The Thinking Story may be used at any time throughout the chapter. Read the Thinking Story "Half a Job" to your class. As you read the story, give students time to think about each question, but not so much that they forget the point being made.

Math TEKS
Number, operation, and quantitative reasoning 2.2.A
Use concrete models to represent and name fractional parts of a whole object (with denominators of 12 or less).
Underlying processes and mathematical tools 2.12.A
Identify the mathematics in everyday situations.

Half a Job

Year by year, things grew worse in Mr. Muddle's museum. "Everything needs to be fixed, everything needs to be painted," he groaned. "There's so much work to be done that I can't get started."

"I'll tell you how I handle problems like that," said Ms. Eng. "When a job is so big that I don't feel like starting it, I just do half the job each day. That way it isn't so hard."

How long does it take Ms. Eng to do the job?   two days

"Half the job each day," said Mr. Muddle. "That sounds like an excellent idea. I'm going to try it. I think I'll start today with painting the walls in this room."

"Good luck," said Ms. Eng. "I'll be back in a week, and I expect I'll find this museum in much better shape if you follow my advice and do half a job every day."

Mr. Muddle got out paint, brushes, and a roller, and he started painting the walls in that room.

How many walls should he paint the first day if he is going to do half the job?   two

Mr. Muddle figured that half of 4 is 2. And so the first day he painted two walls.

The next day Mr. Muddle got out his painting materials again and was ready to start work. "Now, what was it Ms. Eng told me to do?" he asked himself. "Ah, yes, I remember. Do half the job each day. There are two walls that need painting, so if I do half the job today, that means I paint one wall." Mr. Muddle painted one of the walls.

Do you think that is what Ms. Eng meant? no

What should Mr. Muddle have done instead? do the other half of the job by painting both walls

The next day Mr. Muddle said, "This idea of doing only half the job each day really makes life easy. It didn't take me very long at all to do my painting yesterday, and today it should take even less time."

How many walls are left to be painted in the room? one

How much do you think Mr. Muddle will paint today? probably half of the wall

Mr. Muddle noticed that only one wall in the room needed to be painted. Because the rule was to do half a job each day, he painted only half the wall that day.

How many walls has Mr. Muddle painted so far? three and a half

How much painting is left to do? half a wall

Do you think Mr. Muddle will finish the room the next day? no

Why or why not? If he does half of the remaining half, he will still have one-fourth of the wall left to paint.

The next day Mr. Muddle had a very easy job. There was only half a wall left to paint. So his job was to paint half a wall. But he remembered that he was supposed to do only half the job that day.

How much did Mr. Muddle paint that day? one-fourth of the wall

How much of the last wall is still not painted? one-fourth

About how wide would a fourth of the wall in an ordinary room be? maybe one meter

By the next day there was only a strip of wall left to be painted, and it took Mr. Muddle just a few minutes to paint half of it. Every day the strip of wall that was unpainted grew narrower. Every day Mr. Muddle painted only half of what was left.

Do you think Mr. Muddle will ever finish painting the wall? no

Why or why not? He will keep painting only half of what's left.

Ms. Eng stopped by to see how Mr. Muddle was coming with his work on the museum. "What have you been doing?" she asked.

"Just painting the walls in this one room," said Mr. Muddle.

"That's strange," said Ms. Eng. "I thought that job would take you only two days."

Why did Ms. Eng think it would take only two days to paint the room? She thought he would paint one-half of the room one day and the other half of the room the second day.

"You've done a beautiful job of painting this room," said Ms. Eng, "but you seem to have missed a little strip on this wall."

Why is there still a little strip that isn't painted? It's the half left over from what he painted the day before.

"I haven't missed it," said Mr. Muddle. "I'm still working on it. I'm following your good advice and doing half a job each day. For a while the work kept getting easier and easier because every day I had less to paint. But now it's getting harder. The strip is so narrow that it's difficult to paint only half of it. I have to go very slowly, because if I'm not careful I'll make a mistake and paint the whole strip at once."

What would happen if Mr. Muddle painted the whole strip at once? He'd finish painting the room.

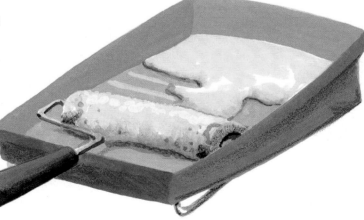

"I'm afraid I didn't explain my idea well enough," said Ms. Eng. "I meant that you should do half the job the first day and the rest of it the next day. That way you do the whole job in two days."

"That's a hard rule to follow," Mr. Muddle said. "You have to remember what the whole job is. It's easier for me if I look each day and see what needs to be done and then do half of it."

"Then I think you'd better forget about my advice and try to do a whole job in one day," said Ms. Eng. "Otherwise it will take you forever to finish one job."

Why would it take Mr. Muddle forever to finish?   He would always leave half of what there was yet to do.

The End

Teaching the Lesson

Guided Discussion

As students answer the questions in the story, ask them to communicate how they chose their answers. Allow students to debate the answers if necessary.

Using Student Pages 283–284

Have students follow the instructions and complete the **Student Edition** activities. Read the instructions aloud if students are having difficulty.

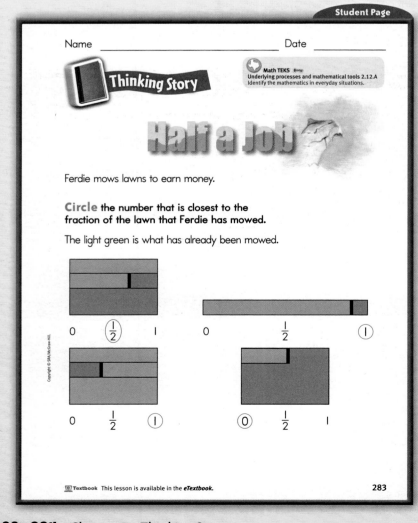

Student Page

Name _____   Date _____

Thinking Story

Math TEKS
Underlying processes and mathematical tools 2.12.A
Identify the mathematics in everyday situations.

Half a Job

Ferdie mows lawns to earn money.

Circle the number that is closest to the fraction of the lawn that Ferdie has mowed.

The light green is what has already been mowed.

0   (½)   1

0   ½   (1)

0   ½   (1)

(0)   ½   1

Textbook This lesson is available in the *eTextbook*.

283

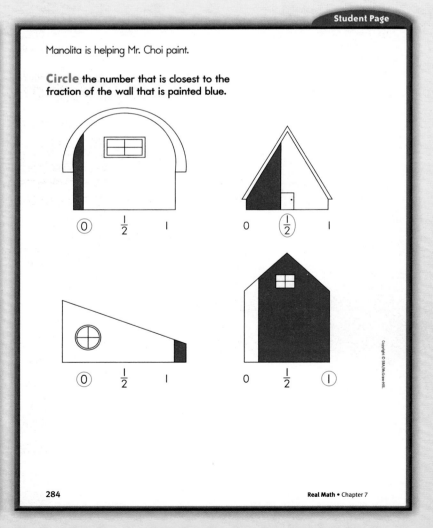

Student Page

Manolita is helping Mr. Choi paint.

Circle the number that is closest to the fraction of the wall that is painted blue.

0   ½   1

0   (½)   1

(0)   ½   1

0   ½   (1)

284

Real Math • Chapter 7

Teacher Reflection

Reflect on each of the lessons you taught in this chapter. Rate each one on the following scale, and then consider ways to maintain or improve positive teaching experiences in the future.

Lessons	Very Effective	Effective	Less Effective	What Worked	Ways to Improve
7.1 Halves and Fourths					
7.2 Writing Fractions					
7.3 Halves, Fourths, and Thirds					
7.4 Sixths and Eighths					
7.5 Fractions of a Set					
7.6 Fifths					
7.7 Equivalent Fractions					
7.8 Fractions of Numbers					
7.9 Telling Time— Hour and Half Hour					
7.10 Telling Time— Quarter Hour					
7.11 Fractions Greater than One					

★ = 120-Day Plan for TAKS

Geometry

Teaching for Understanding

In this chapter students are introduced to plane figures and space figures. Attributes of plane figures are introduced through exploration with pattern blocks. Students explore tessellations, congruency, and symmetry. Paper-folding techniques are used to demonstrate the relationship between flat plane figures and three-dimensional space figures.

Prerequisite Skills and Concepts

- Counting Sides and Angles • Recognizing Equal Parts • Recognizing Basic Shapes

Geometry Skills Trace

Before Grade 2	Grade 2	After Grade 2
Grades K–1 Informally and formally introduced to plane figures and space figures	**This chapter** introduces plane figures, space figures, angles, congruence, and symmetry.	Formal introduction to more plane figures and space figures. Formal introduction to measurement of angles

BIG Ideas! in Chapter 8

This chapter develops the following ideas running throughout elementary mathematics:

- Two- and three-dimensional objects with or without curved surfaces can be described, classified, and analyzed by their attributes.

  In this chapter, plane and solid geometric shapes are explored further, focusing on identifying and describing attributes such as number of sides, faces, and vertices. Students are reintroduced to basic shapes and are given the opportunity to develop greater understanding of spatial relationships between geometric figures. Knowledge and understanding of fractions is integrated in Lesson 8.2 where students are informally introduced to the concept of area. Area will be covered more formally in Chapter 11.

- Polygons can be constructed from or decomposed into other polygons. In Lesson 8.3, students use pattern blocks to put geometric shapes together and take them apart to form other shapes.

  Students are introduced to irregular polygons and learn to distinguish them from regular polygons. In Lessons 8.9 and 8.10, students apply their knowledge of plane shapes to investigate solid geometric shapes. The attributes of solid shapes, such as number of sides, shapes of faces, and number of vertices or corners is explored. Students gain an understanding of the relationships between plane and solid shapes when they construct three-dimensional shapes from two-dimensional figures.

TEXAS

Math TEKS addressed in each lesson can be found in the Chapter Planner on page 285E.

Math TEKS addressed in Problem-Solving, Review, and Assessment lessons are on page 285G.

Complete text of the standards appears on the Lesson Overview page and first Teaching page of each lesson.

Math Background

Geometry

What is Geometry?

Geometry is the mathematics of the properties and relationships of points, lines, angles, surfaces, and solids. Numbers explain how many or how big something is, and geometry explains where things are and what shape they have.

Geometry can be used to understand and to represent the objects, directions, and locations in our world, and the relationships between them. Geometric shapes can be described, analyzed, transformed and composed and decomposed into other shapes.

(Clements, Douglas and J. Sarama, eds. *Engaging Young Children in Mathematics: Standards for Early Childhood Mathematics Education.* Mahwah, New Jersey: Lawrence Erlbaum Associates, Publishers, 2004, p. 39.)

Plane and Space Figures

- A plane is a geometric concept that cannot be created in our three-dimensional world. In geometry, a plane is a flat surface that extends indefinitely in every direction. A plane has no thickness, nor do geometric figures that lie in a plane.

- People often use the word *solid* to refer to figures in space, such as a cube or sphere. However, in mathematics we generally think of such figures as only the empty shell. (This is why we can represent a space figure using a net that lies in a plane until it is "folded" to create a figure.) Therefore, in **Real Math** we refer to figures in a plane as plane figures and those that cannot be placed in a plane as space figures.

- Note also that a square and a circle are one-dimensional objects in a plane (because they are composed of line segments, which have only the dimension of length) and a cube and sphere are two-dimensional objects in space (because their surfaces have length and width but not depth).

Polygons

- A closed figure separates the plane into two non-connected parts.
  - o This is a closed figure:
  - o This is not a closed figure:

- A polygon is a closed figure with straight (not curved) sides.

- A regular polygon has sides that are the same length and angles that have the same measure. A regular polygon may have any number of sides.

Types of Angles

Although angle measurement is not formally defined in this chapter, students should have an intuitive sense of how angles compare to right angles.

- The measure of an angle can be thought of as the amount of turning required to move from one side of the angle to the other side.

- A right angle represents one-fourth of a complete turn. The corners of pages and pieces of paper are often right angles, so paper can be used to check how angles compare to right angles.

- An obtuse angle represents more of a turn than a right angle. If a right angle is held against an angle so one side of each angle coincides and the other side of the unknown angle is visible, the unknown angle is obtuse.

- An acute angle represents less of a turn than a right angle. If a right angle is held against an angle so one side of each angle coincides and the other side of the unknown angle is not visible because it is under the right angle, then the unknown angle is acute.

What Research Says
About Geometry

How Children Learn Geometry

"Geometry can be used to understand and to represent the objects, directions, and locations in our world, and the relationships between them. Geometric shapes can be described, analyzed, transformed and composed and decomposed into other shapes."

Clements, Douglas and J. Sarama, eds. *Engaging Young Children in Mathematics: Standards for Early Childhood Mathematics Education.* Mahwah, New Jersey: Lawrence Erlbaum Associates, Publishers, 2004, p. 39.

Learning Trajectories for Geometric Thought

Children typically follow an observable developmental progression in learning about shapes with recognizable stages or levels. This developmental path can be described as part of a learning trajectory. Key steps in the learning trajectory for geometry from the first-grade range are described below. For the complete trajectory, see Appendix B.

Level Name	Description
Shape DeComposer with Imagery	A significant sign of development is when a child is able to decompose shapes flexibly using independently generated imagery. For example, given hexagons, the child can break it apart to make shapes such as these.
Shape Composer— Units of Units	Children demonstrate further understanding when they are able to build and apply units of units (shapes made from other shapes). For example, in constructing spatial patterns, the child can extend patterning activity to create a tiling with a new unit shape—a unit of unit shapes that he or she recognizes and consciously constructs.
Congruence Determiner	A sign of development is when a child determines congruence by comparing all attributes and all spatial relationships. For example, a child at this level says that two shapes are the same shape and the same size after comparing every one of their sides and angles.
Pattern Unit Recognizer	At this level, a child can identify the smallest unit of a pattern. For example, given objects in a row with one missing, ABBAB_ABB, identifies and fills in the missing element.

Clements, D. H., J. Sarama, (in press). *Early Childhood Mathematics Learning.* In F. K. Lester, Jr. (Ed.), *Second Handbook of Research on Mathematics Teaching and Learning.* New York: Information Age Publishing.

Research-Based Teaching Techniques

"Overall research indicates that all types of geometric ideas appear to develop over time, becoming increasingly integrated and synthesized. . . . Children's ideas about shapes do not come from passive looking. Instead, they come as children's bodies, hands, eyes, and minds engage in active construction. In addition, children need to explore shapes extensively to fully understand them; merely seeing and naming pictures is insufficient. Finally, they have to explore the parts and attributes of shapes."

Clements, Douglas H. "Teaching and Learning Geometry" in Kilpatrick, Jeremy, W. Gary Martin, and Deborah Schifter, eds. *A Research Companion to Principles and Standards for School Mathematics.* Reston, VA: National Council of Teachers of Mathematics, Inc. 2003, p. 152.

RESEARCH IN ACTION

Geometric Figures Chapter 8 provides students with opportunities to explore, measure, compare, describe, and classify geometric shapes and figures that include points, lines, angles, circles, triangles, polygons, and space figures.

Space Figures In Chapter 8 students will work with various attributes of space figures, including pyramids, prisms, and cones and will classify, measure, compare, and describe the figures.

Language Development In Chapter 8 students will gain greater fluency and awareness of the language of geometry. Students will use the language of geometry to compose, compare, classify, and describe geometric figures.

Patterns In Chapter 8 students will explore patterns formed with shapes and figures including the formations of tessellations.

Vocabulary Cards
Use the *SRA Math Vocabulary Cards*
for the vocabulary words indicated to
introduce, teach, review, and reinforce
key math vocabulary for this chapter.

Academic Vocabulary

area (Lesson 8.2) the interior, or inside, of a figure

congruent (Lesson 8.6) exactly alike in shape and size

line of symmetry (Lesson 8.7) a line on which a figure can be folded into two congruent parts

polygon (Lesson 8.8) a closed plane figure having at least three straight sides

quadrilateral (Lesson 8.3) a polygon with four sides and four angles

regular polygon (Lesson 8.8) a polygon having sides that are all the same length and angles that are all equal

space figures (Lesson 8.9) figures that cannot fit in a plane

tessellation (Lesson 8.1) a pattern of plane figures that does not have any spaces between them

English Learner

Cognates

For English learners, a quick way to acquire new English vocabulary is to build on what is known in the primary language.

English	Spanish
pattern	patrón
classify	clasificar
fractional	fraccional
parallelogram	paralelogramo
rhombus	rombo
angle	ángulo
congruent	congruente
triangle	triángulo
polygons	polígonos
cube	cubo
sphere	esfera
pyramid	pirámide

Access Vocabulary

English learners might understand words in different contexts and might not understand idioms. Review chapter vocabulary for this concern. For example:

pattern	a predictable repetition of colors, numbers, or shapes
figures	shapes
plane figures	flat shapes
train tracks	the rails on which a train travels
identify the angles	tell whether the angles are acute, obtuse, or right
identical	the same
plane	a flat surface; not an airplane or plain
compare	to find the likenesses and differences

Texas Chapter Planner

Lessons	Objectives	NCTM Standards	TEXAS Math TEKS
8.1 Tessellations pages 287A–288A 45–60 minutes	**To review the names and properties of common shapes** and to use those shapes to create tessellating patterns	Algebra, Geometry	2.7.A 2.7.B 2.7.C 
8.2 Parts of Plane Figures pages 289A–290A 45–60 minutes	**To continue to become familiar with the properties of common shapes** while also reviewing fractions and informally introducing area	Geometry, Problem Solving	2.7.C 2.2.A
8.3 Combining Plane Figures pages 291A–292A 45–60 minutes	**To explore the results of combining plane figures** and to continue to become familiar with the properties of common shapes	Geometry, Problem Solving	2.7.C 2.2.A 2.12.D
8.4 Defining Plane Figures— Quadrilaterals pages 293A–294A 45–60 minutes	**To provide formal definitions for different kinds of quadrilaterals** and to study and define parallel and perpendicular lines	Geometry, Problem Solving	2.7.A 2.7.B 2.7.C
8.5 Obtuse, Acute, and Right Angles pages 299A–300A 45–60 minutes	**To introduce the properties of different types of angles** and to review telling time	Connections, Geometry	2.10.B 2.7.A 2.13.B
8.6 Congruence pages 301A–302A 45–60 minutes	**To introduce the concept of congruence** and to provide examples of how congruent objects are created	Geometry, Problem Solving	2.7.B 3.9.A
8.7 Symmetry pages 303A–304A 45–60 minutes	**To review the concept of symmetry** and to demonstrate this concept by drawing lines and using paper-folding techniques	Geometry, Problem Solving, Representation	2.7.A 2.7.B 3.9.C
8.8 Defining Other Plane Figures pages 305A–306A 45–60 minutes	**To introduce definitions of some plane figures, such as right triangles,** and to study the difference between regular and irregular polygons	Geometry, Problem Solving	2.7.A 2.7.B
8.9 Space Figures pages 307A–310B 45–60 minutes	**To introduce space figures** through classification and construction activities	Geometry, Connections	2.7.A 2.7.B
8.10 Space Figures and Plane Figures pages 311A–314B 45–60 minutes	**To compare space figures and plane figures** and to decompose space figures into plane figures	Geometry, Connections	2.7.A 2.7.B

★ = 120-Day Plan for TAKS

🗝 = Key standard

285E Chapter 8 • Geometry

Academic Vocabulary	Manipulatives and Materials	Games to reinforce skills and concepts
plane figure tessellation	• *Number Cubes* • Pattern blocks • Overhead pattern blocks	
✎ area	• *Number Cubes* • Pattern blocks • Overhead pattern blocks • SRA Math Vocabulary Cards	
	• *Number Cubes* • Pattern blocks • Overhead pattern blocks	
✎ quadrilateral	• *Number Cubes* • SRA Math Vocabulary Cards	
	• Straightedge • Pattern blocks • Clock	
✎ congruent	• *Number Cubes* • Attribute blocks • Overhead attribute blocks • Pattern blocks or overhead pattern blocks • Tracing paper • SRA Math Vocabulary Cards	
✎ line of symmetry	• *Number Cubes* • A straightedge or ruler for each student • Paper and scissors for each student • Mirror cards • SRA Math Vocabulary Cards	
✎ polygon regular polygon	• *Number Cubes* • SRA Math Vocabulary Cards	
space figures	• *Number Cubes* • Space figures • A copy of *Practice* page 128 for each student • Everyday objects that are the shape of space figures • Scissors and tape	
	• *Number Cubes* • Space figures	

Additional Resources

Differentiated Instruction

Intervention Support Guide Provides instruction for the following prerequisite skills:

- Lesson 8.A Shapes and Parts–1
- Lesson 8.B Shapes and Parts–2
- Lesson 8.C Shapes and Parts–3

Enrichment Support Guide Extends lesson concepts

Practice Reinforces lesson skills and concepts

Reteach Support Guide Provides alternate instruction for lesson concepts

English Learner Support Guide Previews and reviews lesson concepts and vocabulary for English learners

Special Needs Students Extend the ✋ activities to develop concrete models for special needs students.

Technology

The following electronic resources are available:

ⓔ **Planner** Lessons 8.1–8.10

ⓔ **Presentation** Lessons 8.1–8.10

ⓔ **Textbook** Lessons 8.1–8.10

ⓔ **Assess** Lessons 8.1–8.10

ⓔ **MathTools** *Shape Tool* Lessons 8.1, 8.4, 8.8, 8.10
    Tessellations Lessons 8.1, 8.3
    Net Tool Lessons 8.9, 8.10

Building Blocks *Super Shape 1* Lesson 8.1
    Super Shape 2 Lesson 8.2
    Piece Puzzler 5 Lesson 8.3
    Super Shape 3 Lesson 8.4
    Shape Shop 2 Lesson 8.5
    Shape Parts 3 Lesson 8.6
    Geometry Snapshots 3 Lesson 8.7
    Shape Shop 3 Lesson 8.8

Assessment

Informal Assessment rubrics at the end of each lesson provide daily evaluation of student math proficiency.

Texas Chapter Planner, continued

Problem Solving	When to Use	Objectives	NCTM Standards	Math TEKS
Problem Solving 8.A (pp. 285I–286C) 15–30 minutes	Use after the Chapter 8 Pretest.	To introduce chapter concepts in a problem-solving setting	Problem Solving, Communication	2.7.B, 2.13.A
Problem Solving 8.B (pp. 295–296, 296A) 30–45 minutes	Use anytime during the chapter.	To explore methods of solving nonroutine problems	Problem Solving, Communication	2.12.C
Problem Solving 8.C (pp. 315–316, 316A) 45–60 minutes	Use anytime during the chapter.	To explore methods of solving nonroutine problems	Problem Solving, Communication	2.12.B
Thinking Story—Manolita Changes Things (pp. 327A–327E, 327–328) 20–30 minutes	Use anytime during the chapter.	To develop logical reasoning while integrating reading skills with mathematics	Number and Operations, Connections	2.14

Review	When to Use	Objectives	NCTM Standards	Math TEKS
Cumulative Review (p. 297–298) 15–30 minutes	Use anytime after Lesson 8.4.	To review concepts and skills taught earlier in the year	Number and Operations	2.3.A, 2.3.B, 2.7.C, 2.11.A
Cumulative Review (p. 317–318) 15–30 minutes	Use anytime after Lesson 8.10.	To review concepts and skills taught earlier in the year	Number and Operations	2.1.A, 2.3.A, 2.3.B, 2.6.C, 2.10.B
Chapter 8 Review (pp. 321A, 321–322) 30–45 minutes	Use after Lesson 8.10.	To review concepts and skills taught in the chapter	Number and Operations	2.7.A, 2.7.C, 2.10.B

Assessment	When to Use	Objectives	NCTM Standards	Math TEKS
Pretest (*Assessment* pp. 124-125) 15–30 minutes	**Entry** Use prior to Chapter 8.	To provide assessment of prerequisite and chapter topics	Number and Operations, Problem Solving	2.2.A, 2.7.A, 2.7.B, 2.7.C, 2.10.B, 2.13.B, 3.9.A, 3.9.C
Informal Assessment Rubrics (pp. 288A–314B) 5 minutes per student	**Progress Monitoring** Use at the end of each lesson.	To provide daily evaluation of math proficiency	Number and Operations, Communication	2.2.A, 2.7.A, 2.7.B, 2.7.C, 2.10.B, 2.13.B, 3.9.A, 3.9.C
Individual Oral Assessment (p. 298A) 5 minutes per student	Use after Lesson 8.4.	To provide alternate means of assessing students' progress	Number and Operations	2.7.A, 2.7.B, 2.7.C
Mastery Checkpoint (*Assessment* p. 91–92) 15 minutes	**Progress Monitoring** Use in or after Lesson 8.6.	To provide assessment of mastery of key skills	Number and Operations	2.7.B
Chapter 8 Practice Test (pp. 323–324, 325–326) 30–45 minutes	**Progress Monitoring** Use after or in place of the Chapter 8 Review.	To provide assessment or additional practice with the chapter concepts	Number and Operations, Problem Solving	2.2.A, 2.7.A, 2.7.B, 2.7.C, 2.10.B, 2.13.B, 3.9.A, 3.9.C
Chapter 8 Test (*Assessment* pp. 240–243) 240–243 minutes	**Summative** Use after or in place of the Chapter 8 Review.	To provide assessment on the chapter concepts	Number and Operations, Problem Solving	2.2.A, 2.7.A, 2.7.B, 2.7.C, 2.10.B, 2.13.B, 3.9.A, 3.9.C

Texas Technology Resources

Visit SRAonline.com for online versions of the **Real Math** eSuite.

 Technology for Teachers

e Presentation	**Lessons 8.1–8.10** Use the *ePresentation* to interactively present chapter content.
e Planner	Use the Chapter and Lesson Planners to outline activities and time frames for Chapter 8.
e Assess	Students can take the following assessments in *eAssess:* • Chapter Pretest • Mastery Checkpoint **Lesson 8.6** • Chapter Test Teachers can record results and print reports for all assessments in this chapter.
e MathTools	**Shape Tool Lessons 8.1, 8.4, 8.8, 8.10** **Tessellations Lessons 8.1, 8.3** **Net Tool Lessons 8.9, 8.10**

Technology for Students

e Textbook	An electronic, interactive version of the **Student Edition** is available for all lessons in Chapter 8.
e MathTools	**Shape Tool Lessons 8.1, 8.4, 8.8, 8.10** **Tessellations Lessons 8.1, 8.3** **Net Tool Lessons 8.9, 8.10**
TECH KNOWLEDGE	*TechKnowledge* Level 2 provides lessons that specifically teach the Unit 10 Internet and Unit 4 Drawing and Graphics applications that students can use while working on this chapter's project.
Building Blocks	**Super Shape 1 Lesson 8.1** **Super Shape 2 Lesson 8.2** **Piece Puzzler 5 Lesson 8.3** **Super Shape 3 Lesson 8.4** **Shape Shop 2 Lesson 8.5** **Shape Parts 3 Lesson 8.6** **Geometry Snapshots 3 Lesson 8.7** **Shape Shop 3 Lesson 8.8**

Geometry

Introduce Chapter 8 — 10

Chapter Objectives

Explain that in this chapter they will build on what they already know about geometry. They will

- define and identify plane figures and space figures.
- identify obtuse, acute, and right angles.
- match congruent objects and draw lines of symmetry.

Pretest COMPUTING

Administer the Chapter 8 Pretest, which has similar exercises to the Chapter 8 Test.

- If most students do *not* demonstrate mastery on the Pretest, proceed at a normal pace through the chapter. Use the differentiated instruction suggestions at the beginning and end of each lesson to adapt instruction to and follow up on the needs of each student.

- If most students show mastery of some or all of the concepts and skills in the Chapter 8 Pretest, move quickly through the chapter, de-emphasizing lessons linked to items which most students answered correctly. Use the Individual Oral Assessments to monitor progress, and, if necessary, modify your pacing. These assessments are especially useful because they can help you distinguish among different levels of understanding. For example, a student who has mastered a particular skill but does not show a deep understanding of the relevant concepts still needs thorough coverage of the lesson material.

- If you do move quickly through the chapter, be sure not to skip games, Problem-Solving lessons, and Thinking Stories. These provide practice in skills and nonroutine thinking that will be useful even to students who already understand the chapter content. Also, be alert to application problems embedded within lessons that may show students how math topics are used in daily life.

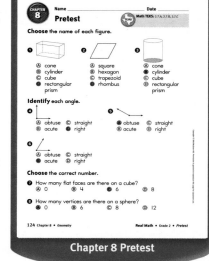

Chapter 8 Pretest

Access Prior Knowledge ✓ UNDERSTANDING

As students look at the photo on page 286, ask questions such as the following:

- **What do you see on this page?**
- **Where might this have been found?**

- **What are some things scientists might learn about dinosaurs by investigating their tracks?**
- **Have you ever seen fossils of dinosaur tracks?**
- **Where did you see them? What did they look like?**

Problem Solving 8.A Introducing Strategie

Tell Students In Today's Lesson They Will

- create pictures of dinosaur tracks.
- put the tracks in categories.
- explain the rules they used to sort the tracks.

Materials

- Scissors
- Glue
- Tracing paper or other thin, translucent paper (several sheets per student)
- Construction paper (several sheets per student)

Guided Discussion

Using Student Pages APPLYING

Explain that a scientist who studies dinosaur tracks and other fossils is called a *paleontologist*. Have students look at page 286, and present this problem:

Imagine that you are a paleontologist who wants to learn about dinosaurs by investigating tracks they left behind. The picture shows one of the tracks you have found in various places. You will use this track as a model to create other tracks with different attributes. As a scientist you want to organize the tracks and make a display to show how they are alike and how they are different. As you observe the tracks closely, think about why some might belong in some categories and others in other categories. Make up a rule or name for each category. Then create a display of the tracks by tracing them, cutting them out, and sorting them according to your categories. On your display, label each category. Try to make categories that will be useful to other paleontologists also.

Guided Discussion UNDERSTANDING

To make sure students understand the problem, ask questions such as the following:

- **What kinds of things do paleontologists learn from observing and sorting dinosaur tracks?** whether different types of dinosaurs lived near each other; how fast the dinosaurs traveled; how big they were; which dinosaurs lived in water; and so on

TEXAS

Geometry and spatial reasoning 2.7.B
Use attributes to describe how 2 two-dimensional figures or 2 three-dimensional geometric figures are alike or different.

Underlying processes and mathematical tools 2.13.A
Explain and record observations using objects, words, pictures, numbers, and technology.

- **What are some different characteristics dinosaur tracks might have?** Many of them have three toes; some seem to have claws; some of the tracks seem wide, and some seem skinny; some have pointy heels, and some have round heels; and so on.
- **What are you supposed to do with the tracks?** Trace them, cut them out, put them in categories, and then make a display.
- **Why do you need to name each category?** so that people who see the display will know how the tracks are organized
- **Could a track be placed into more than one category?** Yes, a skinny track with three toes could be placed into a "skinny" group and also in a "three-toed" group.
- **Could some tracks be placed into one category together but not in another category together?** Yes, if two tracks each have three toes, but one is small and the other is big, both of them could be placed into the "three-toed" category, but both of them could not be placed into the "big" category.

Have each student trace the track on page 286 and use it as a model to create different tracks. Remind students to use as many different characteristics as they can, such as shape of heel and evenness of toes.

While students experiment with categories and sorting to create their displays, encourage them to change their minds as they learn what is useful and not useful for organizing. For example, students might find that categories that are too subjective might not work well because different people would arrange the tracks into these categories in different ways.

Concept/Question Board ☑ APPLYING

Questions
Have students think of and write three questions they have about geometry and how it can be used. Then have them select one question to post on the Question side of the Board.

Concepts
As students work through the chapter, have them collect examples of how geometry is used in everyday situations. For each example, have them write a problem that relates to the item(s). Have them display their examples on the Concept side of the Board. Suggest the following:

- maps
- street signs

Answers
Throughout the chapter, have students post answers to the questions and solutions to the problems on the Board.

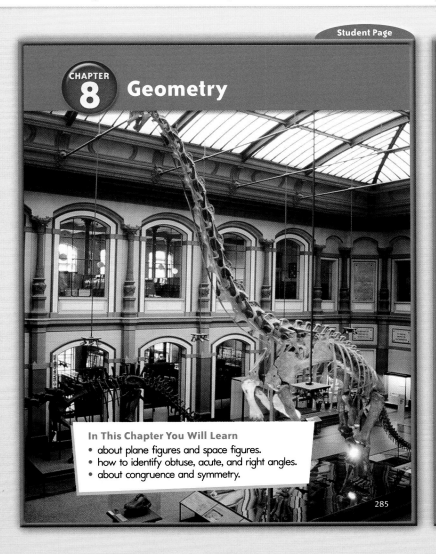

Student Page

CHAPTER 8 Geometry

In This Chapter You Will Learn
- about plane figures and space figures.
- how to identify obtuse, acute, and right angles.
- about congruence and symmetry.

285

Student Page

💡 **Problem Solving** **8·A Introducing Strategies**

Math TEKS
Underlying Processes and Mathematical tools 2.13.A
Explore and record observations using objects, words, pictures, numbers, and technology.

Name _____ Date _____

Trace and cut out the track. Use it as a model to create many tracks with different characteristics.

286 Geometry

Chapter 8 • Problem Solving 8.A

 **Reflect** 20

 Knowledge Age Skills

Effective Communication As students present their displays, have them explain the categories they used, why different tracks belong in one category and not another, and how these categories might help a paleontologist learn about dinosaurs. Ask questions such as the following:

■ **How did you decide what categories to use?** I noticed some tracks were long, and some were short; I decided to make a category for round toes and one for pointy toes; I made a category for the tracks that were fat; and so on.

■ **What categories did you think about that you decided would not be useful?** For example, I made a category of "Tracks I Like," but I decided that would not help a paleontologist learn about dinosaurs; I had a category named "Weird," but Johnny didn't think all the ones I put in that category were weird, so I realized it would be a display of what only I thought about the tracks, not about what another paleontologist would understand.

In discussion, also bring out these points:
● Shapes, even ones that look alike, can have different characteristics.
● When you organize shapes, you can make categories based on the characteristics you want to pay attention to.
● Shapes often fit into more than one category.
● Some categories are "broader" and will include more things than other categories.
● You can think of a category name as a rule that tells you whether something belongs in that group.

Sample Solutions Strategies
Students might use one or more of the following strategies to help them sort the tracks:

Use Measurement
Students might use a ruler or other measurement tool to compare dimensions of the tracks.

Use Direct Comparison
Students might stack the cut-out tracks to see how the shapes compare. They might come up with categories such as "wider than track number 1" or "the same width as track number 1."

Break the Problem into Parts
Students might come up with a large category such as "Three Toes" and then create subgroups such as "pointy" and "round." They could display the tracks in a way that shows this branching organization.

 Home Connection

At this time, you may want to send home the letter on pages 30–33 of **Home Connection.** This letter describes what students will be learning and what activities they can do at home to support their work in school.

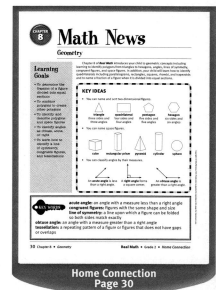

Home Connection Page 30

Assess Use *eAssess* to record and analyze evidence of student understanding.

A Gather Evidence

Use the Daily Class Assessment Records in *Texas Assessment* or *eAssess* to record Informal and Formal Assessments.

Informal Assessment
✓ **Access Prior Knowledge**
Did the student [UNDERSTANDING]
- ❏ make important observations?
- ❏ extend or generalize learning?
- ❏ provide insightful answers?
- ❏ pose insightful questions?

Informal Assessment
✓ **Concept/Question Board**
Did the student [APPLYING]
- ❏ apply learning in new situations?
- ❏ contribute concepts?
- ❏ contribute answers?
- ❏ connect mathematics to real-world situations?

Formal Assessment
✓ **Pretest** [COMPUTING]
Review student answers on the Chapter 8 Pretest.
- ❏ If most students do *not* demonstrate mastery, move at a normal pace through the chapter.
- ❏ If most students answer most questions correctly, move quickly through the chapter, emphasizing those lessons for which students did not answer correctly, as well as games, Problem-Solving lessons, and Thinking Stories.

B Summarize Findings

Analyze and summarize assessment data for each student. Determine which Assessment Follow-Up is appropriate for each student. Use the Student Assessment Record in *Texas Assessment* or *eAssess* to update assessment records.

C Texas Assessment Follow-Up • DIFFERENTIATE INSTRUCTION

Based on your observations of each student, use these teaching strategies for a general approach to the chapter. Look for specific Differentiate Instruction and Monitoring Student Progress strategies in each lesson that relate specifically to the lesson content.

ENRICH	 PRACTICE	RETEACH	INTERVENTION	ENGLISH LEARNER
If . . . students demonstrate a **secure understanding** of chapter concepts, **Then . . .** move quickly through the chapter or use *Enrichment* Lessons 8.1–8.10 as assessment follow-up to extend and apply understanding.	**If . . .** students grasp chapter concepts with **competent understanding,** **Then . . .** use *Practice* Lessons 8.1–8.10 as lesson follow-up to develop fluency.	**If . . .** students have prerequisite understanding but demonstrate **emerging understanding** of chapter concepts, **Then . . .** use *Reteach* assessment follow-up suggestions at the end of each lesson to reteach lesson concepts.	**If . . .** students are not competent with prerequisite skills, **Then . . .** use *Intervention* Lessons 8.A–8.C before each lesson to develop fluency with prerequisite skills.	Use *English Learner Support Guide* Lessons 8.1–8.10 for strategies to preteach lesson vocabulary and concepts.

Math Across the Curriculum

Preview the chapter projects with students. Assign projects or have students choose from the projects to extend and enrich concepts in this chapter.

Create a Map of Dinosaur Locations 3–4 weeks

 SOCIAL STUDIES

TEKS

MATH STANDARD: Geometry and spatial reasoning 2.7 The student uses attributes to identify two- and three-dimensional geometric figures. The student compares and contrasts two- and three-dimensional geometric figures or both.

SOCIAL STUDIES STANDARD: Geography 2.5.A Use symbols, find locations, and determine directions on maps and globes.

TECHNOLOGY STANDARD: Solving Problems 08.B Use electronic tools and research skills to build a knowledge base regarding a topic, task, or assigment.

• •

Have students use mathematics to relate geometric shapes to a map and map key. To broaden the social studies concept, have students study continents, maps, and map keys.

As part of the project, students should consider the following issues:

- areas of Earth that particular dinosaurs inhabited
- time periods in which dinosaurs lived
- eating habits of dinosaurs

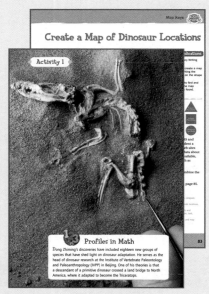

Create a Map of Dinosaur Locations

Activity 1

Profiles in Math

Dong Zhiming's discoveries have included eighteen new groups of species that have shed light on dinosaur adaptation. He serves as the head of dinosaur research at the Institute of Vertebrate Paleontology and Paleanthropology (IVPP) in Beijing. One of his theories is that a descendant of a primitive dinosaur crossed a land bridge to North America, where it adapted to become the Triceratops.

For specific step-by-step instructions for this project, see *Across the Curriculum Math Connections* pages 82–85.

 Knowledge Age Skills

Creative Work with Ideas Students create maps and map keys by using geometric shapes.

Problem Formulation, Planning, and Strategizing Students make maps from textual information.

Use Plane Figures to Draw Dinosaurs 2–3 weeks

 ART WebQuest

TEKS

MATH STANDARD: Geometry and spatial reasoning 2.7 The student uses attributes to identify two- and three-dimensional geometric figures. The student compares and contrasts two- and three-dimensional geometric figures or both.

FINE ARTS STANDARD: Creative expression/performance 2.2.B Create effective compositions, using design elements and principles.

TECHNOLOGY STANDARD: Communication 11.A Publish information in a variety of media including, but not limited to, printed copy or monitor display.

• •

Have students use technology to

- gather information about dinosaurs.
- choose a dinosaur to draw.
- sketch a dinosaur.
- use geometric plane figures to create the shape of a dinosaur.

For this project, students use the Internet to investigate the following information:

- relationships between dinosaur names and body shapes
- the color of dinosaurs' skin
- a database of dinosaur illustrations

Draw Dinosaurs Using Plane Figures

Activity 2

Careers in Math

A scientific illustrator is an artist who draws pictures of things such as the parts of an atom, the life cycle of a flower, or the body shape of a dinosaur. These illustrators carefully research and create scale drawings that realistically represent scientific concepts and wildlife. Scientific illustrators often work for museums or scientific publications.

For specific step-by-step instructions for this project, see *Across the Curriculum Math Connections* pages 86–91.

 Knowledge Age Skills

Creative Work with Ideas Students use plane figures to create dinosaur drawings.

Teamwork Students work in teams to select and draw dinosaurs.

TECH KNOWLEDGE **TechKnowledge** Level 2 provides lessons that specifically teach the Unit 10 Internet and Unit 4 Drawing and Graphics applications that students can use in this project.

TEXAS
Vertical Alignment

Grade 1	Grade 2	Grade 3
1.6.D Use concrete models to combine two-dimensional geometric figures to make new geometric figures.	**2.7.C** Cut two-dimensional geometric figures apart and identify the new geometric figures formed.	**3.8** The student uses formal geometric vocabulary.

Overview LESSON 8.1
TEXAS

Lesson Planner

OBJECTIVES
- To review and familiarize students with the names and some of the properties of common figures such as the triangle, square, trapezoid, rhombus, and hexagon
- To allow students to create and explore tessellation patterns
- To informally introduce how polygons can be put together to create other polygons

MATH TEKS
Applying: Geometry and spatial reasoning 2.7.A
Describe attributes (the number of vertices, faces, edges, sides) of two- and three-dimensional geometric figures such as circles, polygons, spheres, cones, cylinders, prisms, and pyramids.

Geometry and spatial reasoning 2.7.B
Use attributes to describe how 2 two-dimensional figures or 2 three-dimensional geometric figures are alike or different.

Geometry and spatial reasoning 2.7.C
Cut two-dimensional geometric figures apart and identify the new geometric figures formed.

MATH TEKS INTEGRATION
Number, operation, and quantitative reasoning 2.3.B
Model addition and subtraction of two-digit numbers with objects, pictures, words, and numbers.

MATERIALS
- *Number Cubes
- *Pattern blocks
- *Overhead pattern blocks

TECHNOLOGY
- Presentation Lesson 8.1
- MathTools Shape Tool
- MathTools Tessellations
- Building Blocks Super Shape 1

Tessellations ★

Context of the Lesson In this lesson students use pattern blocks to tessellate and become familiar with plane figures. Plane figures were also covered in Grade 1.

See page 285B for Math Background for teachers for this lesson.

Planning for Learning ● DIFFERENTIATE INSTRUCTION

INTERVENTION
If . . . students lack the prerequisite skill of recognizing equal parts,

Then . . . teach *Intervention* Lesson 8.A.

1.2.A, 1.6.4

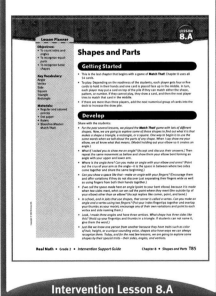

Intervention Lesson 8.A

ENGLISH LEARNER
Preview

If . . . students need language support,

Then . . . use Lesson 8.1 in *English Learner Support Guide* to preview lesson concepts and vocabulary.

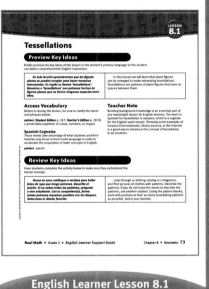

English Learner Lesson 8.1

ENRICH
If . . . students are proficient in the lesson concepts,

Then . . . emphasize exploring *eMathTools*.

PRACTICE
If . . . students would benefit from additional practice,

Then . . . extend Skill Practice before assigning the student pages.

RETEACH
If . . . students are having difficulty understanding tessellations,

Then . . . extend Guided Discussion before assigning the student pages.

Academic Vocabulary
plane figure *n.* a flat shape

tessellation \těsˊə lāˊ shən\ *n.* a pattern of plane figures that does not have any space between them

Access Vocabulary
pattern a predictable repetition of colors, numbers, or shapes

Spanish Cognates
pattern patrón

★ = 120-Day Plan for TAKS

Geometry and spatial reasoning 2.7.A Describe attributes (the number of vertices, faces, edges, sides) of two- and three-dimensional geometric figures such as circles, polygons, spheres, cones, cylinders, prisms, and pyramids.

Geometry and spatial reasoning 2.7.B Use attributes to describe how 2 two-dimensional figures or 2 three-dimensional geometric figures alike or different.

Geometry and spatial reasoning 2.7.C Cut two-dimensional geometric figures apart and identify the new geometric figures formed.

Mental Math   5

 INTEGRATION: TEKS 2.3.B Present exercises such as the following, and have students show their answers using **Number Cubes.**

a. 56 + 29 = 85   **b.** 54 + 39 = 93   **c.** 38 + 47 = 85
d. 63 + 19 = 82   **e.** 38 + 42 = 80   **f.** 28 + 32 = 60

1 Develop   25

Tell Students In Today's Lesson They Will
learn about tessellations and plane figures.

Guided Discussion   ENGAGING   Introductory

Ask the class:

■ **Critical Thinking** **Have you ever seen a pattern in a tile floor?**
Discuss students' responses. Explain that the pattern on a tiled floor is an example of a tessellation.

Divide the class into small groups, and distribute the pattern blocks. Allow time for students to explore and create tessellations. If a digital camera is available, take pictures of the students' patterns, and share them with the class.

Skill Building   UNDERSTANDING   Guided

 After the class has had time to familiarize themselves with the pattern blocks, introduce each figure using **MathTools** the overhead pattern blocks. Name the figure of each pattern block, and point to its attributes as students describe them. The term *parallel* will be formally introduced in Lesson 4 of this chapter. For now, just use the term in context and explain as necessary. Make sure to discuss the information listed below if students do not provide it. Then draw other examples of each figure using the board, overhead projector, or *eMathTools: Shape Tool.*

- **Triangle** All triangles have three sides and three angles. Triangles can have many different figures, but they always have three sides and three angles.
- **Square** All squares have four equal sides. The corners of a square are like the corners of a book. The opposite sides of all squares go in the same direction. All squares have the same shape, but they can be different sizes.
- **Rhombus** All rhombuses (also called *rhombi*) have four equal sides like a square, but the angles are not like the corners of a book. The opposite sides of all rhombuses go in the same direction.
- **Trapezoid** All trapezoids have four sides. Only one set of opposite sides go in the same direction.
- **Hexagon** All hexagons have six sides and six angles. Regular hexagons have six equal sides.

Skill Practice   COMPUTING   Guided

 Do a response drill in which you call out the name of a figure or describe the properties of a figure. Students find, hide, and then show the correct figure. Possible examples include the following:

a. hexagon hexagon
b. triangle triangle
c. figure with three angles triangle
d. figure with two sets of parallel lines square or rhombus
e. figure with one set of parallel lines trapezoid

Progress Monitoring

If . . . students have difficulty identifying the figures during the response drill,

Then . . . plan to spend more time allowing them to explore, create, and share tessellations over the next several days. All students will benefit from this extra exploration time.

2 Use Student Pages   20

Pages 287–288   APPLYING   Independent

Do page 287 as a group activity. Following each problem, repeat part of the pattern on the overhead projector, saying aloud the names of the figures as you place them in the pattern.

Students will need a set of pattern blocks to place within the hexagon figures on page 288. Students should sketch their different tessellations within the hexagon outlines.

As Students Finish

 **Building Blocks** Have students use **Super Shape 1** to explore deconstructing plane figures.

 **MathTools** *Tessellations* Have students use this tool to continue exploring tessellations.

Student Page

Name _____ Date _____

Tessellations

Key Ideas

Math TEKS
Applying: Geometry and spatial reasoning 2.7.C
Cut two-dimensional geometric figures apart and identify
the new geometric figures formed.

These are examples of
plane figures.

hexagon   triangle   square   rhombus   trapezoid

Tessellations are patterns of plane figures
that do not have any spaces or gaps
between them.

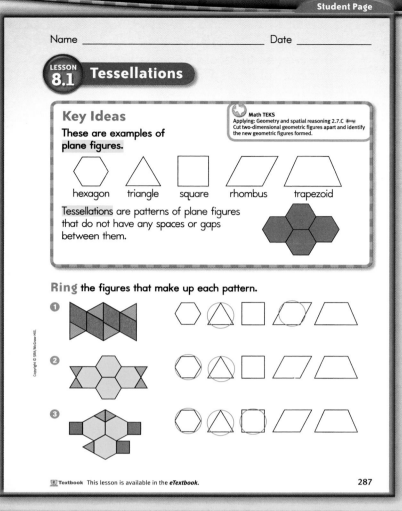

Ring the figures that make up each pattern.

①

②

③

Textbook This lesson is available in the *eTextbook*.

287

---

④ **Use** these figures to fill the hexagons. Can you fill
them six different ways?

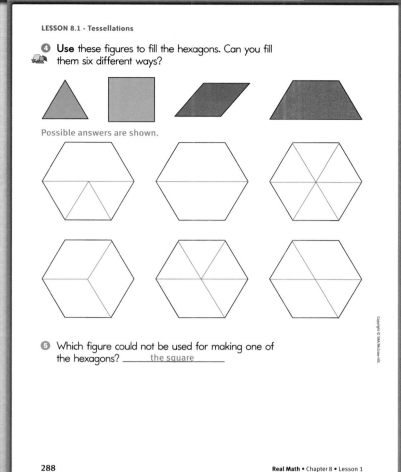

Possible answers are shown.

⑤ Which figure could not be used for making one of
the hexagons? _____the square_____

288

Real Math · Chapter 8 · Lesson 1

---

③ Reflect
5

Guided Discussion ☑ UNDERSTANDING

Allow some time for individual students to show their tessellating
patterns or pictures of their patterns. Have the class identify what
is being repeated in each student's pattern.

■ **Critical Thinking** Can you think of tessellating patterns you may
have seen at home, school, or elsewhere? Tell students to look for
more of these patterns at home and to tell the class about what
they find.

TEXAS TEKS Checkup

**TEKS 2.14 • The student uses logical
reasoning. The student is expected
to justify his or her thinking using
objects, words, pictures, numbers,
and technology.**

Use this problem to assess students'
progress towards standards mastery:

Which shapes make the pattern?

A ▢ △

B ▢ ◣

C ⬠ ▱

D ◺ ▭

Have students choose the correct
answer and then describe how they
knew which choice was correct. In
the discussion, ask questions such
as the following. Be sure to ask
students to explain their reasoning,
because different solution methods
are possible.

■ **How many kinds of shapes make
the pattern?** 2 kinds

■ **Does it matter how many of each
shape there are?** no, just how
many different shapes

Follow-Up
If . . . students need additional
practice with mathematical
reasoning skills,

Then . . . have them complete
*Building Blocks: Legends of the Lost
Shape.*

Assess and Differentiate

 Assess Use *eAssess* to record and analyze evidence of student understanding.

A Gather Evidence

Use the Daily Class Assessment Records in *Texas Assessment* or *eAssess* to record daily observations.

Informal Assessment
☑ **Skill Practice**

Did the student COMPUTING
- ❑ respond accurately?
- ❑ respond quickly?
- ❑ respond with confidence?
- ❑ self-correct?

Informal Assessment
☑ **Guided Discussion**

Did the student UNDERSTANDING
- ❑ make important observations?
- ❑ extend or generalize learning?
- ❑ provide insightful answers?
- ❑ pose insightful questions?

 **TEKS/TAKS Practice**

Use *TEKS/TAKS Practice* pages 59–62 to assess student progress.

B Summarize Findings

Analyze and summarize assessment data for each student. Determine which Assessment Follow-Up is appropriate for each student. Use the Student Assessment Record in *Texas Assessment* or *eAssess* to update assessment records.

C Texas Assessment Follow-Up ● DIFFERENTIATE INSTRUCTION

Based on your observations, use these teaching strategies for assessment follow-up.

INTERVENTION

Review student performance on *Intervention* Lesson 8.A to see if students have mastered prerequisite skills for this lesson.

🔷 **1.2.A** Separate a whole into two, three, or four equal parts and use appropriate language to describe the parts such as three out of four equal parts.

🔷 **1.6.A** Describe and identify two-dimensional geometric figures, including circles, triangles, rectangles, and squares (a special type of rectangle).

ENGLISH LEARNER

Review

Use Lesson 8.1 in *English Learner Support Guide* to review lesson concepts and vocabulary.

ENRICH

If . . . students are proficient in the lesson concepts,

Then . . . encourage them to work on the chapter projects or *Enrichment* Lesson 8.1.

Enrichment Lesson 8.1

PRACTICE

If . . . students would benefit from additional practice,

Then . . . assign *Practice* Lesson 8.1.

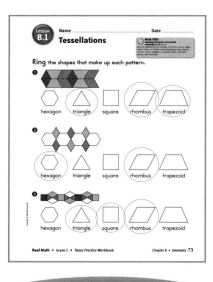

Practice Lesson 8.1

RETEACH

If . . . students are having difficulty making tessellations with multiple figures,

Then . . . have them tessellate with two figures, and then begin to use more figures.

Grade 1	Grade 2	Grade 3
1.6.D Use concrete models to combine two-dimensional geometric figures to make new geometric figures.	**2.7.C** Cut two-dimensional geometric figures apart and identify the new geometric figures formed.	**3.8** The student uses formal geometric vocabulary.

Overview · LESSON 8.2

TEXAS

Lesson Planner

OBJECTIVES
- To continue to familiarize students with some of the properties of common shapes such as triangles, squares, trapezoids, rhombuses, and hexagons
- To informally introduce the term *area* to describe how much space there is inside a polygon
- To review the concept of equivalent fractions

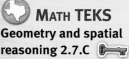

MATH TEKS
Geometry and spatial reasoning 2.7.C
Cut two-dimensional geometric figures apart and identify the new geometric figures formed.
Number, operation, and quantitative reasoning 2.2.A
Use concrete models to represent and name fractional parts of a whole object (with denominators of 12 or less).

MATH TEKS INTEGRATION
Number, operation, and quantitative reasoning 2.3.B
Model addition and subtraction of two-digit numbers with objects, pictures, words, and numbers.
Patterns, relationships, and algebraic thinking 2.6.C
Identify, describe, and extend repeating and additive patterns to make predictions and solve problems.

MATERIALS
- *Number Cubes
- *Pattern blocks
- *Overhead pattern blocks
- *SRA Math Vocabulary Cards*

TECHNOLOGY
Presentation Lesson 8.2
Building Blocks Super Shape 2

Parts of Plane Figures ★

Context of the Lesson This lesson continues the work with pattern blocks from the previous lesson and integrates that work with the study of fractions. Fractions were covered in Chapter 7. The concept of area is informally introduced here. Area will be covered more formally in Chapter 11, where it will be used as a model for understanding multiplication.

See page 285B for Math Background for teachers for this lesson.

Planning for Learning ● DIFFERENTIATE INSTRUCTION

INTERVENTION
If . . . students lack the prerequisite skill of recognizing equal parts,

Then . . . teach *Intervention* Lesson 8.A.

 1.2.A, 1.6.4

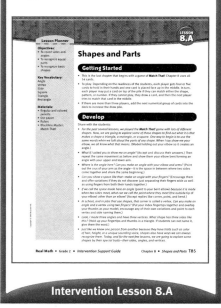

Intervention Lesson 8.A

ENGLISH LEARNER
Preview
If . . . students need language support,

Then . . . use Lesson 8.2 in *English Learner Support Guide* to preview lesson concepts and vocabulary.

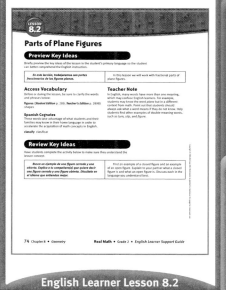

English Learner Lesson 8.2

ENRICH
If . . . students are proficient in the lesson concepts,

Then . . . emphasize *Building Blocks.*

PRACTICE
If . . . students would benefit from additional practice,

Then . . . extend Skill Practice before assigning the student pages.

RETEACH
If . . . students are having difficulty understanding fractions of plane figures,

Then . . . extend Guided Discussion before assigning the student pages.

Academic Vocabulary
✏ **area** \âr´ē ə\ n. the interior, or inside, of a figure

Access Vocabulary
figures shapes

Spanish Cognates
classify clasificar

★ = 120-Day Plan for TAKS

*Manipulative Kit Item ⚷ = Key standard

Geometry and spatial reasoning 2.7.C Cut two-dimensional geometric figures apart and identify the new geometric figures formed.
Number, operation, and quantitative reasoning 2.2.A Use concrete models to represent and name fractional parts of a whole object (with denominators of 12 or less).

Mental Math 5

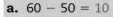 **INTEGRATION: TEKS 2.3.B** Have students subtract and show their answers using **Number Cubes**. Possible examples include the following:

a. 60 − 50 = 10   **b.** 120 − 80 = 40   **c.** 70 − 50 = 20
d. 140 − 90 = 50   **e.** 120 − 60 = 60   **f.** 20 − 10 = 10

1 Develop 25

Tell Students In Today's Lesson They Will
learn about plane figures and area.

Guided Discussion   ENGAGING Introductory

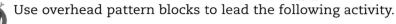 Use overhead pattern blocks to lead the following activity.

■ **What fraction of the blue rhombus can be covered by the green triangle?** $\frac{1}{2}$

Ask for volunteers to come to the overhead projector and show that two green triangles cover the same area as the blue rhombus. Have a discussion that leads students to discover that the area of one triangle is $\frac{1}{2}$ that of the rhombus. Continue to use the term *area* in context without a formal definition at this time. Review fractional notation if necessary.

■ **What fraction of the red trapezoid can be covered by the green triangle?** $\frac{1}{3}$

Have volunteers come to the overhead projector and show that the green triangle covers $\frac{1}{3}$ the area that the red trapezoid covers.

Do several similar problems showing the relationships between the areas of different geometric figures. For example:

- The area of the red trapezoid is $\frac{1}{2}$ the area of the yellow hexagon.
- The area of the blue rhombus is $\frac{1}{3}$ the area of the yellow hexagon.
- The area of the green triangle is $\frac{1}{6}$ the area of the yellow hexagon.

Skill Practice UNDERSTANDING Guided

 Distribute pattern blocks to students. Have students find, hide, and show their answers to the following problems:

■ **Three of these will fill the yellow hexagon. Show one of them.** blue rhombus
■ **Two of these will fill the yellow hexagon. Show one of them.** red trapezoid
■ **Six of these will fill the yellow hexagon. Show one of them.** green triangle
■ **Two of these will fill the blue rhombus. Show one of them.** green triangle
■ **Three of these will fill a red trapezoid. Show one of them.** green triangle

2 Use Student Pages 20

Pages 289–290 APPLYING Independent

Have students complete student pages 289 and 290 individually or in pairs. Allow them to use pattern blocks to complete these exercises.

Progress Monitoring

If . . . students have difficulty determining the fractional areas,

Then . . . work with individual students or small groups using only simple shapes and green triangles to show fractional area. In these cases, the numerator will always be the number of triangles shown, and the denominator will always be the number of triangles that will fit. Gradually work toward more complicated shapes.

As Students Finish

Building Blocks Have students use **Super Shape 2** to continue decomposing shapes.

 RESEARCH IN ACTION

"Overall research indicates that all types of geometric ideas appear to develop over time, becoming increasingly integrated and synthesized. . . . Children's ideas about shapes do not come from passive looking. Instead, they come as children's bodies, hands, eyes, and minds engage in active construction. In addition, children need to explore shapes extensively to fully understand them; merely seeing and naming pictures is insufficient. Finally, they have to explore the parts and attributes of shapes."

Clements, Douglas H. "Teaching and Learning Geometry" in Kilpatrick, Jeremy, W. Gary Martin, and Deborah Schifter, eds. *A Research Companion to Principles and Standards for School Mathematics.* Reston, VA: National Council of Teachers of Mathematics, Inc. 2003, p. 152.

Student Page

Name _____   Date _____

Key Ideas

The smaller shapes have area that is a fraction of the area of the larger shapes.

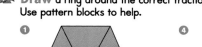

Math TEKS
Geometry and spatial reasoning 2.2.A
Use concrete models to represent and name fractional parts of a whole object (with denominators of 12 or less).

Draw a ring around the correct fraction.
Use pattern blocks to help.

1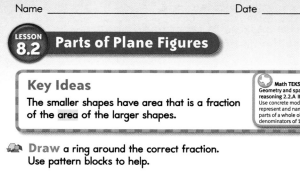
$\frac{1}{3}$ $\frac{2}{3}$ $\boxed{\frac{3}{3}}$ $\frac{1}{6}$

4
$\frac{2}{3}$ $\frac{1}{3}$ $\boxed{\frac{0}{3}}$ $\frac{1}{2}$

2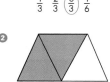
$\frac{1}{3}$ $\boxed{\frac{2}{3}}$ $\frac{3}{3}$ $\frac{1}{6}$

5
$\frac{1}{3}$ $\frac{1}{2}$ $\frac{1}{4}$ $\boxed{\frac{1}{6}}$

3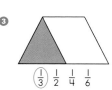
$\boxed{\frac{1}{3}}$ $\frac{1}{2}$ $\frac{1}{4}$ $\frac{1}{6}$

6
$\boxed{\frac{1}{3}}$ $\frac{2}{3}$ $\frac{1}{4}$ $\frac{1}{6}$

@Textbook This lesson is available in the **eTextbook.**

289

290

Student Page

Draw a ring around the correct fraction.
Use pattern blocks to help.

7
$\boxed{\frac{2}{6}}$ $\frac{2}{3}$ $\frac{3}{3}$ $\frac{1}{6}$

11
$\frac{1}{3}$ $\boxed{\frac{1}{2}}$ $\frac{1}{4}$ $\frac{1}{6}$

8
$\boxed{\frac{1}{3}}$ $\frac{2}{3}$ $\frac{3}{3}$ $\frac{4}{6}$

12
$\frac{1}{3}$ $\boxed{\frac{3}{6}}$ $\frac{3}{3}$ $\frac{1}{6}$

9
$\boxed{\frac{2}{6}}$ $\frac{2}{3}$ $\frac{3}{3}$ $\frac{1}{6}$

13
$\frac{1}{3}$ $\boxed{\frac{1}{2}}$ $\frac{1}{4}$ $\frac{2}{3}$

10
$\boxed{\frac{1}{2}}$ $\frac{1}{3}$ $\frac{1}{4}$ $\frac{1}{5}$

14
$\frac{1}{3}$ $\boxed{\frac{1}{2}}$ $\frac{1}{4}$ $\frac{1}{6}$

Real Math • Chapter 8 • Lesson 2

---

③ **Reflect** 5

Guided Discussion REASONING

Discuss Problem 7 on student page 290. Establish that $\frac{2}{6}$ of the hexagon is filled by the two triangles.

■ **Critical Thinking** Can you think of another fraction that correctly describes how much of the hexagon is filled? $\frac{1}{3}$

Lead a discussion that helps students see that the rhombus fills $\frac{1}{3}$ of the hexagon. It then follows that because two triangles fill the rhombus, then two triangles fill $\frac{1}{3}$ of the hexagon. Therefore, $\frac{2}{6}$ and $\frac{1}{3}$ appear to describe the same area of the hexagon.

Call attention to Problem 12. Through discussion, establish that $\frac{3}{6}$ and $\frac{1}{2}$ appear to cover the same area of the hexagon.

Conclude by explaining to students that $\frac{2}{6}$ and $\frac{1}{3}$ are equivalent fractions. Another example of equivalent fractions is $\frac{3}{6}$ and $\frac{1}{2}$.

Review **Cumulative Review:** For cumulative review of previously introduced skills, see page 297–298.

Family Involvement: Assign the **Practice, Reteach,** or **Enrichment** activities depending on the needs of your students.

Concept/Question Board: Have students look for additional examples using geometric figures and post them on the Concept/Question Board.

Math Puzzler: **Integration: 2.6.C** Mr. Ruiz works 5 days per week in an office 3 miles from his house. How many miles does he travel to and from work every week? 30

4 Assess and Differentiate

 **Assess** Use **eAssess** to record and analyze evidence of student understanding.

A Gather Evidence

Use the Daily Class Assessment Records in *Texas Assessment* or *eAssess* to record daily observations.

Informal Assessment
☑ **Guided Discussion**
Did the student [ENGAGING]
- ❏ pay attention to others' contributions?
- ❏ contribute information and ideas?
- ❏ improve on a strategy?
- ❏ reflect on and check the accuracy of his or her work?

Informal Assessment
☑ **Student Pages**
Did the student [APPLYING]
- ❏ apply learning in new situations?
- ❏ contribute concepts?
- ❏ contribute answers?
- ❏ connect mathematics to real-world situations?

 TEKS/TAKS Practice
Use *TEKS/TAKS Practice* pages 65–66 to assess student progress.

B Summarize Findings

Analyze and summarize assessment data for each student. Determine which Assessment Follow-Up is appropriate for each student. Use the Student Assessment Record in *Texas Assessment* or *eAssess* to update assessment records.

C Texas Assessment Follow-Up ● DIFFERENTIATE INSTRUCTION

Based on your observations, use these teaching strategies for assessment follow-up.

INTERVENTION

Review student performance on *Intervention* Lesson 8.A to see if students have mastered prerequisite skills for this lesson.

🔷 **1.2.A** Separate a whole into two, three, or four equal parts and use appropriate language to describe the parts such as three out of four equal parts.

🔷 **1.6.A** Describe and identify two-dimensional geometric figures, including circles, triangles, rectangles, and squares (a special type of rectangle).

ENGLISH LEARNER

Review

Use Lesson 8.2 in *English Learner Support Guide* to review lesson concepts and vocabulary.

ENRICH

If . . . students are proficient in the lesson concepts,

Then . . . encourage them to work on the chapter projects or *Enrichment* Lesson 8.2.

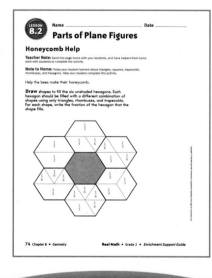

Enrichment Lesson 8.2

PRACTICE

If . . . students would benefit from additional practice,

Then . . . assign *Practice* Lesson 8.2.

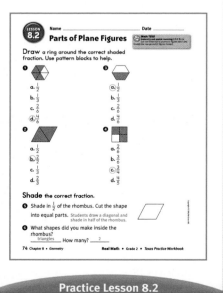

Practice Lesson 8.2

RETEACH

If . . . students are having difficulty finding fractional parts of areas,

Then . . . have them review $\frac{1}{2}$, $\frac{1}{3}$, $\frac{1}{4}$, $\frac{1}{5}$, $\frac{1}{6}$, and $\frac{1}{8}$.

Grade 1	Grade 2	Grade 3
1.6.D Use concrete models to combine two-dimensional geometric figures to make new geometric figures.	**2.7.C** Cut two-dimensional geometric figures apart and identify the new geometric figures formed.	**3.8** The student uses formal geometric vocabulary.

Overview

LESSON 8.3

TEXAS

Lesson Planner

Combining Plane Figures ★

Context of the Lesson This lesson builds on the previous two lessons and allows students to gain more familiarity with the pattern blocks and plane figures.

No further work with tessellations is scheduled for this grade level. However, students would benefit from the opportunity to make interesting tessellation patterns, perhaps as part of the art program.

See page 285B for Math Background for teachers for this lesson.

OBJECTIVES

- To continue to familiarize students with some of the properties of common shapes such as triangles, squares, trapezoids, rhombuses, and hexagons
- To allow students to explore and practice making tessellating patterns

MATH TEKS

Geometry and spatial reasoning 2.7.C
Cut two-dimensional geometric figures apart and identify the new geometric figures formed.
Number, operation, and quantitative reasoning 2.2.A
Use concrete models to represent and name fractional parts of a whole object (with denominators of 12 or less).

MATH TEKS INTEGRATION

Number, operation, and quantitative reasoning 2.3.A
Recall and apply basic addition and subtraction facts (to 18).
Patterns, relationships, and algebraic thinking 2.6.C
Identify, describe, and extend repeating and additive patterns to make predictions and solve problems.

MATERIALS

- *Number Cubes
- *Overhead pattern blocks
- *Pattern blocks

TECHNOLOGY

ⓔ **Presentation** Lesson 8.3
Building Blocks Piece Puzzler 5
ⓔ **MathTools** Tessellations

Planning for Learning ● DIFFERENTIATE INSTRUCTION

INTERVENTION

If . . . students lack the prerequisite skill of recognizing equal parts,

Then . . . teach **Intervention** Lesson 8.A.

1.2.A, 1.6.4

Intervention Lesson 8.A

ENGLISH LEARNER

Preview

If . . . students need language support,

Then . . . use Lesson 8.3 in **English Learner Support Guide** to preview lesson concepts and vocabulary.

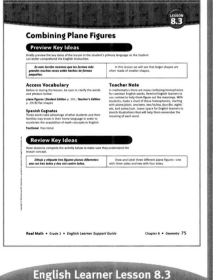

English Learner Lesson 8.3

ENRICH

If . . . students are proficient in the lesson concepts,

Then . . . emphasize **eMathTools.**

PRACTICE

If . . . students would benefit from additional practice,

Then . . . extend Skill Practice before assigning the student pages.

RETEACH

If . . . students are having difficulty understanding combining plane figures,

Then . . . extend Skill Building before assigning the student pages.

Access Vocabulary
plane figures flat shapes

Spanish Cognates
fractional fraccional

★ = 120-Day Plan for TAKS

Teaching Lesson 8.3

TEXAS

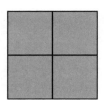
Geometry and spatial reasoning 2.7.C
Cut two-dimensional geometric figures apart and identify the new geometric figures formed.
Number, operation, and quantitative reasoning 2.2.A
Use concrete models to represent and name fractional parts of a whole object (with denominators of 12 or less).

Mental Math   5

   INTEGRATION: TEKS 2.3.A Have students answer addition exercises such as the following, using their **Number Cubes** to respond.

a. 2 + 2 + 3 = 7   **b.** 1 + 8 + 4 = 13   **c.** 9 + 0 + 7 = 16
d. 5 + 0 + 1 = 6   **e.** 3 + 2 + 6 = 11   **f.** 1 + 2 + 1 = 4

1 Develop   20

Tell Students In Today's Lesson They Will
combine plane figures to make other plane figures.

Guided Discussion UNDERSTANDING   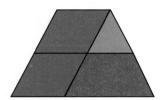 Introductory

  Review the previous lesson with this response exercise. Students use pattern blocks to find, hide, and show their answers. Ask students the following questions:

- Which shape is $\frac{1}{3}$ the area of the yellow hexagon?
  blue rhombus
- Which shape is $\frac{1}{6}$ the area of the yellow hexagon?
  green triangle
- The blue rhombus is $\frac{1}{3}$ the area of what shape?
  yellow hexagon
- **Critical Thinking** Two green triangles are $\frac{2}{3}$ the area of what shape? red trapezoid

Progress Monitoring

If . . . students are hesitant or consistently give incorrect answers during the response exercise,

Then . . . tutor them individually or in small groups as they complete the student pages. As students gain more confidence, they may work alone.

Skill Building APPLYING   Guided

Have students explore combining plane figures with the following exercises. Tell students to make a large hexagon using three blue rhombuses and three yellow hexagons. Tell students to try to make all sides of the large hexagon the same length.

After students have attempted this individually or in small groups, ask a volunteer to come to the overhead projector and to show his or her work.

Give students two or three more exercises of this type. For example:

■ **Make 1 large square from 4 orange squares.**

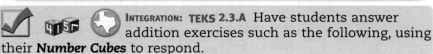

■ **Make a large trapezoid from 1 red trapezoid, 2 blue rhombuses, and 1 green triangle.**

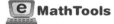

2 Use Student Pages   15

Pages 291–292 APPLYING   Independent

Student pages 291 and 292 contain problems in which students fill the outline of a shape when given a certain number and type of pattern blocks. Offer a lot of encouragement, as these problems will be challenging for students.

As Students Finish

Building Blocks Have students use **Piece Puzzler 5** to practice combining shapes to form new shapes.

 MathTools *Tessellations* Have students use this tool to create tessellations similar to those on the student pages.

Student Page

Name _____ Date _____

LESSON 8.3 Combining Plane Figures

Key Ideas
Larger shapes are often made of smaller shapes.

Math TEKS
Geometry and spatial reasoning 2.7.C
Cut two-dimensional geometric figures apart and identify the new geometric figures formed.

Use pattern blocks to fill these shapes.
Use the blocks shown. Possible answers are shown.

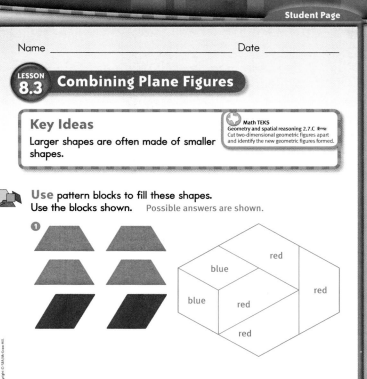

Use pattern blocks to fill these shapes.
Use the blocks shown.

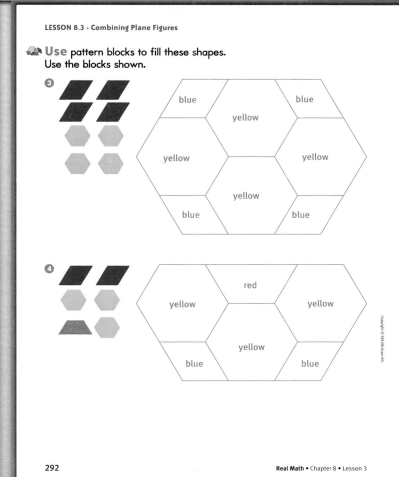

3 Reflect 5

Guided Discussion ✓ REASONING

Have students make a large trapezoid from 1 red trapezoid, 2 blue rhombuses, and 1 green triangle.

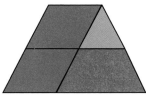

Refer to the large trapezoid, and ask the following questions:

■ **What fraction of the area consists of the green triangle?** $\frac{1}{8}$

Discuss with students how they know that the green triangle is $\frac{1}{8}$ of the area of the large trapezoid. One way is to first determine how many green triangles make up the total area. Each blue rhombus is equal to the area of two green triangles, and the red trapezoid is equal to the area of three green triangles, so the total area of the large trapezoid is eight green triangles.

■ **What fraction of the area consists of the 2 blue rhombuses?** $\frac{4}{8}$, or $\frac{1}{2}$
■ **What fraction of the area consists of the red trapezoid?** $\frac{3}{8}$
■ **Critical Thinking** **What fraction of the area consists of the green triangle, the 2 blue rhombuses, and the red trapezoid?** $\frac{8}{8}$, or 1

Lead a discussion that helps students discover the fact that if you add all the fractional areas, the result will be $\frac{8}{8}$, which is equal to 1.

Cumulative Review: For cumulative review of previously introduced skills, see page 297–298.

Family Involvement: Assign the *Practice, Reteach,* or *Enrichment* activities depending on the needs of your students.

Math Puzzler: Integration: **2.6.C** Hank is 6 years old. He is twice as old as his younger brother, Wally. When Wally is 5, will Hank be 10? Why or why not? no; Hank will always be 3 years older than Wally, but he will not always be twice as old. When Wally is 5, Hank will be 8.

Assess and Differentiate

 **Assess** Use *eAssess* to record and analyze evidence of student understanding.

A Gather Evidence

Use the Daily Class Assessment Records in *Texas Assessment* or *eAssess* to record daily observations.

Informal Assessment
☑ **Mental Math**

Did the student `COMPUTING`
- ❑ respond accurately?
- ❑ respond quickly?
- ❑ respond with confidence?
- ❑ self-correct?

Informal Assessment
☑ **Guided Discussion**

Did the student `REASONING`
- ❑ provide a clear explanation?
- ❑ communicate reasons and strategies?
- ❑ choose appropriate strategies?
- ❑ argue logically?

 TEKS/TAKS Practice

Use *TEKS/TAKS Practice* pages 65–66 to assess student progress.

B Summarize Findings

Analyze and summarize assessment data for each student. Determine which Assessment Follow-Up is appropriate for each student. Use the Student Assessment Record in *Texas Assessment* or *eAssess* to update assessment records.

C Texas Assessment Follow-Up • DIFFERENTIATE INSTRUCTION

Based on your observations, use these teaching strategies for assessment follow-up.

INTERVENTION

Review student performance on *Intervention* Lesson 8.A to see if students have mastered prerequisite skills for this lesson.

🤠 **1.2.A** Separate a whole into two, three, or four equal parts and use appropriate language to describe the parts such as three out of four equal parts.

🤠 **1.6.A** Describe and identify two-dimensional geometric figures, including circles, triangles, rectangles, and squares (a special type of rectangle).

ENGLISH LEARNER

Review

Use Lesson 8.3 in *English Learner Support Guide* to review lesson concepts and vocabulary.

ENRICH

If . . . students are proficient in the lesson concepts,

Then . . . encourage them to work on the chapter projects or *Enrichment* Lesson 8.3.

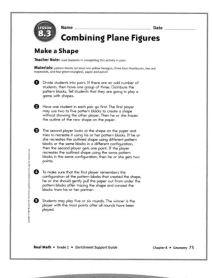

Enrichment Lesson 8.3

TEXAS PRACTICE

If . . . students would benefit from additional practice,

Then . . . assign *Practice* Lesson 8.3.

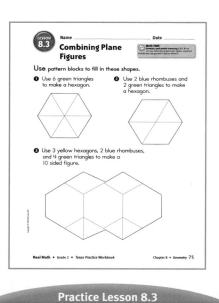

Practice Lesson 8.3

RETEACH

If . . . students are having difficulty combining plane figures to make larger shapes,

Then . . . tell students it is like solving a puzzle. Have them try different placements for the smaller figures until they all fit.

TEXAS **V e r t i c a l   A l i g n m e n t**

Grade 1	Grade 2	Grade 3
1.6.D Use concrete models to combine two-dimensional geometric figures to make new geometric figures.	**2.7.C** Cut two-dimensional geometric figures apart and identify the new geometric figures formed.	**3.8** The student uses formal geometric vocabulary.

Overview   **LESSON 8.4**

TEXAS

OBJECTIVES

- To provide formal definitions for different kinds of four-sided plane figures (quadrilaterals)
- To study and define parallel and perpendicular lines

MATH TEKS

Geometry and spatial reasoning 2.7.A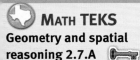
Describe attributes (the number of vertices, faces, edges, sides) of two- and three-dimensional geometric figures such as circles, polygons, spheres, cones, cylinders, prisms, and pyramids.

Geometry and spatial reasoning 2.7.B
Use attributes to describe how 2 two-dimensional figures or 2 three-dimensional geometric figures are alike or different.

Geometry and spatial reasoning 2.7.C
Cut two-dimensional geometric figures apart and identify the new geometric figures formed.

MATH TEKS INTEGRATION

Number, operation, and quantitative reasoning 2.2.B
Use concrete models to represent and name fractional parts of a set of objects (with denominators of 12 or less).

Number, operation, and quantitative reasoning 2.3.C
Select addition or subtraction to solve problems using two-digit numbers, whether or not regrouping is necessary.

MATERIALS

*Number Cubes
- SRA Math Vocabulary Cards

TECHNOLOGY

- Presentation Lesson 8.4
- MathTools Shape Tool
- Building Blocks Super Shape 3

Defining Plane Figures— Quadrilaterals ★

Context of the Lesson Students have been working with plane figures during the previous three lessons. In this lesson we look closely at some of the properties of these figures and develop formal definitions for them.

See page 285B for Math Background for teachers for this lesson.

Planning for Learning ● DIFFERENTIATE INSTRUCTION

INTERVENTION

If . . . students lack the prerequisite skill of recognizing equal parts,

Then . . . teach *Intervention* Lesson 8.A.

   1.2.A, 1.6.4

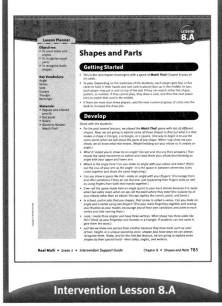

Intervention Lesson 8.A

ENGLISH LEARNER

Preview

If . . . students need language support,

Then . . . use Lesson 8.4 in *English Learner Support Guide* to preview lesson concepts and vocabulary.

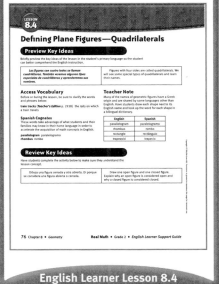

English Learner Lesson 8.4

ENRICH

If . . . students are proficient in the lesson concepts,

Then . . . emphasize *Building Blocks*.

PRACTICE

If . . . students would benefit from additional practice,

Then . . . extend Skill Building before assigning the student pages.

RETEACH

If . . . students are having difficulty understanding quadrilaterals,

Then . . . extend Guided Discussion before assigning the student pages.

Academic Vocabulary

quadrilateral \kwod´rə lat´ər əl\ *n.* a polygon with four sides and four angles

Access Vocabulary

train tracks the rails on which a train travels

Spanish Cognates

parallelogram paralelogramo

rhombus rombo

Teaching Lesson 8.4

 TEXAS

Geometry and spatial reasoning 2.7.A
Describe attributes (the number of vertices, faces, edges, sides) of two- and three-dimensional geometric figures such as circles, polygons, spheres, cones, cylinders, prisms, and pyramids.

Geometry and spatial reasoning 2.7.B
Use attributes to describe how 2 two-dimensional figures or 2 three-dimensional geometric figures are alike or different.

Geometry and spatial reasoning 2.7.C
Cut two-dimensional geometric figures apart and identify the new geometric figures formed.

Mental Math 5

 **INTEGRATION: TEKS 2.2.B** Have students find the fractional parts and show their answers with their *Number Cubes*. Possible examples include the following:

a. $\frac{1}{2}$ of 10 5 **b.** $\frac{1}{2}$ of 12 6 **c.** $\frac{1}{2}$ of 8 4 **d.** $\frac{1}{2}$ of 50 25 **e.** $\frac{1}{2}$ of 16 8

1 Develop 30

Tell Students In Today's Lesson They Will
learn formal definitions for plane figures.

Guided Discussion **UNDERSTANDING** Introductory

Parallel Lines

 Draw two nonparallel lines on the board, and have a student come to the board. Have the student place an X on the board where he or she thinks the lines will meet. Extend the lines to see how close the estimate was.

Draw two parallel lines on the board. Make them parallel to the top and bottom of the board.

Again have a student place an X where he or she thinks they will meet. This should facilitate a discussion noting that the lines will not meet or will meet in a very distant place. Tell students that two lines in a plane that never meet and go on forever are called parallel lines.

Ask students if they can think of examples of parallel lines. Possible answers include railroad tracks, automobile traffic lane markers, and the upper and lower edges of their rulers. Ask:

■ **Critical Thinking** **Can trains run on tracks that are not parallel?**
Allow students to think about this and realize that train tracks must be parallel in order for trains to run on them.

Perpendicular Lines

Draw two pairs of intersecting lines on the board, such as the following:

Have students focus their attention on the second illustration (perpendicular lines). Explain to students that when two lines meet in this way, we say the lines are perpendicular to each other.

Ask students if they see other examples of perpendicular lines in the classroom. There will be many examples. Possible examples include the corners of their desks, the corners of their books, and lines on a calendar.

Classifying Quadrilaterals  **MathTools**

Draw the figures from student page 293 on the board or use *eMathTools: Shape Tool.*

Tell students that all the figures are called quadrilaterals. *Quadrilateral* means "four sides."

Point to and label the trapezoid on the board.
Define *trapezoid*: a quadrilateral that has one pair of parallel lines.

Point to and label the parallelogram on the board.
Define *parallelogram*: a quadrilateral that has two pairs of parallel lines.

Point to and label the rhombus on the board.
Define *rhombus*: a parallelogram with four equal sides.

Point to and label the rectangle on the board.
Define *rectangle*: a parallelogram with two sets of perpendicular lines. The opposite sides of rectangles are always equal in length.

Finally, point to and label the square on the board.
Define *square*: a rectangle that has four sides of equal length.

Skill Building **APPLYING** Guided

Describe the attributes of a quadrilateral, and have students point to the corresponding illustrations of the quadrilaterals on student page 293. Walk around the room to monitor student progress. There will be more than one answer for some descriptions.

2 Use Student Pages 10

Pages 293–294 Independent

Have students complete page 294 independently, using page 293 as a reference.

As Students Finish

Building Blocks Have students use *Super Shape 3* to continue decomposing figures.

 MathTools *Shape Tool* Have student use this tool to practice combining and decomposing figures.

Name _____ Date _____

LESSON 8.4 Defining Plane Figures—Quadrilaterals

Key Ideas

Figures with four sides are called **quadrilaterals**.

This is a quadrilateral.

These are special types of quadrilaterals.

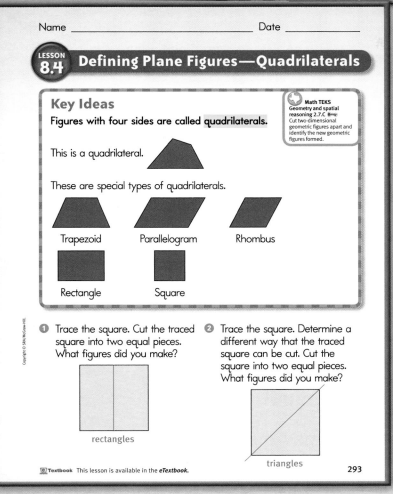

Trapezoid   Parallelogram   Rhombus

Rectangle   Square

Math TEKS
Geometry and spatial reasoning 2.7.C Cut two-dimensional geometric figures apart and identify the new geometric figures formed.

❶ Trace the square. Cut the traced square into two equal pieces. What figures did you make?

rectangles

❷ Trace the square. Determine a different way that the traced square can be cut. Cut the square into two equal pieces. What figures did you make?

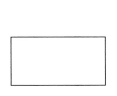

triangles

Textbook This lesson is available in the *eTextbook*.   293

LESSON 8.4 · Defining Plane Figures—Quadrilaterals

❸ Draw a line to make two rectangles.

❹ Draw a line to make two quadrilaterals.

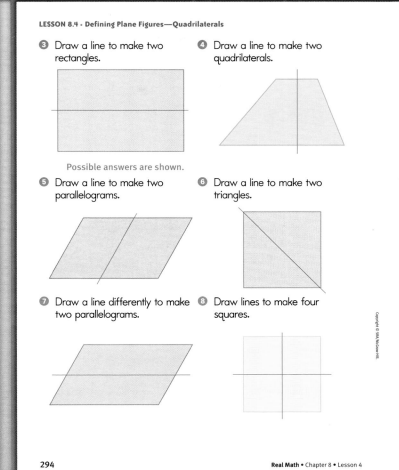

Possible answers are shown.

❺ Draw a line to make two parallelograms.

❻ Draw a line to make two triangles.

❼ Draw a line differently to make two parallelograms.

❽ Draw lines to make four squares.

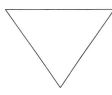

294   **Real Math** · Chapter 8 · Lesson 4

---

3 Reflect   5

Guided Discussion REASONING

Draw or hold up pairs of figures such as the ones below. For each pair, ask and discuss the following questions:

■ **Critical Thinking** How are these figures alike?
■ **Critical Thinking** How are they different?

Sample responses are shown.

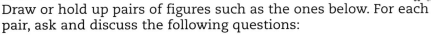

Possible answers include:
There are 4 sides and 4 corners in each figure;
opposite sides are parallel in each figure;
opposite sides are the same length in each figure;
one figure has 4 right angles, the other has none;
one figure is longer than the other

Possible answers include:
The top side is horizontal in each figure;
two sides slant toward each other in each figure;
one figure has 4 sides and 4 corners; the other has 3 sides and 3 corners;
one figure has a pair of parallel sides, the other doesn't

Math Puzzler: Integration: 2.3.C The second-grade classroom has 6 rows of desks. Each row has 4 desks. There is a student at all but 2 desks. How many students are in this class?
22

4 Assess and Differentiate

 Assess Use *eAssess* to record and analyze evidence of student understanding.

A Gather Evidence

Use the Daily Class Assessment Records in *Texas Assessment* or *eAssess* to record daily observations.

Informal Assessment
☑ **Mental Math**

Did the student `COMPUTING`
- ❑ respond accurately?
- ❑ respond quickly?
- ❑ respond with confidence?
- ❑ self-correct?

Informal Assessment
☑ **Guided Discussion**

Did the student `UNDERSTANDING`
- ❑ make important observations?
- ❑ extend or generalize learning?
- ❑ provide insightful answers?
- ❑ pose insightful questions?

🔶 **TEKS/TAKS Practice**

Use *TEKS/TAKS Practice* pages 59–62 to assess student progress.

B Summarize Findings

Analyze and summarize assessment data for each student. Determine which Assessment Follow-Up is appropriate for each student. Use the Student Assessment Record in *Texas Assessment* or *eAssess* to update assessment records.

C Texas Assessment Follow-Up ● DIFFERENTIATE INSTRUCTION

Based on your observations, use these teaching strategies for assessment follow-up.

INTERVENTION

Review student performance on *Intervention* Lesson 8.A to see if students have mastered prerequisite skills for this lesson.

🔶 **1.2.A** Separate a whole into two, three, or four equal parts and use appropriate language to describe the parts such as three out of four equal parts.

🔶 **1.6.A** Describe and identify two-dimensional geometric figures, including circles, triangles, rectangles, and squares (a special type of rectangle).

ENGLISH LEARNER
Review

Use Lesson 8.4 in *English Learner Support Guide* to review lesson concepts and vocabulary.

ENRICH

If . . . students are proficient in the lesson concepts,

Then . . . encourage them to work on the chapter projects or *Enrichment* Lesson 8.4.

Enrichment Lesson 8.4

PRACTICE

If . . . students would benefit from additional practice,

Then . . . assign *Practice* Lesson 8.4.

Practice Lesson 8.4

RETEACH

If . . . students are having difficulty understanding parallel and perpendicular lines,

Then . . . continue to point out examples in the classroom.

Problem Solving 8.B

Comparing Strategies

Objectives

- To explore the Guess and Check and Work Backward strategies
- To prepare students for understanding and working with angles
- To provide practice recognizing fractions of a turn
- To provide practice using a map

Materials

Tracing paper or other translucent paper (optional)

See Appendix A page A24 for instruction and a rubric for problem solving.

Context of the Lesson While providing extended time to work on a nonroutine problem, this lesson illustrates a connection between fractions, which were studied in the previous chapter lesson, and angles, which will be studied later in this chapter.

1 Develop 5

Tell Students In Today's Lesson They Will

find a route to the dinosaur bones and dinosaur tracks.

Guided Discussion

Recall the dinosaur-track activity from the chapter opener.

Have students look at the map at the top of page 295. Ask students to recall maps they have seen and used. Have students discuss the landmarks, locations, and directions they see on this map.

Present this problem to the students:

For Dr. Smith, a paleontologist, this day began like many of his days as he set off from a village to look for dinosaur bones and dinosaur tracks. But today was special. He found an area filled with dinosaur fossils. Some appeared to be large bones embedded deeply in the rock. After studying the site for a while, he headed back to the village. He didn't record how he got from the village to the dinosaur site because he didn't know he was going to find it. But he did record how he got back. By using his directions and the map, can you figure out where all the dinosaur bones are?

Read aloud the directions at the bottom of page 295:

1. Face the sun, and go parallel to the lake for 2 miles.
2. Make a $\frac{1}{4}$ turn to the right.
3. Go 2 miles.
4. Make a $\frac{1}{4}$ turn to the left.
5. Go 3 miles.
6. Make a $\frac{1}{4}$ turn to the left so that you are facing the mountains.
7. Walk 3 miles.
8. Arrive at the village.

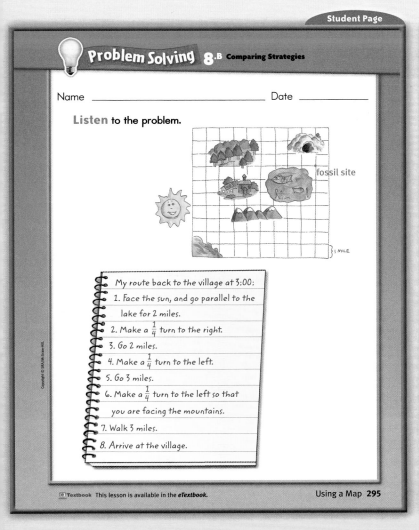

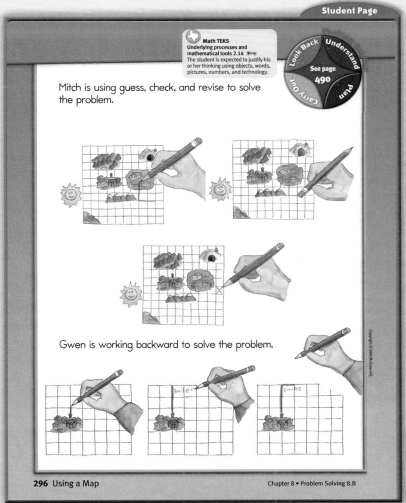

Underlying processes and mathematical tools 2.12.C
Select or develop an appropriate problem-solving plan or strategy including drawing a picture, looking for a pattern, systematic guessing and checking, or acting it out in order to solve a problem.

 **Use Student Pages** 25

Guided Discussion

Analyzing Sample Solution 1

Have students look at the pictures at the top of page 296. Ask questions about his strategy such as the following:

- **Look at the first picture. Why do you think Mitch drew an X on the map?** to show where he thinks the fossil site might be
- **Could Mitch have made his first guess in some other place?** yes
- **Because Mitch has marked a spot for the fossil site, is he finished?** No; he'll have to try out his guess to see if it works and then revise it if it doesn't.
- **How is Mitch showing the first step in Dr. Smith's route back to the village?** He is drawing a line from his X in the direction of the sun. He is making the line 2 spaces long to represent 2 miles.
- **How can Mitch tell which way to go next?** He can pretend he is facing the sun, then he can turn to the right $\frac{1}{4}$ of a complete turn. So the next line should go upward on the map.
- **In the second picture, why is Mitch erasing the lines?** After he ended in the lake, he knew where he started couldn't be correct.
- **In the third picture, why is Mitch drawing another X?** He's making a new guess and starting again.

Analyzing Sample Solution 2

Tell students that Gwen is using a different strategy to try to solve the problem. Have students look at the picture of Gwen's approach at the bottom of page 296. Ask questions such as the following:

- **Look at the first picture. Why is Gwen starting at the village?** She is working backward through Dr. Smith's directions, so she is starting at the end.
- **Why is Gwen drawing a line going up?** Steps 7 and 8 say that if you walk 3 miles facing the mountains, you will arrive at the village. So if Gwen goes the opposite way, she will be following Dr. Smith's path in reverse.
- **Because Gwen is working backward, what step should she look at after Steps 8 and 7?** Step 6
- **Where does Step 6 say to turn?** a $\frac{1}{4}$ turn to the left
- **What would be the opposite of $\frac{1}{4}$ turn to the left?** $\frac{1}{4}$ turn right

Have students work on the problem individually or in pairs by drawing the path on the map on page 295. They may use Gwen's or Mitch's strategy, or one of their own. Provide support as needed, remembering to suggest approaches rather than showing the answer. Remind students they will need to be able to prove they have found the dinosaur fossil site, and they need to draw or describe the path they would take from the village to the site.

 **Reflect** 10

Effective Communication Have students share their solutions and their strategies.

In discussion bring out these points:

- You can use fractions of turns to give directions.
- Left and right depend on which way you are facing.
- In using Guess, Check, and Adjust, it's important to think about and learn from each try.
- Working backward is a good strategy to use when you know how or where a situation ends and how you got there, and you need to find out how or where it began.
- When working backward, you not only do the steps in reverse order but you do the opposite of each step.

Sample Solutions Strategies

Students may use one or more of the following strategies instead of or in conjunction with the strategies presented on student page 296.

Use Spatial Sense

In combination with Guess, Check, and Revise, students might draw Dr. Smith's route on a sheet of tracing paper placed over the map. Then to check other guesses, they can simply move the tracing paper so the path begins at the new guess.

Act It Out/Use a Physical Model

Students might practice walking the path described in the instructions, perhaps laying out a map on the floor to get a feel for how the path will look on the map.

 **Assess** 15

When evaluating student work, focus not only on the correctness of the answer but also on whether the student thought rationally about the problem. Questions to consider include the following:

- Was the student able to navigate using quarter turns and the terms *left* and *right*?
- Could the student understand an instruction enough to show it on the map?
- If the student used Guess, Check, and Revise, did he or she think about what happened with a previous guess before making another guess?
- Did the student check the answer?

Also note which students use particularly sophisticated or creative strategies.

Cumulative Review

Use Pages 297–298

Use the Cumulative Review as a review of concepts and skills that students have previously learned.

Here are different ways that you can assign these problems to your students as they work through the chapter:

- With some of the lessons in the chapter, assign a set of cumulative review problems to be completed as practice or for homework.
  Lesson 8.1—Problems 1–3
  Lesson 8.2—Problems 4–9
  Lesson 8.3—Problem 10
  Lesson 8.4—Problems 11–18

- At any point during the chapter, assign part or all of the cumulative review problems to be completed as practice or for homework.

Cumulative Review
Problems 1–3 review using pictographs, Lesson 4.9. TEKS 2.11.A
Problems 4–9 review adding two-digit numbers, Lesson 5.4. TEKS 2.3.B
Problem 10 reviews creating patterns with plane figures, Lesson 8.3. TEKS 2.7.C
Problems 11–18 review subtraction, Lesson 3.5. TEKS 2.3.A

Progress Monitoring
If . . . students miss more than one problem in a section,   :   **Then . . .** refer to the indicated lesson for remediation suggestions.

Cumulative Review

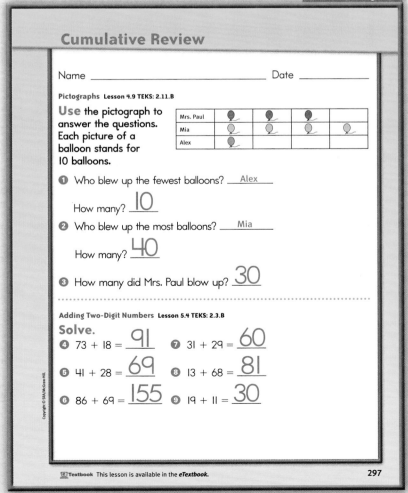

Name _____ Date _____

Pictographs Lesson 4.9 TEKS: 2.11.B

Use the pictograph to answer the questions. Each picture of a balloon stands for 10 balloons.

Mrs. Paul	🎈	🎈	🎈	
Mia	🎈	🎈	🎈	🎈
Alex	🎈			

❶ Who blew up the fewest balloons? __Alex__

How many? __10__

❷ Who blew up the most balloons? __Mia__

How many? __40__

❸ How many did Mrs. Paul blow up? __30__

Adding Two-Digit Numbers Lesson 5.4 TEKS: 2.3.B
Solve.

❹ $73 + 18 = \underline{91}$ ❼ $31 + 29 = \underline{60}$

❺ $41 + 28 = \underline{69}$ ❽ $13 + 68 = \underline{81}$

❻ $86 + 69 = \underline{155}$ ❾ $19 + 11 = \underline{30}$

Cumulative Review

TEKS

Combining Plane Figures Lesson 8.3 TEKS: 2.7.C

Use pattern blocks to fill in the outline.

❿ Use 4 red trapezoids and 2 blue rhombuses to make a hexagon.

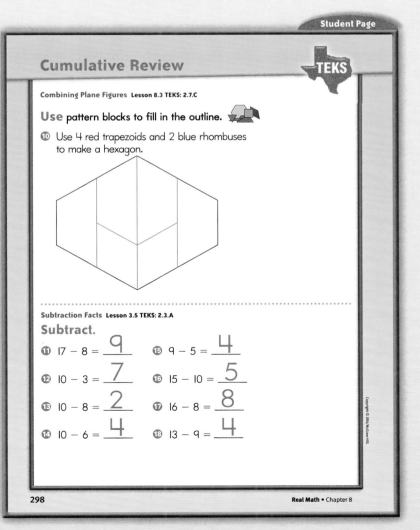

Subtraction Facts Lesson 3.5 TEKS: 2.3.A
Subtract.

⓫ $17 - 8 = \underline{9}$ ⓯ $9 - 5 = \underline{4}$

⓬ $10 - 3 = \underline{7}$ ⓰ $15 - 10 = \underline{5}$

⓭ $10 - 8 = \underline{2}$ ⓱ $16 - 8 = \underline{8}$

⓮ $10 - 6 = \underline{4}$ ⓲ $13 - 9 = \underline{4}$

Individual Oral Assessment

Purpose of the Test

The Individual Oral Assessment is designed to measure students' growing knowledge of chapter concepts. It is administered individually to each student, and it requires oral responses from each student. The test takes about five minutes to complete. See **Assessment** for detailed instructions for administering and interpreting the test, and record students' answers on the Student Assessment Recording Sheet.

Assessment page 142

Directions

Read each question to the student, and record his or her oral response. If the student answers correctly, go to the next question. Stop when the student misses two questions at the same level. Students should not use paper.

Materials

Pattern blocks

Questions

Level 1: Prerequisite 2.7.A

1. (Give student a set of pattern blocks.) Identify a triangle.
2. (Give student a set of pattern blocks.) Identify a trapezoid.
3. (Give student a set of pattern blocks.) Identify a rhombus.
4. (Give student a set of pattern blocks.) Identify a hexagon.

Level 2: Basic 2.7.B

5. (Give student a set of pattern blocks.) Make a pattern using squares and hexagons. any repeating pattern using these shapes
6. (Give student a set of pattern blocks.) Make a pattern using triangles and rhombuses. any repeating pattern using these shapes
7. (Give student a set of pattern blocks.) Make a pattern using trapezoids and triangles. any repeating pattern using these shapes
8. (Give student a set of pattern blocks.) Make a pattern using hexagons and trapezoids. any repeating pattern using these shapes

Level 3: At Level 2.7.C

9. What shape is $\frac{1}{2}$ of a hexagon? trapezoid
10. What shape is $\frac{1}{3}$ of a hexagon? rhombus
11. What shape is $\frac{1}{6}$ of a hexagon? triangle
12. (Show an acute angle.) What kind of angle is this? acute

Level 4: Challenge Application 2.7.A

13. (Give student a set of pattern blocks.) What has all right angles? square
14. (Give student a set of pattern blocks.) What has all acute angles? triangle
15. (Give student a set of pattern blocks.) What has acute and obtuse angles? rhombus, trapezoid
16. (Show a right isosceles triangle.) Identify the angles in this triangle. 1 right, 2 acute

Level 5: Content Beyond Mid-Chapter 2.7.A

17. What space figure looks like a shoe box? rectangular prism
18. What space figure is square on all sides? cube
19. Name any two space figures that will roll. sphere, cone, or cylinder
20. What space figure has a triangle on all sides? triangular pyramid

Grade 1
1.6.D
Read time to the hour and half-hour using analog and digital clocks.

Grade 2
2.10.B
Read and write times shown on analog and digital clocks using five-minute increments.

Grade 3
1.6.D
Tell and write time shown on analog and digital clocks.

Overview

LESSON 8.5

TEXAS

Lesson Planner

OBJECTIVES
- To introduce students to properties of different types of angles
- To teach students to classify angles as obtuse, acute, or right

MATH TEKS
Enriching: Measurement 2.10.B
Read and write times shown on analog and digital clocks using five-minute increments.
Geometry and spatial reasoning 2.7.A
Describe attributes (the number of vertices, faces, edges, sides) of two- and three-dimensional geometric figures such as circles, polygons, spheres, cones, cylinders, prisms, and pyramids.
Underlying processes and mathematical tools 2.13.B
Relate informal language to mathematical language and symbols.

MATH TEKS INTEGRATION
Number, operation, and quantitative reasoning 2.3.B
Model addition and subtraction of two-digit numbers with objects, pictures, words, and numbers.
Number, operation, and quantitative reasoning 2.1.B
Use place value to read, write, and describe the value of whole numbers to 999.

MATERIALS
- *Straightedge
- *Pattern blocks
- Clock

TECHNOLOGY
Presentation Lesson 8.5
Building Blocks Shape Shop 2

Obtuse, Acute, and Right Angles

This is the fifth of a ten-lesson geometry sequence.
Context of the Lesson This lesson integrates the study of angles with classification skills and telling time.
See page 285B for Math Background for teachers for this lesson.

Planning for Learning • DIFFERENTIATE INSTRUCTION

INTERVENTION
If . . . students lack the prerequisite skill of recognizing equal parts,

Then . . . teach *Intervention* Lesson 8.B.

1.2.A, 1.6.4

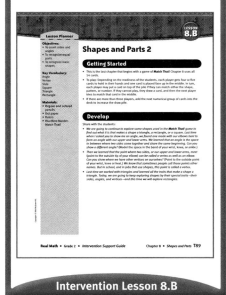

Intervention Lesson 8.B

ENGLISH LEARNER
Preview
If . . . students need language support,

Then . . . use Lesson 8.5 in *English Learner Support Guide* to preview lesson concepts and vocabulary.

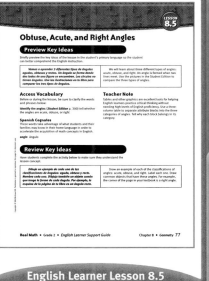

English Learner Lesson 8.5

ENRICH
If . . . students are proficient in the lesson concepts,

Then . . . emphasize chapter projects.

PRACTICE
If . . . students would benefit from additional practice,

Then . . . extend Skill Practice before assigning the student pages.

RETEACH
If . . . students are having difficulty understanding angles,

Then . . . extend Guided Discussion before assigning the student pages.

Access Vocabulary
identifying the angles tell whether the angles are acute, obtuse, or right

Spanish Cognates
angle ángulo

Enriching: Measurement 2.10.B
Read and write times shown on analog and digital clocks using five-minute increments.
Geometry and spatial reasoning 2.7.A
Describe attributes (the number of vertices, faces, edges, sides) of two- and three-dimensional geometric figures such as circles, polygons, spheres, cones, cylinders, prisms, and pyramids.

Underlying processes and mathematical tools 2.13.B
Relate informal language to mathematical language and symbols.

Mental Math 5

 INTEGRATION: TEKS 2.3.B Present students with addition exercises such as the following and have them show their answers using their **Number Cubes**.

a. 20 + 20 40   **b.** 30 + 30 60   **c.** 25 + 25 50
d. 24 + 25 49   **e.** 30 + 19 49   **f.** 30 + 20 50

1 Develop 20

Tell Students In Today's Lesson They Will
learn about obtuse, acute, and right angles.

Guided Discussion UNDERSTANDING

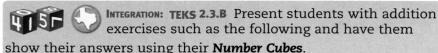 Introductory

 Using a straightedge, draw two lines on the board that are perpendicular but do not meet.

Have two students come to the board and make points where they estimate the lines will meet. Then continue the lines to see how close their estimates were.

Point to the four equal angles that are formed by the intersection of the two perpendicular lines. Tell students these are called right angles.

■ **Critical Thinking** **Can you find other examples of right angles in the classroom?** Some examples might be the corner of the desk, the corner of a piece of paper, and the corner of the board.

Using the pattern blocks, ask:

■ **Which of the polygons have right angles?** the square

Tell students that angles narrower than a right angle are called acute angles. Ask:

■ **Which of the polygons have acute angles?** triangle, rhombus, and parallelogram

Now tell students that angles wider than a right angle are called obtuse angles. Ask:

■ **Which of the polygons have obtuse angles?** hexagon, rhombus, and parallelogram

Skill Practice APPLYING

 Guided

 THUMBS UP Do a response exercise in which you draw an angle on the board. Students show thumbs-up if the angle is obtuse, thumbs-down if acute, and open hand if the angle is a right angle.

2 Use Student Pages 10

Pages 299–300 Independent

Using student page 299 as a guide, review the three types of angles that are defined.

Allow students to complete the rest of student pages 299 and 300 independently.

Progress Monitoring

| **If . . .** students think that angles with longer sides are greater, | **Then . . .** show that extending the lengths of the sides does not change how open an angle is. |

As Students Finish

 Game Allow students to play a game of their choice from any of those previously introduced, or allow students to explore with the pattern blocks to create tessellations.

 Building Blocks Have students use **Shape Shop 2** to practice recognizing properties of figures such as angle measure.

RESEARCH IN ACTION

"To understand angles, students must understand the various aspects of the angle concept. They must overcome difficulties with orientation, discriminate angles as critical parts of geometric figures, and construct and represent the idea of turns, among others. Furthermore, they must construct a high level of integration between these aspects. This difficult task is best begun in the elementary and middle school years, as children deal with corners of figures, comparison of angle size, and turns."

Clements, Douglas H. "Teaching and Learning Geometry" in Kilpatrick, Jeremy, W. Gary Martin, and Deborah Schifter, eds. *A Research Companion to Principles and Standards for School Mathematics*. Reston, VA: National Council of Teachers of Mathematics, Inc. 2003, p. 164.

Name _____ Date _____

LESSON 8.5 Obtuse, Acute, and Right Angles

Key Ideas

Three types of angles are obtuse, acute, and right.

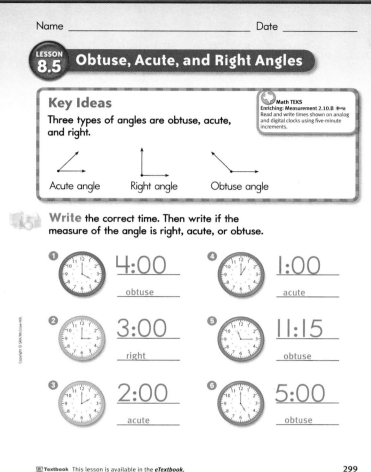

Acute angle   Right angle   Obtuse angle

Math TEKS
Enriching: Measurement 2.10.B
Read and write times shown on analog and digital clocks using five-minute increments.

 Write the correct time. Then write if the measure of the angle is right, acute, or obtuse.

1. 4:00   obtuse

2. 3:00   right

3. 2:00   acute

4. 1:00   acute

5. 11:15   obtuse

6. 5:00   obtuse

LESSON 8.5 · Obtuse, Acute, and Right Angles

7. **TAKS Obj. 1** **Which** clock shows an obtuse angle?

8. **Identify** the angles.

a. _____ obtuse

b. _____ right

c. _____ acute

d. _____ obtuse

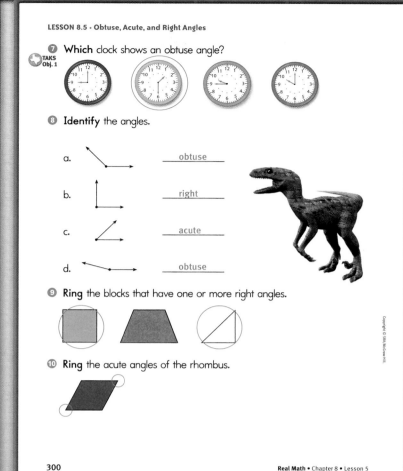

9. **Ring** the blocks that have one or more right angles.

10. **Ring** the acute angles of the rhombus.

---

3 Reflect   5

Guided Discussion ☑ REASONING

Using your classroom clock, show different times, and have students tell whether the angle is acute, obtuse, or right.

After a few examples, show 6 o'clock, and discuss. Most students will say that there is no angle formed, only a straight line. Inform the class that the angle formed at 6 o'clock is called a *straight angle*. Draw a straight angle on the board.

Then draw a line subdividing the straight angle.

Discuss that when you divide a straight angle this way, you always get an acute angle and an obtuse angle. If you divide a straight angle with a perpendicular line, you get two right angles.

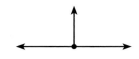

Review **Cumulative Review:** For cumulative review of previously learned skills, see page 317–318.

Family Involvement: Assign the *Practice, Reteach,* or *Enrichment* activities depending on the needs of your students.

Concept/Question Board: Encourage students to continue to post questions, answers, and examples on the Concept/Question Board.

Math Puzzler: **Integration: 2.1.B** Using each digit only once, fill in the blanks with the digits 6, 7, 8, and 9 to make the greatest possible sum: _____ + _____ 97 + 86 or 96 + 87

 **Assess and Differentiate**

 **Assess** Use *eAssess* to record and analyze evidence of student understanding.

A Gather Evidence

Use the Daily Class Assessment Records in *Texas Assessment* or *eAssess* to record daily observations.

Informal Assessment
☑ **Guided Discussion**

Did the student **REASONING**
- ❑ provide a clear explanation?
- ❑ communicate reasons and strategies?
- ❑ choose appropriate strategies?
- ❑ argue logically?

Informal Assessment
☑ **Concept/Question Board**

Did the student **APPLYING**
- ❑ apply learning in new situations?
- ❑ contribute concepts?
- ❑ contribute answers?
- ❑ connect mathematics to real-world situations?

 TEKS/TAKS Practice

Use *TEKS/TAKS Practice* pages 81–82 to assess student progress.

B Summarize Findings

Analyze and summarize assessment data for each student. Determine which Assessment Follow-Up is appropriate for each student. Use the Student Assessment Record in *Texas Assessment* or *eAssess* to update assessment records.

C Texas Assessment Follow-Up • DIFFERENTIATE INSTRUCTION

Based on your observations, use these teaching strategies for assessment follow-up.

INTERVENTION

Review student performance on *Intervention* Lesson 8.B to see if students have mastered prerequisite skills for this lesson.

🔷 **1.2.A** Separate a whole into two, three, or four equal parts and use appropriate language to describe the parts such as three out of four equal parts.

🔷 **1.6.A** Describe and identify two-dimensional geometric figures, including circles, triangles, rectangles, and squares (a special type of rectangle).

ENGLISH LEARNER

Review

Use Lesson 8.5 in *English Learner Support Guide* to review lesson concepts and vocabulary.

ENRICH

If . . . students are proficient in the lesson concepts,

Then . . . encourage them to work on the chapter projects or *Enrichment* Lesson 8.5.

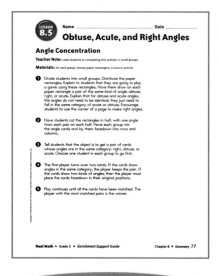

Enrichment Lesson 8.5

TEXAS PRACTICE

If . . . students would benefit from additional practice,

Then . . . assign *Practice* Lesson 8.5.

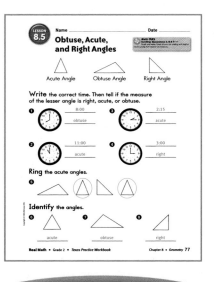

Practice Lesson 8.5

RETEACH

If . . . students confuse acute and obtuse angles on a clock face,

Then . . . show them that each time on the clock face forms either a right angle and an obtuse angle or an acute angle and an obtuse angle. It is not possible to have two right angles, two acute angles, or two obtuse angles.

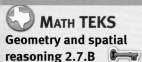

TEXAS Vertical Alignment

Grade 1	Grade 2	Grade 3
1.6.A Describe and identify two-dimensional geometric figures, including circles, triangles, rectangles, and squares (a special type of rectangle).	**2.7.B** Use attributes to describe how 2 two-dimensional figures or 2 three-dimensional geometric figures are alike or different.	**3.8** The student uses formal geometric vocabulary.

Overview LESSON **8.6**

TEXAS

Lesson Planner

OBJECTIVES
- To introduce the concept of congruence
- To provide several examples of how congruent objects are created

MATH TEKS
Geometry and spatial reasoning 2.7.B
Use attributes to describe how 2 two-dimensional figures or 2 three-dimensional geometric figures are alike or different.

Preparing for: Grade 3 Geometry and spatial reasoning 3.9.A
Identify congruent two-dimensional figures.

MATH TEKS INTEGRATION
Number, operation, and quantitative reasoning 2.3.B
Model addition and subtraction of two-digit numbers with objects, pictures, words, and numbers.

Underlying processes and mathematical tools 2.14
The student is expected to justify his or her thinking using objects, words, pictures, numbers, and technology.

MATERIALS
- *Number Cubes
- *Attribute blocks
- *Overhead attribute blocks
- *Pattern blocks or overhead pattern blocks
- Tracing paper
- *SRA Math Vocabulary Cards*

TECHNOLOGY
e Presentation Lesson 8.6
Building Blocks Shape Parts 3

Congruence

Context of the Lesson Congruence was first introduced in the Grade 1 program. Here the concept is integrated with the pattern block studies of the previous geometry lessons. The concept of congruence will become more important when students study the properties of triangles and other polygons in later grades.

See page 285B for Math Background for teachers for this lesson.

Planning for Learning • DIFFERENTIATE INSTRUCTION

INTERVENTION
If . . . students lack the prerequisite skill of recognizing equal parts,

Then . . . teach *Intervention* Lesson 8.B.

 1.2.A, 1.6.4

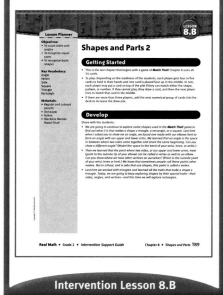

Intervention Lesson 8.B

ENGLISH LEARNER
Preview

If . . . students need language support,

Then . . . use Lesson 8.6 in *English Learner Support Guide* to preview lesson concepts and vocabulary.

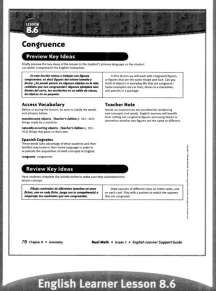

English Learner Lesson 8.6

ENRICH
If . . . students are proficient in the lesson concepts,

Then . . . emphasize chapter projects.

PRACTICE
If . . . students would benefit from additional practice,

Then . . . extend Skill Practice before assigning the student pages.

RETEACH
If . . . students are having difficulty understanding congruence,

Then . . . extend Guided Discussion before assigning the student pages.

Academic Vocabulary
congruent \kən grü´ənt\ *adj.*
exactly alike in shape and size

Spanish Cognates
congruent congruente

 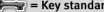

Geometry and spatial reasoning 2.7.B
Use attributes to describe how 2 two-dimensional figures or 2 three-dimensional geometric figures are alike or different.
Preparing for: Grade 3 Geometry and spatial reasoning 3.9.A
Identify congruent two-dimensional figures.

Mental Math 5

 INTEGRATION: TEKS 2.3.B Present students with addition exercises such as the following, and have them show their answers using their **Number Cubes.**

a. 80 + 70 = 150	**b.** 40 + 90 = 130	**c.** 60 + 60 = 120
d. 30 + 50 = 80	**e.** 50 + 70 = 120	**f.** 70 + 70 = 140

1 Develop 20

Tell Students In Today's Lesson They Will

learn about congruent figures.

Guided Discussion ENGAGING

 Introductory

Tell students that two figures the same shape and size are congruent. Using the overhead attribute blocks or by drawing on the board, display a large square. Ask a volunteer to come to the front of the room and to select from the attribute blocks a block congruent to your square. Establish that both squares are the same shape and the same size by placing one on top of the other. Ask:

- ■ **Are these two figures the same shape?** yes
- ■ **Are these two figures the same size?** yes
- ■ **Are these two figures congruent?** yes

Then display a small square next to the large square. Ask the same questions as before. yes, no, no

Repeat with other examples.

Then draw a right triangle, and beside it draw other triangles that are not congruent and one triangle that is congruent. Ask students to identify which triangle is congruent to the first one. Show students how you can trace the first triangle and slide it over each of the others until you find the one that matches exactly. Explain that this is called a slide. Draw another congruent triangle but rotate it by 45 degrees. Demonstrate that in order to match the triangles it is necessary to turn the paper. Explain that this is called a turn. Then model another example that involves a flip (which requires flipping the paper). Demonstrate several more examples of each type of movement.

Skill Practice COMPUTING

 THUMBS UP

Guided

Draw two figures on the board. Tell students to show thumbs-up if they appear congruent. Tell students to show thumbs-down if they do not appear congruent. Use many types of figures, not just polygons. (Make sure that if the figures appear congruent that they are. If not, students may think you are trying to fool you.)

Examples:

a. up **c.** up

 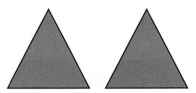

b. down **d.** down

Skill Building ENGAGING

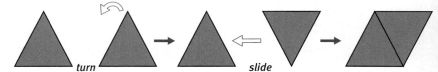

Introduce the activity of using flips, turns, and slides to create new shapes from two or more congruent pattern blocks. Start by presenting a shape-combination puzzle, as follows:

- Take two triangles and place them one next to the other as shown

- ■ **Critical Thinking** **What new pattern-block shape can be made by moving one of these triangles?**
- Show how to turn and slide one of the triangles to create a rhombus. As you do each step, have students describe the movement by saying *slide*, *flip*, or *turn*.

turn   *slide*

Divide the class into small groups and give each group some pattern blocks. Have each group create shape-combination puzzles similar to the one you demonstrated. Explain that they can start with any two or more congruent figures. Tell students that they must be able to use words to describe how to move the block or blocks to create the new shape.

2 Use Student Pages 15

Pages 301–302 APPLYING

 Independent

Have students complete student pages 301 and 302 independently. Provide tracing paper for them to use.

As Students Finish

Building Blocks Have students use **Shape Parts 3** to practice identifying congruence.

 **MathTools** *Pattern Blocks* Have students practice combining congruent shapes to form other shapes.

Student Page

Name _____ Date _____

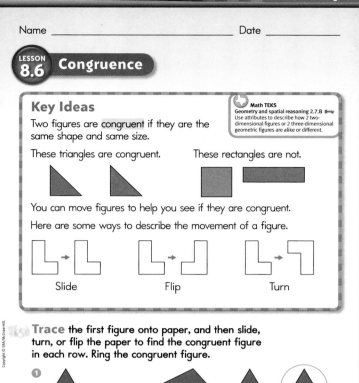

LESSON 8.6 Congruence

Key Ideas

Two figures are **congruent** if they are the same shape and same size.

These triangles are congruent.   These rectangles are not.

You can move figures to help you see if they are congruent.

Here are some ways to describe the movement of a figure.

Slide   Flip   Turn

 **Trace** the first figure onto paper, and then slide, turn, or flip the paper to find the congruent figure in each row. Ring the congruent figure.

❶

❷

Textbook This lesson is available in the *eTextbook*.   301

Math TEKS
Geometry and spatial reasoning 2.7.B
Use attributes to describe how 2 two-dimensional figures or 2 three-dimensional geometric figures are alike or different.

Student Page

LESSON 8.6 · Congruence

Ring the figure that shows what the first figure will look like after you slide, turn, or flip it.

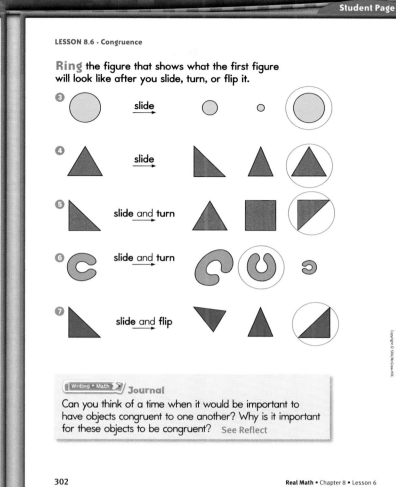

❸   slide →

❹   slide →

❺   slide and turn →

❻   slide and turn →

❼   slide and flip →

Writing + Math   Journal
Can you think of a time when it would be important to have objects congruent to one another? Why is it important for these objects to be congruent?   See Reflect

302   **Real Math** • Chapter 8 • Lesson 6

---

③ Reflect   10

Guided Discussion   REASONING

1. Challenge students to think of congruent figures in their everyday lives. Examples might include cookies, ice cubes, sheets of paper, or building blocks.

Explore the fact that manufactured objects are often congruent, while naturally occurring objects such as leaves, plants, and blades of grass are not. Allow students to present their thoughts about this.

2. Using the pattern blocks or overhead pattern blocks, display a yellow hexagon. Then put two red trapezoids together to make a figures that is congruent to the yellow hexagon, and establish that it is congruent. Then put the two trapezoids together like this:

- **Is this figure the same size as the yellow hexagon?** yes
- **Is this figure a hexagon?** Yes, it has six sides.
- **Critical Thinking   Is this figure congruent to the yellow hexagon?** no

Writing + Math   Journal

One possible answer is that car tires need to be congruent to each other in order for the car to drive smoothly.

☑ Use Mastery Checkpoint 13 found in **Assessment** to evaluate student mastery of congruency. By this time, students should be able to correctly answer eighty percent of the Mastery Checkpoint items.

SOCIAL STUDIES   **Curriculum Connection:** Students may be interested in taking a field trip to a factory or food processing plant that uses mass production techniques to produce congruent objects.

Review   **Cumulative Review:** For cumulative review of previously learned skills, see page 317–318.

Family Involvement: Assign the **Practice, Reteach,** or **Enrichment** activities depending on the needs of your students.

Concept/Question Board: Encourage students to continue to post questions, answers, and examples on the Concept/Question Board.

Math Puzzler: Integration: 2.14 Mr. Muddle noticed that a brick was missing from the foundation of his house. He measured the hole exactly, but he couldn't find a brick that size. He would have to take a brick that was slightly smaller than the hole or one that was slightly larger than the hole. He decided to take the larger brick. Did he make a good choice? Why or why not? no; The larger brick would not fit in the hole, but cement could be filled in around the smaller brick to make it fit.

Chapter 8 • Lesson 6   **301–302**

4 Assess and Differentiate

 **Assess** Use *eAssess* to record and analyze evidence of student understanding.

A Gather Evidence

Use the Daily Class Assessment Records in *Texas Assessment* or *eAssess* to record daily observations.

Formal Assessment

☑ **Mastery Checkpoint**

Did the student
- ❏ use correct procedures?
- ❏ respond with at least 80% accuracy?

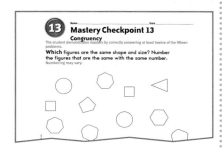

Assessment page 91

🔷 TEKS/TAKS Practice

Use *TEKS/TAKS Practice* pages 63–64 to assess student progress.

B Summarize Findings

Analyze and summarize assessment data for each student. Determine which Assessment Follow-Up is appropriate for each student. Use the Student Assessment Record in *Texas Assessment* or *eAssess* to update assessment records.

C Texas Assessment Follow-Up ● DIFFERENTIATE INSTRUCTION

Based on your observations, use these teaching strategies for assessment follow-up.

 TEXAS

INTERVENTION	ENRICH	PRACTICE	RETEACH
Review student performance on *Intervention* Lesson 8.B to see if students have mastered prerequisite skills for this lesson. 🔷 **1.2.A** Separate a whole into two, three, or four equal parts and use appropriate language to describe the parts such as three out of four equal parts. 🔷 **1.6.A** Describe and identify two-dimensional geometric figures, including circles, triangles, rectangles, and squares (a special type of rectangle).	**If . . .** students are proficient in the lesson concepts, **Then . . .** encourage them to work on the chapter projects or *Enrichment* Lesson 8.6.	**If . . .** students would benefit from additional practice, **Then . . .** assign *Practice* Lesson 8.6.	**If . . .** students are having difficulty recognizing congruent figures, **Then . . .** have them draw pairs of congruent figures on individual index cards. Students can then choose congruent pairs from the pile of cards.

Review

Use Lesson 8.6 in *English Learner Support Guide* to review lesson concepts and vocabulary.

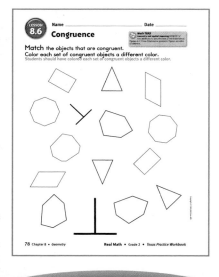

Enrichment Lesson 8.6

Practice Lesson 8.6

Grade 1	Grade 2	Grade 3
1.6.A Describe and identify two-dimensional geometric figures, including circles, triangles, rectangles, and squares (a special type of rectangle).	**2.7.A** Describe attributes of two- and three-dimensional geometric figures.	**3.8** The student is expected to uses formal geometry vocabulary.

Overview

LESSON 8.7

TEXAS

Lesson Planner

OBJECTIVES
- To review the concept of symmetry
- To have students recognize and draw lines of symmetry
- To have students demonstrate an understanding of symmetry by using paper-folding and paper-cutting techniques

MATH TEKS

Geometry and spatial reasoning 2.7.A
Describe attributes (the number of vertices, faces, edges, sides) of two- and three-dimensional geometric figures such as circles, polygons, spheres, cones, cylinders, prisms, and pyramids.

Geometry and spatial reasoning 2.7.B
Use attributes to describe how 2 two-dimensional figures or 2 three-dimensional geometric figures are alike or different.

Preparing for: Grade 3 Geometry and spatial reasoning 3.9.C
Identify lines of symmetry in two-dimensional figures.

MATH TEKS INTEGRATION

Number, operation, and quantitative reasoning 2.3.B
Model addition and subtraction of two-digit numbers with objects, pictures, words, and numbers.

MATERIALS
- *Number Cubes
- *A straightedge or ruler for each student
- *Paper and scissors for each student
- *Mirror Cards
- *SRA Math Vocabulary Cards*

TECHNOLOGY
- Presentation Lesson 8.7
- Building Blocks Geometry Snapshots 3

Symmetry

Context of the Lesson This lesson focuses on symmetry around a line, sometimes called bilateral symmetry. Other types of symmetry include rotational symmetry—the kind we see in figures that look the same when turned around a point, such as the letter S. This type of symmetry will be studied in Grade 5.

See page 285B for Math Background for teachers for this lesson.

Planning for Learning ● DIFFERENTIATE INSTRUCTION

INTERVENTION

If . . . students lack the prerequisite skill of recognizing equal parts,

Then . . . teach *Intervention* Lesson 8.B.

 1.2.A, 1.6.4

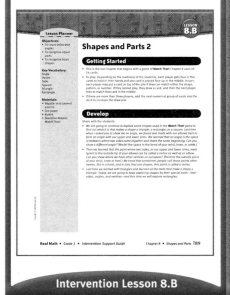

Intervention Lesson 8.B

ENGLISH LEARNER

Preview

If . . . students need language support,

Then . . . use Lesson 8.7 in *English Learner Support Guide* to preview lesson concepts and vocabulary.

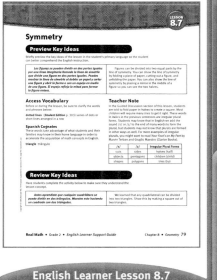

English Learner Lesson 8.7

ENRICH

If . . . students are proficient in the lesson concepts,

Then . . . emphasize *Building Blocks*.

PRACTICE

If . . . students would benefit from additional practice,

Then . . . extend Skill Practice before assigning the student pages.

RETEACH

If . . . students are having difficulty understanding symmetry,

Then . . . extend Skill Building before assigning the student pages.

Academic Vocabulary

✏ **line of symmetry** *n.* a line on which a figure can be folded into two congruent parts

Spanish Cognates
symmetry simetría

Geometry and spatial reasoning 2.7.A
Describe attributes (the number of vertices, faces, edges, sides) of two- and three-dimensional geometric figures such as circles, polygons, spheres, cones, cylinders, prisms, and pyramids.

Geometry and spatial reasoning 2.7.B
Use attributes to describe how 2 two-dimensiona figures or 2 three-dimensional geometric figures a alike or different.
Preparing for: Grade 3 Geometry and spatial reasoning 3.9.C
Identify lines of symmetry in two-dimensional figu

Mental Math 5

  INTEGRATION: TEKS 2.3.B Have students do subtraction exercises such as the following and show their answers using their **Number Cubes.**

a. 140 − 80 = 60   **b.** 130 − 90 = 40   **c.** 90 − 40 = 50
d. 110 − 90 = 20   **e.** 70 − 40 = 30   **f.** 170 − 90 = 80

1 Develop 20

Tell Students In Today's Lesson They Will
learn about symmetry.

Guided Discussion UNDERSTANDING 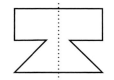 Introductory

Draw three figures on the board, two of which have line symmetry and one that does not. For example:

Demonstrate how you can draw a line of symmetry in one of the figures so it is divided into two congruent figures that are the same size and the same shape. Then ask whether the remaining figures can be divided in that way. Allow a volunteer to come to the board and draw the line of symmetry. Explain that figures that can be divided this way are symmetric and the line dividing the figure is called the line of symmetry.

Repeat with one or two other sets of figures, but include some that have more than one line of symmetry. For example:

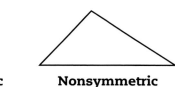

Symmetric   **Symmetric**   **Nonsymmetric**

Skill Building ENGAGING   Guided

 Distribute paper, scissors, and a mirror card to each student. Demonstrate how to fold a sheet of paper in half and cut a triangle on the fold. Unfold the triangle, and explain that the crease is the line of symmetry. Have students spend a few minutes folding paper and cutting shapes.

 Have students show their cutout figures, and note that the crease creates two congruent parts. Show students how to use their mirror cards to check for symmetry. Laying their cutout figures flat, students should hold

the mirror so it touches and is perpendicular to the paper. If they place the mirror on the line of symmetry, it should appear that half of the figure is in the mirror and the other half is on the paper. Demonstrate what it looks like when the mirror is placed somewhere other than the line of symmetry.

Skill Practice   COMPUTING   Guided

 Draw simple figures on the board. Have students show thumbs-up if there is a line of symmetry and thumbs-down if there is not a line of symmetry. After each response, have a volunteer or volunteers come to the board and draw the line of symmetry.

THUMBS UP

Progress Monitoring

If . . . students have difficulty doing the Skill Practice,

Then . . . you may want to do the first part of page 304 in a whole-group session. It might be a good idea to write the letters on the board.

2 Use Student Pages 20

Pages 303–304 Independent

Have students complete pages 303 and 304 independently. Make sure they have mirrors available to check for lines of symmetry. Explain that all of the figures on page 303 and some of the letters on page 304 have more than one line of symmetry, and some of the letters on page 304 do not have any lines of symmetry.

As Students Finish

Building Blocks Have students use **Geometry Snapshots 3** to practice looking for symmetry.

RESEARCH IN ACTION

"Through their everyday activity, children build both intuitive and explicit knowledge of geometric figures . . . young children can learn richer concepts about shape if their educational environment includes four features: varied examples and nonexamples, discussions about shapes and their characteristics, a wider variety of shape classes, and interesting tasks . . . teaching should ensure that children experience many different examples of a type of shape, so that they do not form narrow ideas about any class of shapes. Showing nonexamples and comparing them to similar examples help focus children's attention on the critical attributes of shapes and prompts discussion."

Clements, Douglas and J. Sarama, eds. *Engaging Young Children in Mathematics: Standards for Early Childhood Mathematics Education*. Mahwah, New Jersey: Lawrence Erlbaum Associates Publishers, 2004, p. 38.

Student Page

Name _____ Date _____

Key Ideas

If you can hold a mirror along a line through a polygon and have the figure look the same with and without the mirror, that line is called a line of symmetry.

Math TEKS
Geometry and spatial reasoning 2.7.B
Use attributes to describe how 2 two-dimensional figures or 2 three-dimensional geometric figures are alike or different.

Hold a mirror to each figure, and look for the lines of symmetry. Then draw one of the lines you find.
Possible answers are shown.

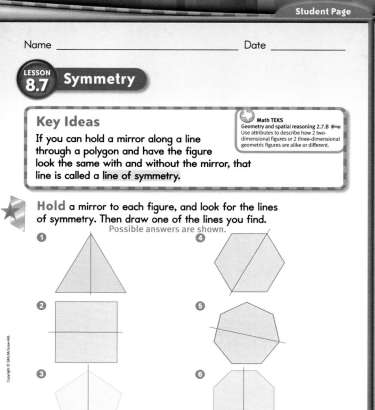

1 2 3 4 5 6

303

Student Page

LESSON 8.7 · Symmetry

Draw lines of symmetry. If a letter has no lines of symmetry, draw a ring around it. Possible answers are shown.

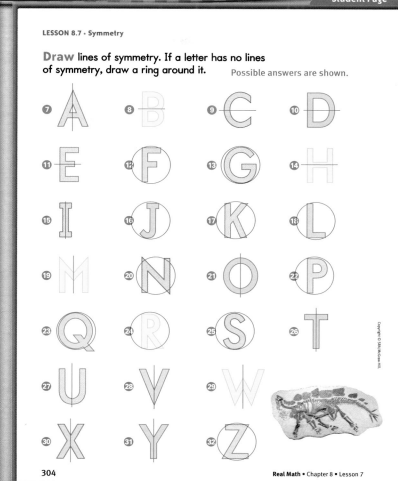

7 A   8 B   9 C   10 D
11 E   12 F   13 G   14 H
15 I   16 J   17 K   18 L
19 M   20 N   21 O   22 P
23 Q   24 R   25 S   26 T
27 U   28 V   29 W
30 X   31 Y   32 Z

304

Real Math · Chapter 8 · Lesson 7

---

③ Reflect

5

Guided Discussion ☑ REASONING

Lead a class discussion on examples of symmetry and near symmetry found in nature.

Many fruits, leaves, plants, and other organisms are approximately symmetrical. Give some common examples of things that are naturally symmetrical, such as butterfly wings, the sun and moon, oranges, and so on. Ask students to come up with some examples on their own.

Draw a circle on the board.

■ **Critical Thinking** **Where are the lines of symmetry on this circle?**
Have students come up to the board and draw lines of symmetry on the circle.

Cumulative Review: For cumulative review of previously learned skills, see page 317–318.

Family Involvement: Assign the *Practice, Reteach,* or *Enrichment* activities depending on the needs of your students.

Concept/Question Board: Encourage students to continue to post questions, answers, and examples on the Concept/Question Board.

Math Puzzler: Integration: **2.2.A** Antonio saved 25¢ on Monday and 5¢ every day after. On which day did he have 50¢?
Saturday

4 Assess and Differentiate

 **Assess** Use *eAssess* to record and analyze evidence of student understanding.

A Gather Evidence

Use the Daily Class Assessment Records in *Texas Assessment* or *eAssess* to record daily observations.

Informal Assessment
☑ **Skill Practice**

Did the student COMPUTING
- ❏ respond accurately?
- ❏ respond quickly?
- ❏ respond with confidence?
- ❏ self-correct?

Informal Assessment
☑ **Guided Discussion**

Did the student REASONING
- ❏ provide a clear explanation?
- ❏ communicate reasons and strategies?
- ❏ choose appropriate strategies?
- ❏ argue logically?

TEKS/TAKS Practice

Use *TEKS/TAKS Practice* pages 63–64 to assess student progress.

B Summarize Findings

Analyze and summarize assessment data for each student. Determine which Assessment Follow-Up is appropriate for each student. Use the Student Assessment Record in *Texas Assessment* or *eAssess* to update assessment records.

C Texas Assessment Follow-Up ● DIFFERENTIATE INSTRUCTION

Based on your observations, use these teaching strategies for assessment follow-up.

INTERVENTION

Review student performance on *Intervention* Lesson 8.B to see if students have mastered prerequisite skills for this lesson.

1.2.A Separate a whole into two, three, or four equal parts and use appropriate language to describe the parts such as three out of four equal parts.

1.6.A Describe and identify two-dimensional geometric figures, including circles, triangles, rectangles, and squares (a special type of rectangle).

Review

Use Lesson 8.7 in *English Learner Support Guide* to review lesson concepts and vocabulary.

ENRICH

If . . . students are proficient in the lesson concepts,

Then . . . encourage them to work on the chapter projects or *Enrichment* Lesson 8.7.

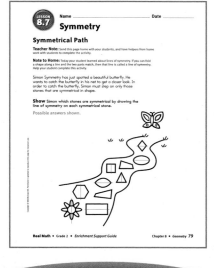

Enrichment Lesson 8.7

PRACTICE

If . . . students would benefit from additional practice,

Then . . . assign *Practice* Lesson 8.7.

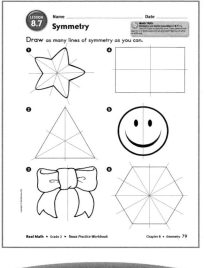

Practice Lesson 8.7

RETEACH

If . . . students are having difficulty recognizing lines of symmetry,

Then . . . have them use paper-folding techniques to determine if figures have lines of symmetry.

TEXAS **Vertical Alignment**

Grade 1	Grade 2	Grade 3
1.6.A Describe and identify two-dimensional geometric figures, including circles, triangles, rectangles, and squares (a special type of rectangle).	**2.7.A** Describe attributes of two- and three-dimensional geometric figures.	**3.8** The student is expected to uses formal geometry vocabulary.

Overview

LESSON 8.8

TEXAS

Lesson Planner

OBJECTIVES
- To introduce definitions of some plane figures such as right triangles and circles
- To study the difference between regular and irregular polygons

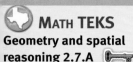 **MATH TEKS**

Geometry and spatial reasoning 2.7.A 🔑
Describe attributes (the number of vertices, faces, edges, sides) of two- and three-dimensional geometric figures such as circles, polygons, spheres, cones, cylinders, prisms, and pyramids.

Geometry and spatial reasoning 2.7.B
Use attributes to describe how 2 two-dimensional figures or 2 three-dimensional geometric figures are alike or different.

MATH TEKS INTEGRATION

Number, operation, and quantitative reasoning 2.3.B
Model addition and subtraction of two-digit numbers with objects, pictures, words, and numbers.

MATERIALS
*Number Cubes 🎲
SRA Math Vocabulary Cards

TECHNOLOGY
ⓔ **Presentation** Lesson 8.8
ⓔ **MathTools** Shape Tool
Building Blocks Shape Shop 3

Looking Ahead
For Lesson 8.9 you should have some everyday objects available that are the shape of space figures, such as a basketball or a shoe box.

Defining Other Plane Figures ⭐

Context of the Lesson In this lesson students learn about plane figures that were not previously introduced or covered. Students are also exposed to irregular polygons. (They have previously worked mostly with regular polygons.) In the next two lessons students will learn about space figures and the relationships between plane figures and space figures.

See page 285B for Math Background for teachers for this lesson.

Planning for Learning ● DIFFERENTIATE INSTRUCTION

INTERVENTION
If . . . students lack the prerequisite skill of recognizing basic shapes,

Then . . . teach *Intervention* Lesson 8.C.

🌎 1.2.A, 1.6.4

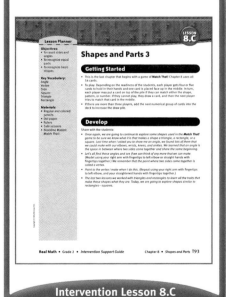

Intervention Lesson 8.C

ENGLISH LEARNER
Preview

If . . . students need language support,

Then . . . use Lesson 8.8 in *English Learner Support Guide* to preview lesson concepts and vocabulary.

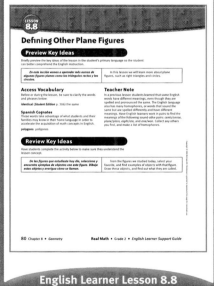

English Learner Lesson 8.8

ENRICH
If . . . students are proficient in the lesson concepts,

Then . . . emphasize chapter projects.

PRACTICE
If . . . students would benefit from additional practice,

Then . . . extend Skill Building.

RETEACH
If . . . students are having difficulty understanding regular and irregular polygons,

Then . . . extend Guided Discussion.

Academic Vocabulary
✏ **polygon** \pol´ē gon´\ *n.* a closed plane figure having at least three straight sides

regular polygon *n.* a polygon having sides that are all the same length and angles that are all equal

Access Vocabulary
identical the same

Spanish Cognates
polygons polígonos

⭐ = 120-Day Plan for TAKS

TEXAS

Geometry and spatial reasoning 2.7.A Describe attributes (the number of vertices, faces, edges, sides) of two- and three-dimensional geometric figures such as circles, polygons, spheres, cones, cylinders, prisms, and pyramids.

Geometry and spatial reasoning 2.7.B Use attributes to describe how 2 two-dimensional figures or 2 three-dimensional geometric figures are alike or different.

Mental Math 5

 INTEGRATION: TEKS 2.3.B Write a number expression on the board, and say it. Students show answers with **Number Cubes.** Possible exercises include the following:

a. 37 + 42 = 79   **b.** 27 + 23 = 50   **c.** 51 + 49 = 100
d. 37 + 52 = 89   **e.** 19 + 21 = 40   **f.** 79 + 11 = 90

1 Develop 20

Tell Students In Today's Lesson They Will
learn about other plane figures.

Introductory

Guided Discussion ☑ e**MathTools** UNDERSTANDING
Write *right angle* on the board or overhead projector.

■ **Critical Thinking** **Can you find and name an example of a right angle?** Possible answer: the corner of a sheet of paper

Then draw a right triangle on the board, overhead projector, or using **eMathTools: Shape Tool.** Ask students to describe what a right triangle is.
Draw several right triangles that are different from each other, such as the following:

Draw some examples to show that not all triangles are right triangles, such as the following:

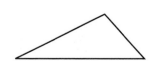

Compare each of the triangles you have drawn, noting differences in the types of angles (acute, obtuse, or right) and the lengths of the sides. Point out that one of the triangles has sides that are the same length and angles that are equal.

Explain that polygons with sides that are the same length and angles that are equal are called *regular polygons.* Draw some examples of regular polygons.

Then explain that polygons that are not regular polygons are called *irregular polygons.* Draw some examples of irregular polygons. Include examples such as the following:

Discuss that these figures are a pentagon, a hexagon, and an octagon, even though they look very different from the regular pentagon, hexagon, and octagon pictured on student page 305.

Skill Building APPLYING
Guided

 Divide students into small groups. Give instructions to the class for a type of polygon to draw such as "Draw a triangle with a right angle" or "Draw an irregular pentagon." Have students draw a polygon that meets your criteria, and then compare similarities and differences among drawings with their group members.

2 Use Student Pages 20

Pages 305–306 APPLYING
Independent

Have students complete page 306 independently. Students can use page 305 as a reference.

As Students Finish

Building Blocks Have students use **Shape Shop 3** to practice identifying polygons.

e**MathTools** **Shape Tool** Have students use this tool to create regular and irregular polygons.

TEXAS
TEKS Checkup

Geometry and spatial reasoning 2.7.C
• **Cut two-dimensional geometric figures apart and identify the new geometric figures formed**

Use this problem to assess students' progress towards standards mastery:

Which shapes form

A
B
C
D

Have students choose the correct answer and then describe how they knew which choice was correct. In the discussion, ask questions such as the following. Be sure to ask students to explain their reasoning, because different solution methods are possible.

■ **Have students draw vertical lines to break the shape into other shapes that are smaller recognizable shapes.**

Follow-Up
If... students need additional practice putting shapes together and taking them apart to form other shapes,

Then... have them complete **Building Blocks: Piece Puzzles 1–5**

Name _____ Date _____

LESSON 8.8 Defining Other Plane Figures

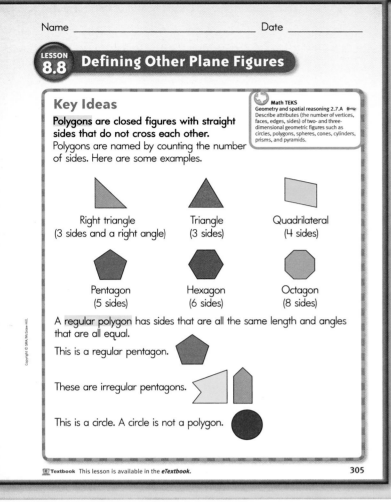

Key Ideas

Polygons are closed figures with straight sides that do not cross each other.

Polygons are named by counting the number of sides. Here are some examples.

Math TEKS
Geometry and spatial reasoning 2.7.A Describe attributes (the number of vertices, faces, edges, sides) of two- and three-dimensional geometric figures such as circles, polygons, spheres, cones, cylinders, prisms, and pyramids.

Right triangle
(3 sides and a right angle)

Triangle
(3 sides)

Quadrilateral
(4 sides)

Pentagon
(5 sides)

Hexagon
(6 sides)

Octagon
(8 sides)

A **regular polygon** has sides that are all the same length and angles that are all equal.

This is a regular pentagon.

These are irregular pentagons.

This is a circle. A circle is not a polygon.

Follow the directions. When you are finished, share your answers with a partner. Then describe how your figures are alike or different.

Possible answers are shown.

① Draw a circle.

② Draw a right triangle.

③ Draw a regular triangle.

④ Draw a triangle with one obtuse angle.

⑤ Draw an irregular hexagon.

⑥ Draw a different irregular hexagon.

⑦ Milo has the following figure on his wall.

Name the figure

A   Octagon

B   Pentagon

Ⓒ   Hexagon

D   Quadrilateral

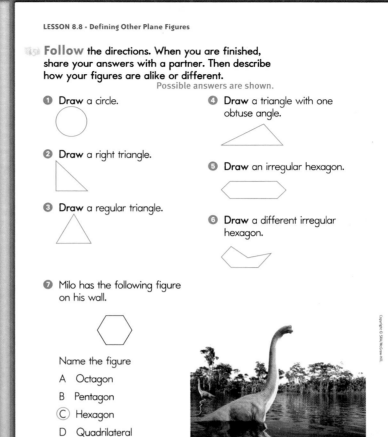

---

③ Reflect   10

Guided Discussion REASONING

Briefly review how polygons are named as students come to the board and draw examples of the polygons named. For example:

■ **What do we call a polygon with 4 sides?** quadrilateral

■ **What do we call a polygon with 5 sides?** pentagon

And so on...

Finally ask,

■ **Critical Thinking   What do we call a polygon with $3\frac{1}{2}$ sides?**
Through discussion, help students see that this is impossible. The half side is really a full side. It makes no sense to talk about a polygon with $3\frac{1}{2}$ sides or with any "half sides."

Cumulative Review: For cumulative review of previously learned skills, see page 317–318.

Family Involvement: Assign the *Practice, Reteach,* or *Enrichment* activities depending on the needs of your students.

Concept/Question Board: Have students attempt to answer any unanswered questions on the Concept/Question Board.

Math Puzzler: **Integration: 2.3.C** There are 21 coins on the floor. There are 3 more heads than tails. How many are heads? 12

4 Assess and Differentiate

 **Assess** Use *eAssess* to record and analyze evidence of student understanding.

A Gather Evidence

Use the Daily Class Assessment Records in *Texas Assessment* or *eAssess* to record daily observations.

Informal Assessment
Guided Discussion

Did the student **UNDERSTANDING**
- ☐ make important observations?
- ☐ extend or generalize learning?
- ☐ provide insightful answers?
- ☐ pose insightful questions?

Informal Assessment
✓Concept/Question Board

Did the student **APPLYING**
- ☐ apply learning in new situations?
- ☐ contribute concepts?
- ☐ contribute answers?
- ☐ connect mathematics to real-world situations?

TEKS/TAKS Practice

Use *TEKS/TAKS Practice* pages 59–62 to assess student progress.

B Summarize Findings

Analyze and summarize assessment data for each student. Determine which Assessment Follow-Up is appropriate for each student. Use the Student Assessment Record in *Texas Assessment* or *eAssess* to update assessment records.

C Texas Assessment Follow-Up ● DIFFERENTIATE INSTRUCTION

Based on your observations, use these teaching strategies for assessment follow-up.

INTERVENTION

Review student performance on *Intervention* Lesson 8.C to see if students have mastered prerequisite skills for this lesson.

1.2.A Separate a whole into two, three, or four equal parts and use appropriate language to describe the parts such as three out of four equal parts.

1.6.A Describe and identify two-dimensional geometric figures, including circles, triangles, rectangles, and squares (a special type of rectangle).

ENGLISH LEARNER

Review

Use Lesson 8.8 in *English Learner Support Guide* to review lesson concepts and vocabulary.

ENRICH

If . . . students are proficient in the lesson concepts,

Then . . . encourage them to work on the chapter projects or *Enrichment* Lesson 8.8.

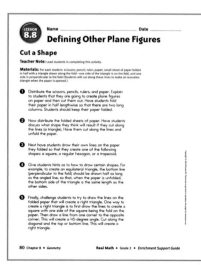

Enrichment Lesson 8.8

PRACTICE

If . . . students would benefit from additional practice,

Then . . . assign *Practice* Lesson 8.8.

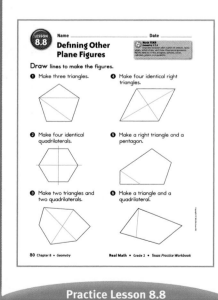

Practice Lesson 8.8

RETEACH

If . . . students are having difficulty identifying polygons by name,

Then . . . remind them that prefixes tri-, quad-, or pent- have meanings that relate to the meaning of the prefix. For example, a tricycle has three wheels.

Grade 1	Grade 2	Grade 3
1.6.A Describe and identify two-dimensional geometric figures, including circles, triangles rectangles, and squares (a special type of rectangle).	**2.7.A** Describe attributes of two-and three-dimensional geometric figures.	**3.8** The student is expected to use formal geometry vocabulary.

Overview LESSON 8.9

TEXAS

Lesson Planner

OBJECTIVES
- To provide informal experience with space figures through classification activities
- To teach students the specific characteristics of certain space figures
- To construct space figures from plane figures

MATH TEKS

Geometry and spatial reasoning 2.7.A
Describe attributes (the number of vertices, faces, edges, sides) of two- and three-dimensional geometric figures such as circles, polygons, spheres, cones, cylinders, prisms, and pyramids.

Geometry and spatial reasoning 2.7.B
Use attributes to describe how 2 two-dimensional figures or 2 three-dimensional geometric figures are alike or different.

MATH TEKS INTEGRATION

Number, operation, and quantitative reasoning 2.3.B
Model addition and subtraction of two-digit numbers with objects, pictures, words, and numbers.

Number, operation, and quantitative reasoning 2.3.C
Select addition or subtraction to solve problems using two-digit numbers, whether or not regrouping is necessary.

MATERIALS
- *Number Cubes
- *Space figures
- Everyday objects that are the shape of space figures
- Scissors and tape
- A copy of *Practice* page 128 for each student

TECHNOLOGY
- **Presentation** Lesson 8.9
- **MathTools** Net Tool

Space Figures ★

TEXAS

Context of the Lesson This lesson builds on the introduction to cubes and tetrahedrons in Grade 1 and prepares students for further exploration into the properties of space figures in Grade 3. In this lesson, students investigate space figures and also construct a space figure. Students will decompose space figures in the next lesson.

Planning for Learning • DIFFERENTIATE INSTRUCTION

INTERVENTION
If . . . students lack the prerequisite skill of recognizing basic shapes,

Then . . . teach *Intervention* Lesson 8.C.

1.2.A, 1.6.4

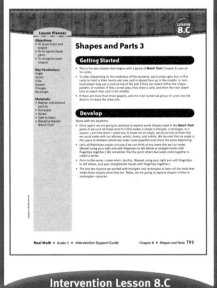

Intervention Lesson 8.C

ENGLISH LEARNER
Preview

If . . . students need language support,

Then . . . use Lesson 8.9 in *English Learner Support Guide* to preview lesson concepts and vocabulary.

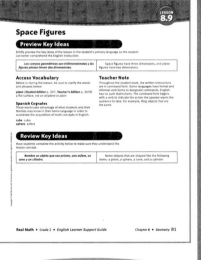

English Learner Lesson 8.9

ENRICH
If . . . students are proficient in the lesson concepts,

Then . . . emphasize chapter projects.

PRACTICE
If . . . students would benefit from additional practice,

Then . . . extend Guided Discussion before assigning the student pages.

RETEACH
If . . . students are having difficulty understanding space figures,

Then . . . extend Guided Discussion before assigning the student pages.

Academic Vocabulary	Access Vocabulary	Spanish Cognates
space figures *n.* figures which cannot fit in a plane	**plane** a flat surface; not an *airplane* or *plain*	**cube** cubo **sphere** esfera

Teaching Lesson 8.9

TEXAS

Geometry and spatial reasoning 2.7.A
Describe attributes (the number of vertices, faces, edges, sides) of two- and three-dimensional geometric figures such as circles, polygons, spheres, cones, cylinders, prisms, and pyramids.
Geometry and spatial reasoning 2.7.B
Use attributes to describe how 2 two-dimensional figures or 2 three-dimensional geometric figures are alike or different.

Mental Math 5

 INTEGRATION: TEKS 2.3.B Have students show answers to subtraction exercises such as the following using their **Number Cubes.**

a. 86 − 28 = 58   **b.** 51 − 33 = 18
c. 70 − 14 = 56   **d.** 87 − 39 = 48
e. 66 − 47 = 19   **f.** 40 − 22 = 18

1 Develop 20

Tell Students In Today's Lesson They Will
learn about space figures.

Guided Discussion ENGAGING   Introductory

Building a Cube

 Remind students that they have previously been studying plane figures. Plane figures exist entirely in a plane, which is a flat surface, such as a table top, that extends forever. Explain that now they are going to learn about space figures. Space figures cannot fit in a plane.

Display the space figures (pyramid, cube, rectangular prism, sphere, cone, and cylinder). Display each figure, tell students its name, and discuss its characteristics. As you describe the space figures, point out that some of them appear to be composed of plane figures. For example, the cylinder appears to have two circles, one on the top and one on the bottom. A cube appears to have six squares put together.

Have students find examples of space figures in the classroom and share their findings with the class. Also display everyday objects that are the shape of space figures, and have students identify them as a pyramid, cube, rectangular prism, sphere, cone, or cylinder. You might, for example, use a **Number Cube** for a cube, a shoe box for a rectangular prism, a ball for a sphere, a can for a cylinder, an ice-cream cone for a cone.

Skill Building APPLYING   Guided

 Distribute a copy of **Practice** page 128 to each student. Ask students what they see on the page. six squares that are joined together Ask students to think about what it would look like if they cut out the figure and folded it. Then have students cut out the figure, fold on the dotted lines, and tape the edges together to form a cube. Students will construct two other space figures from plane figure nets on student page 310.

Name _____ Date _____

LESSON 8.9 · Space Figures

LESSON 8.9 Space Figures

Key Ideas

Space figures cannot fit in a plane. Here are some examples of space figures.

Math TEKS
Geometry and spatial reasoning 2.7.A
Describe attributes (the number of vertices, faces, edges, sides) of two- and three-dimensional geometric figures such as circles, polygons, spheres, cones, cylinders, prisms, and pyramids.

Cone

Pyramid

Sphere

Cylinder

Cube

Rectangular prism

📱 **Match** each figure to the correct name.

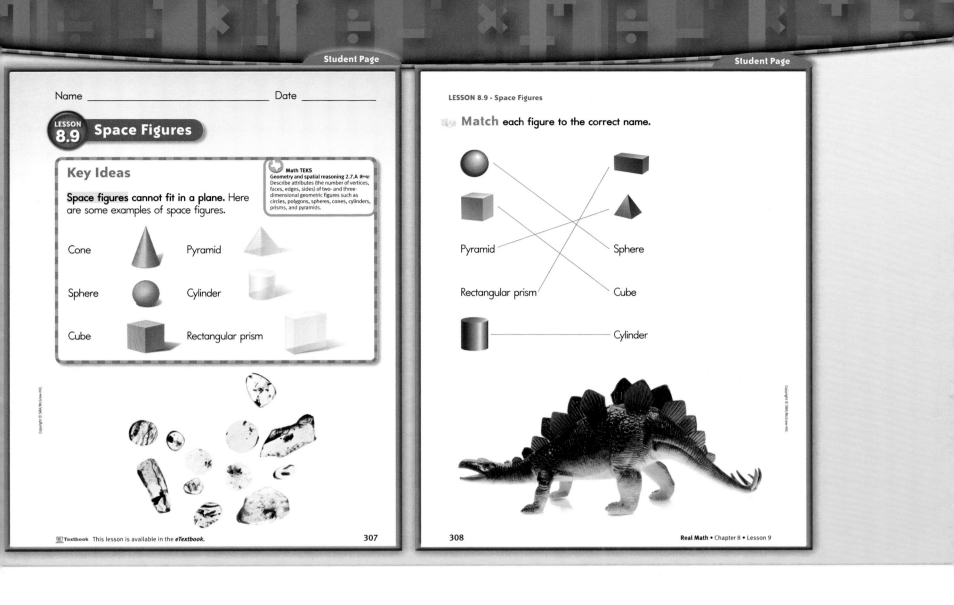

Pyramid

Sphere

Rectangular prism

Cube

Cylinder

Textbook This lesson is available in the *eTextbook*.

307

308

Real Math • Chapter 8 • Lesson 9

---

2 Use Student Pages 20 ⏱

Pages 307–308

👤 Independent

Have students complete page 308 independently, using page 307 as a reference if necessary.

Teacher Reflection

Find the space figures in this picture. Ring the pictures when you find them. Write the names of the figures you find.

pyramid

sphere

cylinder

rectangular prism

cube

LESSON 8.9 · Space Figures

Cut out each figure. Fold and tape to make two different pyramids.

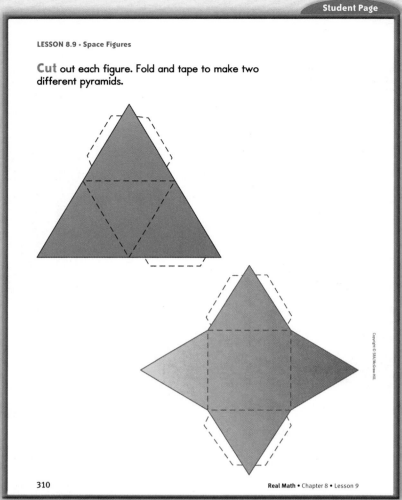

Use Student Pages, continued

Pages 309–310 APPLYING   Independent

Have students complete page 309 by finding the space figures in the picture and writing the names of the figures below the picture. Students can refer to the spellings on page 307.

Then have students cut out the nets on page 310 and construct the square pyramid and triangular pyramid as they constructed the cube earlier.

As Students Finish

MathTools *Net Tool* Have students use this tool to construct their own space figures from plane figure nets.

3 **Reflect** 5

Guided Discussion

Have students examine the space figures they constructed earlier in the lesson. Ask:

■ **What space figures did you construct?** a cube and two pyramids

■ **Critical Thinking** **How are the pyramids different from one another?** One pyramid is constructed of four triangles. Another name for this kind of pyramid is *tetrahedron*. The other pyramid is constructed of four triangles and a square.

Have students imagine taking another of each kind of space figure and attaching it to the bottom of their pyramids and cube. Ask students to predict what the resulting space figures would look like. One would look like it was composed of six triangles, one would look like it was composed of eight triangles, and one would look like it was composed of two squares and four rectangles—it would be a rectangular prism. Have students find a partner, combine the space figures, and see if their predictions were correct.

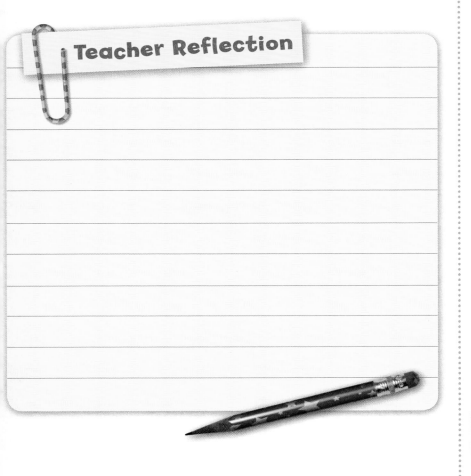

Teacher Reflection

 Cumulative Review: For cumulative review of previously learned skills, see page 317–318.

 Family Involvement: Assign the *Practice, Reteach,* or *Enrichment* activities depending on the needs of your students.

 Concept/Question Board: Have students attempt to answer any unanswered questions on the Concept/Question Board.

 Math Puzzler: Integration: 2.3.C There are 40 buttons in a box. There are 23 red ones. The rest are blue. How many more red buttons than blue buttons are there? 6

4 Assess and Differentiate

 e Assess Use **eAssess** to record and analyze evidence of student understanding.

A Gather Evidence

Use the Daily Class Assessment Records in *Texas Assessment* or *eAssess* to record daily observations.

Informal Assessment
✓ **Mental Math**

Did the student `COMPUTING`
- ❑ respond accurately?
- ❑ respond quickly?
- ❑ respond with confidence?
- ❑ self-correct?

Informal Assessment
✓ **Guided Discussion**

Did the student `ENGAGING`
- ❑ pay attention to others' contributions?
- ❑ contribute information and ideas?
- ❑ improve on a strategy?
- ❑ reflect on and check the accuracy of his or her work?

 TEKS/TAKS Practice

Use *TEKS/TAKS Practice* pages 59–62 to assess student progress.

B Summarize Findings

Analyze and summarize assessment data for each student. Determine which Assessment Follow-Up is appropriate for each student. Use the Student Assessment Record in *Texas Assessment* or *eAssess* to update assessment records.

C Texas Assessment Follow-Up ● DIFFERENTIATE INSTRUCTION

Based on your observations, use these teaching strategies for assessment follow-up.

INTERVENTION

Review student performance on *Intervention* Lesson 8.C to see if students have mastered prerequisite skills for this lesson.

🔷 **1.2.A** Separate a whole into two, three, or four equal parts and use appropriate language to describe the parts such as three out of four equal parts.

🔷 **1.6.A** Describe and identify two-dimensional geometric figures, including circles, triangles, rectangles, and squares (a special type of rectangle).

ENGLISH LEARNER
Review

Use Lesson 8.9 in *English Learner Support Guide* to review lesson concepts and vocabulary.

ENRICH

If . . . students are proficient in the lesson concepts,

Then . . . encourage them to work on the chapter projects or *Enrichment* Lesson 8.9.

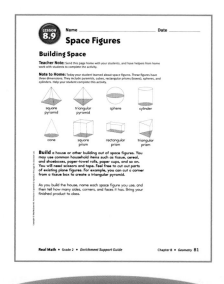

Enrichment Lesson 8.9

PRACTICE

 TEXAS

If . . . students would benefit from additional practice,

Then . . . assign *Practice* Lesson 8.9.

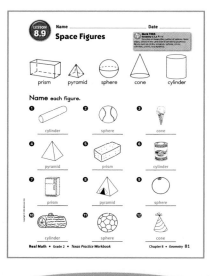

Practice Lesson 8.9

RETEACH

If . . . students are having difficulty identifying space figures,

Then . . . have them continue to identify space figures in the classroom and categorize prisms, cylinders, cubes, spheres, and pyramids.

Grade 1	Grade 2	Grade 3
1.6.A Describe and identify two-dimensional geometric figures, including circles, triangles, rectangles, and squares (a special type of rectangle).	**2.7.A** Describe attributes of two- and three-dimensional geometric figures.	**3.8** The student is expected to uses formal geometry vocabulary.

Overview

LESSON 8.10

TEXAS

Space Figures and Plane Figures ★

Lesson Planner

OBJECTIVES
- To compare space figures and plane figures
- To decompose space figures into plane figures

MATH TEKS

Geometry and spatial reasoning 2.7.A
Describe attributes (the number of vertices, faces, edges, sides) of two- and three-dimensional geometric figures such as circles, polygons, spheres, cones, cylinders, prisms, and pyramids.

Geometry and spatial reasoning 2.7.B
Use attributes to describe how 2 two-dimensional figures or 2 three-dimensional geometric figures are alike or different.

MATH TEKS INTEGRATION

Number, operation, and quantitative reasoning 2.3.A
Recall and apply basic addition and subtraction facts (to 18).

Number, operation, and quantitative reasoning 2.3.B
Model addition and subtraction of two-digit numbers with objects, pictures, words, and numbers.

MATERIALS
- *Number Cubes
- *Space figures

TECHNOLOGY
Presentation Lesson 8.10
MathTools **Net Tool** and **Shape Tool**

Context of the Lesson In the previous lesson students examined the characteristics of space figures and composed them by putting together plane figures. In this lesson students will decompose space figures into plane figures and study the parts of each.

See page 285B for Math Background for teachers for this lesson.

Planning for Learning ● DIFFERENTIATE INSTRUCTION

INTERVENTION
If . . . students lack the prerequisite skill of recognizing basic shapes,

Then . . . teach *Intervention* Lesson 8.C.

1.2.A, 1.6.4

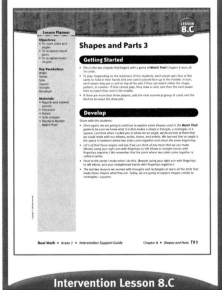

Intervention Lesson 8.C

ENGLISH LEARNER
Preview

If . . . students need language support,

Then . . . use Lesson 8.10 in *English Learner Support Guide* to preview lesson concepts and vocabulary.

English Learner Lesson 8.10

ENRICH
If . . . students are proficient in the lesson concepts,

Then . . . emphasize chapter projects.

PRACTICE
If . . . students would benefit from additional practice,

Then . . . extend Guided Discussion before assigning the student pages.

RETEACH
If . . . students are having difficulty understanding space figures,

Then . . . extend Guided Discussion before assigning the student pages.

Access Vocabulary
compare to find the likenesses and differences

Spanish Cognates
pyramid pirámide

TEXAS

Geometry and spatial reasoning 2.7.A Describe attributes (the number of vertices, faces, edges, sides) of two- and three-dimensional geometric figures such as circles, polygons, spheres, cones, cylinders, prisms, and pyramids.
Geometry and spatial reasoning 2.7.B Use attributes to describe how 2 two-dimensional figures or 2 three-dimensional geometric figures are alike or different.

Mental Math   5

 INTEGRATION: **TEKS 2.3.B** Have students show answers to subtraction exercises such as the following using their **Number Cubes.**

a. 48 − 2 = 46   **b.** 71 − 24 = 47
c. 31 − 24 = 7   **d.** 51 − 43 = 8
e. 80 − 22 = 58   **f.** 39 − 33 = 6

1 Develop   30

Tell Students In Today's Lesson They Will
compare plane figures and space figures.

Guided Discussion e MathTools UNDERSTANDING   Introductory

Draw a picture of a triangle on the board or overhead projector or using **eMathTools: Shape Tool.** Ask students:

■ **How many sides does a triangle have?** 3
■ **How many corners does a triangle have?** 3

Point to each side or corner as you count them. Remind students that plane figures are defined by their number of sides (for instance, all triangles have three sides, all quadrilaterals have four sides, and so on). Explain that space figures are defined in a similar way; by counting the number of faces, edges, and vertices.

Display one of the space figure models, and name and explain each part as you point to it. For example, a cube has six flat faces. The place where two faces meet is an edge: a cube has twelve edges. A vertex is a point where edges come together; a cube has eight vertices.

Strategy Building ENGAGING   Guided

Remind students of the cubes they constructed from nets in the previous lesson. Ask:

■ **What did the net of the cube look like?** six squares
■ **What do the faces of a cube look like?** squares

Take the cube space figure model, and trace each of its faces on the board or overhead projector.

■ **Critical Thinking** **How can you predict what the nets of other space figures would look like?** Discuss that students can predict a net by thinking about which plane figure each face of a space figure looks like.

Skill Building ENGAGING

1. Place an assortment of space figures in a bag or other opaque container. Try to include at least one of each of the following:

Sphere

Cone

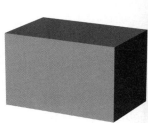
Rectangular Prism

Cylinder

Pyramid

Triangular Prism

2. In each round, choose a student to be the "selector." The selector reaches into the container and grabs an object without removing it or looking into the container.

3. The student describes the attributes of the object that can be felt, such as number of vertices, number of faces, the shape of a face, and so on, to the class.

4. The class tries to name the figure. When most of the students agree, the selector shows the figure he or she is holding. If you think the selector might be switching figures, you can have him or her remove the figure from the container and hold it behind the back while describing it.

Repeat the activity. If time allows and interest warrants, continue with variations, such as the following.

● The class says the name of a figure and the selector tries to pick that figure from the container without looking. The selector is allowed to ask the class questions about the attributes of the figure.

● The class names an attribute, such as *only two edges* or *exactly 5 vertices*. Without looking, the selector tries to pick a figure with that attribute.

● The selector can describe only the type and number of faces. For example: 4 *triangles, 1 square (square pyramid); 1 curved surface, 2 flat circles (cylinder).*

Name _____ Date _____

LESSON 8.10 · Space Figures and Plane Figures

LESSON 8.10 — Space Figures and Plane Figures

Key Ideas

You can compare space figures and plane figures.

Math TEKS
Geometry and spatial reasoning 2.7.A
Describe attributes (the number of vertices, faces, edges, sides) of two- and three-dimensional geometric figures such as circles, polygons, spheres, cones, cylinders, prisms, and pyramids.

❶ Study the plane figures. Complete the table.

Plane Figure		Number of Sides	Number of Corners
	Triangle	3	3
	Square	4	4
	Rectangle	4	4
	Parallelogram	4	4
	Pentagon	5	5

Writing + Math / Journal

Is it possible to draw a polygon with a number of corners that is not equal to the number of sides? Explain.

❷ Study the space figures. Complete the table.

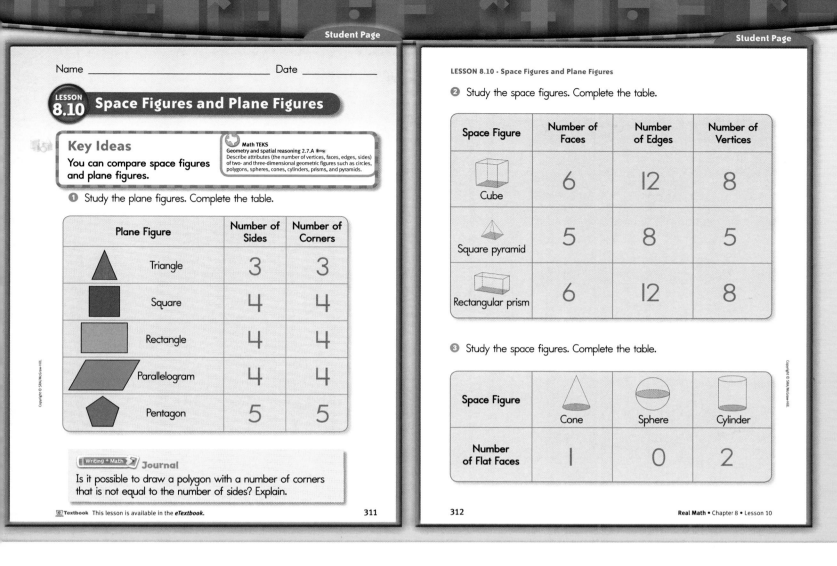

Space Figure		Number of Faces	Number of Edges	Number of Vertices
	Cube	6	12	8
	Square pyramid	5	8	5
	Rectangular prism	6	12	8

❸ Study the space figures. Complete the table.

Space Figure	Cone	Sphere	Cylinder
Number of Flat Faces	1	0	2

2 Use Student Pages — 20

Pages 311–312 UNDERSTANDING

👤 Independent

Have students complete the tables on pages 311 and 312 independently.

TEXAS TEKS Checkup

Geometry and spatial reasoning 2.7.B [b] Use attributes to describe how 2 two-dimensional figures or 2 three-dimensional geometric figures are alike or different.

Use this problem to assess students' progress toward standards mastery:

Which has the same number of corners?

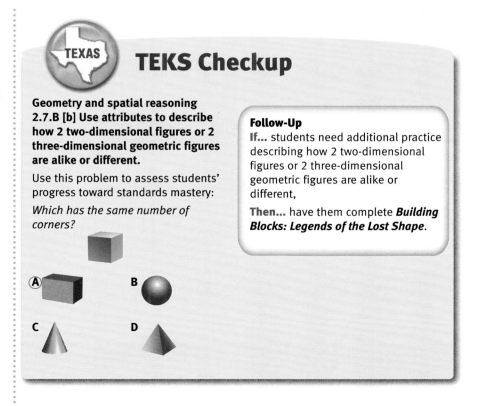

Ⓐ B

C D

Follow-Up

If... students need additional practice describing how 2 two-dimensional figures or 2 three-dimensional geometric figures are alike or different,

Then... have them complete *Building Blocks: Legends of the Lost Shape*.

Teaching Lesson 8.10

LESSON 8.10 · Space Figures and Plane Figures

Draw a line to connect each space figure to the net for that shape.
Trace, cut, and fold the nets to help you.

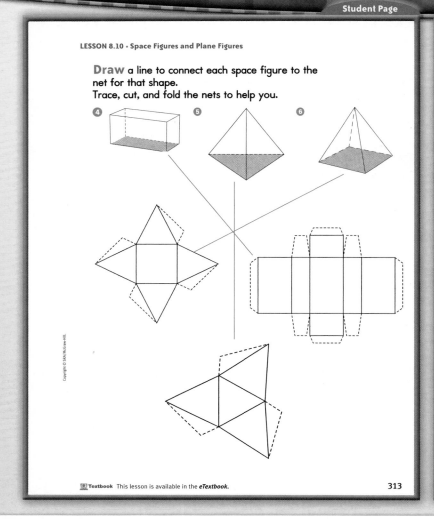

Textbook This lesson is available in the *eTextbook*.

313

LESSON 8.10 · Space Figures and Plane Figures

Different nets can make a cube.
Ring each net that can make a cube.
Draw an X on each net that cannot make a cube.

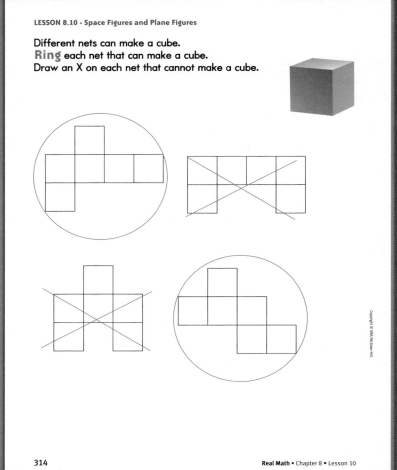

314

Real Math · Chapter 8 · Lesson 10

Use Student Pages, continued

Pages 313–314

👤 Independent

Have students complete pages 313 and 314 independently.

As Students Finish

 **MathTools** *Net Tool* Have students use this tool to continue to explore the relationship between plane figures and space figures.

Teacher Reflection

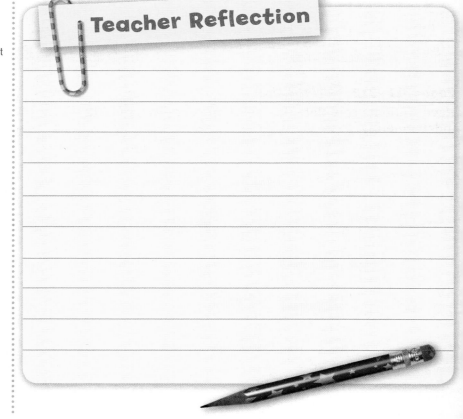

3 **Reflect** 5

Guided Discussion

■ **Critical Thinking** **Why don't we talk about edges, and vertices for cones, spheres, and cylinders?** Have students look at *Student Edition* page 312 for aid.

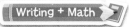 **Journal** ☑

Students may need to make a number of drawings to investigate this but should realize that it is not possible to draw a polygon with a number of corners that is not equal to the number of sides.

 Cumulative Review: For cumulative review of previously learned skills, see page 317–318.

Family Involvement: Assign the *Practice, Reteach,* or *Enrichment* activities depending on the needs of your students.

 Concept/Question Board: Have students attempt to answer any unanswered questions on the Concept/Question Board.

 Math Puzzler: **Integration: 2.3.A** Fifteen people saw a movie. Three more people liked it than did not like it. How many people did not like it? 6

4 Assess and Differentiate

 Assess Use **eAssess** to record and analyze evidence of student understanding.

A Gather Evidence

Use the Daily Class Assessment Records in **Texas Assessment** or **eAssess** to record daily observations.

Informal Assessment
✓ **Mental Math**

Did the student `COMPUTING`
- ❏ respond accurately?
- ❏ respond quickly?
- ❏ respond with confidence?
- ❏ self-correct?

Informal Assessment
✓ **Journal**

Did the student `ENGAGING`
- ❏ pay attention to others' contributions?
- ❏ contribute information and ideas?
- ❏ improve on a strategy?
- ❏ reflect on and check the accuracy of his or her work?

🤠 TEKS/TAKS Practice

Use **TEKS/TAKS Practice** pages 59–62 to assess student progress.

B Summarize Findings

Analyze and summarize assessment data for each student. Determine which Assessment Follow-Up is appropriate for each student. Use the Student Assessment Record in **Texas Assessment** or **eAssess** to update assessment records.

C Texas Assessment Follow-Up • DIFFERENTIATE INSTRUCTION

Based on your observations, use these teaching strategies for assessment follow-up.

INTERVENTION

Review student performance on **Intervention** Lesson 8.C to see if students have mastered prerequisite skills for this lesson.

🤠 **1.2.A** Separate a whole into two, three, or four equal parts and use appropriate language to describe the parts such as three out of four equal parts.

🤠 **1.6.A** Describe and identify two-dimensional geometric figures, including circles, triangles, rectangles, and squares (a special type of rectangle).

ENGLISH LEARNER

Review

Use Lesson 8.10 in **English Learner Support Guide** to review lesson concepts and vocabulary.

ENRICH

If . . . students are proficient in the lesson concepts,

Then . . . encourage them to work on the chapter projects or **Enrichment** Lesson 8.10.

Enrichment Lesson 8.10

PRACTICE

If . . . students would benefit from additional practice,

Then . . . assign **Practice** Lesson 8.10.

Practice Lesson 8.10

RETEACH

If . . . students are having difficulty drawing nets to represent space figures,

Then . . . have them tape individual shapes together or build space figures from flat figures before doing the reverse.

Problem Solving 8.C

Using Strategies

Objectives
- To solve a nonroutine problem involving the relationship between two-dimensional and three-dimensional forms
- To continue to develop spatial sense
- To develop an understanding that problems can have more than one answer

Materials
- Clay, Construction paper, Scissors, tape
- A variety of small, boxes that can be flattened or cut apart (optional)
- Pictures of dinosaur fossils and skeletons (optional)

See Appendix A page A24 for instruction and a rubric for problem solving.

Context of the Lesson While providing a large block of time for students to work on a single problem, this lesson provides an opportunity for students to apply what they have been learning about plane figures and space figures. The lesson also continues the dinosaur theme introduced on pages 285 and 286 and continued on pages 295 and 296.

1 Develop 5

Tell Students In Today's Lesson They Will
- create a clay model of a dinosaur fossil.
- design a box for packing the dinosaur fossil.
- construct the box using the design.

Skill Building

Ask students to think about what a dinosaur fossil might look like. If possible, show pictures of actual dinosaur fossils. Give each student a softball-sized piece of clay. Tell students to use their imaginations to create their own dinosaur fossil. Remind students that dinosaur fossils

- are usually formed from hard parts such as bones or teeth.
- are often found in pieces.
- are often found encased inside rock.

Encourage students to use this information in any way they like as they prepare their models of dinosaur fossils.

Keep the student-made fossils for the next part of the activity.

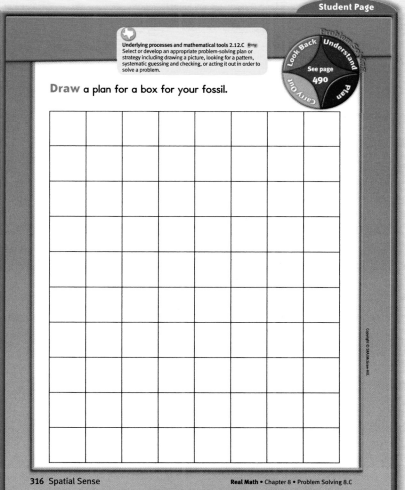

Guided Discussion

Have students look at and discuss the picture on page 315 of paleontologists digging for fossils.

Present this problem:

Out in the desert you have found a rare dinosaur fossil and need to look at it more closely in the lab back in the city. Because fossils break easily, you want to have a special shipping box made to fit the fossil exactly and to protect it. You need to make a plan for the box that you can fax to the museum workshop. The craftspeople at the workshop will construct the box and send it to the site.

Make sure students understand the problem by asking questions such as the following:

- **Why do you need a special box made?** We found a rare fossil and need to ship it to our lab. We don't want it to break while it is being taken back to the lab.
- **What shape are the sides of most boxes?** rectangles
- **How will the workshop know what size and shape box will fit your fossil?** We have to make a plan for a box and fax it to the workshop.
- **If the plan is going to be faxed, how will it have to look?** The plan will have to be flat so it can be put in the fax machine.
- **A box is not flat, so how can you make a plan that is flat?** Write the plan in words; draw rectangles that could be cut out and put together to make a box; make a pattern that could be folded and made into a box; make the box first, and then flatten it and trace it; and so on.
- **Will every group end up with the same plan? Why or why not?** no; because each group has a different fossil to ship
- **What do you have to help you?** We have the fossil model, paper, and tape.

Use Student Pages   25

Guided Discussion

Give students access to paper, scissors, and tape. Have students work together or individually to create a plan for a box for their fossil model. They may build the box first and then make the plan, or they may plan first and then build the box.

Even though students will not be designing boxes with connecting tabs or sections that fold over, they may benefit from flattening or cutting apart actual boxes to see how they are put together.

If students seem to be having difficulty, encourage them to struggle with the problem for a while. When needed, ask guiding questions such as the following:

- **How can you use your fossil model to help you?**
- **Can your plan fit into a fax machine?**
- **If someone else follows your plan, will he or she end up with the same box that you made?**
- **How do you know that your fossil will fit into this box?**

Have students draw a picture of the fossil they made at the bottom of page 315. Then have students copy the plan for a box for the fossil on page 316.

Remind students they will need to be able to prove that the box built from their plan fits their dinosaur fossil model.

Extension

Have students exchange plans and build each other's boxes. They can then try to pack the box with the fossil for which it was designed. Make a class display of fossils and their boxes.

Reflect   10

Problem Formulation, Planning, and Strategizing Have each student or group present the fossil, the plan, and the box made from the plan. Ask questions such as the following:

- **Which was easier: making the plan or making the box? Why?**
- **Which kind of plan did you like best? Why?**
- **How is the plan like the box? How is it different?**

Help students understand the following points:

- The sides of three-dimensional boxes are two-dimensional shapes that can be connected into a continuous pattern or net.
- A three-dimensional form can be constructed by folding its pattern or net.
- You can predict what a three-dimensional shape will look like by looking at its pattern or net.
- When it is difficult to visualize a three-dimensional shape, making a three-dimensional model is often useful.

Assess   15

When evaluating student work, focus on whether students thought rationally about the problem. Questions to consider include the following:

- Did the student understand the problem?
- Was the student able to understand the relationship between the two-dimensional plan and the three-dimensional box?
- Did the student have some organized way of planning and constructing?
- Was the student able to explain his or her thinking?
- Was the student able to prove that the plan resulted in a box that fit the fossil?

Cumulative Review

Use Pages 317–318

Use the Cumulative Review as a review of concepts and skills that students have previously learned.

Here are different ways that you can assign these problems to your students as they work through the chapter:

- With some of the lessons in the chapter, assign a set of cumulative review problems to be completed as practice or for homework.
  Lesson 8.5—Problems 1–3
  Lesson 8.6—Problems 4–6
  Lesson 8.7—Problems 7–12
  Lesson 8.8—Problems 13–14
  Lesson 8.9—Problems 15–16
  Lesson 8.10—Problems 17–18

- At any point during the chapter, assign part or all of the cumulative review problems to be completed as practice or for homework.

Cumulative Review

Problems 1–3 review telling time to the half hour, hour, and quarter hour, Lesson 7.10. TEKS: 2.10.B

Problems 4–6 review obtuse, acute, and right angles, Lesson 8.5. TEKS: 2.10.B

Problems 7–12 review addition facts, Lesson 2.6. TEKS: 2.6.C

Problems 13–14 review addition and subtraction function machines, Lesson 3.3. TEKS: 2.3.A

Problems 15–16 review place value using craft sticks, Lesson 5.1. TEKS: 2.1.A

Problems 17–18 review subtracting tens, Lesson 6.2. TEKS: 2.3.A, 2.3.B

Progress Monitoring

If . . . students miss more than one problem in a section, : **Then . . .** refer to the indicated lesson for remediation suggestions.

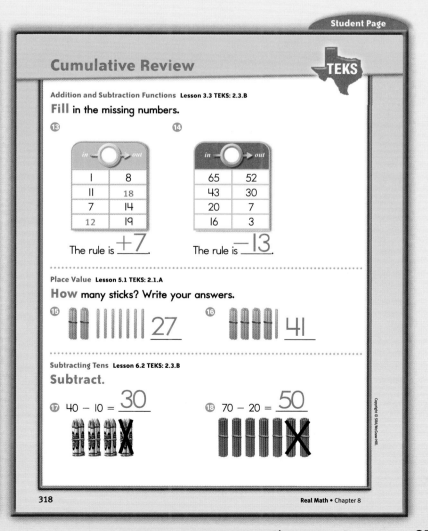

Wrap-Up

1 Discuss

5

Concept/Question Board

Review the Concept/Question Board with students.

- Discuss students' contributions to the Concept side of the Board.
- Have students repose their questions, and lead a discussion to find satisfactory answers.

Chapter Projects APPLYING

Provide an opportunity for students who have worked on one or more of the projects outlined on page 286C to share their work with the class. Allow each student or student group five minutes to present or discuss their projects. For formal assessment, use the rubrics found in *Across the Curriculum Math Connections;* the rubric for **Create a Map of Dinosaur Locations** is on page 85, and the rubric for **Use Plane Figures to Draw Dinosaurs** is on page 91. For informal assessment, use the following rubric and questions.

	Exceeds Expectations	Meets Expectations	Minimally Meets Expectations
Applies mathematics in real-world situations:	❏	❏	❏
Demonstrates strong engagement in the activity:	❏	❏	❏

Create a Map of Dinosaur Locations

- What shapes did you use in your map key? What time period did they represent?
- Which color did you use for plant eaters? Which color did you use for meat eaters?
- What information did you find about your dinosaur?
- How many places were fossils of your dinosaur found? What locations on the map were they found?
- Which dinosaur had the most fossils found on the map?
- What other ways could you create a map of dinosaur locations?

Standards

MATH STANDARD: **Geometry and spatial reasoning 2.7** The student uses attributes to identify two- and three-dimensional geometric figures. The student compares and contrasts two- and three-dimensional geometric figures or both.

SOCIAL STUDIES STANDARD: **Geography 2.5.A** Use symbols, find locations, and determine directions on maps and globes.

TECHNOLOGY STANDARD: **Solving Problems 08.B** Use electronic tools and research skills to build a knowledge base regarding a topic, task, or assigment.

Use Plane Figures to Draw Dinosaurs

- What dinosaur did you choose? Why did you choose that dinosaur?
- What information did you find about your dinosaur?
- What distinguishing features did your dinosaur have?
- What shapes did you use to create your plane-figure drawing?
- Was a drawing and graphics program the best way to create a drawing? Why or why not?
- If you could draw a second dinosaur, what dinosaur would you draw? Why?

Standardsf MATH STANDARD: **Geometry and spatial reasoning 2.7** The student uses attributes to identify two- and three-dimensional geometric figures. The student compares and contrasts two- and three-dimensional geometric figures or both.

FINE ARTS STANDARD: **Creative expression/performance 2.2.B** Create effective compositions, using design elements and principles.

TECHNOLOGY STANDARD: **Communication 11.A** Publish information in a varity of media including, but not limited to, printed copy or monitor display.

Key Ideas Review **UNDERSTANDING**

Review the Key Ideas concepts on pages 319-320 with the class. The Key Ideas pages should be used by students and parents as a reference when reviewing the important concepts covered in this chapter. Ask students the following discussion questions to extend their knowledge of the Key Ideas and check their understanding of the ideas.

Discussion Questions

❶ Discuss plane figures with the class. Can they find examples of plane figures in the classroom or think of any plane figures they have seen? Allow students to share their ideas. Any figure printed or drawn, unless it is an illustration representing a space figure, is a plane figure.

❷ What are some other times they have heard the word *plane*? Does it mean the same thing as the word plane in *plane figure*? Students will most likely have heard the word *plane* used in different contexts. For example, *plane* when referring to an airplane is spelled the same way, but means something different. *Plain* sounds the same but means something different as well. Make sure students understand that you do not mean *plain figures*, as in ordinary figures, but *plane figures* existing on a plane. Students may be interested in discussing other homonyms and homophones.

❸ Discuss space figures with the class. Where have students seen space figures? Allow students to discuss. Finding space figures should be easy, as almost every object we encounter is a space figure. Students are familiar with irregular plane figures, do space figures have to be regular? (No)

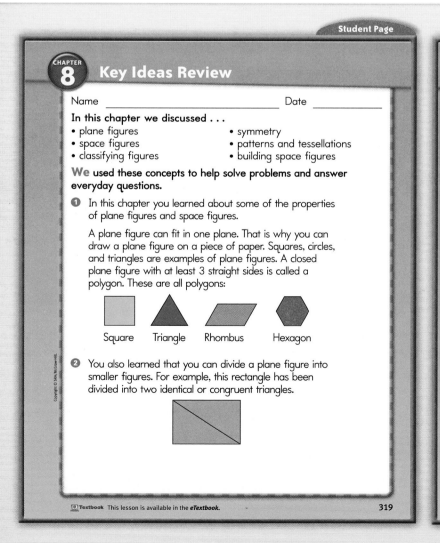

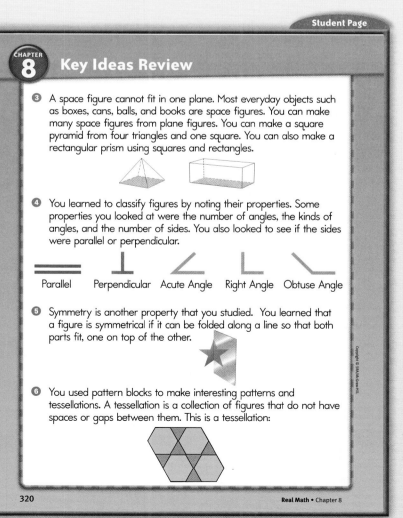

Chapter 8 Error Analysis

Errors Recognizing Figures and Properties

Draw the following figures and answers on the board and allow students to analyze this student's work. Discuss error patterns students find and how to help the student.

Pose this analysis as a challenging problem. When a student thinks he or she might have detected the error pattern, rather than have them tell the answer to the class, write a new exercise on the board and have the student tell you the answer that is consistent with the pattern he or she found. By using this procedure, all students will have a chance to think through the problem—not just the first student to find it.

This student completed some geometry exercises and got the following answers.

1. Place an X under each triangle.

2. Place an X under each figure that is symmetric.

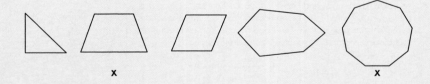

What error is this student making?

This student does not completely understand the definitions for triangles and symmetric figures, and possibly for other geometric figures as well. He or she believes that a figure's orientation, in part, determines what it is. The student needs instruction on the definition of a triangle (a closed figure with 3 line segments) and of a symmetric figure, (a figure is symmetrical if one-half of it is the mirror image of the other half.)

A useful technique for helping this student is to draw an equilateral triangle that he or she does not identify as a triangle. Then rotate it until the base is parallel to the base of the paper it is drawn on and the student sees it as a triangle. Explain that the figure has not changed—only its position has changed.

The same technique can be used with symmetric figures. Start with a symmetric figure that the student does not identify as such and rotate it until the line of symmetry is perpendicular to the base o

TEKS/TAKS Practice

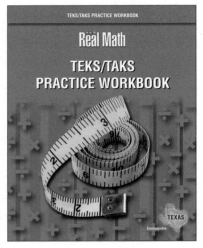

TEKS/TAKS Practice Book

At this time, you may wish to provide practice for standards covered in this chapter.

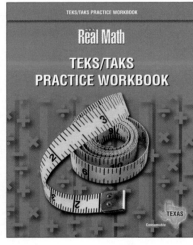

TEKS/TAKS Practice, pp. 65–66, Standard 2.7.C

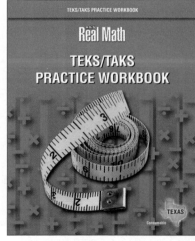

TEKS/TAKS Practice, pp. 59–62, Standard 2.7.A

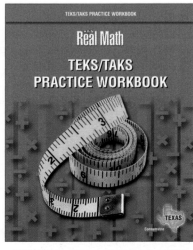

TEKS/TAKS Practice, pp. 63–64, Standard 2.7.B

Chapter Review

Use this Chapter 8 Review to indicate areas in which each student is having difficulty or in which the class may need help. If students do well on the Chapter 8 Review, you may wish to skip directly to the Chapter Test; if not, you may spend a day or so helping students overcome their individual difficulties before taking the Practice Test.

Next to each set of problems is a list of the lessons in the chapter that covered those concepts. If they need help, students can refer to a specific lesson for additional instruction. You can also use this information to make additional assignments based on the previous lesson concepts.

Have students complete pages 321–322 on their own.

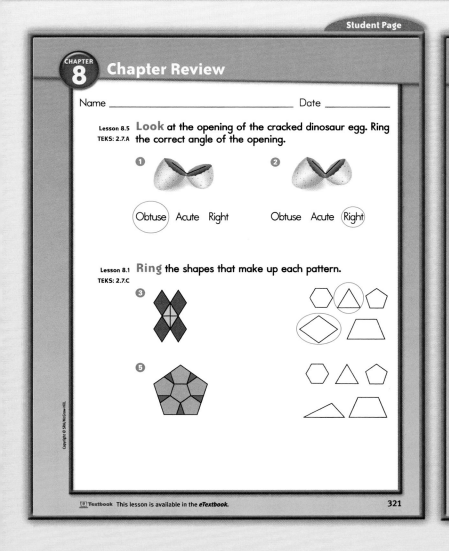

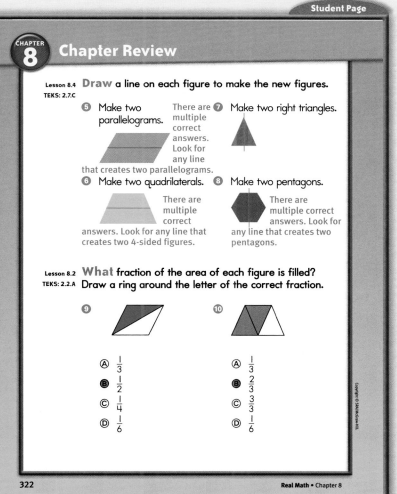

3 Chapter Tests 40

Practice Test

Student Pages 323–326

- The Chapter 8 Practice Test on **Student Edition** pages 323–326 provides an opportunity to formally evaluate students' proficiency with concepts developed in this chapter.
- The content is similar to the Chapter 8 Review, in standardized format.

Practice Test Remediation

Student Pages 323–326

Multiple Choice Questions 3–4 are about measures of angles. If student have difficulty with these problems, then review the terms *acute, obtuse,* and *right* with them. Remind them that many times, the corners of books or pieces of paper make right angles. They can use a right angle as a reference point for determining if an angle is obtuse or acute.

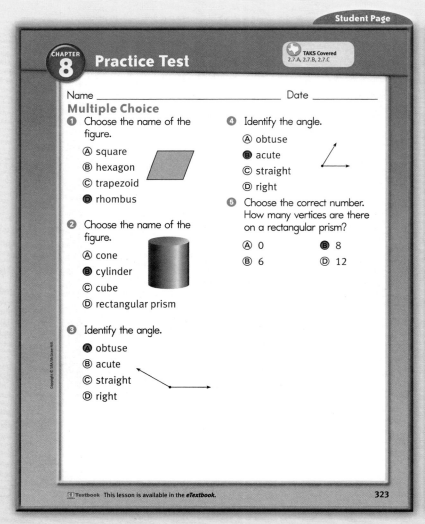

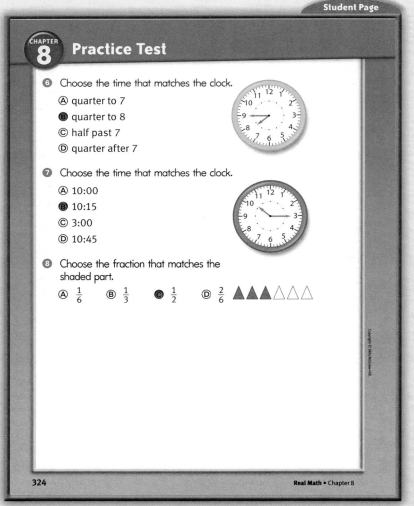

Multiple Choice Questions 8–9 and Short Answer Questions 1–2 are all about determining fractions. If students miss these problems, review the concept of a fraction with them. Also, review how you can have fractions of a figure, fractions of a number, or fractions of a set.

If students have difficulty with Extended Response Question 6, then have them draw a hexagon and cut it out. Then have them fold the paper hexagon to find lines of symmetry.

Multiple Choice Questions 1–2 and 6 all review properties of figures. It students have difficulty with these problems, have them work with pattern blocks and space figure sets so they become more familiar with the figures.

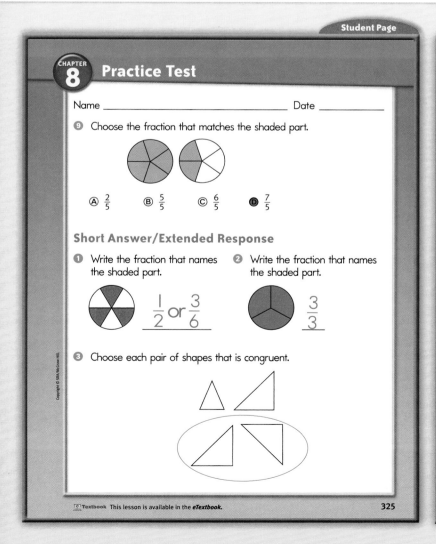

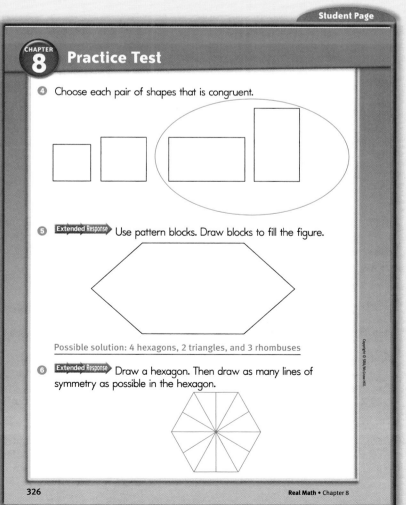

4 Assess and Differentiate

 Assess Use *eAssess* to record and analyze evidence of student understanding.

A Gather Evidence

Use the Daily Class Assessment Records in *Texas Assessment* or *eAssess* to record Informal and Formal Assessments.

Informal Assessment
✓ **Key Ideas Review** UNDERSTANDING

Did the student
❑ make important observations?
❑ extend or generalize learning?
❑ provide insightful answers?
❑ pose insightful questions?

Informal Assessment
✓ **Project** APPLYING

Did the student
❑ meet the project objectives?
❑ communicate clearly?
❑ complete the project accurately?
❑ connect mathematics to real-world situations?

Formal Assessment
✓ **Chapter Test** COMPUTING

Score the test, and record the results.

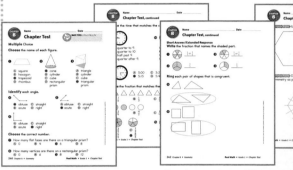

Texas Assessment, pages 240–241   Texas Assessment, pages 242–243

B Summarize Findings

Analyze and summarize assessment data for each student. Determine which Chapter Follow-Up is appropriate for each student. Use the Student Assessment Record in *Texas Assessment* or *eAssess* to update assessment records.

C Chapter Follow-Up • DIFFERENTIATE INSTRUCTION

Based on your observations, use these teaching strategies for chapter follow-up.

ENRICH	PRACTICE	RETEACH	INTERVENTION
If . . . students demonstrate a **secure understanding** of chapter concepts,	**If . . .** students demonstrate **competent understanding** of chapter concepts,	**If . . .** students demonstrate **emerging understanding** of chapter concepts,	**If . . .** students demonstrate **minimal understanding** of chapter concepts,
Then . . . move on to the next chapter.	**Then . . .** move on to the next chapter.	**Then . . .** move on to the next chapter, but continue to provide cumulative review.	**Then . . .** intensive intervention is still needed before they start the next chapter.

Manolita Changes Things

Context of the Thinking Story Manolita changes paper and pictures to make a photo album for her pictures of the dinosaur exhibit at a theme park.

Lesson Planner

OBJECTIVES
To develop logical thinking while integrating reading skills with mathematics

 UNDERLYING PROCESSES AND MATHEMATICAL TOOLS 2.14

The student is expected to justify his or her thinking using objects, words, pictures, numbers, and technology.

 READING/COMPREHENSION 2.9.E
Draw and discuss visual images based on text descriptions.

Reading/comprehension 2.9.F
Make and explain inferences from texts such as determining important ideas and causes and effects, making predictions, and drawing conclusions.

Reading/literary response 2.10.D
Connect ideas and themes across texts.

Using the Thinking Story
The Thinking Story may be used at any time throughout the chapter. Read the Thinking Story "Manolita Changes Things" to your class. As you read the story, give students time to think about each question, but not so much that they forget the point being made.

Manolita Changes Things

Manolita Mudancia wants to be just like her father. Because her father is always changing things, Manolita tries to change things too.

Manolita had 16 photographs of a dinosaur exhibit that she had taken at a theme park. She wanted to make a photo album for them, pasting one photograph onto each page. But all she could find were two square sheets of black construction paper. "I have only enough paper to take care of two pictures," she moaned. Then she added, "Oh, I forgot something. This is enough paper for four pictures."

How can Manolita put four pictures onto two sheets of paper if she puts only one picture on a page? **Answers may vary. Possible answers include pasting one picture on each side of the paper.**

Manolita had forgotten that she could put a picture onto each side of the sheet of paper, just as there are words on both sides of the paper in most books. But she didn't want to put only four pictures in her book. She wanted to put all sixteen pictures in, and she still wanted one picture on each page.

"I think I can change this paper a little to make more pages," Manolita thought. "That's what my dad would do."

How can Manolita make more pages? **She can cut the sheets in half.**

Manolita took a pair of scissors and cut each sheet of paper down the middle.

How many sheets of paper does Manolita have now? **four**

How many pictures can she put onto the sheets now, with one picture on a side?   **eight**

Manolita figured out that she had enough pages for eight of her pictures. "But that doesn't take care of all my pictures," she said.

How many pictures would she still have left?   **eight**

What can Manolita do to get the right number of pages? **She can cut all the sheets in half again.**

Manolita took the four sheets of paper and cut each one across the middle so it made two square sheets.

How many sheets of paper does Manolita have now?   **eight**

How many pictures can she put on the sheets now, with one picture to a side?   **sixteen**

"I did it!" Manolita said happily. "I changed those two sheets of paper a little and now I have eight sheets—just enough to put my sixteen pictures on. And the pages are nice and square like the ones I started with."

Are they exactly like the ones she started with?   **no**

How are they different? **They're smaller.**

But Manolita's troubles were not over. When she tried to put the pictures onto the pages, she found that the pages were a little too small for the pictures. "This is terrible," she said. "I wanted to make more pages. I didn't want to make them smaller."

Why are the pages smaller? **Each one is a part of the sheet of paper she started with.**

Mr. Mudancia came in and asked Manolita what was wrong.

"I'm trying to make a photo album for my pictures," Manolita said, "but the pages are too small. Could you change them a little to make them bigger?"

"Sorry," Mr. Mudancia said. "I don't know any way to do that. But I can change something else a little so your pictures will fit on the pages."

What else can be changed? **the pictures**

How? Encourage students to identify a variety of creative solutions, such as cutting out the main subject of each picture.

Mr. Mudancia took the scissors and cut the edges off one of the pictures. "There," he said. "Now you have a smaller picture, but it fits on the page."

"That's great," Manolita said. "Now I'll have a little book that I can carry in my pocket. We really know how to change things to make them better, don't we, Dad?"

You're getting the idea," Mr. Mudancia said, changing his face a little so it looked proud and happy.

What do you think Mr. Mudancia did to change his face? He smiled.

The End

Copyright © SRA/McGraw-Hill.

Teaching the Lesson

Guided Discussion

As students answer the questions in the story, ask them to communicate how they chose their answers. Allow students to debate the answers if necessary.

Using Student Pages 327–328

Have students follow the instructions and complete the **Student Edition** activities. Read the instructions aloud if students are having difficulty.

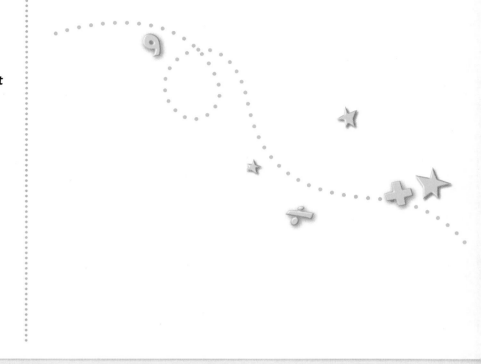

Name _____ Date _____

Thinking Story

🌐 **Math TEKS**
Geometry and spatial reasoning 2.7.B
Use attributes to describe how 2 two-dimensional figures or 2 three-dimensional geometric figures are alike or different.

Manolita Changes Things

Manolita wants to change the appearance of each figure by moving it. Write how she can do it. Trace and move the figures to check.

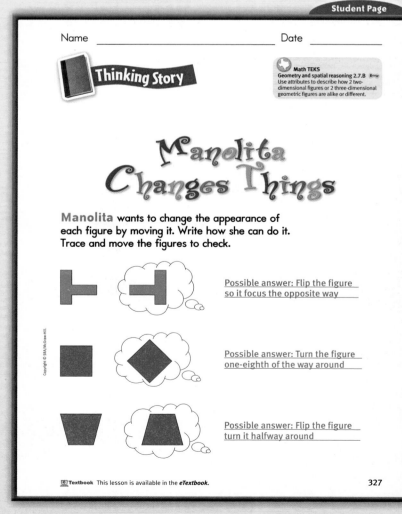

Possible answer: Flip the figure so it focus the opposite way

Possible answer: Turn the figure one-eighth of the way around

Possible answer: Flip the figure turn it halfway around

📖 **Textbook** This lesson is available in the *eTextbook*.

327

Manolita wants to change each figure by cutting it. Draw lines on the quadrilaterals to show how she can do it. Trace and cut to check.

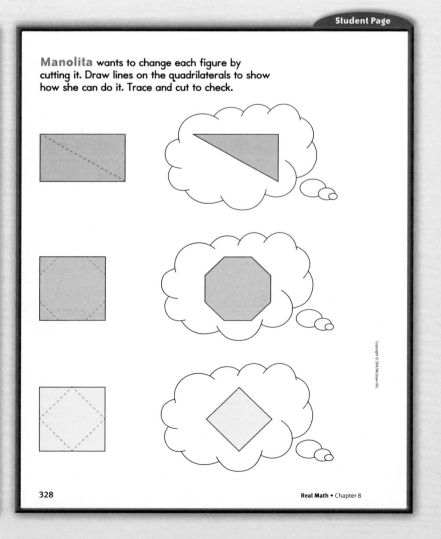

328

Real Math • Chapter 8

Teacher Reflection

Reflect on each of the lessons you taught in this chapter. Rate each one on the following scale, and then consider ways to maintain or improve positive teaching experiences in the future.

Lessons	Very Effective	Effective	Less Effective	What Worked	Ways to Improve
8.1 Tessellations					
8.2 Parts of Plane Figures					
8.3 Combining Plane Figures					
8.4 Defining Plane Figures— Quadrilaterals					
8.5 Obtuse, Acute, and Right Angles					
8.6 Congruence					
8.7 Symmetry					
8.8 Defining Other Plane Figures					
8.9 Space Figures					
8.10 Space Figures and Plane Figures					

Lessons

★ = 120-Day Plan for TAKS

Three-Digit Addition and Subtraction

Teaching for Understanding

This chapter focuses on teaching addition and subtraction with greater numbers. The objective is to use addition and subtraction on a greater scale to elaborate on students' current knowledge of borrowing and regrouping. Students will also continue to develop problem-solving strategies through a variety of real-world situations.

Prerequisite Skills and Concepts

- Adding Two-Digit Numbers
- Subtracting Two-Digit Numbers
- Recognizing Addition and Subtraction Situations

Three-Digit Addition and Subtraction Skills Trace

Before Grade 2	Grade 2	After Grade 2
Grades K–1 Informally and formally introduced addition and subtraction using single-digit numbers	**Chapter 3** developed understanding of single-digit subtraction. **Chapter 6** developed two-digit subtraction and introduced regrouping. **This chapter** develops strategies for three-digit addition and subtraction. The number range is extended to 10,000, and the decimal point is introduced..	Review and mastery of three-digit addition and subtraction with greater numbers Formal introduction of the decimal point

BIG Ideas! in Chapter 9

This chapter develops the following ideas running throughout elementary mathematics:

- The base ten numeration system is a scheme for recording numbers using digits 0-9, groups of ten, and place value. In Lessons 9.1 through 9.3, students learn about place value as a preparation for adding and subtracting three-digit numbers. Students use number lines and Base-ten blocks as ways to visualize the concept of one number being greater than or less than another.

- The operations of addition and subtraction have multiple concrete interpretations, and one operation in related to the other. The main ideas related to addition and subtraction are joining, separating, and comparison numbers. In Lessons 9.4 through 9.7, students extend their knowledge of addition and subtraction to learn the processes for adding and subtracting greater numbers. Real-life situations are provided in the problems to be solved in Lesson 9.8 and in Problem Solving 9.B and 9.C. In Lesson 9.9 students are introduced to the decimal point in the context of dollars and cents to further practice and develop their addition and subtraction skills. In the final lessons of this chapter, 9.10, 9.11, and 9.12, students continue to practice adding and subtracting by approximating and rounding 3-digit numbers.

Math TEKS addressed in each lesson can be found in the Chapter Planner on page 329E.

Math TEKS addressed in Problem Solving, Review, and Assessment lessons are on page 329G.

Complete text of the standards appears on the Lesson Overview page and first Teaching page of each lesson.

TEXAS

Math Background
Addition and Subtraction

Addition and Subtraction Algorithms

"An algorithm is a recipe for computation. . . . Algorithms are important in school mathematics because they can help students understand better the fundamental operations of arithmetic and important concepts such as place value and also because they pave the way for learning more advanced topics."

Kilpatrick, J., J. Swafford, and B. Findell, eds. *Adding It Up: Helping Children Learn Mathematics*. Washington, D.C.: National Research Council/National Academy Press, 2001, p. 103.

- An algorithm is a specific set of steps for completing a procedure.

- Students should not merely memorize the steps of an algorithm, but rather should develop a strong understanding of where the steps come from and why the algorithm works. This helps students remember better and transfer their knowledge more easily to other situations.

- Students were introduced to addition and subtraction algorithms for two-digit numbers in Chapters 5 and 6, through a manipulative-based development that emphasized conceptual understanding. This chapter provides extensive practice with using the algorithms with three-digit numbers.

- The power of the addition and subtraction algorithms reviewed in this chapter is that because of the place value basis for our number system, the same steps work for numbers with any number of digits. Therefore, knowing these algorithms allows students to add and subtract any two positive whole numbers.

Shortcuts

Many computation exercises in this chapter (and throughout *Real Math*) are conducive to using computational shortcuts. Most computation pages contain some items that can be done more easily without the standard algorithm. For example, to find 499 + 499, students can recognize that it must be 2 less than 500 + 500, which is 2 less than 1,000. Also, in problems like 25 + 25 or 75 + 75, students may simply know the answer because these numbers come up often, with money for example. Mixing in such problems helps students learn to recognize when a standard algorithm may be less appropriate than some other method so that they do not go through life unthinkingly using paper and pencil or a calculator every time they need to work with numbers.

Approximation and Detection of Obviously Wrong Answers

Approximation is a major part of using mathematics intelligently. The availability of calculators and computers has made the ability to approximate answers and to recognize obviously wrong answers even more important. Significant as they are, these abilities are not easy to teach. Children and adults seem to prefer precise answers even when a less precise answer is more appropriate and easier to determine. When people get an answer to any question or problem, they tend not to think about the answer but to accept it and go on to the next task. In *Real Math*, we try to overcome people's inclination to avoid approximation and to accept any answer by building into the program a variety of exercises, examples, and activities that focus on the need and usefulness of approximation and detection skills.

What Research Says

About Operations, Place Value, and Rounding

How Children Use Knowledge of Numbers to Perform Multidigit Addition and Subtraction

"The ideas and skills involved in multidigit computation are supported by most of the big ideas of number and operations. Unfortunately, given present-day instruction, many children think of multidigit numbers only as single-digit numbers sitting side by side, ignoring their place value, which invites different kinds of errors. To develop computational methods that they understand, children require strong experience in kindergarten (or earlier) hearing the pattern of repeating tens in the number words and relating them to quantities groups in tens and seeing teen numbers and two-digit numbers as embedded numbers (52 is 50 and 2)."

Clements, Douglas and J. Sarama, eds. *Engaging Young Children in Mathematics: Standards for Early Childhood Mathematics Education*. Mahwah, New Jersey: Lawrence Erlbaum Associates, Publishers, 2004, p. 25.

"Computational estimation takes advantage of important properties of numbers and notational systems, including powers of ten, place value and relations among different operations. It also requires recognizing that the appropriateness of an estimate is related to a problem and its context."

Kilpatrick, J., J. Swafford, and B. Findell, eds. *Adding It Up: Helping Children Learn Mathematics*. Washington, D.C.: National Research Council/National Academy Press, 2001, p. 216.

Learning Trajectories for Comparing and Ordering Numbers and for Performing Addition and Subtraction

The ability to compare and order sets with fluency develops over the course of several years. With instruction and number experience, most children develop foundational understanding of number relationships and place value at ages four and five. Most children follow a natural developmental progression in learning to compare and order numbers with recognizable stages or levels. This developmental path can be described as part of a learning trajectory.

Key steps in the learning trajectory for comparing and ordering numbers from the second-grade range are described below. For the complete trajectory, see Appendix B.

Level Name	Description
Place Value Comparer	Further development is made when a child begins to compare numbers with place-value understanding. For example, a child at this level can explain that "63 is more than 59 because 6 tens is more than 5 tens even if there are more than 3 ones."
Mental Number Line to 100	Children demonstrate the next level in comparing and ordering when they can use mental images and knowledge of number relationships, including ones embedded in tens, to determine relative size and position.
Mental Number Line to 1,000s	About age 8 children begin to use mental images of numbers up to 1,000 and knowledge of number relationships, including place value, to determine relative size and position.
Multidigit +/−	Further development is evidenced when children can use composition of tens and all previous strategies to solve multidigit +/− problems.

Clements, D. H., J. Sarama, & A.-M. DiBiase, eds. *Engaging Young Children in Mathematics: Standards for Early Childhood Mathematics Education*. Mahwah, NJ: Lawrence Erlbaum Associates, 2004.

Research-Based Teaching Strategies

"The written place-value system is an efficient system that lets us write large numbers, but it is also abstract and misleading. The numbers in every position look the same. To understand the meaning of the numbers in the various positions, first- and second-grade children need experience with some kind of size visual quantity supports: manipulatives or drawings that show tens to be collections of 10 ones and show hundreds to be simultaneously 10 tens and 100 ones, and so on."

Fuson, Karen. "Pre-K to Grade 2 Goals and Standards: Achieving 21st Century Mastery for All" in Clements, Douglas and J. Sarama, eds. *Engaging Young Children in Mathematics: Standards for Early Childhood Mathematics Education*. Mahwah, New Jersey: Lawrence Erlbaum Associates, Publishers, 2004, p. 125.

RESEARCH IN ACTION

Place Value Chapter 9 reinforces the development of relational understandings of place value based upon their use of base-ten concepts, language associated with the base-ten number system, and the written expressions of base-ten numbers.

Estimation Throughout Chapter 9 students will reinforce the skills and underlying understandings of the relative size and position of numbers to support their developing skills of estimation. Students will also explore real-world contexts for using estimation skills.

Rounding In Chapter 9 students will use their knowledge of place value and the relative size or position of numbers to support their practice of rounding numbers to form friendly numbers for use in calculations or in determining reasonableness of an answer.

Academic Vocabulary

None

English Learner

Cognates

For English learners, a quick way to acquire new English vocabulary is to build on what is known in the primary language.

English	Spanish
value	valor
models	modelos
equal	igual
example	ejemplo
practice	práctica
subtract	sustraer
practice	practicar
cost	costo
denominations	denominaciones
preparation	preparación
round	ronda
correct	correcto

Access Vocabulary

English learners may understand words in different contexts, or they might not understand idioms. Review chapter vocabulary for this concern. For example:

fill in the table	write the answers in the spaces on the table
draw pictures to show the number	do not draw the numeral
matches the number	goes together or is the same as
rummage sale	a large organized sale of used clothes or items
relationship	the connection between two or more things
$70 off	the price has been reduced by $70
crossed out	eliminated by drawing a line through a number or item
price tags	stickers or tags that tell the price of the item
shortcuts	a solution that takes fewer steps than the standard solution
pick the number	choose the number
check mark	a mark that shows you have reviewed an item

TEXAS Overview

Texas Chapter Planner

Lessons	Objectives	NCTM Standards	TEXAS Math TEKS
⭐ 9.1 **Place Value through 10,000** pages 331A–332A 45–60 minutes	**To study the place value in a four-digit number** by using multiple models	Number and Operations, Communication	2.1.A 2.1.B 🔑 2.5.B 2.8
⭐ 9.2 **Modeling Numbers through 1,000** pages 333A–334A 45–60 minutes	**To understand numbers through 1,000** by creating models and by saying, writing, and recognizing their values	Number and Operations, Representation	2.1.A 2.1.B 🔑 2.5.B
9.3 **Comparing Numbers through 1,000** pages 335A–336A 45–60 minutes	**To show the relation between two-, three-, or four-digit numbers** by using inequality and equality signs	Number and Operations, Algebra, Problem Solving	2.1.C 2.5.B 🔑
9.4 **Adding Multiples of 10** pages 337A–338A 45–60 minutes	**To prepare students to add three-digit numbers** by reviewing and comparing two-digit addition and the regrouping process to three-digit addition	Number and Operations, Algebra, Connections	2.1.A 🔑 2.1.B
⭐ 9.5 **Three-Digit Addition** pages 339A–340A 45–60 minutes	**To develop the three-digit addition algorithm** by applying previous knowledge of place value through 1,000	Number and Operations, Data Analysis and Probability, Connections	2.1.A 🔑 2.1.B 2.3.B
9.6 **Subtracting Multiples of 10** pages 341A–342A 45–60 minutes	**To develop a procedure for subtracting three-digit multiples of ten** by relating them to procedures learned for subtracting two-digit numbers	Number and Operations, Connections	2.1.A 🔑
⭐ 9.7 **Three-Digit Subtraction** pages 343A–344A 45–60 minutes	**To develop a procedure for subtracting any three-digit number** by applying regrouping and subtraction skills	Number and Operations, Problem Solving, Connections	2.1.A 🔑
⭐ 9.8 **Applications of Three-Digit Addition and Subtraction** pages 345A–346A 45–60 minutes	**To develop understanding of adding and subtracting three-digit numbers** by solving exercises and word problems of mixed operations	Data Analysis and Probability, Connections	2.3 2.12.A 🔑
⭐ 9.9 **Adding and Subtracting Money** pages 351A–352A 45–60 minutes	**To apply three-digit addition and subtraction to money situations** by converting dollars and cents into cents and then adding or subtracting	Number and Operations, Connections	2.3.E 🔑
⭐ 9.10 **Shortcuts for Three-Digit Addition and Subtraction** pages 353A–354A 45–60 minutes	**To apply problem-solving strategies,** with a focus on mental-math strategies for addition and subtraction	Number and Operations, Problem Solving	2.3 🔑
9.11 **Round to 10 and 100 with Applications** pages 355A–356A 45–60 minutes	**To estimate sums and differences** by rounding to the nearest hundred	Number and Operations, Communication	2.3.B 2.5.B 🔑 2.8
⭐ 9.12 **Approximating Answers** pages 357A–358A 45–60 minutes	**To approximate sums and differences** by recognizing answers that are obviously incorrect	Number and Operations, Problem Solving	2.1.C

⭐ = 120-Day Plan for TAKS

🔑 = Key standard

Academic Vocabulary	Manipulatives and Materials	Games to reinforce skills and concepts
	• *Number Cubes* • Base-ten materials	
	• *Number Cubes* • Base-ten blocks • Teacher-prepared base-ten cards • Sheets of card stock • Materials such as stickers, stamps, beans, and so on	Harder Counting and Writing Numbers Game
	• *Number Cubes* • Base-ten blocks	Harder Counting and Writing Numbers Game
	• *Number Cubes* • Base-ten blocks • Craft sticks • Play money • **Rummage Sale Game Mat**	Rummage Sale Game
	• *Number Cubes* • Craft sticks • Base-ten blocks	Roll a Problem (Three-Digit Addition) Game
	• *Number Cubes* • Craft sticks • **Rummage Sale Game Mat**	• Rummage Sale Game • Roll a Problem (Three-Digit Addition) Game
	• *Number Cubes* • Base-ten materials • **Checkbook Game Mat**	Checkbook Game
	• *Number Cubes* • **Checkbook Game Mat**	Checkbook Game
	• *Number Cubes* • Play Money	
	Number Cubes	Make 1,000 Game
	• *Number Cubes* • Calculators	
	Number Cubes	

Additional Resources

Differentiated Instruction

Intervention Support Guide Provides instruction for the following prerequisite skills:

- Lesson 9.A Two-Digit Operations–1
- Lesson 9.B Two-Digit Operations–2
- Lesson 9.C Two-Digit Operations–3

Enrichment Support Guide Extends lesson concepts

Practice Reinforces lesson skills and concepts

Reteach Support Guide Provides alternate instruction for lesson concepts

English Learner Support Guide Previews and reviews lesson concepts and vocabulary for English learners

Technology

The following electronic resources are available:

⌨ **Planner** Lessons 9.1–9.12

⌨ **Presentation** Lessons 9.1–9.12

⌨ **Textbook** Lessons 9.1–9.12

⌨ **Assess** Lessons 9.1–9.12

⌨ **MathTools** *Base Ten* Lessons 9.1– 9.7, 9.10–9.12
Coins and Money Lesson 9.9

⌨ **Games** *Make 1,000 Game* Lesson 9.10

Building Blocks *Rocket Blast 3* Lesson 9.1
Multidigit Word Problems with Tools Lessons 9.9, 9.12

Assessment
Informal Assessment rubrics at the end of each lesson provide daily evaluation of student math proficiency.

Problem Solving	When to Use	Objectives	NCTM Standards	TEXAS Math TEKS
Problem Solving 9.A (pp. 329I–330C) 15–30 minutes	Use after the Chapter 9 Pretest.	To introduce chapter concepts in a problem-solving setting	Problem Solving, Communication	2.12.B, 2.14
Problem Solving 9.B (pp. 347–348, 348A) 30–45 minutes	Use anytime during the chapter.	To explore methods of solving nonroutine problems	Problem Solving, Communication	2.12.C
Problem Solving 9.C (pp. 359–360, 360A) 45–60 minutes	Use anytime during the chapter.	To explore methods of solving nonroutine problems	Problem Solving, Communication	2.12.A, 2.12.B
Thinking Story–Loretta the Letter Carrier Chooses Sides (pp. 371A–371E, 371–372) 20–30 minutes	Use anytime during the chapter.	To develop logical reasoning while integrating reading skills with mathematics	Number and Operations, Problem Solving	2.12.A, 2.12.B

Review	When to Use	Objectives	NCTM Standards	Math TEKS
Cumulative Review (p. 349–350) 15–30 minutes	Use anytime after Lesson 9.8.	To review concepts and skills taught earlier in the year	Number and Operations	2.9.A, 2.1.B, 2.1.A, 2.2.B, 2.3.B, 2.5.B, 2.10.B
Cumulative Review (p. 361–362) 15–30 minutes	Use anytime after Lesson 9.12.	To review concepts and skills taught earlier in the year	Number and Operations	2.9.A, 2.2.B, 2.3.B, 2.12.A
Chapter 9 Review (pp. 364A, 365–366) 30–45 minutes	Use after Lesson 9.12.	To review concepts and skills taught in the chapter	Number and Operations	2.5.B, 2.1.B, 2.1.C, 2.5.B, 2.3.E, 2.1.A

Assessment	When to Use	Objectives	NCTM Standards	Math TEKS
Pretest (Assessment pp. 126–127) 15–30 minutes	Entry Use prior to Chapter 9.	To provide assessment of chapter topics	Number and Operations, Problem Solving	2.1.A, 2.1.B, 2.1.C, 2.3, 2.3.E, 2.3.B, 2.5.B, 2.8, 2.12.A
Informal Assessment Rubrics (pp. 332A–358A) 5 minutes per student	Progress Monitoring Use at the end of each lesson.	To provide daily evaluation of math proficiency	Number and Operations, Communication	2.1.A, 2.1.B, 2.1.C, 2.3, 2.3.E, 2.3.B, 2.5.B, 2.8, 2.12.A
Individual Oral Assessment (p. 350A) 5 minutes per student	Progress Monitoring Use after Lesson 9.8.	To provide alternate means of assessing students' progress	Number and Operations	2.3, 2.1
Mastery Checkpoint (Assessment pp. 93–98) 15 minutes	Progress Monitoring Use in or after Lessons 9.2, 9.9, 9.10.	To provide assessment of mastery of key skills	Number and Operations	2.1.C, 2.1.A, 2.3.D, 2.3.E, 2.3
Chapter 9 Practice Test (pp. 367–368, 369–370) 30–45 minutes	Progress Monitoring Use after or in place of the Chapter 9 Review.	To provide assessment or additional practice of the chapter concepts	Number and Operations, Problem Solving	2.1.A, 2.1.B, 2.1.C, 2.3, 2.3.E, 2.3.B, 2.5.B, 2.8, 2.12.A
Chapter 9 Test (Assessment pp. 244–247) 30–45 minutes	Summative Use after or in place of the Chapter 9 Review.	To provide assessment on the chapter concepts	Number and Operations, Problem Solving	2.1.A, 2.1.B, 2.1.C, 2.3, 2.3.E, 2.3.B, 2.5.B, 2.8, 2.12.A

Texas Technology Resources

Visit SRAonline.com for online versions of the *Real Math* eSuite.

TEXAS Technology for Teachers

e Presentation	Lessons 9.1–9.12 Use the *ePresentation* to interactively present chapter content.
e Planner	Use the Chapter and Lesson Planners to outline activities and time frames for Chapter 9.
e Assess	Students can take the following assessments in *eAssess:* • Chapter Pretest • Mastery Checkpoint **Lessons 9.2, 9.9, and 9.10** • Chapter Test Teachers can record results and print reports for all assessments in this chapter.
e MathTools	**Base Ten** Lessons 9.1–9.7, 9.10–9.12 **Coins and Money** Lesson 9.8

TEXAS Technology for Students

e Textbook	An electronic, interactive version of the **Student Edition** is available for all lessons in Chapter 9.
e MathTools	**Base Ten** Lessons 9.1–9.7, 9.10–9.12 **Coins and Money** Lesson 9.8
e Games	Make 1,000 Game Lesson 9.10
TECH KNOWLEDGE	*TechKnowledge* Level 2 provides lessons that specifically teach the Unit 10 Internet and Unit 3 Word Processing, and Unit 4 Drawing and Graphics applications that students can use in this chapter's project.
Building Blocks	**Rocket Blast 3** Lesson 9.1 **Multidigit Word Problems with Tools** Lessons 9.9, 9.12

Three-Digit Addition and Subtraction

Introduce Chapter 9 · 10

Chapter Objectives

Explain to students that in this chapter they will build on what they already know about addition and subtraction. They will

- add and subtract three-digit numbers.
- determine the place value of specific digits for five-digit numbers.

Pretest ☑ COMPUTING

Administer the Chapter 9 Pretest, which has similar exercises to the Chapter 9 Test. :

- If most students do not demonstrate mastery on the Pretest, proceed at a normal pace through the chapter. Use the differentiated instruction suggestions at the beginning and end of each lesson to adapt instruction to and follow up on the needs of each student.

- If most students show mastery of some or all of the concepts and skills in the Chapter 9 Pretest, move quickly through the chapter, de-emphasizing lessons linked to items which most students answered correctly. Use the Individual Oral Assessments to monitor progress, and, if necessary, modify your pacing. These assessments are especially useful because they can help you distinguish among different levels of understanding. For example, a student who has mastered a particular skill but does not show a deep understanding of the relevant concepts still needs thorough coverage of the lesson material.

- If you do move quickly through the chapter, be sure not to skip games, Problem- Solving lessons, and Thinking Stories. These provide practice in skills and nonroutine thinking that will be useful even to students who already understand the chapter content. Also, be alert to application problems embedded within lessons that may show students how math topics are used in daily life.

Chapter 9 Pretest

Access Prior Knowledge ☑ UNDERSTANDING

Have students talk about how postage stamps are used in our lives. If possible, show them a variety of stamps with different pictures and of different values. If any students collect or know someone who collects stamps, ask them to tell the class about the collection.

Problem Solving 9.A Introducing Strategies

Tell Students In Today's Lesson They Will

organize a large pile of stamps to make them easier to count.

Materials

- 2-centimeter or 1-inch graph paper, enough for each student to cut out 100 squares
- Scissors

Guided Discussion UNDERSTANDING  Introductory

Have students look at the photograph on page 329. Ask them if they have ever gone to a post office. Have them talk about what happens at a post office. Guide the conversation by asking questions such as the following:

- **Why do people go to post offices?** to mail things; to pick up mail; to buy stamps
- **What are some of the jobs the postal workers have to do?** determine the amount of postage necessary to mail something; sell stamps; sort mail; deliver mail; and so on
- **If you mail a letter to someone in another city, how do you think it gets from here to there?** Help students visualize a letter coming to the post office mixed in with many other letters that need to be delivered. Postal workers sort it according to where it's going and then load it onto the correct truck or airplane. When the mail gets to the correct city, postal workers there sort through all the mail coming in and then deliver it to the correct address.

Strategy Building REASONING Guided

Have students look at the first illustration on page 330. Ask questions such as the following:

- **What do the students have on the table?** a pile or collection of stamps
- **Can you tell how many stamps there are?** no
- **Would it be easy to count these stamps?** No; there are a lot of them.
- **When the students in the picture count the stamps, what are some ways they could keep track of how many they've already counted?** Accept all reasonable responses such as: they could put them in groups, every minute they could write down how many they've counted, and so on.

TEXAS

Underlying processes and mathematical tools 2.12.B
Solve problems with guidance that incorporates the processes of understanding the problem, making a plan, carrying out the plan, and evaluating the solution for reasonableness.

Underlying processes and mathematical tools 2.14
The student is expected to justify his or her thinking using objects, words, pictures, numbers, and technology.

Guided Discussion APPLYING

Using Student Pages

Give each student enough graph paper so he or she will be able to cut 100 squares that will represent stamps. As students are cutting, ask them how they know they have exactly 100. When most students have finished, put all the stamps in a pile. Organize students into small groups, and give each group a handful (several hundred) to count. Tell students that they will need to present

- how many stamps they have.
- how they know they counted correctly.
- how they organized the stamps to make them easy for others to count.

Concept/Question Board APPLYING

Questions

Have students think of and write three questions they have about three-digit addition and subtraction and how they can be used. Then have them select one question to post on the Question side of the Board.

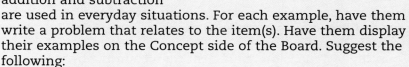

Concepts

As students work through the chapter, have them collect examples of how three-digit addition and subtraction are used in everyday situations. For each example, have them write a problem that relates to the item(s). Have them display their examples on the Concept side of the Board. Suggest the following:

- traveling
- playing music

Answers

Throughout the chapter, have students post answers to the questions and solutions to the problems on the Board.

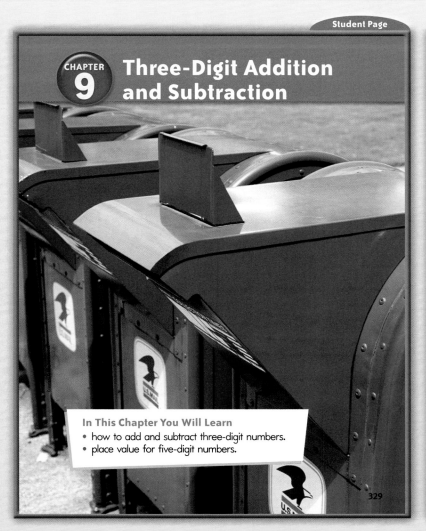

CHAPTER **9**
Three-Digit Addition and Subtraction

In This Chapter You Will Learn
- how to add and subtract three-digit numbers.
- place value for five-digit numbers.

329

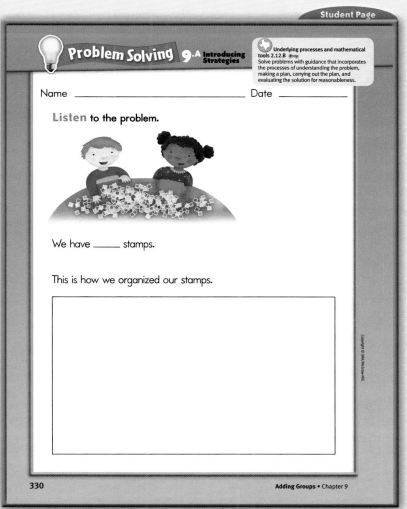

Problem Solving **9.A** Introducing Strategies

Underlying processes and mathematical tools 2.12.B Solve problems with guidance that incorporates the processes of understanding the problem, making a plan, carrying out the plan, and evaluating the solution for reasonableness.

Name _____ Date _____

Listen to the problem.

We have _____ stamps.

This is how we organized our stamps.

330   Adding Groups • Chapter 9

Reflect 20

 Knowledge Age Skills

Effective Communication Have groups present their results. In discussion, bring out the following points:

● Forming groups that are easy to count (twos, fives, tens, twenty-fives) makes it easier to check your counting if you lose track of where you are.

● Counting by tens is more efficient than counting by most other numbers because we are used to tens and our number system is based on ten.

● When people work in groups, they can organize and divide the work so everyone does his or her part.

Sample Solutions Strategies

Students might use one or more of the following strategies to count the stamps.

Grouping/Skip Counting

Students might put their stamps in groups that are easy to count.

Make a Table

Students might make a tally mark for each stamp as they count them.

Use a Physical Model

Students might place each stamp on a numbered square on a 100 Table.

 ## Home Connection

At this time, you may want to send home the letter on pages 34–37 of *Home Connection.* This letter describes what students will be learning and what activities they can do at home to support their work in school.

Home Connection
Page 34

Assess and Differentiate

 Assess   Use *eAssess* to record and analyze evidence of student understanding.

A Gather Evidence

Use the Daily Class Assessment Records in *Texas Assessment* or *eAssess* to record Informal and Formal Assessments.

Informal Assessment

✔ **Access Prior Knowledge**

Did the student   [UNDERSTANDING]
- ❏ make important observations?
- ❏ extend or generalize learning?
- ❏ provide insightful answers?
- ❏ pose insightful questions?

Informal Assessment

✔ **Concept/Question Board**

Did the student   [APPLYING]
- ❏ apply learning in new situations?
- ❏ contribute concepts?
- ❏ contribute answers?
- ❏ connect mathematics to real-world situations?

Formal Assessment

✔ **Pretest**   [COMPUTING]

Review student answers on the Chapter 9 Pretest.
- ❏ If most students do not demonstrate mastery, move at a normal pace through the chapter.
- ❏ If most students answer most questions correctly, move quickly through the chapter, emphasizing those lessons for which students did not answer correctly, as well as games, Problem-Solving lessons, and Thinking Stories.

B Summarize Findings

Analyze and summarize assessment data for each student. Determine which Assessment Follow-Up is appropriate for each student. Use the Student Assessment Record in *Texas Assessment* or *eAssess* to update assessment records.

C Texas Assessment Follow-Up ● DIFFERENTIATE INSTRUCTION

Based on your observations of each student, use these teaching strategies for a general approach to the chapter. Look for specific Differentiate Instruction and Monitoring Student Progress strategies in each lesson that relate specifically to the lesson content.

ENRICH	PRACTICE	RETEACH	INTERVENTION	ENGLISH LEARNER
If . . . students demonstrate a **secure understanding** of chapter concepts, **Then . . .** move quickly through the chapter or use *Enrichment* Lessons 9.1–9.12 as assessment follow-up to extend and apply understanding.	**If . . .** students grasp chapter concepts with **competent understanding,** **Then . . .** use *Practice* Lessons 9.1–9.12 as lesson follow-up to develop fluency.	**If . . .** students have prerequisite understanding but demonstrate **emerging understanding** of chapter concepts, **Then . . .** use *Reteach* Lessons 9.1, 9.3, 9.7, 9.8, and 9.12 to reteach lesson concepts.	**If . . .** students are not competent with prerequisite skills, **Then . . .** use *Intervention* Lessons 9.A–9.C before each lesson to develop fluency with prerequisite skills.	Use *English Learner Support Guide* Lessons 9.1–9.12 for strategies to preteach lesson vocabulary and concepts.

Math Across the Curriculum

Preview the chapter projects with students. Assign projects or have students choose from the projects to extend and enrich concepts in this chapter.

Write about the Historic Iditarod   2–3 weeks

LANGUAGE ARTS WebQuest

TEKS

MATH STANDARD: Number, operation, and quantitative reasoning 2.1 The student understands how place value is used to represent whole numbers. The student understands how place value is used to represent whole numbers.

CROSS CURRICULAR STANDARD (LANGUAGE ARTS): Writing/writing processes 2.18.F Demonstrate understanding of language use and spelling by bringing selected pieces frequently to final form and "publishing" them for audiences.

TECHNOLOGY STANDARD: Solving Problems 07.B Use appropriate software, including the use of word processing and multimedia, to express ideas and solve problems.

Have students use technology to research and key text about the historic Iditarod.

For this project, students use the Internet to investigate the following information:

- photographs and history of the Iditarod
- Iditarod trail maps

For specific step-by-step instructions for this project, see **Across the Curriculum Math Connections** pages 92–97.

Knowledge Age Skills

Creative Work with Ideas Students explore information within the roles of an editor, a writer, and an illustrator.

Teamwork Students work in groups to complete all steps of publishing a book.

 **TechKnowledge** Level 2 provides lessons that specifically teach the Unit 10 Internet, Unit 3 Word Processing, and Unit 4 Drawing and Graphics applications that students can use in this project.

Research the History of Airmail   3 weeks

SOCIAL STUDIES

TEKS

MATH STANDARD: Number, operation, and quantitative reasoning 2.3 The student adds and subtracts whole numbers to solve problems.

CROSS CURRICULAR STANDARD (SOCIAL STUDIES): Government 2.11.B Identify some governmental services in the community such as libraries, schools, and parks and explain their value to the community.

TECHNOLOGY STANDARD: Information acquisition 04 The student uses a variety of strategies to acquire information from electronic resources, with appropriate supervision.

Have students use mathematics to calculate periods of time between events. To broaden the social studies concept, have them study the postal system as an example of a service offered in society.

As part of the project, students should consider the following issues:

- when airmail service was established
- how airmail service was developed
- what service was offered to people after airmail was established

For specific step-by-step instructions for this project, see **Across the Curriculum Math Connections** pages 98–101.

Knowledge Age Skills

Problem Formulation, Planning, and Strategizing Students summarize significant events related to the history of airmail.

Effective Communication Students communicate clearly in summaries of airmail history.

Grade 1	Grade 2	Grade 3
1.1.D Read and write numbers to 99 to describe sets of concrete objects.	**2.1.B** Use place value to read, write, and describe the value of whole numbers to 999.	**3.1.A** Use place value to read, write (in symbols and words), and describe the value of whole numbers through 999,999.

Overview

LESSON 9.1

TEXAS

Lesson Planner

OBJECTIVES
To study the place value in four-digit numbers

MATH TEKS

Number, operation, and quantitative reasoning 2.1.A
Use concrete models of hundreds, tens, and ones to represent a given whole number (up to 999) in various ways.

Number, operation, and quantitative reasoning 2.1.B 🔑
Use place value to read, write, and describe the value of whole numbers to 999.

Patterns, relationships, and algebraic thinking 2.5.B
Use patterns in place value to compare and order whole numbers through 999.

Geometry and spatial reasoning 2.8
The student is expected to use whole numbers to locate and name points on a number line.

MATH TEKS INTEGRATION

Number, operation, and quantitative reasoning 2.3.A
Recall and apply basic addition and subtraction facts (to 18).

Number, operation, and quantitative reasoning 2.3.B
Model addition and subtraction of two-digit numbers with objects, pictures, words, and numbers.

MATERIALS
• *Number Cubes
• *Base-ten materials

TECHNOLOGY
🖳 **Presentation** Lesson 9.1
🖳 **MathTools** Base Ten
Building Blocks Rocket Blast 3

Looking Ahead

You will need to prepare base-ten cards for Lesson 9.2 to demonstrate the place value of three- and four-digit numbers. Create ten cards that illustrate a hundred array (10 columns of 10) and ten cards that illustrate a ten array (2 columns of 5). Also, gather materials such as stickers, beans, stamps, and so on, for students to use when creating their own cards.

*Manipulative Kit Item 🔑 = Key standard

Place Value through 10,000

Context of the Lesson This lesson reviews place value, which was previously covered in Chapter 6, and extends the concept to four-digit numbers. Good understanding of place value is essential for understanding the three-digit addition and subtraction algorithms—the main topic of this chapter. Work with greater numbers is included in the third grade program.

Planning for Learning ● DIFFERENTIATE INSTRUCTION

INTERVENTION

If . . . students lack the prerequisite skill of adding two-digit numbers,

Then . . . teach **Intervention** Lesson 9.A.

   1.3.A, 1.5.D

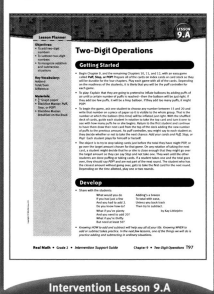

Intervention Lesson 9.A

ENGLISH LEARNER

Preview

If . . . students need language support,

Then . . . use Lesson 9.1 in **English Learner Support Guide** to preview lesson concepts and vocabulary.

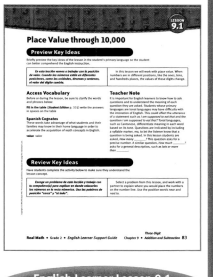

English Learner Lesson 9.1

ENRICH

If . . . students are proficient in the lesson concepts,

Then . . . emphasize chapter projects.

PRACTICE

If . . . students would benefit from additional practice,

Then . . . extend Skill Practice before assigning student pages.

RETEACH

If . . . students are having difficulty understanding the place value of a four-digit number,

Then . . . extend Strategy Building before assigning the student pages.

Access Vocabulary
fill in the table write the answers in the spaces on the table

Spanish Cognates
value valor

⭐ = 120-Day Plan for TAKS

Number, operation and quantitative reasoning 2.1.A Use concrete models of hundreds, tens, and ones to represent a given whole number (up to 999) in various ways.

Number, operation, and quantitative reasoning 2.1.B Use place value to read, write, and describe the value of whole numbers to 999.

Patterns, relationships, and algebraic thinking 2.5.B Use patterns in place value to compare and order whole numbers through 999.

Geometry and spatial reasoning 2.8 The student is expected to use whole numbers to locate and name points on a number line.

Mental Math 5

 INTEGRATION: TEKS 2.3.B Present addition exercises that use multiples of 10 with sums to 100, and have students show their answers using **Number Cubes.** Possible examples include the following:

a. 40 + 30 = 70 **b.** 30 + 60 = 90 **c.** 20 + 50 = 70 **d.** 10 + 90 = 100
e. 40 + 50 = 90 **f.** 70 + 30 = 100 **g.** 80 + 10 = 90 **h.** 100 + 0 = 100

1 Develop 20

Tell Students In Today's Lesson They Will
learn about place value in five-digit numbers.

Guided Discussion UNDERSTANDING  Introductory

Counting by Tens, Hundreds, and Thousands
Review counting by tens to 100.

Have students imagine that they have bought several sheets of postage stamps, and they want to count quickly to see how many stamps they have. There are ten stamps on a sheet, and they have seven sheets. Ask students a question such as the following:

■ **How could you count them?**

Have students count by tens to 70.

Now count by hundreds to 900.

Have three students stand in front of the class and represent the ones, tens, and hundreds places. Have students display the correct fingers as you count by ones, tens, and hundreds as a class.

Call out three-digit numbers, and ask how many fingers each student should put up, for example, 347. 3 hundreds, 4 tens, 7 ones

Try different numbers, ending with 999. Wait for each student to put up nine fingers.

■ **Critical Thinking** **How could you show the number that is one more than 999 without having any student show all ten fingers?** You need another person to be the thousands place; someone should be able to tell you that the next number is 1,000.

Have the class count by thousands to 10,000. Have the students at the front of the room display numbers through 10,000 with their fingers.

Skill Building APPLYING Guided

Place Value Table
Identify each place value in numbers up to four digits by using a place value table.

Draw a place value table on the board that shows up to the thousands place.

Write a three-digit number, and demonstrate placing each number in the correct place on the table. Then write a four-digit number. Call on students to help place each number in the correct place value on the table.

■ **How many thousands, hundreds, tens, and ones are in this number?** In a number such as 1,342, there are 2 ones, 4 tens, 3 hundreds, and 1 thousand.

Repeat this procedure several times.

Skill Practice COMPUTING Guided

 Write a three- or four-digit number on the board. Call out a place value such as the tens place, and have students show the correct digit using their **Number Cubes.** Possible examples include the following:

a. tens in 759 5 **b.** hundreds in 382 3
c. ones in 1,245 5 **d.** thousands in 5,987 5

Strategy Building UNDERSTANDING Guided

Sequence Numbers on a Number Line
Draw a number line on the board, and label 0 and 1,000 as the endpoints. Do not label any other numbers.

■ **Where do you think the number 500 should be on the number line?** Students should suggest in the middle, or halfway.

Have a student mark with a line where the 500 should be on the number line and write the number above. Have other students do the same with other multiples of 100 through 900.

2 Use Student Pages 20

Pages 331–332 UNDERSTANDING Independent
Have students complete pages 331 and 332 independently.

Progress Monitoring

| If . . . students have difficulty understanding place value concepts, | Then . . . use craft sticks, play money, or base-ten blocks to demonstrate the quantities of each digit in a three- or four-digit number. |

As Students Finish

Building Blocks Have students use **Rocket Blast 3** to practice estimating sequencing numbers on an unmarked number line.

 **MathTools** Have students group three-, four-, and five-digit numbers using **Base Ten.**

LESSON 9.1 Place Value through 10,000

Name _____ Date _____

Key Ideas

You can think about blocks or charts to help you understand large numbers.

Example 2,376 *two thousand three hundred seventy-six*

2	3	7	6
thousands	hundreds	Tens	Ones

Math TEKS
Number, operation, and quantitative reasoning 2.1.B
Use place value to read, write, and describe the value of whole numbers to 999.

Write the missing number. You may use *Base-ten blocks* or other materials to help.

1 In 725
How many hundreds? 7
How many tens? 2
How many ones? 5

2 In 304
How many hundreds? 3
How many tens? 0
How many ones? 4

3 In 2,506
How many thousands? 2
How many tens? 0

4 In 4,730
How many thousands? 4
How many hundreds? 7

5 What does the 7 stand for in 4,720? 7 hundreds

6 What does the 3 stand for in 3,500? 3 thousands

Textbook This lesson is available in the *eTextbook*.

331

Mark a point on the number line where you think each number belongs, and label it.

6 5, 7, 9, 4

0   4 5   7   9 10

7 17, 99, 50, 80

0   17   50   80 99 100

8 400; 9,600; 3,000; 7,000

0 400   3,000   7,000   9,600 10,000

9 4,400; 5,600; 5,000; 100

0 100   4,400 5,000 5,600   10,000

10 500, 800, 200, 100

0   100 200   500   800   1,000

11 501, 801, 500, 950, 200

0   200   500 501   801   950 1,000

12 400, 960, 300, 700, 100

0   100   300 400   700   960 1,000

Writing + Math Journal
Use these digits: 2, 3, 4. Write all the possible three-digit numbers. Order them from greatest to least.

332   **Real Math** • Chapter 9 • Lesson 1

---

3 Reflect   10

Guided Discussion   REASONING

Use play money to represent the number 4,765. Use 4 $1,000 bills, 7 $100 bills, 6 $10 bills, and 5 $1 bills.

■ **Critical Thinking** **Can you think of other ways this number can be represented?** Calling on the students' experience with different base-ten materials, show how the number can be represented with base-ten blocks.

Ask if the number can be represented with craft sticks bundled in groups of ten, ten bunches of ten, and so on. Allow that this is possible but that it requires a very large number of sticks.

Conclude the discussion by suggesting that just as craft sticks helped us understand the meaning of 2-digit numbers, play money ($1,000, $100, $10, and $1 bills) can help us understand the meaning of 3- and 4-digit numbers.

Writing + Math Journal

Discuss student answers. There are six number combinations.

432	342	243
423	324	234

TEXAS TEKS Checkup

TEKS 2.1.B • Use place value to read, write, and describe the value of whole numbers to 999.

Use this problem to assess students' progress towards standards mastery:

Which has the correct place values for 586?

A 5 hundreds, 8 tens, 6 ones
B 5 hundreds, 6 tens, 8 ones
C 6 hundreds, 8 tens, 5 ones
D 6 hundreds, 5 tens, 8 ones

Have students choose the correct answer, then describe how they knew which choice was correct. In the discussion, ask questions such as the following. Be sure to ask students to explain their reasoning, since different solution methods are possible.

■ **Which digit is in the ones place?** 6
■ **Which digit is in the tens place?** 8

Follow-Up
If...students have difficulty understanding place value,
Then...reteach the concept using *Reteach* Lesson 9.1.

 Math Puzzler: Integration: TEKS 2.3. A What two numbers have the sum of 7 and the difference of 1? 3 and 4

4 Assess and Differentiate

**Assess**   Use *eAssess* to record and analyze evidence of student understanding.

A Gather Evidence

Use the Daily Class Assessment Records in *Texas Assessment* or *eAssess* to record daily observations.

Informal Assessment
☑ **Skill Practice**

Did the student **COMPUTING**
- ❏ respond accurately?
- ❏ respond quickly?
- ❏ respond with confidence?
- ❏ self-correct?

Informal Assessment
☑ **Student Pages**

Did the student **UNDERSTANDING**
- ❏ make important observations?
- ❏ extend or generalize learning?
- ❏ provide insightful answers?
- ❏ pose insightful questions?

 TEKS/TAKS Practice

Use *TEKS/TAKS Practice* pages 5–8 to assess student progress.

B Summarize Findings

Analyze and summarize assessment data for each student. Determine which Assessment Follow-Up is appropriate for each student. Use the Student Assessment Record in *Texas Assessment* or *eAssess* to update assessment records.

C Texas Assessment Follow-Up ● DIFFERENTIATE INSTRUCTION

Based on your observations, use these teaching strategies for assessment follow-up.

INTERVENTION

Review student performance on *Intervention* Lesson 9.A to see if students have mastered prerequisite skills for this lesson.

1.3.A Model and create addition and subtraction problem situations with concrete objects and write corresponding number sentences.

1.5.D Use patterns to develop strategies to solve basic addition and basic subtraction problems.

ENGLISH LEARNER
Review

Use Lesson 9.1 in *English Learner Support Guide* to review lesson concepts and vocabulary.

ENRICH

If . . . students are proficient in the lesson concepts,

Then . . . encourage them to work on the chapter projects or *Enrichment* Lesson 9.1.

Enrichment Lesson 9.1

PRACTICE

If . . . students would benefit from additional practice,

Then . . . assign *Practice* Lesson 9.1.

Practice Lesson 9.1

RETEACH

If . . . students are having difficulty understanding the place value of four-digit numbers,

Then . . . reteach the concept using *Reteach* Lesson 9.1.

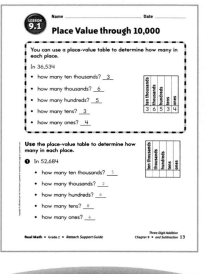

Reteach Lesson 9.1

Grade 1	Grade 2	Grade 3
1.1.B Create sets of tens and ones using concrete objects to describe, compare, and order whole numbers.	**2.1.B** Use place value to read, write, and describe the value of whole numbers to 999.	**3.1.B** Use place value to compare and order whole numbers through 9,999.

Overview

LESSON 9.2

TEXAS

Lesson Planner

OBJECTIVES
- To teach students to understand, say, write, and recognize numbers through 1,000
- To allow students the opportunity to develop a winning strategy for a game that might involve working backwards or finding a pattern

MATH TEKS

Number, operation, and quantitative reasoning 2.1.A
Use concrete models of hundreds, tens, and ones to represent a given whole number (up to 999) in various ways.

Number, operation, and quantitative reasoning 2.1.B
Use place value to read, write, and describe the value of whole numbers to 999.

Patterns, relationships, and algebraic thinking 2.5.B
Use patterns in place value to compare and order whole numbers through 999.

MATH TEKS INTEGRATION

Number, operation, and quantitative reasoning 2.3.A
Recall and apply basic addition and subtraction facts (to 18).

Number, operation, and quantitative reasoning 2.3.B
Model addition and subtraction of two-digit numbers with objects, pictures, words, and numbers.

MATERIALS
- *Number Cubes
- *Base-ten blocks
- Teacher-prepared base-ten cards
- Sheets of card stock
- Materials such as stickers, stamps, beans, and so on

TECHNOLOGY
- Presentation Lesson 9.2
- MathTools Base Ten

Modeling Numbers through 1,000 ⭐

Context of the Lesson This is the second in a series of twelve lessons that develop skills and understanding for working with 2- and 3-digit numbers. In this lesson students will make cards that show sets of 100, 10, and the digits 1 through 9 to create a base-ten device they can use to represent three-digit numbers through 1,000. Students build on their knowledge of place value from Lesson 1.5.

See page 329B for Math Background for teachers for this lesson.

Planning for Learning ● DIFFERENTIATE INSTRUCTION

INTERVENTION
If . . . students lack the prerequisite skill of subtracting two-digit numbers,

Then . . . teach **Intervention** Lesson 9.A.

1.3.A, 1.5.D

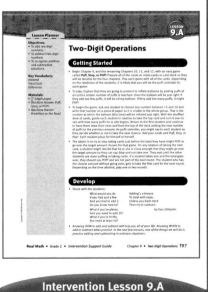

Intervention Lesson 9.A

ENGLISH LEARNER
Preview

If . . . students need language support,

Then . . . use Lesson 9.2 in **English Learner Support Guide** to preview lesson concepts and vocabulary.

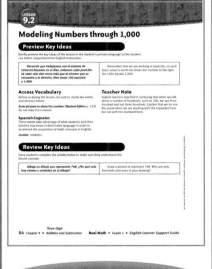

English Learner Lesson 9.2

ENRICH
If . . . students are proficient in the lesson concepts,

Then . . . allow for additional game time.

PRACTICE
If . . . students would benefit from additional practice,

Then . . . extend Skill Building before assigning student pages.

RETEACH
If . . . students are having difficulty understanding numbers to 1,000,

Then . . . extend Guided Discussion before assigning the student pages.

Access Vocabulary
draw pictures to show the number do not draw the numeral

Spanish Cognates
models modelos

Teaching Lesson 9.2

 TEXAS

Number, operation and quantitative reasoning 2.1.A
Use concrete models of hundreds, tens, and ones to represent a given whole number (up to 999) in various ways.
Number, operation, and quantitative reasoning 2.1.B
Use place value to read, write, and describe the value of whole numbers to 999.
Patterns, relationships, and algebraic thinking 2.5.B
Use patterns in place value to compare and order whole numbers through 999.

Mental Math 5

 INTEGRATION: **TEKS 2.3.B** Present exercises that involve subtracting or adding multiples of ten, and have students show their answers using **Number Cubes**. Possible examples include the following:

a. $10 - 10 = 0$ **b.** $20 - 20 = 0$ **c.** $40 - 20 = 20$ **d.** $30 - 10 = 20$
e. $50 - 30 = 20$ **f.** $60 + 40 = 100$ **g.** $80 - 30 = 50$ **h.** $90 - 20 = 70$

1 Develop 20

Tell Students In Today's Lesson They Will
construct and write numbers through 1,000.

Guided Discussion **e MathTools** UNDERSTANDING
 Introductory

Engage students in recognizing and constructing numbers through 1,000.

Organize students into four groups, and distribute base-ten blocks to each group. Write a three-digit number on the board.

■ **Critical Thinking** **How could I show this number using base-ten blocks?** Students should display the correct number using base-ten blocks.

Then display the number using base-ten blocks or **eMathTools: Base Ten.** Have each group work to form the same model using base-ten blocks. Repeat this activity with several examples. Show the correct answer only after students have formed their sets.

Skill Building APPLYING
 Guided

Have students imagine that they are running a bakery and are in charge of making muffins. They can fit 100 muffins on each baking sheet.

- Distribute supplies for students to create their own base-ten cards.
- Give each student one of the sheets of card stock. Have students draw 100 muffins on the sheets to represent the muffins on one of the baking sheets. Encourage students to be creative by using markers, stamps, stickers, beans, or other small materials to create their muffins. Let students attempt the task in their own way. Some may space the muffins so they can't fit them all on a sheet. Others may lose track of how many muffins they have created. Let students who have found a convenient way of arranging the sheets (such as ten rows of 10) show their work to the class. Each student should make one sheet of 100.
- Students who finish early may make a second set of 100, or they may make sets of 10 or numbers from 1 to 10. Put a number label on the bottom of each card. Be sure that sheets of 10 or fewer are labeled to show how many muffins are on

them. As a class, you should end up with at least thirty sets of 100, ten sets of 10, and one each of 1 through 9.

Display a three- or four-digit number using your premade base-ten cards, for example, 2 hundreds cards, 4 tens cards, and a card with 5 ones.

■ **How many muffins do I have?** 245

Write the number on the board, and say it aloud with students. Repeat this activity with more examples, and have students write the number on paper. Practice saying each number after the class has agreed on the correct answer.

a. 1,032   **b.** 489   **c.** 754   **d.** 913   **e.** 309   **f.** 861

Skill and Strategy Building Guided

 Game **The Harder Counting and Writing Numbers Game**

Principal Skills: Students practice counting and writing numbers in the 0–1,000 range.

This game provides practice with counting numbers to 1,000 and using mathematical reasoning. When playing this game, have students use numbers that are no more than 30 apart. It may be easier for students to track the progress of the game if they write in a column.

2 Use Student Pages 20

Pages 333–334 UNDERSTANDING

Before beginning page 333, spend some time showing students how to write the names for numbers. Also, it might be useful to write some of these names on the board so that students have models when they get to the exercises on the bottom of the page.

Many students will remember the game on page 334 from earlier in the year when an easier version was introduced and played in Lesson 1.3.

Progress Monitoring

If . . . students have difficulty making the connection between base-ten blocks and their cards,

Then . . . have students count manually and match various cards to the corresponding number of base-ten blocks.

As Students Finish

 Game Have students play the **Harder Counting and Writing Numbers Game** in pairs.

Student Page

Name _____ **Date** _____

LESSON 9.2 Modeling Numbers through 1,000

Key Ideas
10 hundreds equal
1 thousand.

Math TEKS Number, operation, and quantitative reasoning 2.1.B Use place value to read, write, and describe the value of whole numbers to 999.

Write the number shown.

1. __223__   2. __147__

Draw pictures to show the number.
Instead of drawing 10 or 100 items,
you may show 10 and 100 like this: [10] [100]

3. 253 bells [100] [100] [10] [10] [10] [10] [10] 🔔🔔🔔

4. 302 leaves [100] [100] [100] 🍃🍃

Write the following numbers in words.

5. 782 __seven hundred eighty-two__
6. 361 __three hundred sixty-one__
7. 94 __ninety-four__
8. 7,126 __seven thousand one hundred twenty-six__

Textbook This lesson is available in the eTextbook. 333

Student Page

Game

Math TEKS Number, operation, and quantitative reasoning 2.1.B Use place value to read, write, and describe the value of whole numbers to 999.

Number Sequence and Strategies Practice

Harder Counting and Writing Numbers Game

Players: Two or more
Materials: Paper and pencils

HOW TO PLAY

1. Player One chooses a starting number and an ending number between 0 and 1,000 (for example, 286 and 325). Make sure the numbers are not more than 100 apart.
2. Player Two counts on and writes one, two, or three numbers from the starting number.
3. Player One counts on and writes one, two, or three more numbers.
4. The players take turns counting on and writing. The player who counts to and writes the ending number wins.

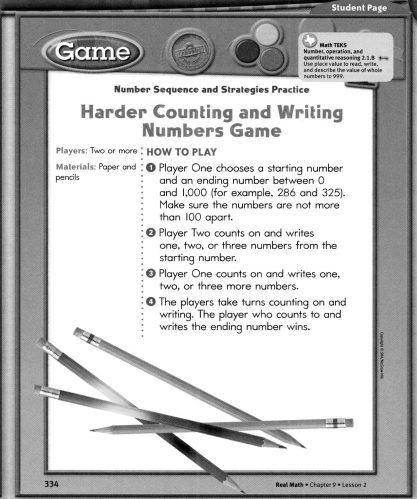

334   Real Math • Chapter 9 • Lesson 2

---

3 Reflect   10

Guided Discussion REASONING

Tell students that you are thinking of a number between 0 and 999. Write the number on a piece of paper that students cannot see. Then tell students that they can ask questions about the number and that you will answer truthfully. Challenge them to guess the number by asking as few questions as possible. Then begin. At first, students are likely to call out numbers without thinking, but gradually the questions should become more focused. For example, let's say your number is 567:

- **Is it more than 500?** (yes)
- **Is it less than 750?** (yes)
- **Is it more than 625?** (no)

At this point, you might want to remind students that they should know your number is less than 625 but more than 500. Continue in this manner until the number is found. Repeat as time and interest warrant.

☑ Use Mastery Checkpoint 14 found in **Texas Assessment** to evaluate student mastery of numerical sequence (1–100). By this time, students should be able to correctly answer eighty percent of the Mastery Checkpoint items.

TEXAS TEKS Checkup

TEKS 2.1.A • Use concrete models of hundreds, tens, and ones to represent a given whole number (up to 999) in various ways.

Use this problem to assess students' progress towards standards masteRY:

Which shows

A
B
C
D

Have students choose the correct answer, then describe how they knew which choice was correct. In the discussion, ask questions such as the following. Be sure to ask students to explain their reasoning, since different solution methods are possible.

- **How many crayons are shown?** 421
- **Which answer can be eliminated because it has the wrong number of hundreds?** Choice D has 1 hundred instead of 4 hundreds

Follow-Up
If...students have difficulty understanding place value,
Then...have students practice the concept using **Practice** Lesson 9.2.

Family Involvement: Assign the **Practice, Reteach,** or **Enrichment** activities depending on the needs of your students.
Have students play the **Harder Counting and Writing Numbers Game** with a family member.

Math Puzzler: **Integration: TEKS 2.3.A** You pay for a $12 toy and a $5 book with two $10 bills. How much change will you get back? $3

4 Assess and Differentiate

 **Assess** Use *eAssess* to record and analyze evidence of student understanding.

A Gather Evidence

Use the Daily Class Assessment Records in *Texas Assessment* or *eAssess* to record daily observations.

Formal Assessment
☑ **Mastery Checkpoint**
Did the student
☐ use correct procedures?
☐ respond with at least 80% accuracy?

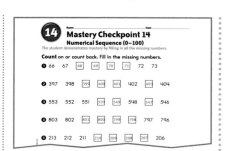

Texas Assessment page 93

 TEKS/TAKS Practice

Use *TEKS/TAKS Practice* pages 5–8 to assess student progress.

B Summarize Findings

Analyze and summarize assessment data for each student. Determine which Assessment Follow-Up is appropriate for each student. Use the Student Assessment Record in *Texas Assessment* or *eAssess* to update assessment records.

C Texas Assessment Follow-Up • DIFFERENTIATE INSTRUCTION

Based on your observations, use these teaching strategies for assessment follow-up.

INTERVENTION

Review student performance on *Intervention* Lesson 9.A to see if students have mastered prerequisite skills for this lesson.

1.3.A Model and create addition and subtraction problem situations with concrete objects and write corresponding number sentences.

1.5.D Use patterns to develop strategies to solve basic addition and basic subtraction problems.

ENGLISH LEARNER
Review

Use Lesson 9.2 in *English Learner Support Guide* to review lesson concepts and vocabulary.

ENRICH

If . . . students are proficient in the lesson concepts,

Then . . . encourage them to work on the chapter projects or *Enrichment* Lesson 9.2.

Enrichment Lesson 9.2

PRACTICE

If . . . students would benefit from additional practice,

Then . . . assign *Practice* Lesson 9.2.

Practice Lesson 9.2

RETEACH

If . . . students are having difficulty modeling four-digit numbers,

Then . . . have them use base-ten materials and a number line to represent a number and then locate it.

Grade 1	Grade 2	Grade 3
1.5.C Compare and order whole numbers using place value..	**2.5.B** Use patterns in place value to compare and order whole numbers through 999.	**3.1.A** Use place value to compare and order whole numbers through 9,999.

Overview

TEXAS

LESSON 9.3

Lesson Planner

OBJECTIVES
To practice using relation signs to compare numbers, sums, and differences with 2-, 3-, and 4-digit numbers.

MATH TEKS

Number, operation, and quantitative reasoning 2.1.C
Use place value to compare and order whole numbers to 999 and record the comparisons using numbers and symbols (<, =, >).

Patterns, relationships, and algebraic thinking 2.5.B
Use patterns in place value to compare and order whole numbers through 999.

MATH TEKS INTEGRATION

Number, operation, and quantitative reasoning 2.3.B
Model addition and subtraction of two-digit numbers with objects, pictures, words, and numbers.

Number, operation, and quantitative reasoning 2.3.D
Determine the value of a collection of coins up to one dollar.

MATERIALS
- *Number Cubes
- *Base-ten blocks

TECHNOLOGY
Presentation Lesson 9.3
MathTools Base Ten

Extended Response
Problem 16

Writing + Math
Journal

Comparing Numbers through 1,000

Context of the Lesson This is the third in a series of twelve lessons that develop skills and understanding for working with 2- and 3-digit numbers. Relation signs were introduced in Lesson 1.9. The use of equalities and inequalities will be applied in this lesson to pairs of three- and four-digit numbers.

See page 329B for Math Background for teachers for this lesson.

Planning for Learning ● DIFFERENTIATE INSTRUCTION

INTERVENTION
If . . . students lack the prerequisite skill of recognizing addition and subtraction situations,

Then . . . teach *Intervention* Lesson 9.A.

1.3.A, 1.5.D

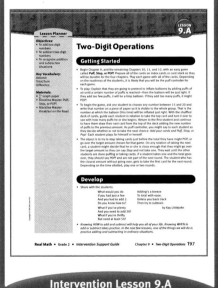

Intervention Lesson 9.A

ENGLISH LEARNER
Preview

If . . . students need language support,

Then . . . use Lesson 9.3 in *English Learner Support Guide* to preview lesson concepts and vocabulary.

English Learner Lesson 9.3

ENRICH
If . . . students are proficient in the lesson concepts,

Then . . . emphasize Reflect.

PRACTICE
If . . . students would benefit from additional practice,

Then . . . extend Skill Practice before assigning student pages.

RETEACH
If . . . students are having difficulty understanding inequalities using three-digit numbers,

Then . . . extend Guided Discussion before assigning the student pages.

Access Vocabulary
matches the number goes together or is the same as

Spanish Cognates
equal igual

Number, operation, and quantitative reasoning 2.1.C
Use place value to compare and order whole numbers to 999 and record the comparisons using numbers and symbols (<, =, >)
Patterns, relationships, and algebraic thinking 2.5.B
Use patterns in place value to compare and order whole numbers through 999.

Mental Math 5

 INTEGRATION: **TEKS 2.3.B** Write pairs of expressions on the board. Have students respond by showing thumbs-up if the expression on the left is greater, thumbs-down if it is less, and open hand if the two expressions are equal. Possible examples include the following:

a. 18 + 5, 19 + 6 down   **b.** 92 + 16, 90 + 16 up
c. 37 + 28, 39 + 20 up   **d.** 74 − 10, 74 − 9 down

1 Develop 20

Tell Students In Today's Lesson They Will

compare numbers through 1,000.

 Introductory

Guided Discussion e MathTools REASONING

 Review the relation signs (<, >, and =). Use the board to demonstrate that the open end of either inequality sign should point to the greater number, and the closed end should point to the smaller number. Explain to students that they can compare the number of digits first. Then they can compare the digits of greatest place value and then the digits to the right as needed.

- Write pairs of three- and four-digit numbers and expressions with a circle between them on the board. Use base-ten blocks or **eMathTools: Base Ten** to demonstrate each number being compared.
- Work through several examples with the students, having them compare the number in the greatest place value first. Give several examples with a single number on each side. Possible examples include the following:

a. 200 < 230   **b.** 204 > 100
c. 890 < 910   **d.** 1,000 > 800
e. 350 + 10 < 350 + 11   **f.** 275 − 5 = 276 − 6

Skill Practice UNDERSTANDING Guided

 THUMBS UP Write pairs of expressions on the board, but this time compare three-digit addition or subtraction expressions that use a multiple of ten. Have students show thumbs-up if the expression on the left is greater, thumbs-down if it is less, and open hand if they are equal. For example:

a. 700 + 80, 700 + 90 down   **b.** 260 − 50, 380 − 50 down
c. 439 − 20, 439 − 60 up   **d.** 622 + 60, 622 + 10 up
e. 183 + 10, 193 + 10 down   **f.** 624 + 30, 614 + 40 open

Students do not need to do the addition and subtraction problems to find the correct answers. Students should decide which side is less without determining the sums and differences. Encourage students to explain and show a way to get the answer without doing the calculation. For example, 260 is less than 380 and if you take away 50 from both, 260 − 50 must be less than 380 − 50. Do several other examples, calling on individual students to offer explanations.

2 Use Student Pages 20

Pages 335–336 UNDERSTANDING   Independent

Have students complete pages 335 and 336 independently.

Progress Monitoring

If . . . students make consistently wrong responses during the Skill Practice,

Then . . . plan to do the student pages with them in small groups. As students catch on, they may work independently.

As Students Finish

Game   Have students play the **Harder Counting and Writing Numbers Game** in pairs.

RESEARCH IN ACTION

"As children work with numbers, they gradually develop flexibility in thinking about numbers, which is a hallmark of number sense . . . Number sense develops as students understand the size of numbers, develop multiple ways of thinking about and representing numbers, use numbers as referents, and develop accurate perceptions about the effects of operations on numbers."

National Council of Teachers of Mathematics. *Principles and Standards for School Mathematics*. Reston, VA: NCTM, 2000, pp. 78–80.

Student Page

Name _____ Date _____

Key Ideas

You can use the greater than sign > and less than sign < to show which number is greater. The wider end of the symbol always points to the greater amount. Use an equal sign = if both sides are the same.

Math TEKS
Patterns, relationships, and algebraic thinking 2.5.B
Use patterns in place value to compare and order whole numbers through 999.

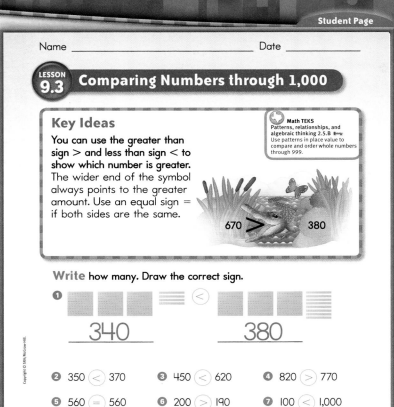

670 > 380

Write how many. Draw the correct sign.

1. 340 $<$ 380

2. 350 $<$ 370
3. 450 $<$ 620
4. 820 $>$ 770
5. 560 $=$ 560
6. 200 $>$ 190
7. 100 $<$ 1,000
8. 400 + 20 $>$ 400 + 10
10. 750 + 30 $<$ 750 + 40
9. 400 − 20 $<$ 400 − 10
11. 750 − 30 $>$ 750 − 40

Write the words *greater than*, *less than*, or *equal to* to make the statements true.

12. Four hundred is __greater than__ three hundred.
13. Two hundred fifty is __less than__ two hundred sixty.

Ring the letter of the number that matches the number shown.

14. 1,000 **TAKS Obj. 1**
   a. one thousand
   b. one hundred
   c. one
   d. ten

15. 930
   a. ninety-three
   b. nine hundred
   c. nine hundred thirty
   d. nine hundred three

16. **Extended Response** Is 589 − 15 greater than, less than, or equal to 588 − 14? How do you know?
   Equal because even though the number you are
   subtracting is one less, the number you are subtracting
   from is also one less.

Game Play the **Harder Counting and Writing Numbers Game** in pairs.

Writing + Math **Journal**
Draw a picture to represent a three-digit number such as 457.

---

3 Reflect
10

Guided Discussion **REASONING**

Put several comparison problems on the board, and have students place the relation signs correctly. Possible problems include the following: 5,785 + 3 $>$ 5,785 + 2

As students choose the correct sign, praise them for being able to calculate with such very large numbers. Many students will probably point out that calculations were not really necessary, only the ability to draw comparisons between the original numbers. Conclude by showing students that with a bit of thinking, many problems that look difficult are really not that difficult.

Extended Response **REASONING**

Problem 16 Discuss students' answers. Students should realize that the expressions are equal. Even though the numbers being subtracted vary by 1, the numbers they are being subtracted from vary by the same amount.

Writing + Math **Journal**

Have students share their drawings. An example would be to draw pictures of base-ten blocks to represent each digit.

TEXAS TEKS Checkup

TEKS 2.1.C Use place value to compare and order whole numbers to 999 and record the comparisons using numbers and symbols (<, =, >).

Which sign is correct? 433 _____ 344

A =   C <

B >   D ÷

Have students choose the correct answer, then describe how they knew which choice was correct. In the discussion, ask questions such as the following. Be sure to ask students to explain their reasoning, since different solution methods are possible.

- How many hundreds are in 433?
  4 hundreds

- Is 4 hundreds equal, greater than, or less than 3 hundreds?
  greater than

TEKS 2.8
The student is expected to use whole numbers to locate and name points on a number line.

Use this problem to assess students' progress towards standards mastery.

Which number is shown on the number line?

0 1 2 3 4 5 6 7 8 9 10

A 2   C 7

B 4   D 9

Follow-Up
If...students have difficulty comparing numbers,

Then...reteach the concept using *Reteach* Lesson 9.3.

Math Puzzler: **Integration: TEKS 2.3. D** Keith has two quarters and two nickels. Kendra has one quarter and five nickels. Who has more money? Keith

4 Assess and Differentiate

 **Assess** Use *eAssess* to record and analyze evidence of student understanding.

A Gather Evidence

Use the Daily Class Assessment Records in *Texas Assessment* or *eAssess* to record daily observations.

Informal Assessment
☑ **Guided Discussion**

Did the student **REASONING**
- ❏ provide a clear explanation?
- ❏ communicate reasons and strategies?
- ❏ choose appropriate strategies?
- ❏ argue logically?

Portfolio Assessment
☑ **Extended Response**

Did the student **REASONING**
- ❏ provide a clear explanation?
- ❏ communicate reasons and strategies?
- ❏ choose appropriate strategies?
- ❏ argue logically?

 TEKS/TAKS Practice

Use *TEKS/TAKS Practice* pages 43–46 to assess student progress.

B Summarize Findings

Analyze and summarize assessment data for each student. Determine which Assessment Follow-Up is appropriate for each student. Use the Student Assessment Record in *Texas Assessment* or *eAssess* to update assessment records.

C Texas Assessment Follow-Up ● DIFFERENTIATE INSTRUCTION

Based on your observations, use these teaching strategies for assessment follow-up.

TEXAS

INTERVENTION	ENRICH	PRACTICE	RETEACH

INTERVENTION

Review student performance on *Intervention* Lesson 9.A to see if students have mastered prerequisite skills for this lesson.

1.3.A Model and create addition and subtraction problem situations with concrete objects and write corresponding number sentences.

1.5.D Use patterns to develop strategies to solve basic addition and basic subtraction problems.

ENGLISH LEARNER

Review

Use Lesson 9.3 in *English Learner Support Guide* to review lesson concepts and vocabulary.

ENRICH

If . . . students are proficient in the lesson concepts,

Then . . . encourage them to work on the chapter projects or *Enrichment* Lesson 9.3.

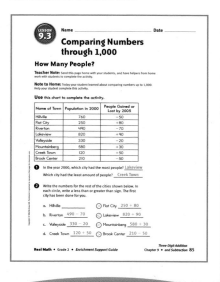

Enrichment Lesson 9.3

PRACTICE

If . . . students would benefit from additional practice,

Then . . . assign *Practice* Lesson 9.3.

Practice Lesson 9.3

RETEACH

If . . . students are having difficulty understanding comparing numbers through 1,000,

Then . . . reteach the concept using *Reteach* Lesson 9.3.

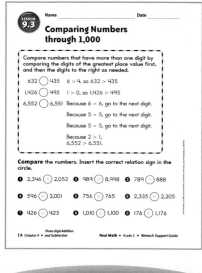

Reteach Lesson 9.3

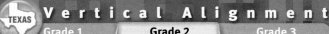

TEXAS
Vertical Alignment

Grade 1	Grade 2	Grade 3
1.1.B Create sets of tens and ones using concrete objects to describe, compare, and order whole numbers.	**2.1.A** Use concrete models of hundreds, tens, and ones to represent a given whole number (up to 999) in various ways.	**3.1.B** Use place value to compare and order whole numbers through 9,999.

Overview

LESSON 9.4

TEXAS

Lesson Planner

OBJECTIVES
- To prepare students to add two three-digit numbers
- To demonstrate working with money up to $1,000

MATH TEKS

Number, operation, and quantitative reasoning 2.1.A
Use concrete models of hundreds, tens, and ones to represent a given whole number (up to 999) in various ways.

Number, operation, and quantitative reasoning 2.1.B
Use place value to read, write, and describe the value of whole numbers to 999.

MATH TEKS INTEGRATION

Number, operation, and quantitative reasoning 2.3.A
Recall and apply basic addition and subtraction facts (to 18).

Number, operation, and quantitative reasoning 2.3.B
Model addition and subtraction of two-digit numbers with objects, pictures, words, and numbers.

MATERIALS
- *Number Cubes
- *Craft sticks
- *Base-ten blocks
- *Play money
- Rummage Sale Game Mat

TECHNOLOGY
- Presentation Lesson 9.4
- MathTools Base Ten

Writing + Math
Journal

Adding Multiples of 10

Context of the Lesson This is the fourth in a series of twelve lessons that develop skills and understanding for working with 2- and 3-digit numbers. This is the introductory lesson for three-digit addition, which is the topic of the next several lessons. Students will review the addition algorithm as well as the regrouping process. Students will compare and relate the process of two-digit addition to three-digit addition. The algorithm for 3-digit addition is taught in the next lesson before exploring 3-digit subtraction.

See page 329B for Math Background for teachers for this lesson.

Planning for Learning ● DIFFERENTIATE INSTRUCTION

INTERVENTION

If . . . students lack the prerequisite skill of adding two-digit numbers,

Then . . . teach **Intervention** Lesson 9.A.

 1.3.A, 1.5.D

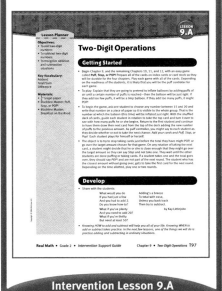

Intervention Lesson 9.A

ENGLISH LEARNER

Preview

If . . . students need language support,

Then . . . use Lesson 9.4 in **English Learner Support Guide** to preview lesson concepts and vocabulary.

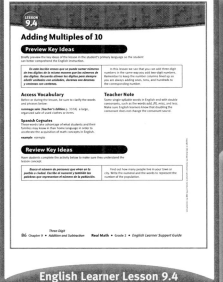

English Learner Lesson 9.4

ENRICH

If . . . students are proficient in the lesson concepts,

Then . . . emphasize additional game time.

PRACTICE

If . . . students would benefit from additional practice,

Then . . . extend Skill Practice before assigning student pages.

RETEACH

If . . . students are having difficulty understanding three-digit addition,

Then . . . extend Guided Discussion before assigning the student pages.

Access Vocabulary
rummage sale a large organized sale of used clothes or items

Spanish Cognates
example ejemplo

Number, operation, and quantitative reasoning 2.1.A Use concrete models of hundreds, tens, and ones to repres[ent] given whole number (up to 999) in various ways.
Number, operation, and quantitative reasoning 2.1.B Use place value to read, write, and describe the value of w[hole] numbers to 999.

Mental Math 5

  INTEGRATION: TEKS 2.3.A Present two-digit addition exercises, and have students show their answers using **Number Cubes.** Possible exercises include the following:

a. $10 + 40 = 50$

b. $40 + 50 = 90$

c. $80 + 20 = 100$

d. $10 + 60 = 70$

e. $30 + 50 = 80$

f. $50 + 40 = 90$

1 Develop 20

Tell Students In Today's Lesson They Will

add three-digit numbers.

 Introductory

Guided Discussion  MathTools UNDERSTANDING

Relate the process of two-digit addition to three-digit addition.

- Write a related set of single-, two-, and three-digit addition exercises on the board, and have students find the sums. Possible problems include the following:

a.
$$\begin{array}{r} 3 \\ +\ 5 \\ \hline 8 \end{array}$$

b.
$$\begin{array}{r} 30 \\ +\ 50 \\ \hline 80 \end{array}$$

c.
$$\begin{array}{r} 300 \\ +\ 500 \\ \hline 800 \end{array}$$

- Demonstrate the answer to the exercises by using three and five groups of one hundred bundled sticks or **eMathTools: Base Ten.**

■ **How are these three exercises similar?** Each adds 3 and 5 of something and gets 8 of them.

■ **How are they different?** The things added are ones, tens, and hundreds.

-  Now demonstrate the same procedure with craft sticks and an exercise that will require regrouping, such as the following:

a.
$$\begin{array}{r} 1 \\ 57 \\ +\ 38 \\ \hline 95 \end{array}$$

b.
$$\begin{array}{r} 1 \\ 570 \\ +\ 380 \\ \hline 950 \end{array}$$

- Guide students to recognize that 57 tens + 38 tens (570 + 380) has an answer related to 57 + 38. Then use craft sticks to show how to find 487 + 389. 876

Ask students a question such as the following:

■ **Critical Thinking** **How is this similar to two-digit addition?** You may have to regroup numbers in the same way, but this time you may need to regroup in both the hundreds place and tens place.

Skill Practice COMPUTING Guided

 Integration: TEKS 2.3.B Have students work in small groups using bundled craft sticks or base-ten blocks to practice three-digit addition exercises. Provide exercises that do not need regrouping as well as those that do. Possible exercises include the following:

a.
$$\begin{array}{r} 200 \\ +\ 500 \\ \hline 700 \end{array}$$

b.
$$\begin{array}{r} 327 \\ +\ 269 \\ \hline 596 \end{array}$$

c.
$$\begin{array}{r} 434 \\ +\ 656 \\ \hline 1{,}090 \end{array}$$

d.
$$\begin{array}{r} 147 \\ +\ 352 \\ \hline 499 \end{array}$$

Strategy Building APPLYING

 Game **Rummage Sale Game Mat** Guided

This game provides practice with regrouping money amounts into tens, hundreds, and thousands.

Introduce this game by playing several turns with a student in front of the class. Complete directions are found on the game mat and in this **Teacher's Edition.**

2 Use Student Pages 20

Pages 337–338 UNDERSTANDING Independent

 Allow students to use play money, craft sticks or base-ten blocks to complete pages 337 and 338 independently.

Progress Monitoring

If . . . students have difficulty regrouping while adding,

Then . . . provide individual practice adding two three-digit numbers with base-ten materials, emphasizing trading ten sets for one larger set (ones for ten, tens for hundred) whenever possible.

As Students Finish

 Game Have students play the **Rummage Sale Game.**

 MathTools Have students create sets representing three-digit numbers by using **Base Ten** and then add two sets together.

Student Page

Name _____ Date _____

LESSON 9.4 — Adding Multiples of 10

Key Ideas

You can add three-digit numbers in the same way you add two-digit numbers.

> **Math TEKS**
> Number, operation, and quantitative reasoning 2.1.A Use concrete models of hundreds, tens, and ones to represent a given whole number (up to 999) in various ways.

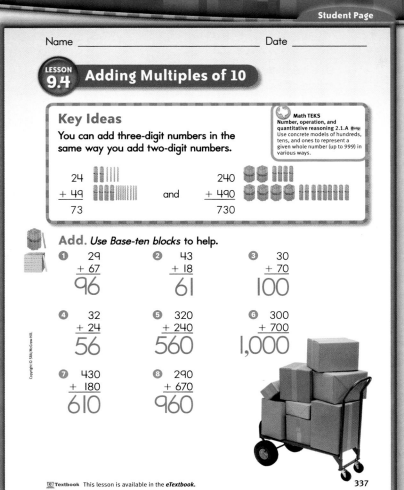

$$24 + 49 = 73 \qquad \text{and} \qquad 240 + 490 = 730$$

Add. *Use Base-ten blocks to help.*

1. $29 + 67 = 96$
2. $43 + 18 = 61$
3. $30 + 70 = 100$
4. $32 + 24 = 56$
5. $320 + 240 = 560$
6. $300 + 700 = 1,000$
7. $430 + 180 = 610$
8. $290 + 670 = 960$

Fill in the missing numbers.

9.

in → +10 → out	
70	80
100	110
130	140
160	170

10.

in → +100 → out	
300	400
500	600
750	850
900	1,000

Write the number.

11. Four hundred twenty-five — 425
12. Nine hundred forty-seven — 947
13. Two hundred sixty-three — 263
14. Which number sentence has a sum of 360? **TAKS Obj. 1**

   a. 18 + 18
   b. 180 + 18
   (c.) 180 + 180
   d. 300 + 80

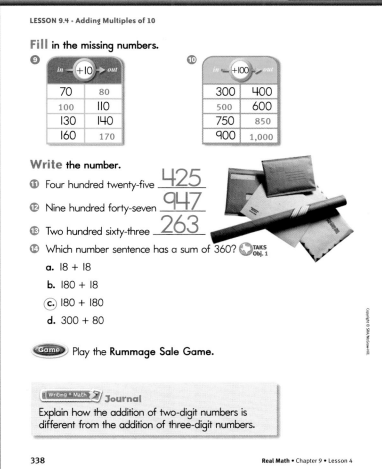

Game Play the **Rummage Sale Game**.

Writing + Math **Journal**

Explain how the addition of two-digit numbers is different from the addition of three-digit numbers.

---

3 Reflect 10

Guided Discussion REASONING

Write the following incorrect number sentence on the board as you explain that a second-grade student had made the mistake shown:

320 + 50 = 820

■ **Critical Thinking** **What mistake did the student make and how would you help this student if you were the teacher?**

The discussion should focus on two things. Foremost is that the answer is contrary to reason. If you add 50 to 320, the answer cannot possibly be 400. Also focus on the importance of lining up the digits correctly in both numbers. In this case, there is a big difference between placing the 5 in the hundreds place compared with the tens place.

Do one or two more similar problems if time and interest permit.

Writing + Math **Journal**

Students should note that two-digit addition is different from three-digit addition because in three-digit addition, you also use the hundreds place.

TEXAS TEKS Checkup

TEKS 2.7.A • Describe attributes (the number of vertices, faces, edges, sides) of two- and three dimensional geometric figures such as circles, polygons, spheres, cones, cylinders, prisms, and pyramids, etc.

Use this problem to assess students' progress toward standards mastery:

Which have the same number of corners?

A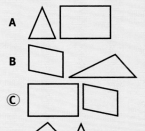

B

C

D

Have students choose the correct answer and then describe how they knew which choice was correct. In the discussion, ask questions such as the following. Be sure to ask students to explain their reasoning, because different solution methods are possible.

■ **How many corners does the triangle have?** 3

Follow-Up

If... students need additional practice describing attributes of two- and three-dimensional geometric figures,

Then... have them complete **Building Blocks: Shape Parts 1–7**.

4 Assess and Differentiate

 Assess Use *eAssess* to record and analyze evidence of student understanding.

A Gather Evidence

Use the Daily Class Assessment Records in *Texas Assessment* or *eAssess* to record daily observations.

Informal Assessment
☑ **Skill Practice**

Did the student **COMPUTING**
- ❑ respond accurately?
- ❑ respond quickly?
- ❑ respond with confidence?
- ❑ self-correct?

Performance Assessment
☑ **Game**

Did the student **APPLYING**
- ❑ apply learning in new situations?
- ❑ contribute concepts?
- ❑ contribute answers?
- ❑ connect mathematics to real-world situations?

 **TEKS/TAKS Practice**

Use *TEKS/TAKS Practice* pages 1–4 to assess student progress.

B Summarize Findings

Analyze and summarize assessment data for each student. Determine which Assessment Follow-Up is appropriate for each student. Use the Student Assessment Record in *Texas Assessment* or *eAssess* to update assessment records.

C Texas Assessment Follow-Up ● DIFFERENTIATE INSTRUCTION

Based on your observations, use these teaching strategies for assessment follow-up.

INTERVENTION

Review student performance on *Intervention* Lesson 9.A to see if students have mastered prerequisite skills for this lesson.

1.3.A Model and create addition and subtraction problem situations with concrete objects and write corresponding number sentences.

1.5.D Use patterns to develop strategies to solve basic addition and basic subtraction problems.

ENGLISH LEARNER
Review

Use Lesson 9.4 in *English Learner Support Guide* to review lesson concepts and vocabulary.

ENRICH

If . . . students are proficient in the lesson concepts,

Then . . . encourage them to work on the chapter projects or *Enrichment* Lesson 9.4.

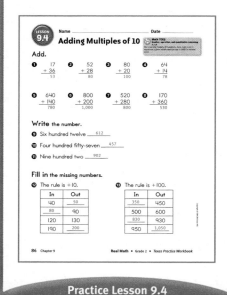

Enrichment Lesson 9.4

PRACTICE

If . . . students would benefit from additional practice,

Then . . . assign *Practice* Lesson 9.4.

Practice Lesson 9.4

RETEACH

If . . . students are having difficulty understanding three-digit addition,

Then . . . have them review place value. Have students show 14 as 1 ten and 4, or show 140 as 1 hundred, 4 tens, and 0.

TEXAS **V e r t i c a l A l i g n m e n t**

Grade 1
1.1.B
Create sets of tens and ones using concrete objects to describe, compare, and order whole numbers.

Grade 2
2.3.B
Model addition and subtraction of two-digit numbers with objects, pictures, words, and numbers.

Grade 3
3.1.B
Use place value to compare and order whole numbers through 9,999.

Overview

LESSON 9.5

TEXAS

Lesson Planner

OBJECTIVES
- To develop the three-digit addition algorithm
- To review the **Roll a Problem Game**, which gives practice with addition, place value, probability, and approximation, from Lesson 5.8

MATH TEKS

Number, operation, and quantitative reasoning 2.1.A
Use concrete models of hundreds, tens, and ones to represent a given whole number (up to 999) in various ways.

Number, operation, and quantitative reasoning 2.1.B
Use place value to read, write, and describe the value of whole numbers to 999.

Number, operation, and quantitative reasoning 2.3.B
Model addition and subtraction of two-digit numbers with objects, pictures, words, and numbers.

MATH TEKS INTEGRATION

Underlying processes and mathematical tools 2.12.A
Identify the mathematics in everyday situations.

MATERIALS
- *Number Cubes
- *Craft sticks
- *Base-ten blocks

TECHNOLOGY
Presentation Lesson 9.5
MathTools Base Ten

Extended Response
Problem 10

Three-Digit Addition ⭐

Context of the Lesson This is the fifth in a series of twelve lessons that develop skills and understanding for working with 2- and 3-digit numbers. The previous lessons were leading to the development of the addition algorithm. In this lesson students will apply their knowledge of place value through 1,000 by adding together two three-digit numbers. After mastering this algorithm, students can add numbers of any place value. The next two lessons lead to the development of the subtraction algorithm.

See page 329B for Math Background for teachers for this lesson.

Planning for Learning • DIFFERENTIATE INSTRUCTION

INTERVENTION

If . . . students lack the prerequisite skill of subtracting two-digit numbers,

Then . . . teach **Intervention** Lesson 9.B.

1.3.A, 1.5.D

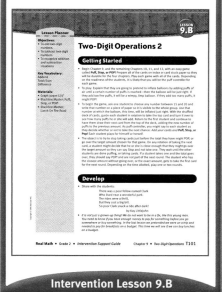

Intervention Lesson 9.B

ENGLISH LEARNER

Preview

If . . . students need language support,

Then . . . use Lesson 9.5 in **English Learner Support Guide** to preview lesson concepts and vocabulary.

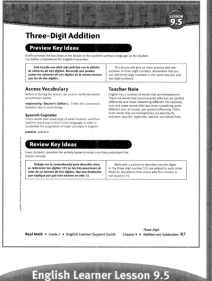

English Learner Lesson 9.5

ENRICH

If . . . students are proficient in the lesson concepts,

Then . . . emphasize additional game time.

PRACTICE

If . . . students would benefit from additional practice,

Then . . . extend Strategy Building before assigning student pages.

RETEACH

If . . . students are having difficulty understanding three-digit addition,

Then . . . extend Guided Discussion before assigning the student pages.

Access Vocabulary
relationship the connection between two or more things

Spanish Cognates
practice práctica

*Manipulative Kit Item = Key standard

⭐ = 120-Day Plan for TAKS

TEXAS

Number, operation and quantitative reasoning 2.1.A 🔑
Use concrete models of hundreds, tens, and ones to represent a given whole number (up to 999) in various ways.
Number, operation, and quantitative reasoning 2.1.B
Use place value to read, write, and describe the value of whole numbers to 999.

Mental Math 5

  **INTEGRATION: TEKS 2.1.B** Present exercises in which you say a two-digit number in expanded form and the students show the number in standard form on their **Number Cubes.** Possible exercises include the following:

a. Two tens and five 25
b. Five tens and six 56
c. Eight tens and two 82
d. Six tens and seven 67
e. Four tens and thirteen 53
f. Three tens and fifteen 45

1 Develop 20

Tell Students In Today's Lesson They Will
add three-digit numbers.

Guided Discussion   MathTools UNDERSTANDING

Introductory

Explain to students that adding 3-digit numbers is like adding 2-digit numbers. Work through the example on student page 339 with the class.

Write several three-digit addition exercises on the board, and have students explain how to answer them. Possible problems include the following:

a.
```
   300
 + 700
 ------
 1,000
```
b.
```
   538
 + 269
 ------
   807
```
c.
```
   497
 + 596
 ------
 1,093
```

If students are having difficulty, show how to solve using base-ten materials or **eMathTools: Base Ten.**

Strategy Building

Guided

 Roll a Problem (Three-Digit Addition) Game

Introduce and play three or four rounds of the **Roll a Problem (Three-Digit Addition) Game** with the class. Use the following form:

```
    _____  _____  _____
 + _____  _____  _____
 ---------------------
```

Show your form on an overhead projector, but turn off the projector before playing the game so students won't try to copy you. When the form is filled in, turn on the overhead projector so students can see it. Have students raise their hands if they think they have a sum—without calculating—that is greater than yours. Select a student whose hand is raised, and ask him or her to write his or her numbers on the board and explain why the sum is greater than your sum. Ask other students if they have a still greater sum. If so, have them write their numbers on the board and explain why the sum is greater. Continue until you have the greatest sum and can declare a winner or winners. Calculate only when necessary.

2 Use Student Pages 20

Pages 339–340 UNDERSTANDING

Independent

Walk students through the example on page 339 by using craft sticks or play money.

Have students complete page 340 independently. Allow students to use base-ten materials if needed. Work with students who are having difficulty with regrouping and place value.

Monitoring Student Progress

If . . . students are having difficulty with regrouping and place value,

Then . . . work individually with students on 3-digit addition problems using base-ten materials, such as play money or base-ten blocks.

As Students Finish

Game ✓ Have students play the **Roll a Problem (Three-Digit Addition) Game** in pairs or small groups.

RESEARCH IN ACTION

"Algorithms and their properties are important mathematical ideas that all students need to understand. An algorithm is a reliable step-by-step procedure for solving problems. To perform arithmetic calculations, children must learn how numerical algorithms work. . . . algorithms, when well understood, can serve as a valuable basis for reasoning about mathematics."

Kilpatrick, J., J. Swafford, and B. Findell, eds. *Adding It Up: Helping Children Learn Mathematics.* Washington, D.C.: National Research Council/National Academy Press, 2001, p. 414.

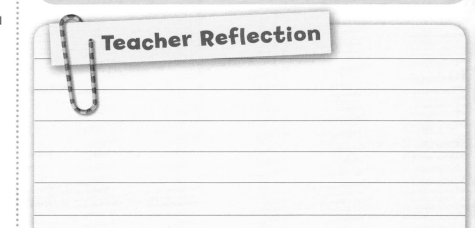
Teacher Reflection

Student Page

Name _____ **Date** _____

LESSON 9.5 Three-Digit Addition

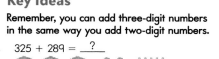

Key Ideas

Remember, you can add three-digit numbers in the same way you add two-digit numbers.

Math TEKS
Number, operation, and quantitative reasoning 2.3.B
Model addition and subtraction of two-digit numbers with objects, pictures, words, and numbers.

325 + 289 = ____?

$$
\begin{array}{r} 325 \\ + 289 \\ \hline \end{array}
$$

$$
\begin{array}{r} \overset{1}{} \\ 325 \\ + 289 \\ \hline 4 \end{array}
$$

$$
\begin{array}{r} \overset{1}{\overset{1}{}} \\ 325 \\ + 289 \\ \hline 14 \end{array}
$$

$$
\begin{array}{r} \overset{1}{\overset{1}{}} \\ 325 \\ + 289 \\ \hline 614 \end{array}
$$

Textbook This lesson is available in the *eTextbook*.

339

Student Page

LESSON 9.5 · Three-Digit Addition

Add.

❶ $\begin{array}{r} 432 \\ + 158 \\ \hline 590 \end{array}$ ❷ $\begin{array}{r} 276 \\ + 395 \\ \hline 671 \end{array}$ ❸ $\begin{array}{r} 403 \\ + 608 \\ \hline 1,011 \end{array}$

❹ $\begin{array}{r} 45 \\ + 17 \\ \hline 62 \end{array}$ ❺ $\begin{array}{r} 63 \\ + 48 \\ \hline 111 \end{array}$ ❻ $\begin{array}{r} 51 \\ + 22 \\ \hline 73 \end{array}$

❼ $\begin{array}{r} 574 \\ + 687 \\ \hline 1,261 \end{array}$ ❽ $\begin{array}{r} 574 \\ + 688 \\ \hline 1,262 \end{array}$ ❾ $\begin{array}{r} 574 \\ + 689 \\ \hline 1,263 \end{array}$

❿ Which number sentence has a sum of 80?
TAKS Obj. 1
(a.) 38 + 42
b. 42 + 81
c. 38 + 24
d. 56 + 80

⓫ What is the sum?
235 + 147
a. 3712
b. 283
(c.) 282
d. 112

⓬ **Extended Response** ➤ **Solve. Explain** how the two are similar.

$\begin{array}{r} 32 \\ + 57 \\ \hline 89 \end{array}$ $\begin{array}{r} 320 \\ + 570 \\ \hline 890 \end{array}$

You are adding the same numbers; only the place value of the numbers has changed.

340

Real Math • Chapter 9 • Lesson 5

---

③ Reflect   10

Guided Discussion **e MathTools** **REASONING**

Write a four-digit addition problem such as the following on the board:

$$
\begin{array}{r} 3527 \\ + 1382 \\ \hline 4909 \end{array}
$$

■ **Critical Thinking** **How can this problem be solved?** Students should relate adding two- and three-digit numbers to the addition of four-digit numbers by continuing the process of adding the digits in the thousands place.

Use base-ten blocks or *eMathTools: Base Ten* to provide a visual representation of this problem.

Extended Response ✔

Problem 12 Discuss students' answers. Students should realize that you are adding the same numbers; only the place value of the numbers has changed.

Cumulative Review: For cumulative review of previously learned skills, see page 349–350.

Family Involvement: Assign the *Practice, Reteach,* or *Enrichment* activities depending on the needs of your students.

Have students play the **Roll a Problem (Three-Digit Addition) Game** with family members.

Concept/Question Board: Encourage students to continue to post questions, answers, and examples on the Concept/Question Board.

Math Puzzler: Integration: TEKS 2.3. A Rowland is not shorter than Jake. Jake is shorter than P.J., who is shorter than Rowland. Write the boys' names in order from shortest to tallest. Jake, P.J., Rowland

4 Assess and Differentiate

 **Assess** Use *eAssess* to record and analyze evidence of student understanding.

A Gather Evidence

Use the Daily Class Assessment Records in *Assessment* or *eAssess* to record daily observations.

Informal Assessment
☑ **Guided Discussion**

Did the student **UNDERSTANDING**
- ☐ make important observations?
- ☐ extend or generalize learning?
- ☐ provide insightful answers?
- ☐ pose insightful questions?

Performance Assessment
☑ **Game**

Did the student **ENGAGING**
- ☐ pay attention to others' contributions?
- ☐ contribute information and ideas?
- ☐ improve on a strategy?
- ☐ reflect on and check the accuracy of his or her work?

 TEKS/TAKS Practice

Use *TEKS/TAKS Practice* page 21 to assess student progress.

B Summarize Findings

Analyze and summarize assessment data for each student. Determine which Assessment Follow-Up is appropriate for each student. Use the Student Assessment Record in *Texas Assessment* or *eAssess* to update assessment records.

C Texas Assessment Follow-Up • DIFFERENTIATE INSTRUCTION

Based on your observations, use these teaching strategies for assessment follow-up.

INTERVENTION

Review student performance on *Intervention* Lesson 9.B to see if students have mastered prerequisite skills for this lesson.

1.3.A Model and create addition and subtraction problem situations with concrete objects and write corresponding number sentences.

1.5.D Use patterns to develop strategies to solve basic addition and basic subtraction problems.

ENGLISH LEARNER

Review

Use Lesson 9.5 in *English Learner Support Guide* to review lesson concepts and vocabulary.

ENRICH

If . . . students are proficient in the lesson concepts,

Then . . . encourage them to work on the chapter projects or *Enrichment* Lesson 9.5.

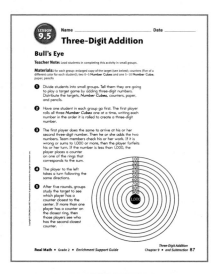

Enrichment Lesson 9.5

PRACTICE

If . . . students would benefit from additional practice,

Then . . . assign *Practice* Lesson 9.5.

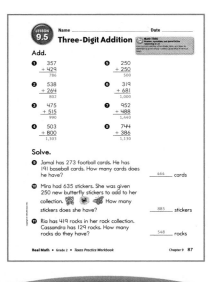

Practice Lesson 9.5

RETEACH

If . . . students are having difficulty understanding three-digit addition,

Then . . . have them use play money to model three-digit addition problems such as $145 + $487.

Grade 1	Grade 2	Grade 3
1.1.B Create sets of tens and ones using concrete objects to describe, compare, and order whole numbers.	**2.1.A** Use concrete models of hundreds, tens, and ones to represent a given whole number (up to 999) in various ways.	**3.1.B** Use place value to compare and order whole numbers through 9,999.

Lesson Planner

OBJECTIVES

To teach a procedure for subtracting three-digit multiples of 10

MATH TEKS

Number, operation, and quantitative reasoning 2.1.A
Use concrete models of hundreds, tens, and ones to represent a given whole number (up to 999) in various ways.

MATH TEKS INTEGRATION

Number, operation, and quantitative reasoning 2.3.A
Recall and apply basic addition and subtraction facts (to 18).

Number, operation, and quantitative reasoning 2.3.B
Model addition and subtraction of two-digit numbers with objects, pictures, words, and numbers.

MATERIALS
- *Number Cubes
- *Craft sticks
- **Rummage Sale Game Mat**
- *Play money

TECHNOLOGY
Presentation Lesson 9.6
MathTools Base Ten

Extended Response
Problem 14

Subtracting Multiples of 10

Context of the Lesson This is the sixth in a series of twelve lessons that develop skills and understanding for working with 2- and 3-digit numbers. This lesson introduces procedures for subtracting three-digit multiples of ten by relating them to procedures learned in Chapter 6 for subtracting two-digit numbers. Lesson 9.7 extends the procedure to subtracting *any* two three-digit numbers. Students will have the opportunity to practice three-digit subtraction and addition in the following lessons. At this point, students should have mastered the algorithm and regrouping process for two-digit numbers.

See page 329B for Math Background for teachers for this lesson.

Planning for Learning • DIFFERENTIATE INSTRUCTION

INTERVENTION

If . . . students lack the prerequisite skill of recognizing addition and subtraction situations,

Then . . . teach *Intervention* Lesson 9.B.

 1.3.A, 1.5.D

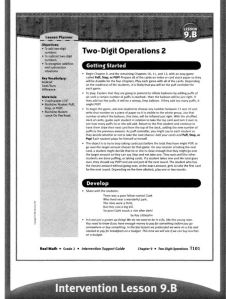

Intervention Lesson 9.B

ENGLISH LEARNER

Preview

If . . . students need language support,

Then . . . use Lesson 9.6 in *English Learner Support Guide* to preview lesson concepts and vocabulary.

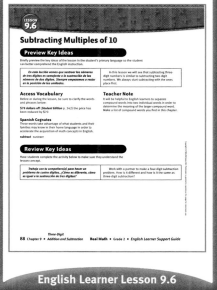

English Learner Lesson 9.6

ENRICH

If . . . students are proficient in the lesson concepts,

Then . . . emphasize additional game time.

PRACTICE

If . . . students would benefit from additional practice,

Then . . . extend Skill Practice before assigning student pages.

RETEACH

If . . . students are having difficulty understanding three-digit subtraction,

Then . . . extend Guided Discussion before assigning the student pages.

Access Vocabulary
$70 dollars off the price has been reduced by $70

Spanish Cognates
subtract sustraer

Teaching Lesson 9.6

 Number, operation, and quantitative reasoning 2.1.A Use concrete models of hundreds, tens, and ones to represent a given whole number (up to 999) in various ways.

Mental Math 5

 INTEGRATION: TEKS 2.3.B Provide students with related subtraction exercises such as the following, and have them show their answers using **Number Cubes.**

a. $9 - 7 = 2$ **b.** $90 - 70 = 20$
c. $6 - 3 = 3$ **d.** $60 - 30 = 30$
e. $5 - 1 = 4$ **f.** $50 - 10 = 40$

1 Develop 20

Tell Students In Today's Lesson They Will
subtract two- and three-digit numbers.

Guided Discussion  **MathTools** UNDERSTANDING · Introductory

Present examples of subtracting multiples of ten from related two- and three-digit numbers. Possible examples include the following:

$$\begin{array}{r} 13 \\ -\ 8 \\ \hline 5 \end{array} \qquad \begin{array}{r} 130 \\ -\ 80 \\ \hline 50 \end{array}$$

Ask students a question such as the following:

■ **Critical Thinking** **How are these two exercises related?** Students should realize that each exercise is subtracting the same numbers, but the place values have changed.

 Next use craft sticks or *eMathTools: Base Ten* to demonstrate the difference in each exercise's place value and the regrouping process of renaming tens as ones and renaming hundreds as tens.

$$\begin{array}{r} 43 \\ -\ 8 \\ \hline 35 \end{array} \qquad \begin{array}{r} 430 \\ -\ 80 \\ \hline 350 \end{array}$$

Write $43 - 8$. Show 4 tens and 3 craft sticks.

■ **How can you take away 8?** by ungrouping a bunch
■ **Now how many loose sticks are there?** 13
■ **How many tens?** 3

Write ³4¹3 to illustrate the regrouping.

■ **When you take away 8, what's left?** 3 tens and 5

Repeat with hundreds.

Skill Practice COMPUTING

 Guided

Distribute craft sticks or other base-ten materials, and have students work in pairs to solve similar subtraction exercises. Encourage students to talk about the process of exchanging or regrouping.

a.
$$\begin{array}{r} 24 \\ -\ 7 \\ \hline 17 \end{array} \qquad \begin{array}{r} 240 \\ -\ 70 \\ \hline 170 \end{array}$$

b.
$$\begin{array}{r} 18 \\ -\ 6 \\ \hline 12 \end{array} \qquad \begin{array}{r} 180 \\ -\ 60 \\ \hline 120 \end{array}$$

2 Use Student Pages 20

Pages 341–342 UNDERSTANDING · Independent

 Have students complete pages 341 and 342 independently. Allow students to use play money or other base-ten materials to regroup if necessary.

Progress Monitoring

If . . . students have difficulty with regrouping,

Then . . . work with students individually, having them rewrite the numbers after exchanging base-ten materials.

As Students Finish

Game Have students play the **Rummage Sale Game** or **Roll a Problem (Three-Digit Addition) Game** in pairs or small groups.

RESEARCH IN ACTION

"The algorithms for multiplication and division depend heavily on fluency with multiplication and addition, and in division, with multidigit subtraction. The difficulties that many students have in subtraction noticeably affect division, so understanding and fluency in multidigit subtraction are very important."

Fuson, Karen F. "Developing Mathematical Power in Whole Number Operations" in Kilpatrick, Jeremy, W. Gary Martin, and Deborah Schifter eds. *A Research Companion to Principles and Standards for School Mathematics.* Reston, VA: National Council of Teachers of Mathematics, Inc. 2003, p. 87.

Student Page

Name _____ Date _____

**LESSON 9.6** Subtracting Multiples of 10

Key Ideas

Subtracting three-digit numbers is similar to subtracting two-digit numbers. **You may regroup.**

Math TEKS
Number, operation, and quantitative reasoning 2.3.B
Model addition and subtraction of two-digit numbers with objects, pictures, words, and numbers.

$24 - 7 = 17$ is like $240 - 70 = 170$

 $- 7 =$

 $- 70 =$

Subtract. Use *Base-ten blocks* to help.

❶
$$\begin{array}{r} 15 \\ -\ 7 \\ \hline 8 \end{array}$$

❷
$$\begin{array}{r} 43 \\ -\ 9 \\ \hline 34 \end{array}$$

❸
$$\begin{array}{r} 62 \\ -\ 5 \\ \hline 57 \end{array}$$

❹
$$\begin{array}{r} 14 \\ -\ 8 \\ \hline 6 \end{array}$$

❺
$$\begin{array}{r} 150 \\ -\ 70 \\ \hline 80 \end{array}$$

❻
$$\begin{array}{r} 620 \\ -\ 50 \\ \hline 570 \end{array}$$

❼
$$\begin{array}{r} 430 \\ -\ 90 \\ \hline 340 \end{array}$$

❽
$$\begin{array}{r} 140 \\ -\ 80 \\ \hline 60 \end{array}$$

Textbook This lesson is available in the *eTextbook*. 341

LESSON 9.6 · Subtracting Multiples of 10

Subtract.

❾
$$\begin{array}{r} 14 \\ -\ 6 \\ \hline 8 \end{array}$$

❿
$$\begin{array}{r} 520 \\ -\ 60 \\ \hline 460 \end{array}$$

⓫
$$\begin{array}{r} 11 \\ -\ 9 \\ \hline 2 \end{array}$$

⓬
$$\begin{array}{r} 140 \\ -\ 60 \\ \hline 80 \end{array}$$

⓭ The regular price for a computer is $943. How much will it cost if it is on sale for $70 off? __$873__

⓮ **Extended Response** Mark lives at 241 East Broadway. Sara lives at 90 East Broadway. How far apart do they live? _cannot tell_

Explain. _Street addresses don't tell how far apart houses are._

⓯ The Edinger family planned to drive 475 miles on the first day of their vacation. They drove 90 miles before lunch. How much farther do they have to drive today? __385__

Game Play the **Rummage Sale Game** in pairs or small groups.

342 **Real Math** • Chapter 9 • Lesson 6

---

③ Reflect 10

Guided Discussion REASONING

Write the following word problem on the board:

Lucille paid $520 for a new computer and received a $50 rebate several weeks later. How much did Lucille pay for the computer?

Then write possible answers on the board, explaining that only one of the answers is correct and that different students gave the incorrect answers. Ask if they can figure out why the students made the mistakes and how they would help the students if they were the teacher. Discuss students' ideas, and be sure to listen to solutions that represent real thinking even if they differ from those given below.

- **$570** This student probably added instead of subtracted. The student should be helped to understand the situation. He or she might also need to learn what a rebate is.
- **$20** This student probably did not line up the digits according to their place value. The student needs help with understanding place value. The student also needs help with detecting answers that are contrary to reason.
- **$460** This student needs help with subtraction facts. He or she thought that the difference between 12 and 5 is 6.
- **$470** This student had the correct answer. We don't know if he or she needs extra help because we have only one problem and answer to study.

Extended Response

Problem 14 Discuss students' answers. Even though addresses don't tell you how far apart things are, they could give you a rough indication.

Cumulative Review: For cumulative review of previously learned skills, see page 349–350.

Family Involvement: Assign the *Practice, Reteach,* or *Enrichment* activities depending on the needs of your students.
Have students play the **Roll a Problem (Three-Digit Addition) Game** with family members.

Concept/Question Board: Encourage students to continue to post questions, answers, and examples on the Concept/Question Board.

Math Puzzler: **Integration: TEKS 2.3. A** Name a three-digit number in which the sum of the digits is 13, the number is greater than 500, and no two digits are the same. Possible answers: 562, 643, 724

Assess and Differentiate

 **Assess**   Use **eAssess** to record and analyze evidence of student understanding.

A Gather Evidence

Use the Daily Class Assessment Records in **Assessment** or **eAssess** to record daily observations.

Informal Assessment
☑ **Guided Discussion**
Did the student **UNDERSTANDING**
- ❑ make important observations?
- ❑ extend or generalize learning?
- ❑ provide insightful answers?
- ❑ pose insightful questions?

Informal Assessment
☑ **Student Pages**
Did the student **UNDERSTANDING**
- ❑ make important observations?
- ❑ extend or generalize learning?
- ❑ provide insightful answers?
- ❑ pose insightful questions?

 TEKS/TAKS Practice

Use *TEKS/TAKS Practice* page 21 to assess student progress.

B Summarize Findings

Analyze and summarize assessment data for each student. Determine which Assessment Follow-Up is appropriate for each student. Use the Student Assessment Record in **Texas Assessment** or **eAssess** to update assessment records.

C Texas Assessment Follow-Up ● DIFFERENTIATE INSTRUCTION

Based on your observations, use these teaching strategies for assessment follow-up.

TEXAS

INTERVENTION

Review student performance on **Intervention** Lesson 9.B to see if students have mastered prerequisite skills for this lesson.

🔘 **1.3.A** Model and create addition and subtraction problem situations with concrete objects and write corresponding number sentences.

🔘 **1.5.D** Use patterns to develop strategies to solve basic addition and basic subtraction problems.

ENGLISH LEARNER

Review

Use Lesson 9.6 in **English Learner Support Guide** to review lesson concepts and vocabulary.

ENRICH

If . . . students are proficient in the lesson concepts,

Then . . . encourage them to work on the chapter projects or **Enrichment** Lesson 9.6.

Enrichment Lesson 9.6

PRACTICE

If . . . students would benefit from additional practice,

Then . . . assign **Practice** Lesson 9.6.

Practice Lesson 9.6

RETEACH

If . . . students struggle with three-digit subtraction,

Then . . . have them use play money to model three-digit subtraction problems.

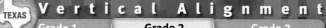

TEXAS Vertical Alignment

Grade 1	Grade 2	Grade 3
1.1.B Create sets of tens and ones using concrete objects to describe, compare, and order whole numbers.	**2.1.A** Use concrete models of hundreds, tens, and ones to represent a given whole number (up to 999) in various ways.	**3.1.B** Use place value to compare and order whole numbers through 9,999.

Overview LESSON **9.7**

TEXAS

Lesson Planner

OBJECTIVES
- To develop a procedure for subtracting any three-digit number
- To provide practice in subtracting three-digit numbers

MATH TEKS

Number, operation, and quantitative reasoning 2.1.A
Use concrete models of hundreds, tens, and ones to represent a given whole number (up to 999) in various ways.

MATH TEKS INTEGRATION

Number, operation, and quantitative reasoning 2.1.C
Use place value to compare and order whole numbers to 999 and record the comparisons using numbers and symbols (<, =, >).

Underlying processes and mathematical tools 2.12.A
Identify the mathematics in everyday situations.

MATERIALS
- *Number Cubes
- *Base-ten materials
- Checkbook Game Mat

TECHNOLOGY
Presentation Lesson 9.7
MathTools Base Ten

Extended Response
Problem 14

Three-Digit Subtraction★

Context of the Lesson This is the seventh in a series of twelve lessons that develop skills and understanding for working with 2- and 3-digit numbers. In this lesson students will learn and practice a procedure for subtracting any two three-digit numbers. Students will practice 3-digit addition and subtraction in the next lessons.

See page 329B for Math Background for teachers for this lesson.

Planning for Learning ● DIFFERENTIATE INSTRUCTION

INTERVENTION
If . . . students lack the prerequisite skill of recognizing addition and subtraction situations,

Then . . . teach *Intervention* Lesson 9.B.

 1.3.A, 1.5.D

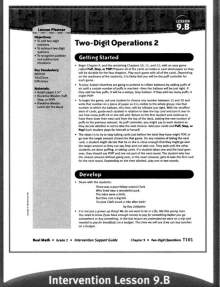

Intervention Lesson 9.B

ENGLISH LEARNER
Preview

If . . . students need language support,

Then . . . use Lesson 9.7 in *English Learner Support Guide* to preview lesson concepts and vocabulary.

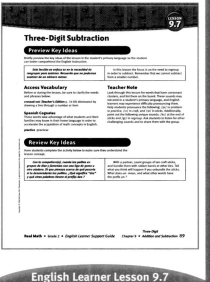

English Learner Lesson 9.7

ENRICH
If . . . students are proficient in the lesson concepts,

Then . . . emphasize additional game time.

PRACTICE
If . . . students would benefit from additional practice,

Then . . . extend Skill Practice before assigning student pages.

RETEACH
If . . . students are having difficulty understanding three-digit addition,

Then . . . extend Guided Discussion before assigning the student pages.

Access Vocabulary
crossed out eliminated by drawing a line through a number or item

Spanish Cognates
practice practicar

TEXAS

Number, operation, and quantitative reasoning 2.1.A
Use concrete models of hundreds, tens, and ones to represent a given whole number (up to 999) in various ways.

Mental Math 5

THUMBS UP

INTEGRATION: TEKS 2.3.B Write pairs of numbers on the board. Have students respond by showing thumbs-up if the number or statement on the left is greater than the number on the right, thumbs-down if it is less, and open hand if the two numbers are equal. Use the same Find, Hide, and Show procedure used previously. Possible examples include the following:

a. 300 + 10, 400 − 10
down

b. 600 + 80, 700 − 10
down

c. 900 − 200, 500
up

d. 1,200 − 0, 200 + 1,000
open hand

e. 700 − 20, 600 + 80
open hand

f. 100 + 600, 800
down

1 Develop 20

Tell Students In Today's Lesson They Will
subtract three-digit numbers.

Guided Discussion   **MathTools** UNDERSTANDING
Introductory

Use base-ten materials or **eMathTools: Base Ten** to show how to subtract numbers that require regrouping and exercises that don't require regrouping. Focus on why regrouping tens and hundreds is sometimes necessary.
Demonstrate with problems such as the following:

$$\begin{array}{r} 531 \\ -228 \\ \hline 303 \end{array}$$

Use craft sticks to demonstrate how to find the answer and regroup. Model how to check answers using addition.
303 + 228 = 531

Skill Practice COMPUTING
Guided

Present several two- and three-digit subtraction exercises. Allow students to work in pairs and use base-ten materials if necessary. Possible exercises include the following:

a. 545 − 237 = 308
b. 490 − 200 = 290
c. 689 − 350 = 339

Skill Building ENGAGING
Guided

Checkbook Game Mat

Game

Demonstrate the **Checkbook Game**. This game provides addition and subtraction applications involving money.

Principal Skills: adding and subtracting two- and three-digit numbers; maintaining a record of money transactions
Players: 2 or 3
Materials: Checkbook Game Mat, 0-5 **Number Cube,** photocopies of the balance sheet, place markers
How to Play:
1. Set up the **Checkbook Game Mat** where all students can see, preferably as a transparency on the overhead projector. Have a bank of play money available.
2. Divide the class into two teams.
3. Have one student from each team take turns going to the front of the room, rolling the cube, and exchanging the appropriate money.
4. Have students count their ongoing amount of money after each turn as you post the score on the board.

2 Use Student Pages 20

Pages 343–344 UNDERSTANDING
Independent

Have student complete pages 343 and 344 independently by using base-ten materials if needed.

Progress Monitoring

If . . . students make errors	**Then . . .** they are probably treating
such as $\begin{array}{r} 412 \\ -386 \\ \hline 174, \end{array}$	each column as a separate subtraction and subtracting the smaller digit from the greater one regardless of location. Encourage them to ask themselves in each place, "Can I subtract, or do I need to regroup?" Modeling with bundled craft sticks or other base-ten materials may be helpful.

As Students Finish

Game

Have students play the **Checkbook Game.**

Teacher Reflection

Student Page

Name _____ Date _____

Three-Digit Subtraction

Key Ideas
When subtracting three-digit numbers, you might need to regroup more than once.

Math TEKS
Number, operation, and quantitative reasoning 2.1.A Use concrete models of hundreds, tens, and ones to represent a given whole number (up to 999) in various ways.

Check the ones column first.

$$676 - 258$$

Regroup if needed. First try the tens place, and then the hundreds place.

$$\begin{array}{r} 616 \\ 67\!\!\!/8 \\ -258 \\ \hline 18 \end{array}$$ detail → $6\ \ 7\!\!\!/\ 16$

Subtract.

$$\begin{array}{r} 676 \\ -258 \\ \hline 418 \end{array} \qquad \begin{array}{r} 676 \text{ letters} \\ -258 \text{ letters} \\ \hline 418 \text{ letters} \end{array}$$

Subtract. The first exercise has been started for you.

1. $\begin{array}{r} 6\ 13 \\ 47\!\!\!/8 \\ -218 \\ \hline 255 \end{array}$ 2. $\begin{array}{r} 675 \\ -384 \\ \hline 291 \end{array}$ 3. $\begin{array}{r} 582 \\ -272 \\ \hline 310 \end{array}$ 4. $\begin{array}{r} 504 \\ -217 \\ \hline 287 \end{array}$

5. $\begin{array}{r} 608 \\ -319 \\ \hline 289 \end{array}$ 6. $\begin{array}{r} 705 \\ -204 \\ \hline 501 \end{array}$ 7. $\begin{array}{r} 600 \\ -357 \\ \hline 243 \end{array}$ 8. $\begin{array}{r} 200 \\ -169 \\ \hline 31 \end{array}$

9. $\begin{array}{r} 410 \\ -328 \\ \hline 82 \end{array}$ 10. $\begin{array}{r} 483 \\ -200 \\ \hline 283 \end{array}$ 11. $\begin{array}{r} 483 \\ -199 \\ \hline 284 \end{array}$ 12. $\begin{array}{r} 483 \\ -198 \\ \hline 285 \end{array}$

13. How can you solve Exercises 10 through 12 in your head?

   Possible answer: To subtract 483 – 200, think of taking away 2 of the 4 hundreds in 483. For 483 – 199, the answer will be 1 more than 483 – 200 because you are taking away 1 less. For 483 – 198, the answer will be 2 more than 483 – 200 because you are taking away 2 less.

14. Explain a way to check your answer to any subtraction exercise.

   Possible answer: Add the answer to the bottom number. If you get the top number, your answer is correct.

15. Rosa is reading a 485-page book. If she is on page 296, how many pages does she have left to read? **TAKS Obj. 1**

   a. 211   **(b.)** 189   c. 198   d. 179

---

3 Reflect   10

Guided Discussion   REASONING

Discuss a problem such as Problem 4 on page 344, which involves a zero in the tens place. Instead of regrouping 100 as 10 tens and ten and then regrouping 1 ten as 10 ones, suggest that students could think of 5 hundreds as 50 tens and change that to 49 tens and 10 ones. This saves one step.

$$\begin{array}{r} 4\ 9\ 14 \\ 5\!\!\!/0\!\!\!/4 \\ -217 \\ \hline 287 \end{array}$$

Have students explain their solution method.

Extended Response

Problem 14 Discuss students' answers. Students should notice that you need to regroup in order to have a large enough number to subtract from.

 Review
Cumulative Review: For cumulative review of previously learned skills, see page 349–350.

 Family Involvement: Assign the *Practice, Reteach,* or *Enrichment* activities depending on the needs of your students.
Have students play the **Checkbook Game** with a family member.

 Concept/Question Board: Encourage students to continue to post questions, answers, and examples on the Concept/Question Board.

 Math Puzzler: Integration: TEKS 2.3. A Grandma came to visit on Monday. She plans to stay for 16 days. On what day of the week will she leave? Wednesday

4 Assess and Differentiate

 Assess Use **eAssess** to record and analyze evidence of student understanding.

A Gather Evidence

Use the Daily Class Assessment Records in **Assessment** or **eAssess** to record daily observations.

Informal Assessment
✓ Guided Discussion

Did the student **UNDERSTANDING**
- ☐ make important observations?
- ☐ extend or generalize learning?
- ☐ provide insightful answers?
- ☐ pose insightful questions?

Informal Assessment
✓ Game

Did the student **ENGAGING**
- ☐ pay attention to others' contributions?
- ☐ contribute information and ideas?
- ☐ improve on a strategy?
- ☐ reflect on and check the accuracy of his or her work?

 TEKS/TAKS Practice

Use **TEKS/TAKS Practice** page 1 to assess student progress.

B Summarize Findings

Analyze and summarize assessment data for each student. Determine which Assessment Follow-Up is appropriate for each student. Use the Student Assessment Record in **Texas Assessment** or **eAssess** to update assessment records.

C Texas Assessment Follow-Up ● DIFFERENTIATE INSTRUCTION

Based on your observations, use these teaching strategies for assessment follow-up.

INTERVENTION

Review student performance on **Intervention** Lesson 9.B to see if students have mastered prerequisite skills for this lesson.

1.3.A Model and create addition and subtraction problem situations with concrete objects and write corresponding number sentences.

1.5.D Use patterns to develop strategies to solve basic addition and basic subtraction problems.

ENGLISH LEARNER

Review

Use Lesson 9.7 in **English Learner Support Guide** to review lesson concepts and vocabulary.

ENRICH

If . . . students are proficient in the lesson concepts,

Then . . . encourage them to work on the chapter projects or **Enrichment** Lesson 9.7.

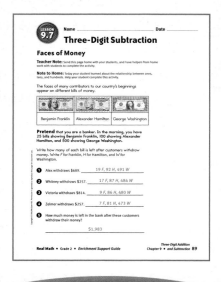

Enrichment Lesson 9.7

PRACTICE

If . . . students would benefit from additional practice,

Then . . . assign **Practice** Lesson 9.7.

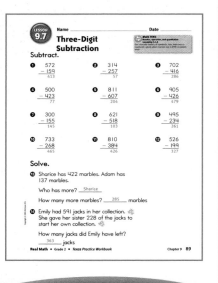

Practice Lesson 9.7

RETEACH

If . . . students are having difficulty understanding three-digit subtraction,

Then . . . reteach the concept using **Reteach** Lesson 9.7.

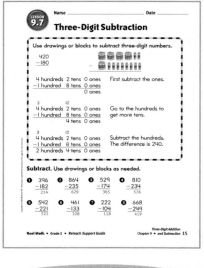

Reteach Lesson 9.7

TEXAS **Vertical Alignment**

Grade 1	**Grade 2**	Grade 3
1.11.A Identify mathematics in everyday situations.	2.12.A Identify the mathematics in everyday situations.	3.14.A Identify the mathematics in everyday situations.

Overview **LESSON 9.8**

TEXAS

Lesson Planner

OBJECTIVES
- To provide practice in adding and subtracting three-digit numbers
- To provide practice in solving word problems

MATH TEKS

Number, operation, and quantitative reasoning 2.3
Add and subtract whole numbers to solve problems.

Underlying processes and mathematical tools 2.12.A
Identify the mathematics in everyday situations.

MATH TEKS INTEGRATION

Number, operation, and quantitative reasoning 2.1.C
Use place value to compare and order whole numbers to 999 and record the comparisons using numbers and symbols ($<$, $=$, $>$).

Underlying processes and mathematical tools 2.12.A
Identify the mathematics in everyday situations.

MATERIALS
- *Number Cubes
- Checkbook Game Mat

TECHNOLOGY
ⓔ Presentation Lesson 9.8

Applications of Three-Digit Addition and Subtraction ★

Context of the Lesson This is the eighth in a series of twelve lessons that develop skills and understanding for working with 2- and 3-digit numbers. In this lesson students will continue to practice three-digit addition and subtraction exercises. Mixing the operations forces students to pay attention to the operation sign in each problem. Students will also apply those skills to word problems.

See page 329B for Math Background for teachers for this lesson.

Planning for Learning ● DIFFERENTIATE INSTRUCTION

INTERVENTION

If . . . students lack the prerequisite skill of adding two-digit numbers,

Then . . . teach *Intervention* Lesson 9.B.

TEXAS 1.3.A, 1.5.D

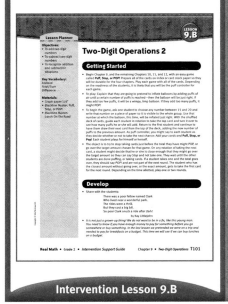

Intervention Lesson 9.B

ENGLISH LEARNER

Preview

If . . . students need language support,

Then . . . use Lesson 9.8 in *English Learner Support Guide* to preview lesson concepts and vocabulary.

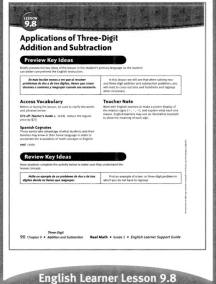

English Learner Lesson 9.8

ENRICH

If . . . students are proficient in the lesson concepts,

Then . . . emphasize additional game time.

PRACTICE

If . . . students would benefit from additional practice,

Then . . . extend Strategy Building before assigning student pages.

RETEACH

If . . . students are having difficulty understanding three-digit addition and subtraction,

Then . . . extend Guided Discussion before assigning the student pages.

Access Vocabulary
$70 off reduce the regular price by $70

Spanish Cognates
cost costo

Teaching Lesson 9.8

 TEXAS

Number, operation, and quantitative reasoning 2.3
Add and subtract whole numbers to solve problems.
Underlying processes and mathematical tools 2.12.A
Identify the mathematics in everyday situations.

Mental Math 5

 THUMBS UP

INTEGRATION: TEKS 2.1.C Write pairs of numbers on the board. Have students respond by showing thumbs-up if the number on the left is greater than the number on the right, thumbs-down if it is less, and open hand if the two numbers are equal. Use the same Find, Hide, and Show procedure used previously. Possible examples include the following:

a. 350 + 90, 450
down

b. 575, 700 − 75
down

c. 930, 530 + 300
up

d. 1,000, 875 + 125
open hand

e. 1,500 − 400, 1,100
open hand

f. 200, 300 + 95
down

1 Develop 20

Tell Students In Today's Lesson They Will
solve three-digit addition and subtraction problems.

Guided Discussion APPLYING Introductory

Have volunteers review how to complete several three-digit addition and subtraction exercises. Possible examples include the following:

a.
```
   1
  327
+ 258
─────
  585
```

b.
```
   1
  472
+ 185
─────
  657
```

c.
```
  71
  382
- 109
─────
  273
```

d.
```
  11
  203
- 142
─────
   61
```

e.
```
  746
- 513
─────
  233
```

f.
```
  522
+ 367
─────
  889
```

Strategy Building UNDERSTANDING Guided

Read word problems aloud to students, and have the class determine whether they need to add, subtract, or neither to solve the problem. Then, have volunteers come to the board and solve the problems if possible. Some examples include the following:

a. There were 350 students who took Spanish in 2006. In 2007, 416 students took Spanish. How many more students took Spanish in 2007? subtract; 416 − 350 = 66

b. Mrs. Okamato is a salesperson. She drove 312 miles on Monday and 287 miles on Tuesday. How far did she drive in the two days? add; 312 + 287 = 599

c. Mr. Ellis has $194. He wants to buy a digital music player that costs $359. How much more money does he need to save? subtract; 359 − 194 = 165

2 Use Student Pages 20

Pages 345–346 UNDERSTANDING Independent

Have students who are able complete pages 345 and 346 independently as you work in small groups with students who still need help.

Progress Monitoring

If . . . students have difficulty seeing the situation for solving the word problems,

Then . . . students should get individual or small-group attention in which they are asked to act out similar problems.

As Students Finish

Game Have students play the **Checkbook Game**.

Teacher Reflection

Student Page

Name _____ Date _____

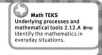
LESSON 9.8 Applications of Three-Digit Addition and Subtraction

Key Ideas

When solving a problem, it is important to understand the situation.

Math TEKS
Underlying processes and mathematical tools 2.12.A Identify the mathematics in everyday situations.

Use the table to answer the questions.

A 15-mile race is held in Big City every year. This chart shows the number of people who started and finished the race this year. It also shows how old the runners were and how many were male and female. Study the chart, and then answer the questions.

Total Number	Male	Female	Age			
			12–17	18–39	40–65	66+
Start: 745	347	398	128	439	165	13
Finish: 525	239	286	88	335	99	3

❶ How many people finished the race? ___525___

❷ How many did not finish? _745 − 525_ = 220

❸ How many people younger than 40 finished? _88 + 335_ = 423

❹ How many 18-year-old boys finished the race? _can't tell_

❺ How many people older than 65 finished? ___3___

❻ How many people older than 65 did not finish? _13 − 3 =_ 10

Textbook This lesson is available in the eTextbook.

345

LESSON 9.8 · Applications of Three-Digit Addition and Subtraction

BIG SALE
This month only.
Take $70 off every price.

$546

$375 $425

$1,230

How much will these cost this month?

❼ Computer _1,230 − 70 = 1,160_

❽ Printer _375 − 70 = 305_

❾ Stereo _425 − 70 = 355_

❿ Television _546 − 70 = 476_

⓫ A computer and a printer _1,160 + 305 = 1,465_
Multistep

⓬ Extended Response How much money would you save by buying the computer and printer now instead of next month? Show two different ways to get your answer. _____
_1,605 − 1,465 = 140, or 70 + 70 = 140_

346

Real Math • Chapter 9 • Lesson 8

---

③ Reflect

10

Guided Discussion REASONING

A newspaper reported the results of the race described on page 345. The newspaper reported that 40 young people (ages 12–17) did not finish, but only ten people over the age of 65 did not finish.

■ Critical Thinking How accurate was the report? Through discussion, help students to see that in one sense the report is accurate. But in another sense it is misleading. More than half of the elderly not finish, but far fewer than half of the young people did not finish.

This may be difficult for some students to understand and it is not important that they fully do so at this time. It is sufficient that they begin to think about how information is reported and that reported information may be incomplete or misleading.

Extended Response

Problem 12 Discuss students' answers. They can use their answer from Problem 11 to help answer Problem 12.

REAL WORLD **Curriculum Connection:** Students may enjoy researching the prices of some of their favorite items.

Review **Cumulative Review:** For cumulative review of previously learned skills, see page 349–350.

Family Involvement: Assign the *Practice, Reteach,* or *Enrichment* activities depending on the needs of your students.

Have students create three-digit addition and subtraction problems with a family member.

Concept/Question Board: Encourage students to continue to post questions, answers, and examples on the Concept/Question Board.

Math Puzzler: Integration: TEKS 2.12. A On Monday, Evan goes to work at 11:00 A.M. He begins work each day one hour earlier than the day before. What time does Evan go to work on Friday? 7:00 A.M.

4 Assess and Differentiate

 Assess Use *eAssess* to record and analyze evidence of student understanding.

A Gather Evidence

Use the Daily Class Assessment Records in *Assessment* or *eAssess* to record daily observations.

Informal Assessment
✓ **Guided Discussion**

Did the student **APPLYING**
- ❑ apply learning in new situations?
- ❑ contribute concepts?
- ❑ contribute answers?
- ❑ connect mathematics to real-world situations?

Informal Assessment
✓ **Student Pages**

Did the student **UNDERSTANDING**
- ❑ make important observations?
- ❑ extend or generalize learning?
- ❑ provide insightful answers?
- ❑ pose insightful questions?

 **TEKS/TAKS Practice**

Use *TEKS/TAKS Practice* page 97 to assess student progress.

B Summarize Findings

Analyze and summarize assessment data for each student. Determine which Assessment Follow-Up is appropriate for each student. Use the Student Assessment Record in *Texas Assessment* or *eAssess* to update assessment records.

C Texas Assessment Follow-Up • DIFFERENTIATE INSTRUCTION

Based on your observations, use these teaching strategies for assessment follow-up.

INTERVENTION	ENRICH	TEXAS PRACTICE	RETEACH
Review student performance on *Intervention* Lesson 9.B to see if students have mastered prerequisite skills for this lesson.	**If . . .** students are proficient in the lesson concepts,	**If . . .** students would benefit from additional practice,	**If . . .** students are having difficulty understanding applications of three-digit addition and subtraction,
1.3.A Model and create addition and subtraction problem situations with concrete objects and write corresponding number sentences.	**Then . . .** encourage them to work on the chapter projects or *Enrichment* Lesson 9.8.	**Then . . .** assign *Practice* Lesson 9.8.	**Then . . .** reteach the concept using *Reteach* Lesson 9.8.
1.5.D Use patterns to develop strategies to solve basic addition and basic subtraction problems.			

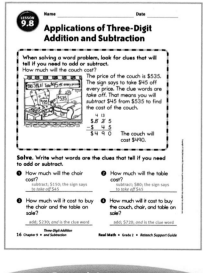

Enrichment Lesson 9.8 · Practice Lesson 9.8 · Reteach Lesson 9.8

ENGLISH LEARNER

Review

Use Lesson 9.8 in *English Learner Support Guide* to review lesson concepts and vocabulary.

Problem Solving 9.B

Comparing Strategies

Objectives

- To explore the Guess, Check, and Revise and Make a Physical Model Strategies
- To provide practice adding two- and three-digit numbers
- To provide practice presenting solutions to nonroutine problems

Materials

- Graph paper
- Scissors

See Appendix A page A24 for instruction and a rubric for problem solving

Context of the Lesson Reasoning and problem solving are prevalent in every *Real Math* lesson. This lesson and other special problem-solving lessons allow more time for students to share and compare their strategies. While continuing the Pony Express theme, this lesson provides additional opportunity for students to use the three-digit addition they have been working on in this chapter.

1 Develop 5

Tell Students In Today's Lesson They Will
balance the mail sacks on a Pony Express horse.

Guided Discussion

 Introductory

Have students look at the picture on page 347 as you describe the following problem to them.

The Pony Express rider is about to load up a fresh horse and head off to the next station. He will ride fast so people get their mail as soon as possible. He has seven sacks of mail to carry. He knows the horse runs best when the weight on it is balanced, so the rider wants to put the same weight in each saddlebag. But he can't move mail from one mail sack into another. He needs to keep the mail in the sack where it is because each sack contains mail for a different frontier settlement. How can the Pony Express rider pack the saddlebags so they weigh the same amount?

To be sure students understand the problem, ask questions such as the following:

- **How many sacks of mail does the rider have to carry?** seven
- **Are all of them the same weight?** No; some of them are heavier than others.
- **What do lbs and oz stand for?** pounds and ounces
- **How much does the first sack weigh?** 4 pounds 6 ounces, or 70 ounces
- **What is the problem asking?** how to pack the bags into two saddlebags so both saddlebags weigh the same amount

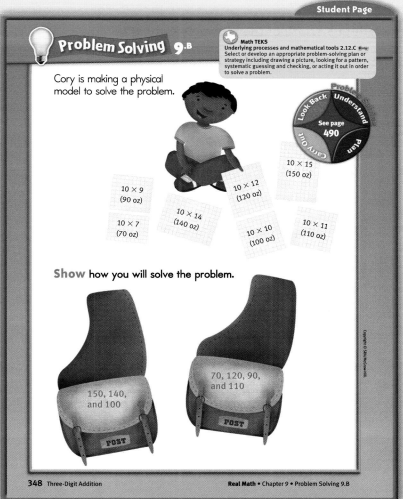

Underlying processes and mathematical tools 2.12.C
Select or develop an appropriate problem-solving plan or strategy including drawing a picture, looking for a pattern, systematic guessing and checking, or acting it out in order to solve a problem.

Number, operation, and quantitative reasoning 2.3.B
addition and subtraction of two-digit numbers with objects, pictures, words and numbers

 Use Student Pages 25

Guided Discussion

 Introductory

Analyzing Sample Solution 1

Have students look at the picture on page 347 of Lucy solving the problem. Ask questions about her strategy, such as the following:

- **What did Lucy do first?** She added the weights of four of the bags.
- **What is she doing now?** She is adding the weights of the other bags.
- **How will this help her solve the problem?** She will check to see if the two groups have the same weight. If they do, then the sacks can be divided this way.
- **If the weights are different, what might she do?** She can try a different combination so there will be more weight on the lighter side and less weight on the heavier side.

Analyzing Sample Solution 2

Tell students that Cory is using a different strategy to try to solve the problem. Have students look at the picture on page 348 of Cory's approach. Ask questions such as the following:

- **What do Cory's cut-out rectangles stand for?** Each rectangle stands for a sack of mail.
- **Why are they different sizes?** because each mail sack is a different weight
- **What is the length and width of the rectangle Cory is holding?** 12 squares long and 10 squares wide
- **Does anyone know how many squares are in that rectangle?** 12 rows of 10 equals 120.
- **Why did Cory make it that size?** to stand for the mail sack that weighs 120 ounces
- **Why is Cory putting rectangles in a line?** Seeing how long a line they make is a way of seeing the total.
- **How will this help him solve the problem?** He will be able to try different combinations until he has two lines that are the same length.
- **How will you work on this problem?** Allow students to share what they like about Lucy's and Cory's strategies and what they would do differently.

Skill Building

Have students work on the problem individually or in pairs. They may use Lucy's strategy, Cory's strategy, or one of their own. Provide support as needed, remembering to suggest approaches rather than showing them the answer. Remind students to check their answers.

 Reflect 10

 Knowledge Age Skills

Effective Communication Ask students to share their solutions and their strategies. In discussion, bring out these points:

- Different strategies can be used to solve the same problem.
- Different people might prefer different strategies for solving problems.
- There are different ways to add a group of large numbers.

Sample Solutions Strategies

Students might use one or more of the following strategies instead of or in conjunction with the strategies presented on student pages 347 and 348.

Act It Out

Students might use base-ten materials to represent the various weights and then use a Guess, Check, and Revise Strategy.

Number Sense

Students could combine all the weights to find the total of all the bags, divide that total into two equal weights, and then try to find combinations that equal those weights.

Assess 15

When evaluating student work, focus not only on the correctness of the answer but also on whether the student thought rationally about the problem. Questions to consider include the following:

- Did the student understand the problem?
- Did the student understand the Sample Solutions Strategies?
- How did the student combine the weights?
- Was the student able to explain his or her strategy?

Cumulative Review

Use Pages 349–350

Use the Cumulative Review as a review of concepts and skills that students have previously learned.

Here are different ways that you can assign these problems to your students as they work through the chapter:

- With some of the lessons in the chapter, assign a set of cumulative review problems to be completed as practice or for homework.
  Lesson 9.1—Problem 1
  Lesson 9.2—Problems 2–3
  Lesson 9.3—Problems 4–7
  Lesson 9.4—Problems 8–9
  Lesson 9.5—Problems 10–15
  Lesson 9.6—Problems 16–18
  Lesson 9.7—Problems 19–22
  Lesson 9.8—Problems 23–24

- At any point during the chapter, assign part or all of the cumulative review problems to be completed as practice or for homework.

Cumulative Review

Problem 1 reviews finding the perimeter, Lesson 4.2. TEKS: 2.9.A

Problems 2–3 review place value through 10,000, Lesson 9.1. TEKS: 2.1.B

Problems 4–7 review fractions of numbers, Lesson 7.8. TEKS: 2.2.B

Problems 8–9 review regrouping for addition, Lesson 5.3. TEKS: 2.3.B

Problems 10–15 review comparing numbers through 1,000, Lesson 9.3. TEKS: 2.5.B

Problems 16–18 review two-digit subtraction, Lesson 6.6. **BIG IDEAS** Number and Operations and Algebra TEKS: 2.3.B

Problems 19–22 review obtuse, acute, and right angles, Lesson 8.5. TEKS: 2.10.B

Problems 23–24 review adding multiples of ten, Lesson 9.4. TEKS: 2.1.A

Progress Monitoring

If . . . students miss more than one problem in a section, **Then . . .** refer to the indicated lesson for remediation suggestions.

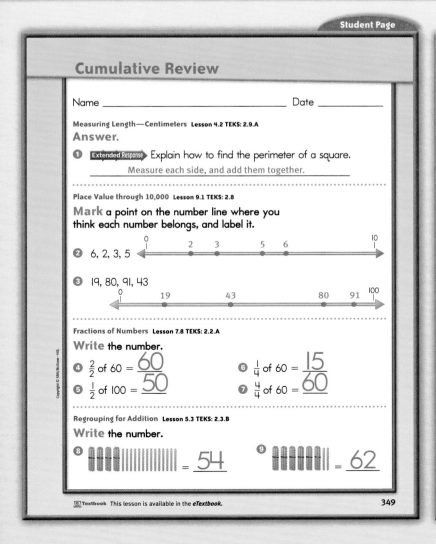

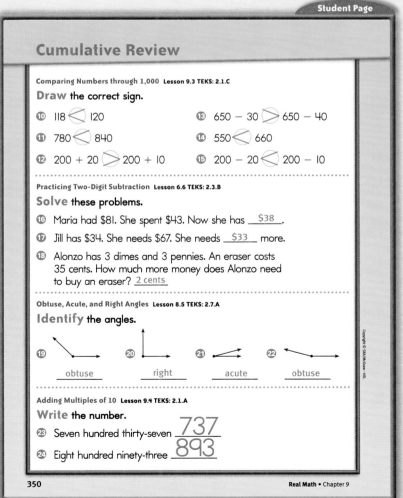

Individual Oral Assessment

Purpose of the Test

The Individual Oral Assessment is designed to measure students' growing knowledge of chapter concepts. It is administered individually to each student, and it requires oral responses from each student. The test takes about five minutes to complete. See *Texas Assessment* for detailed instructions for administering and interpreting the test, and record students' answers on the Student Assessment Recording Sheet.

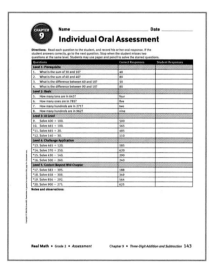

Texas Assessment, page 143

Directions

Read each question to the student, and record his or her oral response. If the student answers correctly, go to the next question. Stop when the student misses two questions at the same level. Students may use paper and pencil to solve the starred questions.

Materials

None

Questions

Level 1: Prerequisite 2.3
1. What is the sum of 30 and 10? 40
2. What is the sum of 40 and 40? 80
3. What is the difference of 60 and 10? 50
4. What is the difference of 90 and 10? 80

Level 2: Basic 2.1
5. How many tens are in 643? 4
6. How many ones are in 785? 5
7. How many hundreds are in 271? 2
8. How many hundreds are in 962? 9

Level 3: At Level 2.3
9. Solve 400 + 100. 500
10. Solve 465 + 100. 565
*11. Solve 465 + 20. 485
*12. Solve 140 − 30. 110

Level 4: Challenge Application 2.3
*13. Solve 465 + 120. 585
*14. Solve 370 + 250. 620
*15. Solve 430 − 140. 290
*16. Solve 500 − 260. 240

Level 5: Content Beyond Mid-Chapter 2.3
*17. Solve 583 − 395. 188
*18. Solve 658 − 309. 349
*19. Solve 856 − 292. 564
*20. Solve 900 − 275. 625

TEXAS

V e r t i c a l   A l i g n m e n t

Grade 1	Grade 2	Grade 3
1.1.c Identify individual coins by name and value and describe relationships among them.	**2.3.E** Describe how the cent symbol, dollar symbol, and the decimal point are used to name the value of a collection of coins.	**3.1.C** Determine the value of a collection of coins and bills.

Overview   **LESSON 9.9**

TEXAS

Lesson Planner

OBJECTIVES
- To provide applications involving dollars and cents
- To introduce the decimal point in the limited context of dollars and cents
- To teach students to convert between dollars and cents and between cents and dollars

 MATH TEKS

Number, operation, and quantitative reasoning 2.3.E
Describe how the cent symbol, dollar symbol, and the decimal point are used to name the value of a collection of coins.

MATH TEKS INTEGRATION

Number, operation, and quantitative reasoning 2.3.B
Model addition and subtraction of two-digit numbers with objects, pictures, words, and numbers.

Underlying processes and mathematical tools 2.12.A
Identify the mathematics in everyday situations.

MATERIALS
- *Number Cubes
- *Play Money (dollars and cents)

TECHNOLOGY
- Presentation Lesson 9.9
- MathTools Coins and Money
- Building Blocks Word Problems 3

Adding and Subtracting Money ★

Context of the Lesson This is the ninth in a series of twelve lessons that develop skills and understanding for working with 2- and 3-digit numbers. In this lesson students will be introduced to the decimal point in the context of dollars and cents. They will apply the addition and subtraction of three-digit numbers to money situations by changing dollars into cents. Place value, addition, and subtraction involving decimals are formally introduced in Grade 3, Chapter 10.

See page 329B for Math Background for teachers for this lesson.

Planning for Learning ● DIFFERENTIATE INSTRUCTION

INTERVENTION

If . . . students lack the prerequisite skill of subtracting two-digit numbers,

Then . . . teach *Intervention* Lesson 9.C.

1.3.A, 1.5.D

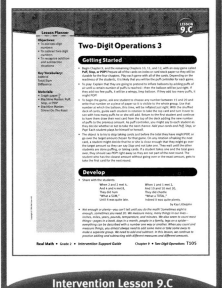

Intervention Lesson 9.C

ENGLISH LEARNER

Preview

If . . . students need language support,

Then . . . use Lesson 9.9 in *English Learner Support Guide* to preview lesson concepts and vocabulary.

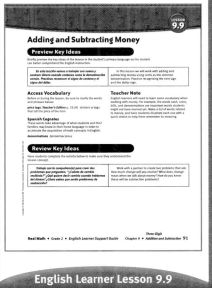

English Learner Lesson 9.9

ENRICH

If . . . students are proficient in the lesson concepts,

Then . . . emphasize additional game time.

PRACTICE

If . . . students would benefit from additional practice,

Then . . . extend Guided Discussion before assigning student pages.

RETEACH

If . . . students are having difficulty understanding three-digit addition,

Then . . . extend Skill Building before assigning the student pages.

Access Vocabulary
price tags stickers or tags that tell the price of the item

Spanish Cognates
denominations denominaciones

Teaching Lesson 9.9

 TEXAS

Number, operation, and quantitative reasoning 2.3.E Describe how the cent symbol, dollar symbol, and the decimal point are used to name the value of a collection of

Mental Math — 5

  INTEGRATION: TEKS 2.3.B Present addition and subtraction exercises involving tens such as the following:

a. 60 − 30 = 30
b. 90 − 90 = 0
c. 90 − 50 = 40
d. 80 −50 = 30
e. 60 + 40 = 100
f. 80 − 0 = 80
g. 70 + 20 = 90
h. 20 + 80 = 100

1 Develop — 20

Tell Students In Today's Lesson They Will
convert dollars into cents.

Guided Discussion MathTools **Introductory** UNDERSTANDING

Skill Building

 Demonstrate converting cents into dollars and cents by using a decimal point and a dollar sign. Use play money or **eMathTools: Coins and Money** to demonstrate money amounts. Tell students that 1 dollar is worth 100 cents. Ask students questions such as the following:

- **How many cents are there in 2 dollars?** 200
- **How many cents are there in 3 dollars?** 300 **In 10 dollars?** 1,000
- **How many dollars are worth 500 cents?** 5 **300 cents?** 3
- **How many whole dollars in 126 cents?** 1 **How many cents left?** 26
- **Critical Thinking** **How would we write it?** Write on the board or overhead projector that 126 cents can also be written $1.26, which is called 1 dollar and 26 cents. Have students practice saying this aloud with you.
- **How many dollars in 475 cents?** 4 **How many cents left?** 75
- **How would we write it?** $4.75 **How do we say this?** four dollars and seventy-five cents

Converting Money **Guided**
Now present dollar and cent amounts, and have students convert them into cents.

Ask students questions such as the following:

- **How would you write 320¢ using the dollar symbol?** $3.20
- **How would your write $5.75 using the cents symbol?** 575¢

Provide several more examples.

Progress Monitoring

If . . . students have difficulty placing the decimal point when writing cents as dollars and cents,

Then . . . encourage them to think, *how many whole dollars is this,* and to place the decimal after the dollars.

2 Use Student Pages — 15

Pages 351–352 **Independent**
Have students complete page 351 independently. Give individual help to those students who are having difficulty. Have students compare page 352 in groups.

When completing these problems, students should realize that to add cents, they must "drop" the decimal point. They must then align the numbers according to place value. Make sure students understand how to correctly align numbers.

For example: $1.50 + $ .50 =   150
                                          + 50

As Students Finish

Game Allow students to play the game of their choice, or assign a game based on student needs.

Building Blocks Have students use **Word Problems 3** to practice word problems.

Student Page

Name _____   Date _____

LESSON 9.9 Adding and Subtracting Money

Key Ideas

$1 = 100 cents $1.25 = 125 cents

Math TEKS
Number, operation, and quantitative reasoning 2.3.E Describe how the cent symbol, dollar symbol, and the decimal point are used to name the value of a collection of coins.

Write how much.

1. __200__ cents = $2.00
2. __1,000__ cents = $10.00
3. __150__ cents = $1.50
4. __96__ cents = $0.96
5. __243__ cents = $2.43
6. __500__ cents = $5.00

7. **Extended Response** How many cents do the horse and the hat cost altogether? __725__ cents

$$\begin{array}{r} 650 \\ + 75 \\ \hline 725 \end{array}$$

Explain how you wrote the answer.
To add cent amounts, you "drop" the decimal, align the two sets of numbers according to their place value, and then add.

 8. Leslie has $10. Suppose she buys the horse and the hat with a $10 bill. How much change will she get? __275__ cents

Multistep

Textbook This lesson is available in the *eTextbook*.   351

LESSON 9.9 · Adding and Subtracting Money

Solve the following problems.

9. John earns $2.75 an hour for working in the garden. How much does he earn in 2 hours? __$5.50, or 550 cents__

10. Jason had $5.50. He spent some of the money. Now he has $2.75. How much did he spend? __$2.75, or 275 cents__

11. A large container of juice costs $2.35. A smaller container costs $1.45. Which is the better buy? __can't tell; It depends on the sizes of the containers and how thirsty the person is.__

12. Regular admission to the ball game is $4.75. Admission for children is $2.30. How much will it cost a father and his young daughter to go to the ball game together? __$7.05, or 705 cents__

13. April bought a book for $3.75. She gave the cashier $5.00. How much change should she get? __$1.25, or 125 cents__

14. Mark bought a puzzle for $3.76 and a pen for $1.25. How much did he pay for both? __$5.01, or 501 cents__

15. **Extended Response** How do you change from cents to dollars?

352   Real Math • Chapter 9 • Lesson 9

---

3 Reflect   10

Guided Discussion e MathTools REASONING

Begin a discussion that focuses attention on the approximate prices of things or events your students find interesting.

One way to do this is to have advertisements from a local newspaper available. Begin by describing something and have students make estimates of what it costs. After some discussion, tell the students what the price is and write that information on the board. When 3 to 5 things are listed on the board, have students make up word problems using that information for their classmates to solve.

Extended Response

Problem 7 Discuss students' answers. Students should have realized that to add cent amounts, you "drop" the decimal, align the two sets of numbers according to their place value, and then add.

Problem 15 Discuss students' answers. Students should have recognized that the number of whole dollars are placed before the decimal and the number of cents left over are placed after the decimal.

✓ Use Mastery Checkpoint 15 found in *Texas Assessment* to evaluate student mastery of familiarity with money. By this time, students should be able to correctly answer eighty percent of the Mastery Checkpoint items.

TEXAS TEKS Checkup

Number, operation, and quantitative reasoning 2.3.E

Describe how the cent symbol, dollar symbol, and the decimal point are used to name the value of a collection of coins.

Use this problem to assess students' progress towards standards mastery:

How much money is

A $4.25   C $5.00
B $4.50   D $5.50

Follow-Up
If...students have difficulty with understanding money,

Then...have students practice the concept using *Practice* Lesson 9.9.

Concept/Question Board: Have students attempt to answer any unanswered questions on the Concept/Question Board.

Math Puzzler: Integration: TEKS 2.12. A Will went on vacation Monday. His vacation lasted 15 days. On which day of the week did his vacation end? Tuesday

4 Assess and Differentiate

 **Assess** Use *eAssess* to record and analyze evidence of student understanding.

A Gather Evidence

Use the Daily Class Assessment Records in *Texas Assessment* or *eAssess* to record daily observations.

Formal Assessment

☑ **Mastery Checkpoint**

Did the student
- ❑ use correct procedures?
- ❑ respond with at least 80% accuracy?

 TEKS/TAKS Practice

Use *TEKS/TAKS Practice* pages 31–33 to assess student progress.

Texas Assessment page 94

B Summarize Findings

Analyze and summarize assessment data for each student. Determine which Assessment Follow-Up is appropriate for each student. Use the Student Assessment Record in *Texas Assessment* or *eAssess* to update assessment records.

C Texas Assessment Follow-Up • DIFFERENTIATE INSTRUCTION

Based on your observations, use these teaching strategies for assessment follow-up.

TEXAS

INTERVENTION	ENRICH	PRACTICE	RETEACH
Review student performance on *Intervention* Lesson 9.C to see if students have mastered prerequisite skills for this lesson. **1.3.A** Model and create addition and subtraction problem situations with concrete objects and write corresponding number sentences. **1.5.D** Use patterns to develop strategies to solve basic addition and basic subtraction problems.	**If . . .** students are proficient in the lesson concepts, **Then . . .** encourage them to work on the chapter projects or *Enrichment* Lesson 9.9.	**If . . .** students would benefit from additional practice, **Then . . .** assign *Practice* Lesson 9.9.	**If . . .** students are having difficulty adding and subtracting money, **Then . . .** have them use bills and coins to make specific amounts of money and make change.

ENGLISH LEARNER

Review

Use Lesson 9.9 in *English Learner Support Guide* to review lesson concepts and vocabulary.

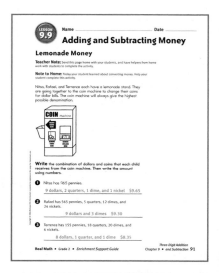

Enrichment Lesson 9.9

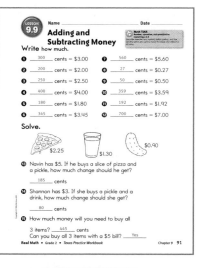

Practice Lesson 9.9

Grade 1	Grade 2	Grade 3
1.3 Recognize and solve problems in addition and subtraction situations.	**2.3** Add and subtract whole numbers to solve problems.	**3.3** Add and subtract to solve meaningful problems involving whole numbers.

Overview — LESSON 9.10

TEXAS

Shortcuts for Three-Digit Addition and Subtraction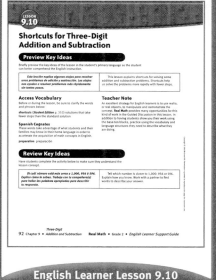

Context of the Lesson This is the tenth in a series of twelve lessons that develop skills and understanding for working with 2- and 3-digit numbers. In this lesson students will continue to practice adding and subtracting and approximating answers.

See page 329B for Math Background for teachers for this lesson.

Planning for Learning ● DIFFERENTIATE INSTRUCTION

INTERVENTION
If . . . students lack the prerequisite skill of adding two-digit numbers,

Then . . . teach *Intervention* Lesson 9.C.

 1.3.A, 1.5.D

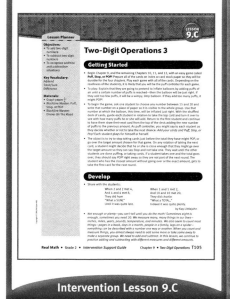

Intervention Lesson 9.C

ENGLISH LEARNER
Preview

If . . . students need language support,

Then . . . use Lesson 9.10 in *English Learner Support Guide* to preview lesson concepts and vocabulary.

English Learner Lesson 9.10

ENRICH
If . . . students are proficient in the lesson concepts,

Then . . . emphasize additional game time.

PRACTICE
If . . . students would benefit from additional practice,

Then . . . extend Skill Building before assigning student pages.

RETEACH
If . . . students are having difficulty understanding three-digit addition and subtraction,

Then . . . extend Guided Discussion before assigning the student pages.

Access Vocabulary
shortcuts a solution that takes fewer steps than the standard solution

Spanish Cognates
preparation preparación

Lesson Planner

OBJECTIVES
To provide practice in using mental math strategies with addition and subtraction

MATH TEKS

Number, operation, and quantitative reasoning 2.3
Add and subtract whole numbers to solve problems.

MATH TEKS INTEGRATION

Number, operation, and quantitative reasoning 2.3.B
Model addition and subtraction of two-digit numbers with objects, pictures, words, and numbers.

Underlying processes and mathematical tools 2.12.A
Identify the mathematics in everyday situations.

MATERIALS
*Number Cubes

TECHNOLOGY
e Presentation Lesson 9.10
e MathTools Base Ten
e Games Make 1,000 Game

Teaching Lesson 9.10

TEXAS

Number, operation, and quantitative reasoning 🔑
Add and subtract whole numbers to solve problems.

Mental Math 5

  INTEGRATION: TEKS 2.3.B Provide addition and subtraction exercises involving tens, such as the following:

a. 30 + 70 = 100   **b.** 80 − 50 = 30   **c.** 40 + 40 = 80
d. 140 − 80 = 60   **e.** 110 − 50 = 60   **f.** 100 − 80 = 20

1 Develop 20

Tell Students In Today's Lesson They Will

use strategies to solve addition and subtraction problems.

Guided Discussion 🖥 MathTools UNDERSTANDING

Introductory

Discuss and practice strategies to solve addition and subtraction problems.

Addition Strategies

 Write a problem on the board or overhead projector, and then use base-ten blocks, interlocking cubes, craft sticks, or **eMathTools: Base Ten** to model the strategy of adding a number to one addend and taking away that number from the other. A possible example includes the following:

- Write 37 + 19 on the board or overhead projector.
- Show three bunches of 10 and 7 more in one pile and one bunch of 10 and 9 more in another pile.
- Then move one counter from the 37 pile to the 19 pile to model 36 + 20.
- Discuss how changing 37 + 19 to 36 + 20 makes it easier to solve the problem mentally.
- Repeat with several three-digit addition problems such as the following:

  399 + 499 400 + 498, or 898

  299 + 215 300 + 214, or 514

Subtraction Strategies

Show how to relate subtraction problems to easier calculations.

Write a problem on the board, and use base-ten blocks or **eMathTools: Base Ten** to demonstrate the strategy of taking away or adding a number to *both* numbers to find the difference. A possible example includes the following:

- Write 37 − 19 on the board.
- Show three bunches of 10 and 7 more in one pile and one bunch of 10 and 9 more in another pile.
- Then add one counter to each pile to make 38 − 20.
- Demonstrate using base-ten blocks or **eMathTools: Base Ten** that the difference is the same for both problems. Show

37 − 19 = 18 with 3 tens rods and 7 cubes minus 1 tens rod and 9 cubes, and then solve. Show 38 − 20 = 18 with 3 tens rods and 8 cubes minus 2 tens rods, and then solve.

Remind students that in subtraction we can add or subtract the same amount to both numbers to keep the difference the same.

Repeat with several three-digit subtraction problems such as the following:

370 − 231 and 369 − 230 = 139

Skill Building APPLYING

Guided

Game Make 1,000 Game

 This game involves estimating sums and using place value to create addends to reach the sum of 1,000. Demonstrate by playing a round with 5 or 6 students. Directions can be found on student page 354. If you want, you may play the whole-class version of this game.

2 Use Student Pages 20

Pages 353–354 ENGAGING

Independent

Have students complete page 353 independently by using shortcuts.

Progress Monitoring

If . . . students insist on using a paper-and-pencil algorithm for the exercises on page 353, or if they have difficulty using a shortcut,

Then . . . do not insist that they use a shortcut. Do, however, try to give mental math exercises from time to time for which students have the opportunity to use shortcuts. These skills will develop gradually and extensive extra teaching is not necessary at this time.

As Students Finish

Game Have students play the **Make 1,000 Game** in pairs.

🖥 Games *Make 1,000 Game*

🖥 MathTools Have students create problems and identify shortcuts by using **Base Ten.**

Student Page

Name _____ Date _____

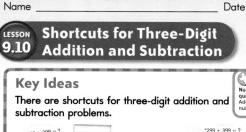

LESSON 9.10 Shortcuts for Three-Digit Addition and Subtraction

Key Ideas

There are shortcuts for three-digit addition and subtraction problems.

Math TEKS
Number, operation, and quantitative reasoning 2.3
Add and subtract whole numbers to solve problems.

"299 + 399 = ?
That's 2 less than 700."

"299 + 399 = ?
That's the same as 300 + 400 − 2."

Use shortcuts if you can.

Add.

1. 300 + 400 = _700_
2. 300 + 399 = _699_
3. 299 + 400 = _699_
4. 299 + 399 = _698_

5. 200 + 500 = _700_
6. 201 + 499 = _700_
7. 499 + 201 = _700_
8. 499 + 202 = _701_

Subtract.

9. 400 − 100 = _300_
10. 400 − 99 = _301_
11. 399 − 99 = _300_
12. 401 − 99 = _302_

13. 375 − 100 = _275_
14. 374 − 99 = _275_
15. 373 − 98 = _275_
16. 372 − 97 = _275_

Textbook This lesson is available in the *eTextbook*.

353

Student Page

 Game

Math TEKS
Number, operation, and quantitative reasoning 2.3
Add and subtract whole numbers to solve problems.

Addition and Strategies Practice

Make 1,000 Game

Players: Two or more

Materials:
- Pencil and paper
- *Number Cubes* (two 0–5 and two 5–10)

HOW TO PLAY

1. Each player chooses and writes down any number between 250 and 750. This is the starting number.
2. Player One rolls all four cubes. All players use the numbers rolled to make a one-, two-, or three-digit number. If a 10 is rolled, that cube is rolled again.
3. All players add the number they made to their starting number. Everyone must do this at the same time without sharing information, and players are not permitted to change numbers after they have been chosen.
4. The goal is to get as close to 1,000 as possible without going over 1,000.
5. The winner of the round is the person who gets closest to 1,000 without going over. That person gets to roll the cubes in the next round of play.

354

Games This game is available as an *eGame*.

---

3 Reflect

10

Guided Discussion REASONING

Present two- or three-digit addition and subtraction exercises on the board, and allow students to find possible shortcuts. As students describe possible shortcuts, allow students to agree, disagree, or provide other interpretations. Possible exercises include the following:

a. 375 + 499 374 + 500
b. 875 − 199 876 − 200
c. 276 + 298 274 + 300
d. 239 − 198 241 − 200
e. 372 + 458 no easy shortcut
f. 873 − 185 no easy shortcut

☑ Use Mastery Checkpoint 16 found in *Assessment* to evaluate student mastery of three-digit addition and subtraction. By this time, students should be able to correctly answer eighty percent of the Mastery Checkpoint items.

 Cumulative Review: For cumulative review of previously learned skills, see page 361–362.

 Family Involvement: Assign the *Practice, Reteach,* or *Enrichment* activities depending on the needs of your students.

Have students play the **Make 1,000 Game** with family members.

 Concept/Question Board: Have students attempt to answer any unanswered questions on the Concept/Question Board.

 Math Puzzler: 🌎 **Integration: TEKS 2.12. A** Leroy saves $1 every day for one year. So far he has saved $187. How much more will he save by the end of the year? $178

4 Assess and Differentiate

 **Assess** Use *eAssess* to record and analyze evidence of student understanding.

A Gather Evidence

Use the Daily Class Assessment Records in *Texas Assessment* or *eAssess* to record daily observations.

Formal Assessment

☑ **Mastery Checkpoint**

Did the student
- ❏ use correct procedures?
- ❏ respond with at least 80% accuracy?

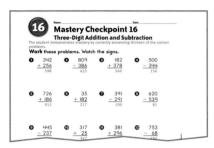

Texas Assessment page 95

TEKS/TAKS Practice

Use *TEKS/TAKS Practice* pages 21–24 to assess student progress.

B Summarize Findings

Analyze and summarize assessment data for each student. Determine which Assessment Follow-Up is appropriate for each student. Use the Student Assessment Record in *Texas Assessment* or *eAssess* to update assessment records.

C Texas Assessment Follow-Up • DIFFERENTIATE INSTRUCTION

Based on your observations, use these teaching strategies for assessment follow-up.

INTERVENTION

Review student performance on *Intervention* Lesson 9.C to see if students have mastered prerequisite skills for this lesson.

1.3.A Model and create addition and subtraction problem situations with concrete objects and write corresponding number sentences.

1.5.D Use patterns to develop strategies to solve basic addition and basic subtraction problems.

ENGLISH LEARNER

Review

Use Lesson 9.10 in *English Learner Support Guide* to review lesson concepts and vocabulary.

ENRICH

If . . . students are proficient in the lesson concepts,

Then . . . encourage them to work on the chapter projects or *Enrichment* Lesson 9.10.

Enrichment Lesson 9.10

PRACTICE

If . . . students would benefit from additional practice,

Then . . . assign *Practice* Lesson 9.10.

Practice Lesson 9.10

RETEACH

If . . . students are having difficulty understanding addition and subtraction shortcuts,

Then . . . review mental math strategies such as adding 1 to a number and taking away 1 from the other.

TEXAS **Vertical Alignment**

Grade 1	Grade 2	Grade 3
1.5.C Compare and order whole numbers using place value	2.5.B Use patterns in place value to compare and order whole numbers through 999.	3.1.B Use place value to compare and order whole numbers through 9,999.

Overview LESSON **9.11**

TEXAS

Lesson Planner

OBJECTIVES

- To introduce rounding to the nearest hundred
- To provide practice using rounding to estimate sums and differences

MATH TEKS

Number, operation, and quantitative reasoning 2.3.B
Model addition and subtraction of two-digit numbers with objects, pictures, words, and numbers.

Patterns, relationships, and algebraic thinking 2.5.B 🗝
Use patterns in place value to compare and order whole numbers through 999.

Geometry and spatial reasoning 2.8
Use whole numbers to locate and name points on a number line.

MATH TEKS INTEGRATION

Number, operation, and quantitative reasoning 2.3.B
Model addition and subtraction of two-digit numbers with objects, pictures, words, and numbers.

Underlying processes and mathematical tools 2.12.A
Identify the mathematics in everyday situations.

MATERIALS

- *Number Cubes 🎲
- *Calculators

TECHNOLOGY

ℯ Presentation Lesson 9.11

Round to 10 and 100 with Applications

Context of the Lesson This is the eleventh in a series of twelve lessons that develop skills and understanding for working with 2- and 3-digit numbers. This is the first lesson on rounding with particular focus on rounding to 10 and 100. More work with rounding within the contexts of estimating measures and making approximate calculations will recur throughout the program. More formal work with rounding will be covered in the third grade.

See page 329B for Math Background for teachers for this lesson.

Planning for Learning ● DIFFERENTIATE INSTRUCTION

INTERVENTION

If . . . students lack the prerequisite skill of recognizing addition and subtraction situations,

Then . . . teach **Intervention** Lesson 9.C.

 1.3.A, 1.5.D

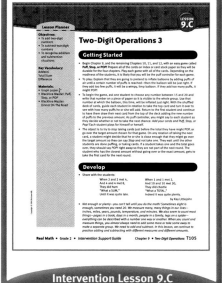

Intervention Lesson 9.C

ENGLISH LEARNER

Preview

If . . . students need language support,

Then . . . use Lesson 9.11 in **English Learner Support Guide** to preview lesson concepts and vocabulary.

English Learner Lesson 9.11

ENRICH

If . . . students are proficient in the lesson concepts,

Then . . . emphasize Guided Discussion in Reflect.

PRACTICE

If . . . students would benefit from additional practice,

Then . . . extend Skill Practice before assigning student pages.

RETEACH

If . . . students are having difficulty understanding rounding to the nearest hundred,

Then . . . extend Skill Building before assigning the student pages.

Access Vocabulary	**Spanish Cognates**
pick the number choose the number	**round** ronda

*Manipulative Kit Item 🗝 = Key standard

Teaching Lesson 9.11

TEXAS

Number, operation, and quantitative reasoning 2.3.B
Model addition and subtraction of two-digit numbers with objects, pictures, words, and numbers.
Patterns, relationships, and algebraic thinking 2.5.B
Use patterns in place value to compare and order whole numbers through 999.
Geometry and spatial reasoning 2.8
Use whole numbers to locate and name points on a numbe

Mental Math 5

 INTEGRATION: TEKS 2.3.B Present two-digit addition or subtraction exercises for students to show the sums or differences. Possible examples include the following:

a. 12 + 19 = 31

b. 26 − 11 = 15

c. 47 − 29 = 18

d. 53 + 39 = 92

e. 35 − 12 = 23

f. 46 − 7 = 39

1 Develop 20

Tell Students In Today's Lesson They Will
learn how and when to round numbers.

Guided Discussion APPLYING   Introductory
Complete the examples on student page 355 with the class. Discuss why rounding is appropriate in some situations but not in others.

Skill Building UNDERSTANDING   Guided

Rounding to 10
Review rounding to 10. Draw a number line from 20 to 50 on the board. Label each multiple of 10 (20, 30, 40, and 50). Then present this scenario: *Julio, Kimberly, and RaShaun work together in an office. Julio is 30 years old and RaShaun is 40 years old. If Kimberly is 37 years old, is she closer in age to Julio or RaShaun?* To aid students in finding the answer to this problem, ask questions such as the following:

■ **Is 37 closer to 30 or 40?** 40

■ **Is there any multiple of 10 that is closer to 37 than 40?** no

Explain to students that they can round numbers to estimate sums and differences.

- Draw a number line from 0 to 100 on the board.
- Demonstrate rounding 58 + 27 as 60 + 30, or about 90.

Repeat the process for differences such as 72 − 39, which rounds to 70 − 40 = 30.

Discuss and practice rounding numbers that have a five in the ones place. Students should see the numbers are equally close to the higher and lower ten.

Rounding to 100
Now draw a number line from 0 to 1,000. Mark each multiple of 100. Demonstrate rounding a three-digit number to the nearest hundred. Ask students a question such as the following:

■ **Is the number 175 closer to 100 or 200?** 200

Discuss and practice rounding numbers that have a fifty in the tens place. Students should notice that the numbers are equally

close to the higher and lower hundred. Repeat this process for more three-digit numbers, emphasizing which hundred the number is closest to.

Skill Practice COMPUTING   Guided
Present a series of two- and three-digit numbers on the board. Have students round to the nearest ten or hundred. Exercises may include the following:

a. 185 200

b. 124 100

c. 47 50

d. 75 70 or 80

e. 210 200

f. 670 700

g. 430 400

h. 890 900

Check for student understanding during this time. Discuss the answers when everyone has finished.

2 Use Student Pages 20

Pages 355–356 UNDERSTANDING Independent
Have students complete pages 355 and 356 independently. Allow students to use calculators to find the exact answers and the differences between their estimates and their exact answers.

Progress Monitoring

If . . . students have difficulty rounding to the nearest hundred,

Then . . . review rounding to the nearest ten, for example, 77 80. Then expand the same number to the hundreds place, for example, 770 800.

As Students Finish

 Allow students to play a game of their choice, or assign a game based on student needs.

Student Page

Name _____ Date _____

LESSON 9.11 **Round to 10 and 100 with Applications**

Key Ideas

Rounding numbers is sometimes useful.

Sometimes we decide to round up.
Sometimes we decide to round down.
Sometimes we decide not to round because
we need an exact answer.

Whether we round up or down or not at all depends on
the situation. It depends on how we will use the numbers.

> **Math TEKS**
> Patterns, relationships, and
> algebraic thinking 2.5.B
> Use patterns in place value to
> compare and order whole
> numbers through 999.

Mario has $700. He wants to
know if he has enough money
to buy the computer and printer.
He rounds up both prices to the
nearest hundred.

479 rounds to 500
134 rounds to 200

❶ 500 + 200 = **700**

Brown's Computer Store	
Computer	$479
Printer	$134
Computer table	$287
DVD case	$45
Super software package	$297

The computer and printer would cost less than $700.
Mario has enough money.

Mrs. Brown owns the computer store. She knows
that she will make a profit if she can sell the
computer and printer for at least $450. To find
out, she rounds down to the nearest hundred.

479 rounds to 400
134 rounds to 100

Textbook This lesson is available in the *eTextbook*. 355

Student Page

LESSON 9.11 · Round to 10 and 100 with Applications

❷ 400 + 100 = **500**
$500 is more than $450. Mrs. Brown will make a profit.

Susan wants to know the approximate cost of the
computer and printer. To find out, she rounds both
prices to the nearest ten.

479 is closer to 480 than to 470. She rounds up to 480.
134 is closer to 130 than to 140. She rounds down to 130.

Susan adds the rounded numbers.

❸ 480 + 130 = **610**
The computer and printer cost about $ **610** .

Susan decides to buy the computer and printer,
so she needs the exact price.

❹ 479 + 134 = **613**
The computer and printer will cost exactly $ **613** .

Round each number to the nearest hundred.
If the number is halfway between, round
up. The first exercise is done for you.

❺ 745 700
❻ 639 **600**
❼ 210 **200**
❽ 453 **500**
❾ 650 **700**
❿ 180 **200**

Round each number to the nearest ten. The first exercise is
done for you. If the number is halfway between, round up.

⓫ 379 380
⓬ 524 **520**
⓭ 671 **670**
⓮ 454 **450**
⓯ 275 **280**
⓰ 823 **820**

356 **Real Math** • Chapter 9 • Lesson 11

③ Reflect   10

Guided Discussion UNDERSTANDING

Using the table on student page 355, ask and discuss the following
scenarios. Decide if they do or do not make sense.

1. Mr. Sanchez wanted to buy the DVD case. He rounded $45 to $0.
   Can he buy the case for $0? Does that make sense? no

2. Mr. Smith wanted to buy the computer table and the printer. So
   he added 134 + 287 = 421. Then he rounded 421 to the nearest
   hundred, or 400. The items cost about $400, he thought. Does that
   make sense? not really; If he has already done the arithmetic, he
   knows the cost. There is no need to round.

If time and interest permit, allow students to think of similar
scenarios and discuss them.

Review **Cumulative Review:** For cumulative review of previously
learned skills, see page 361–362.

Family Involvement: Assign the *Practice, Reteach,* or
Enrichment activities depending on the needs of your students.
Have students play a previously introduced game with family
members.

Concept/Question Board: Have students attempt to
answer any unanswered questions on the Concept/Question
Board.

Math Puzzler: 🌐 Integration: TEKS 2.12. A Bill is 6
years old. He is twice as old as his younger brother Dan. When
Dan is 5, will Bill be 10? Why or why not? no; Bill will always be
3 years older than Dan. When Dan is 5, Bill will be 8.

4 Assess and Differentiate

 **Assess** Use *eAssess* to record and analyze evidence of student understanding.

A Gather Evidence

Use the Daily Class Assessment Records in *Texas Assessment* or *eAssess* to record daily observations.

Informal Assessment
☑ **Skill Building**

Did the student **UNDERSTANDING**
- ❏ make important observations?
- ❏ extend or generalize learning?
- ❏ provide insightful answers?
- ❏ pose insightful questions?

Informal Assessment
☑ **Student Pages**

Did the student **UNDERSTANDING**
- ❏ make important observations?
- ❏ extend or generalize learning?
- ❏ provide insightful answers?
- ❏ pose insightful questions?

TEKS/TAKS Practice

Use *TEKS/TAKS Practice* pages 43–46 to assess student progress.

B Summarize Findings

Analyze and summarize assessment data for each student. Determine which Assessment Follow-Up is appropriate for each student. Use the Student Assessment Record in *Texas Assessment* or *eAssess* to update assessment records.

C Texas Assessment Follow-Up ● DIFFERENTIATE INSTRUCTION

Based on your observations, use these teaching strategies for assessment follow-up.

INTERVENTION

Review student performance on *Intervention* Lesson 9.C to see if students have mastered prerequisite skills for this lesson.

1.3.A Model and create addition and subtraction problem situations with concrete objects and write corresponding number sentences.

1.5.D Use patterns to develop strategies to solve basic addition and basic subtraction problems.

ENGLISH LEARNER

Review

Use Lesson 9.11 in *English Learner Support Guide* to review lesson concepts and vocabulary.

ENRICH

If . . . students are proficient in the lesson concepts,

Then . . . encourage them to work on the chapter projects or *Enrichment* Lesson 9.11.

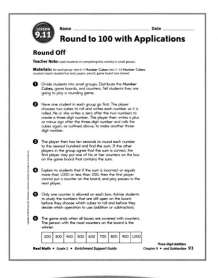

Enrichment Lesson 9.11

PRACTICE

If . . . students would benefit from additional practice,

Then . . . assign *Practice* Lesson 9.11.

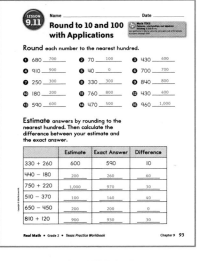

Practice Lesson 9.11

RETEACH

If . . . students have difficulty with approximating sums,

Then . . . write several problems on the board with incorrect sums or differences. Have students estimate to tell why each is wrong.

$324 + 145 = 312$ incorrect because the sum 312 is less than the addend of 324

$450 - 125 = 591$ incorrect because the difference 591 is greater than the minuend 450

Lesson Planner

TEXAS · **Vertical Alignment**

Grade 1	Grade 2	Grade 3
1.1.A Compare and order whole numbers up to 99 (less than, greater than, or equal to) using sets of concrete objects and pictorial models.	**2.1.C** Use place value to compare and order whole numbers to 999 and record the comparisons using numbers and symbols (<, =, >).	**3.1.B** Use place value to compare and order whole numbers through 9,999.

Overview

LESSON 9.12

TEXAS

OBJECTIVES

- To provide practice in approximating sums and differences
- To provide practice recognizing sums and differences that are obviously incorrect and contrary to reason
- To provide practice in solving word problems

MATH TEKS

Number, operation, and quantitative reasoning 2.1.C
Use place value to compare and order whole numbers to 999 and record the comparisons using numbers and symbols (<, =, >).

MATH TEKS INTEGRATION

Number, operation, and quantitative reasoning 2.3.B
Model addition and subtraction of two-digit numbers with objects, pictures, words, and numbers.

Underlying processes and mathematical tools 2.12.A
Identify the mathematics in everyday situations.

MATERIALS
*Number Cubes

TECHNOLOGY
Ⓔ **Presentation** Lesson 9.12
Ⓔ **MathTools** Base Ten
Building **B**locks **Word Problems 4**

Approximating Answers ★

Context of the Lesson This is the last of twelve lessons that develop skills and understanding for working with 2- and 3-digit numbers. This lesson builds on concepts and skills of approximation taught in the previous lesson. The goal is for students to gain a better understanding of number sense by approximating answers to problems and recognizing answers that are obviously incorrect.

See page 329B for Math Background for teachers for this lesson.

Planning for Learning ● DIFFERENTIATE INSTRUCTION

INTERVENTION

If . . . students lack the prerequisite skill of adding two-digit numbers,

Then . . . teach *Intervention* Lesson 9.C.

1.3.A, 1.5.D

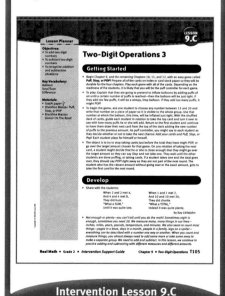

Intervention Lesson 9.C

ENGLISH LEARNER

Preview

If . . . students need language support,

Then . . . use Lesson 9.12 in *English Learner Support Guide* to preview lesson concepts and vocabulary.

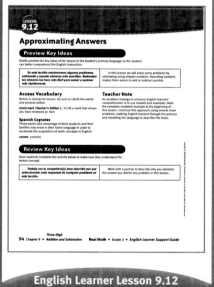

English Learner Lesson 9.12

ENRICH

If . . . students are proficient in the lesson concepts,

Then . . . emphasize additional game time.

PRACTICE

If . . . students would benefit from additional practice,

Then . . . extend Skill Practice before assigning student pages.

RETEACH

If . . . students are having difficulty understanding estimation,

Then . . . extend Guided Discussion before assigning the student pages.

Access Vocabulary
check mark a mark that shows you have reviewed an item

Spanish Cognates
correct correcto

Number, operation, and quantitative reasoning 2.1.C
Use place value to compare and order whole numbers
to 999 and record the comparisons using numbers
and symbols (‹, =, ›).

TEXAS

Mental Math 5

  INTEGRATION: TEKS 2.3.B Present addition and subtraction exercises using multiples of 10, and have students use **Number Cubes** to show their answers. For example:

a. 40 + 60 = 100   **b.** 70 − 20 = 50   **c.** 30 + 70 = 100
d. 50 + 50 = 100   **e.** 90 − 30 = 60   **f.** 90 − 80 = 10

1 Develop 20

Tell Students In Today's Lesson They Will
practice estimating and problem solving.

Guided Discussion    Introductory

Discuss and demonstrate how to approximate sums and differences of three-digit numbers. Write a three-digit addition problem such as the following on the board:

```
  392
+ 206
-----
  598
```

■ **What do you remember about approximation from the previous lesson?**
Remind students that to approximate, you can round numbers to the nearest ten or hundred. Students should recognize that 392 is almost 400, and 206 is a little more than 200; therefore, the sum is about 400 + 200, or 600.

Repeat this procedure for several more addition and subtraction problems.

Next give students word problems that require only an approximate rather than an exact answer, such as the following:

■ **There are 473 students in a school. The lunchroom manager must order enough pears for each student to have 2. About how many pears should the manager order?** Discuss whether the estimate should be *greater than* or *less than* the exact answer. Students should realize that the estimate should be greater than the exact answer to be sure there are enough pears. 500 + 500 = 1,000 is a good estimate.

Continue with several more examples.

Skill Practice UNDERSTANDING Guided

Write several problems on the board with incorrect sums or differences. Have students work together in small groups to explain how they can use mental math or approximation to tell why each sum or difference is incorrect. Present problems similar to the following:

a. 324 + 145 = 312; incorrect because the sum is less than one of the addends

b. 450 − 125 = 521; incorrect because the difference is greater than the minuend

2 Use Student Pages 20

Pages 357–358 ENGAGING
 Independent

Do pages 357 and 358 as a group activity, either as students do the exercises or after they are finished, so that students can express their methods for deciding which answers are correct. For each exercise, two of the answers are clearly wrong, and one is correct. Choose the correct answer.

Progress Monitoring

| **If . . .** students insist on using a paper-and-pencil algorithm for the exercises on page 357, or if they have difficulty detecting obviously wrong answers, | **Then . . .** do not insist that they not use an algorithm. Do, however, give individual or small group instruction in which you think aloud as you determine which possible answers are absurd and contrary to reason. These skills will develop gradually and extensive extra teaching is not necessary at this time. |

As Students Finish

Game Allow students to play the game of their choice, or assign a game based on student needs.

 Building Blocks Have students use **Word Problems 4** to practice word problems.

Teacher Reflection

Approximating Answers

LESSON 9.12

Key Ideas

The answer to some problems can be approximated by using simpler numbers.

297 + 305 =
297 is almost 300, and 305 is just a little more than 300.

We know 300 + 300 = 600.
So the sum of 297 + 305 is about 600.

Math TEKS
Preparing for Numbers, operation and quantitative reasoning 3.5.B Use strategies including rounding and compatible numbers to estimate solutions to addition and subtraction problems.

For each exercise, two of the answers are clearly wrong, and one is correct. Choose the correct answer.

1. 98
    + 103
    a. 101
    b. 201
    c. 301

2. 407
    + 398
    a. 605
    b. 705
    c. 805

3. 489
    + 312
    a. 599
    b. 701
    c. 801

4. 482
    + 312
    a. 694
    b. 704
    c. 794

5. 306
    + 247
    a. 453
    b. 503
    c. 553

6. 694
    + 156
    a. 750
    b. 800
    c. 850

Solve these problems.

7. **Extended Response** Max has $9.00. He will buy flowers for $7.98. How much change should he get? Ring the letter of the correct answer.
   a. $1.02   b. $8.02   c. $10.02   d. $0.02
   Explain how you solved this problem. _____
   Students should explain that they subtracted $7.98 from $9.00.

8. **Extended Response** Karen earned $3.25 yesterday. She earned $4.50 today. How much did she earn in the two days? Ring the letter of the correct answer.
   a. $6.05   b. $7.05   c. $7.75   d. $1.25
   Explain how you solved this problem. ____Students____
   should explain that they added $3.25 and $4.50.

 $1.79 a pound

 75¢ a pound

89¢ a bunch

Jim has $5. Does he have enough money to buy

9. 2 pounds of strawberries? _yes_   11. 3 pounds of pears? _yes_
10. 3 bunches of grapes? _yes_   12. 4 pounds of strawberries? _no_

---

3 Reflect

10

Guided Discussion ✓ REASONING

Present stories in which approximation skills are used correctly and incorrectly. Allow students to discuss the situations. For example:

Mr. Diaz bought a flower pot for $18.70. He gave the clerk $20. The clerk figured that his change should be $1.00. This is incorrect. The change should be exact.

Ms. Ling had a $20 bill. She wanted to know if she had enough money to buy the flower pot that cost $18.70. Did she have enough? This is correct. She needs only an approximate answer.

Extended Response

Problem 7 Discuss students' answers. Students should have realized that they should subtract 7.98 from 9.00.

Problem 8 Students should have realized that to solve this problem, they should add together the two amounts.

Review **Cumulative Review:** For cumulative review of previously learned skills, see page 361–362.

Family Involvement: Assign the *Practice, Reteach,* or *Enrichment* activities depending on the needs of your students.
Have students create approximating problems with family members.

Concept/Question Board: Have students attempt to answer any unanswered questions on the Concept/Question Board.

Math Puzzler: Integration: **TEKS 2.12. A** Mr. Ruiz works 5 days a week in an office 3 miles from his house. How many miles does he travel to and from work every week? 30 miles

4 Assess and Differentiate

 Assess Use **eAssess** to record and analyze evidence of student understanding.

A Gather Evidence

Use the Daily Class Assessment Records in **Texas Assessment** or **eAssess** to record daily observations.

Informal Assessment
☑ **Guided Discussion**

Did the student UNDERSTANDING
- ❏ make important observations?
- ❏ extend or generalize learning?
- ❏ provide insightful answers?
- ❏ pose insightful questions?

Informal Assessment
☑ **Guided Discussion**

Did the student REASONING
- ❏ provide a clear explanation?
- ❏ communicate reasons and strategies?
- ❏ choose appropriate strategies?
- ❏ argue logically?

🌟 **TEKS/TAKS Practice**

Use *TEKS/TAKS Practice* pages 9–12 to assess student progress.

B Summarize Findings

Analyze and summarize assessment data for each student. Determine which Assessment Follow-Up is appropriate for each student. Use the Student Assessment Record in **Texas Assessment** or **eAssess** to update assessment records.

C Texas Assessment Follow-Up ● DIFFERENTIATE INSTRUCTION

Based on your observations, use these teaching strategies for assessment follow-up.

INTERVENTION

Review student performance on **Intervention** Lesson 9.C to see if students have mastered prerequisite skills for this lesson.

🌟 **1.3.A** Model and create addition and subtraction problem situations with concrete objects and write corresponding number sentences.

🌟 **1.5.D** Use patterns to develop strategies to solve basic addition and basic subtraction problems.

ENGLISH LEARNER

Review

Use Lesson 9.12 in **English Learner Support Guide** to review lesson concepts and vocabulary.

ENRICH

If . . . students are proficient in the lesson concepts,

Then . . . encourage them to work on the chapter projects or **Enrichment** Lesson 9.12.

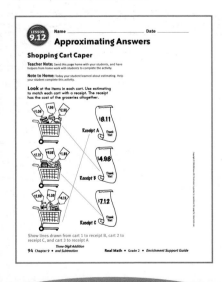

Enrichment Lesson 9.12

PRACTICE

If . . . students would benefit from additional practice,

Then . . . assign **Practice** Lesson 9.12.

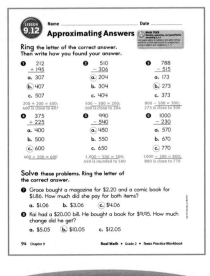

Practice Lesson 9.12

RETEACH

If . . . students are having difficulty understanding approximation,

Then . . . reteach the concept using **Reteach** Lesson 9.12.

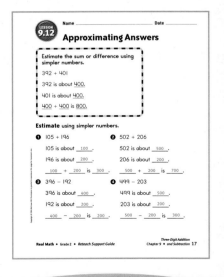

Reteach Lesson 9.12

Problem Solving 9.C

Using Strategies

Objectives

- To provide practice solving and presenting solutions to nonroutine problems
- To explore approximation as a strategy for solving real-world problems
- To provide practice adding several three-digit numbers
- To provide practice using maps

Materials

None

See Appendix A page A24 for instruction and a rubric for problem solving

Context of the Lesson While continuing the Pony Express theme introduced on page 347, this lesson encourages students to consider approximation when solving problems that involve sums of large numbers.

Access Prior Knowledge To help students get a feel for the long distances on the maps in this lesson, talk about riding in a car to different places in your vicinity. Ask students about how long it takes to get to the places. If students don't have much experience with long rides, you might want to display a map of your area and point out familiar destinations with remarks such as "If we left now, we would get there at about the time school is out."

1 Develop
5

Tell Students In Today's Lesson They Will

- decide which route a Pony Express rider should take.
- prove that the route is short enough for the rider to get back in time.

Guided Discussion

Have students look at the map on page 359. Read this problem to the class as the students continue to look at the map.

The railroad brought sacks of mail to Dry Gulch. The Pony Express rider will bring the sacks to Wagon Mound, Redstone, Leadville, Junction City, and Coyote Canyon because the railroad doesn't go to those towns. While he is in each town, the rider will pick up mail to take back to Dry Gulch. To make it back to Dry Gulch in time to get the new mail on the train, he needs to find a route that is less than 1,000 miles long. Can you figure out what route he should take? Remember that he has to start and end at Dry Gulch, go to every town on the map, and travel less than 1,000 miles.

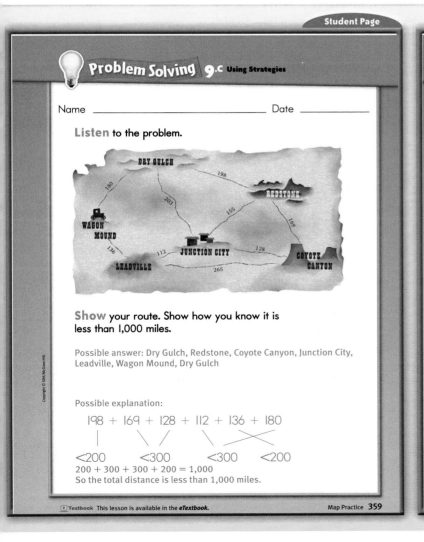

Problem Solving 9.c Using Strategies

Name _____ Date _____

Listen to the problem.

Show your route. Show how you know it is less than 1,000 miles.

Possible answer: Dry Gulch, Redstone, Coyote Canyon, Junction City, Leadville, Wagon Mound, Dry Gulch

Possible explanation:

$$198 + 169 + 128 + 112 + 136 + 180$$

<200   <300   <300   <200
200 + 300 + 300 + 200 = 1,000
So the total distance is less than 1,000 miles.

Textbook This lesson is available in the *eTextbook.*

Map Practice **359**

Problem Solving 9.c

Math TEKS
Underlying processes and mathematical tools 2.12.A
Identify the mathematics in everyday situations.

Start and end at Silver Falls.

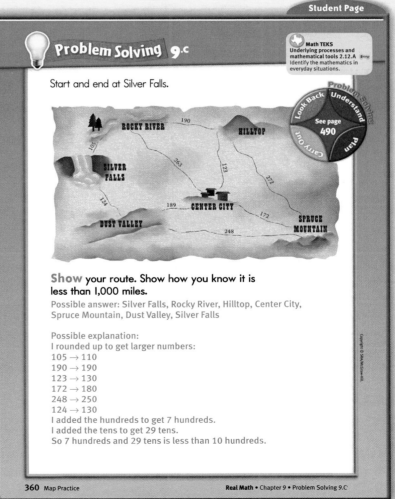

Show your route. Show how you know it is less than 1,000 miles.

Possible answer: Silver Falls, Rocky River, Hilltop, Center City, Spruce Mountain, Dust Valley, Silver Falls

Possible explanation:
I rounded up to get larger numbers:
105 → 110
190 → 190
123 → 130
172 → 180
248 → 250
124 → 130
I added the hundreds to get 7 hundreds.
I added the tens to get 29 tens.
So 7 hundreds and 29 tens is less than 10 hundreds.

360 Map Practice

Real Math • Chapter 9 • Problem Solving 9.C

Underlying processes and mathematical tools 2.12.A
Identify the mathematics in everyday situations.
Underlying processes and mathematical tools 2.12.B
Solve problems with guidance that incorporates the proce
understanding the problem, making a plan, carrying out th
and evaluating the solution for reasonableness.

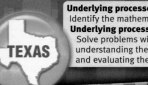

2 Use Student Pages   25

Guided Discussion

Have students work in pairs or small groups to solve the problem. Explain that they can show the route they choose however they like as long as it is clear. As students work, provide support as needed. If students seem to be having difficulty, encourage them to struggle with the problem for a while. When needed, ask guiding questions such as the following:

■ **Have you mapped out possible routes?**
■ **Which route *looks* shorter?**
■ **Can you tell *about* how far it is from (two towns that are not adjacent)?**

Students who finish early may use the map on page 360 to solve a similar problem, or you may assign page 360 as homework. The two problems are the same except for the names of the towns and the distances between them.

Sample Solutions Strategies

Students might use one or more of the following strategies.

Make a Model

Students might use base-ten blocks or a number line to create a linear model of 1,000. Then they might represent sums with blocks or on the number line and compare that to the representation of 1,000.

Use Spatial Sense/Guess, Check, and Revise

Students might decide which route *looks* like it would be the shortest route and then use approximation or computation to check.

Use Number Sense/Use Approximation

Students might round numbers to their nearest 10, 25, or 50 and combine these friendly numbers to get an approximate length of the route.

3 Reflect   10

Effective Communication Ask each group to share their plan and tell how they know their route is less than 1,000 miles. As students present, record their routes on the board by listing the order of the towns visited or by drawing the routes. If groups offer different routes, compare their answers. Ask a representative of the presenting groups if they can prove their answer without actually doing the arithmetic.

Help students understand the following points:

● Some problems can be solved without having to know exact numbers.
● Approximating can save time and be more reliable than exact computation.
● By thinking about friendly numbers (numbers that are easy to work with) you can get an idea of the size of an answer.
● In most situations, there are many ways to approximate. You can use whatever way you like as long as it helps you.

4 Assess   15

When evaluating student work, focus on whether students thought rationally about the problem. Questions to consider include the following:

● Did the student understand the problem?
● Did the student plan his or her route logically?
● Was the student able to explain his or her thinking?
● Was the student able to have confidence in an answer that resulted from an approximation rather than an exact answer?

Cumulative Review

Use Pages 361–362

Use the Cumulative Review as a review of concepts and skills that students have previously learned.

Here are different ways that you can assign these problems to your students as they work through the chapter:

- With some of the lessons in the chapter, assign a set of cumulative review problems to be completed as practice or for homework.
  Lesson 9.9—Problem 1
  Lesson 9.10—Problems 2–5
  Lesson 9.11—Problems 6–7
  Lesson 9.12—Problems 8–11
- At any point during the chapter, assign part or all of the cumulative review problems to be completed as practice or for homework.

Cumulative Review

Problem 1 reviews measuring length in centimeters, Lesson 4.2. **BIG IDEAS** Measurment TEKS: 2.9.A

Problems 2–5 review fractions describing parts of sets, Lesson 7.5. TEKS: 2.2.B

Problems 6–7 review checking subtraction, Lesson 6.7. **BIG IDEAS** Number and Operations and Algebra TEKS: 2.3.B

Problems 8–11 review three-digit addition and subtraction, Lesson 9.8. TEKS: 2.12.A

Progress Monitoring

If . . . students miss more than one problem in a section,

Then . . . refer to the indicated lesson for remediation suggestions.

Cumulative Review

Name _____ Date _____

Measuring Length—Centimeters Lesson 4.2 TEKS: 2.9.A

Solve. Use your centimeter ruler to measure. Write your answers on the lines.

❶ Triangle

	Side	Centimeter
	A	7
	B	4
	C	8

Perimeter   19

Fractions of a Set Lesson 7.5 TEKS: 2.2.B

Write the fraction shown.

❷ ⬤⬤⬤⬤◯◯ $\frac{3}{6}$ or $\frac{1}{2}$

❸ ⬠⬠⬠⬠⬠⬠ $\frac{2}{6}$ or $\frac{1}{3}$

❹ ◼◼◼◼◼◻ $\frac{5}{6}$

❺ ▲△ $\frac{1}{2}$

Cumulative Review

Checking Subtraction Lesson 6.7 TEKS: 2.3.B

Solve these problems.

❻ Jamal's digital camera can hold 90 pictures. He has already taken 39 pictures. How many more pictures can he take? __51__

❼ Keisha is allowed to use her cell phone for 80 minutes each week. She has already used 67 minutes. Can Keisha make a 15-minute phone call? __no__ Explain. _____
She has 13 minutes left to use this week.

Applications of Three-Digit Addition and Subtraction Lesson 9.8 TEKS: 2.12.A

How much will these cost today?

One Day Sale. Take **$93** off every price.

Tractor $1,280. Greenhouse Kit $1,965. Tilling Machine $425. Tractor Cart $360.

❽ tractor __1,280 − 93 = $1,187__

❾ tilling machine __425 − 93 = $332__

❿ tractor cart __360 − 93 = $267__

⓫ a tractor and a tractor cart __1,187 + 267 = $1,454__

Wrap-Up

 **1 Discuss** 5

Concept/Question Board

Review the Concept/Question Board with students.

- Discuss students' contributions to the Concept side of the Board.
- Have students repose their questions, and lead a discussion to find satisfactory answers.

Chapter Projects APPLYING

Provide an opportunity for students who have worked on one or more of the projects outlined on page 330C to share their work with the class. Allow each student or student group five minutes to present or discuss their projects. For formal assessment, use the rubrics found in *Across the Curriculum Math Connections;* the rubric for **Write about the Historic Iditarod** is on page 97, and the rubric for **Research the History of Airmail** is on page 101. For informal assessment, use the following rubric and questions.

	Exceeds Expectations	Meets Expectations	Minimally Meets Expectations
Applies mathematics in real-world situations:	❏	❏	❏
Demonstrates strong engagement in the activity:	❏	❏	❏

Write about the Historic Iditarod

- What did you learn about publishing a book?
- How did you decide what information should be included in your book?
- Which role did you have? Did you enjoy your role?
- What relationships did you find in the distance between checkpoints and the total distance?
- How accurate were your results when you rounded the numbers to add?
- If you had to focus on one thing about the historic Iditarod, what would it be?

TEKS:
Number, operation, and quantitative reasoning 2.1 The student understands how place value is used to represent whole numbers.

LANGUAGE ARTS: **Writing/writing processes 2.18.F** Demonstrate understanding of language use and spelling by bringing selected pieces frequently to final form and "publishing" them for audiences.

TECHNOLOGY: **Solving Problems 07.B.** Use appropriate software, including the use of word processing and multimedia, to express ideas and solve problems.

Research the History of Airmail

- What information did you find about the history of airmail?
- What information did you include in your summary?
- How many years passed between the beginning of the post office and the time when airmail began? How do you know this?
- What else could you have included in your summary?
- Is the Internet a good way to find information? Why or why not?

TEKS:
Number, operation, and quantitative reasoning 2.3 The student adds and subtracts whole numbers to solve problems.

SOCIAL STUDIES: **Government 2.11.B** Identify some governmental services in the community such as libraries, schools, and parks and explain their value to the community.

TECHNOLOGY: **Information acquisition 04** The student uses a variety of strategies to acquire information from electronic resources, with appropriate supervision.

Use Student Pages 25

Key Ideas Review ✓ UNDERSTANDING

Review the Key Ideas concepts on pages 363-364 with the class. The Key Ideas pages should be used by students and parents as a reference when reviewing the important concepts covered in this chapter. Ask students the following discussion questions to extend their knowledge of the Key Ideas and check their understanding of the ideas..

Discussion Questions

① How would students help a friend who was having trouble with three-digit addition or subtraction? Allow students to discuss and share their ideas with the class. One idea, for example, could be to relate three-digit subtraction to two-digit subtraction. Then, break students up into small groups and have them test the ideas that were presented. After students have tried the ideas, have them report on the effectiveness of the different methods. Did then think of any new ideas while trying the other methods?

② Why is it important to consider the situation you are in before you start rounding? Have students ever encountered a situation where rounding would solve their problem? Can they invent a situation where rounding would e the best way to solve the problem? It is important to consider the situation when rounding in order to determine if rounding up or rounding down makes more sense. Allow students to share situations in which they may have had to round, or any situations they invented. Ask students if rounding up or rounding down would better solve the problems they are presenting.

③ Why is it useful to be able to add and subtract dollar and cent amounts? When would students have to do that? By being able to add and subtract dollars and cents, students can save a great amount of time. This way, they can just do the calculations instead of counting the money. Any time students are buying something, or saving money, they will want to be able to keep track of their total. It is important to be able to add and subtract money so you know how much money you should have. This way, people can not take advantage of you and take your money

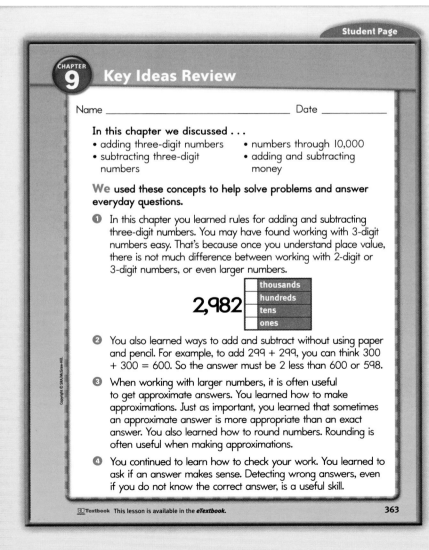

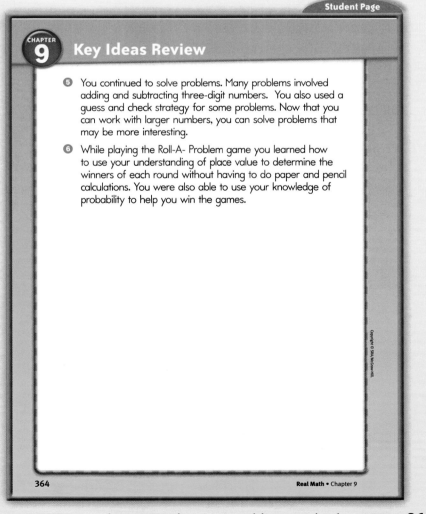

Chapter 9 Error Analysis

Errors with Three-Digit Addition

Write the following problems on the board and allow students to analyze this student's work. Discuss error patterns students find and how to help the student.

Pose this analysis as a challenging problem. When a student thinks he or she might have detected the error pattern, rather than have them tell the answer to the class, write a new exercise on the board and have the student tell you the answer that is consistent with the pattern he or she found. By using this procedure, all students will have a chance to think through the problem – not just the first student to find it.

This student completed some three-digit addition and subtraction exercises and got the following answers.

1. 575 + 273 = 718   **4.** 928 + 71 = 999

2. 456 + 112 = 568   **5.** 376 + 785 = 111

3. 725 + 872 = 197   **6.** 888 + 222 = 111

What error is this student making?

This student knows to add in each column and knows that he or she can only write one digit as an answer in each column. But if a sum is more than one digit he simply writes the first digit and discards the second digit.

This student needs to be interviewed. He or she will need help with understanding place value and with learning the procedure for adding three-digit numbers. Play money using $100, $10 and $1 bills will be a suitable manipulative to help with understanding.

The student also needs to learn to check to see if answers make sense. He or she should have noticed that the technique he or she is using produced the same sum for two very different exercises. That should have made the student realize that the procedure he or she was using could not be correct.

TEKS/TAKS Practice

TEKS/TAKS Practice Book

At this time, you may use the **TEKS/TAKS Practice** to provide practice for standards covered in this chapter.

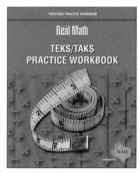

TEKS/TAKS Practice,
pp. 5–8, Standard 2.1.B

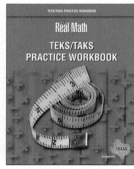

TEKS/TAKS Practice,
pp. 1–4, Standard 2.1.A

TEKS/TAKS Practice,
pp. 9–12, Standard 2.1.C

TEKS/TAKS Practice,
pp. 67–70, Standard 2.8

TEKS/TAKS Practice,
pp. 31–33, Standard 2.3.E

TAKS Preparation Book

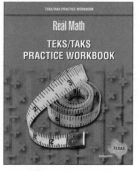

TEKS/TAKS Preparation Book

Use Benchmark Test 3 on pages 17–24 of **TAKS Preparation Book**.

Chapter Review

Use the Chapter 9 Review to indicate areas in which each student is having difficulty or in which the class may need help. If students do well on the Chapter 9 Review, you may wish to skip directly to the Chapter Test; if not, you may want to spend a day or so helping students overcome their individual difficulties before taking the Practice Test.

Next to each set of problems is a list of the lessons in the chapter that covered those concepts. If they need help, students can refer to a specific lesson for additional instruction. You can also use this information to make additional assignments based on the previous lesson concepts.

Have students complete pages 365–366 on their own.

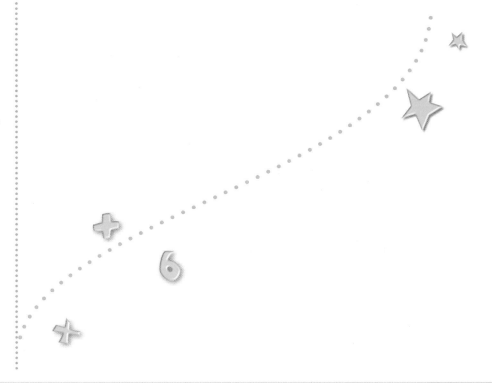

CHAPTER 9 — Chapter Review

Name _____ Date _____

Lesson 9.11
TEKS: 2.5.B

Round to nearest 100.
1. 480 **500**
2. 390 **400**
3. 120 **100**
4. 70 **100**
5. 840 **800**
6. 540 **500**

7. **Extended Response** Is 450 closer to 500 or to 400? Explain.
Students should realize that it is exactly in the middle; either number is an acceptable response.

Lesson 9.1
TEKS: 2.1.B

Write the numbers.
8. In 843
How many hundreds? **8**
How many tens? **4**
How many ones? **3**

9. In 3,184
How many thousands? **3**
How many hundreds? **1**
How many tens? **8**
How many ones? **4**

Lesson 9.12
TEKS: 2.1.C

Ring the best approximate answer.
10. 127
+ 43
(**175**) 150 200

11. 407
+ 398
700 (**800**) 900

12. 512
+ 389
(**915**) 815 715

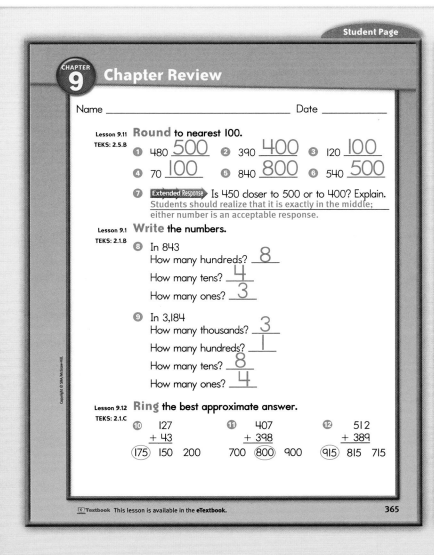

📱Textbook **This lesson is available in the eTextbook.**   365

CHAPTER 9 — Chapter Review

Lesson 9.3
TEKS: 2.5.B

Write the words greater than, less than, or equal to.
13. Five hundred fifty is __greater than__ four hundred sixty.
14. Three hundred is __less than__ five hundred.

Lesson 9.9
TEKS: 2.3.E

Write how much.
15. **1,000** cents
16. 84 cents = **$0.84**
17. 206 cents = **$2.06**
18. $1.21 = **121** cents

Lessons 9.5–9.8
TEKS: 2.1.A

Add or subtract. Watch the signs.
19. 243
+ 621
864

20. 447
+ 293
740

21. 161
+ 820
981

22. 724
+ 893
1,617

23. 12
− 6
6

24. 56
− 4
52

25. 42
− 7
35

26. 420
− 70
350

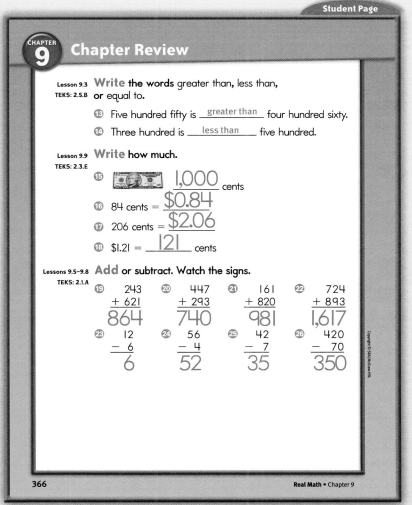

366   **Real Math • Chapter 9**

Chapter 9 • Three-Digit Addition and Subtraction   365–366

Practice Test

Student Pages 367–370

- The Chapter 9 Practice Test on **Student Edition** pages 367–370 provides an opportunity to formally evaluate students' proficiency with concepts developed in this chapter.
- The content is similar to the Chapter 9 Review, in standardized format.

Practice-Test Remediation

Short Answer Questions 1–4 are about ordering large numbers. If students have difficulty with these questions, have them work in groups to create and study number lines. Remind them that large numbers are just like smaller numbers, and they can count in the same way.

If students have difficulty with **Multiple Choice Questions 1–2**, then they probably do not understand place value. Make sure students are reading the details of each question and answer carefully. If they continue to have difficulty, have them write the numbers in a place value chart. This way they should be able to pick out the number words that match the numbers.

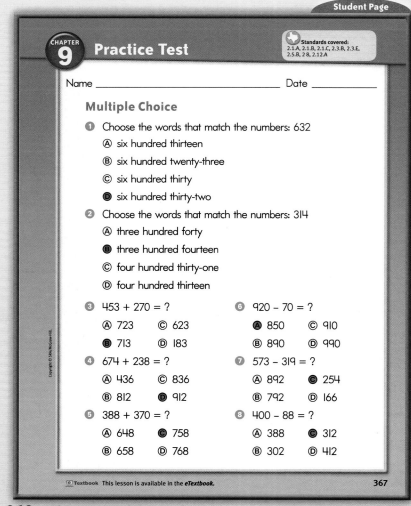

Student Page

CHAPTER 9 Practice Test

Standards covered:
2.1.A, 2.1.B, 2.1.C, 2.3.B, 2.3.E, 2.5.B, 2.8, 2.12.A

Name _____ Date _____

Multiple Choice

1. Choose the words that match the numbers: 632
   - Ⓐ six hundred thirteen
   - Ⓑ six hundred twenty-three
   - Ⓒ six hundred thirty
   - ● six hundred thirty-two

2. Choose the words that match the numbers: 314
   - Ⓐ three hundred forty
   - ● three hundred fourteen
   - Ⓒ four hundred thirty-one
   - Ⓓ four hundred thirteen

3. $453 + 270 = ?$
   - Ⓐ 723   Ⓒ 623
   - ● 713   Ⓓ 183

4. $674 + 238 = ?$
   - Ⓐ 436   Ⓒ 836
   - Ⓑ 812   ● 912

5. $388 + 370 = ?$
   - Ⓐ 648   ● 758
   - Ⓑ 658   Ⓓ 768

6. $920 - 70 = ?$
   - ● 850   Ⓒ 910
   - Ⓑ 890   Ⓓ 990

7. $573 - 319 = ?$
   - Ⓐ 892   ● 254
   - Ⓑ 792   Ⓓ 166

8. $400 - 88 = ?$
   - Ⓐ 388   ● 312
   - Ⓑ 302   Ⓓ 412

Textbook This lesson is available in the *eTextbook*. 367

Student Page

CHAPTER 9 Practice Test

9. Emilio's Bakery made 600 cookies for a fair. They made 180 sugar cookies and 216 peanut butter cookies. All of the rest were chocolate chip. How many cookies were chocolate chip?
   - Ⓐ 160   Ⓑ 204   Ⓒ 384   Ⓓ 396

10. Cameron was in a three-act play at school. The first act was 39 minutes long. The second act was 28 minutes long. The whole play was 100 minutes long. How many minutes long was the third act?
    - Ⓐ 11   Ⓑ 30   ● 33   Ⓓ 43

11. Jalisa sold 211 granola bars to raise money for the school band. Riane sold 187 granola bars. How many more granola bars did Jalisa sell than Riane?
    - ● 24   Ⓑ 36   Ⓒ 116   Ⓓ 398

12. Choose the correct time.
    - Ⓐ half past 4
    - Ⓑ quarter to 5
    - ● quarter to 4
    - Ⓓ quarter after 4

13. Choose the correct time.
    - ● quarter to 11
    - Ⓑ quarter to 10
    - Ⓒ quarter after 10
    - Ⓓ quarter after 11

14. Choose the correct time.
    - Ⓐ 12:15   Ⓑ 9:00   ● 3:00   Ⓓ 2:15

368   **Real Math** • Chapter 9

Short Answer Questions 5–8 involve comparing numbers or expressions. If students have difficulty with these questions, make sure they remember what the relationship symbols stand for. Then, if they are still having difficulty, have students model the numbers with craft sticks or base-ten materials.

If students have difficulty with **Extended Response Question 13 and Short Answer Questions 9–12,** then have them model the problems with play money. Remind them that 100 cents is equivalent to $1.00.

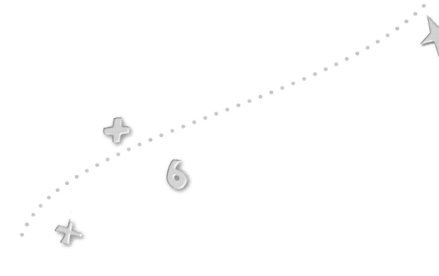

CHAPTER 9 Practice Test

Name _____ Date _____

Short Answer/Extended Response

1. Write the missing numbers. 355, 356, _357_ , _358_ , _359_ , 360

2. Write the missing numbers. 898, 899, _900_ , _901_ , _902_ , 903

3. Write the missing numbers. 1,401, _1,402_ , 1,403, _1,404_ , _1,405_ , 1,406

4. Write the missing numbers. 1,425, _1,426_ , 1,427, _1,428_ , _1,429_ , 1,430

5. Draw >, <, or =. 389 __<__ 409

6. Draw >, <, or =. 723 __>__ 638

7. Draw >, <, or =. 420 + 20 __=__ 410 + 30

8. Draw >, <, or =. 651 + 61 __>__ 551 + 61

9. _212_ cents = $2.12

10. _782_ cents = $7.82

11. _153_ cents = $1.53

12. _400_ cents = $4.00

CHAPTER 9 Practice Test

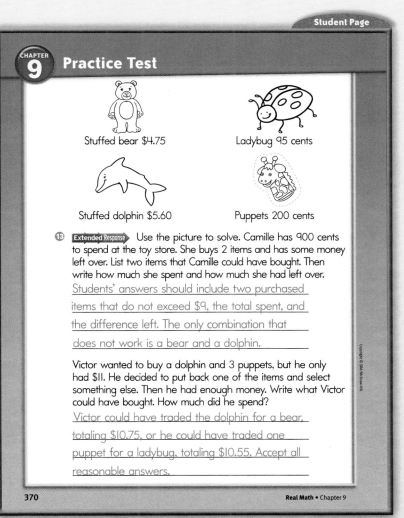

Stuffed bear $4.75   Ladybug 95 cents

Stuffed dolphin $5.60   Puppets 200 cents

13. **Extended Response** Use the picture to solve. Camille has 900 cents to spend at the toy store. She buys 2 items and has some money left over. List two items that Camille could have bought. Then write how much she spent and how much she had left over.
Students' answers should include two purchased
items that do not exceed $9, the total spent, and
the difference left. The only combination that
does not work is a bear and a dolphin.

Victor wanted to buy a dolphin and 3 puppets, but he only had $11. He decided to put back one of the items and select something else. Then he had enough money. Write what Victor could have bought. How much did he spend?
Victor could have traded the dolphin for a bear,
totaling $10.75, or he could have traded one
puppet for a ladybug, totaling $10.55. Accept all
reasonable answers.

4 Assess and Differentiate

 Assess Use *eAssess* to record and analyze evidence of student understanding.

A Gather Evidence

Use the Daily Class Assessment Records in *Texas Assessment* or *eAssess* to record Informal and Formal Assessments.

Informal Assessment

☑ **Key Ideas Review** UNDERSTANDING

Did the student
- ☐ make important observations?
- ☐ extend or generalize learning?
- ☐ provide insightful answers?
- ☐ pose insightful questions?

Informal Assessment

☑ **Project** APPLYING

Did the student
- ☐ meet the project objectives?
- ☐ communicate clearly?
- ☐ complete the project accurately?
- ☐ connect mathematics to real-world situations?

Formal Assessment

☑ **Chapter Test** COMPUTING

Score the test, and record the results.

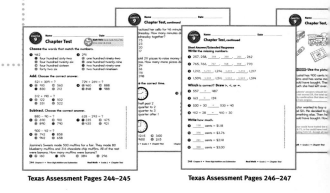

Texas Assessment Pages 244–245   Texas Assessment Pages 246–247

B Summarize Findings

Analyze and summarize assessment data for each student. Determine which Chapter Follow-Up is appropriate for each student. Use the Student Assessment Record in *Texas Assessment* or *eAssess* to update assessment records.

C Chapter Follow-Up • DIFFERENTIATE INSTRUCTION

Based on your observations, use these teaching strategies for chapter follow-up.

ENRICH	PRACTICE	RETEACH	INTERVENTION
If . . . students demonstrate a **secure understanding** of chapter concepts,	**If . . .** students demonstrate **competent understanding** of chapter concepts,	**If . . .** students demonstrate **emerging understanding** of chapter concepts,	**If . . .** students demonstrate **minimal understanding** of chapter concepts,
Then . . . move on to the next chapter.	**Then . . .** move on to the next chapter.	**Then . . .** move on to the next chapter, but continue to provide cumulative review.	**Then . . .** intensive intervention is still needed before they start the next chapter.

Loretta the Letter Carrier Chooses Sides

Context of the Thinking Story Loretta gets a job as a letter carrier and figures out how to make her job easier by understanding odd and even numbers.

Lesson Planner

OBJECTIVES
To develop logical thinking while integrating reading skills with mathematics

 MATH TEKS

Underlying processes and mathematical tools 2.12.A
Identify the mathematics in everyday situations.
Underlying processes and mathematical tools 2.12.B
Solve problems with guidance that incorporates the processes of understanding the problem, making a plan, carrying out the plan, and evaluating the solution for reasonableness.

 Reading/comprehension 2.9.F
Make and explain inferences from texts such as determining important ideas and causes and effects, making predictions, and drawing conclusions.
Reading/literary response 2.10.C
Support interpretations or conclusions with examples drawn from text.
Reading/text structures/literary concepts 2.11.I
Identify the importance of the setting to a story's meaning.

Using the Thinking Story

The Thinking Story may be used at any time throughout the chapter. Read the Thinking Story "Loretta the Letter Carrier Chooses Sides" to your class. As you read the story, give students time to think about each question, but not so much that they forget the point being made.

Loretta the Letter Carrier Chooses Sides

When Loretta was hired as a letter carrier, she was asked a lot of questions, but no one thought to ask her about odd and even numbers. The first day she had a bundle of mail to deliver along Maple Street. She thought, "I'm going to be smart about this." She sorted the mail so 1 Maple Street was first, 2 Maple Street was next, 3 Maple Street was next, and so on. The first house she came to on Maple Street had a number 2 on it. "That's funny," thought Loretta. "There doesn't seem to be a number 1, although I have mail for it."

Why can't Loretta find number 1?
It's on the other side of the street.

Loretta stuffed the mail for 1 Maple Street back into her bag and then delivered the mail to 2 Maple Street. She walked next door with the mail for 3 Maple Street.

Will Loretta find number 3 next door? **no**

Where is number 3? **on the other side of the street**

Loretta knocked on the door. When a man opened it, she handed him the mail.

"This is not my mail," the man said, handing it back to Loretta.

Loretta was confused. "I thought this house is number 3. The house next door is number 2."

What is the number of this house? **4**

"No," the man answered. "This is number 4. Number 3 is across the street."

"Thank you," said Loretta. She started to cross the street, but there was too much traffic.

What will Loretta have to do?
cross at a corner or traffic light

Loretta walked back to the corner and crossed when the traffic light was green. She knocked on the door of the first house.

What is the number of the first house? **1**

When a woman answered, Loretta handed her the mail she was holding in her hand.

What number do you think this mail is for? **3**

"This is not my mail," the woman said. "My house is number 1. This mail is for number 3, next door." Loretta reached into her bag and gave the woman the mail for number 1. Then she delivered the mail to number 3. She was about to go next door when she remembered that number 4 was across the street. She walked back to the corner to cross at the light.

It took Loretta a long time to deliver the mail on Maple Street that day.

Why did it take her so long?
She had to keep going to the corner to cross the street.

Loretta had to keep going back to the corner to cross the street for every new batch of mail she had. If 7 Maple Street was on one side of the street, then, sure enough, 8 Maple Street would be on the other side of the street.

What could Loretta do to deliver the mail faster? sort the mail by odd and even numbers and go down one side of the street at a time

"Those must be even numbers on one side of the street and odd numbers on the other. I wish I knew how to tell which numbers are odd and which numbers are even. I could sort out the odd numbers first and go down one side of the street, and then do the even numbers on the other side. That way I wouldn't have to keep crossing the street. But how am I supposed to know which numbers are odd and which are even?"

How would you help Loretta figure it out? skip count

Loretta finally figured out an easy way to sort the mail. She started with number 1, then skipped the next number, then took number 3, skipped the next number, took number 5, and so on.

What numbers are the ones Loretta took—odd or even? odd

The numbers she skipped were 2, 4, 6, 8, and so on.

Are those numbers odd or even? even

When Loretta sorted her mail that way, she was able to deliver it much faster.

A while later Loretta was given the job of delivering the mail along a street called Park Street. She tried to sort the mail the same way she did for Maple Street—odd numbers first and even numbers second. But there wasn't any mail for 1 Park Street, although there was for 2 Park Street. There wasn't any mail for 3 Park Street either. "That's funny," she said. "There isn't any mail for the odd numbers. All of the mail is for the even numbers. The people on the odd-numbered side of the street must not have any friends who write to them."

Can you think of another reason there might not be any mail for the houses with odd numbers? There are no houses on that side of the street.

When Loretta reached Park Street she discovered the reason she had mail for only one side of the street.

"Now I know why they call this Park Street," Loretta thought.

What do you think Loretta saw on the side of the street that wasn't getting any mail? a park running the full length of the street

The End

Teaching the Lesson

Guided Discussion

As students answer the questions in the story, ask them to communicate how they chose their answers. Allow students to debate the answers if necessary.

Using Student Pages 371–372

Have students follow the instructions and complete the **Student Edition** activities. Read the instructions aloud if students are having difficulty.

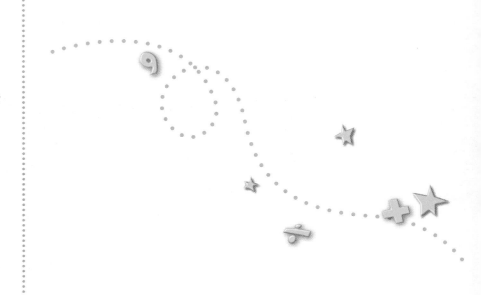

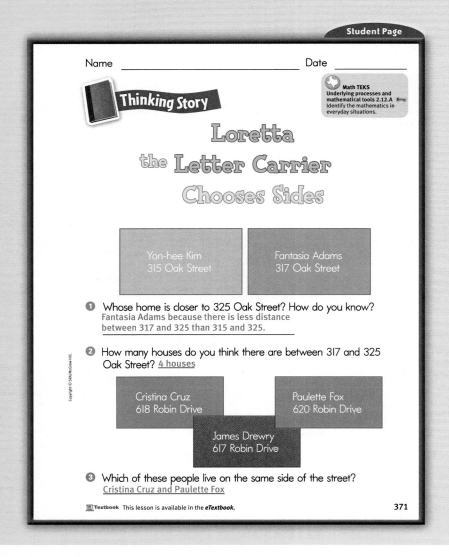

Name _____ Date _____

Thinking Story

Math TEKS
Underlying processes and mathematical tools 2.12.A
Identify the mathematics in everyday situations.

Loretta the Letter Carrier Chooses Sides

Yon-hee Kim 315 Oak Street	Fantasia Adams 317 Oak Street

❶ Whose home is closer to 325 Oak Street? How do you know?
Fantasia Adams because there is less distance between 317 and 325 than 315 and 325.

❷ How many houses do you think there are between 317 and 325 Oak Street? 4 houses

Cristina Cruz 618 Robin Drive	Paulette Fox 620 Robin Drive

James Drewry 617 Robin Drive

❸ Which of these people live on the same side of the street?
Cristina Cruz and Paulette Fox

Textbook This lesson is available in the eTextbook.   371

Complete the pattern.

❶ 2   4   6   8   10   12   **14   16   18**

❷ 17   15   13   11   9   7   **5   3   1**

❸ 5   5   7   7   9   9   **11   11   13**

❹ 10   8   9   8   6   7   **6   4   5**

❺ 1   2   4   7   11   16   **22   29   37**

372   **Real Math** • Chapter 9

Teacher Reflection

Reflect on each of the lessons you taught in this chapter. Rate each one on the following scale, and then consider ways to maintain or improve positive teaching experiences in the future.

Lessons	Very Effective	Effective	Less Effective	What Worked	Ways to Improve
9.1 Place Value through 10,000					
9.2 Modeling Numbers through 1,000					
9.3 Comparing Numbers through 1,000					
9.4 Adding Multiples of 10					
9.5 Three-Digit Addition					
9.6 Subtracting Multiples of 10					
9.7 Three-Digit Subtraction					
9.8 Applications of Three-Digit Addition and Subtraction					
9.9 Adding and Subtracting Money					
9.10 Shortcuts for Three-Digit Addition and Subtraction					
9.11 Round to 10 and 100 with Applications					
9.12 Approximating Answers					

= 120-Day Plan for TAKS

Measurement

Teaching for Understanding

This chapter introduces students to formal measurement. Students measure using temperature, capacity, time, and weight. Students also learn about metric and customary units of measure.

Prerequisite Skills and Concepts

- Measuring Length • Reading and Writing Numbers through 1,000 • Telling Time to the Quarter Hour

Measurement Skills Trace

Before Grade 2	Grade 2	After Grade 2
Grades K–1 Informally and formally introduced measuring capacity, temperature, weight, and length in standard and nonstandard units	**Chapter 4** has students measure length in standard and nonstandard units. Students also use metric and customary scales. **This chapter** has students measure temperature, capacity, and weight using customary and metric units. Students also measure time and calculate elapsed time.	Introduction, review, and mastery of measuring length, weight, capacity, and time. Later grades include formal introduction and mastery of more complex problems using these measurements.

BIG Ideas! in Chapter 10

This chapter develops the following ideas running throughout elementary mathematics:

- Some attributes of objects are measurable and can be quantified using unit amounts. Students can study various attributes of objects through measurement. The lessons in chapter 10 study the various attributes of weight, length, temperature, and time.

- Tools, techniques, and formulas exist for determining measurements. Through the use of tools the attributes of objects can be directly quantified or compared against other objects. Lessons 10.3, 10.4, 10.5, and 10.10 engage students in using tools to quantify the attributes of a number of objects.

Math TEKS addressed in each lesson can be found in the Chapter Planner on page 373E.

Math TEKS addressed in Problem Solving, Review, and Assessment Lessons are on page 373G.

Complete text of the standards appears on the Lesson Overview page and first Teaching page of each lesson.

TEXAS

Math Background

Measurement

What Is Measurement?

"Measurement is one of the main real-world applications of mathematics . . . counting is a type of measurement—it measures how many items in a collection. Measurement of continuous quantities involves assigning a number to attributes such as length, area, and weight. Together, number and measurement are components of quantitative reasoning. In this vein, measurement helps connect the two realms of number and geometry, each providing conceptual support to the other."

Clements, Douglas and J. Sarama, eds. *Engaging Young Children in Mathematics: Standards for Early Childhood Mathematics Education.* Mahwah, New Jersey: Lawrence Erlbaum Associates, Publishers, 2004, pp. 43–50.

Measuring and Comparing Temperature

- Temperature can be measured using the Fahrenheit scale, at which water freezes at 32 degrees and boils at 212 degrees, or using the Celsius scale, at which water freezes at 0 degrees and boils at 100 degrees. The Celsius scale is also known as the Centigrade scale (using the prefix *cent-* meaning hundred) because the span between the two benchmark measures is 100 degrees.

- The other temperature scale that students are likely to someday encounter is the Kelvin scale. This scale uses absolute zero, the coldest possible temperature (−273 degrees Celsius or −459 degrees Fahrenheit), as the zero point. One degree on the Kelvin scale is equivalent to one degree on the Celsius scale, so 100 Kelvin is equivalent to −173 degrees Celsius and so on. The Kelvin scale is used for scientific applications that deal with very low temperatures.

- Comparing temperatures is somewhat different from comparing measurements of other attributes because the zero point is arbitrary. Although temperatures are expressed as numbers, they can only be compared using addition or subtraction, not multiplication and division. Therefore, comparisons such as "twice as warm as" or "half as cold as" are meaningless, although "twice as long as" and "half as heavy as" make perfect sense. The only comparative statements that make sense for temperature reference warmer or colder, or a specific temperature difference (for example, "the temperature went up 10 degrees from noon to 6 pm").

Weight and Mass

- For simplicity *Real Math* follows the common convention of measuring both weight and mass in pounds and kilograms.

- Technically the pound is a unit of weight and a kilogram is a unit of mass. Weight is the amount of heaviness of an object, caused by gravity's pull on it. Mass is the amount of matter an object contains. Mass is measured on a balance scale in kilograms (or slugs, in the customary system), whereas weight is measured on a spring scale in newtons (or pounds in the customary system).

- A person's mass is the same whether it is measured on the earth or on the moon, but his or her weight changes because of the change in gravity. However, this is a subtle distinction, and the effort to teach it to students is typically too great for the potential benefits.

Volume

- In the customary system one fluid ounce is roughly the volume of a quantity of water that weighs one ounce.

- In the metric system the "official" units include meter for length (defined as the length of the path traveled by light in a vacuum during a time interval of 1/299,792,458 of a second) and kilogram for mass (defined as the mass of a specific metal bar in a vault in France). The liter is derived from the meter. Specifically, a volume of 1 milliliter (1/1,000 of a liter) is defined as the volume of 1 cubic centimeter (a cube 1 centimeter on each side). So, a volume of 1 liter is equal to the volume of 1,000 cubic centimeters, or a cube 10 centimeters on each side.

- Technically, volume is the amount of space an object occupies, and capacity is the amount a container can hold. However, as with the difference between weight and mass, this is not a distinction which is necessary to make with students at this level.

What Research Says

About Measurement

How Children Develop Measurement Skills and Concepts

"Measurement involves critical skills including techniques for comparing and measuring, either by iterating copies of a unit or using tools such as rulers. Children's development of these skills is a slow process . . . Recent research suggests that children benefit from using objects and rulers to measure at any age. Not only do children prefer using rulers, but they can use them meaningfully and in combination with manipulable units to develop understanding of length measurement. Even if they do not understand rulers fully or use them accurately, they can use rulers *along with* manipulable units such as centimeter cubes and arbitrary units to develop their measurement skills."

Clements, Douglas and J. Sarama, eds. *Engaging Young Children in Mathematics: Standards for Early Childhood Mathematics Education.* Mahwah, New Jersey: Lawrence Erlbaum Associates, Publishers, 2004, pp. 51–52.

Learning Trajectories for Measurement

Children typically follow an observable developmental progression in learning to measure with recognizable stages or levels. This developmental path can be described as part of a learning trajectory. Key steps in the learning trajectory for measurement from the 2nd grade range are described as follows. For the complete trajectory, see Appendix B.

Strand	Age	Level Name	Level	Description
Measuring	7	Length Unit Iterator	6	A significant change occurs when a child can use a ruler and see the need for identical units.
Measuring	7	Length Unit Relater	7	At the next level, a child can relate size and number of units. For example, the child may explain, "If you measure with centimeters instead of inches, you'll need more of them, because each one is smaller."

Clements, D. H., J. Sarama, and A.-M. DiBiase, eds. *Engaging Young Children in Mathematics: Standards for Early Childhood Mathematics Education.* Mahwah, NJ: Lawrence Erlbaum Associates, 2004.

Research-Based Teaching Techniques

Research has shown that the development of measurement ability and understandings in children is a complex developmental process. The child must develop a recognition that attributes such as length, height, weight and capacity can be measured both formally and informally. They must gain experience in using nonstandard and standard units for measuring and then learn various strategies for using those units to accurately assign values to the attributes being measured.

They gradually acquire knowledge and language associated with standard systems and units of measure. They gain an appreciation of the benefits of using one system or unit over another and become more skillful in using tools of measurement to accurately determine numbers of units when measuring.

Measurement provides children a means to describe, classify and categorize objects in the world around them. It adds richness to their developing sense of space and time.

A foundation in measurement concepts enables students to use measurement systems, tools, and techniques. This foundation needs to be established with the teacher providing children with direct experiences with comparing objects, counting units, and making connections between spatial concepts and number. Children will come to recognize attributes by looking at, touching, or directly comparing objects.

Teachers should guide students' experiences by making the resources for measuring available, planning opportunities to measure, and encouraging students to explain the results of their actions.

National Council of Teachers of Mathematics. *Principles and Standards for School Mathematics.* Reston, VA: NCTM, 2000.

 RESEARCH IN ACTION

Measurement In Chapter 10 students will gain greater awareness of the tools and procedures used to measure and compare attributes of time, temperature, length, weight, and capacity.

Attributes Throughout Chapter 10 students will gain greater awareness of attributes associated with the measurement of time, temperature, length, weight, and capacity.

Communication and Language Development In Chapter 10 students develop greater fluency with and awareness of the language of measurement. Students will use the language of measurement to compare, classify, and describe objects in the world around them.

Academic Vocabulary

capacity (Lesson 10.6) a measure of how much a container can hold

day (Lesson 10.8) a period of twenty-four hours

✎**degree** (Lesson 10.1) a unit of measurement for temperature

✎**hour** (Lesson 10.9) a unit of time equal to sixty minutes

map (Lesson 10.2) a drawing or other representation of Earth's surface, usually showing cities, rivers, oceans, mountains, and other features

midnight (Lesson 10.10) twelve o'clock at night; the middle of the night

✎**minute** (Lesson 10.9) a unit of time equal to sixty seconds

noon (Lesson 10.10) twelve o'clock in the daytime; the middle of the day

✎**perimeter** (Lesson 10.3) the measure of the distance of the path around an object or figure

thermometer (Lesson 10.1) a device or tool for measuring temperature

weight (Lesson 10.4) the amount of heaviness of something

week (Lesson 10.8) a period of seven days, usually considered to begin with Sunday

English Learner

Cognates

For English learners, a quick way to acquire new English vocabulary is to build on what is known in the primary language.

English	Spanish
thermometer	termómetro
distance	distancia
perimeter	perímetro
gram	gramo

Access Vocabulary

English learners might understand words in different contexts and might not understand idioms. Review chapter vocabulary for this concern. For example:

even-numbered	numbers that are even
compass directions	The compass shows four basic directions—north, south, east, and west.
light	In this context, light means "not heavy."

Texas Chapter Planner

Lessons	Objectives	NCTM Standards	TEXAS Math TEKS
⭐ **10.1** Reading a Thermometer pages 375A–376A 45–60 minutes	**To demonstrate how to read thermometers** and to introduce the Fahrenheit and Celsius scales	Number and Operations, Measurement, Algebra, Data Analysis and Probability	2.10.A 🔑 2.8
10.2 Reading a Map pages 377A–378A 45–60 minutes	**To introduce students to maps,** to give practice reading maps, and to introduce north, south, east, and west	Geometry, Algebra, Number and Operations	2.3 🔑 2.12.A
⭐ **10.3** Measuring Perimeter pages 379A–380A 45–60 minutes	**To provide practice finding the perimeter of objects** and to practice measuring length in customary and metric units	Number and Operations, Geometry, Measurement	2.3.B 🔑 2.12.D
⭐ **10.4** Kilograms and Grams pages 381A–382A 45–60 minutes	**To introduce the gram and kilogram as units of weight,** to provide practice measuring in the units, and to teach the relationship between the two units	Measurement	2.9 🔑 2.9.D
⭐ **10.5** Pounds and Ounces pages 383A–384A 45–60 minutes	**To introduce the weights of pounds and ounces** and to provide students with practice measuring in the units	Measurement	2.9 🔑 2.9.D
⭐ **10.6** Measuring Capacity (Customary Units) pages 389A–390A 45–60 minutes	**To introduce customary capacity units** and to teach students how to convert from one unit to another	Measurement, Problem Solving	2.9 🔑 2.9.C
⭐ **10.7** Measuring Capacity (Metric Units) pages 391A–392A 45–60 minutes	**To introduce metric units of measure for capacity** and to demonstrate converting from one unit to another	Measurement, Problem Solving	2.9 🔑 2.9.C
10.8 Units of Time pages 393A–394A 45–60 minutes	**To teach the number and order of the days of the week** and to determine what day of the week it was or will be, given a specific number of days	Measurement, Problem Solving	1.8 2.10.C 🔑
⭐ **10.9** Telling Time to the Minute pages 395A–396A 45–60 minutes	**To introduce telling time to the minute** and to relate analog and digital clocks	Measurement, Problem Solving	2.10.B
⭐ **10.10** Elapsed Time pages 397A–398A 45–60 minutes	**To informally introduce the convention of using 24-hour clock time** and to teach how to determine what hour it was or will be, given a number of hours in the future or past	Measurement, Problem Solving	2.0 🔑 2.10.C 2.10.B

⭐ = 120-Day Plan for TAKS

🔑 = Key standard

Academic Vocabulary	Manipulatives and Materials	Games to reinforce skills and concepts
degree thermometer	• *Number Cubes* • Thermometer • 3 clear glasses, all the same size • Cold water and hot water • *SRA Math Vocabulary Cards*	
map	• *Map Game Mat* • Map of the United States	Map Game (new)
perimeter	• *Number Cubes* • Rulers • *Map Game Mat* • Tape measures • String • Scissors • *SRA Math Vocabulary Cards*	Map Game
weight	• Double-pan balance and metric weights • Classroom objects to weigh • Ice cubes • Insulated cup with lid • *Map Game Mat* • Platform scale	Map Game
	• *Number Cubes* • Double-pan balance and ounce weights • Platform scale • Various objects to weigh	
capacity	• *Number Cubes* • Measuring cup marked in fluid ounces • Clear containers with pint, quart, and gallon capacities • 5 clear, identical containers • Colored water	
	• Transparent liter containers • Transparent measuring cup marked in milliliters • 5 equal-sized transparent containers • Colored water • Small kitchen sponge	
day week	• *Number Cubes* • Monthly calendar of the current month	
hour minute	• *Number Cubes* • Demonstration clock • *Harder Time Game Mat* • *SRA Math Vocabulary Cards*	Harder Time Game
midnight noon	• *Number Cubes* • Demonstration clock • Stopwatches • *Harder Time Game Mat*	Harder Time Game

Additional Resources

Differentiated Instruction

Intervention Support Guide Provides instruction for the following prerequisite skills:

- Lesson 10.A Time and Length–1
- Lesson 10.B Time and Length–2
- Lesson 10.C Time and Length–3

Enrichment Support Guide Extends lesson concepts

Practice Reinforces lesson skills and concepts

Reteach Support Guide Provides alternate instruction for lesson concepts

English Learner Support Guide Previews and reviews lesson concepts and vocabulary for English learners

Technology

The following electronic resources are available:

ⓔ **Planner** Lessons 10.1–10.10

ⓔ **Presentation** Lessons 10.1–10.10

ⓔ **Textbook** Lessons 10.1–10.10

ⓔ **Assess** Lessons 10.1–10.10

ⓔ **Games** *Map Game* Lessons 10.2–10.4

Assessment
Informal Assessment rubrics at the end of each lesson provide daily evaluation of student math proficiency.

Problem Solving	When to Use	Objectives	NCTM Standards	TEXAS Math TEKS
Problem Solving 10.A (pp. 373I–374C) 15–30 minutes	Use before beginning Chapter 10.	To introduce chapter concepts in a problem-solving setting	Problem Solving, Communication	2.12.C, 2.14
Problem Solving 10.B (pp. 385–386, 386A) 30–45 minutes	Use anytime during the chapter.	To explore methods of solving nonroutine problems	Problem Solving, Communication	2.12.C, 2.14, 2.9B
Problem Solving 10.C (pp. 399–400, 400A) 45–60 minutes	Use anytime during the chapter.	To explore methods of solving nonroutine problems	Problem Solving, Communication	2.12.C, 2.13.A, 2.6.B
Thinking Story—Ferdie's Meterstick (pp. 411A–411E, 411–412) 20–30 minutes	Use anytime during the chapter.	To develop logical reasoning while integrating reading skills with mathematics	Measurement	2.9.C, 2.10.C

Review	When to Use	Objectives	NCTM Standards	TEXAS Math TEKS
Cumulative Review (p. 387–388) 15–30 minutes	Use anytime after Lesson 10.5.	To review concepts and skills taught earlier in the year	Number and Operations	2.11.A, 2.3.A, 2.9, 2.13.A
Cumulative Review (p. 401–402) 15–30 minutes	Use anytime after Lesson 10.10.	To review concepts and skills taught earlier in the year	Number and Operations	2.2.A, 2.5.C, 2.1.B, 2.10.C
Chapter 10 Review (pp. 405A, 405–406) 30–45 minutes	Use after Lesson 10.10.	To review concepts and skills taught in the chapter	Number and Operations	2.9, 2.10.A, 2.10.B, 2.3.B, 2.9

Assessment	When to Use	Objectives	NCTM Standards	TEXAS Math TEKS
Pretest (*Assessment* pp. 128–129) 15–30 minutes	**Entry** Use prior to Chapter 10.	To provide assessment of chapter topics	Number and Operations, Problem Solving	1.8, 2.0, 2.3, 2.3.B, 2.8, 2.9, 2.9.C, 2.9.D, 2.10.A, 2.10.B, 2.10.C, 2.12.A, 2.12.D
Informal Assessment Rubrics (pp. 134–135 to 128–129)	**Progress Monitoring** Use at the end of each lesson.	To provide daily evaluation of math proficiency	Number and Operations, Communication	1.8, 2.0, 2.3, 2.3.B, 2.8, 2.9, 2.9.C, 2.9.D, 2.10.A, 2.10.B, 2.10.C, 2.12.A, 2.12.D
Individual Oral Assessment (p. 388A) 5 minutes per student	**Progress Monitoring** Begin after Lesson 10.5.	To provide alternate means of assessing students' progress	Number and Operations	2.9, 2.10, 3.11, 3.12
Chapter 10 Practice Test (pp. 407–408, 409–410) 30–45 minutes	**Progress Monitoring** Use after or in place of the Chapter 10 Review.	To provide assessment or additional practice of the chapter concepts	Data Analysis and Probability, Number and Operations	1.8, 2.0, 2.3, 2.3.B, 2.8, 2.9, 2.9.C, 2.9.D, 2.10.A, 2.10.B, 2.10.C, 2.12.A, 2.12.D
Chapter 10 Test (*Assessment* pp. 248–251) 30–45 minutes	**Summative** Use after or in place of the Chapter 10 Review.	To provide assessment of the chapter concepts	Data Analysis and Probability, Number and Operations	1.8, 2.0, 2.3, 2.3.B, 2.8, 2.9, 2.9.C, 2.9.D, 2.10.A, 2.10.B, 2.10.C, 2.12.A, 2.12.D

Texas Technology Resources

Visit SRAonline.com for online versions of the **Real Math** eSuite.

Technology for Teachers

e Presentation	**Lessons 10.1–10.10** Use the **ePresentation** to interactively present chapter content.
e Planner	Use the Chapter and Lesson Planners to outline activities and time frames for Chapter 10.
e Assess	Students can take the following assessments in **eAssess:** • Chapter Pretest • Chapter Test Teachers can record results and print reports for all assessments in this chapter.

TEXAS **Technology for Students**

e Textbook	An electronic, interactive version of the **Student Edition** is available for all lessons in Chapter 10.
e Games	**Map Game Lessons 10.2–10.4**
TECH KNOWLEDGE	**TechKnowledge** Level 2 provides lessons that specifically teach the Unit 10 Internet and Unit 8 Database applications that students can use in this chapter's projects.

Measurement

Introduce Chapter 10 10 ▶

Chapter Objectives

Explain to students that in this chapter they will build on what they already know about measurement. Explain that in this chapter they will

- read a thermometer and a map.
- measure weight and compare capacity.
- tell time.

Pretest COMPUTING

Administer the Chapter 10 Pretest, which has similar exercises to the Chapter 10 Test.

- If most students do *not* demonstrate mastery on the Pretest, proceed at a normal pace through the chapter. Use the differentiated instruction suggestions at the beginning and end of each lesson to adapt instruction to and follow up on the needs of each student.
- If most students show mastery of some or all of the concepts and skills in the Chapter 10 Pretest, move quickly through the chapter, de-emphasizing lessons linked to items which most students answered correctly. Use the Individual Oral Assessments to monitor progress, and, if necessary, modify your pacing. These assessments are especially useful because they can help you distinguish among different levels of understanding. For example, a student who has mastered a particular skill but does not show a deep understanding of the relevant concepts still needs thorough coverage of the lesson material.
- If you do move quickly through the chapter, be sure not to skip games, Problem-Solving lessons, and Thinking Stories. These provide practice in skills and nonroutine thinking that will be useful even to students who already understand the chapter content. Also, be alert to application problems embedded within lessons that may show students how math topics are used in daily life.

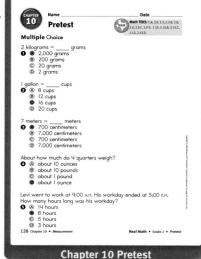

Chapter 10 Pretest

Access Prior Knowledge UNDERSTANDING

Have students talk about why people have gardens and how to create a garden. Have them share any experiences they have had with gardens—community gardens in particular. Discuss things that can be done to

- get ready to plant.
- help the plants grow.

- protect the garden from hungry animals or careless people.

Have students look at the photograph on page 373, and continue the discussion by asking questions such as the following:

- **What are some examples of foods that grow in a garden?** tomatoes, green beans, onions, carrots, beets, lettuce, peas, squash, cucumbers, melons, and so forth
- **What are some of the jobs people have to do to have a successful garden?** till the ground, plant the seeds, fertilize the garden, water the garden, pull the weeds, protect the garden from animals and harmful insects, harvest the produce

 ## Problem Solving 10.A Introducing Strategies

Tell Students In Today's Lesson They Will

- plan the shape of a garden.
- use the fence sections they have to make the largest garden they can.

Materials

- 2-cm or 1-inch graph paper (several sheets for each student)
- Scissors

Guided Discussion

Using Student Pages APPLYING  Introductory

Have students look at the picture on page 374 as you read the following problem:

Mr. Thompson has arranged for his second-grade class to have a section in a community garden to help his students learn about growing plants. The students need to put up a fence around their section before they begin working on the soil. A local business has donated twenty-four sections of fence for them to use. They may put up the fence in any way, but they want their garden to have as much garden space for planting as possible. Help them plan the shape and size of their garden.

Make sure the students understand the problem by asking questions such as the following:

- **What is Mr. Thompson's class going to do?** be responsible for a section of a community garden to help learn about growing plants
- **What must students do before they can start the actual gardening?** put a fence around the section they will use
- **How much fencing do they have?** twenty-four sections
- **Do they want to make the garden as long as possible?** Not necessarily; they want it to have as much room for planting as possible.
- **What is the problem asking you to do?** to plan the shape and size of the garden so it has as much space inside the fence as possible
- **How might you use a grid to help you think about this problem?** A side of each square could equal one section of fence. We can draw different ways to use twenty-four sections of fence to enclose a space.

TEXAS

Underlying processes and mathematical tools 2.12.C
Select or develop an appropriate problem-solving plan or strategy including drawing a picture, looking for a pattern, systematic guessing and checking, or acting it out in order to solve a problem.

Underlying processes and mathematical reasoning 2.14
The student is expected to justify his or her thinking using objects, words, pictures, numbers, and technology.

■ **If you find a way to use all twenty-four sections to make the garden, will you be finished with the problem?** No; we will need to make sure that we've made the garden with the most space. We will probably have to try other designs.

Explain to students that when they present their solutions, they will need to explain

- how they know they used all the fencing.
- how many sides their garden has and how long each side is.
- how many squares are enclosed.

Give each student one or more pieces of graph paper, but have students work on the problem in pairs or small groups. Circulate around the room, and give support as needed. Be sure to allow students plenty of time to struggle with the problem before offering suggestions. If students seem unable to make progress, have them work with a couple of strips of paper or pieces of string as you ask questions such as the following:

■ **Let's pretend this string is all the fence pieces put together. Can you show me a way to surround a garden with this fence?**
■ **Can you show me another way?**
■ **What will this shape look like in a drawing? Show me on the graph paper.**
■ **Can you show me on the graph paper what one section of fence would look like?**
■ **Can you show me what four sections of fence in a straight line would look like?**

Concept/Question Board APPLYING

Questions
Have students think of and write three questions they have about measurement and how it can be used. Then have them select one question to post on the Question side of the Board.

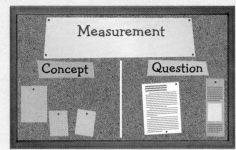

Concepts
As students work through the chapter, have them collect examples of how measurement is used in everyday situations. For each example, have them write a problem that relates to the item(s). Have them display their examples on the Concept side of the Board. Suggest the following:

- arranging furniture
- building a treehouse

Answers
Throughout the chapter, have students post answers to the questions and solutions to the problems on the Board.

CHAPTER 10 Measurement

In This Chapter You Will Learn
- to read a thermometer and a map.
- about weight and capacity.
- to tell time.

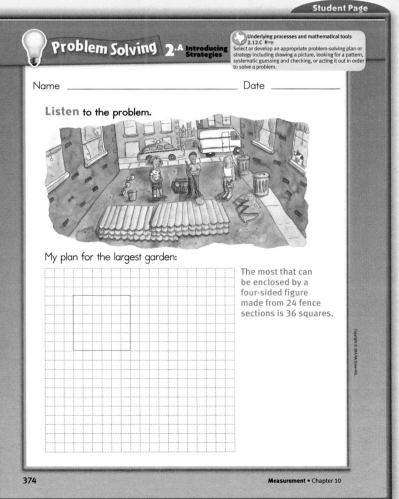

Problem Solving 2·A **Introducing Strategies**

Underlying processes and mathematical tools 2.12.C Select or develop an appropriate problem-solving plan or strategy including drawing a picture, looking for a pattern, systematic guessing and checking, or acting it out to solve a problem.

Name _____ Date _____

Listen to the problem.

My plan for the largest garden:

The most that can be enclosed by a four-sided figure made from 24 fence sections is 36 squares.

374

Measurement • Chapter 10

Reflect 20

Knowledge Age Skills

Effective Communication Have groups present their results. In discussion, bring out these points:

- Figures with different shapes can have the same distance around them.
- Some shapes have more space inside them.
- You can compare size and other attributes by measuring.

If students realize that they can increase the area of the garden by making a shape with more than four sides, commend such thinking, and have the class discuss the possibilities. Students might find it interesting to compare areas by cutting out and superimposing, by counting squares and partial squares, or by other means. If they work carefully, they will find that placing fence sections in a circular arrangement increases the area.

Sample Solutions Strategies

Students might use one or more of the following strategies to solve the problem:

Make a Physical Model

Students might cut out strips of paper or use string, tape, or a geoboard to make it easier for them to experiment with different shapes.

Guess, Check, and Revise

Students might begin by making any figures they can with the twenty-four sections and then counting the squares inside each figure.

Make an Organized List

Students might organize their work by starting with a long, thin rectangle and then moving one section at a time from the long sides to the short sides.

Make a Table

Students might use a table to keep track of the possibilities:

Width	Length	Number of Squares Inside
1	11	11
2	10	20
3	9	27
4	8	32
5	7	35
6	6	36
7	5	35

Home Connection

At this time, you may want to send home the letter on pages 38–41 of *Home Connection.* This letter describes what students will be learning and what activities they can do at home to support their work in school.

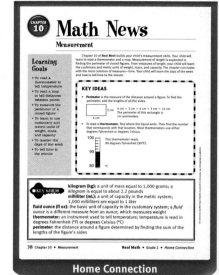

Home Connection Page 38

Assess and Differentiate

 Assess Use *eAssess* to record and analyze evidence of student understanding.

A Gather Evidence

Use the Daily Class Assessment Records in *Texas Assessment* or *eAssess* to record Informal and Formal Assessments.

Informal Assessment

☑ **Access Prior Knowledge**

Did the student UNDERSTANDING

- ❑ make important observations?
- ❑ extend or generalize learning?
- ❑ provide insightful answers?
- ❑ pose insightful questions?

Informal Assessment

☑ **Concept/Question Board**

Did the student APPLYING

- ❑ apply learning in new situations?
- ❑ contribute concepts?
- ❑ contribute answers?
- ❑ connect mathematics to real-world situations?

Formal Assessment

☑ **Pretest** COMPUTING

Review student answers on the Chapter 10 Pretest.

- ❑ If most students do not demonstrate mastery, move at a normal pace through the chapter.
- ❑ If most students answer most questions correctly, move quickly through the chapter, emphasizing those lessons for which students did not answer correctly, as well as games, Problem-Solving lessons, and Thinking Stories.

B Summarize Findings

Analyze and summarize assessment data for each student. Determine which Assessment Follow-Up is appropriate for each student. Use the Student Assessment Record in *Texas Assessment* or *eAssess* to update assessment records.

C Texas Assessment Follow-Up ● DIFFERENTIATE INSTRUCTION

Based on your observations of each student, use these teaching strategies for a general approach to the chapter. Look for specific Differentiate Instruction and Monitoring Student Progress strategies in each lesson that relate specifically to the lesson content.

ENRICH	PRACTICE	RETEACH	INTERVENTION	ENGLISH LEARNER
If . . . students demonstrate a **secure understanding** of chapter concepts, **Then . . .** move quickly through the chapter or use *Enrichment* Lessons 10.1–10.10 as assessment follow-up to extend and apply understanding.	**If . . .** students grasp chapter concepts with **competent understanding,** **Then . . .** use *Practice* Lessons 10.1–10.10 as lesson follow-up to develop fluency.	**If . . .** students have prerequisite understanding but demonstrate **emerging understanding** of chapter concepts, **Then . . .** use *Reteach* Lesson 10.2 to reteach lesson concepts.	**If . . .** students are not competent with prerequisite skills, **Then . . .** use *Intervention* Lessons 10.A–10.C before each lesson to develop fluency with prerequisite skills.	Use *English Learner Support Guide* Lessons 10.1–10.10 for strategies to preteach lesson vocabulary and concepts.

Math Across the Curriculum

Preview the chapter projects with students. Assign projects or have students choose from the projects to extend and enrich concepts in this chapter.

Plan a Flower Garden

 ART

2–3 weeks

TEKS

MATH STANDARD: Underlying processes and mathematical tools 2.13.A Explain and record observations using objects, words, pictures, numbers, and technology.

CROSS CURRICULAR STANDARD (FINE ARTS): Creative expression/ performance 2.2.B Create effective compositions, using design elements and principles.

TECHNOLOGY STANDARD: Communication 10.B Use font attributes, color, white space, and graphics to ensure that products are appropriate for the communication media including multimedia screen displays and printed materials.

Have students use mathematics to plan a flower garden. To broaden the fine arts concept, have them incorporate elements of color you are currently studying.

As part of the project, students should consider the following issues:

- the perimeter of a given garden space
- the relationships between the height and color of different flowers
- the use of a presentation program

For specific step-by-step instructions for this project, see *Across the Curriculum Math Connections* pages 102–105.

 **Knowledge Age Skills**

Effective Communication Students create presentations that effectively communicate their garden plans.

Creative Work with Ideas Students plan aesthetically pleasing flower gardens by using flower colors and heights.

Grow Bean Plants

 SCIENCE WebQuest

3–4 weeks

TEKS

MATH STANDARD: Measurement 2.10.A Read a thermometer to gather data.

CROSS CURRICULAR STANDARD (SCIENCE): Science concepts 2.7 The student knows that many types of change occur.

TECHNOLOGY STANDARD: Information acquisition 05.A Acquire information including text, audio, video, and graphics.

Have students use technology to

- practice reading a thermometer.
- research information about bean plants.
- enter data in a database about the progress and conditions of bean plants.

For this project, students use the Internet to investigate the following information:

- how to read a thermometer
- the parts of plants
- the life cycle of bean plants
- how to grow bean plants

For specific step-by-step instructions for this project, see *Across the Curriculum Math Connections* pages 106–111.

 **Knowledge Age Skills**

Problem Formulation, Planning, and Strategizing Students plan how to grow and care for bean plants.

High-Level Responsibility Students are responsible for finding out how to successfully grow bean plants and record relevant data based upon their observations.

TECHKNOWLEDGE *TechKnowledge* Level 2 provides lessons that specifically teach the Unit 10 Internet and Unit 8 Database applications that students can use in this project.

TEXAS **Vertical Alignment**

Grade 1	Grade 2	Grade 3
1.7.G Compare and order two or more objects according to relative temperature (from hottest to coldest).	2.10.A Read a thermometer to gather data.	3.12.A Use a thermometer to measure temperature.

Overview LESSON **10.1**

TEXAS

OBJECTIVES
- To demonstrate how to read thermometers
- To introduce the Fahrenheit and Celsius scales

 MATH TEKS

Measurement 2.10.A
Read a thermometer to gather data.

Geometry and spatial reasoning 2.8
The student is expected to use whole numbers to locate and name points on a number line.

 MATH TEKS

Preparing for: Grade 3 Number, operation, and quantitative reasoning 3.5.B
Use strategies including rounding and compatible numbers to estimate solutions to addition and subtraction problems.

Underlying processes and mathematical tools 2.14
The student is expected to justify his or her thinking using objects, words, pictures, numbers, and technology.

MATERIALS
- *Number Cubes
- *Thermometers
- 3 clear glasses, all the same size
- Cold water, hot water
- *SRA Math Vocabulary Cards*

TECHNOLOGY
Presentation Lesson 10.1

TEST PREP
Cumulative Review
Mental Math reviews three-digit addition (Lessons 9.4–9.5).

Reading a Thermometer ⭐

Context of the Lesson This is the first lesson in a series that covers different aspects of measurement: weight, length, capacity, temperature, and time. Both metric and customary units are discussed, but students do not convert measurements from one system to the other. In this lesson students learn to read thermometers using the Fahrenheit and Celsius scales.

See page 373B for Math Background for teachers for this lesson.

Planning for Learning ● DIFFERENTIATE INSTRUCTION

INTERVENTION
If . . . students lack the prerequisite skill of measuring length,

Then . . . teach *Intervention* Lesson 10.A.

1.7, 1.8

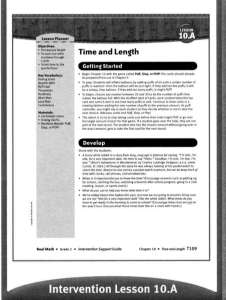

Intervention Lesson 10.A

ENGLISH LEARNER
Preview

If . . . students need language support,

Then . . . use Lesson 10.1 in *English Learner Support Guide* to preview lesson concepts and vocabulary.

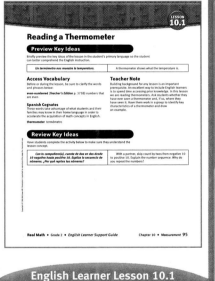

English Learner Lesson 10.1

ENRICH
If . . . students are proficient in the lesson concepts,

Then . . . emphasize Guided Discussion in Reflect.

PRACTICE
If . . . students would benefit from additional practice,

Then . . . extend Skill Practice before assigning the student pages.

RETEACH
If . . . students are having difficulty understanding reading a thermometer,

Then . . . extend Guided Discussion.

Academic Vocabulary
degree \di grē\ n. a unit of measurement for temperature

thermometer \thər mom´i tər\ n. a device or tool for measuring temperature

Access Vocabulary
even-numbered numbers that are even

Spanish Cognates
thermometer termómetro

Teaching Lesson 10.1

Measurement 2.10.A
Read a thermometer to gather data.
Geometry and spatial reasoning 2.8
The student is expected to use whole numbers to
locate and name points on a number line.

TEXAS

Mental Math 5

  INTEGRATION: TEKS 3.5.B Present addition sentences to students. Have them show thumbs-up if the answer is correct and thumbs-down if the answer is incorrect. Possible examples include the following:

a. 40 + 50 = 90
up

b. 45 + 45 = 90
up

c. 35 + 40 = 80
down

d. 20 + 35 = 65
down

e. 25 + 35 = 60
up

f. 74 + 16 = 80
down

1 Develop 25

Tell Students In Today's Lesson They Will
learn to measure temperature.

Guided Discussion UNDERSTANDING

 Introductory

Have students look at their thermometers and lead a discussion about Fahrenheit and Celsius.

■ **Critical Thinking** **Why do you think two different sets of numbers are on the thermometer?** because the thermometer is showing two different temperature scales

Explain to students that the numbers below the F show the Fahrenheit scale, and the numbers below the C show the Celsius scale. Make sure students notice that the 0° on the two scales do not line up.

Explain that in the United States the Fahrenheit scale is more commonly used. For instance, instructions in recipes and on ovens are Fahrenheit. Also when the outdoor temperature is reported on the news, it is usually Fahrenheit. However, in most countries, the Celsius scale is used. The Celsius scale is also commonly used in the United States in the sciences.

Show students how to measure temperature using a thermometer. Explain to students that they should take the reading where the liquid in the thermometer ends. Draw a Fahrenheit (from −10 to 100) and Celsius (from −20 to 40) thermometer on the board or overhead projector. Shade the Fahrenheit thermometer to 65°.

■ **What temperature does this thermometer show?** 65°

Now shade the Celsius thermometer to 15°.

■ **What temperature does this thermometer show?** 15°

Discuss negative temperatures with students. Explain that when the temperature drops below zero, we count the number of degrees below zero that the temperature is and say it is negative, or minus, that temperature. For example, if the temperature were 10 degrees below zero, we would say it is negative ten, or minus ten. Show students how to write a negative temperature, such as −10.

Now shade the Fahrenheit thermometer to –5°.

■ **What temperature does this thermometer show?** −5°

Skill Practice ✓ COMPUTING

 Guided

 Continue shading temperatures on the thermometers you drew on the board or overhead projector and have students show what the correct temperature is using their **Number Cubes.** Avoid using negative temperatures, as students have no way to display the answer. Possible examples include the following:

a. 15° F

b. 32° F

c. 78° F

d. 0° F

e. 25° F

f. 47° F

Strategy Building ENGAGING

Guided

Show the class two glasses containing the same volume of water. One should contain cold ice water (but do not have any ice cubes in the glass), and the other should contain hot water (but not so hot that it is not safe for students to touch). Have a volunteer come to the front of the room, feel the water with his or her fingers, measure the temperature of the first glass, and announce the temperature to the class. The class should then record this temperature by filling in the first thermometer on student page 375. Have a second volunteer come to the front of the room and repeat this procedure for the second glass of water. As students watch, mix together equal parts of the first glass and second glass of water into a third empty glass. Have the class predict what they think the temperature of the third glass will be and write their predictions on page 375.

> **Integration: TEKS 2.14**
>
> ■ **Critical Thinking** **Do you think it will be warmer or colder than the other temperatures?** It will probably be between the other two temperatures.

Have a third volunteer repeat the measuring procedure for the third glass.

Progress Monitoring

If . . . students are consistently answering with the wrong temperature,

Then . . . check to make sure they are reading the appropriate side of the thermometer (either Fahrenheit or Celsius) when they give their answers.

2 Use Student Pages 20

Pages 375–376 ✓ UNDERSTANDING

 Independent

Have students complete pages 375 as a class and 376 individually.

As Students Finish

 Allow students to choose a game from among those previously introduced, or assign games based on needed skill practice.

Student Page

Name _____ Date _____

LESSON 10.1 Reading a Thermometer

Key Ideas

A **thermometer** measures temperature.
Temperature is measured in **degrees**.

Math TEKS Measurement
2.10.A
Read a thermometer to gather data.

Measure the temperature to complete the activity.

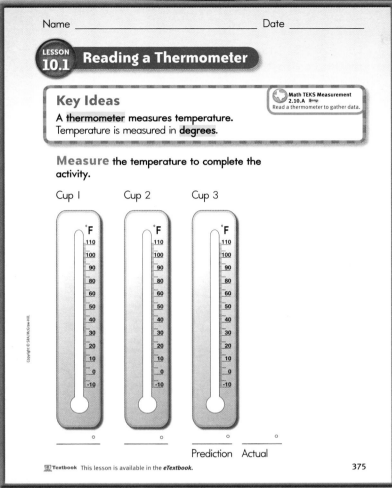

Cup 1   Cup 2   Cup 3

_____°   _____°   _____°
                          Prediction   Actual

Textbook This lesson is available in the *eTextbook*.   375

Student Page

LESSON 10.1 · Reading a Thermometer

Write or show the temperature.

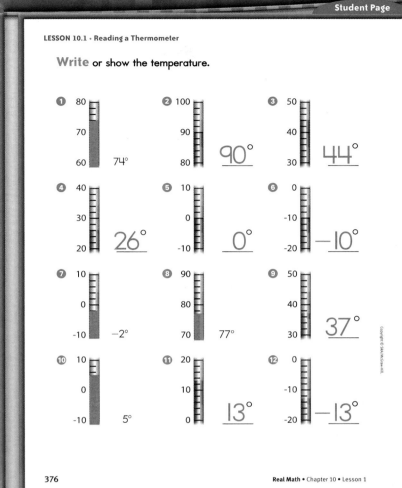

① 80 70 60   74°
② 100 90 80   90°
③ 50 40 30   44°
④ 40 30 20   26°
⑤ 10 0 -10   0°
⑥ 0 -10 -20   −10°
⑦ 10 0 -10   −2°
⑧ 90 80 70   77°
⑨ 50 40 30   37°
⑩ 10 0 -10   5°
⑪ 20 10 0   13°
⑫ 0 -10 -20   −13°

376   **Real Math** · Chapter 10 · Lesson 1

---

 ③ **Reflect**   10

Guided Discussion REASONING

Have students determine the outdoor temperature, either by measurement or by using resources such as the Internet.

- **Do you think the temperature will change over time?** yes
- **Will the temperature be higher or lower at night?** lower
- **Will the temperature be higher or lower tomorrow?** depends on season and weather conditions
- **What about next week or next year?** These answers depend greatly on conditions.

Allow students to discuss their ideas about changing temperatures and how these changes affect their daily lives. If there is interest, have students keep track of the daily outdoor temperatures. After a while you may have students try to predict the next day's temperature.

 Math Puzzler: The high temperature for yesterday was 71 degrees. The low temperature was 6 degrees below the high. What was yesterday's low temperature? 65 degrees

---

TEXAS **TEKS Checkup**

TEKS 2.10.A • Read a thermometer to gather data.

Use this problem to assess students' progress toward standards mastery:

What temperature is shown?

100
90
80

A 80°   **B** 85°
C 90°   **D** 95°

Have students choose the correct answer and describe how they knew which choice was correct. In the discussion, ask questions such as the following. Be sure to ask students to explain their reasoning because different solution methods are possible.

- How do you know the scale on the thermometer? look at the thermometer and count how many spaces are between 80 and 90

- Is the higher temperature near the top or the bottom of the thermometer? the temperatures rise as you go closer to the top of the thermometer

Follow-Up

If...students have difficulty reading thermometers

Then...provide the students with blank thermometers, such as the ones found on page 375 in their Student Edition. Give them temperatures to find on the Fahrenheit scale and watch to ensure the students are using the scale properly.

4 Assess and Differentiate

 Assess Use *eAssess* to record and analyze evidence of student understanding.

A Gather Evidence

Use the Daily Class Assessment Records in *Texas Assessment* or *eAssess* to record daily observations.

Informal Assessment
☑ **Skill Practice**
Did the student COMPUTING
- ❏ respond accurately?
- ❏ respond quickly?
- ❏ respond with confidence?
- ❏ self-correct?

Informal Assessment
☑ **Student Pages**
Did the student UNDERSTANDING
- ❏ make important observations?
- ❏ extend or generalize learning?
- ❏ provide insightful answers?
- ❏ pose insightful questions?

 TEKS/TAKS Practice
Use *TEKS/TAKS Practice* page 79 to assess student progress.

B Summarize Findings

Analyze and summarize assessment data for each student. Determine which Assessment Follow-Up is appropriate for each student. Use the Student Assessment Record in *Texas Assessment* or *eAssess* to update assessment records.

C Texas Assessment Follow-Up • DIFFERENTIATE INSTRUCTION

Based on your observations, use these teaching strategies for assessment follow-up.

INTERVENTION

Review student performance on *Intervention* Lesson 10.A to see if students have mastered prerequisite skills for this lesson.

Measurement 1.7 The student directly compares the attributes of length, area, weight/mass, capacity, and temperature. The student uses comparative language to solve problems and answer questions. The student selects and uses nonstandard units to describe length.

ENGLISH LEARNER
Review
Use Lesson 10.1 in *English Learner Support Guide* to review lesson concepts and vocabulary.

ENRICH

If . . . students are proficient in the lesson concepts,

Then . . . encourage them to work on the chapter projects or *Enrichment* Lesson 10.1.

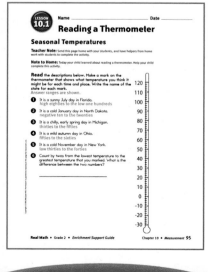
Enrichment Lesson 10.1

PRACTICE

If . . . students would benefit from additional practice,

Then . . . assign *Practice* Lesson 10.1.

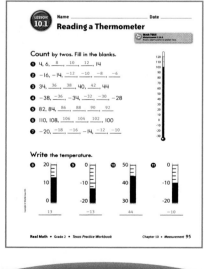
Practice Lesson 10.1

RETEACH

If . . . students are having difficulty reading a thermometer that has markings for even numbers,

Then . . . have them practice skip counting by 2s.

TEXAS
Vertical Alignment

Grade 1	Grade 2	Grade 3
1.3 The student recognizes and solves problems in addition and subtraction situations.	**2.3.B** The student adds and subtracts whole numbers to solve problems.	**3.3.B** Select addition or subtraction and use the operation to solve problems involving whole numbers through 999.

Overview **LESSON 10.2**

TEXAS

Lesson Planner

OBJECTIVES
- To introduce students to maps
- To provide practice in reading maps
- To introduce north, south, east, and west

MATH TEKS

Number, operation, and quantitative reasoning 2.3.B
The student adds and subtracts whole numbers to solve problems.
Underlying processes and mathematical tools 2.12.A Identify the mathematics in everyday situations.
Underlying processes and mathematical tools 2.13.A
Explain and record observations using objects, words, pictures, numbers, and technology.

MATH TEKS INTEGRATION

Preparing for Grade 3 Number, operation, and quantitative reasoning 3.5.B
Use strategies including rounding and compatible numbers to estimate solutions to addition and subtraction problems.

MATERIALS
- **Map Game Mat**
- Map of the United States

TECHNOLOGY
- ⓔ **Presentation** Lesson 10.2
- ⓔ **Games Map Game**

Reading a Map

Context of the Lesson Students have encountered maps in previous lessons in Grade 2, so they should be familiar with them. Grade 1 also had lessons that covered maps and map reading. This lesson has students use a map to determine which route is shortest. This lesson also includes a formal introduction of north, south, east, and west.

See page 373B for Math Background for teachers for this lesson.

Planning for Learning ● DIFFERENTIATE INSTRUCTION

INTERVENTION

If . . . students lack the prerequisite skill of reading and writing numbers through 1,000,

Then . . . teach *Intervention* Lesson 10.A.

 1.7, 1.8

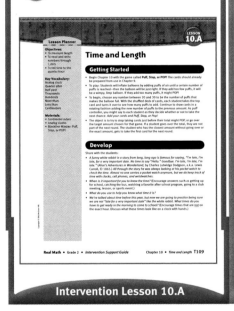

Intervention Lesson 10.A

ENGLISH LEARNER

Preview

If . . . students need language support,

Then . . . use Lesson 10.2 in *English Learner Support Guide* to preview lesson concepts and vocabulary.

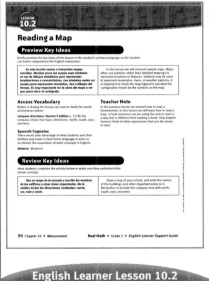

English Learner Lesson 10.2

ENRICH

If . . . students are proficient in the lesson concepts,

Then . . . emphasize additional game time and variations.

PRACTICE

If . . . students would benefit from additional practice,

Then . . . extend Skill Building.

RETEACH

If . . . students are having difficulty understanding reading a map,

Then . . . extend Guided Discussion.

Academic Vocabulary
map \map\ *n.* a drawing or other representation of Earth's surface, usually showing cities, rivers, oceans, mountains, and other features

Access Vocabulary
compass directions the compass shows four basic directions—north, south, east, and west

Spanish Cognates
distance distancia

Teaching Lesson 10.2

 TEXAS

Number, operation, and quantitative reasoning 2.3 The student adds and subtracts whole numbers to solve problems

Underlying processes and mathematical tools 2.12.A Identify the mathematics in everyday situations.

Underlying processes and mathematical tools 2.1 Explain and record observations using objects, words, pictures, numbers, and technology.

Mental Math

 **5**

 INTEGRATION: TEKS 3.5.B Present three-digit subtraction sentences to students. Have them show thumbs-up if the answer is correct and thumbs-down if the answer is incorrect. Possible examples include the following:

a. 60 − 40 = 20
up

b. 30 − 10 = 30
down

c. 45 − 25 = 20
up

d. 70 − 15 = 55
up

e. 52 − 22 = 20
down

f. 67 − 32 = 25
down

1 Develop **25**

Tell Students In Today's Lesson They Will

practice reading maps.

Guided Discussion Introductory

Show students a map of the United States or of your local area and introduce them to north, south, east, and west. Ask questions using the map and the directional words. For example:

- **Can you name a state that is north of Texas?** Kansas
- **Can you name a state that is east of Kansas?** Virginia
- **Can you name a state that is south of Virginia?** Florida
- **Can you name a state that is west of Florida?** California

Use the map on page 377 to introduce road distances, cities, and directions on maps. Explain that the squares on the map represent cities. Ask questions to provide practice in finding distances. Make sure students understand they must drive on the road.

- **How far is it from Chippewa Falls to Deer River?** 83 km

Ask questions to provide practice in figuring out compass directions.

- **In which direction do you travel to go from Castle City to Webster?** south or south southwest

Point out that the distance between two places is the same regardless of which direction you are traveling. For example, you could show that the distance from Deer River to Webster (95 km) is the same as the distance from Webster to Deer River.

Skill Building ENGAGING Guided

Briefly review the terms left and right with students. Face various walls in your classroom. Ask students a series of questions about facing new directions, and have volunteers answer. Explain that you want to face each new direction by turning as little as possible. Possible examples include the following:

- **I am facing north; if I want to face west, which way should I turn?** left
- **I am facing south; if I want to face west, which way should I turn?** right
- **I am facing east; if I want to face north, which way should I turn?** left

- **I am facing south; if I want to face east, which way should I turn?** left
- **I am facing north; if I want to face south, which way should I turn?** either way; It will take you the same amount of time to turn both left or right because north and south are opposite directions.

Skill and Strategy Building APPLYING Guided

Game Map Game

Demonstrate the **Map Game** by playing a round with a student. Besides giving practice in compass directions, this game is helpful in getting students used to associating a direction with a number. As you demonstrate this game, mention the compass directions. Complete directions can be found on the game mat.

2 Use Student Pages **20**

Pages 377–378 UNDERSTANDING

Have students complete page 378, using page 377 for reference.

Progress Monitoring

If . . . students have difficulty reading the map on page 377,

Then . . . work with students individually or in small groups as they do the problems on page 378.

 Integration: TEKS 2.13.A, Journal

As Students Finish

Game Map Game

 Games *Map Game*

RESEARCH IN ACTION

"Spatial sense includes two main spatial abilities: spatial orientation and spatial visualization and imagery. Other important knowledge includes how to represent ideas in drawing and how and when to use such abilities. . . . Neither students nor adults actually have "maps in their heads"—that is, their "mental maps" are not like a mental picture of a paper map. Instead, they are filled with private knowledge and idiosyncrasies and actually consist of many kinds of ideas and processes, which may be organized into several frames of reference. . . . Developing students' ability to make and use mental maps is important, and so is developing geometric ideas from experiences with maps."

Clements, Douglas H. "Teaching and Learning Geometry" in Kilpatrick, Jeremy, W. Gary Martin, and Deborah Schifter, eds. *A Research Companion to Principles and Standards for School Mathematics.* Reston, VA: National Council of Teachers of Mathematics, Inc. 2003, p. 165.

Student Page

Name _____ Date _____

LESSON 10.2 Reading a Map

Key Ideas

Maps show how different places are related in terms of direction and distance.

Math TEKS Underlying processes and mathematical tools 2.13.A Explain and record observations using objects, words, pictures, numbers, and technology.

Study the map.

North
Chippewa Falls
96 km
White Horse
83 km
93 km
86 km
Castle City
115 km
Deer River
West
East
88 km
95 km
99 km
New Manila
Webster
103 km
South

Textbook This lesson is available in the *eTextbook*.

377

LESSON 10.2 · Reading a Map

Complete the table. Use the map on page 377 to find the shortest distances.

Towns	Shortest Distance (kilometers)
① Chippewa Falls and New Manila	211
② New Manila and Deer River	181
③ White Horse and Webster	185
④ Chippewa Falls and Webster	178

Write your answers.

⑤ Which town is farthest from Castle City? _____ Chippewa Falls

⑥ Which town is farthest from Webster? _____ White Horse

⑦ Which town is closest to White Horse? _____ Castle City

⑧ Which town is closest to Deer River? _____ Chippewa Falls

⑨ Which is the shortest way to get to Deer River from White Horse? _____ through Chippewa Falls or Castle City

Writing + Math Journal

Write directions to tell a friend how to get from Chippewa Falls to Castle City. See Reflect

378

Real Math • Chapter 10 • Lesson 2

---

3 Reflect

10

Guided Discussion REASONING

Discuss giving directions to people and how we use maps to find our way from one place to another. Sketch a rough map of the classroom on the board where each student's desk is a different "city." Have students practice giving directions from one "city" to another. For example:

To get from Raul's desk to Tiffany's desk, travel north and turn left at Amir's desk. Head west until you reach Tiffany's desk.

If interest permits, have students sketch a rough map of the classrooms in the school and give similar directions.

Writing + Math Journal

Discuss students' answers. Answers will vary based on what kind of route students took or what directional words they used. For example: Head south to Deer River, turn left and go east until you reach Castle City.

REAL WORLD **Curriculum Connection:** Display a local map, and point out the location of landmarks. Encourage students to locate points of interest on the map. Have students tell which direction they would travel to get to each place from their town.

Review **Cumulative Review:** For cumulative review of previously learned skills, see page 387–388.

Family Involvement: Assign the *Practice, Reteach,* or *Enrichment* activities depending on the needs of your students. Have students play the **Map Game** with a family member.

Concept/Question Board: Have students look for additional examples using measurement and post them on the Concept/Question Board.

Math Puzzler: Jorge lives 14 miles from school. Jenna lives 8 miles farther from school than Jorge does. How far does Jenna live from school? 22 miles

4 Assess and Differentiate

 Assess Use *eAssess* to record and analyze evidence of student understanding.

A Gather Evidence

Use the Daily Class Assessment Records in *Texas Assessment* or *eAssess* to record daily observations.

Informal Assessment

 Skill Building

Did the student **ENGAGING**
- ❏ pay attention to others' contributions?
- ❏ contribute information and ideas?
- ❏ improve on a strategy?
- ❏ reflect on and check the accuracy of his or her work?

Performance Assessment

☑ **Game**

Did the student **APPLYING**
- ❏ apply learning in new situations?
- ❏ contribute concepts?
- ❏ contribute answers?
- ❏ connect mathematics to real-world situations?

TEKS/TAKS Practice

Use *TEKS/TAKS Practice* page 107 to assess student progress.

B Summarize Findings

Analyze and summarize assessment data for each student. Determine which Assessment Follow-Up is appropriate for each student. Use the Student Assessment Record in *Texas Assessment* or *eAssess* to update assessment records.

C Texas Assessment Follow-Up ● DIFFERENTIATE INSTRUCTION

Based on your observations, use these teaching strategies for assessment follow-up.

INTERVENTION

Review student performance on *Intervention* Lesson 10.A to see if students have mastered prerequisite skills for this lesson.

Measurement 1.7 The student directly compares the attributes of length, area, weight/mass, capacity, and temperature. The student uses comparative language to solve problems and answer questions. The student selects and uses nonstandard units to describe length.

ENGLISH LEARNER

Review

Use Lesson 10.2 in *English Learner Support Guide* to review lesson concepts and vocabulary.

ENRICH

If . . . students are proficient in the lesson concepts,

Then . . . encourage them to work on the chapter projects or *Enrichment* Lesson 10.2.

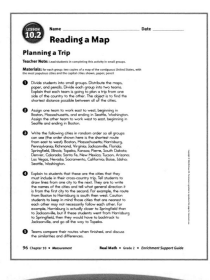

Enrichment Lesson 10.2

TEXAS PRACTICE

If . . . students would benefit from additional practice,

Then . . . assign *Practice* Lesson 10.2.

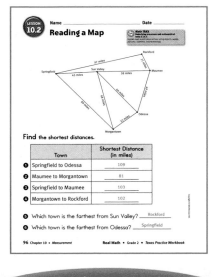

Practice Lesson 10.2

RETEACH

If . . . students are having difficulty understanding reading a map,

Then . . . reteach the concept using *Reteach* Lesson 10.2.

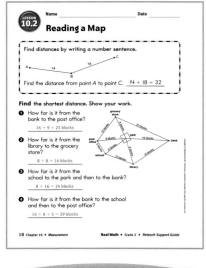

Reteach Lesson 10.2

TEXAS

Vertical Alignment

Grade 1	Grade 2	Grade 3
1.6.A Describe and identify two-dimensional geometric figures, including circles, triangles, rectangles, and squares (a special type of rectangle	**2.3.B** Model addition and subtraction of two-digit numbers with objects, pictures, words, and numbers.	**3.11.B** Use standard units to find the perimeter of a shape.

Overview

LESSON 10.3

TEXAS

Lesson Planner

OBJECTIVES

- To provide practice in finding the perimeter of objects
- To provide practice in measuring length in both customary and metric units
- To reintroduce students to the idea that when converting from a larger unit of measure to a smaller one, the number of units will be greater

MATH TEKS

Number, operation, and quantitative reasoning 2.3.B
Model addition and subtraction of two-digit numbers with objects, pictures, words, and numbers.

Underlying processes and mathematical tools 2.12.D
Use tools such as real objects, manipulatives, and technology to solve problems

MATH TEKS INTEGRATION

Geometry and spatial reasoning 2.7.A
Describe attributes (the number of vertices, faces, edges, sides) of two- and three- dimensional geometric figures such as circles, polygons, spheres, cones, cylinders, prisms, and pyramids, etc.

Underlying processes and mathematical tools 2.14
The student is expected to justify his or her thinking using objects, words, pictures, numbers, and technology.

MATERIALS

- *Number Cubes
- *Rulers
- *Map Game Mat
- Tape measures
- String
- Scissors
- *SRA Math Vocabulary Card*

TECHNOLOGY

e Presentation Lesson 10.3
e Games Map Game

Measuring Perimeter

Context of the Lesson This is the third lesson in a series which covers different aspects of measurement: weight, length, capacity, temperature, and time. Both metric and customary units are discussed, but students do not convert measurements from one system to the other. This lesson reviews perimeter, Which was introduced in Lesson 2.7 as an application of adding with multiple addends. Students will also measure the perimeter of objects in the classroom using centimeters and inches, which were introduced in Chapter 4.

See page 373B for Math Background for teachers for this lesson.

Planning for Learning ● DIFFERENTIATE INSTRUCTION

INTERVENTION

If . . . students lack the prerequisite skill of telling time to the quarter hour,

Then . . . teach **Intervention** Lesson 10.A.

 1.7

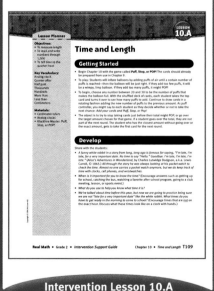

Intervention Lesson 10.A

ENGLISH LEARNER

Preview

If . . . students need language support,

Then . . . use Lesson 10.3 in **English Learner Support Guide** to preview lesson concepts and vocabulary.

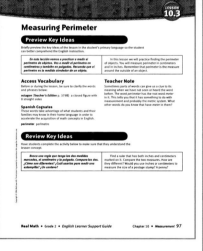

English Learner Lesson 10.3

ENRICH

If . . . students are proficient in the lesson concepts,

Then . . . emphasize chapter projects.

PRACTICE

If . . . students would benefit from additional practice,

Then . . . extend Skill Building.

RETEACH

If . . . students are having difficulty understanding measuring perimeter,

Then . . . extend Guided Discussion.

Academic Vocabulary
✏ **perimeter \pə ri´ mə tər\ n.** the measure of the distance of the path around an object or figure

Spanish Cognates
perimeter perímetro

Number, operation, and quantitative reasoning 2.3.B
Model addition and subtraction of two-digit numbers
with objects, pictures, words, and numbers.
Underlying processes and mathematical tools 2.12.D
Use tools such as real objects, manipulatives, and
technology to solve problems.

Mental Math 5

 INTEGRATION: TEKS 2.7.A Say the name of a plane figure aloud, and have students display how many sides that figure has using their **Number Cubes**. Possible examples include the following:

a. octagon 8	**b.** hexagon 6	**c.** triangle 3
d. trapezoid 4	**e.** pentagon 5	**f.** rhombus 4

1 Develop 25

Tell Students In Today's Lesson They Will

measure perimeter in centimeters and in inches.

Guided Discussion UNDERSTANDING

Introductory

Describe, compare, and name the following figures shown on page 379: triangle, square, octagon, rectangle, and parallelogram.

Remind students that *perimeter* is the measure of the length of the path around a figure. Ask students how they would measure the perimeter of a figure. Explore students' ideas and how they could work or not work. Explain that if the figure is a polygon, the perimeter is the sum of the lengths of its sides.

Skill Building APPLYING

Guided

As a class, pick an object in the classroom, and measure the sides so students can calculate the perimeter. Have a separate volunteer measure each of the sides and report the measurement to the class. If the object is three dimensional, have students discuss which edges they are going to measure to calculate the perimeter. For example, if measuring a computer monitor, students could measure the screen size or the size of the monitor casing.

■ **Critical Thinking** **What would happen if one side were measured in inches and another in centimeters?** The measurement of perimeter would not be accurate because the units would not be the same.

After all the measurements have been reported, have students calculate the perimeter of the object individually or in small groups and discuss their answers.

After students have measured an object with straight sides, have them try to calculate the perimeter of an object with a curved side or several curved sides. In order to do this, students can either use a tape measure or measure a piece of string the length of the side, cut the string, and measure it on a straight edge. Have students try both methods on the same side of an object. Then have them discuss which method is more accurate.

2 Use Student Pages 20

Pages 379–380 APPLYING

Independent

Have students complete page 379 independently. Make sure they understand that the figures are not drawn to scale. Then have students work with a partner to complete page 380. Have the class agree on exactly what objects are going to be measured before students begin filling in the table. Make sure rulers are available for students to complete their work.

As Students Finish

Game Have students play the **Map Game** in pairs.

Games *Map Game*

RESEARCH IN ACTION

"Measurement is one of the main real-world applications of mathematics . . . counting is a type of measurement—it measures how many items in a collection. Measurement of continuous quantities involves assigning a number to attributes such as length, area, and weight. Together, number and measurement are components of quantitative reasoning. In this vein, measurement helps connect the two realms of number and geometry, each providing conceptual support to the other."

Clements, Douglas and J. Sarama, eds. *Engaging Young Children in Mathematics: Standards for Early Childhood Mathematics Education.* Mahwah, New Jersey: Lawrence Erlbaum Associates Publishers, 2004, pp. 43–50.

Teacher Reflection

Student Page

Name _____ Date _____

LESSON 10.3 Measuring Perimeter

Key Ideas

The **perimeter** is the measure of the distance on a path around a figure.

> **Math TEKS** Number, operation, and quantitative reasoning 2.3.B ← Model addition and subtraction of two-digit numbers with objects, pictures, words, and numbers.

Find the perimeter.

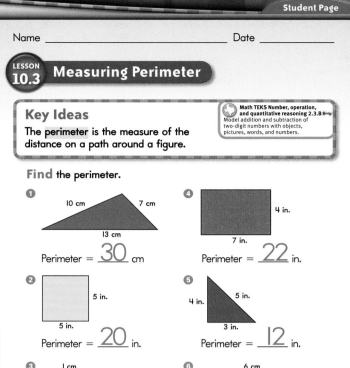

❶
10 cm 7 cm
13 cm
Perimeter = __30__ cm

❹
4 in.
7 in.
Perimeter = __22__ in.

❷
5 in.
5 in.
Perimeter = __20__ in.

❺
4 in. 5 in.
3 in.
Perimeter = __12__ in.

❸
1 cm ... (octagon, each side 1 cm)
Perimeter = __8__ cm

❻
6 cm
3 cm   3 cm
6 cm
Perimeter = __18__ cm

Ⓔ **Textbook** This lesson is available in the *eTextbook*.

379

LESSON 10.3 · Measuring Perimeter

Measure objects in your classroom. Fill in the table.

Object	Perimeter in Centimeters	Perimeter in Inches
❼		
❽		
❾		

What is the perimeter of the combined figures?

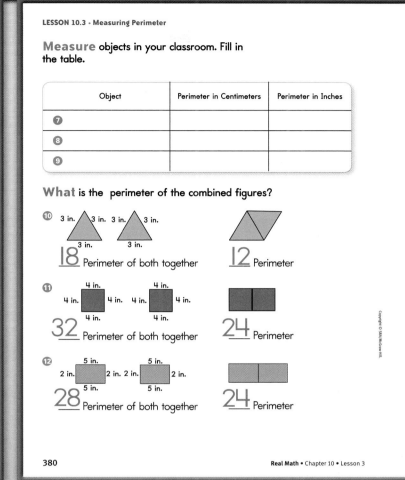

❿
3 in. 3 in. 3 in. 3 in.
3 in. 3 in.
__18__ Perimeter of both together
__12__ Perimeter

⓫
4 in. 4 in.
4 in. 4 in. 4 in. 4 in.
4 in. 4 in.
__32__ Perimeter of both together
__24__ Perimeter

⓬
5 in. 5 in.
2 in. 2 in. 2 in. 2 in.
5 in. 5 in.
__28__ Perimeter of both together
__24__ Perimeter

380

Real Math · Chapter 10 · Lesson 3

---

3 Reflect

10

Guided Discussion ✓ REASONING

Have students look at the table they completed on student page 380.

INTEGRATION: TEKS 2.14

- **Critical Thinking** Which measurements are greater, the number of inches in the perimeter or the number of centimeters in the perimeter? the number of centimeters
- **Why do you think so?** because inches are longer than centimeters, so it takes less of them to cover the same distance

Curriculum Connection: Students might be interested in finding the perimeter of paintings or drawings they have done and then using the measurements to design a frame.

Cumulative Review: For cumulative review of previously learned skills, see page 387–388.

Family Involvement: Assign the *Practice, Reteach,* or *Enrichment* activities depending on the needs of your students. Have students measure the perimeter of objects at home with a family member.

Concept/Question Board: Have students look for additional examples using measurement and post them on the Concept/Question Board.

Math Puzzler: Mrs. Ming wants to put a fence around her pool. She wants to fence an area 6 yards long and 3 yards wide. She plans on buying 20 yards of fence. Is that enough? How can you tell? yes; the perimeter is 18 yards

4 Assess and Differentiate

 Assess Use *eAssess* to record and analyze evidence of student understanding.

A Gather Evidence

Use the Daily Class Assessment Records in *Texas Assessment* or *eAssess* to record daily observations.

Informal Assessment
☑ **Using the Student Pages**

Did the student APPLYING
- ❏ apply learning in new situations?
- ❏ contribute concepts?
- ❏ contribute answers?
- ❏ connect mathematics to real-world situations?

Informal Assessment
☑ **Guided Discussion**

Did the student REASONING
- ❏ provide a clear explanation?
- ❏ communicate reasons and strategies?
- ❏ choose appropriate strategies?
- ❏ argue logically?

 TEKS/TAKS Practice

Use *TEKS/TAKS Practice* page 21 to assess student progress.

B Summarize Findings

Analyze and summarize assessment data for each student. Determine which Assessment Follow-Up is appropriate for each student. Use the Student Assessment Record in *Texas Assessment* or *eAssess* to update assessment records.

C Texas Assessment Follow-Up • DIFFERENTIATE INSTRUCTION

Based on your observations, use these teaching strategies for assessment follow-up.

INTERVENTION

Review student performance on *Intervention* Lesson 10.A to see if students have mastered prerequisite skills for this lesson.

Measurement 1.7 The student directly compares the attributes of length, area, weight/mass, capacity, and temperature. The student uses comparative language to solve problems and answer questions. The student selects and uses nonstandard units to describe length.

ENGLISH LEARNER

Review

Use Lesson 10.3 in *English Learner Support Guide* to review lesson concepts and vocabulary.

ENRICH

If . . . students are proficient in the lesson concepts,

Then . . . encourage them to work on the chapter projects or *Enrichment* Lesson 10.3.

Enrichment Lesson 10.3

TEXAS PRACTICE

If . . . students would benefit from additional practice,

Then . . . assign *Practice* Lesson 10.3.

Practice Lesson 10.3

RETEACH

If . . . students are having difficulty understanding perimeter,

Then . . . help them understand measuring the distance around an object by walking the perimeter of the playground.

TEXAS Vertical Alignment

Grade 1	Grade 2	Grade 3
1.7.F Describe and identify two-dimensional geometric figures, including circles, triangles, rectangles, and squares (a special type of rectangle).	**2.9** The student directly compares the attributes of length, area, weight/mass, and capacity, and uses comparative language to solve problems and answer questions.	**3.11** Use standard units to find the perimeter of a shape.

Overview · LESSON 10.4

TEXAS

Lesson Planner

OBJECTIVES
- To introduce the gram and kilogram as standard units of weight
- To teach the relationship between grams and kilograms
- To provide experience in measuring weight in metric units
- To review how to count in thousands by converting kilograms into grams

MATH TEKS
Measurement 2.9  The student directly compares the attributes of length, area, weight/mass, and capacity, and uses comparative language to solve problems and answer questions. The student selects and uses nonstandard units to describe length, area, capacity, and weight/mass. The student recognizes and uses models that approximate standard units (from both SI, also known as metric, and customary systems) of length, weight/mass, capacity, and time.
Measurement 2.9.D Select a non-standard unit of measure such as beans or marbles to determine the weight/mass of a given object.

MATH TEKS
Preparing for: Grade 3 Number, operation, and quantitative reasoning 3.5.B Use strategies including rounding and compatible numbers to estimate solutions to addition and subtraction problems.
Underlying processes and mathematical tools 2.14 The student is expected to justify his or her thinking using objects, words, pictures, numbers, and technology.

MATERIALS
- *Double-pan balance scale with metric weights
- A variety of objects to weight.
- Ice cubes
- Insulated cup with lid
- *Map Game Mat
- *Platform scale

TECHNOLOGY
- ⓔ **Presentation** Lesson 10.4
- ⓔ **Games** Map Game

*Manipulative Kit Item  = Key standard

Kilograms and Grams ★

Context of the Lesson This is the fourth lesson in a series that cover different aspects of measurement: weight, length, capacity, temperature, and time. Both metric and customary units are discussed, but students do not convert measurements from one system to the other. This lesson is the first of two lesson on measuring weight in standard units and particularly focuses on measuring weight in metric units. Measuring weight in grams was first introduced in Grade 1. The next lesson introduces weight measurement in standard customary units.

See page 373B for Math Background for teachers for this lesson.

Planning for Learning ● DIFFERENTIATE INSTRUCTION

INTERVENTION
If . . . students lack the prerequisite skill of measuring length,

Then . . . teach **Intervention** Lesson 10.B.

 1.7, 1.8

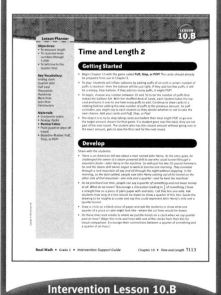

Intervention Lesson 10.B

ENGLISH LEARNER
Preview

If . . . students need language support,

Then . . . use Lesson 10.4 in **English Learner Support Guide** to preview lesson concepts and vocabulary.

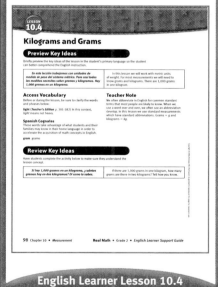

English Learner Lesson 10.4

ENRICH
If . . . students are proficient in the lesson concepts,

Then . . . emphasize Guided Discussion in Reflect.

PRACTICE
If . . . students would benefit from additional practice,

Then . . . extend Guided Discussion before assigning the student pages.

RETEACH
If . . . students are having difficulty understanding measuring weight in grams,

Then . . . extend Guided Discussion before assigning the student pages.

Academic Vocabulary	Access Vocabulary	Spanish Cognates
weight \wāt\ *n.* the amount of heaviness of something	**light** In this context, light means not heavy.	**gram** gramo

★ = 120-Day Plan for TAKS

Teaching Lesson 10.4

  TEXAS

Measurement 2.9 The student directly compares the attributes of length, area, weight/mass, and capacity, and uses comparative language to solve problems and answer questions. The student selects and uses nonstandard units to describe length, area, capacity, and weight/mass. The student recognizes and uses models that approximate standard units (from both SI, also known as metric, and customary systems) of length, weight/mass, capacity, and time.

Measurement 2.9.D Select a non-standa measure such as beans or marbles to d weight/mass of a given object.

Mental Math 5

 THUMBS UP **INTEGRATION: TEKS 3.5.D** Present students with addition and subtraction exercises. Have them show thumbs-up if the sum or difference is even and thumbs-down if the sum or difference is odd. Possible examples include the following:

a. $10 + 70 = 90$
down

b. $90 - 20 = 70$
up

c. $55 - 20 = 35$
up

d. $20 + 34 = 36$
down

e. $65 - 20 = 45$
up

f. $23 + 32 = 85$
down

1 Develop 25

Tell Students In Today's Lesson They Will

learn about grams and kilograms.

Guided Discussion UNDERSTANDING

 Introductory

Prepare in advance a number of objects to be weighed (pack of crayons, box of staples, plastic cups, glue bottles, etc.) as well as a double-pan balance scale.

Have students come to the front of the class and demonstrate how the balance works. Then, have the students list nonstandard units that a specific object could be weighed in, for example a highlighter may be weighed using beans or marbles. Next, select volunteers to come to the front of the class and weigh the objects using the nonstandard units (e.g., washers). After that, select another student to come to the front of the room and weigh the object using a different nonstandard unit (e.g., base-ten blocks). Discuss with the students what they notice. Ask questions such as the following:

■ **Which unit of measurement had the greater number?**

■ **Critical Thinking** **Why do you think it took more of that unit than the other?**

Go on to explain to the students the difficulties that come from comparing the weights of objects using different units. Then, point out to students that this is the reason for standard units, such as grams and kilograms. Mention to the students that they will soon learn about other units to measure weight in, but in this lesson they will work with grams and kilograms.

Explain that there are 1,000 grams in 1 kilogram.

■ **How many grams are in 2 kilograms?** 2,000

Write 2,000 on the board, and say "two thousand."

■ **How many grams are in 10 kilograms?** 10,000

Show students how to use the double-pan balance scale to weigh objects. Demonstrate this by weighing several objects found in the classroom. Explain that they will use a similar scale to weigh objects in the classroom to complete page 382.

Strategy Building APPLYING

Guided

Fill an insulated cup with ice cubes, and put the lid on the cup. Then place the cup on one side of the double-pan balance. Have a volunteer come to the front of the room and balance the scale with the appropriate amount of weights. Then have the other students come and examine the scale to verify that it is indeed balanced.

 INTEGRATION: TEKS 2.14

■ **Critical Thinking** **What do you think will happen as the ice melts? Will the scale stay balanced?** Keep the cup and weights on the scale throughout the day in order to examine what will happen. Because the insulated cup with a lid is a closed system, the weight should stay the same. If the cup were not insulated, then condensation would make the cup heavier throughout the day. Allow students to make their predictions at this time.

After all of the ice has melted, have students see if their predictions were correct. The double-pan balance and weights will be needed for the lesson, so have students record the amount of weights on the scale. Remove the cup and weights for the remainder of the lesson, but place them back on as soon as the balance is free.

2 Use Student Pages 20

Pages 381–382 APPLYING

Guided

Have students complete page 381 independently. After the class has completed the page, help them see that all the answers are multiples of 1,000.

Set up a weigh station with the double-pan balance and platform scale. Have the class choose several objects in the classroom to weigh. Students should decide which units to use to weigh the object. Let each student come up with an estimate and record it on his or her table. Then have a volunteer weigh the object and announce the weight to the class. Then have students calculate the difference between their measurements and estimates. By making students estimate based on earlier measures, students are acting on feedback that helps to improve their later estimates.

Provide a variety of objects for students to weigh, and complete page 382 as a class.

As Students Finish

 Have students play the **Map Game** in pairs or assign games based on needed skill practice.

 **Games** *Map Game*

Student Page

Name _____ Date _____

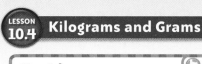
LESSON 10.4 Kilograms and Grams

Key Ideas

The kilogram and the gram are units of weight. There are 1,000 grams in 1 kilogram.

Math TEKS Measurement 2.9 The student directly compare the attributes of length, area, weight/mass, and capacity, and uses comparative language to solve problems and answer questions. The student selects and uses nonstandard units to describe length, area, capacity, and weight/mass. The student recognizes and uses models that approximate standard units of length, weight/mass, capacity, and time.

I kilogram

22 kilograms

How many?

❶ 1 kilogram = **1,000** grams   ❹ 4 kg = **4,000** g

❷ 2 kg = **2,000** g   ❺ 5 kg = **5,000** g

❸ 3 kg = **3,000** g   ❻ 6 kg = **6,000** g

 Textbook This lesson is available in the *eTextbook.*   381

Student Page

LESSON 10.4 · Kilograms and Grams

How much does it weigh?

Record your answers on the table.

Object	Estimated Weight	Measured Weight	Difference

Writing + Math ▶ Journal

If a book is measured in grams and kilograms, which unit would have the greater number? Why?   *See Reflect*

382   Real Math • Chapter 10 • Lesson 4

③ Reflect   10

Guided Discussion   REASONING

Lead a discussion about the table on student page 382.

■ **Critical Thinking Did your estimates get better after the first two or three weighings?** Allow students to discuss, but their estimates probably got more accurate.

■ **Why do you think that happened?** Allow students to discuss. For example, it may have been easier to make estimates after you knew the actual weight of a commonly used object.

Writing + Math ▶ Journal

Discuss students' answers. Students should say that the amount of grams would be greater because grams are smaller than kilograms. Therefore, it would take more grams to equal the same weight in kilograms.

 Cumulative Review: For cumulative review of previously learned skills, see page 387–388.

 Family Involvement: Assign the **Practice, Reteach,** or **Enrichment** activities depending on the needs of your students.

 Concept/Question Board: Encourage students to continue to post questions, answers, and examples on the Concept/Question Board.

 Math Puzzler: In her cupboard Ms. Eng had three cans. They were all sealed shut, they looked alike, and none of them had a label. "I need some cotton," she said. "I know that one of these cans is filled with cotton, another is filled with air that I brought back from my vacation, and another is filled with soup. I wish I didn't have to open all of them to find the one that is filled with cotton." How can Ms. Eng tell which can is filled with cotton without opening any cans? by choosing the one that is neither the heaviest nor the lightest

4 Assess and Differentiate

 Assess Use **eAssess** to record and analyze evidence of student understanding.

A Gather Evidence

Use the Daily Class Assessment Records in *Texas Assessment* or *eAssess* to record daily observations.

Informal Assessment
☑ **Mental Math**

Did the student COMPUTING
- ❑ respond accurately?
- ❑ respond quickly?
- ❑ respond with confidence?
- ❑ self-correct?

Informal Assessment
☑ **Concept/Question Board**

Did the student APPLYING
- ❑ apply learning in new situations?
- ❑ contribute concepts?
- ❑ contribute answers?
- ❑ connect mathematics to real-world situations?

🤠 TEKS/TAKS Practice

Use *TEKS/TAKS Practice* page 77 to assess student progress.

B Summarize Findings

Analyze and summarize assessment data for each student. Determine which Assessment Follow-Up is appropriate for each student. Use the Student Assessment Record in *Texas Assessment* or *eAssess* to update assessment records.

C Texas Assessment Follow-Up ● DIFFERENTIATE INSTRUCTION

Based on your observations, use these teaching strategies for assessment follow-up.

INTERVENTION

Review student performance on *Intervention* Lesson10.B to see if students have mastered prerequisite skills for this lesson.

🤠 **Measurement 1.7** The student directly compares the attributes of length, area, weight/mass, capacity, and temperature. The student uses comparative language to solve problems and answer questions. The student selects and uses nonstandard units to describe length.

ENGLISH LEARNER

Review

Use Lesson 10.4 in *English Learner Support Guide* to review lesson concepts and vocabulary.

ENRICH

If . . . students are proficient in the lesson concepts,

Then . . . encourage them to work on the chapter projects or *Enrichment* Lesson 10.4.

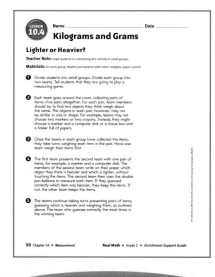

Enrichment Lesson 10.4

🤠 PRACTICE

If . . . students would benefit from additional practice,

Then . . . assign *Practice* Lesson 10.4.

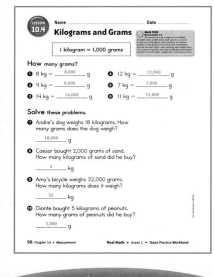

Practice Lesson 10.4

RETEACH

If . . . students are having difficulty deciding whether to weigh objects in grams or kilograms,

Then . . . remind them 1,000 grams are in a kilogram.

TEXAS Vertical Alignment

Grade 1	Grade 2	Grade 3
1.7.F Compare and order two or more objects according to weight/mass (from heaviest to lightest).	**2.9** The student directly compares the attributes of length, area, weight/mass, and capacity, and uses comparative language to solve problems and answer questions.	**3.11** The student selects and uses standard units to describe length, area, capacity/volume, and weight/mass.

Overview

LESSON 10.5

TEXAS

OBJECTIVES

- To introduce standard units of measure for weight
- To help students develop an understanding of weight in pounds and ounces
- To teach students how to convert pounds into ounces and vice versa

 ## MATH TEKS

Measurement 2.9 The student directly compares the attributes of length, area, weight/mass, and capacity, and uses comparative language to solve problems and answer questions. The student selects and uses nonstandard units to describe length, area, capacity, and weight/mass. The student recognizes and uses models that approximate standard units (from both SI, also known as metric, and customary systems) of length, weight/mass, capacity, and time. **Measurement 2.9.D** Select a nonstandard unit of measure such as beans or marbles to determine the weight/mass of a given object.

MATH TEKS INTEGRATION

Extending: Number, operation, and quantitative reasoning 2.2 The student describes how fractions are used to name parts of whole objects or sets of objects. **Underlying processes and mathematical tools 2.12.A** Identify the mathematics in everyday situations.

MATERIALS

- *Number Cubes
- *Double-pan balance and ounce weights
- *Platform scale
- Various objects for students to weigh

TECHNOLOGY

Presentation Lesson 10.5

Looking Ahead

Yor will need clear containers with pint, quart, and gallon capacities for Lesson 10.6.

Pounds and Ounces ⭐

Context of the Lesson This is the fifth lesson in a series that covers different aspects of measurement: weight, length, capacity, temperature, and time. Both metric and customary units are discussed, but students do not convert measurements from one system to the other. This lesson is the second of two lessons on measuring weight in standard units and particularly focuses on measuring weight in customary units. Measuring weight in pounds was first introduced in Grade 1. The next two lessons focus on measuring capacity.

See page 373B for Math Background for teachers for this lesson.

Planning for Learning ● DIFFERENTIATE INSTRUCTION

INTERVENTION

If . . . students lack the prerequisite skill of reading and writing numbers through 1,000,

Then . . . teach *Intervention* Lesson 10.B.

1.7, 1.8

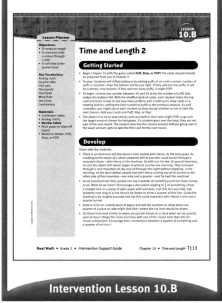

Intervention Lesson 10.B

ENGLISH LEARNER

Preview

If . . . students need language support,

Then . . . use Lesson 10.5 in *English Learner Support Guide* to preview lesson concepts and vocabulary.

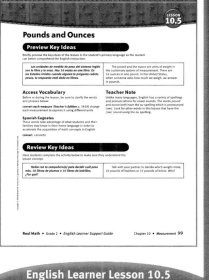

English Learner Lesson 10.5

ENRICH

If . . . students are proficient in the lesson concepts,

Then . . . emphasize Reflect.

PRACTICE

If . . . students would benefit from additional practice,

Then . . . extend Skill Building before assigning the student pages.

RETEACH

If . . . students are having difficulty understanding measuring weight in pounds,

Then . . . extend Guided Discussion before assigning the student pages.

Access Vocabulary
convert each measure change each measurement to express it using different units

Spanish Cognates
convert convertir

Measurement 2.9 The student directly compares the attributes of length, area, weight/mass, and capacity, and uses comparative language to solve problems and answer questions. The student selects and uses nonstandard units to describe length, area, capacity, and weight/mass. The student recognizes and uses models that approximate standard units (from both SI, also known as metric, and customary systems) of length, weight/mass, capacity, and time.

 Measurement 2.9.D Select a non-standard unit of measure s... as beans or marbles to determine the we... mass of a given object.

Mental Math 5

  INTEGRATION: TEKS 2.2 Present students with fraction problems, and have them show their answers using their **Number Cubes.** Possible examples include the following:

a. What is $\frac{1}{4}$ of 12? 3
b. What is $\frac{1}{3}$ of 3? 1
c. What is $\frac{1}{5}$ of 15? 3
d. What is $\frac{1}{2}$ of 12? 6
e. What is $\frac{1}{2}$ of 6? 3
f. What is $\frac{1}{4}$ of 4? 1

1 Develop 25

Tell Students In Today's Lesson They Will

learn about pounds and ounces.

Guided Discussion UNDERSTANDING Introductory

Lead students in a discussion of pounds and ounces.

■ **Do you know what a *pound* is?** a unit of weight

> **INTEGRATION: TEKS 2.12.A**
>
> ■ **Can you name some things that are commonly measured in pounds?** people, food, and packages

Explain that weight is also measured in a unit smaller than a pound, called an *ounce.* Explain that there are 16 ounces in 1 pound.

Point out to the students that both units are used interchangeably in real-world settings when expressing the weight of some objects; for example a steak could weigh 1 pound or 16 ounces. Since weights can be used interchangeably we sometimes need to convert the measurements. Explain to students that converting units is not something confined to measurements of weight alone, but are used when referring to any measurement. The most recognizable to the students is probably height; for example on amusement rides children need to be a certain height to ride, such as 4 feet or 48 inches.

Next, create a chart similar to the following, in which the students explain how to find the equivalent ounces for each pound:

1 pound = 16 ounces
2 pounds = 32 ounces
3 pounds = 48 ounces
6 pounds = 96 ounces

Note that for this lesson students will only be converting pounds to ounces.

Skill Building REASONING Guided

Set up a weigh station with the double-pan balance, the ounce weights, and the platform scale to weigh pounds.

Show several objects to the class, and ask if they would measure them in pounds or ounces. Ordinarily, heavier objects are measured in pounds and lighter objects in ounces to make the answer a reasonable number. For example, a pencil would probably be measured in ounces, not pounds.

Allow volunteers to weigh the objects. Have students try weighing an object that would normally be weighed in ounces (such as an eraser) using the platform scale. Then have them measure the same object using the double-pan balance.

■ **Which measurement is more accurate?** the double-pan balance
■ **Why do you think so?** because that scale and unit of measure is more appropriate for what we are measuring

2 Use Student Pages 20

Pages 383–384 APPLYING Independent

Have students complete page 383 individually. After students finish, complete page 384 together as a class. Use the weigh station you set up earlier to complete page 384. Follow the same procedures used in Lesson 10.4, allowing a volunteer to weigh the object and having each student come up with their own estimate. By making estimate based on earlier measures, students are acting on feedback that helps improve their later estimates.

As Students Finish

 Game Allow students to choose a game from among those previously introduced, or assign games based on needed skill practice.

TEXAS TEKS Checkup

TEKS 2.9.D • Select a non-standard unit of measure such as beans or marbles to determine the weight/mass of a given object.

Use this problem to assess students' progress toward standards mastery:

If two beans weigh about the same as one penny, how many beans would weigh the same as ten pennies?

A about 2   B about 20
C about 50   D about 100

Have students choose the correct answer and describe how they knew which choice was correct. In the discussion, ask questions such as the following. Be sure to ask students to explain their reasoning because

different solution methods are possible.

■ What information are you given? two beans weigh about one penny

■ What is the problem asking? How much would ten pennies weigh?

■ How could you solve this problem? Possible answers: Add two ten times or count by twos ten times.

Follow-Up

If...students have difficulty with non-standard units of measurement,

Then...provide opportunities for students to measure real-world objects (e.g., erasers, crayons, markers, etc.) using non-standard units (e.g., base-ten blocks, marbles, interconnecting cubes, etc.).

Name _____   Date _____

LESSON
10.5   **Pounds and Ounces**

Key Ideas

Pounds and ounces are units of weight. There are 16 ounces in 1 pound.

⭐ **Math TEKS Measurement 2.9** ✋
The student directly compare the attributes of length, area, weight/mass, and capacity, and uses comparative language to solve problems and answer questions. The student selects and uses nonstandard units to describe length, area, capacity, and weight/mass. The student recognizes and uses models that approximate standard units of length, weight/mass, capacity, and time.

about 1 pound

...between 1 and 2 ounces...

Complete

① How many ounces in 1 pound?   16

② How many ounces in 2 pounds?   32

③ How many ounces in 4 pounds?   64

④ How many ounces in 8 pounds?   128

⑤ How many ounces in 16 pounds?   256

📖 **Textbook** This lesson is available in the *eTextbook*.

383

Feathers   Bricks   Clothes

Write your answers.

⑥ Which box probably weighs the most?
   bricks

⑦ Which box probably weighs the least?
   feathers

How much does it weigh? Record your answers on the table.

Object	Estimated Weight	Measured Weight	Difference

---

3 Reflect   10

Guided Discussion ✓ REASONING

Have students use the double-pan balance to try to measure an object using a nonstandard unit. For example, they may try to see how many marbles an eraser weighs.

■ **Critical Thinking** Why is it easier to use standard units when measuring? If you are measuring in standard units, then you can easily explain to other people what you are measuring, and people will have a better idea of what your measurement means.

 Curriculum Connection: Have students look at supermarket ads to find examples of foods that are sold by pounds or ounces.

 Cumulative Review: For cumulative review of previously learned skills, see page 387–388.

 Family Involvement: Assign the *Practice, Reteach,* or *Enrichment* activities depending on the needs of your students.

 Concept/Question Board: Encourage students to continue to post questions, answers, and examples on the Concept/Question Board.

 Math Puzzler: Ferdie packed his suitcase to take to camp. "I wonder if I'll have trouble carrying that," he thought. He put the suitcase on the scale. "Twenty pounds!" he said. "That's one-third of what I weigh. I'd better not take so much stuff." How much does Ferdie weigh? 60 pounds

4 Assess and Differentiate

 Assess Use **eAssess** to record and analyze evidence of student understanding.

A Gather Evidence

Use the Daily Class Assessment Records in **Texas Assessment** or **eAssess** to record daily observations.

Informal Assessment
✓ **Guided Discussion**

Did the student **UNDERSTANDING**

- ❏ make important observations?
- ❏ extend or generalize learning?
- ❏ provide insightful answers?
- ❏ pose insightful questions?

Informal Assessment
✓ **Guided Discussion**

Did the student **REASONING**

- ❏ provide a clear explanation?
- ❏ communicate reasons and strategies?
- ❏ choose appropriate strategies?
- ❏ argue logically?

 TEKS/TAKS Practice

Use **TEKS/TAKS Practice** page 77 to assess student progress.

B Summarize Findings

Analyze and summarize assessment data for each student. Determine which Assessment Follow-Up is appropriate for each student. Use the Student Assessment Record in **Texas Assessment** or **eAssess** to update assessment records.

C Texas Assessment Follow-Up ● DIFFERENTIATE INSTRUCTION

Based on your observations, use these teaching strategies for assessment follow-up.

INTERVENTION

Review student performance on **Intervention** Lesson 10. B to see if students have mastered prerequisite skills for this lesson.

Measurement 1.7 The student directly compares the attributes of length, area, weight/mass, capacity, and temperature. The student uses comparative language to solve problems and answer questions. The student selects and uses nonstandard units to describe length.

ENGLISH LEARNER

Review

Use Lesson 10.5 in **English Learner Support Guide** to review lesson concepts and vocabulary.

ENRICH

If . . . students are proficient in the lesson concepts,

Then . . . encourage them to work on the chapter projects or **Enrichment** Lesson 10.5.

Enrichment Lesson 10.5

PRACTICE

If . . . students would benefit from additional practice,

Then . . . assign **Practice** Lesson 10.5.

Practice Lesson 10.5

RETEACH

If . . . students are having difficulty deciding if objects should be measured in pounds or ounces,

Then . . . have students look through magazines and find objects. Then have students work in groups to determine whether each object should be weighed in ounces or pounds.

Problem Solving 10.B

Comparing Strategies

Objectives

- To explore the Make a Physical Model and Draw a Diagram strategies
- To provide practice working with standard units of weight
- To continue to develop proportional reasoning
- To explore solving and presenting solutions to multistep problems

Materials

- Scissors
- Centimeter grid paper

See Appendix A page A24 for instructions and a rubric for problem solving.

Context of the Lesson While providing an opportunity to work for an extended time on a single nonroutine problem, this lesson also provides practice working with pounds and ounces. Proportional reasoning is developed throughout the *Real Math* program.

1 Develop

 5

Tell Students In Today's Lesson They Will
figure out how many bags of fertilizer they need for their garden.

Guided Discussion

Have students look at the illustration at the top of page 385. Read this problem to them:

Mr. Thompson's students have been working hard on their section of the community garden. They put up the fence, tilled the ground, planted the seeds, watered the seeds, and thinned the seedlings. Now they have to fertilize the garden. One of the neighbors let the students use the eight ounces of fertilizer he had left over. The area it covered is shown in the picture. The students plan to fertilize the whole garden the same way they did the first part, but they will have to buy more fertilizer to do that. The fertilizer comes in three-pound bags. How many bags of fertilizer will they need to buy?

Make sure students understand the problem by asking questions such as the following:

- **How much of the garden did the fertilizer cover?** the part that is shaded in the picture; 25 squares on the grid

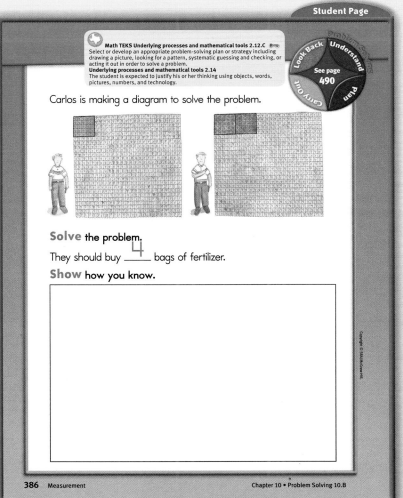

TEXAS

Math TEKS Underlying processes and mathematical tools 2.12.C	Underlying processes and mathematical tools 2.14	Measurement 2.9.B
Select or develop an appropriate problem-solving plan or strategy including drawing a picture, looking for a pattern, systematic guessing and checking, or acting it out in order to solve a problem.	The student is expected to justify his or her thinking using objects, words, pictures, numbers, and technology.	Select a non-standard unit of measure such as square tiles to determine the area of a two-dimensional surface.

- **What is the problem asking you to do?** to find out how many bags of fertilizer they need to cover the rest of the garden
- **How much fertilizer is in each bag?** 3 pounds
- **How might you work to solve the problem?** Allow students to offer approaches. See Sample Solutions Strategies under Reflect.

Exploring Problem Solving 25

Using Student Pages

Analyzing Sample Solution 1

Have students look at the picture on page 385 of Linda solving the problem. Ask questions about her strategy, such as the following:

- **What is Linda doing in the first picture?** She is cutting out the section of the garden that is already fertilized.
- **Why do you think she is doing that?** She is showing how much garden area is covered by 8 ounces of fertilizer. She won't have to fertilize that part because it has been done already.
- **What is Linda doing in the second picture?** She is tracing around the section she cut out.
- **How much fertilizer will be needed to cover the area she is tracing?** It will take 8 ounces, because it's the same size as the section that was fertilized already.
- **What do you think Linda will do next?** continue to trace more sections on the rest of the garden until she has covered the whole garden
- **How can this help her solve the problem?** She will know how many times she will have to use 8 ounces of fertilizer. Then she can use the total number of ounces to figure out how many bags of fertilizer are needed.

Analyzing Sample Solution 2

Tell students that Carlos is using a different strategy to try to solve the problem. Have students look at the picture on page 386 of Carlos's approach. Ask questions such as the following:

- **What is Carlos doing in the first picture?** shading 25 more squares on the grid
- **What is Carlos doing in the second picture?** shading another 25-square section on the grid
- **Why do you think he is shading sections of 25 squares?** He knows that 8 ounces of fertilizer will cover 25 squares.
- **What do you think Carlos will do next?** Allow students to offer ideas. Carlos probably will continue to shade 25-square sections until the whole garden is shaded.
- **Why do you think Carlos has outlined each section of 25 squares?** to help keep track of how many sections of 25 squares there are
- **Why does he need to know how many sections of 25 there are?** so he can figure out how much fertilizer is needed
- **How is Carlos's strategy like Linda's?** Like Linda, Carlos is finding out how many groups of 25 squares need to be fertilized.
- **How is Carlos's strategy different from Linda's?** Carlos is using the grid lines to help him draw each section instead of using a cutout to trace around.
- **How will you try to solve this problem?** Allow students to share what they like about Linda's and Carlos' strategies and what they would do differently. Many may prefer Carlos's method because it takes less time.

Reflect 10

Knowledge Age Skills

Effective Communication Ask students to share their solutions and their strategies.

Sample Solutions Strategies

Students may use one or more of the following strategies instead of or in conjunction with the strategies presented on student pages 385 and 386.

Act It Out

Students might cut out enough 25-square grids to cover the entire garden, group them into pairs to find how many pounds are needed, and then place those into groups of three pairs to show how many bags are needed.

Make a Table

Students might make a table such as the following to determine the number of pounds needed:

Amount of Fertilizer	Number of Squares Covered
8 ounces	25
1 pound	50
3 pounds	150
6 pounds	300
9 pounds	450

Assess 15

When evaluating student work, focus not only on the correctness of the answer but also on whether the student thought rationally about the problem. Questions to consider include the following:

- Did the student understand the problem and the Sample Solutions Strategies?
- Was the student able to explain his or her strategy?
- Did the student use units of weight in sensible ways?
- Could the student explain why he or she chose to buy 3 bags rather than 2 bags?

Also note which students use particularly sophisticated or creative strategies.

Cumulative Review

Review

Use Pages 387–388

Use the Cumulative Review as a review of concepts and skills that students have previously learned.

Here are different ways that you can assign these problems to your students as they work through the chapter:

- With some of the lessons in the chapter, assign a set of cumulative review problems to be completed as practice or for homework.
  Lesson 10.1—Problems 1–2
  Lesson 10.2—Problems 3–4
  Lesson 10.3—Problems 5–6
  Lesson 10.4—Problems 7–13
  Lesson 10.5—Problems 14–17
- At any point during the chapter, assign part or all of the cumulative review problems to be completed as practice or for homework.

Cumulative Review

Problems 1–2 review reading pictographs, Lesson 4.9. TEKS: 2.11.A

Problems 3–4 review applications of addition and subtraction, Lesson 3.6. TEKS: 2.3.A

Problems 5–6 review weight in kilograms and grams, Lesson 10.4. TEKS: 2.9

Problems 7–13 review reading maps, Lesson 10.2. TEKS: 2.13.A

Problems 14–17 review grouping by tens in addition, Lesson 5.9.
BIG IDEAS Number and operations and Algebra TEKS: 2.13.A

Progress Monitoring

If . . . students miss more than one problem in a section,

Then . . . refer to the indicated lesson for remediation suggestions.

Student Page

Cumulative Review

Name _____ Date _____

Pictographs Lesson 4.9 TEKS: 2.11.B

Use the pictograph to answer the questions below.

Each gas can stands for 10 gallons of gas.

Ava Island to Murphy	🛢️🛢️🛢️🛢️🛢️🛢️🛢️🛢️🛢️
Murphy to Brushy Fork	🛢️🛢️🛢️🛢️🛢️🛢️
Brushy Fork to Flint	🛢️🛢️🛢️

1. According to the pictograph, which trip takes the least gas? __Brushy Fork to Flint__

2. How many gallons are used on a trip from Murphy to Brushy Fork? __60__

Applications of Addition and Subtraction Lesson 3.6 TEKS: 2.3.A
Solve.

3. Shelly can walk from her house to Pat's house in 4 minutes. About how many minutes will it take her to walk back? _____
   about 4 minutes

4. About how many minutes will it take her to walk to Pat's house and back? _____
   about 8 minutes; 4 + 4 = 8

Kilograms and Grams Lesson 10.4 TEKS: 2.9

How many?
5. 1 kilogram = __1,000__ g   6. 5 kg = __5,000__ g

Cumulative Review

Reading a Map Lesson 10.2 TEKS: 2.13.A

Use the map to complete the table. Then use the table to answer the questions.

Nita marked towns on a map. She makes deliveries to the plant stores in these towns.

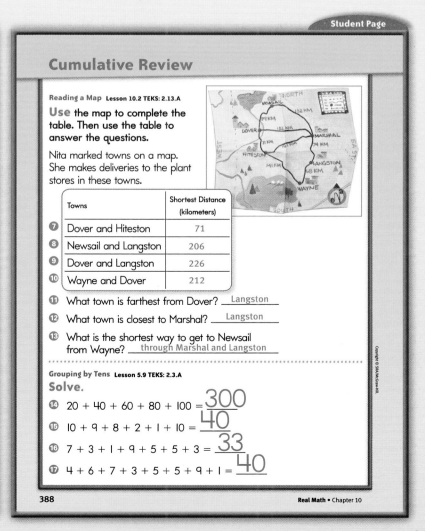

	Towns	Shortest Distance (kilometers)
7	Dover and Hiteston	71
8	Newsail and Langston	206
9	Dover and Langston	226
10	Wayne and Dover	212

11. What town is farthest from Dover? __Langston__

12. What town is closest to Marshal? __Langston__

13. What is the shortest way to get to Newsail from Wayne? __through Marshal and Langston__

Grouping by Tens Lesson 5.9 TEKS: 2.3.A
Solve.

14. $20 + 40 + 60 + 80 + 100 =$ __300__

15. $10 + 9 + 8 + 2 + 1 + 10 =$ __40__

16. $7 + 3 + 1 + 9 + 5 + 5 + 3 =$ __33__

17. $4 + 6 + 7 + 3 + 5 + 5 + 9 + 1 =$ __40__

Individual Oral Assessment

Purpose of the Test

The Individual Oral Assessment is designed to measure students' growing knowledge of chapter concepts. It is administered individually to each student, and it requires oral responses from each student. The test takes about five minutes to complete. See *Texas Assessment* for detailed instructions for administering and interpreting the test, and record students' answers on the Student Assessment Recording Sheet.

Texas Assessment page 144

Directions

Read each question to the student, and record his or her oral response. If the student answers correctly, go to the next question. Stop when the student misses two questions at the same level. Students should not use scrap paper.

Materials

Ruler with inches and centimeters, thermometer, math textbook, clock

Questions

Level 1: Prerequisite 2.9

1. (Give student a ruler.) Show 4 inches on a ruler. 4 in.
2. Which weighs more, a pencil or a book? book
3. Which is shorter, 1 inch or 1 centimeter? 1 centimeter
4. Name an animal that weighs less than you weigh. various, such as cat or bird

Level 2: Basic 2.9

5. (Give student a ruler.) Show 4 centimeters on a ruler. 4 cm
6. Which weighs more, a tiger or a pet cat? tiger
7. Which weighs more, a golf ball or a basketball? basketball
8. Which is longer, 10 inches or 10 centimeters? 10 inches

Level 3: At Level 2.9, 2.10

9. Which weighs more, 1 ounce or 1 pound? 1 pound
10. How many grams are in 1 kilogram? 1,000
11. (Show student a thermometer.) What is the temperature? Answers will vary.
12. Which temperature is colder, 10 or −10? −10

Level 4: Challenge Application 3.11

13. How many ounces are in 1 pound? 16
14. How many grams are in 4 kilograms? 4,000
15. If an object weighs 32 ounces, how many pounds does it weigh? 2
16. About how much does your math book weigh? Answer should be between 2 pounds and 5 pounds.

Level 5: Content Beyond Mid-Chapter

3.11, 3.12

17. How many cups are in 1 pint? 2
18. Which is larger, 2 pints or 2 quarts? 2 quarts
19. How many days are in a week? 7
20. Look at the classroom clock. What time is it?

TEXAS Grade 1	Grade 2	Grade 3
1.7 The students selects and uses non-standard units to describe length.	**2.9** The student directly compares the attributes of length, area, weight/mass, and capacity, and uses comparative language to solve problems and answer questions.	**3.11** The student selects and uses standard units to describe length, area, capacity/volume, and weight/mass.

Overview

LESSON 10.6

TEXAS

Measuring Capacity (Customary Units) ★

Context of the Lesson This is the sixth lesson in a series that covers different aspects of measurement: weight, length, capacity, temperature, and time. Both metric and customary units are discussed, but students do not convert measurements from one system to the other. This lesson is the first of two lessons on measuring capacity in standard units. Measuring capacity in quarts was first introduced in Grade 1. The next lesson explores measuring capacity in metric units.

See page 373B for Math Background for teachers for this lesson.

Planning for Learning ● DIFFERENTIATE INSTRUCTION

Lesson Planner

OBJECTIVES
- To introduce customary capacity units
- To teach students how to convert one customary unit of capacity into another

MATH TEKS
Measurement 2.9 The student directly compares the attributes of length, area, weight/mass, and capacity, and uses comparative language to solve problems and answer questions. The student selects and uses nonstandard units to describe length, area, capacity, and weight/mass. The student recognizes and uses models that approximate standard units (from both SI, also known as metric, and customary systems) of length, weight/mass, capacity, and time.
Measurement 2.9.C Select a non-standard unit of measure such as a bathroom cup or a jar to determine the capacity of a given container.

MATH TEKS INTEGRATION
Number, operation, and quantitative reasoning 2.3.B Model addition and subtraction of two-digit numbers with objects, pictures, words, and numbers.
Underlying processes and mathematical tools 2.12.A Identify the mathematics in everyday situations.

TECHNOLOGY
Presentation Lesson 10.6

INTERVENTION

If . . . students lack the prerequisite skill of telling time to the quarter hour,

Then . . . teach *Intervention* Lesson 10.B.

 1.7, 1.8

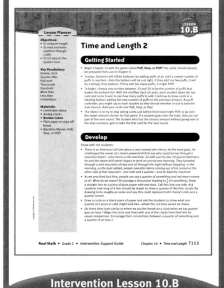

Intervention Lesson 10.B

ENGLISH LEARNER

Preview

If . . . students need language support,

Then . . . use Lesson 10.6 in *English Learner Support Guide* to preview lesson concepts and vocabulary.

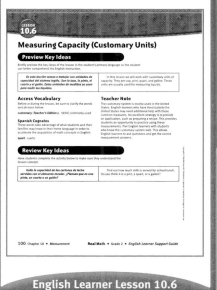

English Learner Lesson 10.6

ENRICH

If . . . students are proficient in the lesson concepts,

Then . . . emphasize Guided Discussion in Reflect.

PRACTICE

If . . . students would benefit from additional practice,

Then . . . extend Skill Building before assigning the student pages.

RETEACH

If . . . students are having difficulty understanding measuring capacity in customary units,

Then . . . extend Guided Discussion before assigning the student pages.

Academic Vocabulary	**Access Vocabulary**	**Spanish Cognates**
capacity \kə pas´i tē\ *n.* a measure of how much a container can hold	customary commonly used	quart cuarto

---

Teaching Lesson 10.6

 TEXAS

Measurement 2.9
The student directly compares the attributes of length, area, weight/mass, and capacity, and uses comparative language to solve problems and answer questions.

Measurement 2.9.C Select a non-standard unit of measure such as a bathroom cup or a jar to determine the capacity of a given container.

Mental Math   5

 INTEGRATION: TEKS 3.3.B Present addition and subtraction exercises. Have students respond using their *Number Cubes*. Possible examples include the following:

a. $170 - 80 = 90$ **b.** $70 + 50 = 120$ **c.** $50 + 90 = 140$
d. $120 - 30 = 90$ **e.** $160 + 80 = 240$ **f.** $70 + 90 = 160$

1 Develop   25

Tell Students In Today's Lesson They Will
learn about measuring capacity.

Guided Discussion   UNDERSTANDING   Introductory

Show students a baby food jar and quart container. Ask students how many full baby food jars they think it will take to fill the quart container. After each baby food jar of water is added ask students if they would like to change their estimate. When the quart container is full ask students how many jars full of water it took to fill the quart.

Next, Display and identify a transparent 1-gallon container and a 1-pint container. Ask students how many pints they think it will take to fill the gallon container. Pour 1 pint of water into the gallon container. Allow students to change their estimates if they wish to. Continue to fill the gallon container, one pint at a time. When the container is full ask how many pints it took to fill the gallon container. 8 Repeat with the pint and quart containers.

Then, show the students an 8 fluid ounce measuring cup. Explain that in this instance, *cup* refers to a unit of measure, not a vessel used for drinking. Ask students if they can think of everyday objects that hold about 1 cup. Possible answers: a mug, a drinking glass

Students learned about ounces as a measure of weight in Lesson 10.5. Be sure students understand that a fluid ounce is a different measurement used for capacity.

Skill Building   APPLYING   Guided

 Lead students in a capacity estimation activity.

Show the class five identical transparent containers. Pour some colored water in the first container, and have students estimate how many fluid ounces of water the container is holding. Then, measure the number of fluid ounces using the fluid ounce container. Label the container with the number of fluid ounces of water it is holding, and pour the measured water back into the container. Repeat for the other containers, leaving the water in each container so students can make comparisons.

2 Use Student Pages   20

Pages 389–390   APPLYING   Guided

Discuss the first few problems on page 389, and solve them together as a class. Demonstrate how to use addition to solve the problems. For example, for Problem 1, explain that because there are 16 ounces in a pint and 2 pints in a quart, then there are $16 + 16$, or 32, ounces in a quart. Then have students complete the rest of pages 389 and 390 independently.

As Students Finish

Game   Allow students to choose a game from among those previously introduced, or assign games based on needed skill practice.

Name _____ Date _____

LESSON 10.6 Measuring Capacity (Customary Units)

Key Ideas

Capacity is a measure of the amount a container can hold. Ounces, cups, pints, quarts, and gallons are units of capacity.

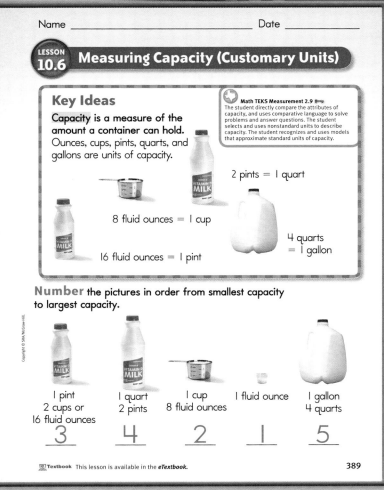

★ **Math TEKS Measurement 2.9**
The student directly compare the attributes of capacity, and uses comparative language to solve problems and answer questions. The student selects and uses nonstandard units to describe capacity. The student recognizes and uses models that approximate standard units of capacity.

2 pints = 1 quart

8 fluid ounces = 1 cup

16 fluid ounces = 1 pint

4 quarts = 1 gallon

Number the pictures in order from smallest capacity to largest capacity.

1 pint 2 cups or 16 fluid ounces	1 quart 2 pints	1 cup 8 fluid ounces	1 fluid ounce	1 gallon 4 quarts
3	4	2	1	5

 Textbook This lesson is available in the *eTextbook*.

389

LESSON 10.6 · Measuring Capacity (Customary Units)

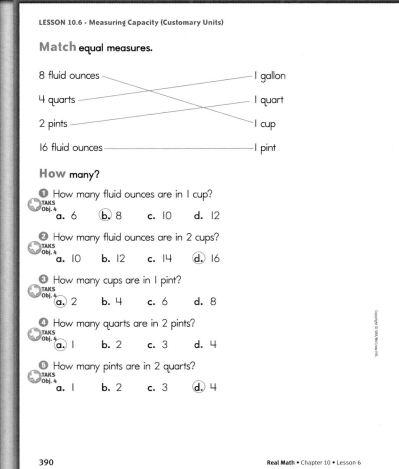

Match equal measures.

8 fluid ounces ——————— 1 gallon

4 quarts ——————— 1 quart

2 pints ——————— 1 cup

16 fluid ounces ——————— 1 pint

How many?

1 How many fluid ounces are in 1 cup?
★ TAKS Obj. 4
  a. 6   **(b.)** 8   c. 10   d. 12

2 How many fluid ounces are in 2 cups?
★ TAKS Obj. 4
  a. 10   b. 12   c. 14   **(d.)** 16

3 How many cups are in 1 pint?
★ TAKS Obj. 4
  (a.) 2   b. 4   c. 6   d. 8

4 How many quarts are in 2 pints?
★ TAKS Obj. 4
  (a.) 1   b. 2   c. 3   d. 4

5 How many pints are in 2 quarts?
★ TAKS Obj. 4
  a. 1   b. 2   c. 3   **(d.)** 4

390   **Real Math** • Chapter 10 • Lesson 6

---

③ Reflect

10

Guided Discussion UNDERSTANDING

Show the class three different bottles of various sizes. Then, show students a large bucket or other large container. Have students estimate how many filled bottles it would take to fill the large bucket. Do this for each of the bottles and record each estimate on the board. Next, ask students to explain how much the bucket can hold. Guide students to see that the number of full bottles it takes to fill the bucket changes from container to container. Go on to ask students to name some advantages of using standard units of capacity. Create a list of the advantages that students present. The greatest advantage of standard units is to communicate more effectively the capacity of containers to others.

★ Integration: TEKS 2.12.A

Finally, ask students to give examples of everyday items that come in a quart, pint, or gallon container.
Possible answers: gallon of milk, quart of oil, pint of ice cream

Curriculum Connection: Have students research the number of ounces of milk they should drink in a day to get the number of recommended daily servings.

Cumulative Review: For cumulative review of previously learned skills, see pages 401–402.

Family Involvement: Assign the *Practice, Reteach,* or *Enrichment* activities depending on the needs of your students.

Concept/Question Board: Encourage students to continue to post questions, answers, and examples on the Concept/Question Board.

Math Puzzler: You can buy 32 ounces of juice for $1.25 or 1 quart of the same juice for $1.50. Which is the best buy? Why?
32 ounces; 1 quart is the same amount, but it costs more.

4 Assess and Differentiate

 **Assess** Use *eAssess* to record and analyze evidence of student understanding.

A Gather Evidence

Use the Daily Class Assessment Records in *Texas Assessment* or *eAssess* to record daily observations.

Informal Assessment
☑ **Student Pages**
Did the student **APPLYING**
- ❑ apply learning in new situations?
- ❑ contribute concepts?
- ❑ contribute answers?
- ❑ connect mathematics to real-world situations?

Informal Assessment
☑ **Concept/Question Board**
Did the student **ENGAGING**
- ❑ pay attention to others' contributions?
- ❑ contribute information and ideas?
- ❑ improve on a strategy?
- ❑ reflect on and check the accuracy of his or her work?

TEKS/TAKS Practice
Use *TEKS/TAKS Practice* pages 75–76 to assess student progress.

B Summarize Findings

Analyze and summarize assessment data for each student. Determine which Assessment Follow-Up is appropriate for each student. Use the Student Assessment Record in *Texas Assessment* or *eAssess* to update assessment records.

C Texas Assessment Follow-Up ● DIFFERENTIATE INSTRUCTION

Based on your observations, use these teaching strategies for assessment follow-up.

INTERVENTION
Review student performance on *Intervention* Lesson 10.B to see if students have mastered prerequisite skills for this lesson.

Measurement 1.7 The student directly compares the attributes of length, area, weight/mass, capacity, and temperature. The student uses comparative language to solve problems and answer questions. The student selects and uses nonstandard units to describe length.

Measurement 1.8 The student understands that time can be measured. The student uses time to describe and compare situations.

ENGLISH LEARNER
Review
Use Lesson 10.6 in *English Learner Support Guide* to review lesson concepts and vocabulary.

ENRICH
If . . . students are proficient in the lesson concepts,

Then . . . encourage them to work on the chapter projects or *Enrichment* Lesson 10.6.

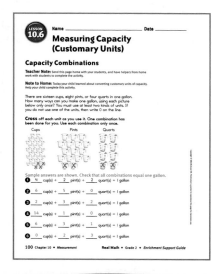
Enrichment Lesson 10.6

PRACTICE
If . . . students would benefit from additional practice,

Then . . . assign *Practice* Lesson 10.6.

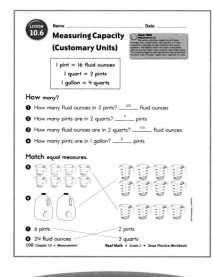
Practice Lesson 10.6

RETEACH
If . . . students have difficulty determining whether to measure in fluid ounces, pints, quarts, or gallons,

Then . . . have them collect cans and bottles and jars of drinks to read the labels. Have students place their liquids from smallest to largest capacity. Students may want to donate their drinks to a local food bank.

TEXAS Vertical Alignment

Grade 1	Grade 2	Grade 3
1.7 The students selects and uses nonstandard units to describe length.	2.9 The student directly compares the attributes of length, area, weight/mass, and capacity, and uses comparative language to solve problems and answer questions.	3.11 The student selects and uses standard units to describe length, area, capacity/volume, and weight/mass.

Overview

LESSON 10.7

TEXAS

Lesson Planner

OBJECTIVES
- To introduce metric units of measurement for capacity
- To demonstrate ways to convert one metric unit of capacity into another

 MATH TEKS

Math TEKS Measurement 2.9 🗝
The student directly compares the attributes of length, area, weight/ mass, and capacity, and uses comparative language to solve problems and answer questions. The student selects and uses nonstandard units to describe length, area, capacity, and weight/mass. The student recognizes and uses models that approximate standard units (from both SI, also known as metric, and customary systems) of length, weight/mass, capacity, and time.
Measurement 2.9.C Select a non-standard unit of measure such as a bathroom cup or a jar to determine the capacity of a given container.

MATH TEKS INTEGRATION

Number, operation, and quantitative reasoning 2.3.B Model addition and subtraction of two-digit numbers with objects, pictures, words, and numbers.

MATERIALS
- Transparent liter containers
- Transparent measuring cup marked in milliliters
- Five equal-sized transparent containers
- Colored water
- Small kitchen sponge

TECHNOLOGY
Presentation Lesson 10.7

Measuring Capacity (Metric Units) ★

Context of the Lesson This is the seventh lesson in a series that covers different aspects of measurement: weight, length, capacity, temperature, and time. Both metric and customary units are discussed, but students do not convert measurements from one system to the other. This lesson is the second of two lessons on measuring capacity in standard units. Measuring capacity in liters was first introduced in Grade 1. The next three lessons explore measuring in units of time.
See page 373B for Math Background for teachers for this lesson.

Planning for Learning • DIFFERENTIATE INSTRUCTION

INTERVENTION

If . . . students lack the prerequisite skill of measuring length,

Then . . . teach *Intervention* Lesson 10.C.

 1.7, 1.8

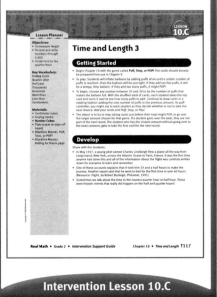

Intervention Lesson 10.C

ENGLISH LEARNER

Preview

If . . . students need language support,

Then . . . use Lesson 10.7 in *English Learner Support Guide* to preview lesson concepts and vocabulary.

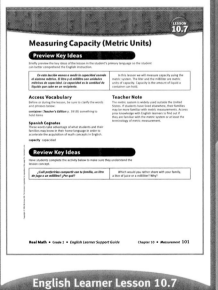

English Learner Lesson 10.7

ENRICH

If . . . students are proficient in the lesson concepts,

Then . . . emphasize chapter projects.

PRACTICE

If . . . students would benefit from additional practice,

Then . . . extend Skill Building before assigning the student pages.

RETEACH

If . . . students are having difficulty understanding measuring capacity in metric units,

Then . . . extend Guided Discussion before assigning the student pages.

Access Vocabulary
container something to hold items

Spanish Cognates
capacity capacidad

Measurement 2.9
The student directly compares the attributes of length, area, weight/mass, and capacity, and uses comparative language to solve problems and answer questions.

Measurement 2.9.C Select a non-standard unit of measure such as a bathroom cup or a jar to determine the capacity of a given container.

Mental Math 5

  THUMBS UP

 INTEGRATION: TEKS 2.3.B Present students with addition and subtraction exercises. Have them show thumbs-up if the answer is correct and thumbs-down if the answer is incorrect. Possible examples include the following:

a. 25 − 15 = 5
down

b. 30 + 30 = 60
up

c. 45 + 15 = 60
up

d. 50 + 20 = 80
down

e. 60 − 20 = 80
down

f. 60 − 15 = 45
up

1 Develop 25

Tell Students In Today's Lesson They Will
learn about liters and milliliters.

Guided Discussion **UNDERSTANDING**

 Introductory

Repeat the Guided Discussion from Lesson 10.6, but now use containers of metric-unit capacity rather than customary units. For example, you might have students estimate how many times you need to soak a kitchen sponge to fill a 250-milliter container. Then use a measuring cup that measures in milliliters to gauge whether their estimates were accurate. As in the previous lesson, allow students to adjust their estimates after you squeeze the first sponge full.

Skill Building **APPLYING**

 Guided

Lead students in a capacity estimation activity.

Show the class five identical transparent containers. Pour some colored water in the first container, and have students estimate how many milliliters of water the container is holding. Then measure the number of milliliters using the milliliter container. Label the container with the number of milliliters of water it is holding, and pour the measured water back into the container. Repeat for the other containers, leaving the water in each container so students can make comparisons.

2 Use Student Pages 20

Pages 391–392 **APPLYING**

 Guided

Read the equivalences on page 391 with the class. Then have students complete pages 391 and 392 in small groups.

As Students Finish

 Game

Allow students to choose a game from among those previously introduced, or assign games based on needed skill practice.

TEXAS   TEKS Checkup

TEKS 2.9.C Select a non-standard unit of measure such as a bathroom cup or a jar to determine the capacity of a given container.

Use this problem to assess students' progress toward standards mastery:

If five bottles of a liquid fill a one gallon bucket, how many bottles would be needed to fill a five gallon bucket?

A about 3

B about 5

C about 25

D about 80

Have students choose the correct answer and then describe how they knew which choice was correct. In the discussion, ask questions such as the following. Be sure to ask students to explain their reasoning because different solution methods are possible

■ What information are you given? five bottles of a liquid fills a one gallon bucket

■ What is the problem asking? How many bottles would be needed to fill a five gallon bucket?

■ How could you solve this problem? Possible answers: Add five, five times or count by fives, five times.

Follow-Up
If...students have difficulty with non-standard units of measurement, **Then...**provide opportunities for students to measure the capacity of real-world objects (e.g., buckets, jars, cups, etc.) using non-standard units (e.g., small cups, eye drops, etc.).

Student Page

Name _____ Date _____

LESSON 10.7 Measuring Capacity (Metric Units)

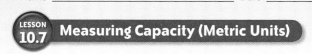

Key Ideas

Milliliters and liters are also units of capacity. There are 1,000 milliliters in 1 liter.

Math TEKS Measurement 2.9 ✦
The student directly compare the attributes of length, area, weight/mass, and capacity, and uses comparative language to solve problems and answer questions. The student selects and uses nonstandard units to describe length, area, capacity, and weight/mass. The student recognizes and uses models that approximate standard units of length, weight/mass, capacity, and time.

How many?

1. __2,000__ milliliters = 2 liters

2. 4 liters = __4,000__ milliliters

3. 5,000 milliliters = __5__ liters

4. ½ liter = __500__ milliliters

5. 3 liters = __3,000__ milliliters

6. __6__ liters = 6,000 milliliters

Textbook This lesson is available in the *eTextbook*.   391

Student Page

Ring the better estimate for the capacity of each object.

7.   about 300 milliliters

about 3 liters

8.  about 2 liters

about 200 liters

9.   about 200 milliliters

about 2 liters

10.   about 90 milliliters

about 900 milliliters

392   Real Math · Chapter 10 · Lesson 7

---

3 Reflect

10

Guided Discussion ✓ REASONING

Rosa, Tariq, Keagan, and Ron each filled a 100-milliliter container with a sponge full of water. Rosa said it took her 4 soaked sponges to fill the container. Tariq said it took him 3 soaked sponges to fill the container. Keagan said it took her 5 soaked sponges to fill the container. Ron then said it took him 6 soaked sponges to fill the container.

■ **Critical Thinking** **If the sponges were different sizes, which student had the largest sponge?** Tariq

Who had the smallest sponge? Ron

Cumulative Review: For cumulative review of previously learned skills, see page 401–402.

Family Involvement: Assign the *Practice, Reteach,* or *Enrichment* activities depending on the needs of your students.

Concept/Question Board: Have students attempt to answer any unanswered questions on the Concept/Question Board.

Math Puzzler: When Ms. Eng put ten packages of beans in a jar, she knew that each package held about 300 beans. Ferdie guessed that there were 532 beans in the jar. Manolita guessed 2,143. Willy guessed 2,800. Marcus guessed 5,000. Who came closest to the correct number? Willy How many beans were in the jar? 3,000

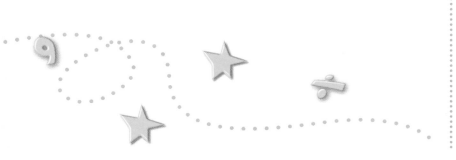

4 Assess and Differentiate

 **Assess** Use *eAssess* to record and analyze evidence of student understanding.

A Gather Evidence

Use the Daily Class Assessment Records in *Texas Assessment* or *eAssess* to record daily observations.

Informal Assessment
☑ **Mental Math**

Did the student `COMPUTING`
- ❑ respond accurately?
- ❑ respond quickly?
- ❑ respond with confidence?
- ❑ self-correct?

Informal Assessment
☑ **Guided Discussion**

Did the student `REASONING`
- ❑ provide a clear explanation?
- ❑ communicate reasons and strategies?
- ❑ choose appropriate strategies?
- ❑ argue logically?

 TEKS/TAKS Practice

Use *TEKS/TAKS Practice* pages 75–76 to assess student progress.

B Summarize Findings

Analyze and summarize assessment data for each student. Determine which Assessment Follow-Up is appropriate for each student. Use the Student Assessment Record in *Texas Assessment* or *eAssess* to update assessment records.

C Texas Assessment Follow-Up ● DIFFERENTIATE INSTRUCTION

Based on your observations, use these teaching strategies for assessment follow-up.

INTERVENTION

Review student performance on *Intervention* Lesson 10.C to see if students have mastered prerequisite skills for this lesson.

🔶 **Measurement 1.7** The student directly compares the attributes of length, area, weight/mass, capacity, and temperature. The student uses comparative language to solve problems and answer questions. The student selects and uses nonstandard units to describe length.

🔶 **Measurement 1.8** The The student understands that time can be measured. The student uses time to describe and compare situations.

ENGLISH LEARNER
Review

Use Lesson 10.7 in *English Learner Support Guide* to review lesson concepts and vocabulary.

ENRICH

If . . . students are proficient in the lesson concepts,

Then . . . encourage them to work on the chapter projects or *Enrichment* Lesson 10.7.

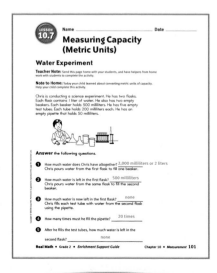

Enrichment Lesson 10.7

TEXAS PRACTICE

If . . . students would benefit from additional practice,

Then . . . assign *Practice* Lesson 10.7.

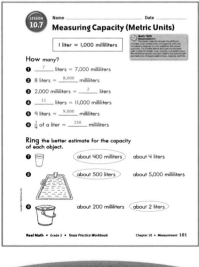

Practice Lesson 10.7

RETEACH

If . . . students struggle converting metric units of capacity,

Then . . . write the following on the board:

$\underline{2,000}$ ml = 2 L

4 L = $\underline{4,000}$ ml

5,000 ml = $\underline{5}$ L

$\frac{1}{2}$ L = $\underline{500}$ ml

Have students complete the problem and correct their answers together.

TEXAS

Vertical Alignment

Grade 1	Grade 2	Grade 3
1.8.B Read time to the hour and half-hour using analog and digital clocks.	**Grade 2** Review of 2.10.C Describe activities that take approximately one second, one minute, and one hour.	**3.12.B** Tell and write time shown on analog and digital clocks.

Overview **LESSON 10.8**

TEXAS

Lesson Planner

OBJECTIVES
- To teach students the order and number of the days of the week
- To teach students how to determine what day of the week it was or will be, given a number of days in the future or past

MATH TEKS
Review of Measurement 1.8 The student understands that time can be measured. The student uses time to describe and compare situations.
Measurement 2.10.C Describe activities that take approximately one second, one minute, and one hour.

MATH TEKS INTEGRATION
Number, operation, and quantitative reasoning 2.3 The student adds and subtracts whole numbers to solve problems.

MATERIALS
- *Number Cubes
- Monthly calendar of the current month

TECHNOLOGY
Presentation Lesson 10.8

Units of Time

Context of the Lesson This is the eighth lesson in a series that covers different aspects of measurement: weight, length, capacity, temperature, and time. Both metric and customary units are discussed, but students do not convert measurements from one system to the other. This lesson reviews measuring time with a calendar, which was covered in Lesson 1.6. The next two lessons further explore measuring in units of time.

See page 373B for Math Background for teachers for this lesson.

Planning for Learning ● DIFFERENTIATE INSTRUCTION

INTERVENTION

If . . . students lack the prerequisite skill of telling time to the quarter hour,

Then . . . teach *Intervention* Lesson 10.C.

1.7, 1.8

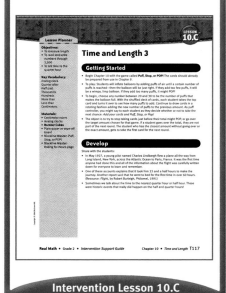

Intervention Lesson 10.C

ENGLISH LEARNER

Preview

If . . . students need language support,

Then . . . use Lesson 10.8 in *English Learner Support Guide* to preview lesson concepts and vocabulary.

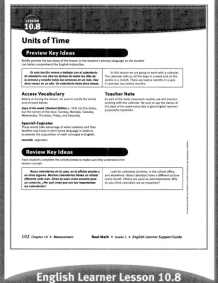

English Learner Lesson 10.8

ENRICH

If . . . students are proficient in the lesson concepts,

Then . . . emphasize Reflect.

PRACTICE

If . . . students would benefit from additional practice,

Then . . . extend Skill Building.

RETEACH

If . . . students are having difficulty understanding units of time,

Then . . . extend Guided Discussion before assigning the student pages.

Academic Vocabulary
day \dā\ *n.* a period of twenty-four hours

week \wēk\ *n.* a period of seven days, usually considered to begin with Sunday

Access Vocabulary
days of the week not the dates, but the names of the days: Sunday, Monday, Tuesday, Wednesday, Thursday, Friday, and Saturday

Spanish Cognates
seconds segundos

Teaching Lesson 10.8

  TEXAS

Review of Measurement 1.8
The student understands that time can be measured. The student uses time to describe and compare situations.

Measurement 2.10.C Describe activities that take approximately one second, one minute, and one hour.container.

Mental Math   5

  INTEGRATION: TEKS 2.3. Present addition and subtraction exercises such as the following to students, and have them use their **Number Cubes** to show their answers.

a. 20 + 30 = 50   **b.** 50 − 20 = 30   **c.** 30 + 40 = 70
d. 35 + 35 = 70   **e.** 55 − 20 = 35   **f.** 50 − 15 = 35

1 Develop   25

Tell Students In Today's Lesson They Will
learn about measuring time.

Guided Discussion UNDERSTANDING Introductory

 Display the current month's calendar. Tell students the current day and date. Ask students to identify each of the following days: today, yesterday, two days ago, five days ago. Have the preceding and following months' calendars available if necessary. Discuss how the pattern of days of the week is similar to a clock—when you reach the end, you start over again. The cycle never breaks or skips a day.

Skill Building APPLYING Guided

Discuss time equivalencies with students. For example, seven days equals one week. Discuss other common time equivalencies. Have students think about the unit of time they are given and try to guess what the equivalent time period is. Ask volunteers to answer questions and discuss the time equivalencies as a class.

- **365 days is the same as** one year, with the exception of a leap year
- **60 seconds is the same as** one minute
- **Name something you can do in one second.** say a small word, blink, clap once
- **60 minutes is the same as** one hour
- **Name something you can do in one minute.** say the alphabet, write a small word, do 20 jumping jacks
- **3,600 seconds is the same as** one hour
- **Name something you can do in one hour.** grocery shopping, watch 2 television shows, play a game of soccer
- **52 weeks is the same as** one year
- **12 months is the same as** one year
- **4 weeks is the same as** approximately one month. However, discuss with students how each month has a different number of days. There is no standard length of a month.

2 Use Student Pages   20

Pages 393–394 APPLYING Guided

Using the current week as a model, complete page 393 with the class. Discuss how the numbers can help identify the days. Ask questions such as, "What is the second day of the week?" Help students see the same day of the week occurs every seven days.

Have students complete page 394 in pairs or small groups. They should complete one column before going on to the next column. You might want to go over several examples with the class before assigning students to work in groups.

As Students Finish

Game Allow students to choose a game from among those previously introduced, or assign games based on needed skill practice.

 TEXAS   TEKS Checkup

TEKS 2.10.C Describe activities that take approximately one second, one minute, and one hour.

Use this problem to assess students' progress toward standards mastery:

How long would this take?

A about one minute
B about one second
C about one hour
D about one day

Have students choose the correct answer and then describe how they knew which choice was correct. In the discussion, ask questions such as the following. Be sure to ask students to explain their reasoning because different solution methods are possible.

- What does it mean when you run a race and the finish line is close? The race is almost complete.
- Is this race almost complete? How do you know? Yes, because the runner is close to the finish line.
- Will it take a long time or a small amount of time to cross the finish line? A small amount of time

Follow-Up
If…students have difficulty estimating the amount of time an activity will take,

Then…have students perform a few activities, such as saying the alphabet, while you time them.

Student Page

Student Page

Name _____ Date _____

LESSON 10.8 Units of Time

Key Ideas
There are seven **days** in one **week**.

★ **Review Math TEKS Measurement 1.8** The student understands that time can be measured. The student uses time to describe and compare situations.

Fill in the missing days.

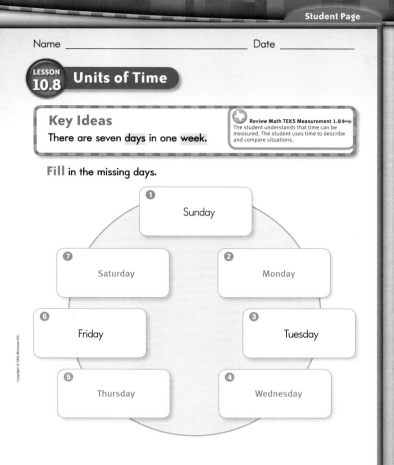

① Sunday
② Monday
③ Tuesday
④ Wednesday
⑤ Thursday
⑥ Friday
⑦ Saturday

Textbook This lesson is available in the *eTextbook*.

393

LESSON 10.8 · Units of Time

What day is it today?

Sunday
Saturday → Monday
Friday → Tuesday
Thursday → Wednesday

Answers shown are examples only.

Use today to complete the table. Write the day it was and the day it will be.

Number of Days	Day It Was	Day It Will Be
1	⑧ Monday	⑨ Wednesday
3	⑩ Saturday	⑪ Friday
6	⑫ Wednesday	⑬ Monday
7	⑭ Tuesday	⑮ Tuesday
8	⑯ Monday	⑰ Wednesday
14	⑱ Tuesday	⑲ Tuesday
21	⑳ Tuesday	㉑ Tuesday
69	㉒ Wednesday	㉓ Monday
70	㉔ Tuesday	㉕ Tuesday
71	㉖ Monday	㉗ Wednesday

394

Real Math • Chapter 10 • Lesson 8

---

 3 **Reflect** 10

Guided Discussion ✓ REASONING

Present this challenging problem for class discussion.

What is the most number of Mondays there can be in one year?

As students at first guess or make reasonable and unreasonable estimates, remind them 365 days are in one year.

Many students might suggest that the answer is $\frac{1}{7}$th of 365, but they won't know how to calculate the answer. Praise students if they arrive at this solution. Then through a series of questions, give the following hints.

1. How many Mondays are in 35 days? 5
2. How many Mondays are in 70 days? 10
3. How many Mondays are in 350 days? 50
4. How many Mondays are in 357 days? 51
5. How many Mondays are in 364 days? 52

If January 1st is a Monday, how many Mondays will be in that year? 53 Can there be more than 53? no Can there be fewer than 53? Yes, there can be 52.

Cumulative Review: For cumulative review of previously learned skills, see pages 401–402.

Family Involvement: Assign the *Practice, Reteach,* or *Enrichment* activities depending on the needs of your students.

Concept/Question Board: Have students attempt to answer any unanswered questions on the Concept/Question Board.

Math Puzzler: Mr. Muddle works every day except for those days that start with *S* or *T*. How many days a week does he work? 3

4 Assess and Differentiate

 **Assess**   Use *eAssess* to record and analyze evidence of student understanding.

A Gather Evidence

Use the Daily Class Assessment Records in *Texas Assessment* or *eAssess* to record daily observations.

Informal Assessment
☑ **Guided Discussion**

Did the student **UNDERSTANDING**
- ❑ make important observations?
- ❑ extend or generalize learning?
- ❑ provide insightful answers?
- ❑ pose insightful questions?

Informal Assessment
☑ **Guided Discussion**

Did the student **REASONING**
- ❑ provide a clear explanation?
- ❑ communicate reasons and strategies?
- ❑ choose appropriate strategies?
- ❑ argue logically?

 TEKS/TAKS Practice

Use *TEKS/TAKS Practice* pages 83–84 to assess student progress.

B Summarize Findings

Analyze and summarize assessment data for each student. Determine which Assessment Follow-Up is appropriate for each student. Use the Student Assessment Record in *Texas Assessment* or *eAssess* to update assessment records.

C Texas Assessment Follow-Up • DIFFERENTIATE INSTRUCTION

Based on your observations, use these teaching strategies for assessment follow-up.

INTERVENTION

Review student performance on *Intervention* Lesson 10.C to see if students have mastered prerequisite skills for this lesson.

Measurement 1.8 The student understands that time can be measured. The student uses time to describe and compare situations.

ENGLISH LEARNER

Review

Use Lesson 10.8 in *English Learner Support Guide* to review lesson concepts and vocabulary.

ENRICH

If . . . students are proficient in the lesson concepts,

Then . . . encourage them to work on the chapter projects or *Enrichment* Lesson 10.8.

Enrichment Lesson 10.8

PRACTICE

If . . . students would benefit from additional practice,

Then . . . assign *Practice* Lesson 10.8.

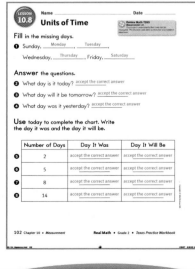

Practice Lesson 10.8

RETEACH

If . . . students have difficulty filling in days of the week,

Then . . . have them recite the days in order starting with Monday. Then have students recite all seven days starting with another day such as Thursday.

TEXAS **V e r t i c a l   A l i g n m e n t**

Grade 1	Grade 2	Grade 3
1.8.B Read time to the hour and half-hour using analog and digital clocks.	**2.10.B** Read and write times shown on analog and digital clocks using five-minutes increments.	**3.12.B** Tell and write time shown on analog and digital clocks.

Overview **LESSON 10.9**

TEXAS

Lesson Planner

OBJECTIVES
- To introduce telling time to the nearest minute
- To relate the time shown on an analog clock face to the time displayed on a digital clock

MATH TEKS
Measurement 2.10.B Read and write times shown on analog and digital clocks using five-minutes increments.

MATH TEKS INTEGRATION
Number, operation, and quantitative reasoning 2.3 The student adds and subtracts whole numbers to solve problems.
Underlying processes and mathematical tools 2.12A Identify the mathematics in everyday situations.

MATERIALS
- *Number Cubes
- *Demonstration clock
- Harder Time Game Mat
- SRA Math Vocabulary Card

TECHNOLOGY
Presentation Lesson 10.9

Telling Time to the Minute

Context of the Lesson This is the ninth lesson in a series that covers different aspects of measurement: weight, length, capacity, temperature, and time. Both metric and customary units are discussed, but students do not convert measurements from one system to the other. This lesson introduces telling time to the minute. Telling time to the hour, half hour, and quarter hour was introduced in Chapter 7 of Grade 1. The next lesson further explores measuring in units of time.

See page 373B for Math Background for teachers for this lesson.

Planning for Learning ● DIFFERENTIATE INSTRUCTION

INTERVENTION
If . . . students lack the prerequisite skill of reading and writing numbers through 1,000,

Then . . . teach *Intervention* Lesson 10.C.

1.7, 1.8

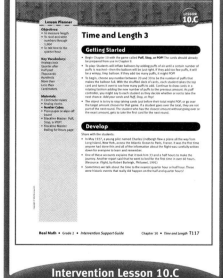

Intervention Lesson 10.C

ENGLISH LEARNER
Preview

If . . . students need language support,

Then . . . use Lesson 10.9 in *English Learner Support Guide* to preview lesson concepts and vocabulary.

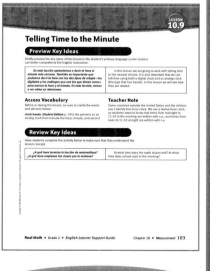

English Learner Lesson 10.9

ENRICH
If . . . students are proficient in the lesson concepts,

Then . . . emphasize additional game time.

PRACTICE
If . . . students would benefit from additional practice,

Then . . . extend Skill and Strategy Building before assigning the student pages.

RETEACH
If . . . students are having difficulty understanding telling time to the minute,

Then . . . extend Guided Discussion before assigning the student pages.

Academic Vocabulary
hour \our\ *n.* a unit of time equal to sixty minutes

minute \min´ it\ *n.* a unit of time equal to sixty seconds

Access Vocabulary
clock hands the pointers on an analog clock that indicate the hour, minute, and second

Teaching Lesson 10.9

 TEXAS

Measurement 2.10.B Read and write times shown on analog and digital clocks using five-minutes increments.

Mental Math   5

  INTEGRATION: TEKS 2.3.   Read aloud the following missing-addend problems, and have students show answers with **Number Cubes.** Say the problems as "30 + what equals 60?"

a. 30 + <u>30</u> = 60   **b.** 20 + <u>40</u> = 60   **c.** 50 + <u>10</u> = 60
d. 10 + <u>50</u> = 60   **e.** 40 + <u>20</u> = 60   **f.** 55 + <u>5</u> = 60

1 Develop   25

Tell Students In Today's Lesson They Will
learn to tell time to the minute.

Guided Discussion UNDERSTANDING   Introductory

Explain to students that each mark on the demonstration clock represents one minute. Ask the following:

- **How many minutes are there in an hour?** 60
- **So how many marks on the clock are there?** 60

Write several different times on the board, such as 8:00, 8:01, and 8:06. Tell students that these times are read as *eight o'clock, eight oh one,* and *eight oh six.* Write on the board 8:09, and ask students how they would read the time. eight oh nine Then display those times on the clock, one at a time, and have students tell what time it is.

Set the clock so the minute hand is on the line just before the 12, and the hour hand is almost at the 9, and discuss how students can tell that time. Explain that because there are 60 minutes in an hour, when the minute hand points at the line 1 minute before the hour, it is at 59 minutes. Students should see that 59 minutes past the hour is the same as one minute before the next hour.

Ask the following:

- **How can you tell times such as 8:33 without counting from the top of the hour?** by knowing that the 6 corresponds to 30 minutes and counting on from 30

Skill and Strategy Building ENGAGING   Guided

 Harder Time Game

Demonstrate the **Harder Time Game.** Students will play as they finish the student pages. Refer to the game mat for materials and rules.

2 Use Student Pages   20

Pages 395–396 UNDERSTANDING   Independent

Have students complete pages 395 and 396 independently. Explain that on page 395 they must write the time each clock shows, but on page 396 they must show the time by drawing or writing on each clock.

As Students Finish

 Game   Have students play the **Harder Time Game** in groups.

TEXAS   TEKS Checkup

TEKS 2.10.B Read and write times shown on analog and digital clocks using five-minute increments.

Use this problem to assess students' progress toward standards mastery:

What time is it?

(A) 4:45   **B** 4:50
C 5:40   **D** 9:25

Have students choose the correct answer and then describe how they knew which choice was correct. In the discussion, ask questions such as the following. Be sure to ask students to explain their reasoning because different solution methods are possible.

- Which hand identifies the hour? the shorter hand
- Which hand identifies the minute? the longer hand
- How many minutes are between each number? five

Follow-Up
If...students have difficulty with reading times on an analog or digital clock,

Then...have students use blank copies of clock faces to draw a time given by a partner.

Student Page

Name _____ Date _____

LESSON 10.9 Telling Time to the Minute

Key Ideas

Each line on the clock represents **1 minute.** There are 60 minutes in **1 hour.** The minute hand takes five minutes to travel from one number to the next.

Math TEKS
Measurement 2.10.B
Read and write times shown on analog and digital clocks using five-minute increments.

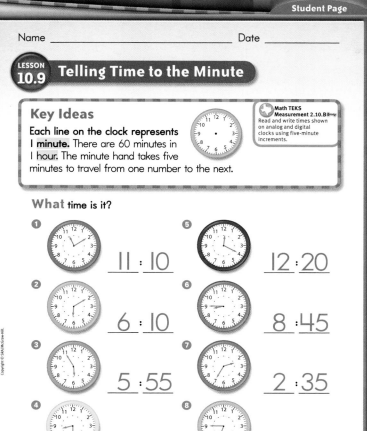

What time is it?

① 11 : 10

② 6 : 10

③ 5 : 55

④ 8 : 30

⑤ 12 : 20

⑥ 8 : 45

⑦ 2 : 35

⑧ 6 : 45

⊡Textbook This lesson is available in the *eTextbook*.

395

Match the analog clock on the left with the digital clock on the right.

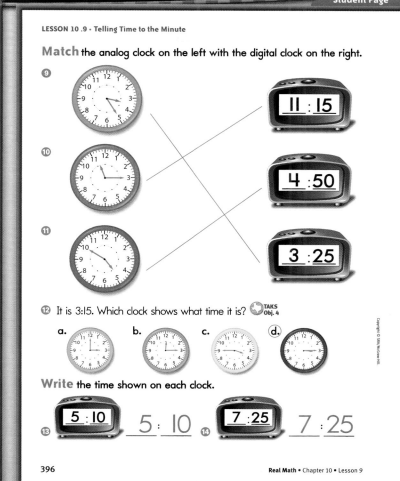

⑨ 11 : 15

⑩ 4 : 50

⑪ 3 : 25

⑫ It is 3:15. Which clock shows what time it is?
TAKS Obj. 4

a.   b.   c.   d.

Write the time shown on each clock.

⑬ 5 : 10   5 : 10   ⑭ 7 : 25   7 : 25

396

Real Math • Chapter 10 • Lesson 9

---

③ Reflect

10 ◖

Guided Discussion UNDERSTANDING

Show a clock that is set to 5:45. Discuss three different ways to say this time. five forty-five, a quarter to six, 15 minutes to six

Then ask students to answer the following question:

Integration: TEKS 2.12.A

It was 5:45 P.M. when John began an activity. It was 6:15 P.M. when John ended this activity. Name some things that John could have done.

As students become more experienced in telling time, you may want to do the following activity occasionally throughout the school year. With all the clocks in the classroom covered or with students' eyes closed, have students estimate the time of day. For example, stop an activity, have students close their eyes, and then ask "What time do you think it is?"

Students will learn to associate certain noises and activities with certain times of the day.

Cumulative Review: For cumulative review of previously learned skills, see pages 401–402.

Family Involvement: Assign the *Practice, Reteach,* or *Enrichment* activities depending on the needs of your students.

Concept/Question Board: Have students attempt to answer any unanswered questions on the Concept/Question Board.

Math Puzzler: Ms. Eng was in charge of the school track meet. After the first race she took the children's names to the judges. "Manolita ran it in 5 minutes, Ferdie took 2 minutes less, and Willy was 1 minute slower than Ferdie." How long did it take Ferdie? 3 minutes How long did it take Willy? 4 minutes

4 Assess and Differentiate

 Assess Use *eAssess* to record and analyze evidence of student understanding.

A Gather Evidence

Use the Daily Class Assessment Records in *Texas Assessment* or *eAssess* to record daily observations.

Performance Assessment
☑ **Game**

Did the student **APPLYING**
- ❑ apply learning in new situations?
- ❑ contribute concepts?
- ❑ contribute answers?
- ❑ connect mathematics to real-world situations?

Informal Assessment
☑ **Student Pages**

Did the student **UNDERSTANDING**
- ❑ make important observations?
- ❑ extend or generalize learning?
- ❑ provide insightful answers?
- ❑ pose insightful questions?

 **TEKS/TAKS Practice**

Use *TEKS/TAKS Practice* pages 81–82 to assess student progress.

B Summarize Findings

Analyze and summarize assessment data for each student. Determine which Assessment Follow-Up is appropriate for each student. Use the Student Assessment Record in *Texas Assessment* or *eAssess* to update assessment records.

C Texas Assessment Follow-Up ● DIFFERENTIATE INSTRUCTION

Based on your observations, use these teaching strategies for assessment follow-up.

INTERVENTION

Review student performance on *Intervention* Lesson 10.C to see if students have mastered prerequisite skills for this lesson.

Measurement 1.8 The student understands that time can be measured. The student uses time to describe and compare situations.

ENGLISH LEARNER

Review

Use Lesson 10.9 in *English Learner Support Guide* to review lesson concepts and vocabulary.

ENRICH

If . . . students are proficient in the lesson concepts,

Then . . . encourage them to work on the chapter projects or *Enrichment* Lesson 10.9.

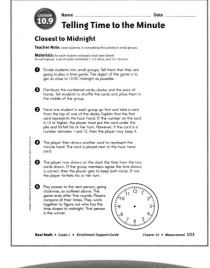

Enrichment Lesson 10.9

PRACTICE

If . . . students would benefit from additional practice,

Then . . . assign *Practice* Lesson 10.9.

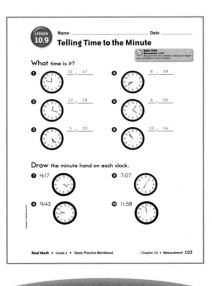

Practice Lesson 10.9

RETEACH

If . . . students struggle with telling time to the minute,

Then . . . have them use blank copies of clock faces to draw a time given by a partner. If the student draws an incorrect time, then have them correct their clock face.

Grade 1	Grade 2	Grade 3
1.8.B Read time to the hour and half-hour using analog and digital clocks.	**2.10** The student uses standard tools to estimate and measure time and temperature.	**3.12.B** Tell and write time shown on analog and digital clocks.

Overview · LESSON 10.10

TEXAS

Lesson Planner

OBJECTIVES
- To informally introduce the convention of using 24-hour clock time
- To teach students how to determine what hour it was or will be, given a number of hours in the future or past

MATH TEKS

Measurement 2.10 The student uses standard tools to estimate and measure time and temperature.
Measurement 2.10.B Read and write times shown on analog and digital clocks using five-minutes increments.
Measurement 2.10.C Describe activities that take approximately one second, one minute, and one hour.

MATH TEKS INTEGRATION
Underlying processes and mathematical tools 2.12A Identifying the mathematics in everyday situations.

MATERIALS
- *Number Cubes
- *Demonstration clock
- *Stopwatches
- Harder Time Game Mat

TECHNOLOGY
Presentation Lesson 10.10

Elipsed Time ★

Elapsed Time ★

Context of the Lesson This is the final lesson in a series that covers different aspects of measurement: weight, length, capacity, temperature, and time. Both metric and customary units are discussed, but students do not convert measurements from one system to the other. This is the last of three lessons in this chapter on telling time and elapsed time. This lesson introduces figuring out what time it was or what time it will be, based on how much time has or will have elapsed.
See page 373B for Math Background for teachers for this lesson.

Planning for Learning ● DIFFERENTIATE INSTRUCTION

INTERVENTION
If . . . students lack the prerequisite skill of telling time to the quarter hour,
Then . . . teach **Intervention** Lesson 10.C.
1.7, 1.8

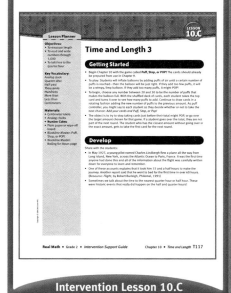

Intervention Lesson 10.C

ENGLISH LEARNER
Preview
If . . . students need language support,
Then . . . use Lesson 10.10 in **English Learner Support Guide** to preview lesson concepts and vocabulary.

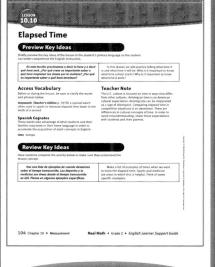

English Learner Lesson 10.10

ENRICH
If . . . students are proficient in the lesson concepts,
Then . . . emphasize Reflect.

PRACTICE
If . . . students would benefit from additional practice,
Then . . . extend Skill Building before assigning the student pages.

RETEACH
If . . . students are having difficulty understanding telling time,
Then . . . extend Guided Discussion before assigning the student pages.

Academic Vocabulary
midnight \mid´ nīt *n.* twelve o'clock at night; the middle of the night

noon \nün *n.* twelve o'clock in the daytime; the middle of the day

Access Vocabulary
stopwatch a special watch often used in sports to measure elapsed time to the tenth of a second

Spanish Cognates
time tiempo

Measurement 2.10
The student uses standard tools to estimate and measure time and temperature.
Measurement 2.10.B Read and write times shown on analog and digital clocks using five-minute increments.

Measurement 2.10.C
Describe activities that take approximately one second, one minute, and one hour.

Mental Math   5

 INTEGRATION: TEKS 2.10 Set the hands of the demonstration clock to various times, and have students use their **Number Cubes** to show the number of minutes after the hour. Possible times include the following:

a. 10:20 20	**b.** 3:40 40	**c.** 7:05 5
d. 8:05 5	**e.** 12:35 35	**f.** 9:15 15

1 Develop   25

Tell Students In Today's Lesson They Will

learn more about telling time.

Guided Discussion UNDERSTANDING   Introductory

Explain to students they are going to talk about the length of time it takes to do certain activities. Explain this is called elapsed time. Go on to ask students questions such as the following:

> **Integration: TEKS 2.12.A**
>
> ■ **What activities take about a minute?** Possible answers: tie both shoe laces, brush your teeth, run 2 laps around the gym
> ■ **What activities take about an hour?** Possible answers: play a game of basketball, household chores, play a video game

Next, display the demonstration clock, and set the time to 12:00. Work with students to calculate what time it will be in 1 hour, 2 hours, 5 hours, 12 hours, and 24 hours. Be sure students understand the difference between A.M. and P.M. and how they apply to the answers. Repeat to find out what time it was 1 hour ago, 2 hours ago, and so on.

2 Use Student Pages   20

Pages 397–398   APPLYING   Independent

Work with students to complete the first column in the table on page 397. Discuss how to arrive at each answer. Have students work independently to complete the second column. Have students use stopwatches and work in small groups to complete the problems and to time the activities on page 398. Make sure students complete the table one row at a time so they can estimate using their previous answers. Then have students name things that might take approximately 1 second, 1 minute, or 1 hour to complete.

As Students Finish

 **Game** Have students play the **Harder Time Game,** or assign games based on needed skill practice.

Name _____ Date _____

LESSON 10.10 Elapsed Time

Key Ideas

You can figure out what time it was in the past or what time it will be in the future.

Times between midnight and noon are A.M. Times between noon and midnight are P.M.

Math TEKS
Measurement 2.10
The student uses standard tools to estimate and measure time and temperature.

The time is now 4:00 P.M.
Complete the table.

Number of Hours	Time It Was	Time It Will Be
1	3:00 P.M.	5:00 P.M.
2	❶ 2:00 P.M.	❷ 6:00 P.M.
4	❸ 12:00 P.M.; noon	❹ 8:00 P.M.
8	❺ 8:00 A.M.	❻ 12:00 A.M.; midnight
12	❼ 4:00 A.M.	❽ 4:00 A.M.
24	❾ 4:00 P.M.	❿ 4:00 P.M.
36	⓫ 4:00 A.M.	⓬ 4:00 A.M.
48	⓭ 4:00 P.M.	⓮ 4:00 P.M.
72	⓯ 4:00 P.M.	⓰ 4:00 P.M.
73	⓱ 3:00 P.M.	⓲ 5:00 P.M.

📱 **Textbook** This lesson is available in the *eTextbook*. 397

⓳ Mrs. Fontana gave her class an assignment on Friday and said it must be finished in eight days. What day of the week will that be?
__Saturday__

⓴ What's wrong with Mrs. Fontana's assignment?
She made the assignment due on a weekend when no one is in school.

How many seconds does it take?
First estimate. Fill in the table below.

Task	Estimate (in seconds)	Measure (in seconds)
㉑ Count to 50.		
㉒ Count to 25.		
㉓ Say the sentence at the bottom of the page clearly.		
㉔ Say the sentence at the bottom of this page clearly twice.		

She sells seashells by the seashore.

---

3 Reflect

10

Guided Discussion REASONING

Tell students that in many parts of the world
- people eat dinner at 1900 hours.
- people wake up at 0600.
- students are in school from 0800 to 1500 hours.
- students go to sleep at 2100 hours.

Through discussion, help students to see that these are times on a 24 hour clock. In this type of system, it is not necessary to use AM or PM to describe morning or afternoon. Instead of starting over again after 12, the numbers continue on until 24.

To make sure students understand, ask them questions such as:

■ **What time does 1300 correspond to?** 1:00 P.M.
■ **What time does 1530 correspond to?** 3:30 P.M.
■ **What time does 0830 correspond to?** 8:30 A.M.

If students are interested, have them write their daily schedules using 24-hour time.

Curriculum Connection: Students may be interested in learning about time zones. Discuss questions such as "If it is 9 A.M. in California, what time is it in New York?"

Cumulative Review: For cumulative review of previously learned skills, see pages 401–402.

Family Involvement: Assign the *Practice, Reteach,* or *Enrichment* activities depending on the needs of your students.

Concept/Question Board: Have students attempt to answer any unanswered questions on the Concept/Question Board.

Math Puzzler: It took Matt 1 hour to get to the mall from his house. He shopped for 3 hours and left the mall at noon. What time had he left his house to go to the mall? 8:00 A.M.

4 Assess and Differentiate

 **Assess** Use *eAssess* to record and analyze evidence of student understanding.

A Gather Evidence

Use the Daily Class Assessment Records in *Texas Assessment* or *eAssess* to record daily observations.

Informal Assessment
☑ **Mental Math**

Did the student `COMPUTING`
- ❑ respond accurately?
- ❑ respond quickly?
- ❑ respond with confidence?
- ❑ self-correct?

Informal Assessment
☑ **Guided Discussion**

Did the student `UNDERSTANDING`
- ❑ make important observations?
- ❑ extend or generalize learning?
- ❑ provide insightful answers?
- ❑ pose insightful questions?

🌟 TEKS/TAKS Practice

Use *TEKS/TAKS Practice* pages 83–84 to assess student progress.

B Summarize Findings

Analyze and summarize assessment data for each student. Determine which Assessment Follow-Up is appropriate for each student. Use the Student Assessment Record in *Texas Assessment* or *eAssess* to update assessment records.

C Texas Assessment Follow-Up ● DIFFERENTIATE INSTRUCTION

Based on your observations, use these teaching strategies for assessment follow-up.

INTERVENTION

Review student performance on *Intervention* Lesson 10.C to see if students have mastered prerequisite skills for this lesson.

🌟 **Measurement 1.8** The student understands that time can be measured. The student uses time to describe and compare situations.

ENGLISH LEARNER

Review

Use Lesson 10.10 in *English Learner Support Guide* to review lesson concepts and vocabulary.

ENRICH

If . . . students are proficient in the lesson concepts,

Then . . . encourage them to work on the chapter projects or *Enrichment* Lesson 10.10.

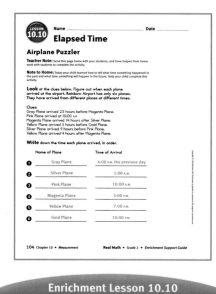

Enrichment Lesson 10.10

🌟 PRACTICE

If . . . students would benefit from additional practice,

Then . . . assign *Practice* Lesson 10.10.

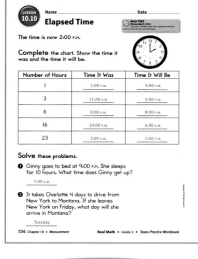

Practice Lesson 10.10

RETEACH

If . . . students have difficulty solving application problems involving time,

Then . . . have them use estimation to determine if their answers are reasonable.

Problem Solving 10·C

Objectives

- To solve a real-world problem involving measurement and elapsed time
- To provide practice solving and presenting solutions to nonroutine problems
- To continue to develop proportional reasoning and using patterns

See Appendix A page A24 for instruction and a rubric for problem solving.

Context of the Lesson This lesson gives students an opportunity to apply what they've been learning about fractions, time, and measurement to a real-world, nonroutine problem. Using patterns and proportional reason are two of the fundamental thinking skills inherent in many lessons throughout the program.

Tell Students In Today's Lesson They Will
find out if a job will be finished in time for lunch.

Guided Discussion

Have students look at the pictures at the top of page 399. Read the following problem to them:

Joey's dad is going to surprise Mr. Thompson's class with a fresh blueberry pie made with blueberries from their community garden. The recipe calls for 8 cups of blueberries. Joey started picking blueberries at 10:30 this morning. By 10:35 he had picked half a cup of blueberries. He wants to be finished by 12:00 in time for a special lunch his dad is making. If Joey continues picking blueberries at the same rate, will he finish in time?

Make sure students understand the problem by asking questions such as the following:

- **What is Joey's dad going to do?** bake a blueberry pie
- **How many blueberries does he need?** 8 cups
- **How is he going to get them?** Joey is picking them.
- **How much has Joey picked so far?** half a cup
- **How long has it taken Joey to pick half a cup of blueberries?** 5 minutes
- **What are you being asked to do?** to find out if Joey will pick 8 cups of blueberries by 12:00 if he keeps working at the same rate
- **What are some ways you might work to solve this problem?** Allow students to suggest and explain methods without going through entire solutions. See Sample Solutions Strategies under Reflect.

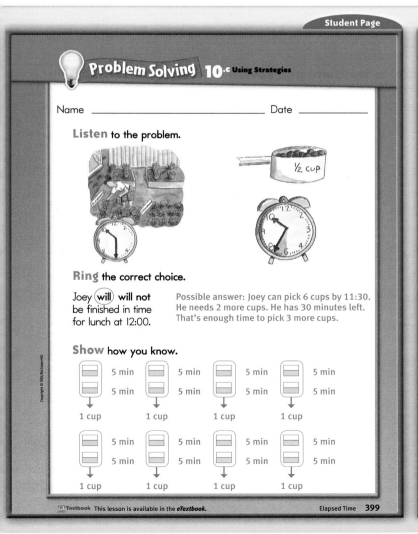

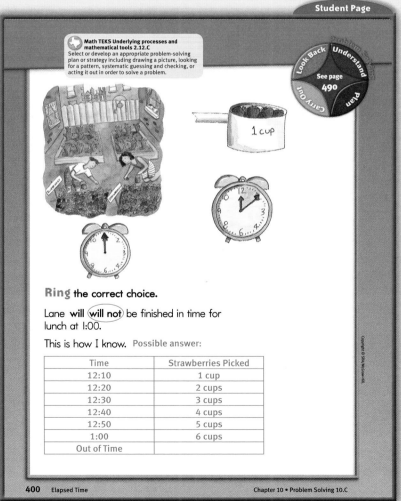

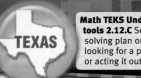

Math TEKS Underlying processes and mathematical tools 2.12.C Select or develop an appropriate problem-solving plan or strategy including drawing a picture, looking for a pattern, systematic guessing and checking, or acting it out in order to solve a problem.

Underlying processes and mathematical tools 2.13.A Explain and record observations using objects, words, pictures, numbers, and technology.
Patterns, relationships, and algebraic thinking 2.6.B Identify patterns in a list of related number pairs based on real-life situation and extend the list.

2 Exploring Problem Solving 25

Have students work in pairs or small groups to solve the problem. Provide support as needed. If students seem to be having difficulty, encourage them to struggle with the problem for a while. When needed, ask guiding questions such as the following:

- How might you use clock faces to help solve this problem?
- How could you draw a simple picture to show the amount of blueberries that Joey's dad needs?
- How many blueberries has Joey picked so far?
- How many blueberries will Joey pick in the next 5 minutes? What time will it be then?
- How can you keep track of the blueberries Joey picks and of the time?

Students who finish early may solve the problem on page 400, or you may assign page 400 as homework. You will need to explain that on page 400, Lane needs to pick 8 cups of strawberries, and she has picked 1 cup from 12:00 to 12:10.

3 Reflect 10

Effective Communication Ask each group to share their solution and their strategies for solving the problem. Help students understand the following points:

- People sometimes use different strategies to find the same answer.
- Some problems don't require finding an exact number. In this problem, students need to determine only whether Joey will finish by noon; they don't need to predict his exact finishing time.
- The problem is asking the students to assume that Joey continues at the same rate, so they can extend the pattern of half a cup every 5 minutes. But they should be aware that not all patterns continue. Certainly Joey couldn't continue picking blueberries at that rate all day; he would get tired and thirsty, need to stop for a break, and so on.

Sample Solutions Strategies

Students may use one or more of the following strategies to help solve the problem.

Make a Diagram

To keep track of what time it is when Joey has picked 8 cups, students might make a diagram using clock faces to show that every 5 minutes he picks another half a cup of blueberries.

Students might make a diagram like the one in the sample response shown on reduced student page 399.

Use Number Sense

Students might realize that Joey picks a cup of blueberries every 10 minutes. Then starting at 10:30, they might say what the time would be 10 minutes later, then 10 minutes later again, and so on until they can see what the time would be after eight 10-minute intervals.

Make a Table

Students might make a table similar to the sample response shown on reduced student page 400.

Use Proportional Reasoning

Students might streamline their use of any strategy by thinking proportionally. For example, if Joey picks 1 cup in a 10-minute period, then he needs 8 such periods to pick 8 cups.

Act It Out/Use a Physical Model

Students might find containers and counters to represent Joey's containers and the blueberries. They might also use a demonstration clock or any clock with a movable minute hand to keep track of time.

Break the Problem into Parts

Students might figure that there are 3 half hours from 10:30 to 12:00. Then after figuring out that Joey picks 3 cups in half an hour, they can figure that he can pick 3 + 3 + 3, or 9 cups from 10:30 to 12:00.

4 Assess 15

When evaluating student work, focus on whether students thought rationally about the problem. Questions to consider include the following:

- Did the student understand the problem?
- Did the student use measurement concepts and units in reasonable ways?
- Did the student explain his or her thinking clearly enough?
- Could the student figure out what happens when a rate is continued?
- Could the student understand other strategies?

Cumulative Review

Use Pages 401–402

Use the Cumulative Review as a review of concepts and skills that students have previously learned.

Here are different ways that you can assign these problems to your students as they work through the chapter:

- With some of the lessons in the chapter, assign a set of cumulative review problems to be completed as practice or for homework.
  Lesson 10.6—Problems 1–3
  Lesson 10.7—Problems 4–5
  Lesson 10.8—Problems 6–7
  Lesson 10.9—Problems 8–12
  Lesson 10.10—Problems 13–22

- At any point during the chapter, assign part or all of the cumulative review problems to be completed as practice or for homework.

Cumulative Review

Problems 1–3 review writing fractions, Lesson 7.2. TEKS: 2.2.A

Problems 4–5 review subtraction applications, Lesson 3.2. TEKS: 2.5.C

Problems 6–7 review place value through 10,000, Lesson 9.1. TEKS: 2.1.B

Problems 8–12 review units of time as days of the week, Lesson 10.8. TEKS: 2.10.C

Problems 13–22 review telling time, Lesson 10.10. TEKS: 2.10.C

Progress Monitoring

If . . . students miss more than one problem in a section, **Then . . .** refer to the indicated lesson for remediation suggestions.

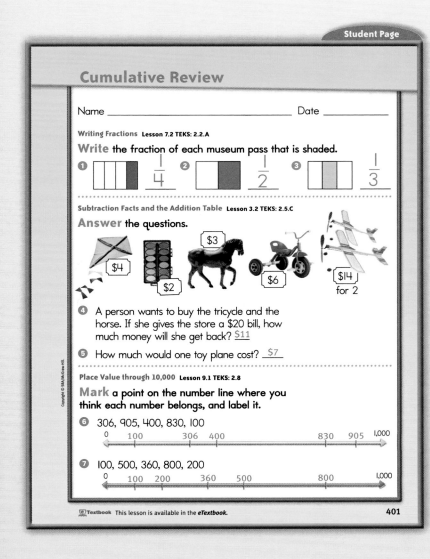

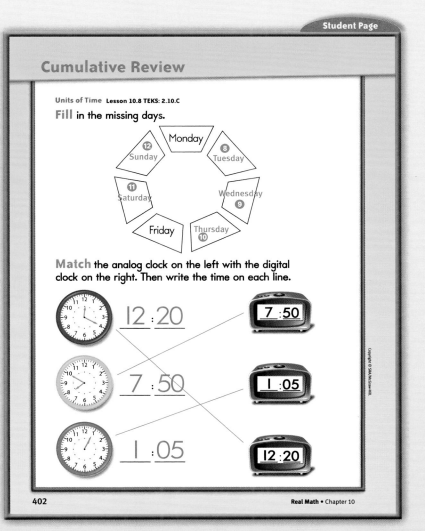

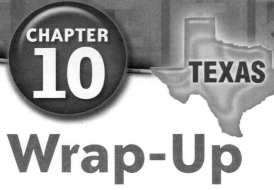
Wrap-Up

1 Discuss 5

Concept/Question Board

Review the Concept/Question Board with students.

- Discuss students' contributions to the Concept side of the Board.
- Have students repose their questions, and lead a discussion to find satisfactory answers.

Chapter Projects APPLYING

Provide an opportunity for students who have worked on one or more of the projects outlined on page 374C to share their work with the class. Allow each student or student group five minutes to present or discuss their projects. For formal assessment, use the rubrics found in *Across the Curriculum Math Connections;* the rubric for **Plan a Flower Garden** is on page 105, and the rubric for **Grow Bean Plants** is on page 111. For informal assessment, use the following rubric and questions.

	Exceeds Expectations	Meets Expectations	Minimally Meets Expectations
Applies mathematics in real-world situations:	❏	❏	❏
Demonstrates strong engagement in the activity:	❏	❏	❏

Plan a Flower Garden

- What flowers did you choose for your flower garden?
- What colors were the flowers you selected?
- What was the perimeter of your garden?
- How did you create a design for your garden?
- Was a presentation program the best way to present the plan for your garden? Why or why not?
- What else could you have included in your flower garden?

 TEKS

MATH STANDARD: **Underlying processes and mathematical tools 2.13.A** Explain and record observations using objects, words, pictures, numbers, and technology.

CROSS CURRICULAR STANDARD (FINE ARTS): **Creative expression/ performance 2.2.B** Create effective compositions, using design elements and principles.

TECHNOLOGY STANDARD: **Communication 10.B** Use font attributes, color, white space, and graphics to ensure that products are appropriate for the communication media including multimedia screen displays and printed materials.

Grow Bean Plants

- What information did you record in your database?
- What was the air temperature around your plants each day?
- Did the temperature of the air affect the growth of your plants? How?
- What changes did you notice in your plants?
- Was a database program a good way to record the changes? Why or why not?
- What factors besides temperature might cause differences in the growth of bean plants?

 TEKS

MATH STANDARD: **Measurement 2.10.A** Read a thermometer to gather data.

CROSS CURRICULAR STANDARD (SCIENCE): **Science concepts 2.7** The student knows that many types of change occur.

TECHNOLOGY STANDARD: **Information acquisition 05.A** Acquire information including text, audio, video, and graphics.

Key Ideas Review UNDERSTANDING

Review the Key Ideas concepts on pages 403-404 with the class. The Key Ideas pages should be used by students and parents as a reference when reviewing the important concepts covered in this chapter. Ask students the following discussion questions to extend their knowledge of the Key Ideas and check their understanding of the ideas.

Discussion Questions

❶ Why would you want to convert between units within the same system of measurement? Could you think of a time where this would be useful? [anno: Allow students to discuss this and present their ideas. For example, if you were trying to convey a measurement to someone, say 60 inches, and the person was having a hard time visualizing that, you could also say that it was 5 feet. That way the person would have an additional point of reference.

❷ Can you think of situations where knowing the elapsed time of an event would be important? [anno: Allow students to share ideas with the class. Some examples would be a track meet, a movie time, or creating a CD of music, where the lengths of songs are important.

❸ Why don't we use a double-pan balance to measure very heavy objects? [anno: Allow students to think about this and discuss it. You may even wish to have them experiment, while supervised, by putting heavy items in the double-pan balance. If you have a heavy object on one side, you would need many weights, or equally heavy weights to get an accurate weight of the object. This may not be practical due to either size or the volume of weights needed.

CHAPTER 10 Key Ideas Review

Name _____ Date _____

In this chapter we discussed . . .
- reading thermometers
- reading maps
- kilograms and grams
- pounds and ounces
- capacity
- telling time
- elapsed time

We used these concepts to help solve problems and answer everyday questions.

❶ You used rulers to measure length in the metric system using centimeters.

❷ You also used rulers to measure length in the customary system using inches.

❸ You used a double-pan balance to measure weight in the metric system using grams and kilograms. There are 1000 grams in one kilogram.

Double-pan Balance

❹ You used a spring scale to measure weight in the customary system using ounces and pounds. There are 16 ounces in 1 pound.

Spring Scale

❺ You measured capacity in the metric system using milliliters and liters. Capacity is the amount a container can hold. There are 1,000 milliliters in 1 liter

---

CHAPTER 10 Key Ideas Review

❻ You measured capacity in the customary system using cups, pints, quarts and gallons. There are 2 cups in 1 pint, 2 pints in a quart, and 4 quarts in a gallon.

❼ The time difference between the beginning of an event and the end of an event is called the elapsed time. Elapsed time tells you how long it takes to do something.

Elapsed Time = 15 minutes

❽ Temperature is measured with a thermometer. You can measure temperature using the Celsius scale or the Fahrenheit scale. In the United States, the Fahrenheit scale is more common.

Chapter 10 Error Analysis

Errors Finding Perimeter

Write the following problems on the board and allow students to analyze this student's work. Discuss error patterns students find and how to help the student.

Pose this analysis as a challenging problem. When a student thinks he or she might have detected the error pattern, rather than have them tell the answer to the class, write a new exercise on the board and have the student tell you the answer that is consistent with the pattern he or she found. By using this procedure, all students will have a chance to think through the problem – not just the first student to find it.

This student completed a page of perimeter problems and got the following answers.

1.

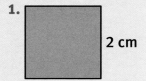

2 cm

The perimeter is __2__ centimeters

2.

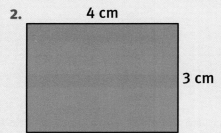

4 cm

3 cm

The perimeter is __7__ centimeters

3.

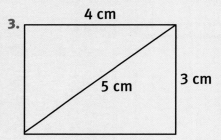

4 cm

5 cm   3 cm

The perimeter is __12__ centimeters

What error is this student making?

Through discussion help students see that this student either does not understand the meaning of perimeter or does not understand the properties of these figures. This student simply adds all of the given numbers.

The student needs instruction on the meaning of perimeter and practice determining the perimeter of figures. He or she might also need instruction on the properties of squares and rectangles. The student needs to be shown that if you know the length of one side of a square, you also know the lengths of the other sides. Similarly, if you know the different lengths of two sides of a rectangle, you also know the lengths of the other sides.

TEKS/TAKS Practice

TEKS/TAKS PRACTICE WORKBOOK

Real Math

TEKS/TAKS PRACTICE WORKBOOK

TEXAS
Consumable

TEKS/TAKS Practice Book

At this time, you may wish to provide practice for standards covered in this chapter.

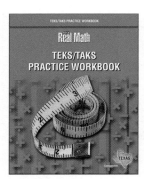

TEKS/TAKS PRACTICE WORKBOOK
Real Math
TEKS/TAKS PRACTICE WORKBOOK
TEXAS

TEKS/TAKS Practice, pp. 79–80, Standard 2.10.A

TEKS/TAKS PRACTICE WORKBOOK
Real Math
TEKS/TAKS PRACTICE WORKBOOK
TEXAS

TEKS/TAKS Practice, pp. 77–78, Standard 2.9.D

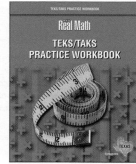

TEKS/TAKS PRACTICE WORKBOOK
Real Math
TEKS/TAKS PRACTICE WORKBOOK
TEXAS

TEKS/TAKS Practice, pp. 75–76, Standard 2.9.C

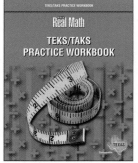

TEKS/TAKS PRACTICE WORKBOOK
Real Math
TEKS/TAKS PRACTICE WORKBOOK
TEXAS

TEKS/TAKS Practice, pp. 83–84, Standard 2.10.C

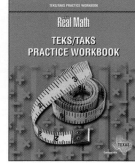

TEKS/TAKS PRACTICE WORKBOOK
Real Math
TEKS/TAKS PRACTICE WORKBOOK
TEXAS

TEKS/TAKS Practice, pp. 81–82, Standard 2.10.B

Chapter Review

Use this Chapter 10 Review to indicate areas in which each student is having difficulty or in which the class may need help. If students do well on the Chapter 10 Review, you may wish to skip directly to the Chapter Test; if not, you may spend a day or so helping students overcome their individual difficulties before taking the Practice Test.

Next to each set of problems is a list of the lessons in the chapter that covered those concepts. If they need help, students can refer to a specific lesson for additional instruction. You can also use this information to make additional assignments based on the previous lesson concepts.

Have students complete pages 405–406 on their own.

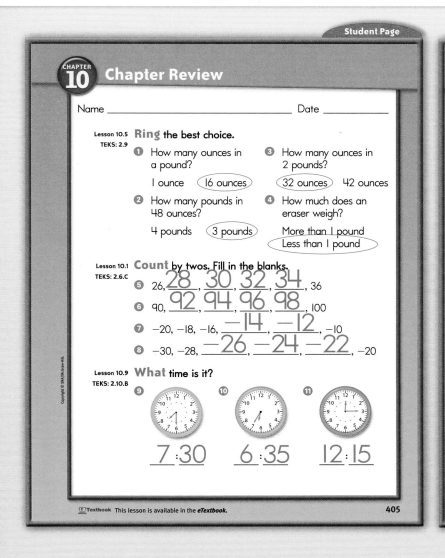

Student Page

CHAPTER 10 Chapter Review

Name _____ Date _____

Lesson 10.5
TEKS: 2.9

Ring the best choice.

1. How many ounces in a pound?
   1 ounce   (16 ounces)

2. How many pounds in 48 ounces?
   4 pounds   (3 pounds)

3. How many ounces in 2 pounds?
   (32 ounces)   42 ounces

4. How much does an eraser weigh?
   More than 1 pound
   (Less than 1 pound)

Lesson 10.1
TEKS: 2.6.C

Count by twos. Fill in the blanks.

5. 26, **28**, **30**, **32**, **34**, 36

6. 90, **92**, **94**, **96**, **98**, 100

7. −20, −18, −16, **−14**, **−12**, −10

8. −30, −28, **−26**, **−24**, **−22**, −20

Lesson 10.9
TEKS: 2.10.B

What time is it?

9. **7**:**30**

10. **6**:**35**

11. **12**:**15**

Textbook This lesson is available in the *eTextbook*.   405

Student Page

CHAPTER 10 Chapter Review

Lesson 10.3
TEKS: 2.3.B

Find the perimeter.

12. Perimeter = **42**

13. Perimeter = **24**

14. Perimeter = **18**

15. You must dig a square hole with a perimeter of at least 32 cm. Draw the hole on the picture. What is the length of each side? **8**

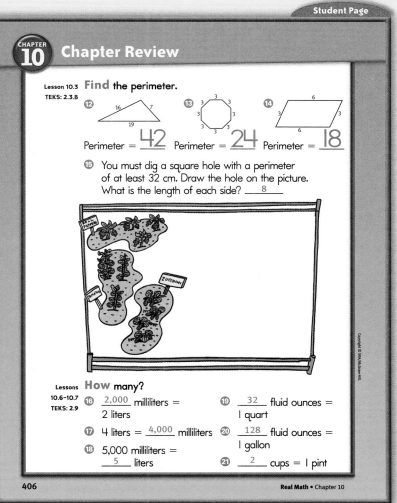

Lessons 10.6–10.7
TEKS: 2.9

How many?

16. **2,000** milliliters = 2 liters

17. 4 liters = **4,000** milliliters

18. 5,000 milliliters = **5** liters

19. **32** fluid ounces = 1 quart

20. **128** fluid ounces = 1 gallon

21. **2** cups = 1 pint

406   **Real Math** • Chapter 10

Chapter 10 • Measurement   **405–406**

3 Chapter Tests   40

Practice Test

Student Pages 407–410

- The Chapter 10 Practice Test on **Student Edition** pages 407–410 provides an opportunity to formally evaluate students' proficiency with concepts developed in this chapter.
- The content is similar to the Chapter 10 Review, in standardized format.

Practice Test Remediation

Multiple Choice Questions 1–8, and **13–14** are all about either converting or estimating measurements. If students have difficulty with the conversion problems, have them review the different units of measure (which are smaller, which are larger) and actually do the conversions using concrete objects and measurement tools.

If students are having difficulty with the estimating problems, ask them to visualize the objects. Some problems may be arising merely because students aren't familiar with the objects being measured (e.g. a medium-sized dog.) Have students practice estimating measures by finding an object in the room, estimating its weight, and then checking to see if they are correct.

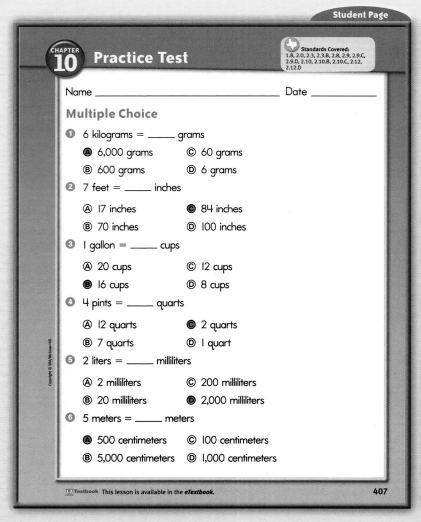

Student Page

CHAPTER 10 Practice Test

Standards Covered:
1.8, 2.0, 2.3, 2.3.B, 2.8, 2.9, 2.9.C, 2.9.D, 2.10, 2.10.B, 2.10.C, 2.12, 2.12.D

Name _____ Date _____

Multiple Choice

1. 6 kilograms = _____ grams
   - Ⓐ 6,000 grams
   - Ⓒ 60 grams
   - Ⓑ 600 grams
   - Ⓓ 6 grams

2. 7 feet = _____ inches
   - Ⓐ 17 inches
   - Ⓒ 84 inches
   - Ⓑ 70 inches
   - Ⓓ 100 inches

3. 1 gallon = _____ cups
   - Ⓐ 20 cups
   - Ⓒ 12 cups
   - Ⓑ 16 cups
   - Ⓓ 8 cups

4. 4 pints = _____ quarts
   - Ⓐ 12 quarts
   - Ⓒ 2 quarts
   - Ⓑ 7 quarts
   - Ⓓ 1 quart

5. 2 liters = _____ milliliters
   - Ⓐ 2 milliliters
   - Ⓒ 200 milliliters
   - Ⓑ 20 milliliters
   - Ⓓ 2,000 milliliters

6. 5 meters = _____ meters
   - Ⓐ 500 centimeters
   - Ⓒ 100 centimeters
   - Ⓑ 5,000 centimeters
   - Ⓓ 1,000 centimeters

📖Textbook This lesson is available in the *eTextbook*.   407

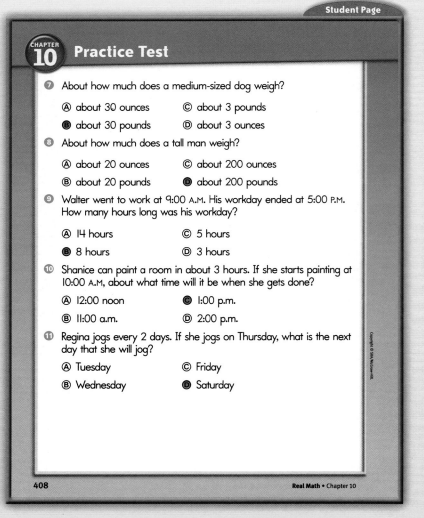

Student Page

CHAPTER 10 Practice Test

7. About how much does a medium-sized dog weigh?
   - Ⓐ about 30 ounces
   - Ⓒ about 3 pounds
   - Ⓑ about 30 pounds
   - Ⓓ about 3 ounces

8. About how much does a tall man weigh?
   - Ⓐ about 20 ounces
   - Ⓒ about 200 ounces
   - Ⓑ about 20 pounds
   - Ⓓ about 200 pounds

9. Walter went to work at 9:00 A.M. His workday ended at 5:00 P.M. How many hours long was his workday?
   - Ⓐ 14 hours
   - Ⓒ 5 hours
   - Ⓑ 8 hours
   - Ⓓ 3 hours

10. Shanice can paint a room in about 3 hours. If she starts painting at 10:00 A.M, about what time will it be when she gets done?
    - Ⓐ 12:00 noon
    - Ⓒ 1:00 p.m.
    - Ⓑ 11:00 a.m.
    - Ⓓ 2:00 p.m.

11. Regina jogs every 2 days. If she jogs on Thursday, what is the next day that she will jog?
    - Ⓐ Tuesday
    - Ⓒ Friday
    - Ⓑ Wednesday
    - Ⓓ Saturday

408   **Real Math • Chapter 10**

Multiple Choice Questions 9–12 are about elapsed time. If students have difficulty with these questions, then have them work in pairs using their clock faces. Have one student set a time, and the other student call out how much time has elapsed. Then the first student sets the clock to the new time. Have students switch roles and repeat.

Short Answer Questions 5–6 involve finding perimeter. If students miss these questions, then have them write number sentences to represent each perimeter before trying to write the answer. This way, you can see if the difficulty is an adding mistake, or if it shows a lack of understanding of perimeter.

CHAPTER 10 · Practice Test

Name _____ Date _____

12 Mario started writing a story the day before Sunday. What day did he begin writing the story?

Ⓐ Saturday   Ⓒ Tuesday

Ⓑ Monday   Ⓓ Friday

13 Which object is closest to 1 meter long?

Ⓐ bookshelf   Ⓒ pencil

Ⓑ paperclip   Ⓓ computer keyboard

14 Which object is closest to 10 inches long?

Ⓐ crayon   Ⓒ motorcycle

Ⓑ math book   Ⓓ car

15 `4:30` Which is not a way to write the time shown on this clock?

Ⓐ half past four   Ⓒ 4:30

Ⓑ four thirty   Ⓓ quarter past four

Textbook This lesson is available in the *eTextbook*.   409

CHAPTER 10 · Practice Test

Short Answer/Extended Response

Write the temperature for each thermometer.

1 50 / 40 / 30   __44__

2 90 / 80 / 70   __77__

3 0 / -10 / -20   __−10__

4 10 / 0 / -10   __5__

5 Evelyn cut a rectangular board 54 inches long. The width of the board is 20 inches. What is the perimeter of the board? __148__ inches

6 Write the time. __12__ : __25__

7 Write the time. __1__ : __35__

8 Write the time. __4__ : __10__

9 Write the time. __9__ : __50__

Write the time shown on each clock.

10 `5:15` __5__ : __15__

11 `12:00` __12__ : __00__ noon, midnight

410   **Real Math • Chapter 10**

4 Assess and Differentiate

 Assess Use **eAssess** to record and analyze evidence of student understanding.

A Gather Evidence

Use the Daily Class Assessment Records in **Texas Assessment** or **eAssess** to record Informal and Formal Assessments.

Informal Assessment
☑ **Key Ideas Review** UNDERSTANDING

Did the student
- ❏ make important observations?
- ❏ extend or generalize learning?
- ❏ provide insightful answers?
- ❏ pose insightful questions?

Informal Assessment
☑ **Project** APPLYING

Did the student
- ❏ meet the project objectives?
- ❏ communicate clearly?
- ❏ complete the project accurately?
- ❏ connect mathematics to real-world situations?

Formal Assessment
☑ **Chapter Test** COMPUTING

Score the test, and record the results.

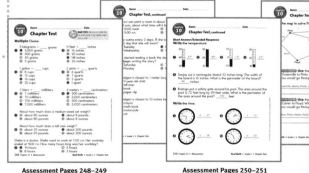

Assessment Pages 248–249   Assessment Pages 250–251

B Summarize Findings

Analyze and summarize assessment data for each student. Determine which Chapter Follow-Up is appropriate for each student. Use the Student Assessment Record in **Texas Assessment** or **eAssess** to update assessment records.

C Chapter Follow-Up ● DIFFERENTIATE INSTRUCTION

Based on your observations, use these teaching strategies for chapter follow-up.

ENRICH	PRACTICE	RETEACH	INTERVENTION
If . . . students demonstrate a **secure understanding** of chapter concepts,	**If . . .** students demonstrate **competent understanding** of chapter concepts,	**If . . .** students demonstrate **emerging understanding** of chapter concepts,	**If . . .** students demonstrate **minimal understanding** of chapter concepts,
Then . . . move on to the next chapter.	**Then . . .** move on to the next chapter.	**Then . . .** move on to the next chapter, but continue to provide cumulative review.	**Then . . .** intensive intervention is still needed before they start the next chapter.

Ferdie's Meterstick

Context of the Thinking Story Ferdie breaks twenty centimeters off his meterstick and uses it to measure and compare various lengths.

Lesson Planner

OBJECTIVES
To develop logical thinking while integrating reading skills with mathematics

MATH TEKS
Measurement 2.9.C
Select a non-standard unit of measure such as a bathroom cup or a jar to determine the capacity of a given container.

Measurement 2.10.C
Describe activities that take approximately one second, one minute, and one hour.

ENGLISH LANGUAGE ARTS AND READING TEKS
Reading Comprehension 2.5 Restate facts and details in the text to clarify and organize ideas.

Reading Comprehension 2.6 Recognize cause-and-effect relationships in a text.

Listening and Speaking Strategies 1.8 Retell stories, including characters, setting, and plot.

Using the Thinking Story

The Thinking Story may be used at any time throughout the chapter. Read the Thinking Story "Ferdie's Meterstick" to your class. As you read the story, give students time to think about each question, but not so much that they forget the point being made.

Measurement 2.9.C Select a non-standard unit of measure such as a bathroom cup or a jar to determine the capacity of a given container.
Measurement 2.10.C Describe activities that take approximately one second, one minute, and one hour.

TEXAS

Ferdie's Meterstick

One day Ms. Arthur gave every child in the class a wooden ruler. "This is a meterstick," she said. "Do you know how many centimeters are in a meter?"

Do you know?   100

"One hundred!" shouted all the students in the class except Ferdie.

"Eighty!" shouted Ferdie.

"One hundred is right," said Ms. Arthur. "There are 100 centimeters in a meter."

"Well, there should be 80," said Ferdie, who never liked to admit that he was wrong. "Eighty is a smaller number, and a meterstick with 80 centimeters is easier to measure with."

Do you think that a measuring stick with 80 centimeters is easier to measure with than a stick with 100 centimeters? Why or why not?   Answers will vary. Possible answers include that it is easier to add 100s than 80s.

"You can take these metersticks home with you tonight and measure things around the house with them," Ms. Arthur said. "Be sure to bring them back in good condition tomorrow, though, because we're going to do a lot of work with them."

That night Ferdie had an idea. He broke 20 centimeters off his meterstick.

How long was Ferdie's measuring stick then?   80 cm

"Eighty centimeters is a better length for a measuring stick," Ferdie said to himself. "Who needs those extra 20 centimeters anyway?"

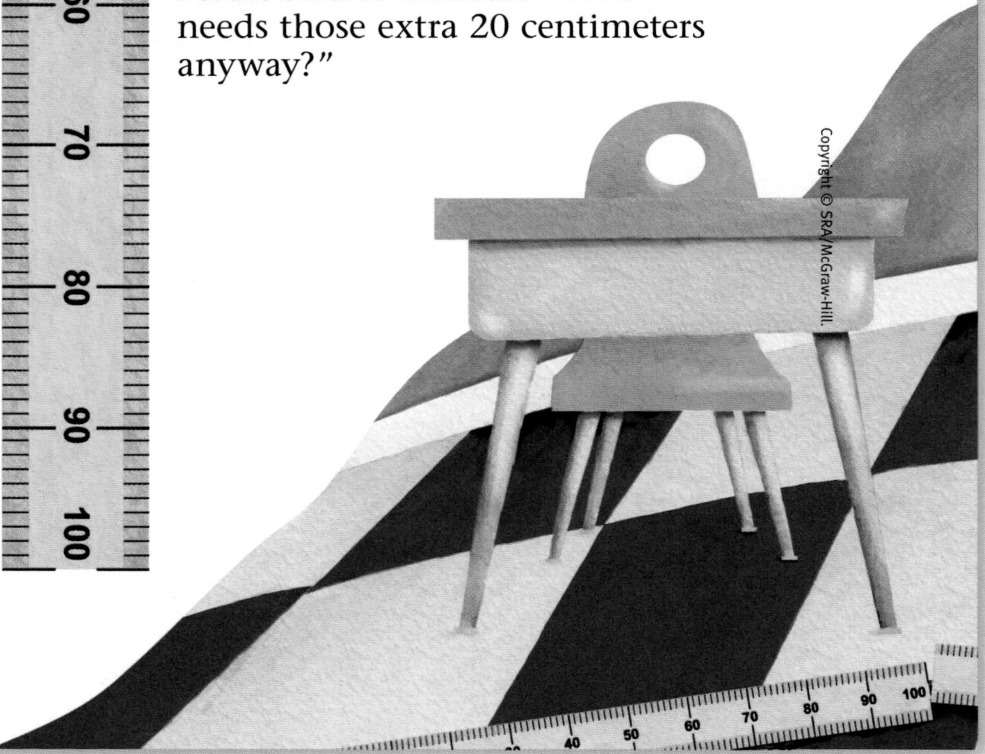

Copyright © SRA/McGraw-Hill.

The next day Ms. Arthur gave the students their first measuring job. They were to find out how many meters wide the room was. The students got down on the floor and moved their metersticks, counting the number of meters. Everyone agreed that the room was about 8 meters across—except Ferdie.

Why would Ferdie get a different answer? His measuring stick is shorter.

Would he find that the room was more or fewer meters across? more

"This room is 10 meters across," said Ferdie. "The rest of you must have counted wrong."

The next measuring job was more fun. Each child measured how far his or her desk was from the classroom door.

"My desk is the farthest from the door!" Ferdie bragged.

"No, it isn't," said Marcus. "See, our desks are next to each other, but mine is farther out than yours."

"I measured, and my desk is 3 meters from the door," said Ferdie. "How far away is yours?"

"Just $2\frac{1}{2}$ meters," Marcus said sadly. "But I still think my desk is farther."

Whose desk is really farther from the door? Marcus's

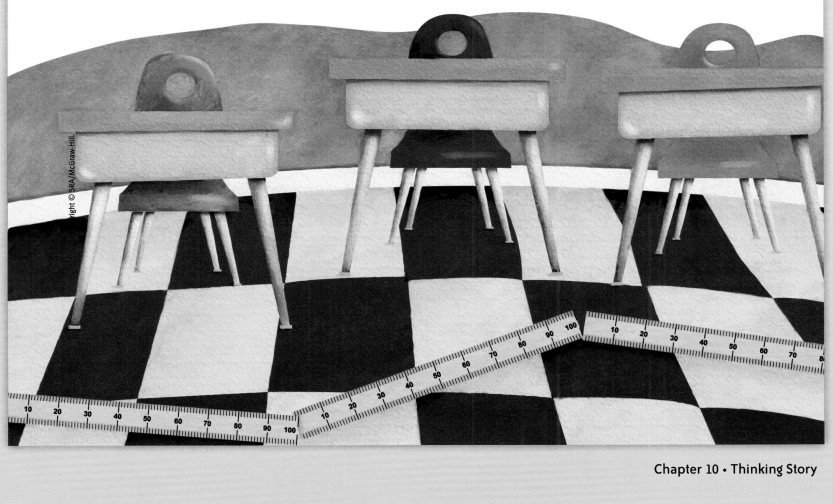

How do you know? Marcus's desk is farther out.

Why does it seem to Ferdie that his desk is farther? Ferdie measured the distance with his shorter measuring stick.

The last thing the children did was the most fun. Each child stood behind a line, ran a few steps, and jumped as far as possible. A chalk mark was made to show where each child landed.

"I jumped $2\frac{1}{2}$ meters," Ferdie announced.

"That can't be true," said Manolita, "because my chalk mark is just as far from the line as yours. And I jumped only 2 meters."

"You might think that you jumped as far as I did, but this proves you didn't," said Ferdie. "Metersticks don't lie."

"If you don't believe me, come and measure my chalk mark yourself," said Ferdie.

Manolita took her meterstick and measured from the starting line to the chalk mark that showed where Ferdie landed.

About what will the distance be, according to Manolita's meterstick? 2 meters

"Just as I thought!" said Manolita. "Two meters—the same distance that I jumped. And you said $2\frac{1}{2}$ meters. That's crazy!"

"You didn't do it right," said Ferdie. "You measured my jump with your meterstick. We're supposed to measure our jumps with our own metersticks. That's what Ms. Arthur said."

Does it usually make any difference which meterstick you use? a little, because not all metersticks are exactly the same length, but generally not enough to notice

"Something does seem a little strange here," said Ms. Arthur. "Could I have a look at that meterstick of yours, Ferdie?"

At first Ferdie didn't want to show it to her, but then he did and explained what he had done. "Did I ruin my meterstick?" he asked.

"Not if you use it right," Ms. Arthur said. "Let's try a little experiment. I want you and Manolita to measure how many centimeters you jumped. Each of you should use your meterstick."

Manolita measured the distance from the starting line to her chalk mark. It was exactly two meterstick lengths.

How many centimeters is that?   200

How can you figure that out?
100 + 100 = 200

Ferdie measured the distance from the starting line to his chalk mark. It was two lengths of his meterstick and 40 centimeters more.

How many centimeters is that?   200

How can you figure that out?
80 + 80 is 160, and 40 more is 200.

"We jumped 200 centimeters," Ferdie and Manolita said.

"Now," said Ms. Arthur, "I'd like you to trade metersticks and measure your jumps again in centimeters."

What answers do you think they will get this time?   the same

"It's 200 centimeters no matter which meterstick you use!" said Ferdie. "My meterstick works. Yipee!"

Why do you get the same answer with both metersticks?   They both measure in centimeters.

On whose meterstick were the centimeters easier to figure out?   Manolita's

Why?   It's easier to add 100 + 100 than 80 + 80 + 40.

The End

Guided Discussion

As students answer the questions in the story, ask them to communicate how they chose their answers. Allow students to debate the answers if necessary.

Using Student Pages 411–412

Have students follow the instructions and complete the **Student Edition** activities. Read the instructions aloud if students are having difficulty.

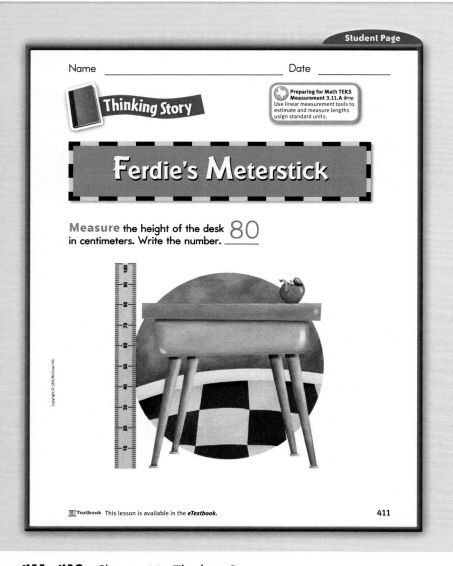

Student Page

Name _____   Date _____

Thinking Story

Preparing for Math TEKS
Measurement 3.11.A
Use linear measurement tools to estimate and measure lengths using standard units.

Ferdie's Meterstick

Measure the height of the desk in centimeters. Write the number. _80_

Student Page

Ring the items that are about 1 meter tall.

Teacher Reflection

Reflect on each of the lessons you taught in this chapter. Rate each one on the following scale, and then consider ways to maintain or improve positive teaching experiences in the future.

Lessons	Very Effective	Effective	Less Effective	What Worked	Ways to Improve
10.1 Reading a Thermometer					
10.2 Reading a Map					
10.3 Measuring Perimeter					
10.4 Kilograms and Grams					
10.5 Pounds and Ounces					
10.6 Measuring Capacity (Customary Units)					
10.7 Measuring Capacity (Metric Units)					
10.8 Units of Time					
10.9 Telling Time to the Minute					
10.10 Elapsed Time					

= 120-Day Plan for TAKS

Introducing Multiplication and Division

Teaching for Understanding

This chapter introduces students to multiplication and division of whole numbers. Students explore how multiplication and division are related and develop an understanding of the principles of multiplication and division using concrete manipulatives.

Prerequisite Skills and Concepts

- Adding a One-Digit to a Two-Digit Number
- Subtraction Facts
- Using a Function Table

Before Grade 2	Grade 2	After Grade 2
Grades K–1 Informally and formally introduced skip counting, arrays, and dividing groups of objects to find fractions of a set or number	**This chapter** develops fluency with multiplication and division notation and the inverse properties of multiplication and division.	Introduction, review, and mastery of multiplication and division facts Later grades include formal introduction and mastery of more complex operations using multiplication and division facts.

BIG Ideas! in Chapter 11

This chapter develops the following ideas running throughout elementary mathematics:

- Operations can be represented in various models. Multiplication of whole numbers can be modeled using various methods. This chapter teaches students multiplication through skip counting, arrays, area models, and repeated addition.

- Each operation is related to other operations. This chapter introduces multiplication and division by focusing on what the two operations have in common as inverse operations. Lesson 11.7 deals with missing factors in an attempt to demonstrate to the students that if they know multiplication they also know division.

Math TEKS addressed in each lesson can be found in the Chapter Planner on page 413E.

Math TEKS addressed in Problem Solving, Review, and Assessment Lessons are on page 413G.

Complete text of the standards appears on the Lesson Overview page and first Teaching page of each lesson.

Math Background

Multiplication and Division

What Are Multiplication and Division?

- Multiplication can be used as a shortcut for repeated addition, adding the same number over and over.

- Division is the inverse of multiplication, just as subtraction is the inverse of addition.

- Unlike multiplication of whole numbers, division of whole numbers does not always result in a whole number. However, since this chapter is merely an introduction to the concept of division, we present only problems that are related to multiplication facts, so that all answers are whole numbers.

Division Symbol

The sign ÷ means "divided by" and is appropriate to use in number sentences ($18 ÷ 6 = 3$, $12 ÷ n = 4$, and so on). The symbol $\overline{)}$ is not appropriate for number sentences; it is used primarily as an aid in calculation when a division algorithm is used. However, as preparation for such division in later grades, we occasionally give exercises in the form $3\overline{)12}$, $7\overline{)19}$, and so on. You might tell the students that the symbol $\overline{)}$ and the corresponding arrangement of divisor, dividend, and quotient will be very helpful later when they do more complicated division problems.

Models for Multiplication

This chapter is designed as an informal introduction to multiplication concepts, and speedy recall of multiplication facts is not expected. Rather, students should understand the meaning of multiplication and some situations in which it is useful. Multiplication is introduced and explored in a variety of contexts.

- Repeated addition and skip counting
Repeated addition and skip counting were introduced in Grade 1 of **Real Math.** In this chapter students learn that a repeated addition expression such as $3 + 3 + 3 + 3 + 3$ can be calculated by skip counting by 3 (that is, saying every third number after 0) and looking at the fifth number—3, 6, 9, 12, 15. The expression can be also be written more efficiently using multiplication, as $5 × 3$.

- Arrays
The number of items in arrays (pictures or objects arranged into rows with the same number in each row) can be counted using skip counting. Each number said while skip counting represents a cumulative total after counting the next row. The number of items in an array can also be written using a multiplication sentence.

- Area
Area is a similar model to arrays but somewhat more abstract. The number of square units in a region can be thought of as an array of squares. Area is a more powerful model for multiplication than arrays since it can involve factors that are not whole numbers, as students will see in later grades.

- Multiplication Table
The multiplication table is used not as a model for multiplication but rather as way of organizing and looking for patterns in multiplication facts. Patterns within the multiplication table are explored in more detail in Grade 3, as students systematically learn strategies to develop fluency.

What Research Says

About Mathematical Operations

How Children Develop an Understanding of Mathematical Operations

Learning Trajectories for Understanding Multiplication and Division

Multiplication and division builds on addition and subtraction understandings and is dependent upon counting and place value concepts. As children begin to learn to multiply they make equal groups and count them all. They then learn skip counting and derive related products from products they know. Finding and using patterns aids in learning multiplication and division facts with understanding. Children typically follow an observable developmental progression in learning to multiply and divide numbers with recognizable stages or levels. This developmental path can be described as part of a learning trajectory. Key steps from the learning trajectory for multiplication and division are described below. For the complete trajectory, see Appendix B.

Level Name	Description
Concrete Modeler ×/÷	As children develop, they are able to solve small-number multiplying problems by grouping—making each group and counting all. At this level a child can solve division/sharing problems with informal strategies, using concrete objects; up to 20 objects and 2-5 people, although the child may not understand equivalence of groups.
Parts and Wholes ×/÷	A new level is evidenced when the child understands the inverse relation between divisor and quotient. For example, this child understands that "If you share with more people, each person gets fewer."
Skip Counter ×/÷	As children develop understanding in multiplication and division they begin to use skip counting for multiplication and for measurement division (finding out how many groups).
Deriver ×/÷	At the next level, children use strategies and derived combinations and solve multidigit problems by operating on tens and ones separately. For example, a child at this level may explain "7 × 6, 5 7s is 35, so 7 more is 42."

Clements, D. H., J. Sarama, & A.-M. DiBiase, eds. *Engaging Young Children in Mathematics: Standards for Early Childhood Mathematics Education.* Mahwah, NJ: Lawrence Erlbaum Associates, 2004.

Clements, D. H., and J. Sarama, (in press). *Early Childhood Mathematics Learning.* In F. K. Lester, Jr. (Ed.), *Second Handbook of Research on Mathematics Teaching and Learning.* New York: Information Age Publishing.

Research-Based Teaching Strategies

Research has shown that students should focus on developing the meanings of and relationship between multiplication and division. It is important for students to understand what each number in a multiplication or division expression represents, and that the two operations act as inverse functions for one another.

Meaning for multiplication will develop as students build and make discoveries from using area models or arrays which help to show how a product is related to its factors. The area model is important because it helps students develop an understanding of properties of multiplication such as the commutativity of multiplication.

Students should become fluent when computing with whole numbers. *Computational fluency* refers to having efficient and accurate methods for computing. Fluency with whole-number computation depends, in large part, on fluency with basic number combinations, such as multiplication pairs and their counterparts for division. Fluency with the basic number combinations develops from well-understood meanings for the four operations and from a focus on thinking strategies. Providing students with opportunities to use skip-counting, area models, and opportunities to reason through relating unknown combinations to known ones all result in deeper understanding of the operations of multiplication and division.

National Council of Teachers of Mathematics. *Principles and Standards for School Mathematics.* Reston, VA: NCTM, 2000.

RESEARCH IN ACTION

Multiplication and Division Throughout Chapter 11 students will recognize patterns and develop strategies, concepts, and procedures for understanding and performing multiplication and division.

Function Machines In Chapter 11 students will work with function machines in order to develop an appreciation of the functional relationships that affect ordered pairs of numbers when operations that involve multiplication or division are performed.

Vocabulary Cards

Use the *SRA Math Vocabulary Cards* for the vocabulary words indicated to introduce, teach, review, and reinforce key math vocabulary for this chapter.

Academic Vocabulary

area (Lesson 11.4) the number of units that the surface of a defined figure measures

array (Lesson 11.3) an orderly arrangement of items into columns and rows

division (Lesson 11.8) the process of seeing how many times one number contains another number; the inverse of multiplication

factor (Lesson 11.7) any number that is multiplied to get a product

multiplication (Lesson 11.2) adding a number to itself a certain number of times using the multiplication symbol ×

repeated addition (Lesson 11.2) adding the same number many times to find a sum

skip counting (Lesson 11.1) counting on by specific intervals and leaving out the numbers that fall between

English Learner

Cognates

For English learners, a quick way to acquire new English vocabulary is to build on what is known in the primary language.

English	Spanish
group	grupo
balance	balanza
multiplication	multiplicación
units	unidades
multiply	multiplicar
compare	comparar
pizza	pizza
function machine	máquina de funciones

Access Vocabulary

English learners might understand words in different contexts and might not understand idioms. Review chapter vocabulary for this concern. For example:

fill in the missing numbers	write the numbers that are needed
predict	to say what you think the answer will be
row	a horizontal straight line in an array
a figure	a shape
products	the answers to multiplication problems
operation	an action such as addition, subtraction, multiplication, or division
table	In this context a table is not furniture; it is a visual organizer of data and information that makes a large amount of information easy to see.
output	the number that comes out of a function machine after an operation like addition, subtraction, multiplication, or division has been applied

Texas Chapter Planner

Lessons	Objectives	NCTM Standards	Math TEKS
⭐ **11.1** Skip Counting and Repeated Addition pages 415A–416A 45–60 minutes	To provide experience with intuitive multiplication through repeated addition	Number and Operations, Connections	2.6.C 🔑 2.4.A 2.8
⭐ **11.2** Introduction to Multiplication pages 417A–418A 45–60 minutes	To gain fluency in repeated addition and skip counting and to introduce the multiplication symbol	Number and Operations, Connections	2.6.C 🔑 2.4.A
⭐ **11.3** Multiplication and Arrays pages 419A–420A 45–60 minutes	To introduce students to array and to provide practice for solving multiplication problems as arrays.	Number and Operations, Communication	2.4.A 🔑 2.13.B
⭐ **11.4** Arrays and Area pages 421A–422A 45–60 minutes	To find area by counting square units and to provide an application for using repeated addition and multiplication	Number and Operations, Measurement	2.9.B 🔑
⭐ **11.5** Using the Multiplication Table pages 423A–424A 45–60 minutes	To use the Multiplication Table and to provide practice learning the multiplication facts	Number and Operations, Communication	2.4 🔑 2.5.A
11.6 Applying Multiplication pages 425A–426A 45–60 minutes	To provide practice with basic multiplication facts	Number and Operations, Problem Solving	2.12 🔑 2.4
⭐ **11.7** Missing Factors pages 431A–432A 45–60 minutes	To introduce missing factor problems and to prepare students for the introduction of division	Number and Operations, Problem Solving	2.4 2.6.B 🔑
⭐ **11.8** Division and Multiplication pages 433A–434A 45–60 minutes	To formally introduce the division sign and to study the inverse properties of multiplication and division	Number and Operations, Problem Solving	2.4.B 🔑 2.6.B
11.9 Division and Multiplication Functions pages 435A–436A 45–60 minutes	To provide practice in multiplying and dividing and to use function tables with multiplication and division	Number and Operations, Problem Solving	2.5 🔑 2.4.B

⭐ = 120-Day Plan for TAKS

🔑 = Key standard

Academic Vocabulary	Manipulatives and Materials	Games to reinforce skills and concepts
skip counting	• *Number Cubes* • Craft sticks • Desktop number lines	
repeated addition multiplication	• *Number Cubes* • Double-pan balance • Ten 5-gram weights • Classroom objects for weighing • *SRA Math Vocabulary Cards*	
array	• *Number Cubes* • Poster board and markers • *SRA Math Vocabulary Cards*	
area	• *Number Cubes* • Graph paper • Rulers • *SRA Math Vocabulary Cards*	
	• *Number Cubes* • Overhead transparency of the 10×10 Multiplication Table • Multiplication Table for each student • *Multiplication Table Game Mat* • *SRA Math Vocabulary Cards*	Multiplication Table Game
	• *Number Cubes* • *Multiplication Table Game Mat* • Multiplication Tables	Multiplication Table Game
	• *Number Cubes* • Counters • *Multiplication Table Game Mat* • *SRA Math Vocabulary Cards*	Multiplication Table Game
division	• *Number Cubes* • Play money • Counters • Multiplication Table • *Multiplication Table Game Mat* • *SRA Math Vocabulary Cards*	Multiplication Table Game
	• *Number Cubes* • Multiplication Table • *Multiplication Table Game Mat* • Function machine	Multiplication Table Game

Additional Resources

Differentiated Instruction

Intervention Support Guide Provides instruction for the following prerequisite skills:

- Lesson 11.A Addition and Subtraction Operations–1
- Lesson 11.B Addition and Subtraction Operations–2
- Lesson 11.C Addition and Subtraction Operations–3

Enrichment Support Guide Extends lesson concepts

Practice Reinforces lesson skills and concepts

Reteach Support Guide Provides alternate instruction for lesson concepts

English Learner Support Guide Previews and reviews lesson concepts and vocabulary for English learners

Technology

The following electronic resources are available:

e **Planner** Lessons 11.1–11.9

e **Presentation** Lessons 11.1–11.9

e **Textbook** Lessons 11.1–11.9

e **Assess** Lessons 11.1–11.9

e **MathTools** *Number Line* Lesson 11.1
        Array Tool Lessons 11.3, 11.4
        Multiplication Table Lessons 11.5, 11.6
        Sets Former Lesson 11.8
        Function Machine Lesson 11.9

e **Games** *Multiplication Table Game* Lessons 11.5–11.9

Building Blocks *Clean the Plates* Lesson 11.1
Comic Book Shop Lesson 11.2
Arrays in Area Lesson 11.4

Assessment
Informal Assessment rubrics at the end of each lesson provide daily evaluation of student math proficiency.

Problem Solving

Problem Solving	When to Use	Objectives	NCTM Standards	TEXAS Math TEKS
Problem Solving 11.A (pp. 413I–414C) 15–30 minutes	Use before beginning Chapter 11.	To introduce chapter concepts in a problem-solving setting	Problem Solving, Communication	2.13.A, 2.14, 2.12.A, 2.12.B
Problem Solving 11.B (pp. 427–428, 428A) 30–45 minutes	Use anytime during the chapter.	To explore methods of solving nonroutine problems	Problem Solving, Communication	2.12.C, 2.14, 2.4.A
Problem Solving 11.C (pp. 437–438, 438A) 45–60 minutes	Use anytime during the chapter.	To explore methods of solving nonroutine problems	Problem Solving, Communication	2.4, 2.12.B, 2.14
Thinking Story—The Amazing Number Machine Makes Mistakes (pp. 449A–449E, 449–450) 20–30 minutes	Use anytime during the chapter.	To develop logical reasoning while integrating reading skills with mathematics	Number and Operations, Problem Solving	2.4, 2.12.B

Review

Review	When to Use	Objectives	NCTM Standards	Math TEKS
Cumulative Review (p. 429–430) 15–30 minutes	Use anytime after Lesson 11.6.	To review concepts and skills taught earlier in the year	Number and Operations	2.3, 2.3.B, 2.4, 2.5.B, 2.7.C, 2.10.C
Cumulative Review (p. 439–440) 15–30 minutes	Use anytime after Lesson 11.9.	To review concepts and skills taught earlier in the year	Number and Operations	2.2.A, 2.4.B, 2.11.A
Chapter 11 Review (pp. 443A, 443–444) 30–45 minutes	Use after Lesson 11.9.	To review concepts and skills taught in the chapter	Number and Operations	2.4, 2.4.B, 2.6.B, 2.6.C

Assessment

Assessment	When to Use	Objectives	NCTM Standards	Math TEKS
Pretest (*Assessment* pp. 130–131) 15–30 minutes	**Entry** Use prior to Chapter 11.	To provide assessment of chapter topics	Number and Operations, Problem Solving	2.4, 2.4.A, 2.4.B, 2.5, 2.5.A, 2.6.B, 2.6.C, 2.9.B, 2.12, 2.13.B
Informal Assessment Rubrics (pp. 416A–436A) 5 minutes per student	**Progress Monitoring** Use at the end of each lesson.	To provide daily evaluation of math proficiency	Number and Operations, Communication	2.4, 2.4.A, 2.4.B, 2.5, 2.5.A, 2.6.B, 2.6.C, 2.9.B, 2.12, 2.13.B
Individual Oral Assessment (p. 430A) 5 minutes per student	**Progress Monitoring** Begin after Lesson 11.6.	To provide alternate means of assessing students' progress	Number and Operations	Individual Oral Assessment
Mastery Checkpoint (*Assessment* pp. 96–97) 15 minutes	**Progress Monitoring** Use in or after Lesson 11.6.	To provide assessment of mastery of key skills	Number and Operations	2.4
Chapter 11 Practice Test (pp. 445–446, 447–448) 30–45 minutes	**Progress Monitoring** Use after or in place of the Chapter 11 Review.	To provide assessment or additional practice of the chapter concepts	Data Analysis and Probability, Number and Operations	2.4, 2.4.A, 2.4.B, 2.5, 2.5.A, 2.6.B, 2.6.C, 2.9.B, 2.12, 2.13.B
Chapter 11 Test (*Assessment* pp. 252–255) 30–45 minutes	**Summative** Use after or in place of the Chapter 11 Review.	To provide assessment of the chapter concepts	Data Analysis and Probability, Number and Operations	2.4, 2.4.A, 2.4.B, 2.5, 2.5.A, 2.6.B, 2.6.C, 2.9.B, 2.12, 2.13.B

Texas Technology Resources

Visit SRAonline.com for online versions of the *Real Math* eSuite.

TEXAS Technology for Teachers

e Presentation	**Lessons 11.1–11.9** Use the *ePresentation* to interactively present chapter content.
e Planner	Use the Chapter and Lesson Planners to outline activities and time frames for Chapter 11.
e Assess	Students can take the following assessments in *eAssess:* • Chapter Pretest • Mastery Checkpoint **Lesson 11.6** • Chapter Test Teachers can record results and print reports for all assessments in this chapter.
e MathTools	**Number Line Lesson 11.1** **Array Tool Lessons 11.3, 11.4** **Multiplication Table Lessons 11.5, 11.6** **Sets Former Lesson 11.8** **Function Machine Lesson 11.9**

TEXAS Technology for Students

e Textbook	An electronic, interactive version of the **Student Edition** is available for all lessons in Chapter 11.
e MathTools	**Number Line Lesson 11.1** **Array Tool Lessons 11.3, 11.4** **Multiplication Table Lessons 11.5, 11.6** **Sets Former Lesson 11.8** **Function Machine Lesson 11.9**
e Games	**Multiplication Table Game Lessons 11.5–11.9**
	TechKnowledge Level 2 provides lessons that specifically teach the Unit 10 Internet and Unit 2 Keyboarding applications that students can use in this chapter's projects.
Building Blocks	**Clean the Plates Lesson 11.1** **Comic Book Shop Lesson 11.2** **Arrays in Area Lesson 11.4**

Introducing Multiplication and Division

Introduce Chapter 11   10

Chapter Objectives

Explain that in this chapter they will

- use repeated addition and arrays.
- learn what multiplication and division are.
- multiply and divide.

Pretest COMPUTING

Administer the Chapter 11 Pretest, which has similar exercises to the Chapter 11 Test.

- If most students do not demonstrate mastery on the Pretest, proceed at a normal pace through the chapter. Use the differentiated instruction suggestions at the beginning and end of each lesson to adapt instruction and follow-up to the needs of each student.
- If most students show mastery of some or all of the concepts and skills in Chapter 11, move quickly through the chapter, de-emphasizing lessons linked to items which most students answered correctly. Use the *Individual Oral Assessments* to monitor progress, and, if necessary, modify your pacing. The oral assessments are especially useful because they can help you distinguish among different levels of understanding. For example, a student who has mastered a particular skill but does not show a deep understanding of the relevant concepts still needs thorough coverage of the lesson material.
- If you do move quickly through the chapter, be sure not to skip games, Problem Solving lessons, and Thinking Stories. These provide practice in skills and nonroutine thinking that will be useful even to students who already understand the chapter content. Also, be alert to application problems embedded within lessons that may show students how math topics are used in daily life.

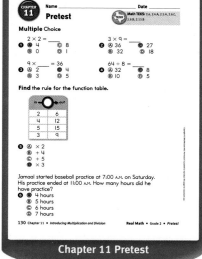

Chapter 11 Pretest

Access Prior Knowledge UNDERSTANDING

Ask students if they have ever eaten foods from different countries. Discuss the types of food they have eaten at home and in restaurants and where these dishes originate.

Problem Solving 11·A Introducing Strategies

Tell Students In Today's Lesson They Will

find out how much a club spent on lunch at a multicultural festival.

Materials

- Countable objects (about 80 per group)

See Appendix A page A24 for rubric for problem solving.

Guided Discussion Introductory

Using Student Pages APPLYING

Have students look at the picture on page 414 while you read this problem to them:

Students in the Diversity Club meet after school to learn about countries around the world. They are learning how to count in several languages, and they are learning about the foods people eat in different countries. One day the club went to a multicultural festival. There were folk dancing, singing, games, posters, and lots of food. Different meals cost different amounts of money. Some of the students bought Mexican meals for $5, some bought Vietnamese meals for $3, and some bought Indian meals for $6. The picture shows the meals 12 of the students bought. How much did these meals cost altogether?

Guided Discussion UNDERSTANDING Guided

To be sure students understand the problem, ask questions such as the following:

- **Where did the students in the club go?** to a multicultural festival
- **What were some things happening at the festival?** folk dancing, singing, games, eating
- **What did the students buy?** foods from different countries

TEXAS

Underlying processes and mathematical tools 2.13.A
Explain and record observations using objects, words, pictures, numbers, and technology.

Underlying processes and mathematical tools 2.14
The student is expected to justify his or her thinking using objects, words, pictures, numbers, and technology.

Underlying processes and mathematical tools 2.12.A
Identify the mathematics in everyday situations.

Underlying processes and mathematical tools 2.12.B
Solve problems with guidance that incorporates the processes of understanding the problem, making a plan, carrying out the plan, and evaluating the solution for reasonableness.

- **Did all of them buy the same thing?** No, some bought Mexican food, some bought Vietnamese food, and some bought Indian food.
- **Did all the meals cost the same amount?** No, the Mexican meal cost $5, the Vietnamese meal cost $3, and the Indian meal cost $6.
- **How can you tell which kinds of meals the students bought?** by looking at the picture
- **What is the problem asking you to do?** find out how much the 12 meals on the table cost altogether
- **How might you work on this problem?** Allow students to suggest methods without giving answers.

Have students work in pairs or small groups to solve the problem. Circulate around the room as they work, offering support as needed. Allow students to use whatever method seems to make sense to them, but remind them to be prepared to explain their methods to the class.

Concept/Question Board APPLYING

Have students think of and write three questions they have about multiplication and division and how they can be used. Then have them select one question to post on the Question side of the Board.

Concepts
As students work through the chapter, have them collect examples of how multiplication and division are used in everyday situations. For each example, have them write a problem that relates to the item(s). Have them display their examples on the Concept side of the Board. Suggest the following:
- shopping
- sightseeing

Answers
Throughout the chapter, have students post answers to the questions and solutions to the problems on the Board.

Student Page

CHAPTER 11 Introducing Multiplication and Division

In This Chapter You Will Learn
- how to use repeated addition and arrays.
- what multiplication and division are.
- how to multiply and divide.

413

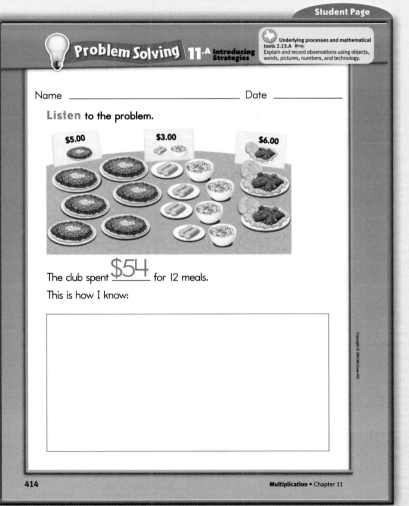

Student Page

💡 **Problem Solving 11.A Introducing Strategies**

Underlying processes and mathematical tools 2.13.A Explain and record observations using objects, words, pictures, numbers, and technology.

Name _____ Date _____

Listen to the problem.

$5.00 $3.00 $6.00

The club spent $54 for 12 meals.

This is how I know:

414

Multiplication • Chapter 11

Reflect
20

Knowledge Age Skills

Effective Communication Have groups present their results. In discussion, bring out the following points:

- Grouping the same numbers together makes it easier to work with them.
- There are different ways to combine groups of numbers and still get the same total.
- There are different strategies that can be used to solve the same problem.

Sample Solutions Strategies

Students might use one or more of the following strategies to solve the problem.

Act It Out

Students might use cubes to stand for dollars and place 5 cubes on each Mexican meal, 3 cubes on each Vietnamese meal, and 6 cubes on each Indian meal. Then they can count the cubes.

Draw a Picture/Add to a Picture

Students might draw money beside each plate to show how much each plate costs and then combine the money.

Write a Number Sentence

Students might write several number sentences or one long one:

$5 + 5 + 3 + 6 + 5 + 3 + 6 + 5 + 3 + 5 + 3 + 5 = $ _____

They might count on for each succeeding number, or they might group the numbers to make them easier to add.

Home Connection

At this time, you may want to send home the letter on pages 42–45 of *Home Connection.* This letter describes what students will be learning and what activities they can do at home to support their work in school.

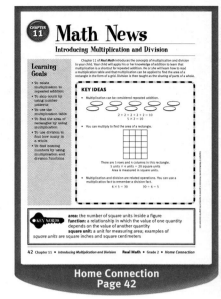

**Home Connection
Page 42**

Extending the Problem

Have students create another problem that could be solved by using the information on page 414. Have students work with a partner to describe how they could use counters or other objects to solve the problem. Possible answer: Place sets of different numbers of colored counters to represent the cost of each type of meal.

Assess and Differentiate

 Assess Use *eAssess* to record and analyze evidence of student understanding.

A Gather Evidence

Use the Daily Class Assessment Records in *Texas Assessment* or *eAssess* to record Informal and Formal Assessments.

Informal Assessment	Informal Assessment	Formal Assessment
☑ **Access Prior Knowledge**	☑ **Concept/Question Board**	☑ **Pretest** `COMPUTING`
Did the student `UNDERSTANDING`	Did the student `APPLYING`	Review student answers on the Chapter 11 Pretest.
❑ make important observations?	❑ apply learning in new situations?	❑ If most students do not demonstrate mastery, move at a normal pace through the chapter.
❑ extend or generalize learning?	❑ contribute concepts?	
❑ provide insightful answers?	❑ contribute answers?	❑ If most students answer most questions correctly, move quickly through the chapter, emphasizing those lessons for which students did not answer correctly, as well as games, Problem-Solving lessons, and Thinking Stories.
❑ pose insightful questions?	❑ connect mathematics to real-world situations?	

B Summarize Findings

Analyze and summarize assessment data for each student. Determine which Assessment Follow-Up is appropriate for each student. Use the Student Assessment Record in *Texas Assessment* or *eAssess* to update assessment records.

C Texas Assessment Follow-Up • DIFFERENTIATE INSTRUCTION

Based on your observations of each student, use these teaching strategies for a general approach to the chapter. Look for specific Differentiate Instruction and Monitoring Student Progress strategies in each lesson that relate specifically to the lesson content.

ENRICH	 PRACTICE	RETEACH	INTERVENTION	ENGLISH LEARNER
If . . . students demonstrate a **secure understanding** of chapter concepts, **Then . . .** move quickly through the chapter or use *Enrichment* Lessons 11.1–11.9 as assessment follow-up to extend and apply understanding.	**If . . .** students grasp chapter concepts with **competent understanding,** **Then . . .** use *Practice* Lessons 11.1–11.9 as lesson follow-up to develop fluency.	**If . . .** students have prerequisite understanding but demonstrate **emerging understanding** of chapter concepts, **Then . . .** use *Reteach* Lessons 11.8 and 11.9 to reteach lesson concepts.	**If . . .** students are not competent with prerequisite skills, **Then . . .** use *Intervention* Lessons 11.A–11.C before each lesson to develop fluency with prerequisite skills.	Use *English Learner Support Guide* Lessons 11.1–11.9 for strategies to preteach lesson vocabulary and concepts.

Math Across the Curriculum

Preview the chapter projects with students. Assign projects or have students choose from the projects to extend and enrich concepts in this chapter.

Compare Diets from Other Cultures 1 week

 TEKS:

MATH STANDARD: Number, operation, and quantitative reasoning 2.4 The student models multiplication and division.

CROSS CURRICULAR STANDARD (SCIENCE): Scientific processes 2.3.A Make decisions using information.

TECHNOLOGY STANDARD: Information acquisition 05.A Acquire information including text, audio, video, and graphics

Have students use mathematics to compare the Food Guide Pyramid to diets from other cultures. To broaden the science concept, have students identify the nutritional values of the types of foods they choose.

As part of the project, students should consider the following issues:

- what types of foods fit into the different categories of the Food Guide Pyramid
- what combinations of food make nutritional meals
- how foods in different cultures compare with foods in American culture

For specific step-by-step instructions for this project, see *Across the Curriculum Math Connections* pages 112–115.

Problem Formulation, Planning, and Strategizing Students plan nutritional meals for a day.

Effective Communication Students explain how nutritional meals from two cultures are similar and different.

Write a Story about Ethnic Food 1–2 weeks

 TEKS:

MATH STANDARD: Number, operation, and quantitative reasoning 2.4 The student models multiplication and division.

CROSS CURRICULAR STANDARD (LANGUAGE ARTS): Writing/purposes 2.14.D Write in different forms for different purposes such as lists to record, letters to invite or thank, and stories or poems to entertain.

TECHNOLOGY STANDARD: Foundations 02.D Produce documents at the keyboard, proofread, and correct errors.

Have students use technology to
- research ideas for a story about ethnic food.
- print a recipe from the Internet.
- write a story on the computer.

For this project, students use the Internet to investigate the following information:

- fun facts about food from around the world
- ethnic food recipes
- information on the country from which the ethnic food originated
- cooking terms

For specific step-by-step instructions for this project, see *Across the Curriculum Math Connections* pages 116–121.

Problem Formulation, Planning, and Strategizing Students adjust recipes and choose setting, plot, and characters for their stories.

Creative Work with Ideas Students explore the information within the role of a fiction writer.

TechKnowledge Level 2 provides lessons that specifically teach the Unit 10 Internet and Unit 2 Keyboarding applications that students can use in this project.

TEXAS **V e r t i c a l   A l i g n m e n t**

Grade 1	Grade 2	Grade 3
1.5.A Use patterns to skip count by twos, fives, and tens.	**2.6.C** Identify, describe, and extend repeating and additive patterns to make predictions and solve problems.	**3.4.A** Learn and apply multiplication facts through 12 by 12 using concrete models and objects.

Overview **LESSON 11.1**

OBJECTIVES
To provide experience with intuitive multiplication through repeated addition

MATH TEKS

Patterns, relationships, and algebraic thinking 2.6.C
Identify, describe, and extend repeating and additive patterns to make predictions and solve problems.

Number, operation, and quantitative reasoning 2.4.A
Model, create, and describe multiplication situations in which equivalent sets of concrete objects are joined.

Geometry and Spatial Reasoning 2.8
The student is expected to use whole numbers to locate and name points on a number line.

MATH TEKS INTEGRATION

Number, operation, and quantitative reasoning 2.3
The student adds and subtracts whole numbers to solve problems.

MATERIALS
- *Number Cubes
- *Craft sticks
- *Desktop Number Lines

TECHNOLOGY
- 🖥 Presentation Lesson 11.1
- 🖥 MathTools Number Line
- Building Blocks Clean the Plates

Looking Ahead
You will need sheets of poster board in Lesson 11.3.

TEXAS
Skip Counting and Repeated Addition ★

Context of the Lesson This is the first of six lessons introducing multiplication. The purpose of this lesson is to use skip counting as one of the three models of multiplication. Note that at this time mastery of the multiplication facts is not expected in the second grade, though students should be encouraged to be fluent in basic multiplication facts as they progress through this chapter.

See page 413B for Math Background for teachers for this lesson.

Planning for Learning ● DIFFERENTIATE INSTRUCTION

INTERVENTION
If . . . students lack the prerequisite skill of using a function table,

Then . . . teach *Intervention* Lesson 11.A.

 1.3.A, 1.5.D

Intervention Lesson 11.A

ENGLISH LEARNER
Preview

If . . . students need language support,

Then . . . use Lesson 11.1 in *English Learner Support Guide* to preview lesson concepts and vocabulary.

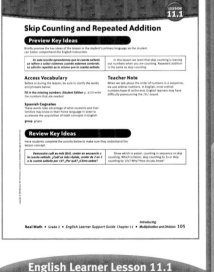

English Learner Lesson 11.1

ENRICH
If . . . students are proficient in the lesson concepts,

Then . . . emphasize Reflect.

PRACTICE
If . . . students would benefit from additional practice,

Then . . . extend Skill Practice before assigning the student pages.

RETEACH
If . . . students are having difficulty understanding repeated addition,

Then . . . extend Guided Discussion before assigning the student pages.

Academic Vocabulary	Access Vocabulary	Spanish Cognates
skip counting counting on by specific intervals and leaving out the numbers that fall between	**fill in the missing numbers** write the numbers that are needed	**group** grupo

Teaching Lesson 11.1

TEXAS

Patterns, relationships, and algebraic thinking 2.6.C 🔑
Identify, describe, and extend repeating and additive patterns to make predictions and solve problems.
Number, operation, and quantitative reasoning 2.4.A
Model, create, and describe multiplication situations in which equivalent sets of concrete objects are joined.

Geometry and Spatial Reasoning 2.8
The student is expected to use whole numbers locate and name points on a number line.

Mental Math | 5

THUMBS UP

INTEGRATION: TEKS 2.3 Present students with three–digit addition exercises, and have them use **thumbs up** if the answers is correct and **thumbs down** if it is incorrect. Possible answers include the following:

a. 200 + 500 = 700   thumbs up
b. 300 + 400 = 700   thumbs up
c. 200 + 400 = 500   thumbs down
d. 400 + 600 = 1,000   thumbs up
e. 400 + 300 = 600   thumbs down
f. 500 + 300 = 800   thumbs up

1 Develop | 20

Tell Students In Today's Lesson They Will

skip count and solve for repeated addition exercises.

Guided Discussion MathTools   UNDERSTANDING

Skip Counting

Tell students to put up their hands with all their fingers up as you point to them one at a time. Have the rest of the class announce how many fingers are up, so the class should say: 10, 20, 30, 40, 50, 60, 70, 80, 90, 100. Tell the class they have just counted by tens to 100. This is sometimes called skip counting because you skip the numbers between the numbers you say.

Now, skip count by fives using fingers again, saying the numbers in unison as you count. Students may wish to quietly whisper the numbers they are skipping when they skip count.

Demonstrate to students skip counting by fives using a number line or *eMathTools: Number Line.* After drawing the skips from 0 and ending with 20, ask students:

■ **What is the third number?** 15

Show students that the third number is 15. Demonstrate with several more examples.

The Commutative Law

Students learned about the Commutative Law in Chapter 2, but the following activity will give them an intuitive reintroduction.

Have two students come to the front of the class.

■ **Can you show three groups of 5 fingers?** One student should hold up both hands, and the other should hold up one hand.

Now have the same two students try to show five groups of 3 fingers. For every one finger one student holds up (the student that held up only one hand before), the other student (the one that held up two hands before) should hold up two fingers to make a "group" of 3 fingers. The two students continue raising fingers until they are holding up the same number of fingers that they held up before. Lead students to see that if they count by fives to 3 fives, that is the same as counting by threes to 5 threes.

Skill Practice COMPUTING   Guided

Use skip counting to have students show their answers to questions such as the following. Write the sequences on the board as you say them aloud.

In the sequence 10, 20, 30, . . .

■ **What is the seventh number?** 70
■ **What is the fifth number?** 50
■ **What is the tenth number?** 100

In the sequence 5, 10, 15, . . .

■ **What is the fourth number?** 20
■ **What is the eighth number?** 40
■ **What is the tenth number?** 50

In the sequence 2, 4, 6, . . .

■ **What is the tenth number?** 20
■ **What is the ninth number?** 18
■ **What is the eighth number?** 16
■ **What is the seventh number?** 14

2 Use Student Pages | 20

Pages 415–416 UNDERSTANDING   Independent

Have students complete pages 415 and 416 independently or in small groups.

Progress Monitoring

If . . . students have difficulty understanding skip counting using a given number,

Then . . . use a number line to show each group of numbers being skipped, and then count the number of skips or terms.

As Students Finish

Building Blocks
Have students use *Clean the Plates* to practice skip counting.

 MathTools
Number Line Have students practice skip counting by using various numbers.

Name _____ Date _____

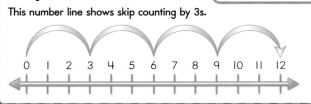

LESSON 11.1 · Skip Counting and Repeated Addition

Key Ideas

Skip counting is counting on in groups and leaving out the numbers in between.

Math TEKS
Patterns, relationships, and algebraic thinking 2.6.C
Identify, describe, and extend repeating and additive patterns to make predictions and solve problems.

This number line shows skip counting by 3s.

Skip count and fill in the missing numbers.

❶ 0 2 __4__ __6__ 8 10

❷ 0 5 10 __15__ __20__ 25

❸ 0 3 6 __9__ __12__ 15

❹ 0 4 __8__ 12 __16__ 20

❺ If 3 tennis balls are in a can, use skip counting by threes to figure out how many tennis balls are in 5 cans. __15; 3, 6, 9, 12, 15__

Some problems can be solved with repeated addition.

Each slice of pizza has three sides. How many sides are there?

❻ 3 + 3 + 3 + 3 + 3 = __15__

How many 3s did you add? __5__

Each plate has four bagels. How many bagels are there?

❼ 4 + 4 + 4 + 4 = __16__

How many 4s did you add? __4__

❽ A sushi chef prepares orders for customers. She counts the orders in groups of 6. Which list shows numbers the chef would count? **TAKS Obj. 1**

  A 6, 16, 26, 36, 46
  B 6, 10, 14, 18, 22
  Ⓒ 6, 12, 18, 24, 30
  D 6, 12, 16, 22, 28

Writing + Math Journal

Write a problem in which you add equal groups. Then solve your problem using concrete objects, such as counters.

See Reflect

---

3 Reflect

10

Guided Discussion REASONING

Modeling Repeated Addition

Write the following problem on the board, and ask students to find the sum by modeling the problems with base-ten blocks.

4 + 4 + 4 + 4 + 4 + 4 = 24

Now write this problem, and have students find the sum.

6 + 6 + 6 + 6 = 24

■ **How are these problems the same?** The sums are the same.
■ **How are these problems different?** The numbers added to get the sum are different.

Help students see that the first problem can be described as 6 groups of 4 things, and that the second problem can be described as 4 groups of 6 things.

So, 4 groups of 6 things is the same as 6 groups of 4 things.

Writing + Math Journal

Discuss student answers. Students may use skip counting or repeated addition to find the sum.

Review **Cumulative Review:** For cumulative review of previously learned skills, see page 429–430.

Family Involvement: Assign the *Practice, Reteach,* or *Enrichment* activities depending on the needs of your students.

Have students practice skip counting and repeated addition with a family member.

Concept/Question Board: Have students look for additional examples that use multiplication and division and post them on the Concept/Question Board.

Math Puzzler: What is the greatest five-digit even number you can write? 99998 What is the least five-digit odd number you can write? 10001

4 Assess and Differentiate

 **Assess** Use **eAssess** to record and analyze evidence of student understanding.

A Gather Evidence

Use the Daily Class Assessment Records in **Texas Assessment** or **eAssess** to record daily observations.

Informal Assessment
☑ **Skill Practice**

Did the student **COMPUTING**
- ❑ respond accurately?
- ❑ respond quickly?
- ❑ respond with confidence?
- ❑ self-correct?

Informal Assessment
☑ **Student Pages**

Did the student **UNDERSTANDING**
- ❑ make important observations?
- ❑ extend or generalize learning?
- ❑ provide insightful answers?
- ❑ pose insightful questions?

TEKS/TAKS Practice

Use *TEKS/TAKS Practice* pages 55–58 to assess student progress.

B Summarize Findings

Analyze and summarize assessment data for each student. Determine which Assessment Follow-Up is appropriate for each student. Use the Student Assessment Record in **Texas Assessment** or **eAssess** to update assessment records.

C Texas Assessment Follow-Up • DIFFERENTIATE INSTRUCTION

Based on your observations, use these teaching strategies for assessment follow-up.

INTERVENTION

Review student performance on **Intervention** Lesson 11.A to see if students have mastered prerequisite skills for this lesson.

1.3.A Model and create addition and subtraction problem situations with concrete objects and write corres-ponding number sentences.

1.5.D Use patterns to develop strategies to solve basic addition and basic subtraction problems.

ENGLISH LEARNER

Review

Use Lesson 11.1 in **English Learner Support Guide** to review lesson concepts and vocabulary.

ENRICH

If . . . students are proficient in the lesson concepts,

Then . . . encourage them to work on the chapter projects or **Enrichment** Lesson 11.1.

Enrichment Lesson 11.1

PRACTICE

If . . . students would benefit from additional practice,

Then . . . assign **Practice** Lesson 11.1.

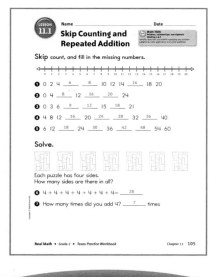

Practice Lesson 11.1

RETEACH

If . . . students struggle with skip counting,

Then . . . have them use calculators to add numbers in a series.

TEXAS Vertical Alignment

Grade 1
1.5.A
Use patterns to skip count by twos, fives, and tens.

Grade 2
2.6.C
Identify, describe, and extend repeating and additive patterns to make predictions and solve problems.

Grade 3
3.4.A
Learn and apply multiplication facts through 12 by 12 using concrete models and objects.

Overview **LESSON 11.2**

Introduction to Multiplication ★

TEXAS

Lesson Planner

OBJECTIVES
- To gain fluency in repeated addition and skip counting
- To introduce the multiplication symbol

MATH TEKS

Patterns, relationships, and algebraic thinking 2.6.C
Identify, describe, and extend repeating and additive patterns to make predictions and solve problems.

Number, operation, and quantitative reasoning 2.4.A
Model, create, and describe multiplication situations in which equivalent sets of concrete objects are joined.

MATH TEKS INTEGRATION

Underlying processes and mathematical tools 2.13.B
Relate informal language to mathematical language and symbols.

MATERIALS
- *Number Cubes
- *Double-pan balance
- *Ten 5-gram weights
- Classroom objects for weighing
- *SRA Math Vocabulary Cards*

TECHNOLOGY
Presentation Lesson 11.2
Building Blocks Comic Book Shop

Context of the Lesson This is the second of six lessons that introduces multiplication. In this lesson students will be introduced to the multiplication symbol and will also relate repeated addition, another model presented in this chapter, to multiplication. Students are encouraged to reach fluency in basic multiplication facts as they move through this chapter.

Planning for Learning ● DIFFERENTIATE INSTRUCTION

INTERVENTION

If . . . students lack the prerequisite skill of adding a one-digit to a two-digit number,

Then . . . teach *Intervention* Lesson 11.A.

 1.3.A, 1.5.D

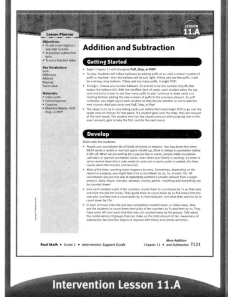

Intervention Lesson 11.A

ENGLISH LEARNER

Preview

If . . . students need language support,

Then . . . use Lesson 11.2 in *English Learner Support Guide* to preview lesson concepts and vocabulary.

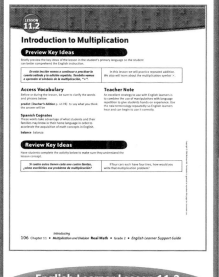

English Learner Lesson 11.2

ENRICH

If . . . students are proficient in the lesson concepts,

Then . . . emphasize chapter projects.

PRACTICE

If . . . students would benefit from additional practice,

Then . . . extend Skill Practice before assigning the student pages.

RETEACH

If . . . students are having difficulty understanding skip counting,

Then . . . extend Guided Discussion before assigning the student pages.

Academic Vocabulary
repeated addition adding the same number many times to find a sum

✏ **multiplication** \mul´tə pli kā´shən\ *n.* adding a number to itself a certain number of times using the multiplication symbol ×

Access Vocabulary
predict to say what you think the answer will be

Spanish Cognates
balance balanza

Teaching Lesson 11.2

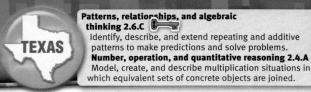

Patterns, relationships, and algebraic thinking 2.6.C Identify, describe, and extend repeating and additive patterns to make predictions and solve problems. **Number, operation, and quantitative reasoning 2.4.A** Model, create, and describe multiplication situations in which equivalent sets of concrete objects are joined.

Mental Math 5

 INTEGRATION: TEKS 2.6.C Present a series of skip counting exercises, and have students show the next number using **Number Cubes.** Possible examples include the following:

a. 2, 4, 6, _8_, 10 _12_
b. 10, 12, _14_, 16, 18, _20_
c. 5, 10, 15, 20, _25_, _30_
d. 30, 35, _40_, 45, 50, _55_
e. 20, 30, 40, _50_, 60, _70_
f. 8, 10, _12_, 14, 16, _18_

1 Develop 20

Tell Students In Today's Lesson They Will
- practice skip counting.
- be introduced to the multiplication symbol.

Guided Discussion  UNDERSTANDING Introductory

Skip Counting and Multiplication

Place an object that weighs about 40 grams on one side of the double-pan balance (a board eraser should be about right).

Place 5-gram weights in the other pan, one at a time, having the students count with you by 5s to see about how much the object weighs (5, 10, 15, . . . 40). Do not try to weigh the object precisely; stop counting when the balance tips. Then say that the weight is about 40 grams.

- **How many times was a 5-gram weight placed on the double-pan balance?** 8 times

Repeat the procedure with a few other objects that weigh between 10 and 50 grams. Each time count by 5s, and ask students how many 5-gram weights were needed to balance or almost balance the scale.

- **How much do eight 5s equal?** 40 If students have trouble, count with them by 5s through 40, and write each number on the board. Tell students as you write on the board that eight 5s is written as $8 \times 5 = 40$. Point out the multiplication symbol emphasizing that 5 was added eight times.

Skill Practice UNDERSTANDING Guided

Do several similar problems, skip counting in unison and then writing the entire multiplication fact on the board. For example:

a. 2, 4, 6, 8; $4 \times 2 = 8$
b. 3, 6, 9, 12; $4 \times 3 = 12$
c. 6, 12, 18, 24; $4 \times 6 = 24$

Have students predict how many fives, for instance, there will be in a given number (say, 30). Use the double-pan balance, and ask a question such as the following:

- **I have something that weighs 45 grams. How many 5-gram weights do I need to put into the pan to balance it?** 9

Demonstrate that the answer is correct.

Then ask another question in terms of length.

- **I have some tiles that measure 3 centimeters each. How many tiles do I need to make a row that is 15 centimeters long?** 5

Demonstrate that the answer is correct by drawing a 15-inch line on the board and dividing it into five 3-inch segments.

Say that repeated addition is the same as multiplication.

- **How many fingers are on one hand?** 5

Have four students hold up their hands.

- **How many fingers are on eight hands?** 40

Explain that they can find out by adding 5 eight times or by multiplying 8×5.

If students hesitate, ask someone to explain that three students would hold up both hands to get six 5s. If your class finds this easy, try seven 5s, and have students hold up the corresponding number of fingers.

2 Use Student Pages 20

Student Pages 417–418 COMPUTING Independent

Have students complete pages 417 and 418 independently.

Progress Monitoring

If . . . students have difficulty understanding repeated addition,

Then . . . use counters to demonstrate the quantities being added.

As Students Finish

Building Blocks Have students use **Comic Book Shop** to practice skip counting and creating multiplication expressions.

Name _____ Date _____

Key Ideas

There is a shorter way to write **repeated addition** problems

$2 + 2 + 2 = 6$

You can use multiplication.

$\times$ means "times."
2 is added 3 times
3 times 2 = 6
$3 \times 2 = 6$

number of times the number is repeated

number being added or repeated

It is also the same as multiplying 2 times 3:
$2 \times 3 = 6$.

🌀 Math TEKS
Patterns, relationships, and algebraic thinking 2.6.C ⬤—
Identify, describe, and extend repeating and additive patterns to make predictions and solve problems.

Solve.

❶ $8 + 8 + 8 + 8 + 8 + 8 + 8 =$ __56__

How many times did you add 8? __7__ times

So, $7 \times 8 =$ __56__.

417

Textbook This lesson is available in the *eTextbook*.

418

❷ $3 + 3 + 3 + 3 + 3 =$ __15__

How many times did you add 3? __5__ times

__5__ $\times$ __3__ = __15__

❸ $5 + 5 + 5 =$ __15__

How many times did you add 5? __3__ times

__3__ $\times$ __5__ = __15__

❹ $3 =$ __3__

How many times did you add 3? __1__ times

__1__ $\times$ __3__ = __3__

❺ $1 + 1 + 1 =$ __3__

How many times did you add 1? __3__ times

__3__ $\times$ __1__ = __3__

❻ $3 + 3 + 3 + 3 =$ __12__

How many times did you add 3? __4__ times

__4__ $\times$ __3__ = __12__

❼ $4 + 4 + 4 =$ __12__

How many times did you add 4? __3__ times

__3__ $\times$ __4__ = __12__

Writing + Math 📝 Journal

The number of counters is the same in each pair.

Use counters to model the additions in Problems 2 and 3, 4 and 5, and 6 and 7. Describe what you notice about the number of counters in each pair of arrays.

Real Math • Chapter 11 • Lesson 2

---

3 Reflect   10 ⏱

Guided Discussion REASONING

🤝

🌟 **Integration: TEKS 2.13.B**

Pose this problem for discussion.

■ **Pencils are sold 4 to a package. How many pencils will there be in 7 packages?** 28 Discuss solutions and be sure to include these three methods:

Fast adding:

$4 + 4 + 4 + 4 + 4 + 4 + 4 = 28$

Skip counting:

4, 8, 12, 16, 20, 24, 28

Multiplying:

$7 \times 4 = 28$

Finally, point out that although each of the methods can be used, the quickest method is to multiply, but only if you remember that $7 \times 4 = 28$.

Writing + Math 📝 Journal ✅

Discuss students' answers.

🌟 TEXAS TEKS Checkup

Number Sense 3.1 Use repeated addition, arrays, and counting by multiples to do multiplication.

Use this problem to assess students' progress towards standards mastery:

Which would be an equation for the array below?

Ⓐ $3 \times 3 = 9$ **B** $1 \times 3 = 3$

C $3 \times 2 = 6$ **D** $9 \times 1 = 9$

Have students choose the correct answer, then describe how they

knew which choice was correct. In the discussion, ask questions such as the following. Be sure to ask students to explain their reasoning, since different solution methods are possible.

■ **How do you write an equation?** use the dimensions of the array as your factors

Follow-Up
If... students have difficulty with arrays to do multiplication,

Then... have students use the *eMathTools: Array Tool* to explore arrays.

---

4 Assess and Differentiate

 **Assess** Use *eAssess* to record and analyze evidence of student understanding.

A Gather Evidence

Use the Daily Class Assessment Records in *Texas Assessment* or *eAssess* to record daily observations.

Informal Assessment
☑ **Guided Discussion**

Did the student **UNDERSTANDING**
- ❏ make important observations?
- ❏ extend or generalize learning?
- ❏ provide insightful answers?
- ❏ pose insightful questions?

Portfolio Assessment
☑ **Journal**

Did the student **APPLYING**
- ❏ apply learning in new situations?
- ❏ contribute concepts?
- ❏ contribute answers?
- ❏ connect mathematics to real-world situations?

🔲 TEKS/TAKS Practice
Use *TEKS/TAKS Practice* pages 55–58 to assess student progress.

B Summarize Findings

Analyze and summarize assessment data for each student. Determine which Assessment Follow-Up is appropriate for each student. Use the Student Assessment Record in *Texas Assessment* or *eAssess* to update assessment records.

C Texas Assessment Follow-Up ● DIFFERENTIATE INSTRUCTION

Based on your observations, use these teaching strategies for assessment follow-up.

INTERVENTION

Review student performance on *Intervention* Lesson 11.A to see if students have mastered prerequisite skills for this lesson.

🔲 **1.3.A** Model and create addition and subtraction problem situations with concrete objects and write corres-ponding number sentences.

🔲 **1.5.D** Use patterns to develop strategies to solve basic addition and basic subtraction problems.

ENGLISH LEARNER
Review

Use Lesson 11.2 in *English Learner Support Guide* to review lesson concepts and vocabulary.

ENRICH

If . . . students are proficient in the lesson concepts,

Then . . . encourage them to work on the chapter projects or *Enrichment* Lesson 11.2.

(Enrichment worksheet)

LESSON 11.2
Name _____ Date _____
Introduction to Multiplication

Salads

Teacher Note: Send this page home with your students, and have helpers from home work with students to complete the activity.

Note to Home: Today your student learned about repeated addition, skip counting, and multiplication. Help your student complete this activity.

Salad chef Lief Lettis has just received his first order of the night from the biggest table in the restaurant.

Use skip counting to figure out how many of each ingredient he needs. Listed below are the ingredients, not including lettuce, for each salad.

Chef Salad	Total Needed
5 pieces of chicken	10
2 strips of turkey	4
8 chunks of cheddar cheese	16
3 chopped up eggs	6
9 black olives	18

Caesar Salad	Total Needed
7 crunchy croutons	35
9 chunks of parmesan cheese	45

Side Salad	Total Needed
4 cherry tomatoes	12
8 cucumber slices	24
2 radishes	6
6 carrot strips	18

Introducing Multiplication
106 Chapter 11 • and Division   **Real Math • Grade 2 • Enrichment Support Guide**

Enrichment Lesson 11.2

🔲 TEXAS PRACTICE

If . . . students would benefit from additional practice,

Then . . . assign *Practice* Lesson 11.2.

(Practice worksheet)

LESSON 11.2
Name _____ Date _____
Introduction to Multiplication

Solve.

❶ 7 + 7 + 7 + 7 + 7 = ___35___
How many times did you add 7? ___5___ times.
So 5 × 7 = ___35___

❷ 3 + 3 + 3 + 3 + 3 + 3 + 3 = ___21___
How many times did you add 3? ___7___ times.
So 7 × 3 = ___21___

❸ 8 + 8 + 8 + 8 + 8 + 8 = ___48___
How many times did you add 8? ___6___ times.
So 6 × 8 = ___48___

❹ 6 + 6 + 6 + 6 + 6 + 6 = ___36___
How many times did you add 6? ___6___ times.
So 6 × 6 = ___36___

❺ 5 + 5 + 5 + 5 = ___20___
How many times did you add 5? ___4___ times.
___4___ × ___5___ = ___20___

106 Chapter 11   **Real Math • Grade 2 • Texas Practice Workbook**

Practice Lesson 11.2

RETEACH

If . . . students have difficulty with skip counting,

Then . . . have them count aloud by 2s or 3s by adding mentally to get the next number in the sequence.

Grade 1	Grade 2	Grade 3
1.5.A Use patterns to skip count by twos, fives, and tens.	**2.4.A** Model, create, and describe multiplication situations in which equivalent sets of concrete objects are joined.	**3.4.A** Learn and apply multiplication facts through 12 by 12 using concrete models and objects.

Overview · LESSON 11.3

TEXAS

Lesson Planner

OBJECTIVES
- To introduce arrays as a model for understanding multiplication
- To begin to practice multiplication facts

MATH TEKS

Number, operation, and quantitative reasoning 2.4.A
Model, create, and describe multiplication situations in which equivalent sets of concrete objects are joined.

Underlying processes and mathematical tools 2.13.B
Relate informal language to mathematical language and symbols.

MATH TEKS INTEGRATION 2.3.A
Recall and apply basic addition and subtraction facts (to 18).

Preparing for Patterns, relationships, and algebraic thinking 3.6.B
Identify patterns in multiplication facts using concrete objects, pictorial models, or technology.

MATERIALS
- *Number Cubes
- Poster board (or large sheets of paper) and markers
- *SRA Math Vocabulary Cards*

TECHNOLOGY
- Presentation Lesson 11.3
- MathTools Array Tool

Multiplication and Arrays ★

Context of the Lesson This is the third of six lessons that introduces multiplication. In this lesson students will learn how to represent multiplication expressions using arrays, the final model presented in this chapter. The study of arrays as a model for multiplication leads naturally to the use of area models. Area models will be used in later grades to help students understand the algorithms for multiplying two- and three-digit numbers. Students are encouraged to develop fluency in basic multiplication facts as they work through this chapter.

See page 413B for Math Background for teachers for this lesson.

Planning for Learning • DIFFERENTIATE INSTRUCTION

INTERVENTION

If . . . students lack the prerequisite skill of subtraction facts,

Then . . . teach *Intervention* Lesson 11.A.

1.3.A, 1.5.D

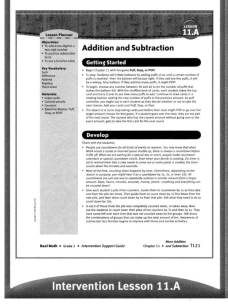

Intervention Lesson 11.A

ENGLISH LEARNER

Preview

If . . . students need language support,

Then . . . use Lesson 11.3 in *English Learner Support Guide* to preview lesson concepts and vocabulary.

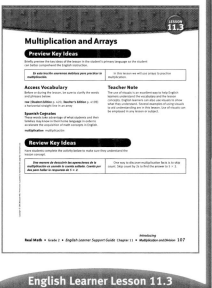

English Learner Lesson 11.3

ENRICH

If . . . students are proficient in the lesson concepts,

Then . . . emphasize Reflect.

PRACTICE

If . . . students would benefit from additional practice,

Then . . . extend Strategy Building before assigning the student pages.

RETEACH

If . . . students are having difficulty understanding multiplication and arrays,

Then . . . extend Guided Discussion before assigning the student pages.

Academic Vocabulary
array \ə rā´\ *n.* an orderly arrangement of items into columns and rows

Access Vocabulary
row a horizontal straight line in an array

Spanish Cognates
multiplication multiplicación

TEXAS

Number, operation, and quantitative reasoning 2.4.A Model, create, and describe multiplication situations in which equivalent sets of concrete objects are joined. **Underlying processes and mathematical tools 2.13.B** Relate informal language to mathematical language and symbols.

Mental Math 5

 INTEGRATION: TEKS 2.3.A Present repeated addition exercises, and have students use **Number Cubes** to show their answers. Possible examples include the following:

a. $1 + 1 + 1 + 1 = 4$
b. $2 + 2 + 2 = 6$
c. $3 + 3 + 3 + 3 = 12$
d. $4 + 4 = 8$
e. $5 + 5 + 5 = 15$
f. $1 + 1 + 1 = 3$
g. $4 + 4 + 4 = 12$
h. $2 + 2 = 4$

1 Develop 20

Tell Students In Today's Lesson They Will

use arrays to practice multiplication.

 Introductory

Guided Discussion MathTools REASONING

Review that one way to discover multiplication facts is repeated addition, so if students want to know what 7×5 is, they can add 5 seven times. Have students hold up five fingers each as you point at them, and have the class announce the total number of fingers showing. Do this slowly so students can count rapidly in between if they choose.

Discuss how to create an array. Draw a row of five Xs on a piece of poster board or use **eMathTools: Array Tool.**

■ **How many Xs would be in four rows?** 20 Draw to check answers.

```
X  X  X  X  X
X  X  X  X  X
X  X  X  X  X
X  X  X  X  X
```

Turn the poster board on its side to show that five rows of four Xs is the same as four rows of five Xs. Again show that 4×5 and $5 + 5 + 5 + 5$ both equal 20.

Have students try to create an array for a $\times 0$ problem such as $10 \times 0 = 0$.

Show that despite how many groups of 0 you have, you still have 0.

Strategy Building UNDERSTANDING

 Guided

 Integration: 3.6.B

Draw a row of five Xs on a sheet of poster board while the students count them. Then draw another row under the first one; students should count out the five new Xs. Repeat until you have five rows of five Xs each.

■ **How many are in the first two rows?** 10
■ **How many are in the first three rows?** 15 **four rows?** 20 **five rows?** 25

Repeat several of the questions in this form:

■ **How many Xs are in 3 rows of 5 Xs?** 15
■ **How many are in 4 rows of 5 Xs?** 20

● On a separate sheet of poster board repeat the exercise for rows of four, up to five rows of four Xs.
● Repeat the activity using rows of three Xs, two Xs, and one X, with five rows in each case.
● Go back, and look at the five rows of three Xs with students.

■ **What are five 3s?** 15
■ **What are three 5s?** 15
■ **How can we get both answers from the figures on the paper?** Students may remember that if you rotate the poster board to its side, there appear to be three rows of five Xs each, instead of five rows of three Xs each.

Modeling Arrays

Distribute 30 counters to pairs of students. Have students use the counters to create an array of 5 rows of 4, counting the total number after they place each row in order to model multiplication situations with equivalent sets. Then have them create an array with 4 rows of 5 counters. Ask questions such as the following.

■ **Is the total number of counters the same in both arrays?** yes
■ **Describe how you could show both 5 × 4 and 4 × 5 with one array.** They could turn the array sideways.

Have students repeat the activity for three rows of 4 and four rows of 3.

2 Use Student Pages 20

Pages 419–420 COMPUTING

 Guided

Have students complete student pages 419 and 420 as a whole class.

Progress Monitoring

If . . . students have difficulty understanding how to relate arrays to multiplication,

Then . . . provide students with more opportunities to create arrays of multiplication facts.

As Students Finish

Game Allow students to play any previously introduced game, or assign a game based on student needs.

 MathTools Have students explore arrays using **Array Tool.**

Student Page

Name _____ Date _____

LESSON 11.3 Multiplication and Arrays

Key Ideas

Multiplication can be shown by arranging pictures in **arrays**.

$4 + 4 + 4 = 12$

So, $3 \times 4 = 12$.

Math TEKS
Number, operation, and quantitative reasoning 2.4.A
Model, create, and describe multiplication situations in which equivalent sets of concrete objects are joined.

Use these pictures to solve the problems.

1. $\underline{5} \times 4 = 20$

3. $\underline{3} \times 3 = 9$

2. $\underline{3} \times 4 = 12$

4. $\underline{3} \times 2 = 6$

Textbook This lesson is available in the *eTextbook*.

419

LESSON 11.3 · Multiplication and Arrays

Use these pictures to solve the problems.

5. $1 \times 4 = \underline{4}$

6. $2 \times 4 = \underline{8}$

7. $3 \times 4 = \underline{12}$

8. $4 \times 4 = \underline{16}$

9. $5 \times 4 = \underline{20}$

10. $1 \times 3 = \underline{3}$

11. $2 \times 3 = \underline{6}$

12. $3 \times 3 = \underline{9}$

13. $4 \times 3 = \underline{12}$

14. $5 \times 3 = \underline{15}$

15. **Extended Response** How many scones do you think this tray can hold? ___12___
Explain why you think there are that many.
Possible answer: I see 2 rows of 3 scones; it looks like there can be 2 more rows of 3 scones each. That would make 4 rows of 3 scones each, which is 12.

420

Real Math • Chapter 11 • Lesson 3

 Reflect 10

Guided Discussion REASONING

Have students create several arrays that consist of ten rows (ten rows of four, ten rows of five, ten rows of six, and so on) and the corresponding multiplication facts ($10 \times 4 = 40$, $10 \times 5 = 50$, $10 \times 6 = 60$).

■ **Do you notice any pattern when you multiply a number by 10?** Yes; each number has a zero written at the end of it.

Have students try making a large array such as ten rows of twelve, or ten rows of twenty.

■ **Does the pattern you found still work for these arrays?** yes; 120 and 200

Extended Response

Problem 15 Discuss students' answers. Students should have realized that if they see 2 rows of 3 scones, it looks like there are 2 more rows of 3 scones each. That would make 4 rows of 3 scones each, which is 12.

Review **Cumulative Review:** For cumulative review of previously learned skills, see page 429–430.

Family Involvement: Assign the **Practice, Reteach,** or **Enrichment** activities depending on the needs of your students.

Have students make flash cards with an array on one side and the two corresponding multiplication facts on the other side.

Concept/Question Board: Have students look for additional examples using multiplication and division and post them on the Concept/Question Board.

Math Puzzler: I am a two-digit even number. If you add my digits you get 13. If you subtract my digits you get 5. What number am I? 94

4 Assess and Differentiate

 **Assess** Use *eAssess* to record and analyze evidence of student understanding.

A Gather Evidence

Use the Daily Class Assessment Records in *Texas Assessment* or *eAssess* to record daily observations.

Informal Assessment
☑ **Strategy Building**

Did the student **UNDERSTANDING**
- ❏ make important observations?
- ❏ extend or generalize learning?
- ❏ provide insightful answers?
- ❏ pose insightful questions?

Portfolio Assessment
☑ **Extended Response**

Did the student **REASONING**
- ❏ provide a clear explanation?
- ❏ communicate reasons and strategies?
- ❏ choose appropriate strategies?
- ❏ argue logically?

TEKS/TAKS Practice

Use *TEKS/TAKS Practice* pages 34–36 to assess student progress.

B Summarize Findings

Analyze and summarize assessment data for each student. Determine which Assessment Follow-Up is appropriate for each student. Use the Student Assessment Record in *Texas Assessment* or *eAssess* to update assessment records.

C Texas Assessment Follow-Up • DIFFERENTIATE INSTRUCTION

Based on your observations, use these teaching strategies for assessment follow-up.

INTERVENTION

Review student performance on *Intervention* Lesson 11.A to see if students have mastered prerequisite skills for this lesson.

1.3.A Model and create addition and subtraction problem situations with concrete objects and write corres-ponding number sentences.

1.5.D Use patterns to develop strategies to solve basic addition and basic subtraction problems.

ENGLISH LEARNER

Review

Use Lesson 11.3 in *English Learner Support Guide* to review lesson concepts and vocabulary.

ENRICH

If . . . students are proficient in the lesson concepts,

Then . . . encourage them to work on the chapter projects or *Enrichment* Lesson 11.3.

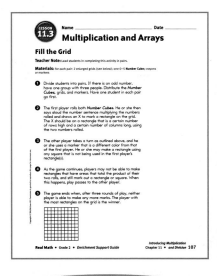

Enrichment Lesson 11.3

TEXAS PRACTICE

If . . . students would benefit from additional practice,

Then . . . assign *Practice* Lesson 11.3.

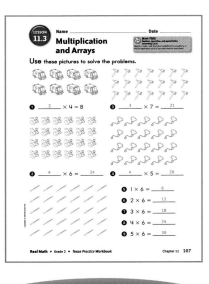

Practice Lesson 11.3

RETEACH

If . . . students struggle with drawing an array of objects or numbers,

Then . . . have them use grid paper to draw an array and then use objects to model an array.

Grade 1	Grade 2	Grade 3
1.7.D Compare and order the area of two or more two-dimensional surfaces.	**2.9.B** Select a non-standard unit of measure such as square tiles to determine the area of a two-dimensional surface.	**3.11.C** Use concrete and pictorial models of square units to determine the area of two-dimensional surfaces.

Overview LESSON 11.4

TEXAS

Lesson Planner

OBJECTIVES

- To demonstrate how to find area by counting the number of square units
- To provide students with an application for using repeated addition and multiplication

MATH TEKS

Measurement 2.9.B
Select a non-standard unit of measure such as square tiles to determine the area of a two-dimensional surface.

MATH TEKS INTEGRATION 2.3.A
Recall and apply basic addition and subtraction facts (to 18).

Preparing for Patterns, relationships, and algebraic thinking 3.11.A
Use linear measurement tools to estimate and measure lengths using standard units.

MATERIALS
- *Number Cubes
- Graph paper
- *Rulers
- **SRA Math Vocabulary Cards**

TECHNOLOGY
- **Presentation** Lesson 11.4
- **MathTools** Array Tool
- **Building Blocks** Arrays in Area

Looking Ahead

In Lesson 11.7 you will need sets of numbers to play the Numbers on the Back Activity.

Arrays and Area

Context of the Lesson This is the fourth of six lessons that introduces multiplication. The last lesson focused on modeling multiplication with arrays. In this lesson students apply their knowledge by finding area using multiplication and arrays. The next two lessons formally introduce students to the Multiplication Table and then to applications of multiplication. Students should be encouraged to be fluent in the basic multiplication facts as they progress through this chapter. See page 413B for Math Background for teachers for this lesson.

Planning for Learning • DIFFERENTIATE INSTRUCTION

INTERVENTION

If . . . students lack the prerequisite skill of adding a one-digit to a two-digit number,

Then . . . teach *Intervention* Lesson 11.B.

 1.3.A, 1.5.D

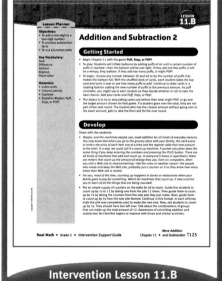

Intervention Lesson 11.B

ENGLISH LEARNER

Preview

If . . . students need language support,

Then . . . use Lesson 11.5 in *English Learner Support Guide* to preview lesson concepts and vocabulary.

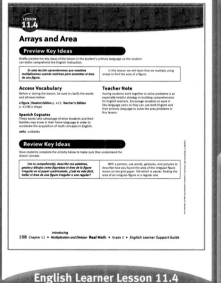

English Learner Lesson 11.4

ENRICH

If . . . students are proficient in the lesson concepts,

Then . . . emphasize Guided Discussion in Reflect.

PRACTICE

If . . . students would benefit from additional practice,

Then . . . extend Skill Building before assigning the student pages.

RETEACH

If . . . students are having difficulty understanding the skill of finding area,

Then . . . extend Guided Discussion before assigning the student pages.

Academic Vocabulary
area \âr´ē ə\ *n.* the number of units that the surface of a defined figure measures

Access Vocabulary
a figure a shape

Spanish Cognates
units unidades

TEXAS

Measurement 2.9.B
Select a non-standard unit of measure such as square tiles to determine the area of a two-dimensional surface.

Mental Math 5

INTEGRATION: TEKS 2.3.A Present repeated addition exercises, and have students show their answers using **Number Cubes.** Possible examples include the following:

a. $3 + 3 + 3 = 9$ **b.** $2 + 2 + 2 + 2 = 8$ **c.** $4 + 4 + 4 = 12$
d. $2 + 2 + 2 = 6$ **e.** $5 + 5 + 5 + 5 = 20$ **f.** $3 + 3 + 3 + 3 + 3 = 15$

1 Develop 20

Tell Students In Today's Lesson They Will
use arrays and multiplication to find area.

Guided Discussion UNDERSTANDING
Introductory

- Draw a 3×4 unit grid on the board or overhead projector. Discuss how to find the area of the rectangular grid by asking the following questions:
- **How many units tall is the figure?** 3
- **How many units wide is the figure?** 4

Explain that the area is the total number of units.

- **What is the area?** 12
- **How did you find the area?** Possible responses: count all the units; multiply 3×4
- **Is the area 3×4?** yes

Discuss the relation of finding area to multiplication.

Demonstrate the Commutative Law by showing that a grid can be turned sideways and that, for instance, $3 \times 4 = 4 \times 3$.

Next draw an irregular figure within the grid. Have students estimate the area of the irregular figure. Discuss whether various estimates are sensible. Help students see that some squares are entirely covered by the figure, so estimates should be at least as great as the number of complete squares, but less than the total area of the grid.

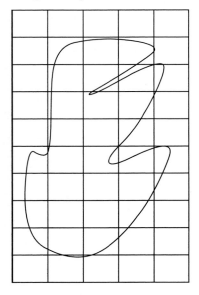

Skill Building ENGAGING
Guided

Provide students with an opportunity to find areas of figures they create.

Distribute a piece of graph paper to each student. Have students work in pairs.

- One student should draw a regular figure such as a square or rectangle on the grid. Then, both students should work together to find the area.
- The other student should draw an irregular shape on a grid. Then, both students should work together to find the area for that figure.

Allow enough time to share several examples, encouraging students to explain how they found the areas of their figure. Students could add the total number of square units within their figures or multiply the number of square units within the length by the number of square units within the width, and then adjust for partially covered squares.

2 Use Student Pages 20

Student Pages 421–422 UNDERSTANDING
Independent

Complete page 421 as a class. Have students complete page 422 independently or in pairs.

Progress Monitoring

If . . . students have difficulty estimating area for partially irregular figures,

Then . . . present an irregular figure on a grid and an erroneous estimate of its area. Ask the student why the estimated area cannot be correct. Think aloud to demonstrate this, if necessary.

As Students Finish

 Have students play a previously introduced game, or assign a game based on student needs.

Building Blocks Have students use **Arrays in Area** to practice finding area.

e MathTools Have students explore arrays using **Array Tool.**

Student Page

Name _____ Date _____

LESSON 11.4 Arrays and Area

Key Ideas

You can understand area by studying arrays.

Area is the total number of square units within a figure.

> ★ **Math TEKS**
> **Math TEKS Measurement**
> **2.9.B**
> Select a non-standard unit of measure such as square tiles to determine the area of a two-dimensional surface.

❶ How many vegetable plants are in Marie's garden? __15__

She built a fence around her garden.

❷ What shape is Marie's garden? __rectangle__

❸ How many vegetables tall is it? __3__

How many vegetables wide is it? __5__

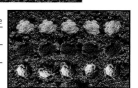

Then Marie installed sprinklers to water all her plants. Marie's garden is now divided into square units.

❹ How many square units is Marie's garden? __15__

❺ What is the area of Marie's garden? __15__ square units

❻ Write a multiplication sentence to show how to find the area of Marie's garden.

__3 × 5 = 15, or 5 × 3 = 15__

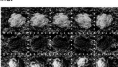

📘 **Textbook** This lesson is available in the *eTextbook*.

421

LESSON 11.4 · Arrays and Area

Use the squares to solve these problems.

❼ Area __100__ square units

10 × 10 = __100__

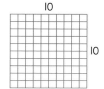
10

10

❽ Area __15__ square units

5 × 3 = __15__

5

3

❾ Area __42__ square units

3 × 14 = __42__

❿ **Extended Response** Explain how you found the area.

Possible answers: counted all the squares; skip counted by threes 14 times; multiplied 3 × 14

422

Real Math • Chapter 11 • Lesson 4

---

3 Reflect

10

Guided Discussion

 **e MathTools** **REASONING**

Integration: TEKS 3.11.A

Have students use rulers to measure rectangular objects in the classroom and then find the area of the objects by creating a corresponding array. For example, if students were to measure a crayon box and find it to be 4 inches by 5 inches, the array would look like this:

```
X  X  X  X
X  X  X  X
X  X  X  X
X  X  X  X
X  X  X  X
```

The corresponding multiplication fact would be 5 × 4 = 20, so the area of the crayon box would be 20 square inches. Students can also create the array using *eMathTools: Array Tool.*

Extended Response

Problem 10 Discuss students' answers. Students should have realized that they can count all the squares, skip count by 3 fourteen times, or multiply 3 × 14.

TEKS Checkup

Measurement 2.9.B Select a non-standard unit of measure such as square tiles to determine the area of a two-dimensional surface.

Use this problem to assess students' progress towards standards mastery:

Which shows the area of the squares?

Ⓐ 10 × 5   **B** 5 × 5
C 10 × 10   **D** 5 × 2

Have students choose the correct answer, then describe how they knew which choice was correct. In the discussion, ask questions such as the following. Be sure to ask students to

explain their reasoning, since different solution methods are possible.

■ **How many squares wide and long is the diagram?** 5 by 10

■ **Why use multiplication?** counting the area by counting the squares is more difficult as the rectangles get larger

Follow-Up

If... students have difficulty with determining the area of a two-dimensional surface,

Then... have students use *Building Block: Arrays in Area* to practice finding area.

4 Assess and Differentiate

 e Assess Use *eAssess* to record and analyze evidence of student understanding.

A Gather Evidence

Use the Daily Class Assessment Records in *Texas Assessment* or *eAssess* to record daily observations.

Informal Assessment
✓ **Student Pages**

Did the student UNDERSTANDING
- make important observations?
- extend or generalize learning?
- provide insightful answers?
- pose insightful questions?

Informal Assessment
✓ **Guided Discussion**

Did the student REASONING
- provide a clear explanation?
- communicate reasons and strategies?
- choose appropriate strategies?
- argue logically?

 **TEKS/TAKS Practice**

Use *TEKS/TAKS Practice* pages 75–78 to assess student progress.

B Summarize Findings

Analyze and summarize assessment data for each student. Determine which Assessment Follow-Up is appropriate for each student. Use the Student Assessment Record in *Texas Assessment* or *eAssess* to update assessment records.

C Texas AsseTexasssment Follow-Up ● DIFFERENTIATE INSTRUCTION

Based on your observations, use these teaching strategies for assessment follow-up.

INTERVENTION

Review student performance on *Intervention* Lesson 11.B to see if students have mastered prerequisite skills for this lesson.

1.3.A Model and create addition and subtraction problem situations with concrete objects and write corres-ponding number sentences.

1.5.D Use patterns to develop strategies to solve basic addition and basic subtraction problems.

ENGLISH LEARNER
Review

Use Lesson 11.4 in *English Learner Support Guide* to review lesson concepts and vocabulary.

ENRICH

If . . . students are proficient in the lesson concepts,

Then . . . encourage them to work on the chapter projects or *Enrichment* Lesson 11.4.

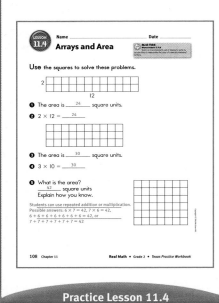

Enrichment Lesson 11.4

PRACTICE

If . . . students would benefit from additional practice,

Then . . . assign *Practice* Lesson 11.4.

Practice Lesson 11.4

RETEACH

If . . . students struggle with area,

Then . . . have them color a pair of figures, one of which has a greater area. Have students identify which figure took longer to color and relate that to the figure with the larger area.

TEXAS Vertical Alignment

Grade 1	Grade 2	Grade 3
1.5.A Use patterns to skip count by twos, fives, and tens.	**2.4** The student models multiplication and division.	**3.4.A** Learn and apply multiplication facts through 12 by 12 using concrete models and objects.

Overview

LESSON 11.5

TEXAS

Using the Multiplication Table ★

OBJECTIVES

- To provide students with the opportunity to use the Multiplication Table
- To provide students with practice learning the multiplication facts

MATH TEKS

Number, operation, and quantitative reasoning 2.4
The student models multiplication and division.

Patterns, relationships, and algebraic thinking 2.5.A
Find patterns in numbers such as in 100s chart.

MATH TEKS INTEGRATION

Number, operation, and quantitative reasoning 2.3
The student adds and subtracts whole numbers to solve problems.

Number, operation, and quantitative reasoning 2.3.D
Determine the value of a collection of coins up to one dollar.

MATERIALS

- *Number Cubes
- Overhead transparency of the Multiplication Table (10 × 10)
- Multiplication Table for each student
- Multiplication Table Game Mat
- *SRA Math Vocabulary Cards*

TECHNOLOGY

- **Presentation** Lesson 11.5
- **MathTools** Multiplication Table
- **Games** Multiplication Table Game

Context of the Lesson This is the fifth of six lessons that introduces multiplication. In this lesson students will begin to build experience with the multiplication facts for factors 0 through 10 and will use the Multiplication Table as a tool. Students will gain more practice with multiplication in the next lesson. Students are now strongly encouraged to gain fluency in the basic multiplication facts.

See page 413B for Math Background for teachers for this lesson.

Planning for Learning ● DIFFERENTIATE INSTRUCTION

INTERVENTION

If . . . students lack the prerequisite skill of using a function table,

Then . . . teach *Intervention* Lesson 11.B.

1.3.A, 1.5.D

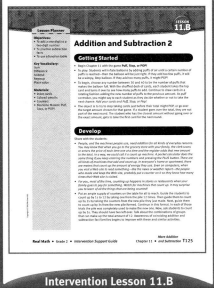

Intervention Lesson 11.B

ENGLISH LEARNER

Preview

If . . . students need language support,

Then . . . use Lesson 11.5 in *English Learner Support Guide* to preview lesson concepts and vocabulary.

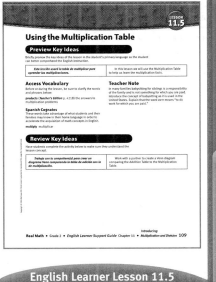

English Learner Lesson 11.5

ENRICH

If . . . students are proficient in the lesson concepts,

Then . . . emphasize additional game time.

PRACTICE

If . . . students would benefit from additional practice,

Then . . . extend Strategy Building before assigning the student pages.

RETEACH

If . . . students are having difficulty understanding the Multiplication Table,

Then . . . extend Guided Discussion before assigning the student pages.

Access Vocabulary
✎ **products** the answers to multiplication problems

Spanish Cognates
multiply multiplicar

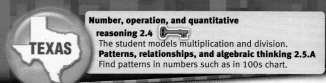

Teaching Lesson 11.5

 TEXAS

Number, operation, and quantitative reasoning 2.4
The student models multiplication and division.
Patterns, relationships, and algebraic thinking 2.5.A
Find patterns in numbers such as in 100s chart.

Mental Math   5

 INTEGRATION: TEKS 2.3 Present three-digit addition and subtraction exercises, and have students show their answers using **Number Cubes.** Possible examples include the following:

a. 100 + 500 = 600   **b.** 220 + 320 = 540
c. 130 + 620 = 750   **d.** 360 − 40 = 320
e. 400 − 100 = 300   **f.** 550 + 130 = 680
g. 800 − 400 = 400   **h.** 330 + 330 = 660

1 Develop   20

Tell Students In Today's Lesson They Will
use the Multiplication Table to find products.

 Introductory

Guided Discussion   MathTools UNDERSTANDING

The Multiplication Table

- Distribute a Multiplication Table to each student. Remind students that they already know how to use an Addition Table. Display a Multiplication Table or **eMathTools: Multiplication Table.** A copy of the Multiplication Table can be found in **Practice** on page 127.

- ■ **Can you figure out how to use this Multiplication Table to find 3 × 4 without being told?** Allow one or two students to share their ideas on how this is done. Through discussion and with student input, demonstrate how to use the table to find 3 × 4.

- Find the 3 along the left side of the table.
- Move your finger to the right until it is under the 4. (Check for student understanding of finger placement at this time.)
- Bring both fingers together . . . slide your fingers across and down until they meet. They should land on the 12. (Check student answers.)

Continue to practice finding the products of several multiplication facts using the Multiplication Table as a tool. Include some with factors through 10 and be sure to circulate the room and check for understanding.

Strategy Building Games ENGAGING

 Multiplication Table Game

Demonstrate the game, which provides practice with multiplication facts in the 0–5 range. Complete instructions are on the game mat. This game is also available as an eGame.

2 Use Student Pages   20

Pages 423–424 UNDERSTANDING   Independent

Have students use the Multiplication Table to complete student pages 423 and 424.

As Students Finish

Game ✓ Allow enough time for students to play the **Multiplication Table Game** in small groups.

e MathTools Have students practice finding factors for given products using the **Multiplication Table.**

e Games **Multiplication Table Game**

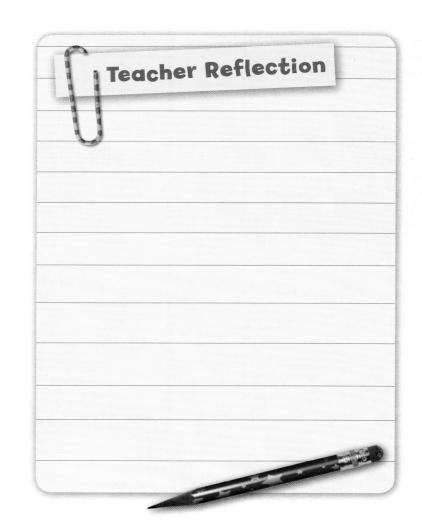

Teacher Reflection

Student Page

Name _____   Date _____

LESSON 11.5 Using the Multiplication Table

Key Ideas

Multiplication facts can be found on the Multiplication Table.

$3 \times 4 = 12$

Math TEKS
Number, operation, and quantitative reasoning 2.4 — The student models multiplication and division.

×	0	1	2	3	4	5
0	0	0	0	0	0	0
1	0	1	2	3	4	5
2	0	2	4	6	8	10
3	0	3	6	9	12	15
4	0	4	8	12	16	20
5	0	5	10	15	20	25

Use the Multiplication Table to solve.

1. $3 \times 5 = 15$ 2. $2 \times 3 = 6$ 3. $4 \times 4 = 16$
4. $5 \times 5 = 25$ 5. $3 \times 3 = 9$ 6. $2 \times 4 = 8$
7. $0 \times 5 = 0$ 8. $1 \times 2 = 2$ 9. $0 \times 3 = 0$

This lesson is available in the *eTextbook*.   423

LESSON 11.5 · Using the Multiplication Table

10. **Extended Response** Carmen earns $4 each day for watching her younger brother after school. How much money does she earn for 3 days? _____ $12
Explain how you know. ___ $4 + 4 + 4 = 12 ___

11. Heide, Hilla, and Heike each have $4. How many dollars do they have altogether? $12

12. Tomatoes are sold 4 to a box. How many tomatoes are in 5 boxes? 20

13. A square measures 5 centimeters on each side.
What is its perimeter? 20 centimeters
What is its area? 25 square centimeters

14. Chester, Ms. Heather's cat, eats about 4 cans of cat food each week. About how many cans of cat food will Heather need for 3 weeks? 12

15. Amy and Sara are best friends. They are 7 years old. How old will they be in 2 years? 9

Solve the following without using the Multiplication Table.

16. A furniture store has 7 tables that each have 2 chairs. How many chairs are there altogether? **TAKS Obj. 1**
A 27   B 9   **C 14**   D 12

17. Gina has 8 dimes. How much money does she have? **TAKS Obj. 1**
A 10¢   **B 80¢**   C 8¢   D 90¢

18. Nate has 10 nickels. How much money does he have? **TAKS Obj. 1**
A 10¢   B 5¢   C 55¢   **D 50¢**

424   **Real Math · Chapter 11 · Lesson 5**

---

3 Reflect   10

Guided Discussion **REASONING**

Have students study the Multiplication Table. Encourage students to make up problems using the facts on the table that are similar to the problems on student page 424. Then have students trade problems and solve.

Extended Response

Problem 10 Discuss students' answers. Students should have realized that to find the answer, they should add 4 three times; $3 \times 4 = 12$.

Cumulative Review: For cumulative review of previously learned skills, see page 429–430.

Family Involvement: Assign the *Practice, Reteach,* or *Enrichment* activities depending on the needs of your students. Have students play the **Multiplication Table Game** with a family member.

Concept/Question Board: Encourage students to continue to post questions, answers, and examples on the Concept/Question Board.

Integration: TEKS 2.3.D Math Puzzler: If you saved a nickel each day for a week, would you have more or less than 50¢ at the end of the week? How can you tell? less, because 5¢ each day for a week is $5 \times 7 = 35$¢

4 Assess and Differentiate

 **Assess** Use *eAssess* to record and analyze evidence of student understanding.

A Gather Evidence

Use the Daily Class Assessment Records in *Texas Assessment* or *eAssess* to record daily observations.

Informal Assessment
✓ Guided Discussion
Did the student **UNDERSTANDING**
- make important observations?
- extend or generalize learning?
- provide insightful answers?
- pose insightful questions?

Performance Assessment
✓ Game
Did the student **ENGAGING**
- pay attention to others' contributions?
- contribute information and ideas?
- improve on a strategy?
- reflect on and check the accuracy of his or her work?

TEKS/TAKS Practice
Use *TEKS/TAKS Practice* pages 34–36 to assess student progress.

B Summarize Findings

Analyze and summarize assessment data for each student. Determine which Assessment Follow-Up is appropriate for each student. Use the Student Assessment Record in *Texas Assessment* or *eAssess* to update assessment records.

C Texas Assessment Follow-Up • DIFFERENTIATE INSTRUCTION

Based on your observations, use these teaching strategies for assessment follow-up.

INTERVENTION
Review student performance on *Intervention* Lesson 11.B to see if students have mastered prerequisite skills for this lesson.

1.3.A Model and create addition and subtraction problem situations with concrete objects and write corres-ponding number sentences.

1.5.D Use patterns to develop strategies to solve basic addition and basic subtraction problems.

ENGLISH LEARNER
Review
Use Lesson 11.5 in *English Learner Support Guide* to review lesson concepts and vocabulary.

ENRICH
If . . . students are proficient in the lesson concepts,

Then . . . encourage them to work on the chapter projects or *Enrichment* Lesson 11.5.

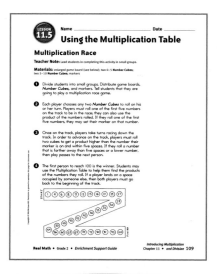

Enrichment Lesson 11.5

PRACTICE
If . . . students would benefit from additional practice,

Then . . . assign *Practice* Lesson 11.5.

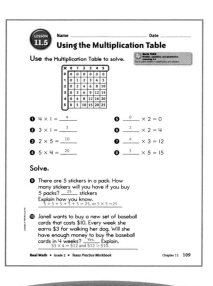

Practice Lesson 11.5

RETEACH
If . . . students struggle with the Multiplication Table,

Then . . . have them review their facts using flash cards to speed up their recall of basic facts.

TEXAS **Vertical Alignment**

Grade 1	Grade 2	Grade 3
1.11.B Solve problems with guidance that incorporates the processes of understanding the problem, making a plan, carrying out the plan, and evaluating the solution for reasonableness.	**2.12** The student is expected applies Grade 2 mathematics to solve problems connected to everyday experiences and activities in and outside of school.	**3.4** The student recognizes and solves problems in multiplication and division situations.

Overview **LESSON 11.6**

TEXAS

Lesson Planner

OBJECTIVES
- To provide more practice with the basic multiplication facts
- To solve word problems, some of which involve multiplication.

MATH TEKS

Underlying processes and mathematical tools 2.12
The student is expected applies Grade 2 mathematics to solve problems connected to everyday experiences and activities in and outside of school.

Number, operation, and quantitative reasoning 2.4
The student models multiplication and division.

MATH TEKS INTEGRATION
Recall and apply basic addition and subtraction facts (to 18).

Number, operation, and quantitative reasoning 2.3
The student adds and subtracts whole numbers to solve problems.

Number, operation, and quantitative reasoning 2.4.A
Model, create, and describe multiplication situations in which equivalent sets of concrete objects are joined.

Underlying processes and mathematical tools 2.12.A
Identify the mathematics in everyday situations.

MATERIALS
- *Number Cubes
- Multiplication Table Game Mat
- Multiplication Tables

TECHNOLOGY
- Presentation Lesson 11.6
- MathTools Multiplication Table
- Games Multiplication Table Game

Looking Ahead
You will need the function machine you created and used in Chapter 2 for Lesson 11.9.

*Manipulative Kit Item = Key standard

Applying Multiplication

Context of the Lesson This is the last of six lessons that introduces multiplication. This lesson helps students understand multiplication by solving word problems using multiplication. The next three lessons introduce students to division.

See page 413B for Math Background for teachers for this lesson.

Planning for Learning • DIFFERENTIATE INSTRUCTION

INTERVENTION
If . . . students lack the prerequisite skill of subtraction facts,

Then . . . teach **Intervention** Lesson 11.B.

1.3.A, 1.5.D

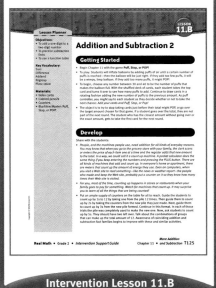

Intervention Lesson 11.B

ENGLISH LEARNER
Preview

If . . . students need language support,

Then . . . use Lesson 11.6 in **English Learner Support Guide** to preview lesson concepts and vocabulary.

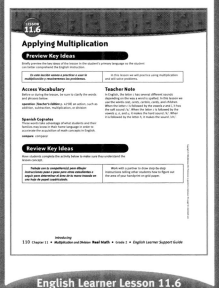

English Learner Lesson 11.6

ENRICH
If . . . students are proficient in the lesson concepts,

Then . . . emphasize additional game time.

PRACTICE
If . . . students would benefit from additional practice,

Then . . . extend Skill Practice before assigning the student pages.

RETEACH
If . . . students are having difficulty understanding applying multiplication,

Then . . . extend Guided Discussion before assigning the student pages.

Access Vocabulary
operation an action such as addition, subtraction, multiplication, or division

Spanish Cognates
compare comparar

Underlying processes and mathematical tools 2.12 The student is expected applies Grade 2 mathematics to solve problems connected to everyday experiences and activities in and outside of school.
Number, operation, and quantitative reasoning 2.4 The student models multiplication and division.

Mental Math · 5

INTEGRATION: TEKS 2.3 Present three-digit addition and subtraction exercises, and have students display their answers using **Number Cubes.** Possible examples include the following:

a. 130 + 705 = 835 · **b.** 210 + 390 = 600 · **c.** 120 − 30 = 90
d. 110 − 70 = 40 · **e.** 107 + 803 = 910 · **f.** 308 + 402 = 710

1 Develop · 20

Tell Students In Today's Lesson They Will
solve word problems that use multiplication.

Guided Discussion UNDERSTANDING
 Introductory

Present word problems, one at a time, that involve applications of multiplication. Include an occasional problem that requires a different operation. Illustrate each problem on the board and with materials if necessary. Encourage students to solve before assisting them with guidance. Write the appropriate equation on the board, and have students discuss how they solved each problem.

Problems might include:

INTEGRATION: TEKS 2.4.A

- The Noshos want to buy all new tires for each of their 3 cars. How many tires will they have to buy? 3 × 4 = 12 tires
- Mr. Sleeby wants to buy 7 apples. Each apple costs 9¢. How much money will Mr. Sleeby need? 7 × 9 = 63¢
- Sharon wants to buy a bag of peanuts that costs 10¢ and an apple that costs 9¢. How much money will she need? 10 + 9 = 19; 19¢
- Ferdie wanted to estimate the height of a 5-story building. He estimated each story to be about 4 meters high. What do you think Ferdie's estimate for the height of the building was? 5 × 4 = 20 meters high
- In the Mudanzas' bathroom, tiles cover the floor. There are 7 tiles in each row, and there are 8 rows. How many tiles are there in the room? 7 × 8 = 56 tiles

Skill Practice MathTools COMPUTING

Display a Multiplication Table or *eMath Tools: Multiplication Table.*

Present multiplication number sentences on the board or overhead projector. Have students display the correct answer on their **Number Cubes.** Possible examples include the following:

a. 7 × 4 = 28 · **b.** 7 × 7 = 49 · **c.** 10 × 8 = 80 · **d.** 5 × 8 = 40
e. 6 × 3 = 18 · **f.** 4 × 6 = 24 · **g.** 8 × 6 = 48 · **h.** 7 × 8 = 56

2 Use Student Pages · 20

Pages 425–426 COMPUTING · Independent

Have students complete student pages 425 and 426 independently. Help students who have trouble reading the problems.

As Students Finish

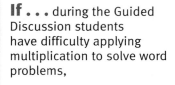 Allow students to play the **Multiplication Table Game** in small groups. When students are ready, they can play the Harder Multiplication Table Game, which provides practice up to the 10s facts.

Games *Multiplication Table Game*

Progress Monitoring

If . . . during the Guided Discussion students have difficulty applying multiplication to solve word problems,

Then . . . plan to work individually or in small groups with these students as they complete the pages in the Student Edition. Thinking aloud and acting out the problems will help many students catch on.

Student Page

Name _____ Date _____

LESSON 11.6 Applying Multiplication

Key Ideas

Multiplication can be used to solve everyday problems.

There are 6 marbles in one bag.

How many marbles are in 3 bags?

$3 \times 6 = 18$

There are 18 marbles.

Math TEKS
Underlying processes and mathematical tools 2.12
The student applies Grade 2 mathematics to solve problems connected to everyday experiences and activities in and outside of school.

Solve these problems.

One bag of cat food weighs 8 pounds and costs 4 dollars.

1. How much will 5 bags cost? $20

2. How much will 6 bags weigh? 48 pounds

3. Bonnie has 2 cats. Each cat eats $\frac{1}{4}$ pound of food per day. About how many days will one bag last? about 16 days

4. About how many bags will Bonnie need each month? about 2 bags

---

Solve these problems.

5. CDs are sold in packages of 5. How many CDs are in 7 packages? 35

6. Charlie walks 4 blocks to school every day and walks home the same way. How many blocks does Charlie walk to and from school in 5 days? 40

7. Sally works 2 hours every morning and 3 hours every afternoon. How many hours does she work in 10 days? 50

8. Julia and Finn rode their bicycles 2 kilometers to the library. Each of them checked out 3 books. If they returned home the same way, how many kilometers was the round-trip? 4

9. Harriet bought 7 bottles of juice. Each bottle contained 8 ounces of juice and cost $3.
How many ounces of juice did she buy? 56
How much did the juice cost? $21

10. In football a touchdown is worth 6 points. How many points are 6 touchdowns? 36

11. In basketball some baskets are worth 1 point, some baskets are worth 2 points, and some are worth 3 points.
Katie made five 3-point baskets and six 2-point baskets. How many points did she score? 27
Amy made two 3-point baskets and seven 2-point baskets. How many points did she score? 20

12. It costs $3 to rent a bike for one hour. How much will a 7-hour rental cost? $21 (TAKS Obj. 1)

   (A) $21   **B** $18   **C** $7   **D** $3

---

3 Reflect   10

Guided Discussion   REASONING

Integration: TEKS 2.12.A

Write the following three equations on the board:

1. $8 \times 3 = 24$

2. $8 + 3 = 11$

3. $8 - 3 = 5$

Now ask a volunteer to make up a word problem that can be solve by only one of the equations. Ask the rest of the class to identify the correct equation. Use a find-hide-show response technique so that students answer together, showing a 1, 2, or 3 on their 0-5 *Number Cubes*. Repeat with other volunteers as time and interest permits.

✓ Use Mastery Checkpoint 17 found in **Assessment** to evaluate student mastery of multiplication facts. By this time, students should be able to correctly answer eighty percent of the Mastery Checkpoint items.

Cumulative Review: For cumulative review of previously learned skills, see page 429–430.

Family Involvement: Assign the *Practice, Reteach,* or *Enrichment* activities depending on the needs of your students. Have students play the **Multiplication Table Game** with a family member.

Concept/Question Board: Encourage students to continue to post questions, answers, and examples on the Concept/Question Board.

Math Puzzler: There are 24 students in Mr. Luker's class and the same number in Mr. Yanok's class. There are 27 students in Mr. Meier's class. How many students are there altogether? 75

4 Assess and Differentiate

 **Assess** Use *eAssess* to record and analyze evidence of student understanding.

A Gather Evidence

Use the Daily Class Assessment Records in *Texas Assessment* or *eAssess* to record daily observations.

Formal Assessment

✓ **Mastery Checkpoint**

Did the student
- ☐ use correct procedures?
- ☐ respond with at least 80% accuracy?

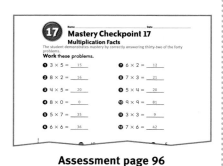

Assessment page 96

🟠 TEKS/TAKS Practice

Use *TEKS/TAKS Practice* pages 97–98 to assess student progress.

B Summarize Findings

Analyze and summarize assessment data for each student. Determine which Assessment Follow-Up is appropriate for each student. Use the Student Assessment Record in *Texas Assessment* or *eAssess* to update assessment records.

C Texas Assessment Follow-Up • DIFFERENTIATE INSTRUCTION

Based on your observations, use these teaching strategies for assessment follow-up.

INTERVENTION

Review student performance on *Intervention* Lesson 11.B to see if students have mastered prerequisite skills for this lesson.

🟠 **1.3.A** Model and create addition and subtraction problem situations with concrete objects and write corres-ponding number sentences.

🟠 **1.5.D** Use patterns to develop strategies to solve basic addition and basic subtraction problems.

ENGLISH LEARNER

Review

Use Lesson 11.6 in *English Learner Support Guide* to review lesson concepts and vocabulary.

ENRICH

If . . . students are proficient in the lesson concepts,

Then . . . encourage them to work on the chapter projects or *Enrichment* Lesson 11.6.

Enrichment Lesson 11.6

🟠 TEXAS PRACTICE

If . . . students would benefit from additional practice,

Then . . . assign *Practice* Lesson 11.6.

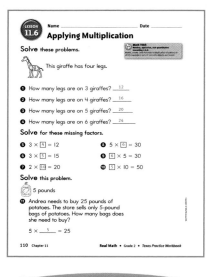

Practice Lesson 11.6

RETEACH

If . . . students are having difficulty understanding applying multiplication,

Then . . . reteach the concept.

Problem Solving

Comparing Strategies

Objectives
- To explore the Guess and Check, Make a Table, and Use Logical Reasoning strategies
- To provide practice applying concepts of multiplication in real-world situations
- To provide practice in solving and presenting solutions to multistep problems

Materials
Countable objects (about 60 per group)

See Appendix A page A24 for instruction and a rubric for problem solving.

Context of the Lesson Reasoning and problem solving are prevalent in every *Real Math* lesson. This lesson and other special problem-solving lessons allow more time for students to share and compare their strategies. While continuing the ethnic-food theme, this lesson provides additional opportunity for students to continue to develop their understanding of multiplication.

1 Develop

5

Tell Students In Today's Lesson They Will
find the least expensive way to buy a special food.

Guided Discussion

Introductory

Remind students about the problem they solved earlier on page 414 about the students in the Diversity Club. Tell them they are going to hear more about the club today.

You may want to discuss the traditional Greek foods mentioned in the story problem below: kabob, spanakopita (spinach pie), and dolmades (stuffed grape leaves).

Have students look at the picture on page 427 as you read this problem to them:

The students in the Diversity Club decided to prepare a Greek dinner for their parents. They decided to serve lamb kabobs, spanakopita, and dolmades. There will be 34 people at the dinner. When the students went shopping, they found that dolmades come in cans of 3 for $5 or in cans of 8 for $10. They want to buy enough dolmades so that each person can have one, but they want to spend the least amount of money as possible.

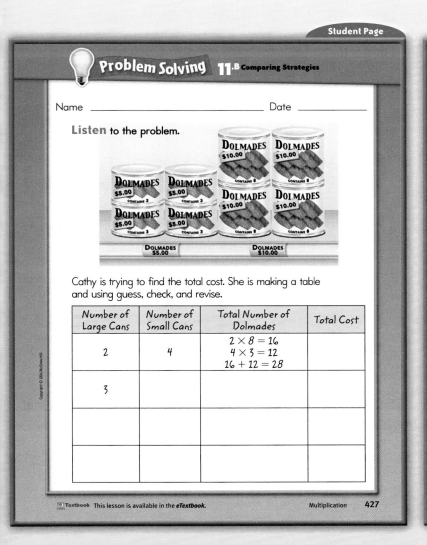

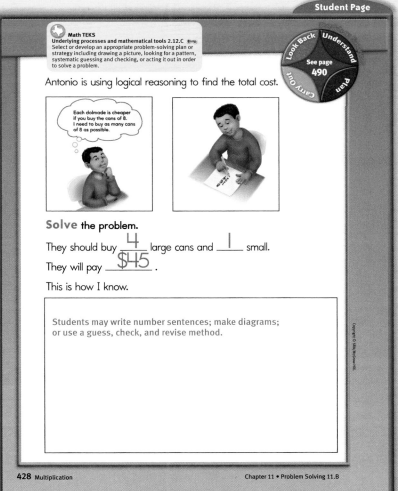

How many large cans and how many small cans should they buy? How much will that cost?

Tell students they are going to have a chance to solve the problem, but first they will look at how two other students are trying to solve it.

 2 Exploring Problem Solving 25

Using Student Pages

 Guided

Analyzing Sample Solution 1

Have students look at the picture on page 427 of Cathy solving the problem. Ask questions about her strategy, such as the following:

■ **Look at the table Cathy made. What is Cathy's first guess?** buying 2 large cans and 4 small cans

■ **Is Cathy sure these are the right numbers of each can to buy?** No, she made a guess, and she is going to check it.

■ **In the third column, what does each number sentence show?** 2 × 8 = 16 shows there are 16 dolmades in 2 large cans; 4 × 3 = 12 shows there are 12 dolmades in 4 small cans; 16 + 12 = 28 shows there are 28 dolmades altogether in 2 large cans and 4 small cans.

■ **What is the fourth column for?** to figure out how much that combination of cans would cost

■ **Why do you think she skipped the fourth column?** She found out there wouldn't be enough dolmades in 2 large cans and 4 small cans, so there was no point in figuring out how much it would cost.

■ **What can Cathy do next?** She can try a combination with more cans. She can try different numbers of cans until she has a combination that has at least 34 dolmades.

■ **If Cathy finds a combination that has exactly 34 dolmades, can she be sure she has the right answer?** No, it may be enough dolmades, but it may not be the cheapest way to buy them.

Analyzing Sample Solution 2

Tell students that Antonio is using a different strategy to try to solve the problem. Have students look at the picture on page 428 of Antonio's approach. As you ask and discuss questions such as the ones below, you may want to use objects and play money to help students understand Antonio's reasoning.

■ **Look at the first picture. What has Antonio figured out?** The large cans are a better buy than the small cans; you get more for your money with the large cans.

■ **How do you know that 8 dolmades for $10 is a better deal than 3 dolmades for $5?** If you spend $10 on small cans, you can buy 2 cans, and you get 6 dolmades. If you spend the same amount on a large can, you get more dolmades; you get 8 dolmades.

■ **What is Antonio doing in the second picture?** He is counting by 8s. He is figuring out how many dolmades he will have if he buys 1 large can, 2 large cans, 3 large cans, and so on.

■ **Why is he doing that?** In order to help figure out how many large cans to buy; he wants to get as close as he can to 34.

■ **Does Antonio need to buy exactly 34 dolmades in large cans?** No, he can buy some small cans too. Or he can buy more than 34 dolmades and have some extra if that turns out to be the least expensive way.

■ **How will you work on this problem?** Allow students to share what they like about Cathy's and Antonio's strategies and what they would do differently.

 **3 Reflect** 10

 **Knowledge Age Skills**

Effective Communication Ask students to share their solutions and their strategies. In discussion bring out these points:

● Some strategies are more efficient than others. Cathy's strategy may ultimately lead to the best combination, but it may involve a lot of guessing and checking to do so. By using logical reasoning, Antonio saves a lot of time and computation.

● When you get a result, think about what it means. The problem asks for the least expensive way to buy enough dolmades. If Cathy finds a combination of cans that provides exactly 34 dolmades, that doesn't mean that this is the least expensive combination.

Sample Solutions Strategies

Students might use one or more of the following strategies instead of or in conjunction with the strategies presented on student pages 427 and 428.

Act It Out

Students might use counters to represent the dolmades, group them into eights and threes and assign prices to these groups.

Using Number Sense/Write a Number Sentence

Students might subtract to determine how many large cans they can buy without exceeding 34 dolmades.

Using a Physical Model/Skip Counting

To determine the cost of a given number of large or small cans, students might skip count by 5 or 10 on a number line.

 4 Assess 15

When evaluating student work, focus not only on the correctness of the answer but also on whether the student thought rationally about the problem. Questions to consider include the following:

● Did the student understand the problem?
● Did the student understand the Sample Solutions Strategies?
● Was the student able to use multiplication in appropriate ways?
● Did the student keep track of what he or she was doing in an understandable way?
● Was the student able to explain his or her strategy?

Cumulative Review

Use Pages 429–430

Use the Cumulative Review as a review of concepts and skills that students have previously learned.

Here are different ways that you can assign these problems to your students as they work through the chapter:

- With some of the lessons in the chapter, assign a set of cumulative review problems to be completed as practice or for homework.
  Lesson 11.1—Problems 1–2
  Lesson 11.2—Problems 3–8
  Lesson 11.3—Problems 9–10
  Lesson 11.4—Problems 11–14
  Lesson 11.5—Problems 15–20
  Lesson 11.6—Problems 21–29

- At any point during the chapter, assign part or all of the cumulative review problems to be completed as practice or for homework.

Cumulative Review

Problems 1–2 review time in days and weeks, Lesson 10.10. TEKS: 2.10.C

Problems 3–8 review subtracting two-digit numbers, Lesson 6.4. TEKS: 2.3.B

Problems 9–10 review fractions and parts of plane figures, Lesson 8.2. TEKS: 2.7.C

Problems 11–14 review three-digit addition and subtraction, Lesson 9.10. TEKS: 2.3

Problems 15–20 review comparing numbers through 1,000, Lesson 9.3. TEKS: 2.5.B

Problems 21–29 review multiplication and the Multiplication Table, Lesson 11.5. TEKS: 2.4

Progress Monitoring

If . . . students miss more than one problem in a section,

Then . . . refer to the indicated lesson for remediation suggestions.

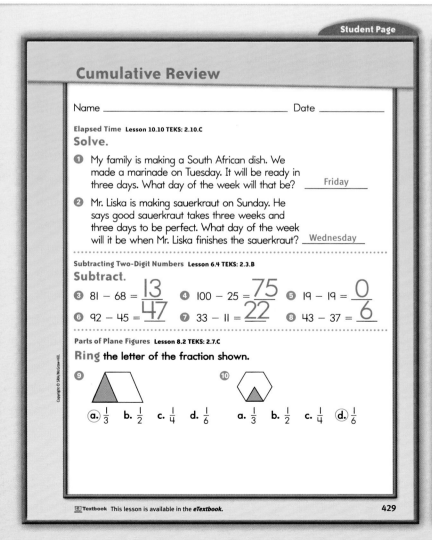

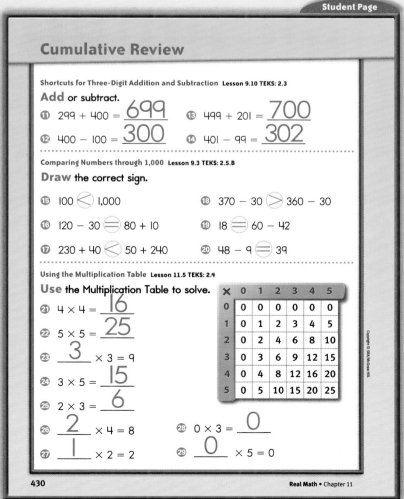

Individual Oral Assessment

Purpose of the Test

The Individual Oral Assessment is designed to measure students' growing knowledge of chapter concepts. It is administered individually to each student, and it requires oral responses from each student. The test takes about five minutes to complete. See *Texas Assessment* for detailed instructions for administering and interpreting the test, and record students' answers on the Student Assessment Recording Sheet.

Texas Assessment page 145

Directions

Read each question to the student, and record his or her oral response. If the student answers correctly, go to the next question. Stop when the student misses two questions at the same level. Students should not use scrap paper.

Materials

Questions

Level 1: Prerequisite   1.3

1. What is 2 + 2? 4
2. What is 3 + 3? 6
3. What is 6 + 6? 12
4. What is 8 + 8? 16

Level 2: Basic   1.5.A

5. Skip count. What is the next number: 2, 4, 6, ? 8
6. Skip count. What is the next number: 3, 6, 9, ? 12
7. Skip count. What are the next two numbers: 5, 10, 15, ? 20, 25
8. Skip count. What are the next two numbers: 10, 20, 30, ? 40, 50

Level 3: At Level   2.4.A

9. Multiply, skip count, or use repeated addition. What is 2 × 7? 14
10. Multiply, skip count, or use repeated addition. What is 2 × 4? 8
11. Multiply, skip count, or use repeated addition. What is 5 × 3? 15
12. Multiply, skip count, or use repeated addition. What is 5 × 4? 20

Level 4: Challenge Application   2.4.A

13. What is 4 × 4? 16
14. What is 6 × 4? 24
15. What is 5 × 7? 35
16. What is 3 × 9? 27

Level 5: Content Beyond Mid-Chapter   2.4.B

17. What number is half of 12? 6
18. What is 12 divided by 2? 6
19. What is 12 divided by 3? 4
20. What is 25 divided by 5? 5

TEXAS

Vertical Alignment

Grade 1	Grade 2	Grade 3
1.5.A Use patterns to skip count by twos, fives, and tens.	**2.6.B** Identify patterns in a list of related number pairs based on a real-life situation and extend the list.	**3.7.A** Generate a table of paired numbers based on a real-life situation such as insects and legs

Overview

LESSON 11.7

TEXAS

Lesson Planner

OBJECTIVES
- To introduce missing-factor problems
- To prepare students for the introduction of division
- To provide additional practice with multiplication facts

MATH TEKS

Number, operation, and quantitative reasoning 2.4
The student models multiplication and division.

Patterns, relationships, and algebraic thinking 2.6.B 🔑
Identify patterns in a list of related number pairs based on a real-life situation and extend the list.

MATH TEKS INTEGRATION

Preparing for Grade 3 3.4.A
Number, operation, and quantitative reasoning
Learn and apply multiplication facts through 12 by 12 using concrete models and objects.

Number, operation, and quantitative reasoning 2.4.A
Model, create, and describe multiplication situations in which equivalent sets of concrete objects are joined

Underlying processes and mathematical tools 2.12.A
Identify the mathematics in everyday situations.

MATERIALS
- *Number Cubes
- *Counters
- *Multiplication Table Game Mat
- *SRA Math Vocabulary Cards* ✏️

TECHNOLOGY
- ⒺPresentation Lesson 11.7
- ⒺGames Multiplication Table Game

Missing Factors ⭐

Context of the Lesson This is the first of three lessons that introduces students to division. In this lesson students solve missing-factor problems. In the next two lessons, students are formally introduced to division before relating multiplication to division.

See page 413B for Math Background for teachers for this lesson.

Planning for Learning • DIFFERENTIATE INSTRUCTION

INTERVENTION

If . . . students lack the prerequisite skill of adding a one-digit number to a two-digit number,

Then . . . teach *Intervention* Lesson 11.C.

 1.3.A, 1.5.D

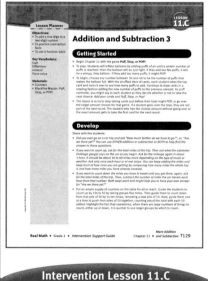

Intervention Lesson 11.C

ENGLISH LEARNER

Preview

If . . . students need language support,

Then . . . use Lesson 11.7 in *English Learner Support Guide* to preview lesson concepts and vocabulary.

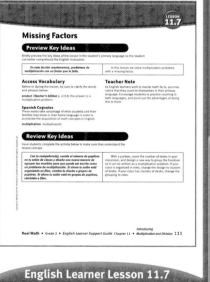

English Learner Lesson 11.7

ENRICH

If . . . students are proficient in the lesson concepts,

Then . . . emphasize additional game time.

PRACTICE

If . . . students would benefit from additional practice,

Then . . . extend Skill Practice before assigning the student pages.

RETEACH

If . . . students are having difficulty understanding the place value of a four-digit number,

Then . . . extend Guided Discussion before assigning the student pages.

Academic Vocabulary
✏️ **factor** \fak´ tər\ *n.* any number that is multiplied to get a product

Access Vocabulary
product the answer to a multiplication problem

Spanish Cognates
multiplication multiplicación

Teaching Lesson 11.7

TEXAS

Number, operation, and quantitative reasoning 2.4
The student models multiplication and division.
Patterns, relationships, and algebraic thinking 2.6.B
Identify patterns in a list of related number pairs based on a real-life situation and extend the list.

Mental Math 5

 INTEGRATION: TEKS 3.4.A Present multiplication exercises, and have students use **Number Cubes** to show their answers. Possible answers include the following:

a. $2 \times 8 = 16$ **b.** $1 \times 5 = 5$ **c.** $8 \times 0 = 0$ **d.** $4 \times 10 = 40$
e. $3 \times 5 = 15$ **f.** $5 \times 3 = 15$ **g.** $2 \times 4 = 8$ **h.** $3 \times 2 = 6$

1 Develop 20

Tell Students In Today's Lesson They Will
solve missing-factor problems.

Guided Discussion UNDERSTANDING
 Introductory

Missing Factors
Present multiplication number sentences with missing factors on the board or overhead projector. Have students explain how they would solve each problem. Possible examples include the following:

 Integration: TEKS 2.4.A

■ If I multiply 5 times a certain number, I will get 35. What is that number? $5 \times \underline{\quad} = 35$? 7
■ Erasers cost 8¢ each. How many erasers can I buy for 40¢? $\underline{\quad} \times 8 = 40$? 5 erasers
■ If 5 children are going to share the baseball cards they have and together they have 40 cards, how many cards will each child get? $5 \times \underline{\quad} = 40$? 8 cards each

Skill Practice COMPUTING
 Guided

 Continue to present exercises, focusing attention on the idea that if a wrong answer is given, it can easily be spotted because the number sentence will be wrong. Thus, a student who gives 6 as an answer to the first exercises shown below should see that it is wrong. Have students show their answers using their **Number Cubes.**

a. $3 \times \underline{5} = 15$ **b.** $\underline{4} \times 8 = 32$ **c.** $5 \times \underline{1} = 5$

Skill and Strategy Building ENGAGING
 Guided

Numbers on the Back
Building with the following text:
• Students will remember this game from Chapter 3.
• You will need pairs of slips of paper, each with numbers written on them - two slips with 0, two slips with 1, two slips with 2, and so on through 10.

1. Call two students to the front of the room, have them stand with their backs to the class, and attach a number to each student's back.
2. Allow each student to see the number on the other student's back.
3. Tell students that they are to determine the number on their own back but that first they will need a clue from the class.
4. Tell the class to give the product of the two numbers as the clue. Each student is to determine the number on his or her back. Remind students to use skip counting or the Multiplication Table to solve.
5. Repeat with other students, adjusting the difficulty level each time to the ability of the students.

2 Use Student Pages 20

Student Pages 431–432   UNDERSTANDING   Independent
Have students work alone or in small groups to complete the problems on student pages 431 and 432.

Progress Monitoring

If . . . a student has difficulty determining the number on his or her back in the front of the class. : **Then . . .** help the student by thinking aloud as you write the problem on the board. For example, $8 \times \underline{\quad} = 16$.

As Students Finish

 Allow enough time for students to play the **Multiplication Table Game.**

e Games *Multiplication Table Game*

Teacher Reflection

Student Page

Name _____ Date _____

LESSON 11.7 **Missing Factors**

Key Ideas

Missing-factor exercises are similiar to missing-addend exercises.

4 + _____ = 7

4 × _____ = 12

Math TEKS
Patterns, relationships, and algebraic thinking 2.6.B Identify patterns in a list of related number pairs base on a real-life situation and extend the list.

Solve these problems. Use materials to help you solve.

① I paid $21 for 7 candles.
How much would 1 candle cost? **$3**

There are 7 days in 1 week.

② How many weeks are in 14 days? **2**

③ How many weeks are in 35 days? **5**

④ How many weeks are in 49 days? **7**

⑤ How many weeks are in 28 days? **4**

January

SUN	MON	TUE	WED	THU	FRI	SAT
1	2	3	4	5	6	7
8	9	10	11	12	13	14
15	16	17	18	19	20	21
22	23	24	25	26	27	28
29	30	31				

Textbook This lesson is available in the *eTextbook*. 431

LESSON 11.7 · Missing Factors

Paul sells blueberries for $3 a basket.

Help Paul by completing this table.

Number of Baskets	1	2	3	4	5	6	7	8	9	10
Price (dollars)	3	6	9	12	15	18	21	24	27	30

Use the table to answer these questions.

⑥ Megan paid $24. How many baskets did she buy?
8 × 3 = 24

⑦ Late in the season Paul raised his prices. Five baskets of blueberries cost $20. How much was 1 basket? **$4 per basket**
5 × **4** = 20

Solve.

⑧ 4 × **2** = 8

⑨ 5 × **3** = 15

⑩ 5 × **4** = 20

⑪ 10 × **5** = 50

⑫ Nancy wants to buy 15 eggs. They come 5 to a box. How many boxes must she buy? 5 × **3** = 15

⑬ Tanisha spent $16 for 4 movie tickets. How much was 1 ticket?

Ⓐ $4 C $6
B $5 D $7

432 **Real Math** • Chapter 11 • Lesson 7

---

3 Reflect 5

Guided Discussion REASONING

Integration: TEKS 2.12.A

Write a missing factor sentence on the board and have students make up word problems to match the sentence.

For example: 6 × ____ = 18

Ben Bought 6 boxes of paper for $18. How much was one box? $3

Anna rode her bicycle around the park 6 times. Her odometer shows that she rode 18 kilometers. How many kilometers is it around the park? 3

Laura needed $18. She could earn $6 each week. How many weeks will it take her to earn $18? 3

Cumulative Review: For cumulative review of previously learned skills, see page 439–440.

Family Involvement: Assign the *Practice, Reteach,* or *Enrichment* activities depending on the needs of your students. Have students create missing-factor problems with a family member.

Concept/Question Board: Have students attempt to answer any unanswered questions on the Concept/Question Board.

Math Puzzler: Using each digit only once, fill in the blanks with the digits 6, 7, 8, and 9 to make the greatest possible sum: **97** + **86** or 96 + 87

4 Assess and Differentiate

 Assess — Use *eAssess* to record and analyze evidence of student understanding.

A Gather Evidence

Use the Daily Class Assessment Records in *Texas Assessment* or *eAssess* to record daily observations.

Informal Assessment
☑ **Skill Practice**

Did the student `COMPUTING`
- ☐ respond accurately?
- ☐ respond quickly?
- ☐ respond with confidence?
- ☐ self-correct?

Informal Assessment
☑ **Student Pages**

Did the student `UNDERSTANDING`
- ☐ make important observations?
- ☐ extend or generalize learning?
- ☐ provide insightful answers?
- ☐ pose insightful questions?

 **TEKS/TAKS Practice**

Use *TEKS/TAKS Practice* pages 51–54 to assess student progress.

B Summarize Findings

Analyze and summarize assessment data for each student. Determine which Assessment Follow-Up is appropriate for each student. Use the Student Assessment Record in *Texas Assessment* or *eAssess* to update assessment records.

C Texas Assessment Follow-Up • DIFFERENTIATE INSTRUCTION

Based on your observations, use these teaching strategies for assessment follow-up.

INTERVENTION

Review student performance on *Intervention* Lesson 11.C to see if students have mastered prerequisite skills for this lesson.

Number, operation, and quantitative reasoning 1.3.A Model and create addition and subtraction problem situations with concrete objects and write corresponding number sentences.

Patterns, relationships, and algebraic thinking 1.5.D Use patterns to develop strategies to solve basic addition and basic subtraction problems.

ENGLISH LEARNER

Review
Use Lesson 11.7 in **English Learner Support Guide** to review lesson concepts and vocabulary.

ENRICH

If . . . students are proficient in the lesson concepts,

Then . . . encourage them to work on the chapter projects or *Enrichment* Lesson 11.7.

Enrichment Lesson 11.7

PRACTICE

If . . . students would benefit from additional practice,

Then . . . assign *Practice* Lesson 11.7.

Practice Lesson 11.7

RETEACH

If . . . students are having difficulty understanding missing factors,

Then . . . remind them about fact families and the Commutative Law.

Vertical Alignment TEXAS

Grade 1	Grade 2	Grade 3
1.5.A Use patterns to skip count by twos, fives, and tens.	2.4.B Model, create, and describe division situations in which a set of concrete objects is separated into equivalent sets.	3.6.C Identify patterns in related multiplication and division sentences (fact families) such as 2 x 3 = 6, 3 x 2 = 6, 6 ÷ 2 = 3, 6 ÷ 3 = 2.

Overview LESSON **11.8**
TEXAS

Lesson Planner

OBJECTIVES
- To provide an initial experience with division
- To help students see division as the inverse of multiplication
- To introduce the division sign ÷

MATH TEKS

Number, operation, and quantitative reasoning 2.4.B

Model, create, and describe division situations in which a set of concrete objects is separated into equivalent sets.

Patterns, relationships, and algebraic thinking 2.6.B

Identify patterns in a list of related number pairs based on a real-life situation and extend the list.

MATH TEKS INTEGRATION

Preparing for Grade 3 3.4.A Number, operation, and quantitative reasoning

Learn and apply multiplication facts through 12 by 12 using concrete models and objects.

Number, operation, and quantitative reasoning 2.4.A

Model, create, and describe multiplication situations in which equivalent sets of concrete objects are joined

Underlying processes and mathematical tools 2.12.A

Identify the mathematics in everyday situations.

MATERIALS
- *Number Cubes
- *Play money
- *Counters
- Multiplication Table
- Multiplication Table Game Mat
- *SRA Math Vocabulary Cards*

TECHNOLOGY
- e Presentation Lesson 11.8
- e MathTools Sets Former
- e Games Multiplication Table Game

Division and Multiplication ★

Context of the Lesson This is the second of three lessons that introduces students to division. In this lesson students are formally introduced to the division sign. Students also study the inverse properties of multiplication and division. In the next lesson, students further explore the relationship between multiplication and division.

See page 413B for Math Background for teachers for this lesson.

Planning for Learning ● DIFFERENTIATE INSTRUCTION

INTERVENTION

If . . . students lack the prerequisite skill of subtraction facts,

Then . . . teach *Intervention* Lesson 11.C.

1.3.A, 1.5.D

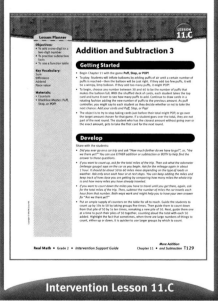

Intervention Lesson 11.C

ENGLISH LEARNER

Preview

If . . . students need language support,

Then . . . use Lesson 11.8 in *English Learner Support Guide* to preview lesson concepts and vocabulary.

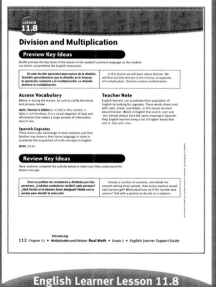

English Learner Lesson 11.8

ENRICH

If . . . students are proficient in the lesson concepts,

Then . . . emphasize Guided Discussion in Reflect.

PRACTICE

If . . . students would benefit from additional practice,

Then . . . extend Skill Practice before assigning the student pages.

RETEACH

If . . . students are having difficulty understanding division,

Then . . . extend Guided Discussion before assigning the student pages.

Academic Vocabulary
✎ division \di vizh´ ən\ *n.* the process of seeing how many times one number contains another number; the inverse of multiplication

Access Vocabulary
table In this context a table is not furniture; it is a visual organizer of data and information that makes a large amount of information easy to see.

Spanish Cognates
pizza pizza

---

*Manipulative Kit Item = Key standard

★ = 120-Day Plan for TAKS

Teaching Lesson 11.8

 TEXAS

Number, operation, and quantitative reasoning 2.4
The student models multiplication and division.
Patterns, relationships, and algebraic thinking 2.6.B
Identify patterns in a list of related number pairs based on real-life situation and extend the list.

Mental Math 5

 INTEGRATION: **TEKS 3.4.A** Present the following multiplication exercises, and have students show their answers using **Number Cubes.**

a. $2 \times 1 = 2$ **b.** $5 \times 5 = 25$ **c.** $4 \times 5 = 20$
d. $3 \times 5 = 15$ **e.** $10 \times 0 = 0$ **f.** $2 \times 8 = 16$

1 Develop 20

Tell Students In Today's Lesson They Will
learn about division.

Guided Discussion   MathTools UNDERSTANDING Introductory

Distributing and Division

- Display 30 counters or use **eMathTools: Sets Former** to display 30 objects.
- Tell five students that you want to divide the objects evenly among them.
- Have students predict how many each will receive; then distribute the objects to each of the five students to check their answers. Guide students to see that each will get 6 objects; $5 \times 6 = 30$.
- Write $30 \div 5 = 6$ on the board, and explain what each number in the number sentence represents: 5 students each get 6 objects out of 30.
- Repeat with other numbers, including numbers that have some objects left over. Problems may include the following:
1. 25 objects shared among 5 students; each student will get 5 objects; $25 \div 5 = 5$.
2. 24 objects shared among 6 students; each student will get 4 objects; $24 \div 6 = 4$.
3. 27 objects shared among 6 students; each student will get 4 objects, and 3 will be left over.

Discuss how some numbers can be divided equally, and others cannot. Explain that the number left over is called the *remainder*. Make sure students understand that every number will not divide evenly into a specific number of parts. Remind students to think about odd numbers and how they cannot be divided equally by 2.

Skill Building   MathTools UNDERSTANDING Introductory

Integration: TEKS 2.4.A

Use counters or **eMathTools: Sets Former** to demonstrate related multiplication and division problems. As you demonstrate one fact, keep a table of each fact on the overhead projector or board. For example, show $5 \times 4 = 20$ and $20 \div 4 = 5$. Continue, allowing students to contribute to the related facts being presented.

Skill Practice COMPUTING   Guided

Missing Factors

 Repeat the missing-factor Skill Practice from the previous lesson (Lesson 11.7). This time rewrite each missing-factor equation as a division sentence. Have students show their answers using **Number Cubes.** For example:

a. $3 \times \underline{4} = 12$ and $12 \div 4 = \underline{3}$
b. $3 \times \underline{2} = 6$ and $6 \div 2 = \underline{3}$
c. $5 \times \underline{4} = 20$ and $20 \div 4 = \underline{5}$
d. $7 \times \underline{3} = 21$ and $21 \div 3 = \underline{7}$
e. $4 \times \underline{6} = 24$ and $24 \div 6 = \underline{4}$
f. $5 \times \underline{1} = 5$ and $5 \div 1 = \underline{5}$

2 Use Student Pages 15

Student Pages 433–434   Independent

Have students complete page 433 with partners using play money to solve the problems. Have students complete page 434 independently.

Progress Monitoring

If . . . students have difficulty understanding related multiplication and division problems,	**Then . . .** use manipulatives to demonstrate how multiplication and division are inverse operations.

As Students Finish

Game Have students play the **Multiplication Table Game.**

Games *Multiplication Table Game*

RESEARCH IN ACTION

"The algorithms for multiplication and division depend heavily on fluency with multiplication and addition, and in division, with multidigit subtraction. The difficulties that many students have in subtraction noticeably affect division, so understanding and fluency in multidigit subtraction are very important."

Fuson, Karen F. "Developing Mathematical Power in Whole Number Operations" in Kilpatrick, Jeremy, W. Gary Martin, and Deborah Schifter, eds. *A Research Companion to Principles and Standards for School Mathematics.* Reston, VA: National Council of Teachers of Mathematics, Inc., 2003, p. 87.

Student Page

Name _____ Date _____

LESSON **11.8** **Division and Multiplication**

Key Ideas

Division is used to share parts of a whole.

I have 8 fortune cookies to share with 4 friends.
How many cookies will each friend get? 2

$8 \div 4 = 2$

Division and multiplication are inverse operations.
This is the symbol for division: ÷.

Math TEKS
Number, operation, and quantitative reasoning 2.4.B ● Model, create, and describe division situations in which a set of concrete objects is separated into equivalent sets.

Solve.

1 Twelve dollars are to be divided equally among 3 students. How many dollars will each student get?

$12 \div 3 = \underline{4}$

2 Twenty-four dollars are to be divided equally among 4 students. How many dollars will each student get?

$24 \div 4 = \underline{6}$

3 Thirty-two dollars are to be divided equally among 8 students. How many dollars will each student get?

$32 \div 8 = \underline{4}$

4 Fifteen cents are to be divided equally among 3 cups. How many cents will be in each cup?

$15 \div 3 = \underline{5}$

Textbook This lesson is available in the *eTextbook*.

433

434

LESSON 11.8 · Division and Multiplication

Solve these problems. Use counters and a Multiplication Table if you need help.

5 $50 \div 10 = \underline{5}$ **11** $40 \div 5 = \underline{8}$

6 $5 \times 10 = \underline{50}$ **12** $8 \times 5 = \underline{40}$

7 $60 \div 6 = \underline{10}$ **13** $40 \div 8 = \underline{5}$

8 $10 \times 6 = \underline{60}$ **14** $5 \times 8 = \underline{40}$

9 $20 \div 5 = \underline{4}$ **15** $48 \div 8 = \underline{6}$

10 $4 \times 5 = \underline{20}$ **16** $6 \times 8 = \underline{48}$

Rich and Gail each need 40 stickers for a project.
There are 8 stickers in a package.
How many packages should they each buy?

Gail's Solution   Rich's solution

17 $8 \times \underline{5} = 40$ **18** Subtract 8 until you reach 0. $\underline{5}$

19 How many packages of stickers should Gail and Rich each buy? $\underline{5}$

20 Terrell has a bag of 26 pretzels. If the pretzels are shared equally with two other people, how many will be left over?

A 1   C 3

Ⓑ 2   D 4

Real Math · Chapter 11 · Lesson 8

---

3 Reflect   10

Guided Discussion REASONING

Integration: TEKS 2.12.A

Provide students with a problem, such as the following:

Jennifer has $40. Each day she buys the same lunch, which costs her $5. How many days will her $40 buy her lunch?

Explain to students how this situation involves repeated subtraction. Money is subtracted from a whole amount each day.

Then, provide students with a problem such as the following:

Jennifer has $40. She has 5 favorite charities she would like to give the money to. How much will each charity receive?

Explain to students how this situation involves equal sharing. The money is equally shared among a certain amount of people. Go on to ask students how the situations are different and how they are the same.

Finally, ask students to come up with examples of situations involving repeated subtraction or equal sharing.

TEKS Checkup

Number, operation, and quantitative reasoning 2.4.B

Model, create, and describe division situations in which a set of concrete objects is separated into equivalent sets.

Use this problem to assess students' progress towards standards mastery:

Which shows two equal sets?

A ◯ = ◯ ◯

B (set) = (set)

Ⓒ (set) = (set)

D (set) = (set)

Have students choose the correct answer, then describe how they knew

which choice was correct. In the discussion, ask questions such as the following. Be sure to ask students to explain their reasoning, since different solution methods are possible.

■ **How many counters must be on each side to have equal sets?** an equal number

■ **Which has the same on one side and the other side?** choice C

Follow-Up
If…students have difficulty with determining describing division situations,

Then…have students review fact families by using the eMathTools: Multiplication Table.

Math Puzzler: There are six rows of desks in the second-grade classroom. Each row has four desks. There is a student at every desk except two. How many students are in this class? 22

4 Assess and Differentiate

 Assess Use *eAssess* to record and analyze evidence of student understanding.

A Gather Evidence

Use the Daily Class Assessment Records in *Texas Assessment* or *eAssess* to record daily observations.

Informal Assessment
☑ **Guided Discussion**

Did the student **UNDERSTANDING**
- ☐ make important observations?
- ☐ extend or generalize learning?
- ☐ provide insightful answers?
- ☐ pose insightful questions?

Informal Assessment
☑ **Skill Building**

Did the student **UNDERSTANDING**
- ☐ make important observations?
- ☐ extend or generalize learning?
- ☐ provide insightful answers?
- ☐ pose insightful questions?

 **TEKS/TAKS Practice**

Use *TEKS/TAKS Practice* pages 37–38 to assess student progress.

B Summarize Findings

Analyze and summarize assessment data for each student. Determine which Assessment Follow-Up is appropriate for each student. Use the Student Assessment Record in *Texas Assessment* or *eAssess* to update assessment records.

C Texas Assessment Follow-Up ● DIFFERENTIATE INSTRUCTION

Based on your observations, use these teaching strategies for assessment follow-up.

 TEXAS

INTERVENTION

Review student performance on *Intervention* Lesson 11.C to see if students have mastered prerequisite skills for this lesson.

Number, operation, and quantitative reasoning 1.3.A Model and create addition and subtraction problem situations with concrete objects and write corresponding number sentences.

Patterns, relationships, and algebraic thinking 1.5.D Use patterns to develop strategies to solve basic addition and basic subtraction problems.

ENGLISH LEARNER
Review

Use Lesson 11.8 in *English Learner Support Guide* to review lesson concepts and vocabulary.

ENRICH

If . . . students are proficient in the lesson concepts,

Then . . . encourage them to work on the chapter projects or *Enrichment* Lesson 11.8.

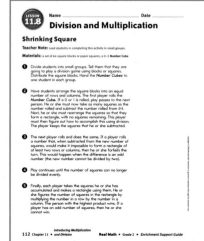

Enrichment Lesson 11.8

PRACTICE

If . . . students would benefit from additional practice,

Then . . . assign *Practice* Lesson 11.8.

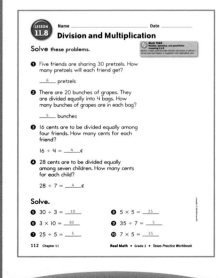

Practice Lesson 11.8

RETEACH

If . . . students have difficulty solving multiplication and division problems,

Then . . . reteach the concept using *Reteach* Lesson 11.8.

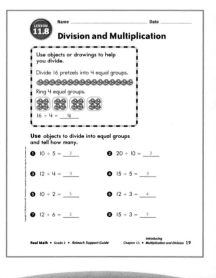

Reteach Lesson 11.8

Vertical Alignment

Grade 1	Grade 2	Grade 3
1.5 The student recognizes patterns in numbers and operations.	**2.5** The student uses patterns in numbers and operations.	**3.6** The student uses patterns to solve problems.

Overview

LESSON 11.9

TEXAS

OBJECTIVES

- To provide practice in multiplying and dividing
- To demonstrate how to identify patterns in determining a function machine rule

MATH TEKS

Patterns, relationships, and algebraic thinking 2.5
The student uses patterns in numbers and operations.

Number, operation, and quantitative reasoning 2.4.B
Model, create, and describe division situations in which a set of concrete objects is separated into equivalent sets.

MATH TEKS INTEGRATION

Preparing for Grade 3, 3.6.C
Identify patterns in related multiplication and division sentences (fact families) such as $2 \times 3 = 6$, $3 \times 2 = 6$, $6 \div 2 = 3$, $6 \div 3 = 2$.

Underlying processes and mathematical tools 2.12.A
Identify the mathematics in everyday situations.

MATERIALS

- *Number Cubes
- Multiplication Table Game Mat*
- Multiplication Tables
- Function machine

TECHNOLOGY

- e Presentation Lesson 11.9
- e MathTools Function Machine
- e Games Multiplication Table Game

Division and Multiplication Functions

Context of the Lesson This is the third of three lessons that introduces students to division and is the final lesson on multiplication and division. Students will use the function machine in this lesson to reinforce multiplication and division skills.

See page 413B for Math Background for teachers for this lesson.

Planning for Learning • DIFFERENTIATE INSTRUCTION

INTERVENTION

If . . . students lack the prerequisite skill of using a function table,

Then . . . teach *Intervention* Lesson 11.C.

 1.3.A, 1.5.D

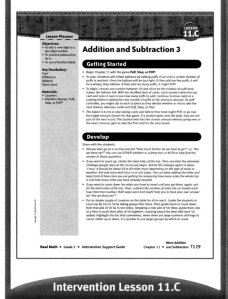

Intervention Lesson 11.C

ENGLISH LEARNER

Preview

If . . . students need language support,

Then . . . use Lesson 11.9 in *English Learner Support Guide* to preview lesson concepts and vocabulary.

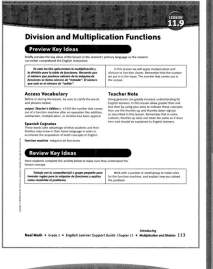

English Learner Lesson 11.9

ENRICH

If . . . students are proficient in the lesson concepts,

Then . . . emphasize additional game time.

PRACTICE

If . . . students would benefit from additional practice,

Then . . . extend Skill Practice before assigning the student pages.

RETEACH

If . . . students are having difficulty understanding division,

Then . . . extend Guided Discussion before assigning the student pages.

Access Vocabulary
output the number that comes out of a function machine after an operation like addition, subtraction, multiplication, or division has been applied

Spanish Cognates
function machine máquina de funciones

TEXAS

Patterns, relationships, and algebraic thinking 2.5
The student uses patterns in numbers and operations.
Number, operation, and quantitative reasoning 2.4.B
Model, create, and describe division situations in which
a set of concrete objects is separated into equivalent sets.

Mental Math   5

  Integration: TEKS 3.6.C Present multiplication and division exercises, and have students use **Number Cubes** to show their answers. Possible examples include the following:

a. $6 \times 4 = 24$

b. $15 \div 5 = 3$

c. $24 \div 4 = 6$

d. $3 \times 6 = 18$

e. $3 \times 5 = 15$

f. $18 \div 6 = 3$

1 Develop   20

Tell Students In Today's Lesson They Will

apply multiplication and division to function tables.

Introductory

Guided Discussion   **MathTools** UNDERSTANDING

Draw a function table on the board or use **eMathTools: Function Machine** to lead an activity for applying multiplication and division facts.

 Integration: TEKS 2.12.A

Present students with a situation such as the following: Odell spends money each day to ride the subway to school. After 2 days, he has spent $4. After 3 days, he has spent $6. After 5 days, he has spent $10. How can a function machine show the amount of money Odell spends to ride the subway each day? Share with the students the numbers for the input and output. Then, have the students find the rule and explain how they came to that conclusion. Be sure to display a Multiplication Table during this exercise. When using division rules to create function tables and operate the function machine, make sure that the rules work with any number ($\div 1$) or that the numbers chosen are divisible without having remainders.

Skill Building ENGAGING

Guided

Use the function machine you created and used in Chapter 2.

Choose one student to be first to operate the machine. Secretly discuss a simple multiplication or division rule with this student, such as always multiplying a number by 1. Have the rest of the class write numbers on slips of paper and put them into the machine one at a time. The student operating the machine applies the rule to each number and feeds the altered slip of paper through the opposite slot. Have a Multiplication Table available to the student operating the machine and students feeding in numbers. Students try to determine the rule so they can predict what number they will get back. Let other students have turns operating the machine.

Skill Practice   COMPUTING

Guided

Supply multiplication and division rules, and have students provide the input and output values on function tables. Allow students to work in small groups for each rule. Then have one group at a time share the values they solved for. Possible rules include the following:

a. $\times 0$

b. $\div 1$

c. $\times 2$

d. $\times 10$

e. $\div 2$

f. $\times 1$

2 Use Student Pages   20

Pages 435–436 COMPUTING

Individual

Have students complete student pages 435 and 436 independently.

As Students Finish

 Game Have students play the **Multiplication Table Game.**

e Games *Multiplication Table Game*

e MathTools *Function Machine* Have students practice multiplication and division functions.

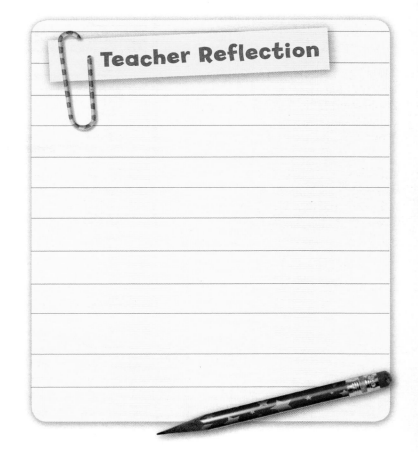

Teacher Reflection

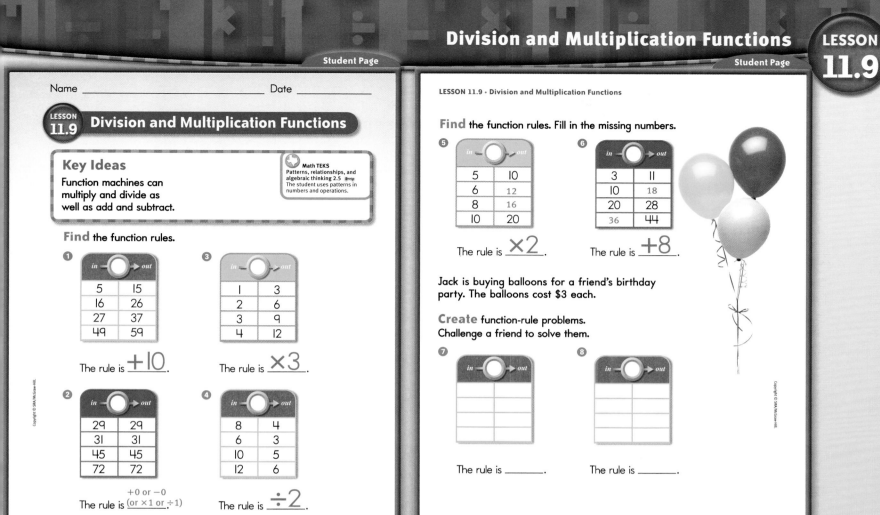

Student Page

Name _____ Date _____

LESSON 11.9 · Division and Multiplication Functions

Key Ideas

Function machines can multiply and divide as well as add and subtract.

Math TEKS
Patterns, relationships, and algebraic thinking 2.5
The student uses patterns in numbers and operations.

Find the function rules.

①
in ○ → out	
5	15
16	26
27	37
49	59

The rule is $+10$.

③
in ○ → out	
1	3
2	6
3	9
4	12

The rule is $\times 3$.

②
in ○ → out	
29	29
31	31
45	45
72	72

The rule is $\dfrac{+0 \text{ or } -0}{\text{(or } \times 1 \text{ or } \div 1)}$

④
in ○ → out	
8	4
6	3
10	5
12	6

The rule is $\div 2$.

Textbook This lesson is available in the *eTextbook*.

435

436

Find the function rules. Fill in the missing numbers.

⑤
in ○ → out	
5	10
6	12
8	16
10	20

The rule is $\times 2$.

⑥
in ○ → out	
3	11
10	18
20	28
36	44

The rule is $+8$.

Jack is buying balloons for a friend's birthday party. The balloons cost $3 each.

Create function-rule problems. Challenge a friend to solve them.

⑦
in ○ → out	

The rule is _____.

⑧
in ○ → out	

The rule is _____.

Real Math · Chapter 11 · Lesson 9

---

③ Reflect

10

Guided Discussion REASONING

Refer to student page 436, and have a few students share their examples of making up rules for a function machine. Have students explain how they completed this activity. Encourage students to give reasons for their answers.

Cumulative Review: For cumulative review of previously learned skills, see page 439–440.

Family Involvement: Assign the *Practice, Reteach,* or *Enrichment* activities depending on the needs of your students. Have students create multiplication and division function tables with a family member.

Concept/Question Board: Have students attempt to answer any unanswered questions on the Concept/Question Board.

Math Puzzler: How many different pairs of factors can you write that have a product of 12? 3 pairs of factors: 1×12; 2×6; 3×4

4 Assess and Differentiate

 **Assess** Use **eAssess** to record and analyze evidence of student understanding.

A Gather Evidence

Use the Daily Class Assessment Records in **Texas Assessment** or **eAssess** to record daily observations.

Informal Assessment
☑ **Guided Discussion**

Did the student [UNDERSTANDING]

❑ make important observations?
❑ extend or generalize learning?
❑ provide insightful answers?
❑ pose insightful questions?

Informal Assessment
☑ **Skill Practice**

Did the student [COMPUTING]

❑ respond accurately?
❑ respond quickly?
❑ respond with confidence?
❑ self-correct?

TEKS/TAKS Practice

Use **TEKS/TAKS Practice** pages 39–42 to assess student progress.

B Summarize Findings

Analyze and summarize assessment data for each student. Determine which Assessment Follow-Up is appropriate for each student. Use the Student Assessment Record in **Texas Assessment** or **eAssess** to update assessment records.

C Texas Assessment Follow-Up ● DIFFERENTIATE INSTRUCTION

Based on your observations, use these teaching strategies for assessment follow-up.

TEXAS

INTERVENTION

Review student performance on **Intervention** Lesson 11.C to see if students have mastered prerequisite skills for this lesson.

🔷 **Number, operation, and quantitative reasoning 1.3.A** Model and create addition and subtraction problem situations with concrete objects and write corresponding number sentences.

🔷 **Patterns, relationships, and algebraic thinking 1.5.D** Use patterns to develop strategies to solve basic addition and basic subtraction problems.

ENGLISH LEARNER
Review

Use Lesson 11.9 in **English Learner Support Guide** to review lesson concepts and vocabulary.

ENRICH

If . . . students are proficient in the lesson concepts,

Then . . . encourage them to work on the chapter projects or **Enrichment** Lesson 11.9.

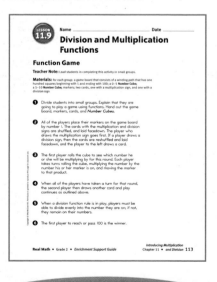

Enrichment Lesson 11.9

PRACTICE

If . . . students would benefit from additional practice,

Then . . . assign **Practice** Lesson 11.9.

Practice Lesson 11.9

RETEACH

If . . . students are having difficulty understanding multiplication and division functions,

Then . . . reteach the concept using **Reteach** Lesson 11.9.

Reteach Lesson 11.9

Problem Solving 11·C

Using Strategies

Objectives
- To provide practice applying multiplication and division to real-world problems
- To provide practice solving and presenting solutions to nonroutine problems

Materials
None

See Appendix A page A24 for instruction and a rubric for problem solving.

Context of the Lesson This lesson continues the theme of ethnic foods from pages 413–414 and 427–428. Students will have an opportunity to apply what they've been learning about multiplication and division to a real-world, nonroutine problem.

1 Develop
5

Tell Students In Today's Lesson They Will
figure out how to share Indian crackers in a fair way.

Guided Discussion

Introductory

Remind students about previous activities in this chapter relating to ethnic foods (pages 413–414 and 427–428). Also remind them about the students in the Diversity Club who study different countries around the world.

Have students look at the picture on page 437. Ask questions such as the following:

- **What are the students in the picture doing?** getting ready to eat
- **What are they going to eat?** Possible answer: some stew and some crackers

Have students continue to look at the picture while you read the following story:

The students in the Diversity Club decided to try some traditional Indian food to help them learn about India. Mr. Smith, the teacher in charge of the club, went to an Indian restaurant and bought some Chicken Korma and 3 packages of puppodums, a traditional Indian cracker. There are 8 puppodums in each package. There are 4 students in the club today, and they want to share the 3 packages of puppodums. How many puppodums can each of them get?

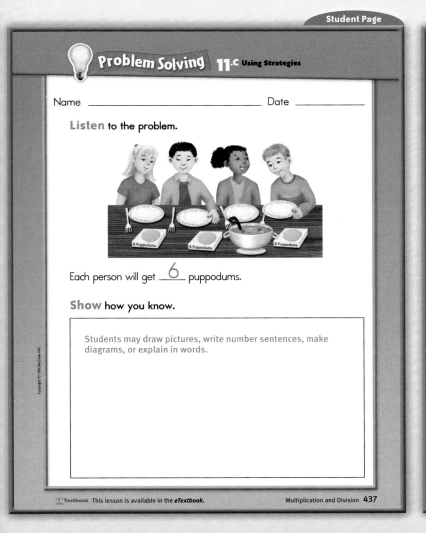

Underlying processes and mathematical tools 2.14
The student is expected to justify his or her thinking using objects, words, pictures, numbers, and technology.
Underlying processes and mathematical reasoning 2.12.B
Solve problems with guidance that incorporates the

processes of understanding the problem, making a plan, and evaluating the solution for reasonableness.
Number, operation, and quantitative reasoning 2.4.A
Model, create, and describe multiplication situations in which equivalent sets of concrete objects are joined.

 **Exploring Problem Solving**   25 ⏱

Using Student Pages

 Independent

Have students work in pairs or small groups to solve the problem. Provide support as needed. If students seem to be having difficulty, encourage them to struggle with the problem for a while. When needed, ask guiding questions such as the following:

- **Have you ever shared a group of things with others? How did you share?**
- **How might using cubes help you solve this problem?**
- **What might you do first with the cubes?**

Students who finish early may solve the problem on page 438, or you may assign page 438 as homework. The two problems are the same except for the number of students and the number of puppodums.

 Reflect   10 ⏱

 Knowledge Age Skills

Effective Communication Ask each group to share their plan and their strategies for solving the problem. Help students understand the following points:

- People can use different strategies and get the same answer.
- If you get the same answer using different strategies, that's a good sign that the answer is correct.
- It is a good idea to think about what a reasonable answer might be before you start to work on a problem. Then you can check your answer to see if it is reasonable.

Sample Solutions Strategies

Students might use one or more of the following strategies to help solve the problem:

Draw a Picture

Students might draw a picture of all the puppodums and then assign them to 4 groups and count how many are in each group.

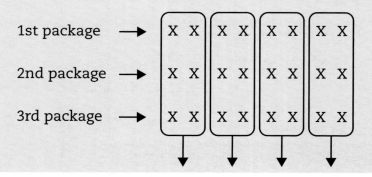

1st package →
2nd package →
3rd package →

Write Number Sentences

Students might first find the total number of puppodums by multiplying the number of packages by the number of puppodums in each package: $3 \times 8 = 24$.

Then they could divide the total by the number of students sharing: $24 \div 4 = 6$.

Or they might think and write $4 \times \underline{\quad} = 24$.

Use a Physical Model

Students might use cubes or other counters to represent the puppodums, form 3 packages of 8, and then deal them into 4 equal groups.

Use Number Sense

Students might realize that each student will get 2 puppodums from each package and realize that because there are 3 packages, each student will get 6 puppodums.

Use Guess, Check, and Revise

To figure out how to share the 24 objects among 4 children, students might try different numbers until they find one that works.

 Assess   15 ⏱

When evaluating student work, focus on whether students thought rationally about the problem. Questions to consider include the following:

- Did the student understand the problem?
- If the student used multiplication or division concepts, did she or he use these in reasonable ways?
- Was the student able to explain his or her thinking?
- Did the student check the answer?

Cumulative Review

Use Pages 439–440

Use the Cumulative Review as a review of concepts and skills that students have previously learned.

Here are different ways that you can assign these problems to your students as they work through the chapter:

- With some of the lessons in the chapter, assign a set of cumulative review problems to be completed as practice or for homework.
  Lesson 11.7—Problems 1–5
  Lesson 11.8—Problems 6–8
  Lesson 11.9—Problems 9–13

- At any point during the chapter, assign part or all of the cumulative review problems to be completed as practice or for homework.

Cumulative Review

Problems 1–5 review writing fractions and fractions of plane figures, Lesson 7.2. TEKS: 2.2.A

Problems 6–8 review reading graphs on a grid, Lesson 4.12. TEKS: 2.11.A

Problems 9–13 review division and multiplication, Lesson 11.8. TEKS: 2.4.B

Progress Monitoring

If . . . students miss more than one problem in a section,

Then . . . refer to the indicated lesson for remediation suggestions.

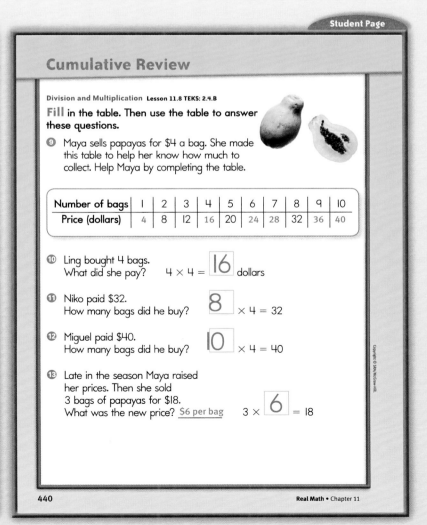

Cumulative Review

Student Page

Name _____ Date _____

Writing Fractions Lesson 7.2 TEKS: 2.2.A

Use the picture to answer the questions.

Jana and Min are riding the high-wire bikes at the museum. The wire is 20 meters long.

1. Jana has gone $\frac{3}{4}$ of the way. How many meters has she gone? **15**

2. Min has gone $\frac{1}{4}$ of the way. How many meters has she gone? **5**

3. Draw a J to show where Jana is.

4. Draw an M to show where Min is.

5. How many more meters does Min have to ride to reach the landing platform? **15**

Graphs on a Grid Lesson 4.12 TEKS: 2.11.A

Use the graph to answer the questions.

This restaurant has food from Central America. Use the graph to see how many customers have visited each day.

6. Connect the points on the graph.

7. About how many customers visited on day 1? **40**

8. Which day had about 100 customers? **day 5**

439

Cumulative Review

Student Page

Division and Multiplication Lesson 11.8 TEKS: 2.4.B

Fill in the table. Then use the table to answer these questions.

9. Maya sells papayas for $4 a bag. She made this table to help her know how much to collect. Help Maya by completing the table.

Number of bags	1	2	3	4	5	6	7	8	9	10
Price (dollars)	4	8	12	16	20	24	28	32	36	40

10. Ling bought 4 bags. What did she pay? $4 \times 4 = $ **16** dollars

11. Niko paid $32. How many bags did he buy? **8** $\times 4 = 32$

12. Miguel paid $40. How many bags did he buy? **10** $\times 4 = 40$

13. Late in the season Maya raised her prices. Then she sold 3 bags of papayas for $18. What was the new price? **$6 per bag** $3 \times $ **6** $ = 18$

440

Real Math • Chapter 11

Wrap-Up

1 Discuss  5

Concept/Question Board

Review the Concept/Question Board with students.

- Discuss students' contributions to the Concept side of the Board.
- Have students repose their questions, and lead a discussion to find satisfactory answers.

Chapter Projects APPLYING

Provide an opportunity for students who have worked on one or more of the projects outlined on page 414C to share their work with the class. Allow each student or student group five minutes to present or discuss their projects. For formal assessment, use the rubrics found in *Across the Curriculum Math Connections;* the rubric for **Compare Diets from Other Cultures** is on page 115, and the rubric for **Write a Story about Ethnic Food** is on page 121. For informal assessment, use the following rubric and questions.

	Exceeds Expectations	Meets Expectations	Minimally Meets Expectations
Applies mathematics in real-world situations:	❑	❑	❑
Demonstrates strong engagement in the activity:	❑	❑	❑

Compare Diets from Other Cultures

- Which culture did you pick? Why did you pick that culture?
- What foods did you choose? Why?
- How many servings of each food would you eat in one day? In one week?
- What equations did you write to calculate the servings you would have in one week?
- How is the food from the culture you chose similar to or different from the food in your culture?
- Was using the table a useful tool? Why or why not?
- Would you like to visit the culture you chose and try the food? Why or why not?

TEKS:
MATH STANDARD: **Number, operation, and quantitative reasoning 2.4** The student models multiplication and division.

CROSS CURRICULAR STANDARD (SCIENCE): **Scientific processes 2.3.A** Make decisions using information.

TECHNOLOGY STANDARD: **Information acquisition 05.A.** Acquire information including text, audio, video, and graphics.

Write a Story about Ethnic Food

- What food did you write about? Why did you choose that food?
- What recipe did you choose to include in your story?
- What else did you include in your story?
- What function did you write to adjust the recipe? Was this function useful?
- Was your story based more on experience or imagination?
- How did you use the Internet to find ideas for your story?

TEKS:
MATH STANDARD: **Number, operation, and quantitative reasoning 2.4** The student models multiplication and division.

CROSS CURRICULAR STANDARD (LANGUAGE ARTS): **Writing/purposes 2.14.D** Write in different forms for different purposes such as lists to record, letters to invite or thank, and stories or poems to entertain.

TECHNOLOGY STANDARD: **Foundations 02.D** Produce documents at the keyboard, proofread, and correct errors.

Key Ideas Review ✓ UNDERSTANDING

Review the Key Ideas concepts on pages 441–442 with the class. The Key Ideas pages should be used by students and parents as a reference when reviewing the important concepts covered in this chapter. Ask students the following discussion questions to extend their knowledge of the Key Ideas and check their understanding of the ideas.

Discussion Questions

❶ **Can you think of some situations where you would use multiplication to solve a problem? What are they?** Allow the class to discuss. Multiplication can be used when you know you have to add the same number over and over again. For example, if there were 672 students participating in a school field day, and the principal needed to buy 3 ribbons for each student, it would be much easier to multiply 672 × 3 than to add three 672 times.

❷ **Why would you want to know the area of a rectangle?** If you are covering the surface of something, you need to know the area. For example, if you wanted to put carpet in a rectangular room, you would need to know how much carpet to buy. Have students work together to figure out the area of a desk or table.

❸ **Why is it inefficient to use skip counting instead of memorizing multiplication facts?** Allow students to discuss. Skip counting takes much longer, and is sometimes awkward. Skip counting by 2s is not difficult, but skip counting by 7s would be hard to remember.

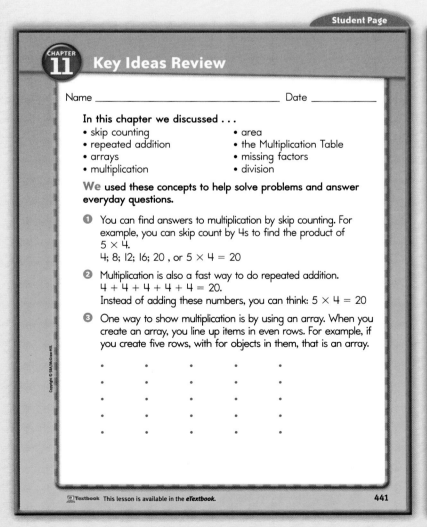

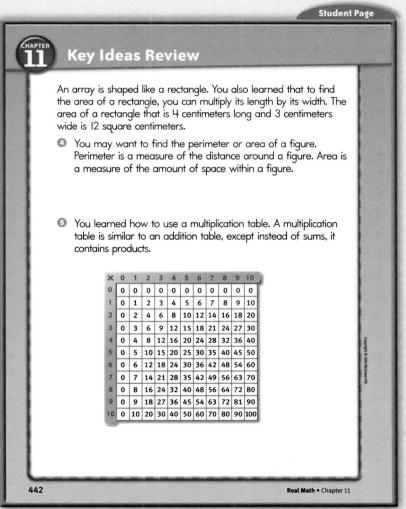

Chapter 2 Error Analysis

Errors Reading Problems

Write the following problems on the board and allow students to analyze this student's work. Discuss error patterns students find and how to help the student.

Pose this analysis as a challenging problem. When a student thinks he or she might have detected the error pattern, rather than have them tell the answer to the class, write a new exercise on the board and have the student tell you the answer that is consistent with the pattern he or she found. By using this procedure, all students will have a chance to think through the problem – not just the first student to find it.

This student completed a page of problems and got the following answers.

1. **One week has 7 days. How many days are in 3 weeks?** 21
2. **Marcia works 5 days in one week and 4 days in the next week. How many days did she work?** 20
3. **Charles has 4 dollars. Then he earned 3 more dollars. How many dollars does Charles have now?** 12
4. **Amy is 10 years old. How old was she 2 years ago?** 20
5. **A garden has 5 rows each with 6 tomato plants. How many tomato plants are in the garden?** 30
6. **If one car can hold 5 people, how many people will 3 cars hold?** 15

What error is this student making?

This student always multiplies the two numbers in each problem, even if multiplying is not called for. It's possible that the student knows better but because this set of problems came right after a multiplication lesson, he or she just assumed that the problems called for multiplication and didn't bother to read the problems.

It's also possible that the student needs instruction on when multiplication is called for (when several of identical objects or events are added.)

TEKS/TAKS Practice

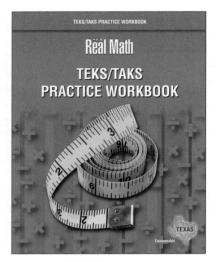

TEKS/TAKS Practice Book

At this time, you may wish to provide practice for standards covered in this chapter.

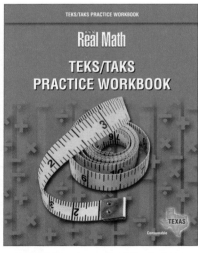

TEKS/TAKS Practice, pp. 34-36, Standard 2.4.A

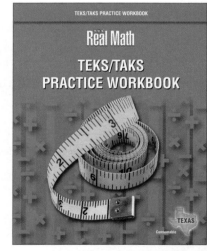

TEKS/TAKS Practice, pp. 73-74, Standard 2.9.B

TEKS/TAKS Practice, pp. 37-38, Standard 2.4.B

Chapter Review

Use this Chapter 11 Review to indicate areas in which each student is having difficulty or in which the class may need help. If students do well on the Chapter 11 Review, you may wish to skip directly to the Chapter Test; if not, you may spend a day or so helping students overcome their individual difficulties before taking the Practice Test.

Next to each set of problems is a list of the lessons in the chapter that covered those concepts. If they need help, students can refer to a specific lesson for additional instruction. You can also use this information to make additional assignments based on the previous lesson concepts.

Have students complete pages 443–444 on their own.

CHAPTER 11 Chapter Review

Name _____ Date _____

Lesson 11.1
TEKS: 2.6.C
Skip count and fill in the missing numbers.

① 0 6 12 18 **24** 30

② | 2 | 4 | 6 | **8** | 10 | **12** | 14 | **16** | **18** | 20 |

Lesson 11.9
TEKS: 2.4.B
Find the function rules. Fill in the missing numbers.

③
in	out
8	4
12	6
16	8
22	11

The rule is **÷2**.

④
in	out
98	93
107	102
83	78
62	57

The rule is **−5**.

⑤
in	out
8	24
9	27
10	30
11	33

The rule is **×3**.

⑥
in	out
18	6
9	3
12	4
24	8

The rule is **÷3**.

CHAPTER 11 Chapter Review

Lesson 11.5
TEKS: 2.4
Use the squares to solve these problems.

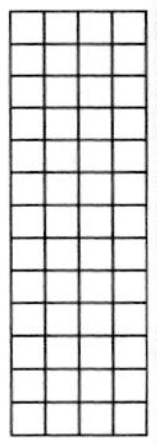

⑦ The area is **52** square units.

⑧ $4 \times 13 = $ **52**

Lesson 11.7
TEKS: 2.6.B
Solve these problems.

⑨ I paid $21 for seven candles. How much would one candle cost? $ **3**

⑩ $54 is to be divided equally among nine people. How many dollars for each person?

$54 \div 9 = $ **6**

Lessons 11.7
TEKS: 2.4
Solve.

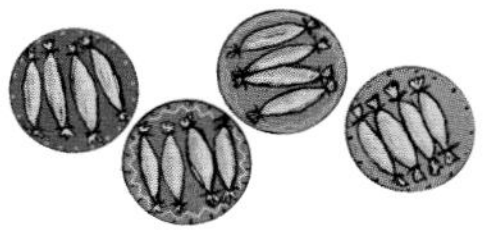

Each plate has four tamales.

⑪ How many tamales are there? **4 + 4 + 4 + 4 = 16**

⑫ $5 \times$ **3** $= 15$

⑬ **2** $\times 4 = 8$

⑭ $5 \times$ **4** $= 20$

⑮ $4 \times$ **2** $= 8$

⑯ Mira wants to make a Greek salad for 35 people. Her recipe makes enough for 7 people. How many times will she use her recipe?

$7 \times$ **5** $= 35$

---

3 Chapter Tests
40

Practice Test

Student Pages 445–448

- The Chapter 11 Practice Test on *Student Edition* pages 445–448 provides an opportunity to formally evaluate students' proficiency with concepts developed in this chapter.
- The content is similar to the Chapter 11 Review, in standardized format.

Practice-Test Remediation

Short Answer Questions 1–3 are all about skip counting. If students have difficulty with these problems, then have them practice skip counting using a number line until they become more confident.

Short Answer Questions 4–10 all involve repeated addition and multiplication. If students miss these problems then have them work with manipulatives to solve these or similar problems. After several rounds, they should see the connection between multiplication and repeated addition.

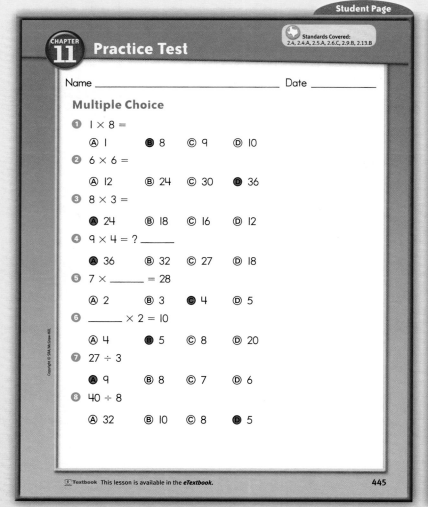

Student Page

CHAPTER 11 Practice Test

Standards Covered:
2.4, 2.4.A, 2.5.A, 2.6.C, 2.9.B, 2.13.B

Name _____ Date _____

Multiple Choice

1. $1 \times 8 =$
   - Ⓐ 1
   - Ⓑ 8
   - Ⓒ 9
   - Ⓓ 10

2. $6 \times 6 =$
   - Ⓐ 12
   - Ⓑ 24
   - Ⓒ 30
   - ● 36

3. $8 \times 3 =$
   - ● 24
   - Ⓑ 18
   - Ⓒ 16
   - Ⓓ 12

4. $9 \times 4 = ?$ _____
   - Ⓐ 36
   - Ⓑ 32
   - Ⓒ 27
   - Ⓓ 18

5. $7 \times$ _____ $= 28$
   - Ⓐ 2
   - Ⓑ 3
   - ● 4
   - Ⓓ 5

6. _____ $\times 2 = 10$
   - Ⓐ 4
   - ● 5
   - Ⓒ 8
   - Ⓓ 20

7. $27 \div 3$
   - ● 9
   - Ⓑ 8
   - Ⓒ 7
   - Ⓓ 6

8. $40 \div 8$
   - Ⓐ 32
   - Ⓑ 10
   - Ⓒ 8
   - ● 5

📖Textbook This lesson is available in the *eTextbook*.

445

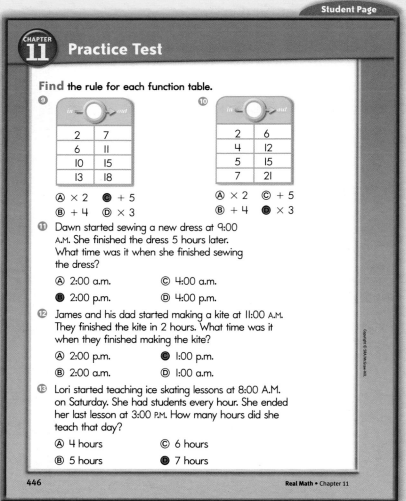

Student Page

CHAPTER 11 Practice Test

Find the rule for each function table.

9.

in	out
2	7
6	11
10	15
13	18

   - Ⓐ $\times 2$
   - ● $+ 5$
   - Ⓑ $+ 4$
   - Ⓓ $\times 3$

10.

in	out
2	6
4	12
5	15
7	21

   - Ⓐ $\times 2$
   - Ⓒ $+ 5$
   - Ⓑ $+ 4$
   - ● $\times 3$

11. Dawn started sewing a new dress at 9:00 A.M. She finished the dress 5 hours later. What time was it when she finished sewing the dress?
    - Ⓐ 2:00 a.m.
    - Ⓒ 4:00 a.m.
    - ● 2:00 p.m.
    - Ⓓ 4:00 p.m.

12. James and his dad started making a kite at 11:00 A.M. They finished the kite in 2 hours. What time was it when they finished making the kite?
    - Ⓐ 2:00 p.m.
    - ● 1:00 p.m.
    - Ⓑ 2:00 a.m.
    - Ⓓ 1:00 a.m.

13. Lori started teaching ice skating lessons at 8:00 A.M. on Saturday. She had students every hour. She ended her last lesson at 3:00 P.M. How many hours did she teach that day?
    - Ⓐ 4 hours
    - Ⓒ 6 hours
    - Ⓑ 5 hours
    - ● 7 hours

446

Real Math • Chapter 11

445–446   Chapter 11 • Introducing Multiplication and Division

Multiple Choice Questions 1–10 and Extended Response Question 11 are about multiplication and division facts. If students have difficulty with these questions, have them practice their multiplication and division facts with a partner using flashcards or the Multiplication Table.

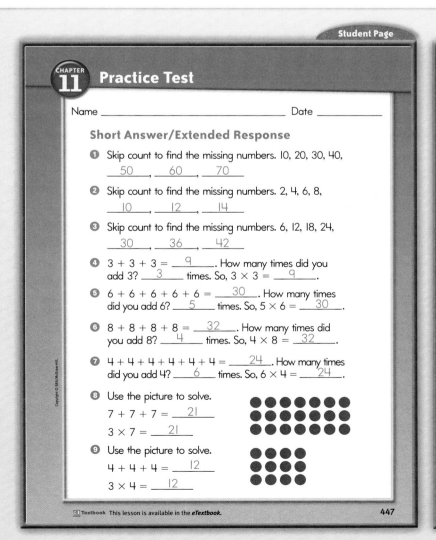

CHAPTER 11 Practice Test

Name _____ Date _____

Short Answer/Extended Response

1. Skip count to find the missing numbers. 10, 20, 30, 40, __50__, __60__, __70__

2. Skip count to find the missing numbers. 2, 4, 6, 8, __10__, __12__, __14__

3. Skip count to find the missing numbers. 6, 12, 18, 24, __30__, __36__, __42__

4. $3 + 3 + 3 =$ __9__. How many times did you add 3? __3__ times. So, $3 \times 3 =$ __9__.

5. $6 + 6 + 6 + 6 + 6 =$ __30__. How many times did you add 6? __5__ times. So, $5 \times 6 =$ __30__.

6. $8 + 8 + 8 + 8 =$ __32__. How many times did you add 8? __4__ times. So, $4 \times 8 =$ __32__.

7. $4 + 4 + 4 + 4 + 4 + 4 =$ __24__. How many times did you add 4? __6__ times. So, $6 \times 4 =$ __24__.

8. Use the picture to solve.
   $7 + 7 + 7 =$ __21__
   $3 \times 7 =$ __21__

9. Use the picture to solve.
   $4 + 4 + 4 =$ __12__
   $3 \times 4 =$ __12__

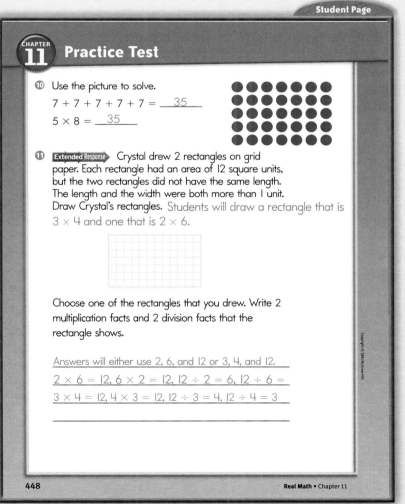

CHAPTER 11 Practice Test

10. Use the picture to solve.
    $7 + 7 + 7 + 7 + 7 =$ __35__
    $5 \times 8 =$ __35__

11. **Extended Response** Crystal drew 2 rectangles on grid paper. Each rectangle had an area of 12 square units, but the two rectangles did not have the same length. The length and the width were both more than 1 unit. Draw Crystal's rectangles. Students will draw a rectangle that is 3×4 and one that is 2×6.

Choose one of the rectangles that you drew. Write 2 multiplication facts and 2 division facts that the rectangle shows.

Answers will either use 2, 6, and 12 or 3, 4, and 12.
$2 \times 6 = 12$, $6 \times 2 = 12$, $12 \div 2 = 6$, $12 \div 6 =$
$3 \times 4 = 12$, $4 \times 3 = 12$, $12 \div 3 = 4$, $12 \div 4 = 3$

4 Assess and Differentiate

 Assess Use **eAssess** to record and analyze evidence of student understanding.

A Gather Evidence

Use the Daily Class Assessment Records in **Texas Assessment** or **eAssess** to record Informal and Formal Assessments.

Informal Assessment
☑ **Key Ideas Review** `UNDERSTANDING`

Did the student
- ❑ make important observations?
- ❑ extend or generalize learning?
- ❑ provide insightful answers?
- ❑ pose insightful questions?

Informal Assessment
☑ **Project** `APPLYING`

Did the student
- ❑ meet the project objectives?
- ❑ communicate clearly?
- ❑ complete the project accurately?
- ❑ connect mathematics to real-world situations?

Formal Assessment
☑ **Chapter Test** `COMPUTING`

Score the test, and record the results.

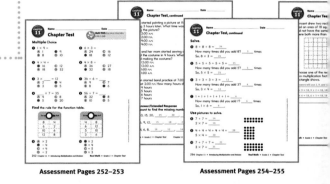

Assessment Pages 252–253   Assessment Pages 254–255

B Summarize Findings

Analyze and summarize assessment data for each student. Determine which Chapter Follow-Up is appropriate for each student. Use the Student Assessment Record in **Texas Assessment** or **eAssess** to update assessment records.

C Chapter Follow-Up • DIFFERENTIATE INSTRUCTION

Based on your observations, use these teaching strategies for chapter follow-up.

ENRICH	PRACTICE	RETEACH	INTERVENTION
If . . . students demonstrate a **secure understanding** of chapter concepts,	**If . . .** students demonstrate **competent understanding** of chapter concepts,	**If . . .** students demonstrate **emerging understanding** of chapter concepts,	**If . . .** students demonstrate **minimal understanding** of chapter concepts,
Then . . . move on to the next chapter.	**Then . . .** move on to the next chapter.	**Then . . .** move on to the next chapter, but continue to provide cumulative review.	**Then . . .** intensive intervention is still needed before they start the next chapter.

The Amazing Number Machine Makes Mistakes

Context of the Thinking Story Ferdie and Manolita use a number machine to help plan a party, but the machine keeps making mistakes.

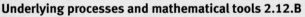

Lesson Planner

OBJECTIVES
To develop logical thinking while integrating reading skills with mathematics

 ### MATH TEKS

Number, operation, and quantitative reasoning 2.4
The student models multiplication and division.

Underlying processes and mathematical tools 2.12.B
Solve problems with guidance that incorporates the processes of understanding the problem, making a plan, carrying out the plan, and evaluating the solution for reasonableness.

ENGLISH LANGUAGE ARTS AND READING TEKS

Reading/comprehension 2.9.A
Use prior knowledge to anticipate meaning and make sense of texts.
Reading/comprehension 2.9.G
Identify similarities and differences across texts such as in topics, characters, and problems.
Reading/literary response 2.10.C
Support interpretations or conclusions with examples drawn from text.

Using the Thinking Story
The Thinking Story may be used at any time throughout the chapter. Read the Thinking Story "The Amazing Number Machine Makes Mistakes" to your class. As you read the story, give students time to think about each question, but not so much that they forget the point being made.

Number, operation, and quantitative reasoning 2.4
The student models multiplication and division.
Underlying processes and mathematical tools 2.12.B
Solve problems with guidance that incorporates the process
understanding the problem, making a plan, carrying out the
and evaluating the solution for reasonableness.

TEXAS

The Amazing Number Machine
Makes Mistakes

Ferdie decided to have a surprise party for Portia. It would be an extra-surprising surprise party because her birthday wasn't until December, and he planned to have the party in May.

How many months early will the party be?   seven

Ferdie knew it was seven months early, but once he got the idea he couldn't wait that long to have the party. The first person he invited was Manolita.

"That's a great idea, but you'll need some help to plan the party. I know just the machine for the job," said Manolita.

"Machine?" asked Ferdie. "What machine?"

"Didn't you know?" asked Manolita. "I've built an extra-special, super-duper number machine that knows everything. Anything you want to know it can tell you. If you need to know anything about a party, it can tell you that too. Let's go to my house. I'll show it to you and we can get started."

"Let's stop and get Marcus," said Ferdie.

"He's not at home right now," said Manolita. "But he might stop by my house later."

Manolita took Ferdie to the basement of her house and showed him the Amazing Number Machine. "What do you want to know first?" she asked.

"Let's figure out how much food we need. I'm inviting 15 guests, and we need two tacos for each guest."

How many tacos do they need? thirty

"Oh Amazing Number Machine," said Manolita. "We will have 15 children at the party…"

"How many tacos do we need if each child will have two?" asked Ferdie.

After a moment, a deep voice came out of the machine. "Seventeen tacos," it said.

Was the machine right? no

Did the machine add 15 and 15? no

What did the machine do? It added 15 and 2.

"It hasn't been working very well lately," said Manolita. "It seems to have a bug in it."

"Let's try it again. Oh Amazing Number Machine," said Ferdie, "fifteen guests and two tacos for each guest."

The machine answered, "Thirteen tacos."

Did the machine add this time? no

What did the machine do? It subtracted 2 from 15.

"Your machine has more than a bug in it," said Ferdie. "I can figure it out faster myself. We need 30 tacos. But the next problem is harder. Tacos come in packages of six each. I think we need six packages."

"Wait," said the machine, "give me another chance."

Manolita started, "Oh Amazing Number Machine, Ferdie thinks we need six packages of tacos to get 30 tacos. There are six tacos in a package. Is he right?"

Is Ferdie right? no

How many packages of tacos do they need? five

The machine answered in an even deeper voice, "Ferdie is wrong. Six packages of tacos makes 12 tacos."

Is the machine right? no

What did it do? It added 6 and 6.

"That silly machine added 6 and 6," said Ferdie. "That's not the way to figure out how many packages we need."

How would you figure out how many packages they need? Answers may vary. Possible answers include skip counting by 6s to get to 30 or finding what number times 6 equals 30.

"The machine is doing about as well as you are," said Manolita. "Let me figure it out. There are six tacos in a package. Six times 5 is 30. We need five packages of tacos."

Is Manolita right? yes

"I just remembered something," said Ferdie. "Two of my guests have measles. They won't be able to come to the party. I wonder how many guests will be there."

How many guests will be at the party? 13

How did you figure that out? Subtract 2 from 15.

"Give me another chance," said the machine, "that's an easy one." Ferdie decided to give the machine one more chance. "Oh Amazing Number Machine, if there are 15 guests and two can't come, how many guests will be there?"

"Thirty," answered the machine.

Did the machine subtract 2 from 15? No

What did it do? It multiplied 15 by 2.

"I'll never trust that machine again!" said Ferdie. "It added 15 and 15. It should have subtracted 2 from 15. Anyone knows that if two guests get sick you have to subtract them from the party. There will be only 13 guests."

"I don't understand what has gotten into that machine," said Manolita. "There must be something wrong with it—listen."

The children were very quiet so they could listen. Strange sounds were coming from inside the machine. They could hear wee voices talking and something that sounded like a crowd shouting in the distance.

"Let's give the machine one more chance," Manolita said. "Oh Amazing Number Machine, here is one more problem for you, and it's an easy one."

Do you have any idea what could be making noises like that? Someone is inside.

"Quiet!" said the machine. "Can't you hear that the bases are loaded and there is only one out?"

"I think I recognize that voice," Ferdie said. "Let me see what's going on here."

Ferdie lifted the lid off the machine. Inside he found Marcus holding a tiny radio to his ear. There was nothing else inside the machine.

How does the machine work? Marcus answers the questions.

"What's wrong with you today?" Manolita asked Marcus. "You always used to give good answers when you were inside the machine."

"Sorry," said Marcus. "I guess I was too busy trying to listen to a baseball game at the same time."

The End

Teaching the Lesson

Guided Discussion

As students answer the questions in the story, ask them to communicate how they chose their answers. Allow students to debate the answers if necessary.

Using Student Pages 449–450

Have students follow the instructions and complete the **Student Edition** activities. Read the instructions aloud if students are having difficulty.

Name _____ Date _____

Thinking Story

Math TEKS
Underlying processes and mathematical tools 2.12.B
Solve problems with guidance that incorporates the processes of understanding the problem, making a plan, carrying out the plan, and evaluating the solution for reasonableness.

The Amazing Number Machine
Makes Mistakes

Draw your own number machine.
Write what it does.

_____
_____
_____
_____

Textbook This lesson is available in the *eTextbook*.   449

Count how many people will be at the party.
Write the number.

8

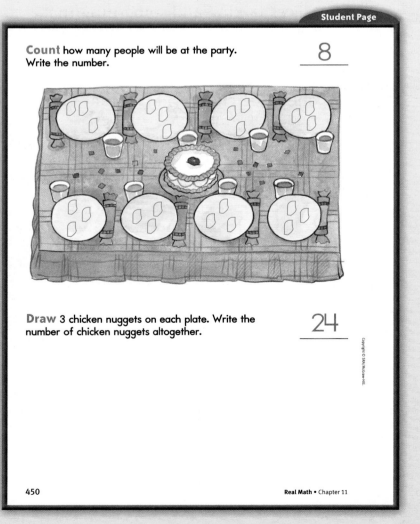

Draw 3 chicken nuggets on each plate. Write the number of chicken nuggets altogether.

24

450   **Real Math • Chapter 11**

Teacher Reflection

Reflect on each of the lessons you taught in this chapter. Rate each one on the following scale, and then consider ways to maintain or improve positive teaching experiences in the future.

Lessons	Very Effective	Effective	Less Effective	What Worked	Ways to Improve
11.1 Skip Counting and Repeated Addition					
11.2 Introduction to Multiplication					
11.3 Multiplication and Arrays					
11.4 Arrays and Area					
11.5 Using the Multiplication Table					
11.6 Applying Multiplication					
11.7 Missing Factors					
11.8 Division and Multiplication					
11.9 Division and Multiplication Functions					

★ = 120-Day Plan for TAKS

Patterns and Algebra

Teaching for Understanding

In this chapter students explore patterns and use numbers in different ways. They learn to solve problems with mixed operations and use variables. Students review the use of function machines and begin to use composite functions.

Prerequisite Skills and Concepts

- Adding Two-Digit Numbers • Recognizing Numbers That Sum to 10 and 100
- Reading Number Sentences

Patterns and Algebra Skills Trace

Before Grade 2	Grade 2	After Grade 2
Grades K–1 Introduced to patterns and functions	**This chapter** develops strategies for identifying number or shape patterns and functions and develops fluency with column addition.	Review and mastery of patterns, functions, and column addition

BIG Ideas! in Chapter 12

This chapter develops the following ideas running throughout elementary mathematics:

- Some mathematical situations have numbers that repeat in predictable ways called patterns. They can be used to identify relationships and make generalizations. Patterns of objects and numbers are the theme for chapter 12. In lessons 12.1 to 12.4 students are encouraged to recognize, describe, and extend patterns of various forms.

- Some mathematical situations have objects or numbers that repeat in predictable ways and can be generalized using algebraic expressions and equations. The use of the function machine, such as in Lessons 12.1 through 12.3, as a way of recognizing and describing patterns helps introduce students to greater algebraic thinking.

⭐ = 120-Day Plan for TAKS

Math TEKS addressed in each lesson can be found in the Chapter Planner on page 451E.

Math TEKS addressed in Problem Solving, Review, and Assessment Lessons are on page 451G.

Complete text of the standards appears on the Lesson Overview page and first Teaching page of each lesson.

TEXAS

Math Background
Patterns and Algebra

What is Algebra?

- Algebra is difficult to describe, even for mathematicians. It has been described as generalized arithmetic, and as the language of mathematics.

- Arithmetic involves the basic operations of addition, subtraction, multiplication, and division. Algebra extends arithmetic through the use of symbols and other notation. Algebraic thinking involves understanding patterns, equations, relationships, and variables.

- A variable is a letter or symbol used to stand for a number. In some situations (such as $x \div 2 = 5$) the letter stands for a specific number (in this case, 10) and is not actually variable, because it does not change. In other situations (such as $x + 8 = y$) the variables can stand for infinitely many numbers that meet the conditions of the number sentence (1 and 9, 2 and 10, 3.5 and 11.5, and so on).

- Algebra is typically offered as a full-year mathematics course in eighth or ninth grade. However, many algebraic ideas, including patterns, functions, and variables, are introduced in the early grades of **Real Math** so that students are very familiar with those topics by the time they reach middle school.

Patterns

- Patterns occur when a rule is applied repeatedly to get the next item in a series. Formally and informally recognizing numerical patterns builds toward a stronger understanding of algebraic functions and function rules.

- Skill in observing, describing, and comparing patterns in pictures and objects is important for identifying the properties of geometric figures and sets of objects or numbers. Identifying patterns and classifying objects according to their properties (attributes) allows us to separate them into groups or sets and allows us to identify the properties that are common to all members of the set. That ability becomes important in areas of mathematics as diverse as geometry and probability.

Algebra and Functions

- One-step functions (functions that perform one operation on every input number, such as adding 3 or multiplying by 5) were introduced in Kindergarten and reviewed in Grade 2 beginning in Chapter 2.

- Lesson 12.2 introduces functions that use two steps, such as "multiply by 2, then subtract 1." In later grades we refer to these as *composite functions* and model them using two function machines in a row, for which the output of the first function becomes the input of the second function.

- A two-step function in which both steps use the same operation can always be written with a single function rule. For example, the rule "add 4, then add 3" will always give the same output as the rule "add 7" because successively adding 4 and 3 is the same as adding 7.

- A two-step function in which the steps are inverse operations (addition and subtraction or multiplication and division) can also be written with a single function rule. For example, the rule "multiply by 6, then divide by 2" will always give the same output as the rule "multiply by 3," because 6 divided by 2 equals 3.

- If a two-step function rule involves multiplication or division, then addition or subtraction, it usually cannot be reduced to a single rule. For example, the rule "multiply by 1, then subtract 7" gives the same output as the rule "subtract 7," and the rule "divide by 3, then add 0" gives the same output as the rule "divide by 3."

What Research Says

About Algebraic Thinking and Functions

How Children Develop Algebraic Thinking through the Use of Functions

Learning Trajectories for Patterns, Functions and Pre-Algebraic Concepts

Algebra begins with a search for patterns. Identifying patterns helps bring order, cohesion, and predictability to seemingly unorganized situations and allows one to make generalizations beyond the information directly available. The recognition and analysis of patterns are important components of the young child's intellectual development because they provide a foundation for the development of algebraic thinking. Although prekindergarten children engage in pattern-related activities and recognize patterns in their everyday environment, research has revealed that an abstract understanding of patterns develops gradually during the early childhood years. Children typically follow an observable developmental progression in learning about patterns with recognizable stages or levels. This developmental path can be described as part of a learning trajectory. Key steps in the learning trajectory for algebra from the 2nd grade range are described below. For the complete trajectory, see Appendix B.

Level Name	Description
Pattern Maker from N	As a child develops patterning, he or she is able to fill in a missing element of pattern. For example, given objects in a row with one missing, ABBAB_ABB, identifies and fills in the missing element.
Pattern Unit Recognizer	At this level, a child can identify the smallest unit of a pattern. For example, given objects in a row with one missing, ABBAB_ABB, identifies and fills in the missing element.
Problem Solver +/−	As children develop their addition and subtraction abilities, they can solve all types of problems, with flexible strategies and many known combinations. For example, when asked, "If I have 13 and you have 9, how could we have the same number?" this child says, "Nine and one is ten, then three more to make 13. One and three is four. I need four more!"

Clements, D. H., J. Sarama, & A.-M. DiBiase, eds. *Engaging Young Children in Mathematics: Standards for Early Childhood Mathematics Education.* Mahwah, NJ: Lawrence Erlbaum Associates, 2004.

Research-Based Teaching Techniques

"The concept of function is one of the big ideas in all of mathematics. Functions are the tool used for mathematically modeling all types of real-world change. Functions can be represented in ways that lead to analysis and understanding of that change. Students experience the function concept whenever they consider how a change in one variable can cause or have a corresponding effect on another. The study of functions should focus on change relationships in contexts that are meaningful and interesting to students . . . Students should develop an understanding of the multiple methods of expressing real-world functional relationships using words, graphs, equations, and tables."

Van de Walle, John A. *Elementary and Middle School Mathematics: Teaching Developmentally,* 5th edition. Boston: Pearson Education, Inc., 2004, p. 436.

RESEARCH IN ACTION

Algebraic Thinking Chapter 12 supports the learner's development of algebraic thinking through the use of functions and variables.

Inverse Functions In Chapter 12 students will gain greater awareness of how inverse functions are function rules that undo each other; for example: addition undoes subtraction and multiplication undoes division.

Function Machines In Chapter 12 students will work with function machines to develop an appreciation of the functional relationships or rules that affect ordered pairs of numbers.

Academic Vocabulary

operation (Lesson 12.2) something done to one or more numbers to produce a single number

pattern (Lesson 12.1) repetition of shapes or numbers in a predictable way

✎**variable** (Lesson 12.7) a letter or other symbol that represents a number

English Learner

Cognates

For English learners, a quick way to acquire new English vocabulary is to build on what is known in the primary language.

English	Spanish
functions	funciones
pattern	patrón
mixed operations	operaciones mixtas
calculator	calculador
geometric figures	figuras geométricas
column	columna
variable	variable
problems	problemas

Access Vocabulary

English learners might understand words in different contexts and might not understand idioms. Review chapter vocabulary for this concern. For example:

mixed operations	two or more different operations
display	the window on the calculator where the numbers are shown
analyze	to think carefully about something
missing	something that is not where it should be
strategy	a plan of action for solving a problem

Texas Chapter Planner

Lessons	Objectives	NCTM Standards	TEXAS Math TEKS
12.1 Patterns and Functions pages 453A–454A 45–60 minutes	**To identify and complete patterns** and to identify inputs, outputs, and rules in function tables	Algebra, Representation	2.5.A 2.5.B
12.2 Functions with Mixed Operations pages 455A–456A 45–60 minutes	**To provide practice with composite functions** and to practice identifying patterns	Number and Operations, Algebra	2.6.C
12.3 More Functions with Mixed Operations pages 457A–458A 45–60 minutes	**To practice solving realistic problems** using mixed operations	Number and Operations, Algebra, Problem Solving	2.6.A 2.12.D
12.4 Patterns and Shapes pages 459A–460A 45–60 minutes	**To recognize and create patterns using plane figures** while reviewing identifying plane figures	Algebra, Geometry	2.6
12.5 Column Addition pages 465A–466A 45–60 minutes	**To review methods for adding columns of numbers**	Number and Operations	2.3
12.6 Number Sentences pages 467A–468A 45–60 minutes	**To introduce different number expressions with mixed operations that represent the same number** and to solve multistep word problems involving mixed operations	Numbers and Operations	2.13.A
12.7 Creating Word Problems pages 469A–470A 45–60 minutes	**To have students create their own word problems from number sentences** and to extract number sentences, using variables, from word problems	Number and Operations	2.12.A

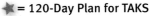 = 120-Day Plan for TAKS

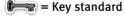 = Key standard

Academic Vocabulary	Manipulatives and Materials	Games to reinforce skills and concepts
pattern	*Number Cubes*	
operation	*Number Cubes*	
	• *Number Cubes* • Calculators (optional)	
	• *Number Cubes* • Pattern blocks	
	Number Cubes	**Roll a Problem (Three-Digit Column Addition) Game**
	Number Cubes	**Harder What's the Problem Game**
✎ variable	• *Number Cubes* • SRA Math Vocabulary Cards	

Additional Resources

Differentiated Instruction

Intervention Support Guide Provides instruction for the following prerequisite skills:

- Lesson 12.A Multidigit Addition–1
- Lesson 12.B Multidigit Addition–2
- Lesson 12.C Multidigit Addition–3

Enrichment Support Guide Extends lesson concepts

Practice Reinforces lesson skills and concepts

Reteach Support Guide Provides alternate instruction for lesson concepts

English Learner Support Guide Previews and reviews lesson concepts and vocabulary for English learners

Technology

The following electronic resources are available:

ⓔ **Planner** Lessons 12.1–12.7

ⓔ **Presentation** Lessons 12.1–12.7

ⓔ **Textbook** Lessons 12.1–12.7

ⓔ **Assess** Lessons 12.1–12.7

ⓔ **MathTools** *Function Machine* Lessons 12.1–12.3

Building Blocks *Function Machine 1* Lesson 12.1
Function Machine 2 Lesson 12.2
Function Machine 3 Lesson 12.3
Marching Patterns 3 Lesson 12.4
Word Problems with Tools 9 Lesson 12.5
Word Problems with Tools 7 Lesson 12.7

Assessment
Informal Assessment rubrics at the end of each lesson provide daily evaluation of student math proficiency.

Problem Solving	When to Use	Objectives	NCTM Standards	TEXAS Math TEKS
Problem Solving 12.A (pp. 451I–452C) 15–30 minutes	Use after the Chapter 12 Pretest.	To introduce chapter concepts in a problem-solving setting	Problem Solving, Communication	2.12.C, 2.13.A, 2.13.B
Problem Solving 12.B (pp. 461–462, 462A) 30–45 minutes	Use anytime during the chapter.	To explore methods of solving nonroutine problems	Problem Solving, Communication	2.6.C, 2.12.C
Problem Solving 12.C (pp. 471–472, 472A) 45–60 minutes	Use anytime during the chapter.	To explore methods of solving nonroutine problems	Problem Solving, Communication	2.6.C, 2.13.B
Thinking Story—Paint Up, Fix Up, Measure Up (pp. 483A–483E, 483–484) 20–30 minutes	Use anytime during the chapter.	To develop logical reasoning while integrating reading skills with mathematics	Number and Operations, Connections	2.3.C, 2.12.C

Review	When to Use	Objectives	NCTM Standards	Math TEKS
Cumulative Review (p. 463–464) 15–30 minutes	Use anytime after Lesson 12.4.	To review concepts and skills taught earlier in the year	Number and Operations	2.3.B, 2.5.A, 2.10.B, 2.12
Cumulative Review (p. 473–474) 15–30 minutes	Use anytime after Lesson 12.7.	To review concepts and skills taught earlier in the year	Number and Operations	2.3, 2.11.B, 2.13.A
Chapter 12 Review (pp. 477A, 477–478) 30–45 minutes	Use anytime after Lesson 12.7.	To review concepts and skills taught in the chapter	Number and Operations	2.3, 2.6, 2.6.A, 2.6.C, 2.13.A

Assessment	When to Use	Objectives	NCTM Standards	Math TEKS
Pretest (*Assessment* p. 132–133) 15–30 minutes	Entry Use prior to Chapter 12.	To provide assessment of chapter topics	Number and Operations, Problem Solving	2.3, 2.5.A, 2.5.B, 2.6, 2.6.A, 2.6.C, 2.12.A, 2.12.D, 2.13.A
Informal Assessment Rubrics (pp. 158–159 to 181–182) 5 minutes per student	Progress Monitoring Use at the end of each lesson.	To provide daily evaluation of math proficiency	Number and Operations, Communication	2.3, 2.5.A, 2.5.B, 2.6, 2.6.A, 2.6.C, 2.12.A, 2.12.D, 2.13.A
Individual Oral Assessment (p. 464A) 5 minutes per student	Progress Monitoring Use after Lesson 12.4.	To provide alternate means of assessing students' progress	Number and Operations	1.3.A, 2.3, 2.4, 2.5.A, 2.6, 3.3.A
Mastery Checkpoint (*Assessment* p. 98–99) 15 minutes	Progress Monitoring Use in or after Lesson 12.5.	To provide assessment of mastery of key skills	Number and Operations	2.3, 2.6.C
Chapter 12 Practice Test (pp. 479–480, 481–482) 30–45 minutes	Progress Monitoring Use after or in place of the Chapter 12 Review.	To provide assessment or additional practice of the chapter concepts	Number and Operations, Problem Solving	2.3, 2.5.A, 2.5.B, 2.6, 2.6.A, 2.6.C, 2.12.A, 2.12.D, 2.13.A
Chapter 12 Test (*Assessment* pp. 256–259) 30–45 minutes	Summative Use after or in place of the Chapter 12 Review.	To provide assessment of the chapter concepts	Number and Operations, Problem Solving	2.3, 2.5.A, 2.5.B, 2.6, 2.6.A, 2.6.C, 2.12.A, 2.12.D, 2.13.A

Texas Technology Resources

Visit SRAonline.com for online versions of the *Real Math* eSuite.

TEXAS Technology for Teachers

e Presentation	**Lessons 12.1–12.7** Use the *ePresentation* to interactively present chapter content.
e Planner	Use the Chapter and Lesson Planners to outline activities and time frames for Chapter 12.
e Assess	Students can take the following assessments in *eAssess:* • Chapter Pretest • Mastery Checkpoint **Lesson 12.5** • Chapter Test Teachers can record results and print reports for all assessments in this chapter.
e MathTools	Function Machine **Lessons 12.1, 12.2, 12.3**

TEXAS Technology for Students

e Textbook	An electronic, interactive version of the *Student Edition* is available for all lessons in Chapter 12.
e MathTools	Function Machine **Lessons 12.1, 12.2, 12.3**
TECH KNOWLEDGE	*TechKnowledge* Level 2 provides lessons that specifically teach the Unit 10 Internet and Unit 7 Spreadsheet applications that students can use in this chapter's project.
Building Blocks	Function Machine 1 **Lesson 12.1** Function Machine 2 **Lesson 12.2** Function Machine 3 **Lesson 12.3** Marching Patterns 3 **Lesson 12.4** Word Problems with Tools 9 **Lesson 12.5** Word Problems with Tools 7 **Lesson 12.7**

Patterns and Algebra

Introduce Chapter 12 10

Chapter Objectives

Explain to students that in this chapter they will build on what they already know about patterns. Explain that is this chapter they will

- create and extend patterns.
- create word problems.

Pretest COMPUTING

Administer the Chapter 12 Pretest, which has similar exercises to the Chapter 12 Test.

- If most students do not demonstrate mastery on the Pretest, proceed at a normal pace through the chapter. Use the differentiated instruction suggestions at the beginning and end of each lesson to adapt instruction and follow-up to the needs of each student.
- If most students show mastery of some or all of the concepts and skills in Chapter 12, move quickly through the chapter, de-emphasizing lessons linked to items which most students answered correctly. Use the *Individual Oral Assessments* to monitor progress, and, if necessary, modify your pacing. The oral assessments are especially useful because they can help you distinguish among different levels of understanding. For example, a student who has mastered a particular skill but does not show a deep understanding of the relevant concepts still needs thorough coverage of the lesson material.
- If you do move quickly through the chapter, be sure not to skip games, Problem Solving lessons, and Thinking Stories. These provide practice in skills and nonroutine thinking that will be useful even to students who already understand the chapter content. Also, be alert to application problems embedded within lessons that may show students how math topics are used in daily life.

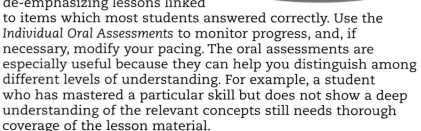

Chapter 12 Pretest

Access Prior Knowledge UNDERSTANDING

As students look at the photograph on page 451 and the diagram on page 452, ask questions such as the following:

- Have you ever seen a village or building like the one in the photo?
- How would you describe the shape of this building?

■ **The diagram gives you an idea of the inside of the building. Why do you think a diagram like this is called a *cross section*?** It shows the section you would see if you cut through it.

Share with students the following information about Native American pueblos:

- Pueblos are ancient Native American villages consisting of buildings made of adobe (earth mixed with water and straw).
- The flat-roofed buildings are made up of many individual homes, built side by side and often stacked.
- In earlier days there were no doors or windows, and people entered only from the top.
- Many pueblos are still occupied today by Native Americans in New Mexico and Arizona.
- Pueblos are considered nations with their own governments, courts, police forces, and school systems. Each pueblo has its own traditional ceremonial activities.

Problem Solving 12.A Introducing Strategies

Tell Students In Today's Lesson They Will

- build and draw their own stair-step patterns.
- describe their patterns so someone else can make it.

Materials

- Linking or snap cubes (40 to 50 per student or pair of students)
- Graph paper
- Crayons or markers

See Appendix A page A24 for instruction and rubric for problem solving.

Guided Discussion UNDERSTANDING

Have students share what they know about Native American homes and talk about what they see in the picture of the pueblo. During the discussion write a list on the board of the words or phrases students use to describe the shape of the pueblo. Guide students by asking questions such as the following:

■ **When you look at the cross section of the pueblo, what do you see?** steps going up; rooms going up; the building getting taller; stacks of rooms; and so on

■ **When you look from left to right, what is the first thing you see?** one room

■ **What do you see next?** two rooms, one stacked on top of the other

■ **What do you see next?** three rooms, one stacked on top of the other

■ **If the stacks kept going this way, what would happen?** There would be four rooms in the next stack; the building would

TEXAS

Underlying processes and mathematical tools 2.13.A
Explain and record observations using objects, words, pictures, numbers, and technology.
Underlying processes and mathematical tools 2.13.B
Relate informal language to mathematical language and symbols

Underlying processes and mathematical tools 2.12.C
Select or develop an appropriate problem-solving plan or strategy including drawing a picture, looking for a pattern, systematic guessing and checking, or acting it out in order to solve a problem.

get taller and taller; there would be many more rooms in the pueblo.

Tell students that an archaeologist is a scientist who studies the people, customs, and life of ancient times. Present this problem:

You are an archaeologist studying ancient pueblos. You notice a stair-step pattern when you look at a cross section of a pueblo. You wonder if you might find other stair-step patterns in ancient homes, so you decide to experiment with different ways the patterns might look. How might you build and describe other kinds of stair-step patterns?

Strategy Building REASONING

Tell students that they are going to use cubes and graph paper to construct and draw their own stair-step patterns. Then they are going to describe their pattern in writing so someone else can build it.

To make sure students understand the problem, ask questions such as the following:

■ **What are you supposed to do?** make a stair-step pattern with cubes and then draw it and write a description of it
■ **How could you make a stair-step pattern with cubes?** You could use different heights of towers or bars of cubes put side by side so it looks like a stair step.
■ **How can the graph paper help you?** You can try drawing different stair-step patterns on it.

■ **Does a stair-step pattern always get bigger?** No, it can start big and get smaller; it can start small and get bigger; it can get bigger and then get smaller again.
■ **Does a stair-step pattern always have to go up or down by 1 with each step?** No, it could go up or down by more than 1. It can go up or down by different quantities with each step.

Give students access to the cubes and graph paper. Have them work alone or with a partner to create a stair-step pattern. Students draw their patterns on the grid on page 452 and then describe the pattern on the same page. If students have included color as part of their patterns, encourage them to include descriptions of the color pattern as well.

If students have difficulty describing their patterns, ask questions such as the following:

■ **How could you describe the stair-step pattern we see in the cross section?** It goes up 1 each time; it goes over 1 and up 1.
■ **How could you describe a stair-step pattern that starts with one room but then goes to three stacked rooms and then 5 stacked rooms?** It goes up 2 each time; it goes over 1 and up 2.

Have students read their descriptions of their patterns to each other and try to build each other's stair-step patterns. Remind students that if someone is not building the pattern correctly, they may need to revise the description to make it clearer. Keep in mind that communicating precisely is difficult and is a skill that continues to develop over time.

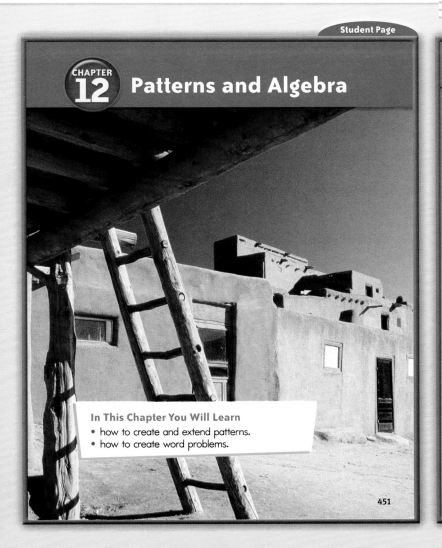

Student Page

CHAPTER 12 Patterns and Algebra

In This Chapter You Will Learn
• how to create and extend patterns.
• how to create word problems.

451

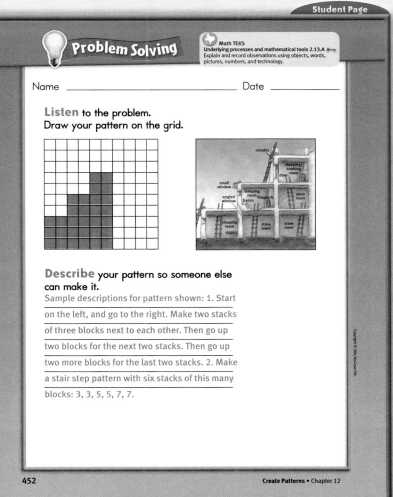

Student Page

💡 **Problem Solving**

Math TEKS
Underlying processes and mathematical tools 2.13.A
Explain and record observations using objects, words, pictures, numbers, and technology.

Name _____ Date _____

Listen to the problem.
Draw your pattern on the grid.

Describe your pattern so someone else can make it.
Sample descriptions for pattern shown: 1. Start on the left, and go to the right. Make two stacks of three blocks next to each other. Then go up two blocks for the next two stacks. Then go up two more blocks for the last two stacks. 2. Make a stair step pattern with six stacks of this many blocks: 3, 3, 5, 5, 7, 7.

452

Create Patterns • Chapter 12

Concept/Question Board APPLYING

Questions
Have students think of and write three questions they have about patterns and algebra and how they can be used. Then have them select one question to post on the Question side of the Board.

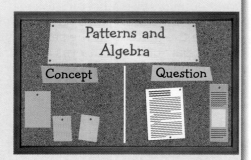

Patterns and Algebra

Concept   Question

Concepts
As students work through the chapter, have them collect examples of how patterns and algebra are used in everyday situations. For each example, have them write a problem that relates to the item(s). Have them display their examples on the Concept side of the Board. Suggest the following:

- gardens
- music

Answers
Throughout the chapter, have students post answers to the questions and solutions to the problems on the Board.

Home Connection

At this time, you may want to send home the letter on pages 46–49 of **Home Connection.** This letter describes what students will be learning and what activities they can do at home to support their work in school.

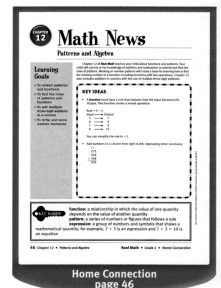

Home Connection page 46

Reflect   20

 Knowledge Age Skills

Effective Communication Have students display and discuss their stair-step patterns. Ask questions such as the following:

■ **How did you use numbers and words to help other students make your pattern?**

■ **What changes did you have to make in your description or in your pattern? Why?**

In discussion, also bring out these points:

- Numbers can help you describe some things more clearly.
- The greater the change is in the pattern from one step to the next, the steeper the steps are.
- Even though patterns involve change, there should be something that stays the same about the way things change in the pattern. In a pattern, someone should be able to see or figure out what comes next or what came before.

Assess and Differentiate

 Assess Use *eAssess* to record and analyze evidence of student understanding.

A Gather Evidence

Use the Daily Class Assessment Records in *Texas Assessment* or *eAssess* to record Informal and Formal Assessments.

Informal Assessment	**Informal Assessment**	**Formal Assessment**
☑ **Access Prior Knowledge**	☑ **Concept/Question Board**	☑ **Pretest** COMPUTING
Did the student UNDERSTANDING	Did the student APPLYING	Review student answers on the Chapter 12 Pretest.
❑ make important observations?	❑ apply learning in new situations?	❑ If most students do not demonstrate mastery, move at a normal pace through the chapter.
❑ extend or generalize learning?	❑ contribute concepts?	❑ If most students answer most questions correctly, move quickly through the chapter, emphasizing those lessons for which students did not answer correctly, as well as games, Problem-Solving lessons, and Thinking Stories.
❑ provide insightful answers?	❑ contribute answers?	
❑ pose insightful questions?	❑ connect mathematics to real-world situations?	

B Summarize Findings

Analyze and summarize assessment data for each student. Determine which Assessment Follow-Up is appropriate for each student. Use the Student Assessment Record in *Texas Assessment* or *eAssess* to update assessment records.

C Texas Assessment Follow-Up ● DIFFERENTIATE INSTRUCTION

Based on your observations of each student, use these teaching strategies for a general approach to the chapter. Look for specific Differentiate Instruction and Monitoring Student Progress strategies in each lesson that relate specifically to the lesson content.

ENRICH	**PRACTICE**	**RETEACH**	**INTERVENTION**	**ENGLISH LEARNER**
If . . . students demonstrate a **secure understanding** of chapter concepts, **Then . . .** move quickly through the chapter or use *Enrichment* Lessons 12.1–12.7 as assessment follow-up to extend and apply understanding.	**If . . .** students grasp chapter concepts with **competent understanding**, **Then . . .** use *Practice* Lessons 12.1–12.7 as lesson follow-up to develop fluency.	**If . . .** students have prerequisite understanding but demonstrate **emerging understanding** of chapter concepts, **Then . . .** use *Reteach* Lessons 12.1 and 12.4 to reteach lesson concepts.	**If . . .** students are not competent with prerequisite skills, **Then . . .** use *Intervention* Lessons 12.A–12.C before each lesson to develop fluency with prerequisite skills.	Use *English Learner Support Guide* Lessons 12.1–12.7 for strategies to preteach lesson vocabulary and concepts.

Math Across the Curriculum

Preview the chapter projects with students. Assign projects or have students choose from the projects to extend and enrich concepts in this chapter.

Compare Native American Homes 3–4 weeks

SOCIAL STUDIES WebQuest

TEKS

MATH STANDARD: Patterns, relationships, and algebraic thinking 2.6 The student uses patterns to describe relationships and make predictions.

CROSS CURRICULAR STANDARD (SOCIAL STUDIES): Geography 2.7.B Explain how people depend on the physical environment and its natural resources to satisfy their basic needs.

TECHNOLOGY STANDARD: Solving Problems 08.B Use electronic tools and research skills to build a knowledge base regarding a topic, task, or assignment.

For this project, students use the Internet to investigate the following information about historical Native American homes:

- regions in which historical Native American homes are located
- different types of historical Native American homes
- materials used for building and design features

For specific step-by-step instructions for this project, see *Across the Curriculum Math Connections* pages 122–127.

Compare Native American Homes

Activity 1

Careers in Math

Anthropologists are scientists who study people. They examine the details that make up everyday life in a society, such as language, food, politics, and religion. They may study the ways of life, archaeological remains, languages, or physical characteristics of people in various parts of the world. Anthropologists use scientific research methods and math to collect and analyze data.

Creative Work with Ideas Students take on the role of an author to provide information.

Effective Communication Students organize research for comparisons.

 **TechKnowledge** Level 2 provides lessons that specifically teach the Unit 10 Internet and Unit 7 Spreadsheet applications that students can use in this project.

Create a Frontier Album Quilt 3–4 weeks

 ART

TEKS

MATH STANDARD: Patterns, relationships, and algebraic thinking 2.6.C Identify, describe, and extend repeating and additive patterns to make predictions and solve problems.

CROSS CURRICULAR STANDARD (FINE ARTS): Perception 2.1.B Identify art elements such as color, texture, form, line, and space and art principles such as emphasis, pattern, and rhythm.

TECHNOLOGY STANDARD: Communication 10.B Use font attributes, color, white space, and graphics to ensure that products are appropriate for the communication media including multimedia screen displays and printed materials.

Have students use mathematics to create a frontier album quilt. To broaden the fine arts concept, have students incorporate elements of pattern you are currently studying.

As part of the project, students should consider the following issues:

- frontier life
- number patterns in quilts
- patterns in the design of a quilt square
- copying and pasting objects in a drawing and graphics document

Create a Frontier Album Quilt

Activity 2

Profiles in Math

Western American settlers brought with them quilting traditions that they shared with Native American tribes. Southwestern Hopi artists took traditional patterns and designs from their pottery and basket weaving and applied them to quilting. Bonnie Nampeyo Chapella, who comes from a family of famous Hopi potters, is an example of a quilter who uses traditional Hopi designs in her quilts.

For specific step-by-step instructions for this project, see *Across the Curriculum Math Connections* pages 128–131.

Teamwork Students work together to create number-pattern quilts.

Group Assessment Students evaluate their work on their group's project.

Grade 1
1.4
The student uses repeating patterns and additive patterns to make predictions.

Grade 2
2.5.A
Find patterns in numbers such as in a 100s chart.

Grade 3
3.6.A
Identify and extend whole-number and geometric patterns to make predictions and solve problems.

Overview

LESSON 12.1

Lesson Planner

OBJECTIVES
- To identify and complete patterns
- To identify inputs, outputs, and rules in function tables

MATH TEKS

Patterns, relationships, and algebraic thinking 2.5.A
Find patterns in numbers such as in a 100s chart.

Patterns, relationships, and algebraic thinking 2.5.B
Use patterns in place value to compare and order whole numbers through 999.

MATH TEKS INTEGRATION
Number, operation, and quantitative reasoning 2.1.C Use place value to compare and order whole numbers to 999 and record the comparisons using numbers and symbols ($<$, $=$, $>$).

Underlying processes and mathematical tools 2.12.A
Identify the mathematics in everyday situations.

MATERIALS
*Number Cubes

TECHNOLOGY
Presentation Lesson 12.1
MathTools Function Machine
Building Blocks Function Machine 1

Patterns and Functions ⭐

Context of the Lesson In this lesson students examine number sequences to find patterns using all previously learned numerical operations. Students also review function tables, which have been used throughout Grade 2 of *Real Math*.

See page 451B for Math Background for teachers for this lesson.

Planning for Learning ● **DIFFERENTIATE INSTRUCTION**

INTERVENTION

If . . . students lack the prerequisite skill of recognizing numbers that sum to 10 and 100,

Then . . . teach *Intervention* Lesson 12.B.

1.3.A, 1.5.D

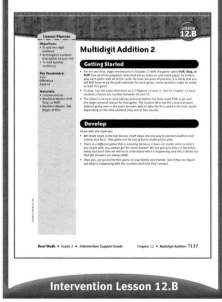

Intervention Lesson 12.B

ENGLISH LEARNER

Preview

If . . . students need language support,

Then . . . use Lesson 12.1 in *English Learner Support Guide* to preview lesson concepts and vocabulary.

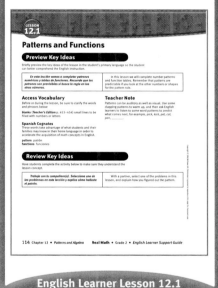

English Learner Lesson 12.1

ENRICH

If . . . students are proficient in the lesson concepts,

Then . . . emphasize exploring *eMathTools*.

PRACTICE

If . . . students would benefit from additional practice,

Then . . . extend Skill Practice before assigning the student pages.

RETEACH

If . . . students are having difficulty understanding number patterns,

Then . . . extend Skill Building before assigning the student pages.

Academic Vocabulary
pattern \pat ´ərn\ *n.* repetition of shapes or numbers in a predictable way

Spanish Cognates
functions funciones

pattern patrón

Patterns, relationships, and algebraic thinking 2.5.A Find patterns in numbers such as in a 100s chart.
Patterns, relationships, and algebraic thinking 2.5.B Use patterns in place value to compare and order whole numbers through 999.

Mental Math 5

THUMBS UP

INTEGRATION: TEKS 2.1.C Present students with inequalities, and have them use thumbs-up (greater than), thumbs-down (less than), or open hand (equal to) to show their answers. Possible examples include the following:

a. 12 − 6 ◯ 7 down
b. 13 − 4 ◯ 9 open hand
c. 3 + 7 ◯ 9 up
d. 7 + 9 ◯ 8 + 8 open hand
e. 15 − 7 ◯ 12 − 5 up
f. 13 − 7 ◯ 3 + 3 open hand

1 Develop 20

Tell Students In Today's Lesson They Will

complete number patterns and work with function tables.

Skill Building APPLYING

 Introductory

Write the following number pattern on the board: 1, 2, 4, 5, 7, 8, 10, 11, 13, _14_, _16_, _17_, _19_, _20_, 22. Discuss how to find the pattern in this series of numbers. Write the students' suggestions beneath each number. Students should see that the pattern for the first nine numbers looks like this: +1 +2 +1 +2 +1 +2 +1 +2.

After students have determined the pattern from the given numbers, they can use the pattern to fill in the blanks. Point out that because the last number is given, they can check to see whether they are correct.

Skill Practice COMPUTING

  Introductory

Write patterns on the board, and have students show the missing number. Make sure to include the last number so students can check that they are correct. Possible exercises include the following:

a. 6, 12, 18, _24_, 30
b. 4, 8, 12, _16_, 20
c. 65, 60, 55, _50_, 45
d. 90, 81, 72, _63_, 54

2 Use Student Pages 20

Pages 453–454 UNDERSTANDING   Independent

Work through the first pattern on page 453 with the class just as you did in Skill Building.

Have students complete the rest of page 453 and page 454 individually.

Progress Monitoring

If . . . students see a pattern that is different from the answer in the book, : **Then . . .** ask them to explain their pattern. Commend them if they have a logical reason for their pattern.

As Students Finish

Game Allow students to play a game of choice, or assign games based on needed skill practice.

 MathTools *Function Machine* Have students review function machines.

Building Blocks Have students use *Function Machine 1* to practice functions.

RESEARCH IN ACTION

"Algebra begins with a search for patterns. Identifying patterns helps bring order, cohesion, and predictability to seemingly unorganized situations and allows one to make generalizations beyond the information directly available. The recognition and analysis of patterns are important components of the young child's intellectual development because they provide a foundation for the development of algebraic thinking."

Clements, Douglas and J. Sarama, eds. *Engaging Young Children in Mathematics: Standards for Early Childhood Mathematics Education.* Mahwah, New Jersey: Lawrence Erlbaum Associates Publishers, 2004, p. 52.

Student Page

LESSON 12.1 Patterns and Functions

Key Ideas

Patterns occur often in the world around us. When you recognize a pattern, you can figure out what comes next.

 Math TEKS
Patterns, relationships, and algebraic thinking 2.5.B
Use patterns in place value in numbers such as in a 100s chart.

Find the patterns. Fill in the blanks.

1. 30, 27, 24, 21, 18, 15, __12__, __9__, __6__, __3__, 0
2. 100, 95, 90, 85, __80__, __75__, __70__, __65__, __60__, __55__, 50
3. 7, 14, 21, 28, __35__, __42__, __49__, __56__, __63__, 70
4. 70, 63, 56, 49, __42__, __35__, __28__, __21__, __14__, __7__, 0
5. 3, 6, 9, 7, 10, 13, 11, __14__, __17__, __15__, __18__, 21
6. 2, 4, 6, 5, 7, 9, 8, 10, __12__, __11__, __13__, __15__, __14__, 16
7. 20, 17, 14, 16, 13, 10, 12, __9__, __6__, __8__, __5__, 2

Textbook This lesson is available in the *eTextbook*.

453

LESSON 12.1 · Patterns and Functions

Fill in the blanks.

8. in → +4 → out

3	7
10	14
0	4
20	24

9. in → -5 → out

10	5
14	9
23	18
5	0

What is the rule? Write it in the box.

10. in → ○ → out

7	9
10	12
81	83

The rule is __+2__.

11. in → ○ → out

70	60
40	30
27	17

The rule is __−10__.

 **Journal**

How are patterns useful when you are trying to solve a problem? **See Reflect**

454 **Real Math** • Chapter 12 • Lesson 1

---

3 Reflect 10

Guided Discussion REASONING

1. Discuss the patterns on student page 453. Write the following pattern on the board:

   11, 13, ____, 17, 19, ____, ____, 25, ____

   ■ **What numbers go in the blanks?** 15, 21, 23, 27

Discuss that because the last number is not given, students have no way of checking the answer to make sure they are correct. For example, the last number could be a 24, which would make the pattern +2, +2, +2, +2, +2, +2, +2, −1.

Have students make a rule for this sequence of numbers and extend the pattern an additional eight numbers. Then have them share sequences and try to guess each others' patterns.

Integration: TEKS 2.12.A

2. Ask students to identify some nonmathematical patterns that occur in their everyday lives. Possible examples include:

   • The sun rises every morning and sets every evening.
   • School classes follow a schedule.
   • The days of the week repeat.

 Journal

Students should recognize that after a pattern in a problem has been identified, one can often predict what will happen next.

TEXAS TEKS Checkup

Patterns, relationships, and algebraic thinking 2.5.A • Find patterns in numbers such as in a 100s chart.
Use this problem to assess students' progress toward standards mastery:
Find the pattern.
48, 42, 36, 30

A +6   C ×3
B ÷2   **D** −6

Have students choose the correct answer and then describe how they knew which choice was correct. In the discussion, ask questions such as the following. Be sure to ask students to explain their reasoning because

different solution methods are possible.

■ **Is 48 greater or less than 42?** greater
■ **What is 48 − 42?** 6
■ **Is 42 − 36 also 6?** yes
■ **What is the pattern for the four numbers shown?** −6

Follow-Up
If...students have difficulty finding patterns,

Then...have students explore *Building Blocks: Function Machine 1.*

 **4 Assess and Differentiate**

 Assess Use *eAssess* to record and analyze evidence of student understanding.

A Gather Evidence

Use the Daily Class Assessment Records in *Texas Assessment* or *eAssess* to record daily observations.

Informal Assessment
☑ **Skill Practice**

Did the student **COMPUTING**
❏ respond accurately?
❏ respond quickly?
❏ respond with confidence?
❏ self-correct?

Portfolio Assessment
☑ **Journal**

Did the student **APPLYING**
❏ apply learning in new situations?
❏ contribute concepts?
❏ contribute answers?
❏ connect mathematics to real-world situations?

 **TEKS/TAKS Practice**

Use *TEKS/TAKS Practice* pages 39–42 to assess student progress.

B Summarize Findings

Analyze and summarize assessment data for each student. Determine which Assessment Follow-Up is appropriate for each student. Use the Student Assessment Record in *Texas Assessment* or *Assess* to update assessment records.

C Texas Assessment Follow-Up • DIFFERENTIATE INSTRUCTION

Based on your observations, use these teaching strategies for assessment follow-up.

INTERVENTION

Review student performance on *Intervention* Lesson 12.B to see if students have mastered prerequisite skills for this lesson.

Number, operation, and quantitative reasoning 1.3. A Model and create addition and subtraction problem situations with concrete objects and write corresponding number sentences.

ENGLISH LEARNER

Review

Use Lesson 12.1 in *English Learner Support Guide* to review lesson concepts and vocabulary.

ENRICH

If . . . students are proficient in the lesson concepts,

Then . . . encourage them to work on the chapter projects or *Enrichment* Lesson 12.1.

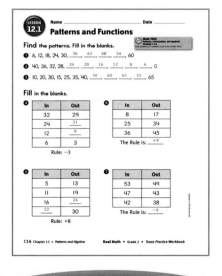

Enrichment Lesson 12.1

PRACTICE

If . . . students would benefit from additional practice,

Then . . . assign *Practice* Lesson 12.1.

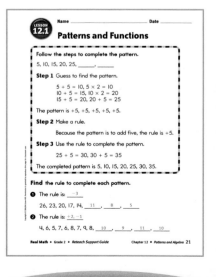

Practice Lesson 12.1

RETEACH

If . . . students are having difficulty understanding number patterns,

Then . . . reteach the concept using *Reteach* Lesson 12.1.

Reteach Lesson 12.1

OBJECTIVES
- To provide practice identifying patterns
- To provide practice with basic operations using function tables
- To identify and demonstrate the use of composite functions (functions involving more than one operation)

MATH TEKS
Patterns, relationships, and algebraic thinking 2.6.C Identify, describe, and extend repeating and additive patterns to make predictions and solve problems.

MATH TEKS INTEGRATION
Number, operation, and quantitative reasoning 2.3.A Recall and apply basic addition and subtraction facts (to 18).

Patterns, relationships, and algebraic thinking 2.5.C Use patterns and relationships to develop strategies to remember basic addition and subtraction facts. Determine patterns in related addition and subtraction number sentences (including fact families) such as $8 + 9 = 17, 9 + 8 = 17, 17 - 8 = 9$, and $17 - 9 = 8$.

MATERIALS
*Number Cubes

TECHNOLOGY
- Ⓔ Presentation Lesson 12.2
- Ⓔ MathTools Function Machine
- Building Blocks Function Machine 2

TEXAS Vertical Alignment

Grade 1	Grade 2	Grade 3
1.5.D Use patterns to develop strategies to solve basic addition and basic subtraction problems.	**2.6.C** Identify, describe, and extend repeating and additive patterns to make predictions and solve problems.	**3.7.B** Identify and describe patterns in a table of related number pairs based on a meaningful problem and extend the table.

Overview **LESSON 12.2**

Functions with Mixed Operations ★

Context of the Lesson In this lesson students will have the opportunity to create rules for the function tables using a variety of operations, including addition, subtraction, multiplication, and division.
See page 451B for Math Background for teachers for this lesson.

Planning for Learning ● DIFFERENTIATE INSTRUCTION

INTERVENTION
If . . . students lack the prerequisite skill of reading number sentences,

Then . . . teach *Intervention* Lesson 12.C.

1.3.A, 1.5.D

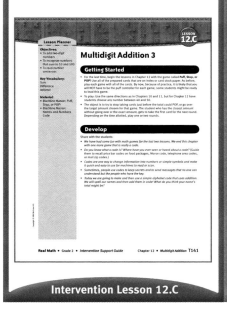

Intervention Lesson 12.C

ENGLISH LEARNER
Preview

If . . . students need language support,

Then . . . use Lesson 12.2 in *English Learner Support Guide* to preview lesson concepts and vocabulary.

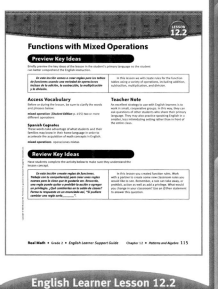

English Learner Lesson 12.2

ENRICH
If . . . students are proficient in the lesson concepts,

Then . . . emphasize exploring *eMathTools*.

PRACTICE
If . . . students would benefit from additional practice,

Then . . . extend Guided Discussion before assigning the student pages.

RETEACH
If . . . students are having difficulty understanding mixed operations,

Then . . . extend Guided Discussion before assigning the student pages.

Academic Vocabulary
operation \op´ə rā´shən\ *n.* something done to one or more numbers to produce a single number

Access Vocabulary
mixed operations two or more different operations

Spanish Cognates
mixed operations operaciones mixtas

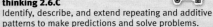

Patterns, relationships, and algebraic thinking 2.6.C
Identify, describe, and extend repeating and additive patterns to make predictions and solve problems.

Mental Math 5

INTEGRATION: TEKS 2.3.A Present students with addition and subtraction exercises, and have them use their **Number Cubes** to show their answers. Possible examples include the following:

a. $13 - 1 = 12$ **b.** $15 + 4 = 19$ **c.** $5 + 9 = 14$ **d.** $7 + 11 = 18$
e. $19 - 6 = 13$ **f.** $11 - 6 = 5$ **g.** $14 - 7 = 7$ **h.** $17 - 10 = 7$

1 Develop 15

Tell Students In Today's Lesson They Will

learn about and use mixed operations.

Guided Discussion UNDERSTANDING

Introductory

 Integration: TEKS 2.5.C

Introduce students to mixed operations. Have students suggest several ways to get from 6 to 11 using addition and subtraction. Guide them to see that they can use a variety of operations, just as they did when they wrote different number sentences with the same solution.

Surround the fist half of the Guided Discussion with a blue frame. Begin frame at the first sentence that reads, "Introduce students to mixed..." and end the blue frame at the sentence that ends with, "...only one operation. +5"

Some possible answers include:

- $6 + 7 - 2$
- $6 + 8 - 3$
- $6 - 3 + 8$

Have students then find a rule that would involve only one operation. +5

Have students practice mixed operations using a function machine table. Copy the following table on the board:

3	6
4	8
5	10

Tell students the rule for this table is $\times 4 \div 2$. Work the problems with the students. Then ask:

■ **Critical Thinking** **How can we simplify this rule and still make it work for the table on the board?** Students should see that $\times 2$ will give the same results.

Repeat the procedure using a different mixed operation.

2 Use Student Pages 15

Pages 455–456 APPLYING

Guided

Divide students into pairs and have them work together to complete the problems on student pages 455 and 456.

As Students Finish

MathTools *Function Machine* Have students use this tool to explore functions with mixed operations.

Building Blocks *Function Machine 2*

RESEARCH IN ACTION

"The relationship among patterns, functions, and algebra is not necessarily obvious. Patterns involve real or potential repetitions (audio, visual, tactile, numeric, and so on). Algebra in its traditional school form involves rules for manipulating symbols. A function, according to the definition all students must memorize, is a particular kind of mapping from one set to another."

Smith, Erik. "Stasis and Change: Integrating Patterns, Functions, and Algebra Throughout the K-12 Curriculum." in Kilpatrick, Jeremy, W. Gary Martin, and Deborah Schifter, eds. *A Research Companion to Principles and Standards for School Mathematics.* Reston, VA: National Council of Teachers of Mathematics, Inc. 2003, p. 136.

TEXAS TEKS Checkup

Patterns, relationships, and algebraic thinking 2.6.A • Generate a list of paired numbers based on a real-life situation such as number of tricycles related to number of wheels.

Use this problem to assess students' progress toward standards mastery:

Which table of pairs shows the number of legs on one grasshopper, two grasshoppers, three grasshoppers, and four grasshoppers?

A
1	6
6	12
12	18
24	24

C
6	4
12	3
18	2
24	1

B
1	6
2	12
3	18
4	24

D
1	3
2	6
3	9
4	12

Patterns, relationships, and algebraic thinking 2.6.B • Identify patterns in a list of related number pairs based on a real-life situation and extend the list.

Use this problem to assess students' progress toward standards mastery:

How many legs would be on 8 grasshoppers?

(A) 48   **C** 54
B 42   **D** 60

Have students choose the correct answer and then describe how they knew which choice was correct. In the discussion, ask questions such as the following. Be sure to ask students to explain their reasoning because different solution methods are possible.

■ **How did you find the answer?**
8×6

Follow-Up
If...students have difficulty solving problems involving patterns,

Then...reteach the lesson using *Reteach* Lesson 12.1.

TEXAS — Statistics, Data Analysis, and Probability 2.0
Students demonstrate an understanding of patterns and how patterns grow and describe them in general ways.

Functions with Mixed Operations

LESSON 12.2

Student Page

Name _____ Date _____

LESSON 12.2 · Functions with Mixed Operations

Key Ideas

A mixed operation is an expression that uses more than one **operation**.

$3 + 8 - 4$ is a mixed operation because it uses addition and subtraction.

$3 + 8 - 4 = 7$

Math TEKS
Patterns, relationships, and algebraic thinking 2.6.C
Identify, describe, and extend repeating and additive patterns to make predictions and solve problems.

Follow the directions.

❶ Kevin is making hard function problems. His rule is $+9 -4$. Fill in the missing numbers.

❷ Write what is difficult about Kevin's problem.

One possible response is that there are two operations to perform.

❸ Write what is easy about Kevin's problem.

One possible response is the rule can be simplified to $+5$.

8	13
20	25
3	8
10	15

❹ Lorena is also making hard function problems. Her rule is $\times 3 -1$. Fill in the missing numbers.

❺ Write what is hard about Lorena's problem.

One possible response is that there are two operations to perform.

❻ Write what is easy about Lorena's problem.

One possible response is that the -1 operation is easy.

3	8
10	29
4	11
2	5

Textbook This lesson is available in the *eTextbook*.

455

Find the mixed operation function.

❼
4	7
5	9
6	11
7	13

The rule is ___$\times 2 -1$___.

❽
6	13
7	15
8	17
9	19

The rule is ___$\times 2 +1$___.

Make your own mixed operation functions. Challenge a friend to solve them. Answers will vary.

❾

The rule is _____.

❿

The rule is _____.

⓫

The rule is _____.

⓬

The rule is _____.

456

Real Math • Chapter 12 • Lesson 2

---

3 Reflect

5

Guided Discussion ✓ REASONING

Ask students,

■ **Which kind of mixed function rules can usually be simplified, and which can't? Give examples.**

In general if the rules involve only addition and subtraction or only multiplication and division, they can be simplified. For example, $+3 -2$ or $\times 4 \div 2$ can be simplified. But when multiplication or division is mixed with addition or subtraction, we can usually not simplify to a single operation. For example, $\times 2 +4$ cannot be reduced to a single operation rule.

Teacher Reflection

Review — **Cumulative Review:** For cumulative review of previously learned skills, see page 463–464.

Family Involvement: Assign the *Practice, Reteach,* or *Enrichment* activities depending on the needs of your students.

Concept/Question Board: Have students look for additional examples of patterns and post them on the Concept/Question Board.

Math Puzzler: A service representative from the phone company called Mr. Muddle and told him that he owed $20 for one month's bill. "I'll pay $2 of it when I pay my bill each month until it's paid," said Mr. Muddle. How much will Mr. Muddle have to pay each month? $22 How long will it take him to pay what he owes? ten months

Chapter 12 • Lesson 2 **455–456**

4 Assess and Differentiate

**Assess** Use *eAssess* to record and analyze evidence of student understanding.

A Gather Evidence

Use the Daily Class Assessment Records in *Texas Assessment* or *eAssess* to record daily observations.

Informal Assessment
☑ **Student Pages**

Did the student **APPLYING**
- ☐ apply learning in new situations?
- ☐ contribute concepts?
- ☐ contribute answers?
- ☐ connect mathematics to real-world situations?

Informal Assessment
☑ **Guided Discussion**

Did the student **REASONING**
- ☐ provide a clear explanation?
- ☐ communicate reasons and strategies?
- ☐ choose appropriate strategies?
- ☐ argue logically?

TEKS/TAKS Practice

Use *TEKS/TAKS Practice* pages 55–58 to assess student progress.

B Summarize Findings

Analyze and summarize assessment data for each student. Determine which Assessment Follow-Up is appropriate for each student. Use the Student Assessment Record in *Texas Assessment* or *eAssess* to update assessment records.

C Texas Assessment Follow-Up ● DIFFERENTIATE INSTRUCTION

Based on your observations, use these teaching strategies for assessment follow-up.

INTERVENTION

Review student performance on *Intervention* Lesson 12.C to see if students have mastered prerequisite skill for this lesson.

Number, operation, and quantitative reasoning 1.3.A Model and create addition and subtraction problem situations with concrete objects and write corresponding number sentences.

ENGLISH LEARNER

Review

Use Lesson 12.2 in *English Learner Support Guide* to review lesson concepts and vocabulary.

ENRICH

If . . . students are proficient in the lesson concepts,

Then . . . encourage them to work on the chapter projects or *Enrichment* Lesson 12.2.

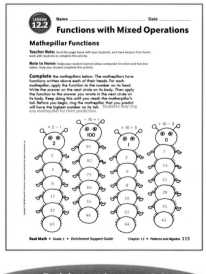

Enrichment Lesson 12.2

PRACTICE

If . . . students would benefit from additional practice,

Then . . . assign *Practice* Lesson 12.2.

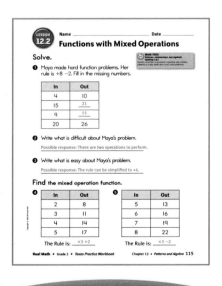

Practice Lesson 12.2

RETEACH

If . . . students are having difficulty solving problems involving mixed operations,

Then . . . demonstrate the composite function rule. Have pairs of students act as human function machines for two different functions, such as −2 and ×3. Write a number on a slip of paper, and hand it to the first student, who crosses it out, performs the function, and writes the answer. The student then hands the paper to his or her partner, who crosses out the answer, performs the second function, and writes the final solution.

Lesson Planner

Vertical Alignment TEXAS

Grade 1	Grade 2	Grade 3
1.5.D Use patterns to develop strategies to solve basic addition and basic subtraction problems.	**2.6.A** Generate a list of paired numbers based on a real-life situation such as number of tricycles related to number of wheels.	**3.7.B** Identify and describe patterns in a table of related number pairs based on a meaningful problem and extend the table.

Overview LESSON 12.3

TEXAS

OBJECTIVES
To practice solving realistic problems using mixed operations

MATH TEKS
Patterns, relationships, and algebraic thinking 2.6.A
Generate a list of paired numbers based on a real-life situation such as number of tricycles related to number of wheels.
Underlying processes and mathematical tools 2.12.D
Use tools such as real objects, manipulatives, and technology to solve problems.

MATH TEKS INTEGRATION
Number, operation, and quantitative reasoning 2.3.A
Recall and apply basic addition and subtraction facts (to 18).
Patterns, relationships, and algebraic thinking 2.6.C
Identify, describe, and extend repeating and additive patterns to make predictions and solve problems.
Patterns, relationships, and algebraic thinking 2.6.B
Identify patterns in a list of related number pairs based on a real-life situation and extend the list.

MATERIALS
- *Number Cubes
- *Calculators (optional)

TECHNOLOGY
Ⓔ Presentation Lesson 12.3
Ⓔ MathTools Function Machine
Building Blocks Function Machine 3

More Functions with ★ Mixed Operations

Context of the Lesson In this lesson students use function tables to solve real-world situations involving mixed operations.
See page 451B for Math Background for teachers for this lesson.

Planning for Learning ● DIFFERENTIATE INSTRUCTION

INTERVENTION
If . . . students lack the prerequisite skill of reading number sentences,

Then . . . teach *Intervention* Lesson 12.C.

1.3.A, 1.5.D

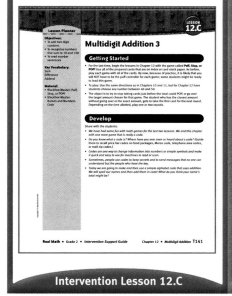

Intervention Lesson 12.C

ENGLISH LEARNER
Preview
If . . . students need language support,

Then . . . use Lesson 12.3 in *English Learner Support Guide* to preview lesson concepts and vocabulary.

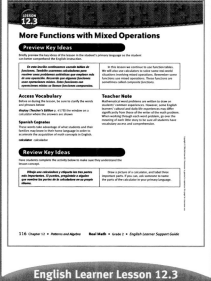

English Learner Lesson 12.3

ENRICH
If . . . students are proficient in the lesson concepts,

Then . . . emphasize exploring *eMathTools*.

PRACTICE
If . . . students would benefit from additional practice,

Then . . . extend Skill Practice before assigning the student pages.

RETEACH
If . . . students are having difficulty understanding composite functions,

Then . . . extend Skill Building before assigning the student pages.

Access Vocabulary
display the window on a calculator where the answers are shown

Spanish Cognates
calculator calculador

---

*Manipulative Kit Item = Key standard

★ = 120-Day Plan for TAKS

Teaching Lesson 12.3

 TEXAS

Patterns, relationships, and algebraic thinking 2.6.A Generate a list of paired numbers based on a real-life situation such as number of tricycles related to number of wheels.

Underlying processes and mathematical tools 2 Use tools such as real objects, manipulatives, and technology to solve problems.

Mental Math 5

 **INTEGRATION: TEKS 2.3.A** Tell students that you are thinking of a function with the rule −2. You will say an input, and students should use **Number Cubes** to display the output. Possible examples include the following:

a. 12 10 **b.** 7 5 **c.** 4 2 **d.** 2 0

1 Develop 30

Tell Students In Today's Lesson They Will

use calculators and function tables to solve mixed operation problems.

Skill Building ENGAGING

 Introductory

Show students how to use a calculator to apply function rules. (Note that the composite function feature may work differently on different calculators. Check the calculators your students will be using, and adjust your instructions accordingly.) Turn on the calculator, clear it, and press [+ 5 =]. Next press [9 =]. Show the display 14. Have another student choose a number and press the number and [=]. Tell the class what the display says. Continue the activity until students can figure out what the display will say before you press the [=] and what the function rule is.

Discuss how calculators can be used to make quick calculations when dealing with difficult mixed operations.

Skill Practice COMPUTING

 Guided

Have students complete this activity in pairs. One student should set a constant function on the calculator without revealing it. The other student then has to guess what the rule is or what the output will be for a given input.

Guided Discussion

Copy the following table on the board:

In	Out
3	6
4	8
5	10

Tell students the rule for this table is ×4 ÷2. Work the problems with students.

■ **How could you simplify this rule and still make it work for the table on the board?** The rule ×2 will give you the same results.

● Allow students to experiment with their calculators to discover how to simplify the rule.

2 Use Student Pages 20

Pages 457–458 APPLYING

 Independent

Have students complete pages 457 and 458 independently. Discuss students' strategies and answers when they finish the exercises.

Integration: TEKS 2.6.B, Problem 1

As Students Finish

e MathTools *Function Machine* Have students use this tool to explore functions with mixed operations.

Building Blocks *Function Machine 2*

Student Page

Name _____ Date _____

LESSON 12.3 More Functions with Mixed Operations

Key Ideas

Mixed operations can help you solve everyday problems quickly.

Math TEKS
Patterns, relationships, and algebraic thinking 2.6.A
Generate a list of paired numbers based on a real-life situation such as number of tricycles related to number of wheels.

Matt charges $3 per hour for mowing lawns, plus $1 to cover the cost of his travel.

❶ Complete the table to show how much Matt should collect.

Matt's Lawn Mowing Service Price Table

Hours	1	2	3	4	5	6	7	8
Charge (dollars)	4	7	10	13	16	19	22	25

Allison also mows lawns. She estimates how long a job will take. Then she charges a fixed price for her service.

❷ **Extended Response** Which method of charging is fairer, Matt's or Allison's? Write why you think so.

See Reflect in Teacher's Edition.

_____

_____

Student Page

LESSON 12.3 · More Functions with Mixed Operations

Kenji is busy making hard function problems.

Complete the tables, and then find an easier rule to see why they are not really that hard. Then write the simplified rule for each problem.

+5 −2	
1	4
0	3
10	13

❸ The simplified rule is __+3__.

+5 +5	
1	11
0	10
18	28

❺ The simplified rule is __+10__.

×2 ÷2	
8	8
1	1
17	17

❹ The simplified rule is __×1, ÷1, +0, or −0__.

×6 ÷2	
1	3
0	0
7	21

❻ The simplified rule is __×3__.

---

③ Reflect 10

Guided Discussion UNDERSTANDING

Integration: TEKS 2.6.C Have students make up their own composite function table by filling in a few inputs and outputs. Have them exchange and complete each other's tables, including the rule.

Extended Response

Problem 2 One possible response is that Matt's method is fairer because he works by the hour. Allison may overestimate the time needed to mow a lawn and therefore might overcharge a customer. Another response is that Allison's method is fairer because the customer knows in advance what the charge will be, while Matt may work more slowly to be paid more. Accept any answer that is supported with a good reason.

Teacher Reflection

Cumulative Review: For cumulative review of previously learned skills, see page 463–464.

Family Involvement: Assign the *Practice, Reteach,* or *Enrichment* activities depending on the needs of your students.

Concept/Question Board: Have students look for additional examples of patterns and post them on the Concept/Question Board.

Math Puzzler: All of Mr. Ridman's cars' tires are flat except for one. He has six cars. How many new tires will he need? 23

4 Assess and Differentiate

 Assess Use *eAssess* to record and analyze evidence of student understanding.

A Gather Evidence

Use the Daily Class Assessment Records in *Texas Assessment* or *eAssess* to record daily observations.

Informal Assessment
☑ **Mental Math**

Did the student **COMPUTING**
- ❏ respond accurately?
- ❏ respond quickly?
- ❏ respond with confidence?
- ❏ self-correct?

Informal Assessment
☑ **Extended Response**

Did the student **REASONING**
- ❏ provide a clear explanation?
- ❏ communicate reasons and strategies?
- ❏ choose appropriate strategies?
- ❏ argue logically?

 **TEKS/TAKS Practice**

Use *TEKS/TAKS Practice* pages 49–50 to assess student progress.

B Summarize Findings

Analyze and summarize assessment data for each student. Determine which Assessment Follow-Up is appropriate for each student. Use the Student Assessment Record in *Texas Assessment* or *eAssess* to update assessment records.

C Texas Assessment Follow-Up • DIFFERENTIATE INSTRUCTION

Based on your observations, use these teaching strategies for assessment follow-up.

INTERVENTION

Review student performance on *Intervention* Lesson 12.C to see if students have mastered prerequisite skill for this lesson.

Number, operation, and quantitative reasoning 1.3.A Model and create addition and subtraction problem situations with concrete objects and write corresponding number sentences.

ENGLISH LEARNER
Review

Use Lesson 12.3 in *English Learner Support Guide* to review lesson concepts and vocabulary.

ENRICH

If . . . students are proficient in the lesson concepts,

Then . . . encourage them to work on the chapter projects or *Enrichment* Lesson 12.3.

Enrichment Lesson 12.3

PRACTICE

If . . . students would benefit from additional practice,

Then . . . assign *Practice* Lesson 12.3.

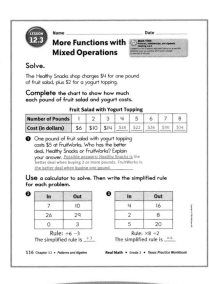

Practice Lesson 12.3

RETEACH

If . . . students are having difficulty with function operations,

Then . . . have students use calculators to keep track of each step.

Lesson Planner

TEXAS **Vertical Alignment**

Grade 1	Grade 2	Grade 3
1.4 The student uses repeating patterns and additive patterns to make predictions	2.6.C Identify, describe, and extend repeating and additive patterns to make predictions and solve problems.	3.6.A Identify and extend whole-number and geometric patterns to make predictions and solve problems.

Overview TEXAS

LESSON 12.4

OBJECTIVES
- To recognize and create patterns using geometric figures
- To review identifying plane figures

 MATH TEKS

Patterns, relationships, and algebraic thinking 2.6.C
Identify, describe, and extend repeating and additive patterns to make predictions and solve problems.

 MATH TEKS INTEGRATION

Number, operation, and quantitative reasoning 2.4.A
Model, create, and describe multiplication situations in which equivalent sets of concrete objects are joined.
Underlying processes and mathematical tools 2.13.A
Identify the mathematics in everyday situations.

MATERIALS
- *Pattern blocks
- *Number Cubes

TECHNOLOGY
Presentation Lesson 12.4
Building Blocks Marching Patterns 3

Patterns and Shapes ★

Context of the Lesson In this lesson students create patterns using geometric figures. Students created tessellations in Lesson 8.1. This lesson also includes a discussion of repeating and growing patterns.

See page 451B for Math Background for teachers for this lesson.

Planning for Learning ● DIFFERENTIATE INSTRUCTION

INTERVENTION

If . . . students lack the prerequisite skill of recognizing numbers that sum to 10 and 100,

Then . . . teach *Intervention* Lesson 12.A.

🌟 1.3.A, 1.5.D

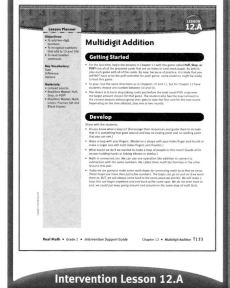

Intervention Lesson 12.A

ENGLISH LEARNER

Preview

If . . . students need language support,

Then . . . use Lesson 12.4 in *English Learner Support Guide* to preview lesson concepts and vocabulary.

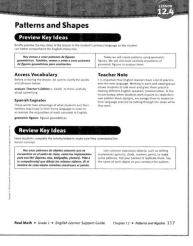

English Learner Lesson 12.4

ENRICH

If . . . students are proficient in the lesson concepts,

Then . . . emphasize chapter projects.

PRACTICE

If . . . students would benefit from additional practice,

Then . . . extend Skill Building before assigning the student pages.

RETEACH

If . . . students are having difficulty understanding shape patterns,

Then . . . extend Skill Building before assigning the student pages.

Access Vocabulary
analyze to think carefully about something

Spanish Cognates
geometric figures figuras geométricas

TEXAS

Patterns, relationships, and algebraic thinking 2.6.C
Identify, describe, and extend repeating and additive patterns to make predictions and solve problems.

Mental Math
5

  INTEGRATION: TEKS 2.4.A Present students with a series of multiplication and division problems. Students should respond with **Number Cubes**, using the find, hide, and show routine. Possible examples include the following:

a. $5 \times 7 = 35$ **b.** $3 \times 8 = 24$ **c.** $4 \times 8 = 32$
d. $4 \times 1 = 4$ **e.** $4 \div 2 = 2$ **f.** $2 \times 2 = 4$

1 Develop
20

Tell Students In Today's Lesson They Will
create and analyze patterns using geometric figures.

Skill Building ENGAGING

Introductory

 Present a simple repeating pattern on the board using squares, rectangles, circles, and triangles. Have students explain what the pattern is. Then draw a second pattern, leaving out two shapes. Discuss how to determine what the missing shapes are by having students say the pattern aloud from the beginning.

Have students create patterns using pattern blocks. Pair students, or have them work in small groups. Have one student begin a pattern and the other students finish it. Review geometric changes from Chapter 8, such as reflections and rotations, and encourage students to use them to make their patterns more complicated.

2 Use Student Pages
20

Pages 459–460 APPLYING

Independent

Have students complete pages 459–460 individually. Have students then exchange their patterns on page 460 to see if they can extend them. For example, if the pattern for Problem 7 is red, blue, green, then the next figure would be a green triangle.

As Students Finish

Building Blocks *Marching Patterns 3*

 RESEARCH IN ACTION

"Geometry can be used to understand and to represent the objects, directions, and locations in our world, and the relationships between them. Geometric shapes can be described, analyzed, transformed and composed and decomposed into other shapes."

Clements, Douglas and J. Sarama, eds. *Engaging Young Children in Mathematics: Standards for Early Childhood Mathematics Education.* Mahwah, New Jersey: Lawrence Erlbaum Associates Publishers, 2004, p. 39.

TEXAS

TEKS Checkup

Underlying processes and mathematical tools 2.12.D • Use tools such as real objects, manipulatives, and technology to solve problems.

Underlying processes and mathematical tools 2.13.A • Explain and record observations using objects, words, pictures, numbers, and technology.

Use this problem to assess students' progress toward standards mastery:

Which is next in the pattern?

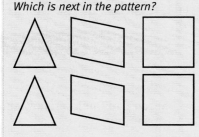

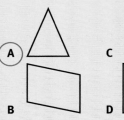

Have students choose the correct answer, then describe how they knew which choice was correct. In the discussion, ask questions such as the following. Be sure to ask students to explain their reasoning, since different solution methods are possible.

- **What is the pattern?** triangle, quadrilateral, square, triangle

- **What is the missing shape?** another triangle

Follow-Up
If...students have difficulty solving problems involving patterns,

Then...reteach the lesson using *Reteach* Lesson 12.4.

Student Page

Name ______________________ Date __________

LESSON 12.4 **Patterns and Shapes**

Key Ideas

Plane figures can be used to make a pattern.

Math TEKS
Patterns, relationships, and algebraic thinking 2.6.C
Identify, describe, and extend repeating and additive patterns to make predictions and solve problems.

Look for the pattern. Draw the missing figures.

1

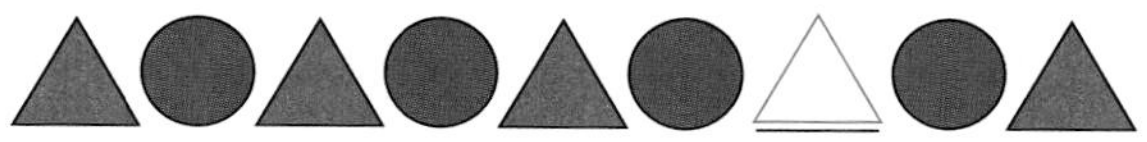

2

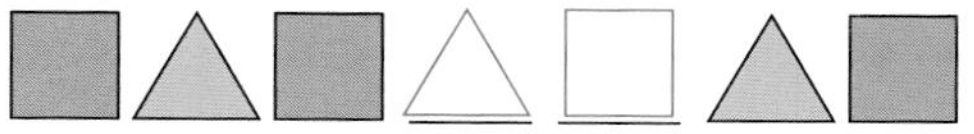

3

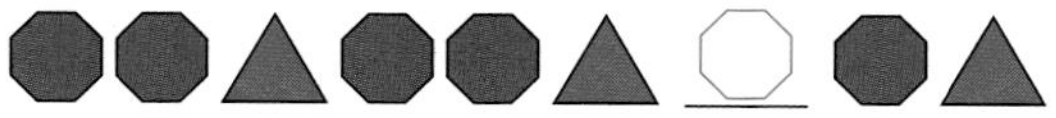

4

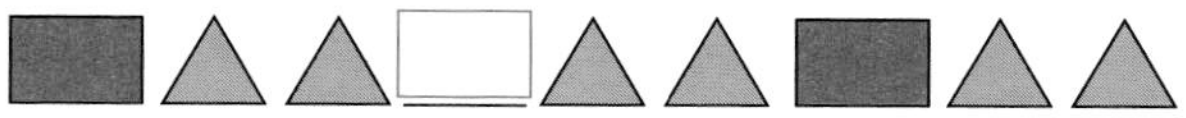

5

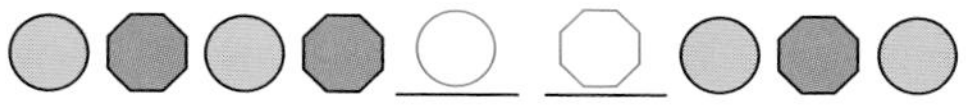

6

Textbook This lesson is available in the *eTextbook*.

Student Page

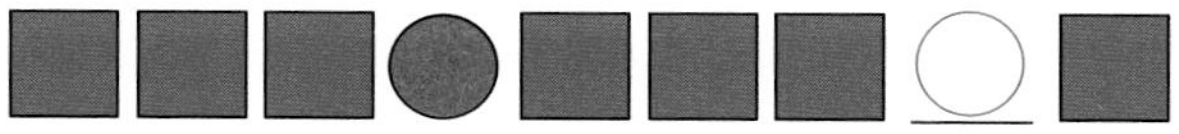

Make your own patterns using colors.

7

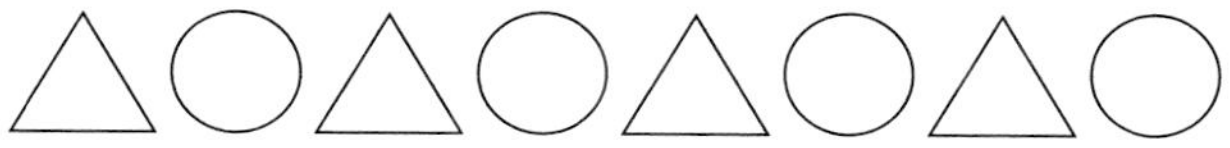

8

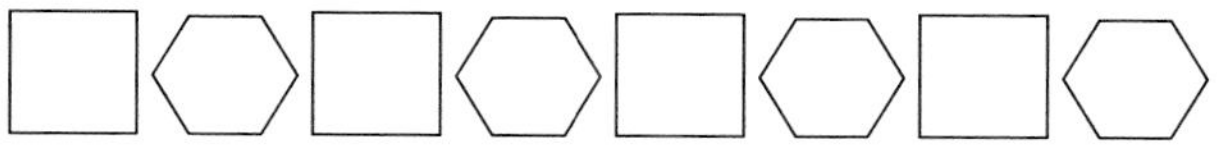

9

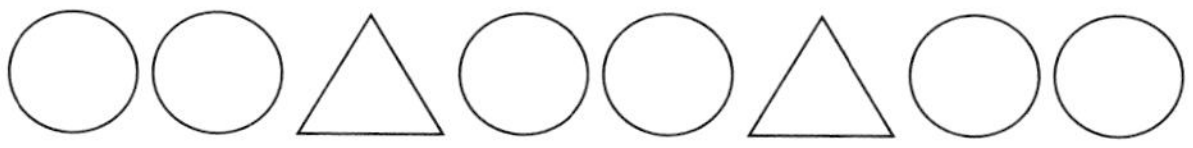

10

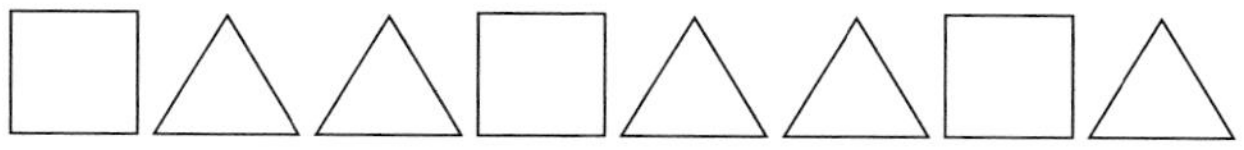

11

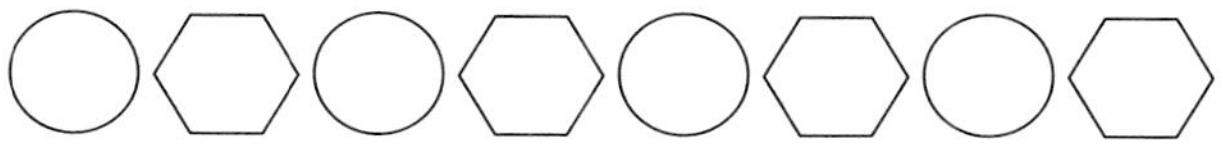

12

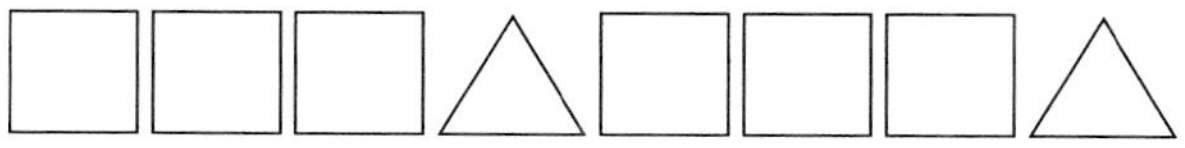

3 Reflect

10

Guided Discussion

REASONING

Integration: TEKS 2.13.A Draw the following pattern on the board:

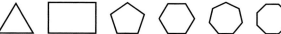

- **What is the pattern?** This is a growing pattern. Each figure has one more side than the previous one.
- **How many sides should the next shape have?** 9

Discuss the difference between a repeating pattern and a growing pattern. Have students create repeating and growing patterns and then share them with the class.

Cumulative Review: For cumulative review of previously learned skills, see page 463–464.

Family Involvement: Assign the ***Practice, Reteach,*** or ***Enrichment*** activities depending on the needs of your students.

Concept/Question Board: Encourage students to continue to post questions, answers, and examples on the Concept/Question Board.

Math Puzzler: On Monday Evan goes to work at 11:00 A.M. He begins work each day one hour earlier than the day before. What time does Evan go to work on Friday? 7:00 A.M.

4 Assess and Differentiate

 **Assess** Use *eAssess* to record and analyze evidence of student understanding.

A Gather Evidence

Use the Daily Class Assessment Records in *Texas Assessment* or *eAssess* to record daily observations.

Informal Assessment
☑ **Guided Discussion**

Did the student **REASONING**
- ❑ provide a clear explanation?
- ❑ communicate reasons and strategies?
- ❑ choose appropriate strategies?
- ❑ argue logically?

Informal Assessment
☑ **Concept/Question Board**

Did the student **APPLYING**
- ❑ apply learning in new situations?
- ❑ contribute concepts?
- ❑ contribute answers?
- ❑ connect mathematics to real-world situations?

 TEKS/TAKS Practice

Use *TEKS/TAKS Practice* pages 55–58 to assess student progress.

B Summarize Findings

Analyze and summarize assessment data for each student. Determine which Assessment Follow-Up is appropriate for each student. Use the Student Assessment Record in *Texas Assessment* or *eAssess* to update assessment records.

C Texas Assessment Follow-Up • DIFFERENTIATE INSTRUCTION

Based on your observations, use these teaching strategies for assessment follow-up.

INTERVENTION

Review student performance on *Intervention* Lesson 12.A to see if students have mastered prerequisite skills for this lesson.

Number, operation, and quantitative reasoning 1.3.A Model and create addition and subtraction problem situations with concrete objects and write corresponding number sentences.

ENGLISH LEARNER

Review

Use Lesson 12.4 in *English Learner Support Guide* to review lesson concepts and vocabulary.

ENRICH

If . . . students are proficient in the lesson concepts,

Then . . . encourage them to work on the chapter projects or *Enrichment* Lesson 12.4.

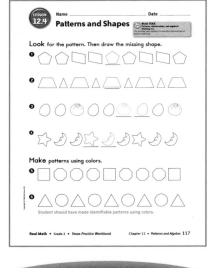

Enrichment Lesson 12.4

PRACTICE

If . . . students would benefit from additional practice,

Then . . . assign *Practice* Lesson 12.4.

Practice Lesson 12.4

RETEACH

If . . . students are having difficulty understanding mixed operations,

Then . . . reteach the concept using *Reteach* Lesson 12.4.

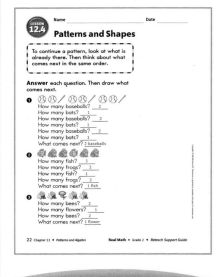

Reteach Lesson 12.4

Problem Solving 12.B

Comparing Strategies

Objectives
- To explore the Make a Physical Model and Draw a Diagram strategies
- To use a function rule to solve a nonroutine problem
- To provide practice generalizing about patterns

Materials
Linking or snap cubes (60–75 per student or pair of students)

See Appendix A page A24 for instruction and rubric for problem solving.

Context of the Lesson While providing extended time to work on a nonroutine problem, this lesson provides a connection between patterns and functions.

1 Develop   5 ⏱

Tell Students In Today's Lesson They Will
figure out how many cubes are needed to build a triangular wall.

Guided Discussion   👥 Introductory

Have students look at the photograph of the ancient Mayan pyramid on page 461.

Present this problem to the students:

You are an archaeologist who has found part of an ancient triangular wall made of cube-shaped blocks. You have uncovered the top four layers of the wall and notice a pattern in how the blocks are stacked. You are going to use the pattern to build a model of the wall that is 10 layers high. How many blocks will you need for your model?

Have students look at the diagram of the wall portion. Make sure students understand the problem by asking questions such as these:

- ■ **What is the problem asking you to do?** to figure out how many cubes we need to build a model of the wall with ten layers
- ■ **What do you have to help you?** the first four layers of the wall
- ■ **How many blocks are in the top layer of the wall?** 1
- ■ **How many blocks are in the second layer?** 2
- ■ **What do you notice about the number of blocks in each layer and the number of the layer?** They are the same. Layer 2 has 2 blocks, layer 3 has 3 blocks, layer 4 has 4 blocks, and so on.
- ■ **If you wanted to build a model of the wall with the top four layers, how many blocks would you need?** 10: 1 for the first layer, 2 for the second, 3 for the third, and 4 for the fourth; 1 + 2 + 3 + 4 = 10

Tell students that they are going to have a chance to figure out the number of blocks needed for the model, but first they will look at how two other students are trying to solve this problem.

Problem Solving 11.B Comparing Strategies

Name _____ Date _____

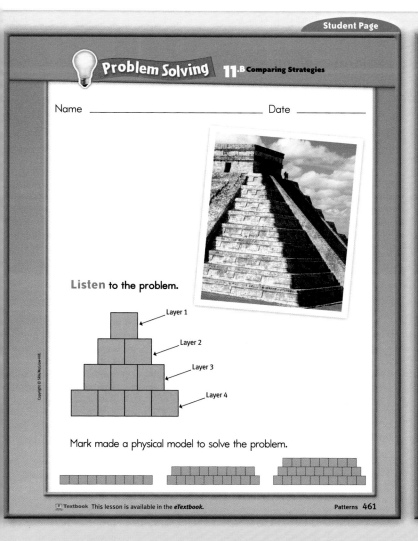

Listen to the problem.

Layer 1
Layer 2
Layer 3
Layer 4

Mark made a physical model to solve the problem.

Math TEKS
Patterns, relationships, and algebraic thinking 2.6.C
Identify, describe, and extend repeating and additive patterns to make predictions and solve problems.

Rebecca used draw a diagram/use a number pattern to solve the problem.

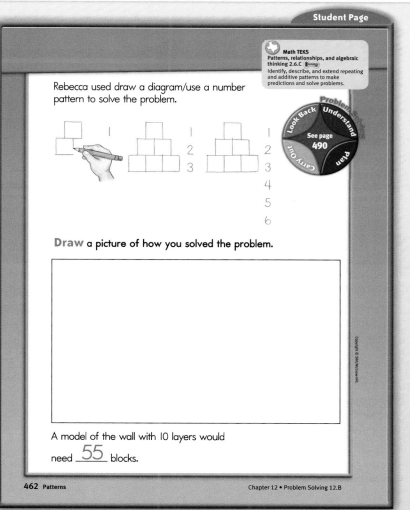

Look Back · Understand · Plan · Carry Out

See page 490

Draw a picture of how you solved the problem.

A model of the wall with 10 layers would need __55__ blocks.

TEXAS

Patterns, relationships, and algebraic thinking 2.6.C
Identify, describe, and extend repeating and additive patterns to make predictions and solve problems.
Underlying processes and mathematical tools 2.12.C
Select or develop an appropriate problem-solving plan or strategy including drawing a picture, looking for a pattern, systematic guessing and checking, or acting it out in order to solve a problem.

 Exploring Problem Solving 25

Using Student Pages

 Guided

Analyzing Sample Solution 1

Have students look at the picture on the bottom of page 461 of Mark solving the problem. Ask questions such as the following:

■ **Look at the first picture. Why is Mark building a row of 10 cubes?** He is building the bottom layer of the model. There will be 10 cubes in the bottom layer.

■ **What is Mark doing in the second picture?** He's adding 9 cubes on top of the 10 cubes. He is building the next layer above the bottom layer.

■ **How do you think Mark will get an answer to the problem?** He will keep building the model from the bottom up and then count all the cubes in the model.

Analyzing Sample Solution 2

Have students look at the picture on the top of page 462 of Rebecca's approach. Ask questions such as the following:

■ **Look at the first picture. Why is Rebecca drawing a square below the one she has already drawn?** She is starting to draw the second layer of the wall. She is making a diagram of the wall starting from the top down.

■ **Look at the second picture. Why is Rebecca writing numbers?** She is writing how many cubes are in each layer. She is writing the number of the layer.

■ **In the third picture, Rebecca is just writing numbers and isn't drawing any more squares. Why is that?** She doesn't need to draw the squares because she is using the pattern.

Have students work on the problem individually or in pairs. They may use Rebecca's strategy, Mark's strategy, or one of their own. Remind students they will need to be able to prove that they have found the correct number of cubes needed to build a model of the wall with 10 layers.

 Reflect 10

Have students share their solutions and their strategies. In discussion, bring out these points:

● A growing pattern changes in the same way repeatedly. For example, in the wall, the number of blocks in a layer increases by 1 as you go from one layer down to the next.

● There can be different ways to use a pattern to solve a problem. You can often use a pattern to save time and effort, as Rebecca did by writing numbers instead of drawing every block.

● When you extend a pattern, you should have a reason for believing that the pattern will continue. What appears to be a pattern may be just coincidence. For example, if one student is absent on Monday, two on Tuesday, and three on Wednesday, that does not mean four students will be absent on Thursday.

Sample Solutions Strategies

Students may use one or more of the following strategies instead of or in conjunction with the strategies presented on student page 462.

Make a Table

Students can make a T table like the one below. They might notice helpful numerical patterns, such as if they add the number of the layer to the number of cubes so far, they get the new total number of cubes in the model.

Number of Layers	Number of Cubes Needed for a Model
1	1
2	3
3	6
4	10
5	15

10 + 5 = 15. The layer number (5) plus the number of cubes so far (10) equals the number of cubes in 5 layers.

Write a Number Sentence/Find a Pattern

Students might write a long number sentence for the total number of blocks. They might find and use a pattern that helps them add the numbers.

For example, each pair of connected numbers equals 10.

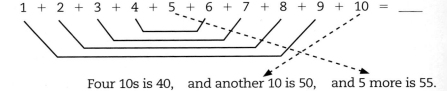

$$1 + 2 + 3 + 4 + 5 + 6 + 7 + 8 + 9 + 10 = \underline{\hspace{1cm}}$$

Four 10s is 40, and another 10 is 50, and 5 more is 55.

Students might instead add the five pairs that make 11 to get 55.

 Assess 15

When evaluating student work, focus not only on the correctness of the answer but also on whether the student thought rationally about the problem. Questions to consider include the following:

● Did the student understand the problem and the Sample Solution Strategies?

● Did the student have an organized method for determining the number of blocks needed?

● Was the student able to explain his or her strategy and convince others that the answer is correct?

Also note which students use particularly sophisticated or creative strategies.

Cumulative Review

Use Pages 463–464

Use the Cumulative Review as a review of concepts and skills that students have previously learned.

Here are different ways that you can assign these problems to your students as they work through the chapter:

- With some of the lessons in the chapter, assign a set of cumulative review problems to be completed as practice or for homework.
  Lesson 12.1—Problems 1–2
  Lesson 12.2—Problems 3–5
  Lesson 12.3—Problems 6–9
  Lesson 12.4—Problems 10–14

- At any point during the chapter, assign part or all of the cumulative review problems to be completed as practice or for homework.

Cumulative Review

Problems 1–2 review applying multiplication, Lesson 11.6. TEKS: 2.12

Problems 3–5 review checking subtraction, Lesson 6.7. TEKS: 2.3.B

Problems 6–9 review identifying patterns and function rules, Lesson 12.1. TEKS: 2.5.A

Problems 10–14 review identifying time and obtuse, acute, and right angles, Lesson 8.5. TEKS: 2.10.B

> ### Progress Monitoring
>
> **If . . .** students miss more than one problem in a section, : **Then . . .** refer to the indicated lesson for remediation suggestions.

Cumulative Review

Name _____ Date _____

Applying Multiplication Lesson 11.6 TEKS: 2.12

Solve these problems.

1 Malin wants to buy 36 cups of salt. There are 4 cups of salt in each bag. How many bags must she buy?

$4 \times \boxed{9} = 36$

2 Jillian made 96 ounces of jam. She wants to store the jam in jars. She can fit 12 ounces in each jar. How many jars will she need?

$12 \times \boxed{8} = 96$

Checking Subtraction Lesson 6.7 TEKS: 2.3.B

Solve these problems.
Explain your answers.

3 Ellie had $83. She bought a kite. She now has __$66__.

Explain. __Subtract 17 from 83.__

4 Aiden bought a basketball. He gave the clerk two $20 bills. How much change did he get? _____ $2

Explain. __Subtract 38 from 40.__

5 Daniel has a $50 bill. He buys two dinosaur models and a kite. How much change should he get? __$15__

Explain. Two dinosaur models at $9 each plus one kite at $17 equals $35 (9 + 9 + 17 = 35). Then 50 − 35 = $15.

STORE

$49 $38 $17 $11

$9 ea.

Book

Cumulative Review

Patterns and Functions Lesson 12.1 TEKS: 2.6.C

Find the patterns. Fill in the blanks.

6

2	4	6	8	10	12	14	16	18	20	22	24

7

3	6	9	12	15	18	21	24	27	30	33	36

8 in → +5 → out

4	9
53	58
9	14
27	32

9 in → −11 → out

60	49
22	11
30	19
18	7

Obtuse, Acute, and Right Angles Lesson 8.5 TEKS: 2.10.B

Write the time. Then write whether the angle is obtuse, acute, or right.

10 1:00 acute

11 4:00 obtuse

12 5:00 obtuse

13 9:00 right

14 Ring the right angles.

Individual Oral Assessment

Purpose of the Test

The Individual Oral Assessment is designed to measure students' growing knowledge of chapter concepts. It is administered individually to each student, and it requires oral responses from each student. The test takes about five minutes to complete. See **Texas Assessment** for detailed instructions for administering and interpreting the test, and record students' answers on the Student Assessment Recording Sheet.

Texas Assessment page 146

Directions

Read each question to the student, and record his or her oral response. If the student answers correctly, go to the next question. Stop when the student misses two questions at the same level. Students may use paper and pencil for the starred questions.

Materials

Paper and pencil, pattern blocks

Questions

Level 1: Prerequisite 1.5.A

1. Skip count. Which number is next? 5, 10, 15, ? 20
2. Skip count. Which number is next? 2, 4, 6, ? 8
3. Skip count. Which number is next? 4, 8, 12, ? 16
4. Skip count. Which number is next? 10, 20, 30, ? 40

Level 2: Basic 2.5.A

5. Which number is next? What is the pattern? 35, 36, 37, ? 38; add 1
6. Which number is next? What is the pattern? 18, 17, 16, ? 15; subtract 1
7. Which number is next? What is the pattern? 10, 12, 14, ? 16; add 2
8. Which number is next? What is the pattern? 80, 70, 60, ? 50; subtract 10

Level 3: At Level 2.3, 2.4

*9. What is $5 \times 2 + 1$? 11
*10. What is $3 \times 2 - 1$? 5
*11. What is $4 \times 4 + 2$? 18
*12. What is $6 \times 6 - 2$? 34

Level 4: Challenge Application 2.6

13. Use pattern blocks. Show a square, rhombus, square, rhombus, and square. What comes next in the pattern? rhombus
14. Use pattern blocks. Show a triangle, triangle, circle, triangle, triangle, circle, and triangle. What comes next in the pattern? triangle
15. Use pattern blocks. Show a square, trapezoid, hexagon, square, trapezoid, hexagon, square, and trapezoid. What comes next in the pattern? hexagon
16. Use pattern blocks. Show a hexagon, rhombus, square, rhombus, hexagon, rhombus, square, rhombus, hexagon, and rhombus. What comes next in the pattern? square

Level 5: Content Beyond Mid-Chapter

3.3.A
*17. What is $100 + 125 + 48$? 273
*18. What is $130 + 210 + 165$? 505
*19. What is $114 + 208 + 301$? 623
*20. What is $221 + 81 + 339$? 641

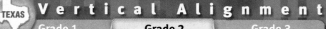
Grade 1	Grade 2	Grade 3
1.3.B Use concrete and pictorial models to apply basic addition and subtraction facts (up to $9 + 9 = 18$ and $18 - 9 = 9$).	**2.3** The student adds and subtracts whole numbers to solve problems.	**3.3.A** Model addition and subtraction using pictures, words, and numbers.

Overview LESSON **12.5**

TEXAS

Lesson Planner

OBJECTIVES
To introduce procedures for adding columns of multidigit numbers

 MATH TEKS
Number, operation, and quantitative reasoning 2.3 The student adds and subtracts whole numbers to solve problems.

 MATH TEKS INTEGRATION
Number, operation, and quantitative reasoning 2.3.B Model addition and subtraction of two-digit numbers with objects, pictures, words, and numbers.

MATERIALS
*Number Cubes

TECHNOLOGY
Presentation Lesson 12.5
Building Blocks Word Problems with Tools 9

Column Addition

Context of the Lesson This is a review of skills learned in previous lessons. In this lesson students will add columns of numbers and solve problems with three or more addends.

See page 451B for Math Background for teachers for this lesson.

Planning for Learning • DIFFERENTIATE INSTRUCTION

INTERVENTION

If . . . students lack the prerequisite skill of recognizing numbers that sum to 10 and 100,

Then . . . teach *Intervention* Lesson 12.A.

 1.3.A, 1.5.D

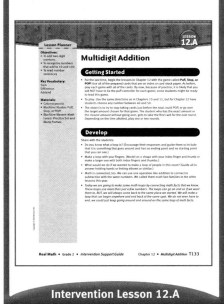

Intervention Lesson 12.A

ENGLISH LEARNER

Preview

If . . . students need language support,

Then . . . use Lesson 12.5 in *English Learner Support Guide* to preview lesson concepts and vocabulary.

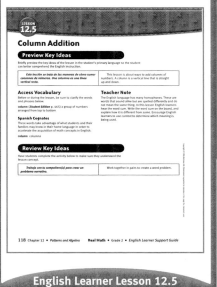

English Learner Lesson 12.5

ENRICH

If . . . students are proficient in the lesson concepts,

Then . . . emphasize game strategies.

PRACTICE

If . . . students would benefit from additional practice,

Then . . . extend Skill and Strategy Building before assigning the student pages.

RETEACH

If . . . students are having difficulty understanding column addition,

Then . . . extend Strategy Building before assigning the student pages.

Spanish Cognates
column columna

Number, operation, and quantitative reasoning 2.3
The student adds and subtracts whole numbers to solve problems.

TEXAS

Mental Math 5

 **INTEGRATION: TEKS 2.3.B** Have students add and subtract using their **Number Cubes** to respond. Possible examples include the following:

a. $8 + 5 = 13$ **b.** $16 - 8 = 8$ **c.** $6 + 7 = 13$ **d.** $11 - 4 = 7$
e. $5 + 4 = 9$ **f.** $11 - 8 = 3$ **g.** $8 + 8 = 16$ **h.** $8 - 5 = 3$

1 Develop 35

Tell Students In Today's Lesson They Will
use column addition to add several large numbers.

Strategy Building UNDERSTANDING

 Introductory

Present students with a word problem that involves several addends. For example:

- **There are 87 students in the second grade, 92 in third grade, 78 in fourth grade, and 81 in fifth grade. How many students are there in the four grades?**

Work with the class to solve the problem. Show the algorithm and the solution on the board, focusing on regrouping the ones and tens. $87 + 92 + 78 + 81 = 338$

Then do a problem that involves three-digit numbers. For example:

- **Mr. Hillman worked three weeks during summer vacation. The first week he earned $550. The second week he earned $567. The third week he earned $620. How much money did he earn in the three weeks?** $1,737

Skill and Strategy Building ENGAGING

Game **Roll a Problem Game: Three-Digit Column Addition Variation**

Demonstrate and then play this variation of the **Roll a Problem Game.** Students should use blank sheets of paper to play games. As with the basic game introduced in previous lessons, this game can also be played by the whole group, with you acting as a leader, or by as few as two students. To play this variation, roll a blue 5–10 **Number Cube.** If you roll a 10, roll again, and don't use the number. Try three three-digit numbers to begin with, and then make the game easier or harder depending on how your class reacts.

2 Use Student Pages 15

Pages 465–466 APPLYING

Independent

Have students complete pages 465 and 466 independently. When students finish, discuss their methods and solutions, focusing particularly on their strategies for solving the word problems on page 466.

Progress Monitoring

If . . . students have difficulty adding columns of numbers or they don't understand why you start at the right,

Then . . . use manipulatives, such as craft sticks bundled in tens and hundreds or play money with $10 and $100 bills, to show how. Have students count the manipulatives to represent each number, then exchange 10 ones for 10 and 10 tens for 100.

As Students Finish

Game Have students play the **Roll a Problem Game: Three-Digit Column Addition Variation** in small groups.

Building Blocks *Word Problems with Tools 9*

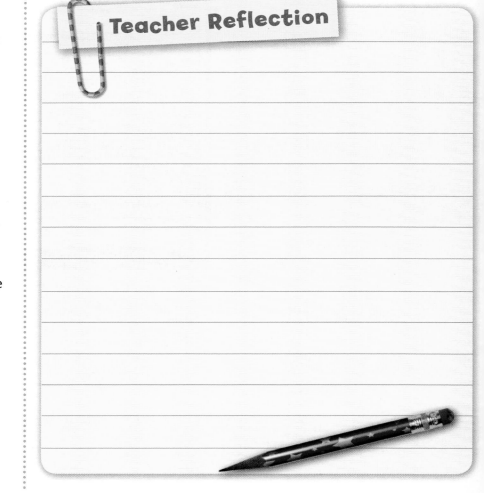

Teacher Reflection

Name _____ Date _____

LESSON 12.5 **Column Addition**

Key Ideas
Adding columns of numbers is similar to adding two numbers.

Math TEKS
Number, operation, and quantitative reasoning 2.3
The student adds and subtracts whole numbers to solve problems.

Add.

①
```
  342
  186
+ 274
━━━━
  802
```

②
```
   98
   76
+  85
━━━━
  259
```

③
```
  343
  297
+ 160
━━━━
  800
```

④
```
  333
  333
+ 334
━━━━
1,000
```

⑤
```
   75
   75
   75
+  75
━━━━
  300
```

⑥
```
  250
  250
  250
+ 250
━━━━
1,000
```

⑦ Antonio's family went on vacation. To spend one night at the hotel costs $78. How much did Antonio's family spend for 3 nights at the hotel?

a. $240   b. $78   c. $234   d. $156

Answer the questions.

⑧ Mr. Li is updating his horse corral. He wants to put a fence around it. What is the perimeter of the corral he wants to fence?

__118 meters__

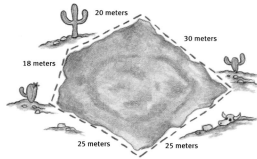

20 meters
30 meters
18 meters
25 meters   25 meters

⑨ Each roll of fencing is 25 meters long. How many rolls of fencing does Mr. Li need? __5__

⑩ The town of Muddleville was founded 96 years ago. There are 87 people now living in Muddleville. There are also 42 cats in Muddleville. How many dogs are there in Muddleville?

__cannot tell from the given information__

Game Play the **Roll a Problem Game**.

---

③ Reflect   10 ⏱

Guided Discussion **REASONING**

Ask if anyone can figure out how to add three four-digit numbers, such as

```
  1074
  4563
+ 2817
```

Students should see that the pattern is the same but now the last step is to add thousands. Tell students that if they can do this, they can add any numbers no matter how great.

☑ Use Mastery Checkpoint 18 found in *Texas Assessment* to evaluate student mastery of column addition. By this time, students should be able to correctly answer eighty percent of the Mastery Checkpoint items.

Cumulative Review: For cumulative review of previously learned skills, see page 473–474.

Family Involvement: Assign the *Practice, Reteach,* or *Enrichment* activities depending on the needs of your students.

Concept/Question Board: Encourage students to continue to post questions, answers, and examples on the Concept/Question Board.

Math Puzzler: Gary flipped a coin 25 times. It landed on heads 3 more times than it landed on tails. How many times did it land on tails? 11

4 Assess and Differentiate

 **Assess** Use *eAssess* to record and analyze evidence of student understanding.

A Gather Evidence

Use the Daily Class Assessment Records in *Texas Assessment* or *eAssess* to record daily observations.

Formal Assessment

✓ **Mastery Checkpoint**

Did the student
- ❑ use correct procedures?
- ❑ respond with at least 80% accuracy?

18 Mastery Checkpoint 18
Column Addition

The student demonstrates mastery by correctly answering at least fourteen of the eighteen problems.
Add.

❶ 24	❷ 8	❸ 50
37	35	50
67	52	50
+ 13	+ 19	+ 50
141	114	200

❹ 44	❺ 17	❻ 3
1	39	60
+ 55	+ 10	20
100	66	+ 10
		93

Assessment page 98

TEKS/TAKS Practice

Use *TEKS/TAKS Practice* pages 19–20 to assess student progress.

B Summarize Findings

Analyze and summarize assessment data for each student. Determine which Assessment Follow-Up is appropriate for each student. Use the Student Assessment Record in *Texas Assessment* or *eAssess* to update assessment records.

C Texas Assessment Follow-Up ● DIFFERENTIATE INSTRUCTION

Based on your observations, use these teaching strategies for assessment follow-up.

INTERVENTION

Review student performance on *Intervention* Lesson 12.A to see if students have mastered prerequisite skills for this lesson.

🔷 **Number, operation, and quantitative reasoning 1.3.A** Model and create addition and subtraction problem situations with concrete objects and write corresponding number sentences.

🔷 **Patterns, relationships, and algebraic thinking 1.5.D** Use patterns to develop strategies to solve basic addition and basic subtraction problems.

ENGLISH LEARNER

Review

Use Lesson 12.5 in *English Learner Support Guide* to review lesson concepts and vocabulary.

ENRICH

If . . . students are proficient in the lesson concepts,

Then . . . encourage them to work on the chapter projects or *Enrichment* Lesson 12.5.

Enrichment Lesson 12.5

PRACTICE

If . . . students would benefit from additional practice,

Then . . . assign *Practice* Lesson 12.5.

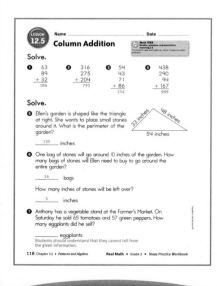

Practice Lesson 12.5

RETEACH

If . . . students are having difficulty with column addition,

Then . . . have them use graph paper to align columns and simplify addition.

TEXAS **Vertical Alignment**

Grade 1	Grade 2	Grade 3
1.12.B Relate informal language to mathematical language and symbols	**2.13.A** Explain and record observations using objects, words, pictures, numbers, and technology.	**3.16.A** Make generalizations from patterns or sets of examples and nonexamples.

Overview **LESSON 12.6**

Lesson Planner

OBJECTIVES
- To show that a number may be represented with many different expressions
- To practice solving word problems, many of which require mixed operations

MATH TEKS
Underlying processes and mathematical tools 2.13.A
Explain and record observations using objects, words, pictures, numbers, and technology.

MATH TEKS INTEGRATION
Number, operation, and quantitative reasoning 2.4.A
Model, create, and describe multiplication situations in which equivalent sets of concrete objects are joined.
Underlying processes and mathematical tools 2.13.B
Relate informal language to mathematical language and symbols.

MATERIALS
*Number Cubes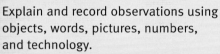

TECHNOLOGY
e Presentation Lesson 12.6

Number Sentences

Context of the Lesson Number sentences and equations involving mixed operations are introduced in this lesson as a challenge. This lesson also serves as an introduction to pre-algebra. Mastery by all students is not expected.

See page 451B for Math Background for teachers for this lesson.

Planning for Learning • DIFFERENTIATE INSTRUCTION

INTERVENTION

If . . . students lack the prerequisite skill of recognizing numbers that sum to 10 and 100,

Then . . . teach *Intervention* Lesson 12.A.

 1.3.A, 1.5.D

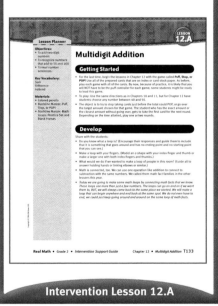

Intervention Lesson 12.A

ENGLISH LEARNER

Preview

If . . . students need language support,

Then . . . use Lesson 12.6 in *English Learner Support Guide* to preview lesson concepts and vocabulary.

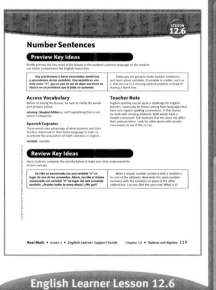

English Learner Lesson 12.6

ENRICH

If . . . students are proficient in the lesson concepts,

Then . . . emphasize chapter projects.

PRACTICE

If . . . students would benefit from additional practice,

Then . . . extend Skill and Strategy Building before assigning the student pages.

RETEACH

If . . . students are having difficulty understanding writing number sentences,

Then . . . extend Skill Building before assigning the student pages.

Access Vocabulary
missing something that is not where it should be

Spanish Cognates
variable variable

TEXAS

Underlying processes and mathematical tools 2.13.A
Explain and record observations using objects, words, pictures, numbers, and technology.

Mental Math 5

 INTEGRATION: TEKS 2.4.A Have students show the answers to addition, subtraction, multiplication, and division problems using their **Number Cubes.** Possible examples include the following:

a. $30 \div 6 = 5$ **b.** $12 \div 6 = 2$ **c.** $5 \times 3 = 15$
d. $6 \times 3 = 18$ **e.** $14 - 8 = 6$ **f.** $12 - 7 = 5$

1 Develop 20

Tell Students In Today's Lesson They Will
make number sentences.

Skill Building ENGAGING Introductory

Ask students to make up an addition expression that has a value of 7. Focus on the fact that there is more than one correct answer $(1 + 6, 5 + 2, 3 + 4,$ and so on). Repeat using different numbers for multiplication, subtraction, and division exercises. Then invite students to create several expressions using mixed operations that represent the same number. For example:

$10 - 4 + 4; 2 \times 3 + 4, 7 + 5 - 2.$

Skill and Strategy Building APPLYING Guided

Game Harder What's the Problem Game

Demonstrate this game, which provides practice with making number sentences and using mathematical reasoning. Students will play in small groups as they finish the student pages.

Players: two to five

Materials: paper and pencil

How to Play: Begin by having Player One write a number sentence, and show it to the other players in the group. Each player in turn then tries to write a different number sentence with the same answer. Each number sentence must have at least two operation signs (same or different). Players then check each other's number sentences for accuracy. Every player with a correct number sentence is a winner in the round. Players repeat rounds, taking turns as the player who writes the first number sentence.

2 Use Student Pages 20

Pages 467–468 UNDERSTANDING

Have students work in pairs to complete pages 467 and 468. Instruct partners that they must agree on each number sentence before writing it. Encourage partners to discuss and share their reasoning for each answer.

A possible solution to the last word problem on page 468 involves subtraction and multiplication. Because students have not yet formally learned how to solve mixed subtraction and multiplication problems, have them explain what they did and why.

Integration: TEKS 2.13.B, Problem 10–13

As Students Finish

Game Harder What's the Problem Game

TEKS Checkup

Underlying processes and mathematical tools 2.13.B • Relate informal language to mathematical language and symbols.

Use this problem to assess students' progress toward standards mastery:

Stephanie earns $25 each hour at her job. Today she earned $75. Which equation could be used to find how many hours Stephanie worked today?

A $75 \times 3 = n$

B $25 \times 75 = n$

C $25 \div 75 = n$

D $75 \div 25 = n$

Have students choose the correct answer and describe how they knew which choice was correct. In the discussion, ask questions such as the following. Be sure to ask students to explain their reasoning because different solution methods are possible.

- Which operation could be used to find the number of hours she worked? division
- Which division is correct? $75 \div 25$

Follow-Up
If...students have difficulty deciding on what mathematical language to use,

Then...have students practice by playing the **Harder What's the Problem Game.**

Name _____ Date _____

LESSON 12.6 Number Sentences

Key Ideas

There are many different ways to combine numbers and operations to represent a given number.

Math TEKS
Underlying processes and mathematical tools 2.13.A
Explain and record observations using objects, words, pictures, numbers, and technology.

Write three number sentences that give the number shown as the answer. *Answers given are examples only.*

10
① $5 + 3 + 6 - 4 = 10$
② $25 - 15 = 10$
③ $5 + 1 + 4 = 10$

8
④ $16 - 8 = 8$
⑤ $18 - 5 - 5 = 8$
⑥ $6 + 4 - 2 = 8$

5
⑦ $15 - 6 - 7 + 3 = 5$
⑧ $25 - 20 = 5$
⑨ $10 - 5 = 5$

Write a number sentence for each situation. Then solve the problem.

⑩ Mary earned $5 on Monday, $7 on Tuesday, and $4 on Wednesday. How many dollars did she earn altogether?

$5 + 7 + 4 = \$16$

⑪ Samantha had 9 marbles. She bought 2 more. Then she gave away 3. Then she got 3 more. How many marbles does Samantha have now?

$9 + 2 - 3 + 3 = 11$

⑫ John earned $3 a day for 7 days. How many dollars has he earned altogether?

$3 \times 7 = \$21$

 ⑬ There were 20 apples on the tree. Abby picked 3 apples a day for 5 days. One apple fell off the tree. How many apples are on the tree now?
Multistep

$3 \times 5 = 15$ and $20 - 15 - 1 = 4$ or $20 - 3 - 3 - 3 - 3 - 3 - 1 = 4$

Game Play the **Harder What's the Problem Game.**

---

3 Reflect 10

Guided Discussion REASONING

Write $10 - 5 - 2$ on the board, and ask whether anybody could get more than one value for the expression. A student might subtract $10 - 5$ and then subtract 2 from that difference, resulting in 3. Or a student might think that 2 should be subtracted from 5 first and then that difference should be subtracted from 10, resulting in 7.

Tell the class that we will work from left to right in such expressions for now but they may wish to use other rules sometimes in the future.

Cumulative Review: For cumulative review of previously learned skills, see page 473–474.

Family Involvement: Assign the *Practice, Reteach,* or *Enrichment* activities depending on the needs of your students.

Concept/Question Board: Have students attempt to answer any unanswered questions on the Concept/Question Board.

Math Puzzler: Each container holds up to 3 tennis balls. You have 20 tennis balls. What is the fewest number of containers you need to put all the tennis balls in containers? 7

4 Assess and Differentiate

 **e Assess** Use *eAssess* to record and analyze evidence of student understanding.

A Gather Evidence

Use the Daily Class Assessment Records in *Texas Assessment* or *eAssess* to record daily observations.

Informal Assessment
☑ **Mental Math**

Did the student **COMPUTING**
- ❏ respond accurately?
- ❏ respond quickly?
- ❏ respond with confidence?
- ❏ self-correct?

Informal Assessment
☑ **Skill Building**

Did the student **ENGAGING**
- ❏ pay attention to others' contributions?
- ❏ contribute information and ideas?
- ❏ improve on a strategy?
- ❏ reflect on and check the accuracy of his or her work?

 TEKS/TAKS Practice

Use *TEKS/TAKS Practice* pages 107–108 to assess student progress.

B Summarize Findings

Analyze and summarize assessment data for each student. Determine which Assessment Follow-Up is appropriate for each student. Use the Student Assessment Record in *Texas Assessment* or *eAssess* to update assessment records.

C Texas Assessment Follow-Up • DIFFERENTIATE INSTRUCTION

Based on your observations, use these teaching strategies for assessment follow-up.

INTERVENTION

Review student performance on *Intervention* Lesson 12.A to see if students have mastered prerequisite skills for this lesson.

🟦 **Number, operation, and quantitative reasoning 1.3.A** Model and create addition and subtraction problem situations with concrete objects and write corresponding number sentences.

🟦 **Patterns, relationships, and algebraic thinking 1.5.D** Use patterns to develop strategies to solve basic addition and basic subtraction problems.

ENGLISH LEARNER
Review

Use Lesson 12.6 in *English Learner Support Guide* to review lesson concepts and vocabulary.

ENRICH

If . . . students are proficient in the lesson concepts,

Then . . . encourage them to work on the chapter projects or *Enrichment* Lesson 12.6.

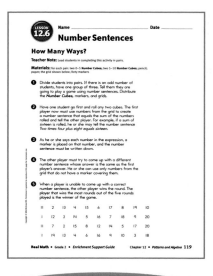

Enrichment Lesson 12.6

TEXAS PRACTICE

If . . . students would benefit from additional practice,

Then . . . assign *Practice* Lesson 12.6.

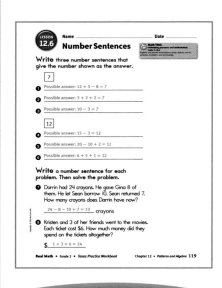

Practice Lesson 12.6

RETEACH

If . . . students are having difficulty understanding writing number sentences,

Then . . . have students make a list of key words for each operation.

TEXAS Vertical Alignment

Grade 1	Grade 2	Grade 3
1.12.B Relate informal language to mathematical language and symbols.	2.12.A Identify the mathematics in everyday situations.	3.15.B Relate informal language to mathematical language and symbols.

Overview LESSON 12.7

OBJECTIVES
- To have students create word problems
- To practice using variables in number sentences
- To practice extracting number sentences from word problems

MATH TEKS
Underlying processes and mathematical tools 2.12.A
Identify the mathematics in everyday situations.

MATH TEKS INTEGRATION
Underlying processes and mathematical tools 2.13.B
Relate informal language to mathematical language and symbols
Preparation for Grade 3: Number, operation, and quantitative reasoning 3.4.A
Learn and apply multiplication facts through 12 by 12 using concrete models and objects.

MATERIALS
- *Number Cubes
- *SRA Math Vocabulary Cards*

TECHNOLOGY
Presentation Lesson 12.7
Building Blocks Word Problems with Tools 7

Creating Word Problems

Context of the Lesson In this lesson students create their own word problems and write number sentences that are derived from the problems. Use of variables and mixed operations should be encouraged but not required. When creating word problems, students should try to think of situations they encounter every day.

See page 451B for Math Background for teachers for this lesson.

Planning for Learning • DIFFERENTIATE INSTRUCTION

INTERVENTION
If . . . students lack the prerequisite skill of recognizing numbers that sum to 10 and 100,

Then . . . teach *Intervention* Lesson 12.A.

1.3.A, 1.5.D

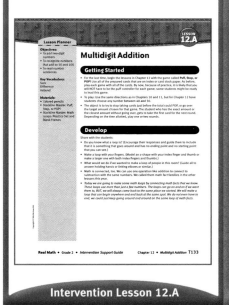

Intervention Lesson 12.A

ENGLISH LEARNER
Preview
If . . . students need language support,

Then . . . use Lesson 12.7 in *English Learner Support Guide* to preview lesson concepts and vocabulary.

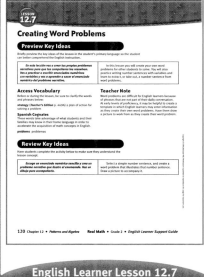

English Learner Lesson 12.7

ENRICH
If . . . students are proficient in the lesson concepts,

Then . . . emphasize chapter projects.

PRACTICE
If . . . students would benefit from additional practice,

Then . . . extend Skill Building before assigning the student pages.

RETEACH
If . . . students are having difficulty understanding variables,

Then . . . extend Skill Building before assigning the student pages.

Academic Vocabulary
variable \vâr´ē ə bəl\ *n.*
a letter or other symbol that represents a number

Access Vocabulary
strategy a plan of action for solving a problem

Spanish Cognates
problems problemas

Teaching Lesson 12.7

 TEXAS **Underlying processes and mathematical tools 2.12.A** Identify the mathematics in everyday situations.

Mental Math ⏱ 5

  INTEGRATION: TEKS 3.4.A Present multiplication facts, and have students show answers with **Number Cubes.** Possible exercises include the following:

a. $3 \times 5 = 15$ **b.** $2 \times 3 = 6$
c. $4 \times 4 = 16$ **d.** $5 \times 5 = 25$
e. $3 \times 3 = 9$ **f.** $2 \times 4 = 8$
g. $0 \times 5 = 0$ **h.** $1 \times 2 = 2$

1 Develop ⏱ 20

Tell Students In Today's Lesson They Will
make their own word problems and solve them.

Skill Building ✓ ENGAGING   Introductory

Present students with a word problem, and have them write a corresponding number sentence. For example,

- **There were 5 birds sitting on a fence. Then 4 more birds came. How many birds are there now?** $5 + 4 = 9$

Then present a problem to introduce the use of variables. For example,

- **There were 5 birds sitting on a fence. Then some more birds came. Now there are 10 birds. How many birds came?**

Explain that students can use a *variable* to represent a number they do not know. They can write $5 + n = 10$. Students can then solve for n, which equals 5.

Explain that a variable can stand for one number as it did in the previous example or it can stand for many numbers. For example,

- **Mrs. King is making sandwiches. For each sandwich she needs 2 slices of bread. How many slices of bread does she need?**

In this situation students can write a number sentence with two variables. In the sentence $x = 2 \times y$, y represents the number of sandwiches Mrs. King is going to make and x represents the number of bread slices she needs for y sandwiches. If you know one of the values of one of the variables, then you can solve for the other variable. For example,

- **If Mrs. King is going to make 4 sandwiches, how many slices of bread does she need?** $x = 2 \times 4$; $x = 8$. She needs 8 slices.
- **If Mrs. King has 10 slices of bread, how many sandwiches can she make?** $10 = 2 \times y$; $y = 5$. She can make 5 sandwiches.

Demonstrate a problem that uses variables and mixed operations. For example,

- **At the beginning of the school year, each student brings 2 boxes of tissues for the classroom. The teacher also likes to buy 3 extra boxes of tissues for the classroom.**

Explain that you can write a number sentence using *a* to represent the number of students and *b* to represent the total number of boxes the classroom will have: $b = 2 \times a + 3$.

- **How many boxes of tissues will the classroom have if there are 17 students?** $b = 2 \times 17 + 3$; $b = 37$

Have students create word problems, trade them with another student, and solve them. Encourage the use of variables and mixed operations.

2 Use Student Pages ⏱ 20

Pages 469–470 APPLYING   Guided

Have students work in pairs to complete pages 469 and 470.

> Integration: TEKS 2.13.B, Problems 5–6

As Students Finish

Game **Roll a Problem** (Introduced in Lesson 12.5)

Building Blocks *Word Problems with Tools 7*

RESEARCH IN ACTION

"Children who have difficulty translating a concept from one representation to another are the same children who have difficulty solving problems and understanding computations. Strengthening their ability to move between and among these representations improves the growth of children's concepts."

Lesh, R.A., T.A. Post, and M.J. Behr. "Representations and Translations among Representations in Mathematics Learning and Problem Solving:" in C. Janver, ed., *Problems of Representation in the Teaching and Learning of Mathematics.* Hillsdale, NJ: Erlbaum, 1987, pp. 33–40.

TEXAS   TEKS Checkup

Underlying processes and mathematical tools 2.12.C • Select or develop an appropriate problem solving plan or strategy including drawing a picture, looking for a pattern, systematic guessing and checking, or acting it out in order to solve a problem.

Use this problem to assess students' progress toward standards mastery:

Which word problem shows this number sentence? $2 + y = 5$

A Maria picked up 2 library books and 5 DVDs.

B Maria picked up 2 library books and then picked up 5 more the next day.

C Maria had 5 library books and $2 in fines.

D Maria had 2 library books at home. She picked up more books at the library and now has 5 library books.

Have students choose the correct answer and describe how they knew which choice was correct. In the discussion, ask questions such as the following. Be sure to ask students to explain their reasoning because different solution methods are possible.

- **If Maria had 2 books and 5 DVDs, what equation is that?** $2 + 5 = y$

- **If the equation equals 5, what does that tell you?** that the sum adds to 5

Follow-Up
If…students have difficulty with selecting or developing an appropriate problem solving plan,

Then…have students practice by using **Building Blocks: Word Problems with Tools 7**.

Student Page

Name _____ Date _____

 LESSON 12.7 Creating Word Problems

Key Ideas

To show a missing number in a problem, you can use an unknown.

Math TEKS
Underlying processes and mathematical tools 2.12.A Identify the mathematics in everyday situations.

Follow the directions for each problem.

Monica invited 12 people to her party. Some of the people didn't come.

❶ Write a number sentence to show how many people came. Use x to stand for the number of people who didn't come and y to stand for the number who came.
$y = 12 - x$

❷ If 4 didn't come, how many came? **8**

Danny is bringing a snack to school. He wants to make sure he brings 2 napkins for each student in his class plus 10 extra napkins in case there is a spill.

❸ Write a number sentence to show how many napkins Danny needs to bring. Use x to stand for the number of students and y to stand for the number of napkins he needs to bring.
$y = 2 \times x + 10$

❹ If 20 students are in his class, how many napkins will Danny need to bring? **50**

Textbook This lesson is available in the *eTextbook*.
469

LESSON 12.7 · Creating Word Problems

Write word problems for each number sentence below.

❺ $y = 5 + x$
Possible answer: Heather is 5 years older than her sister. How old is Heather?

❻ $y = 10 - x$
Possible answer: There were 10 cats at the animal shelter and some were adopted. How many cats are left?

470
Real Math • Chapter 12 • Lesson 7

❸ Reflect
10

Guided Discussion UNDERSTANDING

Have the class work together to create a multistep or extended-response word problem about a real-life situation. For example,

■ I bought some CDs on the Internet. There was a shipping charge of $4 no matter how many I bought and an additional charge of $3 per CD. How much will shipping cost? $x = 3 \times y + 4$
■ How much will shipping cost if I buy 5 CDs? $x = 3 \times 5 + 4$; $x = 19$

Cumulative Review: For cumulative review of previously learned skills, see page 473–474.

Family Involvement: Assign the *Practice, Reteach,* or *Enrichment* activities depending on the needs of your students.

Concept/Question Board: Have students attempt to answer any unanswered questions on the Concept/Question Board.

Math Puzzler: What is the greatest four-digit odd number you can write in which all four digits are different? 9,875

4 Assess and Differentiate

 **Assess** Use *eAssess* to record and analyze evidence of student understanding.

A Gather Evidence

Use the Daily Class Assessment Records in *Texas Assessment* or *eAssess* to record daily observations.

Informal Assessment
☑ **Mental Math**

Did the student COMPUTING
- ❏ respond accurately?
- ❏ respond quickly?
- ❏ respond with confidence?
- ❏ self-correct?

Informal Assessment
☑ **Skill Building**

Did the student ENGAGING
- ❏ pay attention to others' contributions?
- ❏ contribute information and ideas?
- ❏ improve on a strategy?
- ❏ reflect on and check the accuracy of his or her work?

 **TEKS/TAKS Practice**

Use *TEKS/TAKS Practice* pages 97–98 to assess student progress.

B Summarize Findings

Analyze and summarize assessment data for each student. Determine which Assessment Follow-Up is appropriate for each student. Use the Student Assessment Record in *Texas Assessment* or *eAssess* to update assessment records.

C Texas Assessment Follow-Up • DIFFERENTIATE INSTRUCTION

Based on your observations, use these teaching strategies for assessment follow-up.

INTERVENTION

Review student performance on *Intervention* Lesson 12.A to see if students have mastered prerequisite skills for this lesson.

Number, operation, and quantitative reasoning 1.3.A Model and create addition and subtraction problem situations with concrete objects and write corresponding number sentences.

ENGLISH LEARNER

Review

Use Lesson 12.7 in *English Learner Support Guide* to review lesson concepts and vocabulary.

ENRICH

If . . . students are proficient in the lesson concepts,

Then . . . encourage them to work on the chapter projects or *Enrichment* Lesson 12.7.

Enrichment Lesson 12.7

PRACTICE

If . . . students would benefit from additional practice,

Then . . . assign *Practice* Lesson 12.7.

Practice Lesson 12.7

RETEACH

If . . . students are having difficulty creating and writing word problems,

Then . . . have them work in pairs where one student creates the word problem and the other student writes it.

Problem Solving 12.C

Using Strategies

Objectives

- To provide practice using patterns to solve a real-world, nonroutine problem
- To build connections between function rules and visual patterns
- To develop an understanding that problems can have more than one answer

Materials

- Linking or snap cubes (40 to 50 per student or pair of students)
- Graph paper
- Scissors
- Crayons or markers

See Appendix A page A24 for instruction and rubric for problem solving.

Context of the Lesson While providing a large block of time for students to work on a single problem, this lesson provides an opportunity for students to apply what they have been learning about function rules and patterns to actual textile patterns. This lesson involves patterns similar to the ones in the Chapter Introduction, but here the patterns go in more than one direction. The lesson also continues the Native American theme introduced on pages 451–452 and continued on pages 461–462.

1 Develop 5

Tell Students In Today's Lesson They Will

- create their own rug designs.
- describe their design so others can make it.
- figure out which designs go with which descriptions.

Guided Discussion

 Introductory

As students look at the photograph on page 471, ask questions such as the following:

■ **Have you ever seen a rug like this before?**

■ **How would you describe the rug?**

Share with students the following information:

- Navajo weavers are usually women who raise sheep for wool to make the rugs. They shear the sheep, clean and card the wool, and then spin the wool.
- The rug was woven on a loom from different-colored yarns, perhaps wool from sheep the artist owned.
- Sometimes weavers use the different colors of the sheep's natural wool for the different shades and colors in the rug. Sometimes weavers dye the wool using native plants.

Student Page

Problem Solving 12.C Using Strategies

Name _____ Date _____

Listen to the problem.

Textbook This lesson is available in the eTextbook. Patterns **471**

Student Page

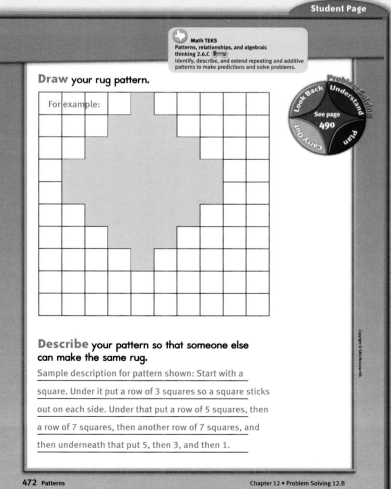

Math TEKS
Patterns, relationships, and algebraic thinking 2.6.C
Identify, describe, and extend repeating and additive patterns to make predictions and solve problems.

Draw your rug pattern.

For example:

Problem Solving
Look Back / Understand
See page 490
Carry Out / Plan

Describe your pattern so that someone else can make the same rug.

Sample description for pattern shown: Start with a
square. Under it put a row of 3 squares so a square sticks
out on each side. Under that put a row of 5 squares, then
a row of 7 squares, then another row of 7 squares, and
then underneath that put 5, then 3, and then 1.

472 Patterns   Chapter 12 • Problem Solving 12.B

TEXAS

Patterns, relationships, and algebraic thinking 2.6.C
Identify, describe, and extend repeating and additive patterns to make predictions and solve problems.
Underlying processes and mathematical tools 2.13.B
Relate informal language to mathematical language and symbols.

- Weavers may spend many months weaving their rug after they do all the work of obtaining and dying the wool.

2 Exploring Problem Solving 25

Using Student Pages
 Guided

Have students look at the photo of the rug on page 471. Ask students to describe the patterns they see in the rug. Encourage them to look closely to find as many patterns as they can, reminding them of the patterns they worked on in the Chapter Introduction on page 452.

Present this problem:

Imagine that you are learning how to weave. You want to create a rug with an interesting pattern. Your grandmother is an accomplished weaver and will help you, but first you must show and explain to her how you want your pattern to look. Make your pattern on a 10-by-10 grid, and write a description of it.

Guided Discussion

To make sure students understand the problem, ask questions such as the following:

■ **What are you supposed to do?** Draw a pattern for a rug design, and then describe it so someone else can make it.

■ **How might the weaver have put together the patterns you see on the rug on page 471?** Help students see that the weaver might have continued the pattern for a while and then changed it in the opposite direction; she might have combined smaller patterns to make a larger one; and so on.

On the board sketch this simple pattern:

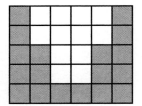

Ask students the following questions:

■ **How could you describe the shaded pattern?** It looks like the letter U; it goes down and then back up; it takes away and then adds on; it goes down by 2, then up by 2; it's two stair-step patterns set face to face; and so on.

■ **What are ways to describe a design so someone else can make it?** You can describe the steps to make it; you can tell a rule for the pattern; you can tell where to put the colors or shading in each row; and so on.

Give students access to the cubes and graph paper. Have them work alone or in pairs to create a pattern or patterns for their rugs. They might do this in a variety of ways:

- Students may make different patterns with cubes or on graph paper and then copy the one they like best on the grid on page 472.

- Students might make and cut out a small pattern, trace around it to make several copies of the pattern, rotate the copies in different ways, and then combine them into one large design.

- Students might color various squares in rows in an organized way so a pattern emerges as is often done in weaving.

Help students as needed to write a description of their patterns. Remind them to think what it would be like to read the description if they knew nothing about the pattern.

Have each student read his or her description to another student, who then tries to draw the design on graph paper. Encourage students to enhance or rewrite their descriptions if they see that it is not communicating their design accurately.

3 Reflect 10

Effective Communication Display the attempted duplicate designs in one area of the classroom. Have students cut out their descriptions from page 472 and place them in another area. Encourage the class to work together to try to match the descriptions with the patterns. Ask questions such as the following:

■ **What was easy and what was difficult about matching the patterns with the descriptions?**

■ **Were there any patterns that could go with more than one description?**

■ **Were there any descriptions that could go with more than one pattern?**

■ **Which descriptions were the easiest to understand? Why?**

In discussion, also bring out these points:

- Patterns can be repeated or combined to make larger patterns.
- Patterns can be viewed in different ways such as horizontally, vertically, or diagonally.
- A design that has a pattern can be communicated by stating the rule or rules of the pattern, the steps for making the design, or some other description of how the parts of the design are organized.

4 Assess 15

When evaluating student work, focus on whether students thought rationally about the problem. Questions to consider include the following:

- Did the student understand the problem?
- Was the student able to relate a visual pattern to the same pattern described in words?
- Was the student able to see smaller patterns within larger ones?
- Could the student describe a visual design clearly enough for someone to duplicate it?
- Was the student able to explain his or her thinking?

Cumulative Review

Use Pages 473–474

Use the Cumulative Review as a review of concepts and skills that students have previously learned.

Here are different ways that you can assign these problems to your students as they work through the chapter:

- With some of the lessons in the chapter, assign a set of cumulative review problems to be completed as practice or for homework.
  Lesson 12.5—Problems 1–4
  Lesson 12.6—Problems 5–6
  Lesson 12.7—Problems 7–15

- At any point during the chapter, assign part or all of the cumulative review problems to be completed as practice or for homework.

Cumulative Review

Problems 1–4 review reading data on a horizontal bar graph, Lesson 4.11. TEKS: 2.11.B

Problems 5–6 review column addition and perimeter, Lesson 12.5.

Problems 7–15 review writing number sentences, Lesson 12.6. TEKS: 2.13.A

Progress Monitoring

If . . . students miss more than one problem in a section,

Then . . . refer to the indicated lesson for remediation suggestions.

Student Page

Cumulative Review

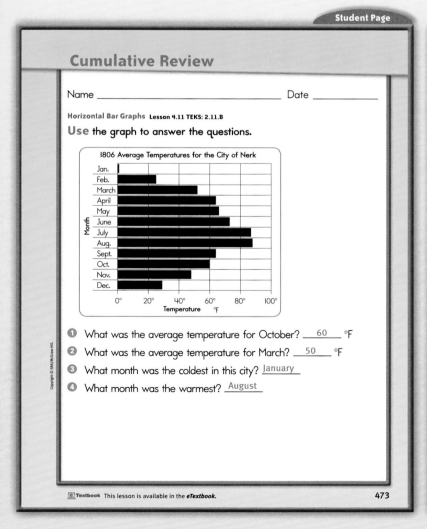

Name _____ Date _____

Horizontal Bar Graphs Lesson 4.11 TEKS: 2.11.B

Use the graph to answer the questions.

1806 Average Temperatures for the City of Nerk

❶ What was the average temperature for October? __60__ °F
❷ What was the average temperature for March? __50__ °F
❸ What month was the coldest in this city? __January__
❹ What month was the warmest? __August__

This lesson is available in the eTextbook.   473

Student Page

Cumulative Review

Column Addition Lesson 12.5 TEKS: 2.3

Use the drawing to answer the questions.

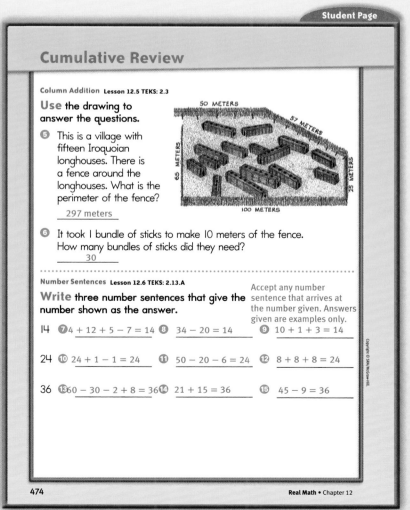

❺ This is a village with fifteen Iroquoian longhouses. There is a fence around the longhouses. What is the perimeter of the fence?
__297 meters__

❻ It took 1 bundle of sticks to make 10 meters of the fence. How many bundles of sticks did they need?
__30__

Number Sentences Lesson 12.6 TEKS: 2.13.A

Write three number sentences that give the number shown as the answer.

Accept any number sentence that arrives at the number given. Answers given are examples only.

14   ❼ $4 + 12 + 5 - 7 = 14$ ❽ $34 - 20 = 14$ ❾ $10 + 1 + 3 = 14$

24   ❿ $24 + 1 - 1 = 24$ ⓫ $50 - 20 - 6 = 24$ ⓬ $8 + 8 + 8 = 24$

36   ⓭ $60 - 30 - 2 + 8 = 36$ ⓮ $21 + 15 = 36$ ⓯ $45 - 9 = 36$

474   **Real Math • Chapter 12**

Wrap-Up

1 Discuss

5

Concept/Question Board

Review the Concept/Question Board with students.

- Discuss students' contributions to the Concept side of the Board.
- Have students repose their questions, and lead a discussion to find satisfactory answers.

Chapter Projects APPLYING

Provide an opportunity for students who have worked on one or more of the projects outlined on page 452C to share their work with the class. Allow each student or student group five minutes to present or discuss their projects. For formal assessment, use the rubrics found in *Across the Curriculum Math Connections;* the rubric for **Compare Native American Homes** is on page 127, and the rubric for **Create a Frontier Album Quilt** is on page 131. For informal assessment, use the following rubric and questions.

	Exceeds Expectations	Meets Expectations	Minimally Meets Expectations
Applies mathematics in real-world situations:	❏	❏	❏
Demonstrates strong engagement in the activity:	❏	❏	❏

Compare Native American Homes

 SOCIAL STUDIES WebQuest

- What Native American homes did you research? What were some of the homes' features?
- What information did you include in your spreadsheets?
- What were some similarities and differences between the homes?
- What numerical patterns in the data did you observe?
- Which homes do you think are interesting? Why?
- What do you think it would be like to live in various Native American homes?

TEKS

MATH STANDARD: **Patterns, relationships, and algebraic thinking 2.6** The student uses patterns to describe relationships and make predictions.

CROSS CURRICULAR STANDARD (SOCIAL STUDIES): **Geography 2.7.B** Explain how people depend on the physical environment and its natural resources to satisfy their basic needs.

TECHNOLOGY STANDARD: **Solving Problems 08.B** Use electronic tools and research skills to build a knowledge base regarding a topic, task, or assignment.

Create a Frontier Album Quilt

 ART

- What object did you choose for your quilt square? Why?
- What number pattern did your group choose for the quilt?
- What part of the number pattern did you use for your quilt square?
- Was a drawing and graphics program a good way to design your quilt square? Why or why not?
- What other design elements did you include on your quilt?
- What story does your quilt tell?

TEKS

MATH STANDARD: **Patterns, relationships, and algebraic thinking 2.6.C** Identify, describe, and extend repeating and additive patterns to make predictions and solve problems.

CROSS CURRICULAR STANDARD (FINE ARTS): **Perception 2.1.B** Identify art elements such as color, texture, form, line, and space and art principles such as emphasis, pattern, and rhythm.

TECHNOLOGY STANDARD: **Communication 10.B** Use font attributes, color, white space, and graphics to ensure that products are appropriate for the communication media including multimedia screen displays and printed materials.

2 Use Student Pages

25

Key Ideas Review UNDERSTANDING

Review the Key Ideas concepts on pages 475–476 with the class. The Key Ideas pages should be used by students and parents as a reference when reviewing the important concepts covered in this chapter. Ask students the following discussion questions to extend their knowledge of the Key Ideas and check their understanding of the ideas.

Discussion Questions

❶ **Where have you seen patterns in everyday situations?** Allow students to discuss. Students may mention shape patterns, such as tessellations found in tiled floors. However, point out that there are also other patterns. For example, the order in which you teach lessons every day may be according to a pattern.

❷ **Can you create your own mixed operation function?** Have students work with partners to create a mixed operation function machine. Then have them create function tables according to their rules without filling in all the inputs and outputs. Have groups trade function tables and try and find each others' functions. Were there any cases where the group had designated one function rule, but the other group found a different rule that also worked for the table?

CHAPTER 12 Key Ideas Review

Name _____ Date _____

In this chapter we discussed . . .
- patterns and numbers
- functions and mixed operations
- patterns and shapes
- making word problems

We used these concepts to help solve problems and answer everyday questions.

❶ In this chapter you practiced finding patterns. You found number patterns such as this one. Can you find the missing numbers?

40, 41, 39, 40, 38, _____, 37, 38, 36, _____, 35, 36

You found patterns using geometric figures. Can you find the missing figure?

You also solved many problems. You were able to use patterns to solve some of them.

Textbook This lesson is available in the *eTextbook*.   475

CHAPTER 12 Key Ideas Review

❷ You extended your understanding of functions to include mixed operations. So now if you see a function rule for

$$\times 3 - 2$$

You can find the output if you know the input as on this function table.

x column	column
2	4
4	10
1	1
5	13
7	19

Finding patterns and function rules are useful tools for solving problems. They are also an important part of knowing mathematics.

476   **Real Math** • Chapter 12

Chapter 12 Error Analysis

Errors with Column Addition

Write the following problems on the board and allow students to analyze this student's work. Discuss error patterns students find and how to help the student.

Pose this analysis as a challenging problem. When a student thinks he or she might have detected the error pattern, rather than have them tell the answer to the class, write a new exercise on the board and have the student tell you the answer that is consistent with the pattern he or she found. By using this procedure, all students will have a chance to think through the problem – not just the first student to find it.

This student completed a page of problems and got the following answers.

1. 38 + 47 + 46 = 122
2. 29 + 17 + 32 = 148
3. 598 + 57 + 79 = 822
4. 57 + 57 + 57 + 100 = 712
5. 25 + 20 +20 + 23 = 88
6. 75 + 75 + 75 + 75 = 282

What error is this student making?

Through discussion help students see that this student appears to know his addition facts, but is not carrying correctly. When the sum of a column is a 2-digit number the student always writes the first number at the bottom of the column and carries the second digit.

This student needs to learn that tens are carried to the tens column and hundreds are carried to the hundreds column. This can be demonstrated using base-ten materials.

TEKS/TAKS Practice

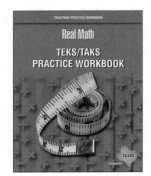

TEKS/TAKS Practice Book

At this time, you may wish to provide practice for standards covered in this chapter.

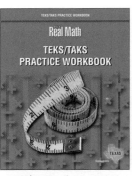

TEKS/TAK Practice, pp. 34–36, Standard 2.5.A

TEKS/TAK Practice, pp. 73–74, Standard 2.6.A

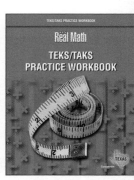

TEKS/TAK Practice, pp. 37–38, Standard 2.6.B

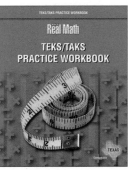

TEKS/TAK Practice, pp. 34–36, Standard 2.12.D

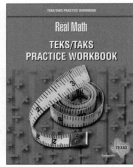

TEKS/TAK Practice, pp. 73–74, Standard 2.13.A

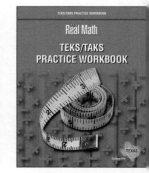

TEKS/TAK Practice, pp. 37–38, Standard 2.6.B

TAKS Preparation Book

TAKS Preparation Book

Use Benchmark Test 4 on pages 25–32 of **TAKS Preparation Book**. You may also want to use **Practice Test** 1 and 2 on pages 33–48.

Chapter Review

Use this Chapter 12 Review to indicate areas in which each student is having difficulty or in which the class may need help. If students do well on the Chapter 12 Review, you may wish to skip directly to the Chapter Test; if not, you may spend a day or so helping students overcome their individual difficulties before taking the Practice Test.

Next to each set of problems is a list of the lessons in the chapter that covered those concepts. If they need help, students can refer to a specific lesson for additional instruction. You can also use this information to make additional assignments based on the previous lesson concepts.

Have students complete pages 477–478 on their own. For review purposes, you may want to do some of the word problems on page 478 as a class.

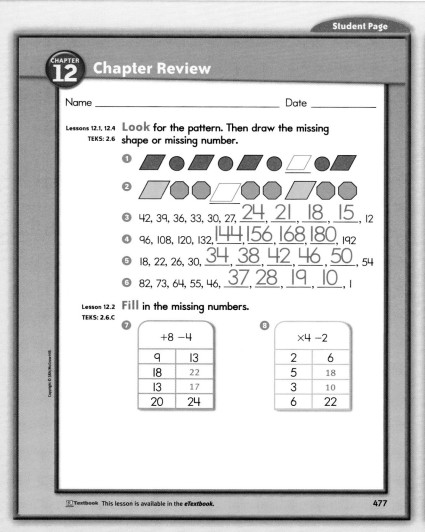

CHAPTER 12 — Chapter Review

Name _____ Date _____

Lessons 12.1, 12.4 **TEKS: 2.6** Look for the pattern. Then draw the missing shape or missing number.

① [pattern of shapes]

② [pattern of shapes]

③ 42, 39, 36, 33, 30, 27, **24**, **21**, **18**, **15**, 12

④ 96, 108, 120, 132, **144**, **156**, **168**, **180**, 192

⑤ 18, 22, 26, 30, **34**, **38**, **42**, **46**, **50**, 54

⑥ 82, 73, 64, 55, 46, **37**, **28**, **19**, **10**, 1

Lesson 12.2 **TEKS: 2.6.C** Fill in the missing numbers.

⑦ +8 −4

9	13
18	22
13	17
20	24

⑧ ×4 −2

2	6
5	18
3	10
6	22

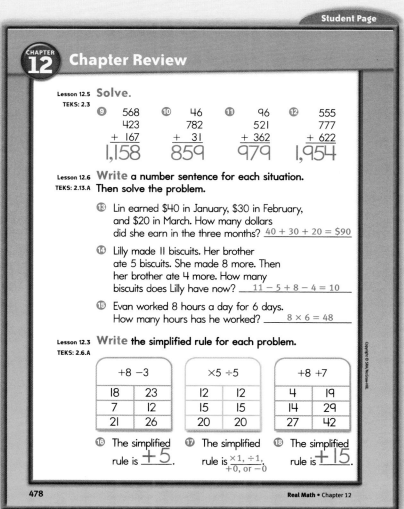

CHAPTER 12 — Chapter Review

Lesson 12.5 **TEKS: 2.3** Solve.

⑨
$$\begin{array}{r} 568 \\ 423 \\ + 167 \\ \hline 1{,}158 \end{array}$$

⑩
$$\begin{array}{r} 46 \\ 782 \\ + 31 \\ \hline 859 \end{array}$$

⑪
$$\begin{array}{r} 96 \\ 521 \\ + 362 \\ \hline 979 \end{array}$$

⑫
$$\begin{array}{r} 555 \\ 777 \\ + 622 \\ \hline 1{,}954 \end{array}$$

Lesson 12.6 **TEKS: 2.13.A** Write a number sentence for each situation. Then solve the problem.

⑬ Lin earned $40 in January, $30 in February, and $20 in March. How many dollars did she earn in the three months? $40 + 30 + 20 = \$90$

⑭ Lilly made 11 biscuits. Her brother ate 5 biscuits. She made 8 more. Then her brother ate 4 more. How many biscuits does Lilly have now? $11 - 5 + 8 - 4 = 10$

⑮ Evan worked 8 hours a day for 6 days. How many hours has he worked? $8 \times 6 = 48$

Lesson 12.3 **TEKS: 2.6.A** Write the simplified rule for each problem.

+8 −3

18	23
7	12
21	26

×5 ÷5

12	12
15	15
20	20

+8 +7

4	19
14	29
27	42

⑯ The simplified rule is **+5**.

⑰ The simplified rule is ×1, ÷1, +0, or −0.

⑱ The simplified rule is **+15**.

3 Chapter Tests   40

Practice Test

Student Pages 479–482
- The Chapter 12 Practice Test on **Student Edition** pages 479–482 provides an opportunity to formally evaluate students' proficiency with concepts developed in this chapter.
- The content is similar to the Chapter 12 Review, in standardized format.

Practice-Test Remediation

Multiple Choice Questions 1–4 are all about determining mixed operation functions. If students have difficulty with these problems, then work through the problems with them and show step-by-step how you found your answer.

Multiple Choice Questions 5–6 are about writing number sentences based on situations. If students have difficulty with these problems then have them work in groups to create situations and practice writing number sentences to match the situations. Also, remind students that they can check their work by performing the operations and seeing if their answers are reasonable.

Short Answer Questions 1–4 and **Extended Response Questions 7–8** are about creating and finding patterns. If students have difficulty with these questions, have them create their own patterns or repeating patterns and share them with the other students.

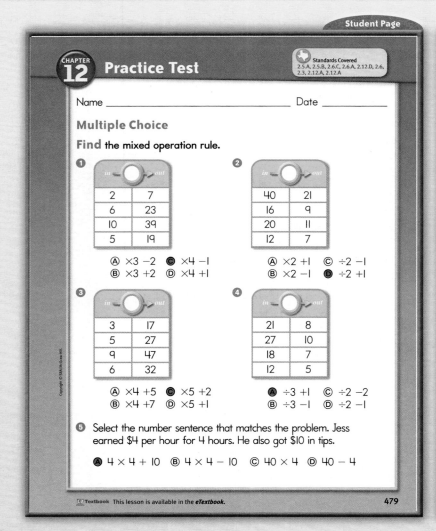

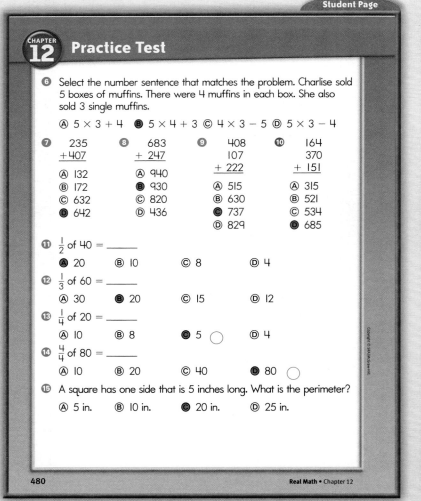

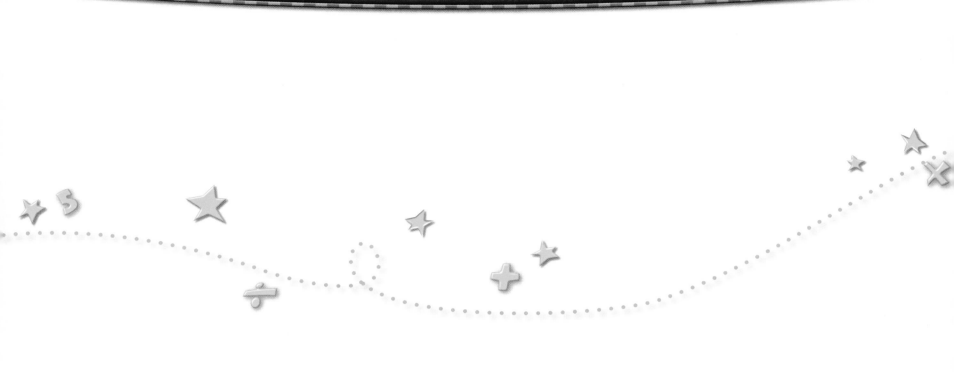

CHAPTER 12 Practice Test

Name _____ Date _____

Short Answer/Extended Response

1. Find the pattern. Fill in the blanks.

   36, 34, 32, 30, _28_, _26_

   The pattern is _−2_.

2. Find the pattern. Fill in the blanks.

   8, 12, 16, 20, _24_, _28_

   The pattern is _+4_.

3. Find the pattern. Fill in the blanks.

   64, 32, 16, 8, _4_, _2_

   The pattern is _÷2_.

4. Find the pattern. Fill in the blanks.

   5, 10, 15, 20, _25_, _30_

   The pattern is _+5_.

5. **Extended Response** Complete the chart. A school supply store sold packages of paper for $5 each. They had a special sale. The first package was $5, and every additional package was $3. Find the cost of 2, 3, 4, 5, and 6 packages of paper.

Paper Prices						
Packages	1	2	3	4	5	6
Cost ($)	5	8	11	14	17	20

CHAPTER 12 Practice Test

6. **Extended Response** Complete the chart. A store had a sale on gift-wrapping paper. The first roll of paper was $3, and every additional roll was $2. Find the cost of 2, 3, 4, 5, and 6 rolls of wrapping paper.

Wrapping Paper Sale						
Rolls	1	2	3	4	5	6
Cost ($)	3	5	7	9	11	13

7. **Extended Response** Place 6 triangles and 3 squares in any order that you choose to make a pattern. Draw the pattern that you made. Draw vertical lines to show where the pattern repeats. Students' patterns should include any combination of 6 triangles and 3 squares.

8. **Extended Response** Angela used 3 different shapes to draw a pattern. One of the shapes was used more often than the other two shapes. Draw a pattern that could be like the one Angela drew. Draw vertical lines to show where the pattern repeats. Students' patterns should include 2 of one shape and 1 each of two additional shapes. The pattern repeats after every fourth item.

4 Assess and Differentiate

 Assess Use *eAssess* to record and analyze evidence of student understanding.

A Gather Evidence

Use the Daily Class Assessment Records in *Texas Assessment* or *eAssess* to record Informal and Formal Assessments.

Informal Assessment

✓ **Key Ideas Review** UNDERSTANDING

Did the student
- ❑ make important observations?
- ❑ extend or generalize learning?
- ❑ provide insightful answers?
- ❑ pose insightful questions?

Informal Assessment

✓ **Project** APPLYING

Did the student
- ❑ meet the project objectives?
- ❑ communicate clearly?
- ❑ complete the project accurately?
- ❑ connect mathematics to real-world situations?

Formal Assessment

✓ **Chapter Test** COMPUTING

Score the test, and record the results.

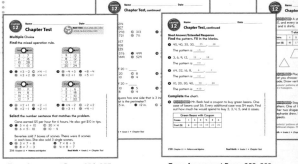

Texas Assessment Pages 256–257   Texas Assessment Pages 258–259

B Summarize Findings

Analyze and summarize assessment data for each student. Determine which Chapter Follow-Up is appropriate for each student. Use the Student Assessment Record in *Texas Assessment* or *eAssess* to update assessment records.

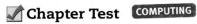

Texas Assessment

C Chapter Follow-Up ● DIFFERENTIATE INSTRUCTION

Based on your observations, use these teaching strategies for chapter follow-up.

ENRICH	PRACTICE	RETEACH	INTERVENTION
If . . . students demonstrate a **secure understanding** of chapter concepts,	**If . . .** students demonstrate **competent understanding** of chapter concepts,	**If . . .** students demonstrate **emerging understanding** of chapter concepts,	**If . . .** students demonstrate **minimal understanding** of chapter concepts,
Then . . . encourage them to explore math and play math games until they start the next level of math.	**Then . . .** encourage them to practice math and play math games to prepare for the next level of math.	**Then . . .** encourage them to play math games and use and practice math before they begin the next level of math. Suggest that these students study and review math to be ready for the next level.	**Then . . .** encourage them to use and practice math until they start the next level of math. Advise taking a remedial math class to be ready for the next level of math.

Paint Up, Fix Up, Measure Up

Context of the Thinking Story Mr. Muddle needs to finish painting his house and put a screen on the back door, but he keeps getting the measurements wrong.

Lesson Planner

OBJECTIVES
To develop logical thinking while integrating reading skills with mathematics

MATH TEKS

Number, operation, and quantitative reasoning 2.3.C Select addition or subtraction to solve problems using two-digit numbers, whether or not regrouping is necessary.

Underlying processes and mathematical tools 2.12.C Select or develop an appropriate problem-solving plan or strategy including drawing a picture, looking for a pattern, systematic guessing and checking, or acting it out in order to solve a problem.

Measurement
• Recognizing the attributes of length and volume
• Comparing objects according to the attributes of length and volume

Reading/comprehension 2.9.E Draw and discuss visual images based on text descriptions.

Reading/literary response 2.10.C Support interpretations or conclusions with examples drawn from text.

Reading inquiry/research 2.12.H Draw conclusions from information gathered.

Using the Thinking Story

The Thinking Story may be used at any time throughout the chapter. Read the Thinking Story "Paint Up, Fix Up, Measure Up" to your class. As you read the story, give students time to think about each question, but not so much that they forget the point being made.

Paint Up, Fix Up, Measure Up

Mr. Muddle's house gets more and more broken down every year. The longer he waits to repair things, the more he forgets the things that need to be repaired.

Last spring he remembered that his house needed to be painted, but he soon forgot that it had four sides. He stopped painting after only one side was finished.

How many sides were left unpainted? **three**

In the summer Mr. Muddle noticed that three sides of his house were still unpainted. All four sides of his house are the same size, and he remembered buying 10 gallons of paint to paint one side.

How much paint will he need to finish painting his house?
30 gallons

Mr. Muddle went to the paint store and bought 10 gallons of paint so he could finish the house.

Will he have enough paint? no

How much of the house will he be able to paint with 10 gallons? one side

How much of the house will still need to be painted? two sides

When he had used the 10 gallons of paint, Mr. Muddle was surprised to find that only one more side of his house was painted and that two sides still needed paint. He went back to the paint store, but he couldn't remember how much paint he needed.

How much more paint does Mr. Muddle need? 20 gallons

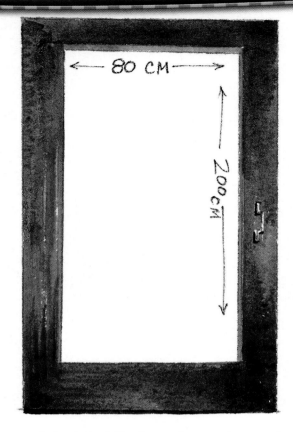

Mr. Muddle decided to go home and check before buying any more paint.

When he got home, he noticed that he needed a new screen for the back door. "I might as well take care of that right now," he thought. He carefully measured the screen and found that it was 80 centimeters wide and 200 centimeters high.

Suggest that the students draw a picture of the screen and write the dimensions along the edges.

Mr. Muddle wrote the measurements so he wouldn't forget them. When he got to the hardware store, he found that the only screening they sold was 100 centimeters wide.

What should Mr. Muddle do? How long a piece of screening should he buy?   200 cm

At first, Mr. Muddle thought he would buy a piece 200 centimeters long. "That would be the right length," he thought, "but it would be too wide." Then he had an idea. "Since this screening is 20 centimeters too wide," he thought, "I'll get it 20 centimeters shorter to make up for it."

How long a piece of screening will Mr. Muddle buy?   180 cm; Suggest that the students draw a picture of the piece of screening Mr. Muddle bought and write the dimensions.

Mr. Muddle bought a piece of screening that was 180 centimeters long and, of course, it was 100 centimeters wide. When he returned home and tried to put it into the door frame, he was surprised to find that it didn't fit.

What was wrong with it?   It was too wide and too short.

The screen stuck out on the sides and didn't reach to the top. "I guess I could cut some off the sides to make it fit," Mr. Muddle thought.

"But my metal-cutting scissors are broken. Besides, I don't know any way to make it longer at the top. I guess I'll just have to put it on the way it is and hope the flies don't notice that something is wrong."

What do you think the flies will find out?   They can get in at the top.

Mr. Muddle was surprised to find that so many flies were getting in through his back door. "I have this nice new screen to keep them out," he said, "but they keep coming in through the top part of the door that isn't covered. Those flies don't seem to appreciate the work I've done."

The End

Teaching the Lesson

Guided Discussion

As students answer the questions in the story, ask them to communicate how they chose their answers. Allow students to debate the answers if necessary.

Using Student Pages 483–484

Have students follow the instructions and complete the **Student Edition** activities. Read the instructions aloud if students are having difficulty.

Name _____ Date _____

Math TEKS
Number, operation, and quantitative reasoning 2.3.C
Select additions or subtraction to solve problems using two-digit numbers, whether or not regrouping is necessary.

Thinking Story

Paint Up, Fix Up, Measure Up

Each side of the house takes 10 gallons of paint. Mr. Muddle has leftover paint. Each bucket holds 5 gallons of paint. Write the name of the color Mr. Muddle will need to use to paint all four walls of his house.

yellow

Textbook This lesson is available in the *eTextbook*.

483

How many centimeters too wide is the screen for the door on each side? Write the number.

10

How many centimeters too short is the screen for the door? Write the number.

20

80 cm
280 cm
100 cm
180 cm

484

Real Math • Chapter 12

Teacher Reflection

Reflect on each of the lessons you taught in this chapter. Rate each one on the following scale, and then consider ways to maintain or improve positive teaching experiences in the future.

Lessons	Very Effective	Effective	Less Effective	What Worked	Ways to Improve
12.1 Patterns and Functions					
12.2 Functions with Mixed Operations					
12.3 More Functions with Mixed Operations					
12.4 Patterns and Shapes					
12.5 Column Addition					
12.6 Number Sentences					
12.7 Creating Word Problems					

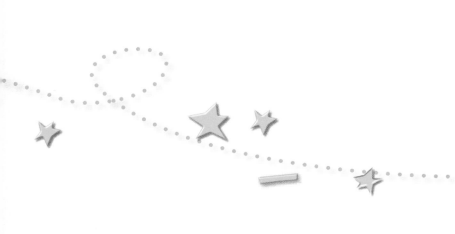

Picture Glossary

A

acute angle

angles

C

cylinder

E

eighth

F

fifth

flip

Picture Glossary

M

mode

the number that appears most often in a set of data

O

obtuse angle

P

parallel

perpendicular

polygon

a closed plane figure with three or more sides

prism

pyramid

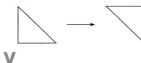

Picture Glossary

Q

quadrilateral

R

range

the lowest and highest numbers in a set of data

rhombus

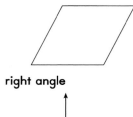

right angle

S

sixth

slide

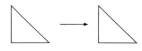

Picture Glossary

T

thermometer

trapezoid

turn

V

variables

$$3 \times n = y$$

Appendix

This appendix provides additional information about key issues in mathematics education and how they are addressed in *Real Math.*

About Mathematics

"Genuine mathematics...constitutes one of the finest expressions of the human spirit. The great areas of mathematics—algebra, real analysis, complex analysis, number theory, combinatorics, probability theory, statistics, topology, geometry, and so on—have undoubtedly arisen from our experience of the world around us, in order to systematize that experience, to give it order and coherence, and thereby to enable us to predict and perhaps control future events."

Hilton, Peter. "Mathematics in Our Culture" in Gullberg, Jan. Mathematics: From the Birth of Numbers. New York: W.W. Norton & Company, 1997.

Mathematics is a way of describing relationships between numbers and other measurable quantities. As the language of science, mathematics communicates ideas in universally accepted terminology. It can express simple equations or explain relationships among the farthest objects in the known universe. Mathematics has helped make advances in medicine, technology, astronomy, meteorology, biology, physics, economics, and political science.

Mathematics has two main branches: pure mathematics, the study of abstract relationships, and applied mathematics, which applies mathematical analysis to real-world problems. The relationship between pure and applied mathematics is a complex one, and is constantly shifting.

Mathematics continues to grow at a phenomenal rate. There is no end in sight, and the application of mathematics to science becomes greater all the time.

Key Events in the Timeline of Mathematics

- Counting was the earliest mathematical activity. Early humans needed counting to keep track of herds and for trade. Early counting systems used the fingers of one or both hands, as evidenced by the predominance of the numbers 5 and 10 as the bases for most number systems today. Advances were in the concept of numbers, the invention of addition, subtraction, multiplication, and division, and concepts such as the line and the circle in geometry.

  - **2000 B.C.** The Babylonians of ancient Mesopotamia and the ancient Egyptians developed principles of arithmetic, measurement, and calculation.

    - **1400 B.C.** The first true evidence of mathematical activity in China can be found in numeration symbols on tortoise shells and oracle bones from the Shang dynasty. These inscriptions contain both tally and code symbols based on a decimal system. Early Chinese mathematics had a great influence on later civilizations.

      - **1000 B.C.** The Maya used a base-20 number system, which probably descended from early times when people counted on both fingers and toes and may have been the first to have a special symbol for zero. The Maya also developed two types of calendars, calculating the length of the lunar month and the solar year with remarkable precision.

- **6th Century B.C.** The Greeks adopted elements of mathematics from the Babylonians and the Egyptians and invented abstract mathematics founded on a logical structure of definitions, axioms (propositions accepted as self-evident), and proofs. Thales and Pythagoras were famous mathematicians.

  - **300 B.C.** Euclid, a Greek mathematician, deduced some 500 theorems comprising all the important results of Greek mathematics to that time. Euclid began by defining terms, such as line, angle, and circle. He stated ten self-evident truths, such as "The whole is greater than any of its parts."

    - **1st Century A.D.** After the decline of Greece and Rome, mathematics flourished for hundreds of years in India and the Islamic world. Their mathematical masterpieces and those of the Greeks were translated into Arabic in the centers of Islamic learning, where mathematical discoveries continued during the Middle Ages. Our present numeration system, with each number having an absolute value and a place value (ones, tens, hundreds, and so forth), is known as the Hindu-Arabic system.

      - **8th Century A.D.** Translators in Baghdad produced Arabic versions of Greek and Indian mathematical works. Many of the ancient Greek works on mathematics were preserved during the Middle Ages through Arabic translations and commentaries. Europe acquired much of this learning during the 12th century, when Greek and Arabic works were translated into Latin, the written language of the educated Europeans.

"Number rules the universe."

—Pythagoras, Greek philosopher and mathematician, 580–520 B.C.

> **"Mathematics is one of humanity's great achievements. By enhancing the capabilities of the human mind, mathematics has facilitated the development of science, technology, engineering, business, and government. Mathematics is also an intellectual achievement of great sophistication and beauty that epitomizes the power of deductive reasoning. For people to participate fully in society, they must know basic mathematics."**
>
> Kilpatrick, J., Swafford, J., and Findell, B. eds. *Adding It Up: Helping Children Learn Mathematics*. Washington, D.C.: National Research Council/National Academy Press, 2001, p. 1.

Real Math and Mathematics

Real Math has been developed with a keen respect for the history and the beauty of mathematics. Careful attention has been paid to developing children's understanding of mathematics in a coherent and logical fashion to demonstrate the connections among the different strands and branches of mathematics. *Real Math* aims for children to develop a positive attitude toward mathematics. Specific abilities and understandings will be of little value to children unless accompanied by two convictions: (a) that mathematics does what it was invented to do —solve real, interesting problems; and (b) that it is a tool that can be used confidently and well. Also, we hope that students will find mathematics enjoyable to do and that they will appreciate it esthetically.

- **9th Century A.D.** Arab mathematician al-Khwārizmī wrote a systematic introduction to algebra. The English word *algebra* comes from *al-jabr* in the title. A 12th-century Latin translation of al-Khwārizmī's treatise was crucial for the later development of algebra in Europe. Al-Khwārizmī's name is the source of the word *algorithm*.

  - **16th Century** Mathematicians began to use symbols to make algebraic thinking and writing more concise. These symbols included $+$, $-$, $\times$, $=$, $>$ (greater than), and $<$ (less than). The most significant innovation, by French mathematician François Viète, was the systematic use of letters for variables in equations.

    - **17th Century** The founders of modern science—Nicolaus Copernicus, Johannes Kepler, Galileo, and Isaac Newton—studied the natural world as mathematicians, and they looked for its mathematical laws. Over time, mathematics grew more and more abstract as mathematicians sought to establish the foundations of their fields logically. The most important development in geometry during the 17th century was the discovery of analytic geometry by René Descartes and Pierre de Fermat, which makes it possible to study geometric figures using algebraic equations. The discovery of differential and integral calculus by Sir Isaac Newton and Gottfried Wilhelm Leibniz ranks as the crowning achievement of 17th-century mathematics. Calculus allowed the solution of many problems that had been previously insoluble, including the determination of the laws of motion and the theory of electromagnetism.

- **18th Century** During the 18th century, calculus became the cornerstone of mathematical analysis on the European continent. Mathematicians applied the discovery to a variety of problems in physics, astronomy, and engineering. In the course of doing so, they also created new areas of mathematics. The greatest mathematician of the 18th century, Leonhard Euler of Switzerland, was also the most prolific writer on mathematical subjects of all time. His treatises covered essentially the entire fields of pure and applied mathematics.

  - **The 19th Century** was a period of intense mathematical activity. It began with German mathematician Carl Friedrich Gauss, considered to be the last complete mathematician because of his contributions to all branches of the field. The century saw a great effort to place all areas of mathematics on firm theoretical foundations. The support for these foundations was logic—the deduction of basic propositions from a limited set of assumptions and definitions. Mathematicians also discovered the existence of additional geometries and algebras, and more than one kind of infinity.

    - **During the 20th Century** mathematics made rapid advances on all fronts. The foundations of mathematics became more solidly grounded in logic, while at the same time mathematics advanced the development of symbolic logic. Philosophy and physics, too, benefited from the contributions of mathematicians to the Relativity Theory and Quantum Theory. Indeed, mathematics achieved broader applications than ever before as new fields developed within mathematics (computational mathematics, game theory, and chaos theory), and other branches of knowledge, including economics and physics, achieved firmer grounding through the application of mathematics. Even the most abstract mathematics seemed to find application, and the boundaries between pure mathematics and applied mathematics grew ever fuzzier.

Content Strands of Mathematics

"One reason why mathematics enjoys special esteem, above all other sciences, is that its laws are absolutely certain and indisputable, while those of other sciences are to some extent debatable and in constant danger of being overthrown by newly discovered facts."

—Albert Einstein, physicist, 1879–1955

Algebra

Algebra is the branch of mathematics that uses symbols to represent arithmetic operations. Algebra extends arithmetic through the use of symbols and other notations, such as exponents and variables. Algebraic thinking involves understanding patterns, equations, and relationships, and includes concepts of functions and inverse operations. Because algebra uses symbols rather than numbers, it can produce general rules that apply to all numbers. What most people commonly think of as algebra involves the manipulation of equations and the solving of equations. Exposure to algebraic ideas can and should occur well before students first study algebra in middle school or high school. Even primary-grade students are capable of understanding many algebraic concepts. Developing algebraic thinking in the early grades smoothes the transition to algebra in middle school and high school and ensures success in future math and science courses, as well as in the workplace.

> **"Algebra begins with a search for patterns. Identifying patterns helps bring order, cohesion, and predictability to seemingly unorganized situations and allows one to make generalizations beyond the information directly available. The recognition and analysis of patterns are important components of the young child's intellectual development because they provide a foundation for the development of algebraic thinking."**
>
> Clements, Douglas and Sarama, J. eds. *Engaging Young Children in Mathematics: Standards for Early Childhood Mathematics Education.* Mahwah, New Jersey: Lawrence Erlbaum Associates, Publishers, 2004. p. 52.

Real Math and Algebra

Goal: Understanding of functional relationships between variables that represents real-world phenomena in a constant state of change. Children should be able to draw the graphs of functions and to derive information about functions from their graphs. They should understand the special importance of linear functions and the connection between the study of functions and the solution of equations and inequalities.

The algebra readiness strand that begins in the PreK level is designed to prepare students for future work in algebra by exposing them to algebraic thinking, including looking for patterns, using variables, working with functions, using integers and exponents, and being aware that mathematics is far more than just arithmetic.

Arithmetic

Arithmetic, one of the oldest branches of mathematics, arises from the most fundamental of mathematical operations: counting. The arithmetic operations—addition, subtraction, multiplication, division, and placeholding—form the basis of the mathematics that we use regularly. Mastery of the basic operations with whole numbers (addition, subtraction, multiplication, and division)

> **"Although some educators once believed that children memorize their 'basic facts' as conditioned responses, research now shows that children do not move from knowing nothing about sums and differences of numbers to having the basic number combinations memorized. Instead, they move through a series of progressively more advanced and abstract methods for working out the answers to simple arithmetic problems. Furthermore, as children get older, they use the procedures more and more efficiently."**
>
> Kilpatrick, J., Swafford, J. and Findell, B. eds. Adding It Up: Helping Children Learn Mathematics. Washington, D.C.: National Research Council/National Academy Press, 2001. p. 182–183.

Real Math and Arithmetic

Goal: Mastery of the basic operations with whole numbers (addition, subtraction, multiplication, and division). Whatever other skills and understandings children acquire, they must have the ability to calculate a precise answer when necessary. This fundamental skill includes not only knowledge of the appropriate arithmetic algorithms, but also mastery of the basic addition, subtraction, multiplication, and division facts and understanding of the positional notation (base ten) of the whole numbers.

Mastery Checkpoints occur throughout the program to indicate when mastery of concepts and skills is expected. Skills are introduced at least one grade level before mastery is expected and then reviewed in Mental Math and subsequent grade levels. Once taught, arithmetic skills are also integrated into other topics, such as functions and geometry.

Data Collection and Organization

Ability to organize information to make it easier to use and the ability to interpret data and graphs.

> "Describing data involves reading displays of data (e.g., tables, lists, graphs); that is, finding information explicitly stated in the display, recognizing graphical conventions, and making direct connections between the original data and the display. The process is essentially what has been called reading the data.... The process of organizing and reducing data incorporates mental actions, such as ordering, grouping, and summarizing. Data reduction also includes the use of representative measures of center (often termed *measures of central tendency*), such as mean, mode, or median, and measures of spread, such as range or standard deviation."
>
> Kilpatrick, J., Swafford, J. and Findell, B. eds. *Adding It Up: Helping Children Learn Mathematics.* Washington, D.C.: National Research Council/National Academy Press, 2001, p. 289.

Real Math and Data Organization

Goal: Ability to organize and arrange data for greater intelligibility. Children should develop not only the routine skills of tabulating and graphing results, but also, at a higher level, the ability to detect patterns and trends in poorly organized data, either before or after reorganization. In addition, children need to develop the ability to extrapolate and interpolate from data and from graphic representations. Children should also know when extrapolation or interpolation is justified and when it is not.

In *Real Math* students work with graphs beginning in PreK. In each grade, the program emphasizes understanding what data shows.

Geometry

Geometry is the branch of mathematics that deals with the properties of space. Plane geometry is the geometry of flat surfaces, and solid geometry is the geometry of three-dimensional space figures. Geometry has many more fields, including the study of spaces with four or more dimensions.

> "Geometry can be used to understand and to represent the objects, directions, and locations in our world, and the relationships between them. Geometric shapes can be described, analyzed, transformed, and composed and decomposed into other shapes."
>
> Clements, Douglas and Sarama, J. eds. *Engaging Young Children in Mathematics: Standards for Early Childhood Mathematics Education.* Mahwah, New Jersey: Lawrence Erlbaum Associates, Publishers, 2004. p. 39.

Real Math and Geometry

Goal: Understanding of and ability to use geometric concepts in a variety of contexts.

To appreciate how geometry can help to explain algebraic concepts.

Measurement

Understanding of what a measurement is and how units relate to measurement.

> "Measurement is one of the main real-world applications of mathematics...counting is a type of measurement—it measures how many items in a collection. Measurement of continuous quantities involves assigning a number to attributes, such as length, area, and weight. Together, number and measurement are components of quantitative reasoning. In this vein, measurement helps connect the two realms of number and geometry, each providing conceptual support to the other."
>
> Clements, Douglas and Sarama, J. eds. *Engaging Young Children in Mathematics: Standards for Early Childhood Mathematics Education.* Mahwah, New Jersey: Lawrence Erlbaum Associates, Publishers, 2004. p. 43–50.

Real Math and Measurement

Goal: Firm understanding of magnitude with respect to measurements and of the role of units in assigning numerical magnitudes to physical quantities. Children should, for example, understand the need for standard units of measurement and know how to use appropriate measurement tools (rulers, balances, liquid volume measures, and thermometers).

In *Real Math,* students work extensively with estimating measures and making actual measurements. They work with both the customary system (inches, pounds, cups) and the metric system (meters, grams, liters) separately so that they develop an intuitive feel for measurements in both systems.

Number Sense and Place Value

Understanding of the significance and use of numbers in counting, measuring, comparing, and ordering.

> "It is very important for teachers to provide children with opportunities to recognize the meaning of mathematical symbols, mathematical operations, and the patterns or relationships represented in the child's work with numbers. For example, the number sense that a child acquires should be based upon an understanding that inverse operations, such as addition and subtraction, undo the operations of the other. Instructionally, teachers must encourage their students to think beyond simply finding the answer and to actually have them think about the numerical relationships that are being represented or modeled by the symbols, words, or materials being used in the lesson."
>
> Kilpatrick, J., Swafford, J. and Findell, B. eds. *Adding It Up: Helping Children Learn Mathematics.* Washington, D.C.: National Research Council/National Academy Press, 2001, p. 270–271.

Real Math and Number Sense

Goal: Firm understanding of the significance and use of numbers in counting, measuring, comparing, and ordering. The ability to think intelligently, using numbers. This basic requirement of numeracy includes the ability to recognize given answers as absurd, without doing a precise calculation, by observing that they violate experience, common sense, elementary logic, or familiar arithmetic patterns. It also includes the use of imagination and insight in using numbers to solve problems. Children should be able to recognize when, for example, a trial-and-error method is likely to be easier to use and more manageable than a standard algorithm.

Developing number sense is a primary goal of *Real Math* in every grade. Numbers are presented in a variety of representations and integrated in many contexts so that students develop thorough understanding of numbers.

Probability and Statistics

Probability and statistics deal with events where outcomes are uncertain, and they assess the likelihood of possible outcomes. Statistics is the organization and analysis of data for the purpose of simplification, comparison, and prediction.

Real Math and Probability and Statistics

Goal: The ability to use probabilistic ideas in ordinary, elementary applications. Children should understand the reasons for (and something of the dangers of) using sampling techniques; they should have the ability to describe a population in terms of some simple statistic (mean, median, range); and they should understand the difference between intelligent risk taking, based on reasonable estimates of probabilities, and foolish risks, based on unsupported guesswork or wishful thinking.

Rational Numbers—Fractions, Decimals, and Percents

Understanding fractions, decimals, and percents and their relationships to each other, including the ability to perform calculations and to use rational numbers in measurement.

> "Children need to learn that rational numbers are numbers in the same way that whole numbers are numbers. For children to use rational numbers to solve problems, they need to learn that the same rational number may be represented in different ways, as a fraction, a decimal, or a percent. Fraction concepts and representations need to be related to those of division, measurement, and ratio. Decimal and fractional representations need to be connected and understood. Building these connections take extensive experience with rational numbers over a substantial period of time. Researchers have documented that difficulties in working with rational numbers can often be traced to weak conceptual understanding....Instructional sequences in which more time is spent at the outset on developing

> meaning for the various representations of rational numbers and the concept of unit have been shown to promote mathematical proficiency."
>
> —Kilpatrick, J., Swafford, J. and Findell, B. eds. *Adding It Up: Helping Children Learn Mathematics.* Washington, D.C.: National Research Council/National Academy Press, 2001, p. 415–416.

Real Math and Rational Numbers

Goal: Understanding of rational numbers and of the relationship of fractions to decimals. Included here are the ability to do appropriate calculations with fractions or decimals (or both, as in fractions of decimals); the use of decimals in (metric unit) measurements; and the multiplication of fractions as a model for the "of" relation and as a model for areas of rectangles.

Goal: Understanding of the meaning of rates and of their relationship to the arithmetic concept of ratio. Children should be able to calculate ratios, proportions, and percentages; understand how to use them intelligently in real-life situations; understand the common units in which rates occur (such as kilometers per hour, cents per gram); understand the meaning of per; and be able to express ratios as fractions.

In *Real Math,* understanding of rational numbers begins in the earliest grades with sharing activities and develops understanding of rational numbers with increasing sophistication at each grade.

The Research Behind *Real Math*

SRA *Real Math* is a standards-and research-based program that has been built to address the future of mathematics education in which research, standards, and testing are aligned to effectively develop student proficiency in mathematics. ***Real Math*** is based on three different types of research.

Foundational Research

Real Math has incorporated curriculum to cover new emphases in standards and a careful review of the landmark compendiums of math educational research.

Adding It Up: Helping Children Learn Mathematics
Kilpatrick, J., Swafford, J., Findell, B. eds. Mathematics Learning Study Committee, National Research Council, 2001.

Research Companion to Principles and Standards for School Mathematics
Kilpatrick, J., Martin, W. G., and Schifter, D. eds., 2002.

SRA's ***Real Math*** is the first math program to fully integrate the five strands of mathematical proficiency as defined by today's research.

Real Math focuses on meeting the current national standards by uniquely adjusting the program to incorporate, lesson by lesson, the five key proficiencies identified by the math research community (Kilpatrick, 2001; Kilpatrick, Martin, Gray, and Schifter, 2003).

> ***Understanding***—*Conceptual Understanding* is comprehending mathematical concepts, operations, and relations—knowing what mathematical symbols, diagrams, and procedures mean.
>
> ***Computing***—*Procedural Fluency* is carrying out mathematical procedures, such as adding, subtracting, multiplying, and dividing numbers flexibly, accurately, efficiently, and appropriately.
>
> ***Applying***—*Strategic Competence* is being able to formulate problems mathematically and devise strategies for solving them using concepts and procedures appropriately.
>
> ***Reasoning***—*Adaptive Reasoning* refers to using logic to explain and justify a solution to a problem or to extend from something known to something not yet known.
>
> ***Engaging***—*Productive Disposition* is seeing mathematics as sensible, useful, and doable.

In addition to the attention to developing all five strands of math proficiency, the program incorporates the following practices supported by the foundational research cited below.

- **Rational Number Concept Development**
  Moss, J. *How Students Learn: Mathematics in the Classroom.* National Academy of Sciences, 2005.
- **Expanded Counting**
  (Fuson, 1990; Geary, 1994; Miller and Paredes, 1996).
- **Finger Sets**
  (Fuson, Perry, and Kwon, 1994).
- **Teaching Addition and Subtraction With and Without Renaming At the Same Time**
  (Fuson, 1990; Fuson, Stigler, and Bartsch, 1988; Usnick, 1992).
- **Games** *Games*
  (Bright, Harvey, and Wheeler, 1979; Schoedler, 1981; Koran and McLaughlin, 1990; Case and Griffin, 1990; Siegler and Ramani, 2006).

- **Intuitive Multiplication Starting Early**
  (Mulligan and Mitchellmore, 1997; Clark and Kamii, 1996).
- **Math Talk—Guided Discussion**
  (Kilpatrick, J., Swafford, J. and Findell, B. eds. *Adding It Up: Helping Children Learn Mathematics.* Washington, D.C.: National Research Council/National Academy Press, 2001, pp. 425–426.)

Field Test Qualitative Research

Real Math is an elementary math curriculum that has been under continual development for 30 years. The program was developed one grade level at a time. As each grade's manuscript was completed, it was field-tested in schools. The authors taught the program as well. Teacher comments, questions, and suggestions were considered and incorporated into the manuscript. The next grade level would then be field-tested. The entire process of development took more than 10 years. As part of the development of the 2007 and 2009 editions of ***Real Math***, the program was field-tested in five schools in different parts of the United States. As chapters were developed, they were tested in classrooms in each school. Teachers filled out daily lesson reports and observers were sent to each site five times throughout the year. The lesson reports were used to refine the lessons and improve the manuscript.

Efficacy Quantitative Research

The Research Behind *Building Blocks* **B**uilding **B**locks

Building Blocks, the PreK level of ***Real Math***, was designed upon research conducted in a well-defined, rigorous, and complete fashion. ***Building Blocks*** software developed as part of this research also is used in Grades K–6 of ***Real Math***. Results indicate strong positive effects, with achievement gains near or exceeding those recorded for individual tutoring.

Learning Trajectories for Primary Grades Mathematics

As part of the work developed for ***Building Blocks***—Foundations for Mathematical Thinking under the National Science Foundation grant number ESI-9730804, Doug Clements and Julie Sarama identified the learning trajectories in key areas of mathematics. Complete learning trajectories describe the goals of learning, the thinking and learning processes of children at various levels, and the learning activities in which they might engage.

The learning trajectory research informs the sequence of activities in grades K–6. The complete trajectories are listed in the Appendix of each ***Teacher's Edition***. They are referenced in the chapter openers in What Research Says.

Clements, D. H., Sarama, J., and DiBiase, A.-M. eds. *Engaging young children in mathematics: Standards for early childhood mathematics education.* Mahwah, N.J.: Lawrence Erlbaum Associates, 2004.

Math Proficiencies

Mathematical proficiency has five strands. These strands are not independent; they represent different aspects of a complex whole.... they are interwoven and interdependent in the development of proficiency in mathematics.

Kilpatrick, J., Swafford, J. and Findell, B. eds. Adding It Up: Helping Children Learn Mathematics. Washington, D.C.: National Research Council/National Academy Press, 2001, p. 115–133.

1. **Understanding** (Conceptual Understanding): Comprehending mathematical concepts, operations, and relations—knowing what mathematical symbols, diagrams, and procedures mean.

   Conceptual Understanding refers to an integrated and functional grasp of mathematical ideas. Students with conceptual understanding know more than isolated facts and methods. They understand why a mathematical idea is important and the kinds of contexts in which it is useful. They have organized their knowledge into a coherent whole, which enables them to learn new ideas by connecting those ideas to what they already know. Conceptual understanding also supports retention. Because facts and methods learned with understanding are connected, they are easier to remember and use, and they can be reconstructed when forgotten. If students understand a method, they are unlikely to remember it incorrectly.

   A significant indicator of conceptual understanding is being able to represent mathematical situations in different ways and knowing how different representations can be useful for different purposes.

   Knowledge that has been learned with understanding provides the basis for generating new knowledge and for solving new and unfamiliar problems. When students have acquired conceptual understanding in an area of mathematics, they see the connections among concepts and procedures and can give arguments to explain why some facts are consequences of others. They gain confidence, which then provides a base from which they can move to another level of understanding.

2. **Computing** (Procedural Fluency): Carrying out mathematical procedures, such as adding, subtracting, multiplying, and dividing numbers flexibly, accurately, efficiently, and appropriately.

   Procedural Fluency refers to knowledge of procedures, knowledge of when and how to use them appropriately, and skill in performing them flexibly, accurately, and efficiently. In the domain of numbers, procedural

Each problem that I solved became a rule which served afterwards to solve other problems.

René Descartes French philosopher and mathematician, 1596–1650

fluency is especially needed to support conceptual understanding of place value and the meanings of rational numbers. It also supports the analysis of similarities and differences between methods of calculating. These methods include, in addition to written procedures, mental methods for finding certain sums, differences, products, or quotients, as well as methods that use calculators, computers, or manipulative materials such as blocks, counters, or beads.

Students need to be efficient and accurate in performing basic computations with whole numbers without always having to refer to tables or other aids. They also need to know reasonably efficient and accurate ways to add, subtract, multiply, and divide multidigit numbers, both mentally and with pencil and paper. A good conceptual understanding of place value in the base-ten system supports the development of fluency in multidigit computation. Such understanding also supports simplified but accurate mental arithmetic and more flexible ways of dealing with numbers than many students ultimately achieve.

3. **Applying** (Strategic Competence): Being able to formulate problems mathematically and to devise strategies for solving them using concepts and procedures appropriately.

   Strategic Competence refers to the ability to formulate mathematical problems, represent them, and solve them. This strand is similar to what has been called *problem solving* and *problem formulation*. Although students are often presented with clearly specified problems to solve in the school setting, outside of school they encounter situations in which part of the difficulty is to figure out exactly what the problem is. Then they need to formulate the problem so that they can use mathematics to solve it. Consequently, they are likely to need experience and practice in problem formulating, as well as in problem solving. They should know a variety of solution strategies, as well as which strategies might be useful for solving a specific problem.

   To represent a problem accurately, students must first understand the situation, including its key

Professional Development

features. They then need to generate a mathematical representation of the problem that captures the core mathematical elements and ignores the irrelevant features.

Students develop procedural fluency as they use their strategic competence to choose among effective procedures. They also learn that solving challenging mathematics problems depends on the ability to carry out procedures readily, and conversely, and that problem-solving experience helps them acquire new concepts and skills.

4. **Reasoning** (Adaptive Reasoning): Using logic to explain and justify a solution to a problem or to extend from something known to something not yet known.

Adaptive Reasoning refers to the capacity to think logically about the relationships among concepts and situations. Such reasoning is correct and valid, stems from careful consideration of alternatives, and includes knowledge of how to justify the conclusions. In mathematics, adaptive reasoning is the glue that holds everything together and guides learning. One uses it to navigate through the many facts, procedures, concepts, and solution methods, and to see that they all fit together in some way, that they make sense. In mathematics, deductive reasoning is used to settle disputes and disagreements. Answers are right because they follow some agreed-upon assumptions through a series of logical steps. Students who disagree about a mathematical answer need not rely on checking with the teacher, collecting opinions from their classmates, or gathering data from outside the classroom. In principle, they need only check that their reasoning is valid.

Research suggests that students are able to display reasoning ability when three conditions are met: they have a sufficient knowledge base, the task is understandable and motivating, and the context is familiar and comfortable.

5. **Engaging** (Productive Disposition): Seeing mathematics as sensible, useful, and doable—if you work at it—and being willing to do the work.

Productive Disposition refers to the tendency to see sense in mathematics, to perceive it as both useful and worthwhile, to believe that steady effort in learning mathematics pays off, and to see oneself as an effective learner and doer of mathematics. If students are to develop conceptual understanding, procedural fluency, strategic competence, and adaptive reasoning abilities, they must believe mathematics is understandable, not arbitrary; that with diligent effort, it can be learned and used; and that they are capable of figuring it out. Developing a productive disposition requires frequent opportunities to make sense of mathematics, to recognize the benefits of perseverance, and to experience the rewards of sense making in mathematics.

Students' dispositions toward mathematics are a major factor in determining their educational success. Students who have developed a productive disposition are confident in their knowledge and ability. They see that mathematics is both reasonable and intelligible, and believe that, with appropriate effort and experience, they can learn.

Real Math and Math Proficiency

The goals of **Real Math** are to develop the five interwoven proficiencies. In every lesson, activities are designed to address understanding, computing, reasoning, applying, and engaging in an integrated fashion. Most games, for example, can be thought of as one or more mathematical problems. Students must first identify that a problem or problems exist, then provide a structure of the problem and use reasoning to arrive at a solution. At the same time, students are developing fluency in arithmetic. There is little question that students demonstrate engagement with mathematics, as well, when they are playing a **Real Math** game. Similarly, many activities in **Real Math** are engaging because the situations are those that are real to students. The students are well-motivated to learn the mathematics involved in each situation.

Real Math Computational Expectations

At every grade level, **Real Math** develops each strand of mathematics with understanding, teaching children to appreciate and think mathematically. Problem solving, communicating mathematically, algebra, measurement, geometry, probability, and statistics, for example, are explored in every grade. Below are the computational expectations that are developed with understanding at each grade level that build fluency with number.

PreK

There are two key ideas emphasized in number.

1. Numbers can be used to tell us how many, describe order, and measure; they involve numerous relations, and can be represented in various ways.

2. Operations with numbers can be used to model a variety of real-world situations and to solve problems; they can be carried out in various ways.

Grade K

- Numbers (cardinal and ordinal) through 100
- Counting; writing numerals
- Measurement with nonstandard units
- One-to-one matching
- Adding and subtracting whole numbers in the 0–100 range

Grade 1

- Numbers 0 through 100
- Addition and subtraction concepts
- Basic addition facts (through 10 + 10)
- Measurement with nonstandard units
- Introductory work with Multiplication, fractions, recording data, maps, and inequalities

Grade 2

- Numbers through 10,000
- Basic addition and subtraction facts
- Multidigit addition and subtraction algorithms
- Introduction to multiplication and division
- Measurement with standard units
- Fractions of area and fractions of numbers
- Reading maps

Grade 3

- Numbers through 1,000,000 and beyond
- Fractions and decimals
- Multiplication and division
- Multiplication facts through 10 × 10
- Multidigit multiplication algorithms
- Measurement
- Graphing and functions
- Adding and subtracting decimals

Grade 4

- General multidigit multiplication algorithm
- Division by a one-digit divisor
- Addition and subtraction of common fractions
- Rounding and approximation
- Linear functions and composite and inverse functions
- Graphing such functions
- Multiplying decimals and whole numbers
- Introduction to mixed numbers

Grade 5

- Multidigit division algorithm
- Rounding
- Linear functions and composite and inverse functions
- Graphing such functions
- Introduction of negative numbers
- Rates, ratios, and percentages
- Relation of fractions and decimals
- Addition, subtraction, and multiplication of fractions, mixed numbers, and decimals
- Division with decimal dividends and quotients

Grade 6

- All operations with whole numbers, fractions, and decimals
- Some operations with negative numbers
- Computational shortcuts
- Compass and ruler constructions
- Nonlinear functions
- Graphing such functions
- Exponents
- Use of hand-held calculators

Basic Facts

> "Although some educators once believed that children memorize their 'basic facts' as conditioned responses, research now shows that children do not move from knowing nothing about sums and differences of numbers to having the basic number combinations memorized. Instead, they move through a series of progressively more advanced and abstract methods for working out the answers to simple arithmetic problems. Furthermore, as children get older, they use the procedures more and more efficiently."
>
> Kilpatrick, J., Swafford, J. and Findell, B. eds. *Adding It Up: Helping Children Learn Mathematics*. Washington, D.C.: National Research Council/National Academy Press, 2001, p. 182–183.

The "basic" computation facts involve addition expressions in which the addends are whole numbers from 0 through 10, the corresponding subtraction expressions, multiplication expressions in which the factors are whole numbers from 0 through 10, and the corresponding division expressions. Fluency with basic facts is the ability to quickly and accurately use facts. Fluency is necessary before students can use multidigit algorithms efficiently. *Real Math* uses a variety of methods to ensure that students become fluent with basic facts by developing an understanding of how facts are related rather than by encouraging rote memorization.

If students have difficulty with some basic facts, you can help them by providing (or helping them discover) specific strategies for the facts they have not mastered. If students use their thinking skills and understand our base-ten number system and relationships between numbers, they can use strategies, such as the following, to help with quick and accurate recall.

Note that *Real Math* teaches the addition and multiplication facts systematically to emphasize the relationships between the facts, but that most of the subtraction and division facts are taught to be the inverses of the addition and multiplication facts, rather than being grouped on their own.

Addition Fact Helpers

These strategies can help with many of the addition facts.

To add:	Think of:
0	No change
1	Counting up 1
2	Counting up 2
4	One less than adding 5
5	Finger sets
6	One more than adding 5
9	One less than adding 10
10	Write 1 in the tens place

Other strategies which may be helpful include the following:

- **Commutative Law** (for example, 6 + 9 and 9 + 6). Students should recognize that if they can add two numbers in one order, they also know the sum in the opposite order. You can demonstrate this using concrete objects that are arranged in two different ways or a picture of two sets that is turned upside down. This realization cuts roughly in half the number of facts students need to learn.

- **Doubles** (for example, 4 + 4 and 7 + 7). Most students find the doubles facts easy to learn, since only one distinct addend is involved in each fact. The **Roll a Double Game** provides targeted practice with doubles facts.

- **Near doubles** (for example, 4 + 5, 8 + 7, and 7 + 9). When the two addends in a fact differ by 1 or 2, students can relate the fact to a doubles fact. For example, 8 + 7 must be 1 more than 7 + 7, so it is 14 + 1, or 15. One way to find 7 + 9 is to recognize that since 7 is 1 less than 8 and 9 is 1 more than 8, we know 7 + 9 = 8 + 8, or 16.

- **Sums of 10** (for example, 3 + 7 and 2 + 8). Students can become familiar with pairs of numbers that add to 10 by thinking of their fingers—raising 3 fingers then 7 fingers results in all 10 fingers being raised. The **Roll a Ten Game** provides targeted practice with the skill of recognizing sums of 10, which is useful for mental computation.

- **Remaining facts**. The strategies above will help with all facts except 8 + 3, 7 + 4, and 8 + 4. If students have trouble with these, you can demonstrate that 8 + 3 and 7 + 4 are both 1 more than 7 + 3, and that 8 + 4 = 8 + 2 + 2 = 10 + 2.

- **Subtraction**. To subtract 10 from a number between 10 and 20, simply remove the tens digit. To subtract 0, leave the number unchanged. For other subtraction facts, think of the corresponding addition fact.

Multiplication Fact Helpers

To multiply by:	Think:
0	The product is 0.
1	The product is the other number.
2	Add the number to itself.
3	Add the number to its double.
4	Double the number and then double that answer.
5	Multiply the number by 10 and take half.
6	Add the number to 5 times the number, or double three times the number.
8	Double four times the number, or double the number three times.
9	Subtract the number from 10 times the number.
10	Write a "0" after the number to indicate that number of tens.

Other strategies which may be helpful include the following:

- **Commutative Law** (for example, 6×9 and 9×6). Students should recognize that if they can multiply two numbers in one order, they also know the product of the numbers in the opposite order. You can demonstrate this using an array that is turned sideways so that rows become columns and columns become rows. This realization cuts roughly in half the number of facts students need to learn.

- **Square facts** (for example, 3×3 and 7×7). Most students find the square facts relatively easy to learn, since only one distinct factor is involved in each fact.

- **Near squares** (for example, 8×7 and 6×8). When the two factors in a fact differ by 1 or 2, students can relate the product to a square fact. When the difference is 1, the product can be found by adding the smaller factor to its square. For example, 8×7 is 7 more than 7×7 — that is, $49 + 7 = 56$. When the difference is 2, students can use the pattern $(n - 1)(n + 1) = n^2 - 1$. They can discover this pattern in the multiplication table even though they cannot prove it algebraically. For example, $6 \times 8 = (7 - 1)(7 + 1) = 49 - 1 = 48$.

- **Multiples of 9**. Once students are familiar with most of the multiplication facts, you may want to point out that the sum of the digits in multiples of 9 is always a multiple of 9. They can use this to check their work, or to recall a product if they can find the first digit. For example, 7×9 is a little less than 7×10, or 70, so the first digit is 6. Since $6 + 3 = 9$, the product is 63. It is best not to introduce this pattern when students are first learning multiplication facts because they may inappropriately apply it to other factors. It is not true, for instance, that the sum of the digits of a multiple of 8 is a multiple of 8 (although the "rule" does also work for 3).

Another quick way to multiply a whole number (0 through 10) by 9 is to spread out fingers and turn down the finger corresponding to the other factor (for example, the third finger to find 3 times 9). The product is "read" by counting the fingers to the left of the folded finger as tens, and the fingers to the right as ones. Two fingers and seven fingers represents 27.

- **Division**. Since the division facts do not fall neatly into patterns, the most efficient way to find division facts is to think of the corresponding multiplication fact. For example, $56 \div 7 = 8$ because $8 \times 7 = 56$.

Ways to Practice Facts

Even after students have learned all the basic facts with understanding, they need practice to retain their fluency. There are several useful ways for students to practice facts at school or at home.

- **Flash Cards**. When used appropriately, flash cards are a good way to provide either targeted practice with certain facts or general practice with all facts. Flash cards should be used by students independently or with a partner (teacher, aide, parent, or another student working on the same facts). If a student answers correctly, he or she should receive positive reinforcement. Incorrect answers should simply receive no reaction — negative reinforcement is counter-productive since it often leads to frustration.

- **Frequent "quizzing."** If a student or class is struggling with just a few facts, ask about those facts frequently throughout the day. For example, when walking around the room checking students' progress, you can say, "What's 6×8?" Encourage parents to do the same before and after school.

- **Games**. Playing appropriate games is an excellent way to provide practice with many facts in a brief period of time, while engaging even those students who are already fluent with basic facts.

  Good games for addition practice include **Roll a 15, Addition Table,** and **Addition Crossing.**

  Good games for multiplication practice include **Multiplication Table, Multiple Crossing,** and **Multigo.**

- **Speed Tests**. Administer speed tests periodically after most students have learned the basic facts to ensure that students are maintaining and improving their skills. Timed exercises are important because decreasing the time to think about an answer encourages automatic recall. Be sure to stress that students should work to improve their own performance, rather than comparing their results to those of others.

Algorithms

> "Step-by-step procedures for adding, subtracting, multiplying, or dividing numbers are called algorithms.... Learning to use algorithms for computation with multidigit numbers is an important part of developing proficiency with numbers. Algorithms are procedures that can be executed in the same way to solve a variety of problems arising from different situations and involving different numbers."
>
> Kilpatrick, J., Swafford, J. and Findell, B. eds. *Adding It Up: Helping Children Learn Mathematics.* Washington, D.C.: National Research Council/National Academy Press, 2001, p. 196.

An algorithm is a set of steps for carrying out a procedure. There are many commonly used algorithms for addition, subtraction, multiplication, and division of multidigit numbers. **Real Math** guides students to discover one standard algorithm for each operation. However, if students have previously learned a different algorithm, or have figured out efficient procedures for some computations on their own, they should not be restricted to the procedures taught in class.

Addition

A standard algorithm for addition is introduced using two sets of sticks bundled in groups of ten.

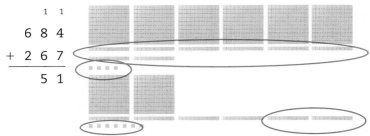

There are 7 tens and 15 ones.

We can regroup 10 ones as 1 ten.

Now there are 8 tens and 5 ones, so 37 + 48 = 85.

To avoid regrouping at the end, we can start adding with the ones place. We can record each step.

Beginning on the rightmost (ones) column, find the sum of the digits in the column. Write the ones digit of the sum below the addition line and carry the tens digit to the top of the tens column. Then repeat this process for the tens, hundreds, and so on.

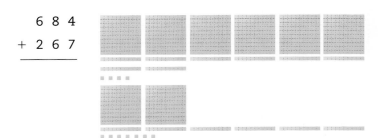

Add the ones: 4 + 7 = 11. Think, 11 ones = 1 ten and 1 one. Write the 1 one below the addition line. Write the 1 ten on top of the tens column.

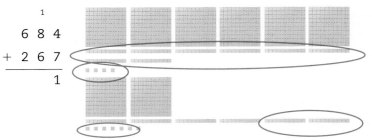

Add the tens: 1 + 8 + 6 = 15. Think, 15 tens = 1 hundred and 5 tens. Write the 5 tens below the addition line. Write the 1 hundred on top of the hundreds column.

Add the hundreds.: 1 + 6 + 2 = 9. Write the 9 hundreds below the hundreds column.

```
  1 1
  6 8 4
+ 2 6 7
-------
  9 5 1
```

Subtraction

As with the addition algorithm, a standard algorithm for subtraction is introduced using a set of sticks bundled in groups of ten.

```
  8 5
− 3 7
_____
```

There are not enough ones to take away 7.

Regroup 1 ten as 10 ones.

```
  8 5
− 3 7
_____
```

There are 4 tens and 8 ones.

$85 − 37 = 48$

It is easiest if we start subtracting with the ones place. We can record each step.

Beginning at the rightmost (ones) column, find the difference of that column. If the difference cannot be found, then rename the number in the next column to the left. Rewrite the tens and ones to reflect renaming. Then repeat this process for the tens, hundreds, and so on.

```
  1 1 6 5
−     4 2 8
_____
```

Since 8 ones cannot be taken from 5 ones, rename 6 tens as 5 tens and 10 ones.

```
        5  15
  1 1 6̶ 5̶
−     4 2 8
_____
```

Subtract the ones.

```
        5  15
  1 1 6̶ 5̶
−     4 2 8
_____
            7
```

Subtract the tens.

```
        5  15
  1 1 6̶ 5̶
−     4 2 8
_____
        3 7
```

Since 4 hundreds cannot be taken from 1 hundred, rename 1 thousand as 10 hundreds.

```
        5  15
  1 1 6̶ 5̶
−     4 2 8
_____
        3 7
```

Subtract the hundreds.

```
        5  15
  1 1 6̶ 5̶
−     4 2 8
_____
      7 3 7
```

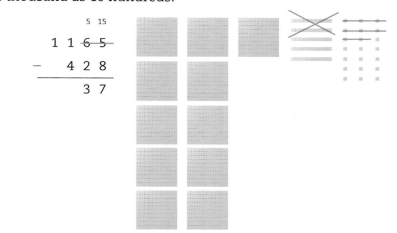

Professional Development

Multiplication

Efficient multiplication of multidigit numbers uses the Distributive Law. To multiply by a multidigit number, you can rewrite the product as a series of partial products. For example, $43 \times 8 = (40 + 3) \times 8 = (40 \times 8) - (3 \times 8) = 320 + 24 = 344$.

Products of two multidigit numbers can be found by writing each factor in expanded form and finding the products of each pair of terms. For example, $46 \times 73 = (40 + 6) \times (70 + 3) = (40 \times 70) + (40 \times 3) + (6 \times 70) + (6 \times 3)$.

Real Math introduces these ideas using area models in which each partial product is shown as a separate area. The product of the numbers (the sum of the areas of each rectangle) is the sum of the partial products.

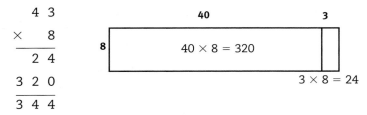

```
    4 3
  ×   8
  ─────
    2 4
  3 2 0
  ─────
  3 4 4
```

```
            4 6
          × 7 3
          ─────
  6 × 3 = 18      1 8
  40 × 3 = 120  1 2 0
  6 × 70 = 420  4 2 0
  40 × 70 = 2,800  2 8 0 0
          ───────
          3, 3 5 8
```

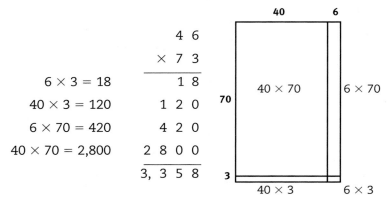

Standard algorithm

Once students understand the idea of partial products, they are introduced to a more efficient way of recording their work.

Beginning at the rightmost column, find the product. Write the ones digit of the product below the line and carry the tens digit to the top of the tens column. Then repeat this process for each digit of the second factor.

```
    4 6
  × 7 3
  ─────
```

Multiply 3 times the ones: $6 \times 3 = 18$.

18 ones = 1 ten and 8 ones

```
      1
    4 6
  × 7 3
  ─────
      8
```

Multiply 3 times the tens and add the carried ten:

$(4 \times 3) + 1 = 13$. Record 13 tens.

```
      1
    4 6
  × 7 3
  ─────
  1 3 8
```

Multiply 7 tens times the ones: $7 \times 6 = 42$.

42 tens = 4 hundreds and 2 tens.

```
      1
    4 6
  × 7 3
  ─────
  1 3 8
      2
```

Multiply 7 tens times 4 tens and add the 4 carried tens:

$(7 \times 4) + 4 = 32$

```
      4
    4 6
  × 7 3
  ─────
  1 3 8
  3 2 2
```

Add the partial products.

```
      4
    4 6
  × 7 3
  ─────
  1 3 8
  3 2 2
  ─────
  3, 3 5 8
```

Division

Division with a multidigit dividend is introduced using an example in which an amount of money (expressed in $100, $10, and $1 bills) is shared as equally as possible by a number of students. As students share the money, they exchange $100 bills for $10 bills and $10 bills for $1 bills as needed.

Share $836 (8 $100-bills, 3 $10-bills, and 6 $1-bills) among 7 students.

Each student gets 1 $100-bill, so write 100 above the dividend. Now $700 has been distributed, so subtract 700 from the total.

$$\begin{array}{r} 100 \\ 7\overline{)836} \\ -700 \\ \hline 136 \end{array}$$

Now there is 1 $100 bill, 3 $10 bills, and 6 $1 bills. Exchange the 1 $100-bill for 10 $10-bills, to leave 13 $1-bills.

Each student gets 1 $10-bill, so write 10 above the dividend and subtract 70.

$$\begin{array}{r} 10 \\ 100 \\ 7\overline{)836} \\ -700 \\ \hline 136 \\ -70 \\ \hline 66 \end{array}$$

Now there are 6 $10-bills and 6 $1-bills left. Exchange the 6 $10 bills for 60 $1-bills, to leave 66 $1-bills.

Each student gets 9 $1-bills, so write 9 above the dividend and subtract 63 (7 × 9).

$$\begin{array}{r} 9 \\ 10 \\ 100 \\ 7\overline{)836} \\ -700 \\ \hline 136 \\ -70 \\ \hline 66 \\ -63 \\ \hline 3 \end{array}$$

The mathematical sciences particularly exhibit order, symmetry, and limitation; and these are the greatest forms of the beautiful.

Aristotle, Greek philosopher, 384–322 B.C.

Since 100 + 10 + 9 = 119, each student gets $119. There will be $3 left over.

This naturally leads to a standard algorithm which involves asking how many times the divisor divides into the thousands, hundreds, tens, and ones of the dividend.

Standard algorithm

Once students understand the steps in division, they are introduced to progressively more efficient ways of writing them. Three different versions of the algorithm are taught. Each uses the same steps, but they differ in the amount of writing they require.

Long Form	Shorter From	Shorter Form
1,276 Remainder 4	With Zeros	Without Zeros

Long Form

$$\begin{array}{r} 6 \\ 70 \\ 200 \\ 1000 \\ 7\overline{)8936} \\ -7000 \\ \hline 1936 \\ -1400 \\ \hline 536 \\ -490 \\ \hline 46 \\ -42 \\ \hline 4 \end{array}$$

Shorter From With Zeros

Be careful to put the answers in the correct column.

$$\begin{array}{r} 1276 \ \text{R4} \\ 7\overline{)8936} \\ -7000 \\ \hline 1936 \\ -1400 \\ \hline 536 \\ -490 \\ \hline 46 \\ -42 \\ \hline 4 \end{array}$$

Shorter Form Without Zeros

Subtract and "bring down" only the next digit. Be careful to put the answers in the correct columns.

$$\begin{array}{r} 1276 \ \text{R4} \\ 7\overline{)8936} \\ -7 \\ \hline 19 \\ -14 \\ \hline 53 \\ -49 \\ \hline 46 \\ -42 \\ \hline 4 \end{array}$$

Technology

> "The purpose of using technology is not to make the learning of mathematics easier, but richer and better."
>
> —Alfinio Flores

Technology has changed the world of mathematics. Technological tools have eliminated the need for tedious calculations and have enabled significant advances in applications of mathematics. Technology also can help to make teaching more engaging, effective, and efficient.

Real Math Technology for Teachers

ePlanner provides a tool to help teachers plan daily lessons and plot out year-long goals.

- Daily lesson plan with lesson and homework detail
- Weekly lesson plan
- Monthly plan
- Yearly plan with lesson detail
- Lesson summaries and electronic lessons from the **ePresentation** that can be accessed at home
- Program resources
- Correlation to state guidelines
- Ability to search for lessons by topic and standard
- Homework site

ePresentation is an electronic presentation of all of the *Real Math* lessons, **eGames,** and **eMathTools.** Teachers can use this daily or periodically to vary instructional presentations.

Presentation

Real Math ePresentation is an interactive chalkboard that

- Presents step-by-step visual, animated, and interactive electronic *Real Math* lessons to the entire class
- Includes the key parts of every lesson
  - Mental Math
  - Develop
    - Guided Discussion
    - Skill and Strategy Building and Practice
    - Hands-On Activities
  - Assign Student Pages
  - Reflect
- Includes key resources from the ***Teacher's Edition*** and Program Resources for easy access
- Links to **eTextbook** and **eMathTools** at point of use
- Engages the entire classroom in actively learning mathematical concepts
- Manages classroom pacing

eAssess enables teachers to record, track, and report on all aspects of students' math performances and progress toward achieving standards.

Professional Development

This unique, comprehensive, and flexible library includes courses designed to teach and model research-based strategies for teaching mathematics to build student math proficiency. Because teachers play such a critical role in students' mathematical achievements, SRA provides these courses to develop teacher efficiency and proficiency.

Current courses include

- Teaching Computational Fluency
- Teaching for Understanding
- Teaching Applications of Mathematics
- Teaching Mathematical Reasoning and Problem Solving
- Engaging Children in Mathematics
- Mathematics Classroom Management
- Strategies for Teaching Math to English Learners
- Math Intervention
- Mathematics Refresher for Elementary Teachers

Computer Math Technology for Students

eTextBook

 **Textbook**

The electronic version of the entire **Real Math** student textbook for use at school or at home

- Helps students complete their homework because they can access it anywhere there is a computer
- Includes key resources, such as
  - glossary terms
  - zoom feature to review problems in isolation
  - electronic index
- Provides all answers for checking homework in a teacher's version of **eTextbook**.

Building Blocks

Building Blocks software provides computer math activities that address specific developmental levels of the math learning trajectories. **Building Blocks** software is critical to the prekindergarten level of **Real Math**, and provides support activities for specific concepts for grades K–6.

Some **Building Blocks** activities have different levels of difficulty, as indicated by ranges in the Activity Names below. The list provides an overview of all of the **Building Blocks** activities, along with the domains, descriptions, and appropriate age ranges.

Building Blocks Activities and Free Explores

This list identifies all of the **Building Blocks** Activities and Free Explore Activities. Use it to determine developmentally appropriate activities that build specific skills and concepts.

Activity	Learning Trajectory	Age Range
Arrays in Area	Multiplication/Division	8–11
Barkley's Bones 1–10	Number: Adding and Subtracting	5–7
Barkley's Bones 1–20	Number: Adding and Subtracting	6–8
Before and After Math	Number: Counting (Verbal)	4–6
Book Stacks	Number: Counting (Objects)	6–8
Bright Idea: Counting On Game	Number: Counting (Strategies)	6–8
Build Stairs 1: Count Steps	Number: Counting (Strategies)	4–6
Build Stairs 2: Order Steps	Number: Counting (Strategies)	4–7
Build Stairs 3: Find the Missing Step	Number: Counting (Strategies)	6–7

Activity	Learning Trajectory	Age Range
Build Stairs Free Explore	Number: Counting (Strategies)	4–7
Clean the Plates	Multiplication/Division	7–9
Comic Book Shop	Multiplication/Division	7–9
Comparisons	Measurement: Length	4–8
Count and Race	Number: Counting (Verbal)	3–6
Count and Race Free Explore	Number: Counting (Verbal)	3–6
Countdown Crazy	Number: Counting (Object)	5–7
Create a Scene	Geometry: Composition/Decomposition	4–12
Deep Sea Compare	Measurement: Length	5–7
Dinosaur Shop 1: Label Boxes	Number: Counting (Object)	4–6
Dinosaur Shop 2: Fill Orders	Number: Counting (Object) and Adding and Subtracting	5–7
Dinosaur Shop 3: Add Dinosaurs (1–5)	Number: Adding and Subtracting	4–6
Dinosaur Shop 3: Add Dinosaurs (1–10)	Number: Adding and Subtracting	4–7
Dinosaur Shop 4: Make It Right?	Number: Adding and Subtracting	5–7
Dinosaur Shop Free Explore	Number: Counting (Object)	4–7
Double Compare 1–10	Number: Adding and Subtracting	5–7
Double Compare 1–20	Number: Adding and Subtracting	5–7
Easy as Pie: Add Numbers	Number: Adding and Subtracting	6–8
Eggcellent: Addition Choice	Number: Adding and Subtracting	6–8
Egg-stremely Equal	Multiplication/Division	4–8
Field Trip	Multiplication/Division	8–11
Figure the Fact: Two-Digit Adding	Number: Adding and Subtracting	7–9
Function Machine 1–5	Number: Adding and Subtracting Multiplication and Division	6–12
Geometry Snapshots 1: Exact Matches	Geometry: Imagery	5–7
Geometry Snapshots 2: Several Shapes	Geometry: Imagery	5–7
Geometry Snapshots 3: Symmetric Shapes	Geometry: Imagery	5–7
Geometry Snapshots 4: Line Segments	Geometry: Imagery	6–8
Geometry Snapshots 5: Arrays	Geometry: Imagery	7–11
Geometry Snapshots 6: Angles	Geometry: Imagery	7–10
Geometry Snapshots 7: Rotated Combinations	Geometry: Imagery	8–11
Geometry Snapshots 8: 3D Shapes	Geometry: Imagery	8–12
Kitchen Counter	Number: Counting (Verbal)	3–6
Legends of the Lost Shape	Geometry: Shapes (Properties)	8–12
Lots O'Socks: Adding Game	Number: Adding and Subtracting	6–8
Marching Patterns 1: Extend AB	Patterning	5–7
Marching Patterns 2: Extend	Patterning	5–7

Activity	Learning Trajectory	Age Range
Marching Patterns 3: Extend	Patterning	5–7
Math-O-Scope	Number: Counting (Strategies)	7–9
Memory Geometry 1: Exact Matches	Geometry: Shapes (Identifying)	3–5
Memory Geometry 2: Turned Shapes	Geometry: Shapes (Identifying)	3–5
Memory Geometry 3: Shapes-A-Round	Geometry: Shapes (Matching)	3–5
Memory Geometry 4: Shapes of Things	Geometry: Shapes (Matching)	3–5
Memory Geometry 5: Shapes in the World	Geometry: Shapes (Matching)	3–5
Memory Number 1: Counting Cards	Number: Counting (Object)	4–6
Memory Number 2: Counting Cards to Numerals	Number: Counting (Object)	4–6
Memory Number 3: Dots to Dots	Number: Counting (Object)	4–6
Mystery Pictures 1: Match Shapes	Geometry: Shapes (Matching)	3–5
Mystery Pictures 2: Name Shapes	Geometry: Shapes (Matching)	3–5
Mystery Pictures 3: Match New Shapes	Geometry: Shapes (Matching)	3–6
Mystery Pictures 4: Name New Shapes	Geometry: Shapes (Matching)	5–7
Mystery Pictures Free Explore	Geometry: Shapes (Matching)	3–7
Number Compare 1: Dots and Numerals	Number: Comparing	4–6
Number Compare 2: Dots to 7	Number: Comparing	5–7
Number Compare 3: Dots to 10	Number: Comparing	6–8
Number Compare 4: Numerals to 100	Number: Comparing	7–9
Number Compare 5: Dot Arrays to 100	Multiplication/Division	8–11
Number Snapshots 1: Dot Collections up to 3	Number: Subitizing	3–5
Number Snapshots 2: Dot Collections up to 4	Number: Subitizing	4–6
Number Snapshots 3: Dots to Numerals up to 5	Number: Subitizing	5–7
Number Snapshots 4: Dot Collections up to 5	Number: Subitizing	5–7
Number Snapshots 5: Dot Sums to Numerals up to 5	Number: Subitizing (Conceptual)	5–7
Number Snapshots 6: Dots to Numerals up to 7	Number: Subitizing (Conceptual)	6–8
Number Snapshots 7: Dot Collections up to 10	Number: Subitizing	5–7
Number Snapshots 8: Dots to Numerals up to 10	Number: Subitizing (Conceptual)	6–8
Number Snapshots 9: Dots to Numerals up to 20	Number: Subitizing	6–8
Number Snapshots 10: Dots to Numerals up to 50	Number: Subitizing	7–9
Numeral Train Game	Number: Counting (Object)	4–6
Off the Tree: Add Apples	Number: Adding and Subtracting	5–7
Ordinal Construction Company	Number: Comparing	5–7
Party Time 1: Set the Table	Number: Comparing	4–6
Party Time 2: Count Placemats	Number: Counting (Object)	4–6
Party Time 3: Produce Groups	Number: Counting (Object)	4–6
Party Time Free Explore	Number: Comparing	4–6
Pattern Planes 1: Duplicate AB	Patterning	3–6

Activity	Learning Trajectory	Age Range
Pattern Planes 2: Duplicate	Patterning	3–6
Pattern Planes 3: Duplicate	Patterning	4–6
Pattern Zoo 1: Recognize AB	Patterning	3–5
Pattern Zoo 2: Recognize	Patterning	3–6
Pattern Zoo 3: Recognize	Patterning	4–6
Patterns Free Explore	Patterning	3–5
Piece Puzzler 1: Match Pictures	Geometry: Composition/Decomposition	4–6
Piece Puzzler 2: Assemble Pieces	Geometry: Composition/Decomposition	4–6
Piece Puzzler 3: Make Pictures	Geometry: Composition/Decomposition	5–7
Piece Puzzler 4: Compose Shapes	Geometry: Composition/Decomposition	5–7
Piece Puzzler 5: Substitute Shapes	Geometry: Composition/Decomposition	6–8
Piece Puzzler Free Explore	Geometry: Composition/Decomposition	4–6
Pizza Pizzazz 1: Match Collections	Number: Comparing	3–5
Pizza Pizzazz 2: Make Matches (1–5)	Number: Counting (Object)	4–6
Pizza Pizzazz 2: Make Matches (1–10)	Number: Counting (Object)	5–7
Pizza Pizzazz 3: Make Number Pizzas (1–5)	Number: Counting (Object)	4–6
Pizza Pizzazz 3: Make Number Pizzas (1–10)	Number: Counting (Object)	4–6
Pizza Pizzazz 4: Count Hidden Pepperoni	Number: Adding and Subtracting	3–6
Pizza Pizzazz 5: Make It Right	Number: Adding and Subtracting	6–8
Pizza Pizzazz Free Explore	Number: Comparing	3–5
Reptile Ruler	Measurement: Length	7–10
Road Race: Counting Game	Number: Counting (Object)	3–6
Road Race: Shape Counting	Number: Counting (Object)	4–6
Rocket Blast 1	Number: Comparing	6–8
Rocket Blast 2	Number: Comparing	7–10
Rocket Blast 3	Number: Comparing	8–11
School Supply Shop	Number: Counting (Objects)	6–8
Sea to Shore: Plus One	Number: Counting (Verbal)	6–8
Shape Parts 1–7	Geometry: Shapes (Parts)	5–11
Shape Shop 1–3	Geometry: Shapes (Properties)	5–11
Snack Time	Multiplication/Division	6–8
Space Race: Number Choice	Number: Comparing	4–6
Super Shape 1: Simple Decomposer Introduction	Geometry: Composition/Decomposition	5–7
Super Shape 2: Simple Decomposer with Help	Geometry: Composition/Decomposition	5–7
Super Shape 3: Simple Decomposer	Geometry: Composition/Decomposition	5–7
Super Shape 4: Simple Decomposer Making New Shapes	Geometry: Composition/Decomposition	5–7
Super Shape 5: Shape Decomposer (with Help)	Geometry: Composition/Decomposition	6–8
Super Shape 6: Shape Decomposer with Imagery	Geometry: Composition/Decomposition	7–9

Activity	Learning Trajectory	Age Range
Super Shape 7: Shape Decomposer with Units of Units	Geometry: Composition/Decomposition	8–11
Tidal Tally	Number: Counting (Strategies)	6–8
Tire Recycling	Number: Counting (Objects)	6–8
Word Problems with Tools 1: Find Result or Change	Number: Adding and Subtracting	5–7
Word Problems with Tools 2: Find Result or Change, Counting +/−	Number: Adding and Subtracting	6–8
Word Problems with Tools 3: Part-Whole and Numbers-in-Numbers +/−	Number: Adding and Subtracting	6–8
Word Problems with Tools 4: Multidigit +/− to 100 and Multidigit Solver	Number: Adding and Subtracting	7–9
Word Problems with Tools 5: Parts and Wholes x/÷	Multiplication/Division	7–9
Word Problems with Tools 6: Parts and Wholes x/÷	Multiplication/Division	7–9
Word Problems with Tools 7: Problem Solver +/−	Number: Adding and Subtracting	8–11
Word Problems with Tools 8: Multidigit +/− (Adding Two Groups to 100)	Number: Adding and Subtracting	8–11
Word Problems with Tools 9: Multidigit +/− (Adding Two Groups to 1000)	Number: Adding and Subtracting	8–11
Word Problems with Tools 10: Multidigit X/÷	Multiplication/Division	8–11
Word Problems with Tools 11: Multidigit +/− (Review)	Number: Adding and Subtracting	8–12
Word Problems with Tools 12: Multidigit +/− (Review)	Number: Adding and Subtracting	8–12
Workin' on the Railroad	Measurement: Length	6–9

eGames

This list identifies all of the **eGames** in **Real Math**. Use it to determine engaging, developmentally appropriate activities that build specific skills and concepts. Most **eGames** are designed as solitaire versions, which allow students to try to better their previous scores. In other **eGames**, students play against the computer.

Game	Grade levels
Addition Table	1–3
Anything But 10	4–6
Baseball Game	4–6
Calendar Game	K–2
Circo	5–6
Count to 20 by Ones and Twos	K–2
Count to 20 by Ones and Twos (Expert)	K–2
Cube 100	3–5
Cube 100 Challenge	3–6
Cube 100 Expert	4–6
Don't Go Over 1000	4–6
Don't Take Them All	K-2
Don't Take Them All (Expert)	K-2
Fraction Game	2–5
Fracto	3–5
Get the Point	4–6
Get to 100 by Tens or Ones	2–3
Get to 100 by Tens or Ones (Expert)	2–4

Game	Grade levels
Golf	5–6
Hockey	5–6
Make 1000	2–3
Map Game	1–2
More or Less	3–4
Mul-Tack-Toe	2–3
Multigo 1	3–4
Multigo 2	3–4
Multiple Crossing	3–4
Multiplication Table	3–4
Numbo Jumbo	5–6
Order	4–6
Race from 15 to −15 and Back	4–6
Roll 20 to 5	2–4
Roll a 15	4–6
Roll a 15 Challenge	4–6
Roll a 15 Expert	4–6
Roll a Double	1–2
Roll a 10	1–2
Stolen Treasure	1–3
Tips	5–6
Up to 1	5–6

Real Math eMathTools

Data Organization and Display Tools

Coordinate Grid
Graphing
Pictograph
Spreadsheet
Venn Diagram

Calculation and Counting Tools

100 Table
Addition Table
Array
Base Ten
Calculator
Coins and Money
Fractions
Function Machine
Multiplication Table
Number Line
Number Stairs
Probability
Sets Former

Measurement and Conversion Tools

Calendar
Estimating Proportion
Metric and Customary Conversion
Stopwatch

Geometric Exploration Tools

Geometry Sketch Tool
Net Tool (2D to 3D)
Pythagorean Theorem
Shape Creator
Shape Tool
Tessellations

Using Games

The Role of Games

Games provide practice. They give students a way of becoming proficient in the mathematical skills to which they have been introduced. Many **Real Math** games do more. They offer students a chance to recognize situations, real to the student, that can be understood through mathematical thinking, which leads to the identification and solution of strategy problems. This usually leads to in-depth mathematical communication between students regarding the problem and solution.

A benefit of this development through games is that there is no need to teach students the best solution. The process of trying to find a better strategy is the useful activity.

Games also afford teachers the opportunity to monitor progress. By observing game-playing sessions, teachers can assess students' computational fluency, understanding, reasoning, and engagement.

Games allow students of all levels of ability to compete fairly. Winning games requires a mix of chance, skills, and thinking strategies.

Games and Skills

Each of the games in **Real Math** involves the use of specific math skills. When a lesson plan prescribes a game, it does so because the principal skills involved in that game need attention at that time. Most games provide practice in many skills. For example, nearly all the games help students develop and apply intuitive concepts of probability. Many games afford students the opportunity to apply problem-solving strategies, such as recognizing a problem, working backward, or making an approximation.

Types of Games

Cube Games

These games are included in appropriate lessons in the **Student** and **Teacher's Editions.** The games' rules appear on the student pages. Many of the cube games have variations that extend beyond mathematics or provide applications for new strategies. Variations can be learned quickly, making the cube games even more practical. Directions for all cube games are also reproduced in **Home Connection,** as well as in the **Home Connection Game Kit.**

Mat Games

Mat games can be found in the **Game Mat Kit** and are reproduced in Appendix D of this **Teacher's Edition.** The mat games are referenced in appropriate lessons.

eGames

These games are electronic versions of some of the cube games. They are referenced in appropriate lessons throughout the program. The **eGames** can be accessed online, on the **eGames** CD-ROM, or through the **eTextbook, ePresentation,** or **ePlanner.**

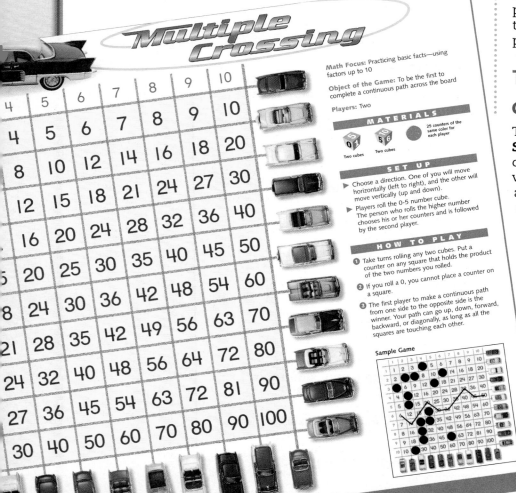

Building Blocks

These electronic games are referenced in appropriate lessons throughout the lower grades of **Real Math.** The Pre–K level of the **Building Blocks** software, which includes the games appropriate for prekindergarten, is a crucial part of the Pre–K curriculum. The **Building Blocks** games referenced in appropriate lessons at the other grade levels reinforce key concepts.

Choosing Games

Some lesson plans suggest a particular game, some suggest that teachers select appropriate games for students based on needed skill practice; and some suggest that students be given a free choice of games. The authors recommend that teachers maintain a balance between selecting games for students and having students choose games for themselves.

To help students choose games, teachers can make a chart of the games that have been introduced to date. The chart can be a simple list or an organized collection of game mats, titles, game rules, materials lists, and illustrations. A group of students might be put in charge of making the display and updating it whenever a new game is introduced.

When you do prescribe games, check the game directory in Appendix D. This listing of the principal skills involved in each game will help you select those games that will give each student an appropriate form of practice.

Learning Game Rules

Rules for each game are given in the lesson in which the game is introduced. The directions for game mats are also found on the game mats. Here are some tips for making sure that games are played correctly:

- Familiarize yourself with each game before showing students how to play it. Read the instructions, and then play the game by yourself or with a colleague or friend.

- Demonstrate—do not tell—how a game is played. Even for straightforward games, oral instructions can sound complicated. Introduce a game by demonstrating it in front of the class, with you playing against the class, with you playing against one student (representing the class), or with two students (representing teams) playing against each other. The **ePresentation** allows teachers to present and demonstrate all games to the entire class at one time. Make sure that each student can see while you demonstrate a game.

- Verbalize the rules as you demonstrate games. End the demonstration when all the rules have been covered.

- Supervise to see that students get off to the right start after you have introduced a game.

- Let students teach other students. Those who have grasped the game rules can help those who have not.

Organizing Successful Game Sessions

- Pair children wisely. There are times when it will be appropriate to pair children of the same ability. However, this rule should not become invariable because most games involve some luck. Furthermore, if a student who is not attentive while playing a game plays with one who is, the first student may realize that paying attention may help.

- Change groupings from day to day. Students can learn different things by playing with different partners.

- Be sure students are challenged by a game. Most games have easier and harder variations.

- Assign a referee to each group. When students get so absorbed in their own efforts that they do not follow the rules, a referee can be useful. This is particularly appropriate for kindergarten through second grade. The referee can see that the rules are followed, remind each player when it is his or her turn, settle disputes, keep track of scores, and in some games, act as a banker.

- Make game mats accessible. Store mats so they are easy for the students to find and to return without your help.

- Encourage students to play games during free time, in school, and at home, as well as during the scheduled game sessions.

- Allow students opportunities to create and name their own variations of the games. In some cases, you may want to describe a student's variation to the entire class and ask him or her to name it. Be alert, however, to avoid student-invented variations that reduce the skill practice or thinking value of the game.

- Get help during game-playing sessions. Likely candidates are parents, grandparents, teacher's aides, or students in upper grades. Be sure the helpers know the rules of the games by having them play the chosen games ahead of time.

Game-Playing Behavior

Establishing the proper atmosphere for game playing makes the sessions more effective and easier to manage. Encourage enjoyment rather than competition. Emphasize sportsmanship, fair play, and taking turns. Beginning with the first game-playing session, teach students to control their excitement and to speak using low voices. Cubes, when rolled, should stay within a confined area. Insisting that students roll cubes on an $11 \times 8\frac{1}{2}$ pad or cardboard field reduces noise and inappropriate exuberance.

Problem Solving

Problem solving and reasoning are fundamental math proficiencies. Without the ability to reason mathematically, identify problems, and devise appropriate strategies to solve them, computational fluency has little relevance. There are several keys to developing students' problem-solving abilities.

1. Use Real Problems

The first and most important step in helping students become good problem solvers is to provide opportunities to identify and solve problems that are genuinely interesting and, therefore, motivating. We call these *real problems*. To help understand what we mean by *real,* we can consider three types of problems: those that are real, those that are realistic, and those that are contrived.

Contrived Problems appear largely in textbooks — never in real life. They often occur when it is difficult to find an application for a particular type of computation, so a forced, contrived situation is invented. When students encounter such problems they learn the wrong lesson — that mathematics is an endeavor that makes work, not one that saves work and solves useful problems.

Realistic Problems mirror the kind of mathematics that people do in real life. Although not as motivating as real problems, they are an important part of a mathematics program. Unit pricing, comparing or combining quantities or measures, balancing a checkbook, and learning to read a telephone bill are all examples of realistic problems.

Real Problems are developed from the reality of the person being asked to solve the problem; they come from the social situation of the problem solver and his or her desire to find a solution. The same problem may be real to one person and realistic to another who is engaged in a different activity, but if a problem is real to one person, then it can never be a contrived problem. Carefully developed activities are another source of real problems.

Finding real problems is one of the more difficult challenges in curriculum development, one that we take seriously and work hard at achieving.

2. Develop Critical-Thinking Skills

Students must have tools that are useful for solving problems. Computational skills are, of course, important, but they are not enough. Students also need an arsenal of critical-thinking skills (sometimes called *problem-solving strategies,* and sometimes called *heuristics*) that they can call upon to solve particular problems. These skills should not be taught in isolation. Rather, students should learn to use them in different contexts. By doing so, students are more likely to recognize in which situations a particular skill will be useful and when it is not likely to be useful.

We can group critical-thinking skills into two categories — those that are useful in virtually all situations and those that are useful in specific contexts.

Problem-Solving Rubric

Use this rubric to evaluate student problem-solving ability.

Criteria	4	3	2	1
Understand Problems	Identifies real problem independently	Recognizes independently there is a problem	Waits for someone else to point out the problem	Cannot identify a problem even when someone points it out
Gathering Facts	Accesses information to obtain all necessary facts	Knows where to look to obtain facts	Able to gather one or two facts independently	Does not realize the need to find facts and uses any set of numbers to calculate
Brainstorm Solutions	Generates several creative solutions independently	Generates a solution independently	Generates ideas with assistance	Does not generate any solution and may ask, "What do I do?"
Problem Solving Strategies	Develops an efficient and workable strategy	Develops a workable strategy	Uses an appropriate strategy some of the time	Uses an inappropriate or unworkable strategy
Evaluate Solutions	Uses reflection to decide what to do differently next time.	Takes time to analyze effectiveness of each possible solution	Recognizes advantages and disadvantages of some solutions with assistance	Does not evaluate the effectiveness of proposed solutions
Persistence	Continues problem solving outside of math class	Persists in class independently	Will try with encouragement and assistance	Gives up easily

Problem-Solving Stages

Understand

The first step in becoming a good problem solver is to learn how to identify when a problem does, in fact, exist. Too often in school mathematics, we give students problems to solve, even many interesting problems, but the problems are always given by the teacher or provided by the textbook—they are never identified by the student as arising from a particular context. That is not the way we encounter problems in the real world.

Without exception, students must understand each problem or physical situation and do only what makes sense to them. Applying rules in unthinking ways, using key words that avoid thinking, or using other shortcuts that subvert or eliminate understanding are all counterproductive, and although they might lead to correct answers in contrived situations, such tactics do not help students become good problem solvers.

Questions to Ask

- Do I really understand the problem?
- Can I explain it in my own words?
- What am I trying to find out?
- What information do I have?
- Do I need more information?

Plan

Students must learn to reflect on problems both before and after solving them. Before a solution is found, students might reflect on problems they have encountered earlier. A solution to a problem encountered earlier might offer a clue about how to structure the solution to the current problem. These connections with familiar problems, skills, and procedures can help students formulate a plan for solving the problem at hand.

Questions to Ask

- How or where can information that might help?
- Have I solved problems like this before? If so, how did I do it?
- Could there be more than one solution? Or no solution at all?

Carry Out

Once students have an idea of steps to take to solve a problem, they then use them to find the answer. Oftentimes this is not simple. Following a plan or procedure by rote that begins to make no sense is not effective. Returning to the problem to make sure of understanding or make adjustments to a plan are strategic steps in effective problem solving.

Look Back

Good problem solvers also reflect on problems after they have been solved. This is a key to effective problem solving and proficiency in mathematics. By thinking about problems after solving them, students are likely to better understand the processes they used and see things the second and third time that they did not see the first time. One of the central roles of games in *Real Math* is to afford students the opportunity to revisit problems. Students do this by replaying games that allow them to formulate and reformulate winning strategies.

Questions to Ask

- Does the answer make sense? Can I check it?
- Is there an easier way to solve the problem?
- What have I learned from this problem that might help with other problems?
- Was there an easier or a more elegant solution?
- Can I think of related problems that I have not yet solved?

Problem-Solving Strategies for Specific Situations

A partial listing of critical-thinking skills that are likely to be useful in specific contexts are the following:

Draw a Picture — Sometimes drawing a picture will help to visualize and hence understand a problem.

Look for a Pattern — Some problems can be solved by looking for and finding patterns.

Guess, Check, and Adjust — If a direct procedure cannot be found, it is sometimes useful to make an educated guess and then check to see if that answer makes sense. This procedure often involves making several successive guesses, each based on feedback from earlier guesses.

Make a Table or Graph — Organizing information in a table or graph will often reveal important trends and patterns.

Work Backward — For some problems, working backward helps to reveal a pattern or patterns.

Work an Easier Problem — If a problem appears too difficult, it sometimes helps to solve a related, but easier, problem. Solving the easier problem will often reveal strategies likely to be useful for solving the more difficult problem.

Detect Absurdities — Spotting answers that are contrary to reason, even if the correct answer is not known, is often an important part of the problem-solving process.

Ask the Right Questions — Knowing when necessary information is missing, knowing how to find the information, and knowing how to ask the right questions to find the information is often useful.

Approximate — Many problems do not require precise answers. Knowing when a precise answer is appropriate and when an approximate answer is appropriate is important, as is sufficient knowledge of the number system in order to make approximations.

3. Involve All Students in Problem Solving

Problem solving is an activity that must involve all students, not just those who are more able or who have mastered particular computational skills. *Real Math* lessons are designed to provide many such opportunities.

4. Include Problem Solving in Every Lesson

If students are to see the usefulness of mathematics for solving interesting problems that are relevant to their own lives, and if they are to have lots of experience solving problems, such activities must be part of every mathematics lesson — not something that is reserved for Fridays or perhaps isolated in one or two chapters of a textbook. That is why we include problem-solving opportunities in every lesson in **Real Math.** There are no exceptions.

Real Math and Problem Solving

Real Math lessons are rich in problem-solving opportunities and are adaptable to many styles of teaching. The principal sources of problem-solving opportunities come from the following:

Games

Real Math games are a principal source of traditional skill practice. Most games do more: they give the student an opportunity to work out important mathematical ideas and strategies. Thus a student might start a game by just getting the skill practice, but after a while he or she might realize that the game involves more than practice — that a winning strategy must be developed. Although students compete with each other during game playing sessions, they often communicate their strategies to each other and discuss them.

Thinking Stories

Thinking Stories found in kindergarten, grades one, two and three are an essential part of the *Real Math* approach to developing problem solving abilities; they develop creativity and common sense in the use of mathematics. The problem-solving skills that are stressed include recognizing absurd answers, recognizing obvious answers (those that don't need calculation), recognizing when a problem can be solved using mathematics and when other, non-mathematical knowledge is needed, and so on.

Exploring Problem Solving

Three sets of explorations in every chapter focus specifically on introducing, comparing, and using strategies for identifying and solving problems. Students analyze solution methods and share other possible solutions.

Mathematics is being lazy. Mathematics is letting the principles do the work for you so that you do not have to do the work for yourself.

George Pólya, mathematician, 1887–1985

Activities

The many whole-class and small-group activities allow students to apply mathematics in different contexts, which are often cross-curricular. Such activities are rich in opportunities for students to communicate their ideas within their small groups and also to others from whom they are seeking information.

Computation Pages

As in most programs, pages that provide needed computation practice are included throughout *Real Math.* But because we frequently include groups of related exercises on these pages, students learn to look for them and use the resulting patterns to avoid tedious computations. For example, an exercise such as $54 + 73 =$ might be followed by $54 + 74 =$ and $54 + 75 =$. Students who notice this pattern can compute the first sum, but then note that each successive sum is one more than the previous sum. Such patterns appear often in *Real Math.*

Word Problems

Realistic word problems appear frequently throughout *Real Math.* They illustrate situations in which mathematics is useful in the real world, and they are a source of much practice. To be certain that students understand the situations described in these problems, we never group problems of the same type together, such as giving problems, all of which call for addition. To do so would allow students to simply look for the numbers and use the indicated operation. They would not have to understand the problem and would not have to think. To encourage thinking, we include problems that include too much information, too little information, problems that can be solved by mathematics, and those that cannot. We do not allow students to rely on key words either, because doing so allows students to avoid thinking and to apply procedures that are likely to only work with problems that appear in textbooks.

Guided Discussion

Mathematical discussions have the potential to greatly advance mathematical understanding. A good discussion provides opportunities for students to explain their thinking, to expand or challenge their understanding by listening to others' contributions, and to justify their reasoning. Good mathematical discussions enable teachers to assess and understand student thinking to inform their future instruction.

Discussion Management

These points will help produce more discussions:

1. Restate some or all of what the student has said, and then ask the student to respond and verify whether or not the teacher's restatement is correct.

2. Ask students to restate someone else's reasoning, which gives the rest of the class another rendition of the first student's contribution and provides evidence that other students could and did hear. It is also evidence for the speaker's points.

3. Ask students to apply and explain their own reasoning to someone else's reasoning. This will involve more students in the discussion and will encourage student interactions.

4. Prompt students by asking for further commentary to support a position.

5. Use free time. This time allows students to think and consider answers to complicated questions before they speak.

Real Math and Guided Discussion

Guided Discussion plays a prominent role in the Develop and Reflect parts of virtually every lesson in *Real Math.* Routines for Guided Discussion are included in the Getting Started section of each grade level to develop effective discussion strategies.

Questions that Promote Learning

Not all questions have the same effect. Questions help teachers learn what students are thinking, and to consider instructional implications of that knowledge. Below are ideas for formulating questions to promote learning during Guided Discussion.

Engaging questions to invite students to participate in a discussion

Identify terms, relationships, and methods already known that are connected to the topic.	What is _____? What does _____ mean?
Share opinions about the topic.	What do you think about _____?
Relate concrete experiences that are pertinent to the topic.	Have you ever been asked to do this before?
Verify the results.	How do you know this is true?

Exploratory questions to help students consider connections and consequences

Identify a specific difficulty, and decide how to solve it.	What was the hardest part of the problem? Is there an easier way to solve it?
Relate personal experience in solving the problem.	What did you do in the past to solve the problem?
Draw analogies to other situations.	How is this the same as or different from other problems?
Process and record results.	Write the steps you used to solve the problem.

Synthesizing questions to help students pull ideas together.

Identify patterns.	What pattern do you see in everyone's results?
Generalize.	What is a good way to solve this problem?
Elaborate rules, definitions, and laws that express the generalization.	Write the steps for solving problems like this.
Argue, prove, or demonstrate assumptions.	Which way is the best way to solve a problem like this? How is it better?
Use references.	Who else solved the problem in this way?

Clarifying questions to help students explain their thinking or to help you understand their thinking

Reflect on examples and analyze results.	Which is the easiest/hardest/most fun way of approaching the problem, and why?
Provide examples.	What is an example of a problem like this?
Describe stages and observations.	What was the thinking process you used to solve the problem?
Understand and accept limitations of personal and peer knowledge, and search for other information sources.	Is there a better way? How could we find out?

Refocusing questions to help students get back on track

Refocusing questions are most useful when students are working in nonproductive ways.	How is this like _____? What does this say about _____?

Manipulatives and How to Use Them

"The use of concrete materials, sometimes termed manipulatives, for teaching mathematics is widely accepted, particularly in elementary grades. Manipulatives should always be seen as a means and not an end in themselves. They require careful use over sufficient time to allow students to build meaning and make connections....Simply putting materials on desks is not enough to guarantee students will learn appropriate mathematics. The relationship between learning and the use of manipulatives is far more complex than many mathematics educators have thought....When students use a manipulative, they need to be helped to see its relevant aspects and to link those aspects to appropriate symbolism and mathematical concepts and operations....If students do not see the connections among object, symbol, language, and idea, using a manipulative becomes just one more thing to learn rather than a process leading to a larger mathematical learning goal....The evidence indicates...that manipulatives can provide valuable support for student learning when teachers interact over time with the students to help them build links between the object, the symbol, and the mathematical idea that both represent."

Kilpatrick, J., Swafford, J. and Findell, B. eds. *Adding It Up: Helping Children Learn Mathematics*. Washington, D.C.: National Research Council/National Academy Press. 2001, p. 353–354.

"The laws of nature are written in the language of mathematics...the symbols are triangles, circles, and other geometrical figures, without whose help it is impossible to comprehend a single word."

Galileo Galilei, Italian astronomer and physicist, 1564–1642

Real Math and Manipulatives

The purpose of using manipulatives is to help students understand mathematics, not to get answers to problems. Too often students know rules, but do not know how or why the rules work. By explaining abstract concepts with manipulatives, students can develop and demonstrate understanding of mathematical concepts. Manipulatives are used whenever appropriate in *Real Math*. Each time they are used, there is also a plan to remove the need for them so that once the understanding is achieved, students focus attention on fluency and the abstract. The power of mathematics is in its abstractness.

Below are common manipulatives and their principal purposes.

Manipulatives	Description	Purpose	Concepts to Develop
Money	Pennies, nickels, dimes, quarters, half dollars, $1-, $5-, $10-, $20-, $50-, and $100-bills	Demonstrate concepts and values of money and applications of base-ten arithmetic	• Number sense • Base-ten system • Place value
Pattern Blocks	Colorful blocks in different geometric shapes (hexagons, squares, trapezoids, triangles, and parallelograms, and rhombi) and colors	Create and demonstrate different types of color and shape patterns and to explore the mathematics of tiling and tesselations	• Number sense • Fractions • Geometry • Proportional reasoning
Attribute Blocks	Blocks in five shapes (circle, hexagon, rectangle, square, and triangle), different sizes, thicknesses, and colors	Build shape identification, logical thinking, and comparing and ordering concepts	• Number sense • Geometry
Platonic Solids	Wooden 3-D cone, cube, pyramid, and sphere	Develop geometric concepts of space figures	• Geometry
Mirror	Small nonbreakable mirror	Develop concepts of symmetry	• Geometry
Geoboard	Plastic board with pegs and rubber bands laid out in a square grid	Explore shapes, area, perimeter, symmetry, design, and fractions of shapes	• Geometry • Measurement
Protractor	Clear protractor in graduations from 0–180 degrees	Measure angles	• Geometry • Measurement
Compass	Center point and pencil	Draw and measure circles	• Geometry • Measurement
Gummed Tape	Adhesive paper tape	Create geometric figures and shapes	• Geometry
Fraction Tiles	Plastic tiles in sets of different fractional increments including $\frac{1}{8}, \frac{1}{4}, \frac{1}{3}, \frac{1}{2}$, and 1.	Explore parts of wholes and adding and subtracting fractions	• Number sense • Fractions and rational numbers • Measurement
Spinners	Plastic spinners	Explore probability	• Probability • Number operations
Counters	Colored plastic disks	Explore patterns and counting	• Number sense • Counting • Probability • Number operations
Base-Ten Blocks	Plastic shapes in cubes, flats, rods, and units	Explore base-ten systems, counting, and number operations	• Number sense • Counting • Number operation
Craft Sticks and Rubber Bands	Wood sticks	Explore place value and standard multidigit addition and subtraction algorithms	• Number sense • Counting • Number operation
Counters	Plastic shapes	Explore counting and ordering numbers	• Number sense • Counting • Number operation
Math-Link Cubes	Plastic cubes that nest together	Explore counting, patterns, number operations, and composing and decomposing numbers	• Number sense • Counting • Patterns • Number operations • Rational number
Ruler and Tape Measure	Plastic customary and metric ruler and tape measure	Explore metric and customary measurements of length	• Measurement •Counting
Measuring Cups and Liter Pitcher	Plastic metric and customary measurement containers	Explore metric and customary measurements of capacity	• Measurement • Geometry • Fractions, decimals, and percents
Double Pan Balance and Platform Scales	Scale and balance and weight set	Explore metric and customary measurements of weight	• Measurement
Thermometer	Metric and Fahrenheit thermometers	Explore temperature measurements	• Measurement
Clock Face	Plastic analog clock face	Explore time measurements	• Measurement
Stopwatch	Electronic stopwatch	Explore time measurements	• Measurement • Fractions, decimals, and percents

Differentiating Instruction

"In the context of education, we define *differentiation as* 'a teacher's reacting responsively to a learner's needs.' A teacher who is differentiating understands a student's need to express humor or work with a group, or to have additional teaching on a particular skill, or to delve more deeply into a particular topic....Differentiation is simply attending to the learning needs of a particular student or small group of students rather than the more typical pattern of teaching the class as though all individuals in it were basically alike. The goal of a differentiated classroom is maximum student growth and individual success."

—Tomlinson, Carol Ann and Allan, Susan Demirsky. *Leadership for Differentiating Schools and Classrooms.* Alexandria, VA: Association for Supervision and Curriculum Development. 2000, p. 4.

All students can benefit from differentiated instruction. Differentiated instruction is dependent on ongoing, daily assessment and an interest in and understanding of how children learn and develop concepts.

How to Differentiate

Instruction can be differentiated in three key ways:

- **Content** What the teacher wants students to learn and the materials or mechanisms through which that is accomplished. Differentiating the content may entail teaching prerequisite concepts to students who need intervention or by asking questions that will cause students to think beyond the concepts covered in the lesson.

- **Process** How or what activities the students do to ensure that they use key skills to make sense of the content. Differentiating the process may include grouping students in different ways, or alternating the pace of the lesson by moving more slowly or more quickly than originally planned. It might also include stressing different modalities: visual, auditory, or kinesthetic.

- **Product** How the student will demonstrate what he or she has come to know. Differentiating the product may include assigning **Enrichment, Practice,** or **Reteach** activities to complete.

Differentiating instruction does not mean chaos or a classroom devoid of structure with everyone working on different goals. Lessons should have clearly defined purposes with students focused on one key understanding.

Analyzing Student Needs

Teachers successful at differentiating instruction are typically in tune with individual student needs. These needs vary, and should be addressed in the context of the key ideas of the lesson. By preparing for differentiation and considering what you might do when you encounter different student needs, teachers can have materials and strategies at the ready.

For a particular concept or lesson, different students may need

- challenge.
- social interaction.
- alternative instruction.
- independence.
- personal attention.
- serious intervention.
- language support.
- creative expression.
- cooperative grouping.
- extra practice.

Real Math and Differentiated Instruction

Every lesson of **Real Math** begins with Planning for Learning: Differentiate Instruction ideas. These include

- *Intervention* that teach prerequisite skills for students who are not ready for the lesson concepts.

- *English Learner Preview* lesson that preview lesson concepts and vocabulary for students learning English.

- *Enrichment* ideas for expanding parts of the lesson if, as you are teaching, you realize students are already confident with the lesson concepts.

- *Practice* strategies for extending parts of the lesson, if you realize during the lesson that students would benefit from more practice.

- *Reteach* ideas for re-presenting and reinforcing the key teaching of the lesson, if you realize that students are not grasping the concepts.

During the lesson, Monitoring Student Progress presents tips for addressing specific concerns.

At the end of the lesson, Assessment Follow-Up provides activities to review, reteach, practice, or enrich lesson concepts depending on student performance.

Key Principles of a Differentiated Classroom

- The teacher is clear about what matters in subject matter.

- The teacher understands, appreciates, and builds upon student differences.

- Assessment and instruction are inseparable.

- The teacher adjusts content, process, and product in response to student readiness, interests, and learning profiles.

- All students participate in respectful work.

- Students and teachers are collaborators in learning.

- Goals of a differentiated classroom are maximum growth and individual success.

- Flexibility is the hallmark of a differentiated classroom.

Tomlinson, Carol Ann and Allan, Susan Demirsky. *Leadership for Differentiating Schools and Classrooms.* Alexandria, VA: Association for Supervision and Curriculum Development. 2000, p. 48.

Assessment

Much has been written about the importance of assessment. The Assessment Standards book from the National Council of Teachers of Mathematics tells us that classroom assessment should

- provide a rich variety of mathematical topics and problem situations.

- give students opportunities to investigate problems in many ways.

- question and listen to students.

- look for evidence of learning from many sources.

- expect students to use concepts and procedures effectively in solving problems.

The goals of assessment are to

- improve instruction by informing teachers of the effectiveness of their lessons.

- promote growth of students by identifying where they need additional instruction and support.

- recognize accomplishments.

Real Math and Assessment

Real Math provides opportunities for formal and informal assessments and convenient ways to record, track, and report on student achievements.

Informal Assessments

Informal assessment involves ongoing observations of student involvement in class activities. Informal assessments are tailored to evaluate students on the five areas of mathematic proficiency: computing, understanding, reasoning, applying, and engaging.

Every lesson includes two **Assessment** checkmarks in the *Teacher's Edition* next to activities tailored to reveal students' math proficiencies. These activities may include Guided Discussion, Skill Building, Strategy Building, Games, or Journals. The checkmarks alert teachers to carefully observe students during the activity. Rubric checklists in Assess and Differentiate of the lesson describe specific positive behaviors to look for as signs of development. As teachers become familiar with the rubric checklists, they can access them through memory. Teachers can record their observations in the Daily Class Assessment Records for each proficiency.

Computing	• respond accurately • respond quickly • respond with confidence • self-correct
Understanding	• make important observations • extend or generalize learning • provide insightful answers • pose insightful questions
Reasoning	• provide a clear explanation • communicate reasons and strategies • chooses appropriate strategies • argue logically
Applying	• apply learning in new situations • contribute concepts • contribute answers • connect mathematics to real-world situations
Engaging	• pay attention to others' contributions • contribute information and ideas • improve on a strategy • reflect on and check the accuracy of his or her work

Daily checklist observations can be summarized in the Student Assessment Record for the chapter or in **eAssess** to provide a long-term holistic view of student proficiency. If teachers record these observations, these daily informal assessments can be powerful indicators of student proficiency, and as such help inform instruction, as well as provide feedback to students and their parents.

Formal Assessment

There are several opportunities for formal assessment in every chapter. All assessments can be recorded further in the Student Assessment Record or in **eAssess** for every chapter to provide a comprehensive view of student achievement.

- **Pretests** test prerequisite and chapter concepts to provide a diagnostic assessment of student understanding for the upcoming chapter.

- **Speed Tests** appear in lessons to test computational fluency.

- **Mastery Checkpoints** provide assessments for skills that should be mastered at particular points in the program. The Mastery Checkpoint Chart provides a class view of student progress toward mastery of particular skills.

- **Oral Assessment** in the middle of the chapter is an opportunity for teachers to interact individually with students to assess their growth in proficiency. An Individual Oral Assessment recording sheet is available in **Assessment** for each Oral Assessment for teacher convenience.

- **Daily Quizzes** are available to provide a quick review and assessment of student understanding of lesson concepts and skills.

- **Chapter Tests** offer a way to assess student understanding of chapter content and skills.

 **Assess**

The **eAssess** program offers a powerful way to record and track student progress. Teachers can enter data on a daily or weekly basis. The more data a teacher inputs—including records of Formal and Informal Assessments, completion of student pages, completion of projects, and additional activities—the more comprehensive and reliable the reports that can be generated will be.

Using **eAssess,** teachers can generate reports that show student performance in reference to the entire class, individual development, and in reference to state and/or national standards. These reports provide a comprehensive view of individual student and class performance that can provide valuable feedback for your instruction and for student and parent conferences.

More information, including masters of recording sheets and tests, can be found in **Assessment.**

Handwriting Models

Starting point, straight down: 1

Starting point, around right, slanting left, and straight across right: 2

Starting point, around right, in at the middle, and around right: 3

Starting point, straight down, and straight across right. Starting point, straight down, and crossing line: 4

Straight down, curve around right and up. Starting point, straight across right: 5

Starting point, slanting left, around the bottom curving up around left and into the curve: 6

Starting point, straight across right, and slanting down left: 7

Starting point, curving left, curving down and around right, slanting up right to starting point: 8

Starting point, curving around left all the way, and straight down: 9

Starting point, straight down. Starting point, curving left all the way around to starting point: 10

*Students follow natural developmental progressions in learning, developing mathematical ideas in their own ways. Curriculum research has revealed sequences of activities that are effective in guiding students through these levels of thinking. These developmental paths can be described as learning trajectories. Each learning trajectory has levels of understanding, each more sophisticated than the last, and with tasks that promote growth from one level to the next. The **Building Blocks** Learning Trajectories give simple labels, descriptions, and examples of each level. Complete learning trajectories describe the goals of learning, the thinking and learning processes of students at various levels, and the learning activities in which they might engage.*

Learning Trajectories for Primary Grades Mathematics

Developmental Levels

The following provides the developmental levels from the first signs of development in different strands of mathematics through approximately age 8. Research shows that when teachers understand how students develop mathematics understanding, they are more effective in questioning, analyzing, and providing activities that further students' development than teachers who are unaware of the development process. Consequently students have a much richer and more successful math experience in the primary grades.

Frequently Asked Questions (FAQ)

1. **When are students "at" a level?** Students are at a certain level when most of their behaviors reflect the thinking—ideas and skills—of that level. Often, they show a few behaviors from the next (and previous) levels as they learn.

2. **Can students work at more than one level at the same time?** Yes, although most students work mainly at one level or in transition between two levels (naturally, if they are tired or distracted, they may operate at a much lower level). Levels are not "absolute." They are "benchmarks" of complex growth that represent distinct ways of thinking. So, another way to think of them is as a sequence of different patterns of thinking. Students are continually learning, within levels and moving between them.

3. **Can students jump ahead?** Yes, especially if there are separate "subtopics." For example, we have combined many counting competencies into one "Counting" sequence with subtopics, such as verbal counting skills. Some students learn to count to 100 at age 6 after

learning to count objects to 10 or more; some may learn that verbal skill earlier. The subtopic of verbal counting skills would still be followed.

4. **How do these developmental levels support teaching and learning?** The levels help teachers, as well as curriculum developers, and assess, teach, and sequence activities. *Teachers who understand learning trajectories and the developmental levels that are at their foundation are more effective and efficient.* Through planned teaching and also by encouraging informal, incidental mathematics, teachers help students learn *at an appropriate and deep level.*

5. **Should I plan to help students develop just the levels that correspond to my students' ages?** No! The ages in the table are typical ages when students develop these ideas. *But these are rough guides only*—students differ widely. Furthermore, the ages below are lower bounds on what students achieve without instruction. So, these are "starting levels," not goals. We have found that students who are provided high-quality mathematics experiences are capable of developing to levels one or more years beyond their peers.

Each column in the table, such as "Counting," represents a main developmental progression that underlies the learning trajectory for that topic.

Clements, D. H., Sarama, J., & DiBiase, A.M. *Engaging Young Students in Mathematics: Standards for Early Childhood Mathematics Education.* Mahwah, NJ: Lawrence Erlbaum Associates.

Clements, D. H., & Sarama, J. "Early Childhood Mathematics Learning." In F. K. Lester, Jr. (Ed.), *Second Handbook of Research on Mathematics Teaching and Learning.* New York: Information Age Publishing.

Learning Trajectories

Developmental Levels for Counting

The ability to count with confidence develops over the course of several years. Beginning in infancy, students show signs of understanding numbers. With instruction and number experience, most students can count fluently by age 8, with much progress in counting occurring in kindergarten and first grade. Most students follow a natural developmental progression in learning to count with recognizable stages or levels. This developmental path can be described as part of a learning trajectory.

Age Range	Level Name	Level	Description
1–2	Precounter	1	A student at the earliest level of counting may name some numbers meaninglessly. The student may skip numbers and have no sense of sequence.
1–2	Chanter	2	At this level, a student may sing-song numbers, but without meaning.
2	Reciter	3	At this level, the student may verbally count with separate words, but not necessarily in the correct order.
3	Reciter (10)	4	A student at this level may verbally count to 10 with some correspondence with objects. They may point to objects to count a few items, but then lose track.
3	Corresponder	5	At this level, a student may keep one-to-one correspondence between counting words and objects—at least for small groups of objects laid in a line. A corresponder may answer "how many" by recounting the objects starting over with one each time.
4	Counter (Small Numbers)	6	At around 4 years of age, students may begin to count meaningfully. They may accurately count objects to 5 and answer the "how many" question with the last number counted. These students may count verbally to 10 and may write or draw to represent 1–5.
4	Producer—Counter to (Small Numbers)	7	The next level after counting small numbers is to produce a group of four objects. When asked to show four of something, for example, this student may give four objects.
4	Counter (10)	8	This student may count structured arrangements of objects to 10. He or she may be able to write or draw to represent 10 and may accurately count a line of nine blocks and say there are 9.
4	Just After/Just Before Counter	9	A student at this level may find the number just after or just before another number, but only by counting up from 1.
5	Counter and Producer—Counter to (10+)	10	Around 5 years of age, students may begin to count out objects accurately to 10 and then beyond to 30. They may keep track of objects that have and have not been counted, even in different arrangements. They may write or draw to represent 1 to 10 and then 20 and 30, and may give the next number to 20 or 30.
5	Counting Error Recognizer	11	The next level in counting is recognizing errors in others' counting and being able to eliminate most errors in one's own counting.

Age Range	Level Name	Level	Description
5	Counter Backward from 10	12	Another milestone at about age 5 is being able to count backward from 10.
6	Counter from N (N+1, N−1)	13	Around 6 years of age, students may begin to count on, counting verbally and with objects from numbers other than 1.
6	Just After/Just Before	14	Another noticeable accomplishment is that students may determine the number immediately before or after another number without having to start back at 1.
6	Skip-Counting by 10s to 100	15	A student at this level may count by tens to 100. They may count through decades knowing that 40 comes after 39, for example.
6	Counter to 100	16	A student at this level may count by ones through 100, including the decade transitions from 39 to 40, 49 to 50, and so on.
6	Counter On Using Patterns	17	At this level, a student may keep track of counting acts by using numerical patterns, such as tapping as he or she counts.
6	Skip-Counter	18	At this level, students can count by 5s and 2s with understanding.
6	Counter of Imagined Items	19	At this level, a student may count mental images of hidden objects.
6	Counter On Keeping Track	20	A student at this level may keep track of counting acts numerically with the ability to count up one to four more from a given number.
6	Counter of Quantitative Units	21	At this level, a student can count unusual units, such as "wholes" when shown combinations of wholes and parts. For example, when shown three whole plastic eggs and four halves, a student at this level will say there are five whole eggs.
6	Counter to 200	22	At this level, a student may count accurately to 200 and beyond, recognizing the patterns of ones, tens, and hundreds.
7	Number Conserver	23	A major milestone around age 7 is the ability to conserve number. A student who conserves number understands that a number is unchanged even if a group of objects is rearranged. For example, if there is a row of ten buttons, the student understands there are still ten without recounting, even if they are rearranged in a long row or a circle.
7	Counter Forward and Back	24	A student at this level may count in either direction and recognize that sequence of decades mirrors single-digit sequence.

Developmental Levels for Comparing and Ordering Numbers

Comparing and ordering sets is a critical skill for students as they determine whether one set is larger than another in order to make sure sets are equal and "fair." Prekindergartners can learn to use matching to compare collections or to create equivalent collections. Finding out how many more or fewer in one collection is more demanding than simply comparing two collections. The ability to compare and order sets with fluency develops over the course of several years. With instruction and number experience, most students develop foundational understanding of number relationships and place value at ages 4 and 5. Most students follow a natural developmental progression in learning to compare and order numbers with recognizable stages or levels. This developmental path can be described as part of a learning trajectory.

Age Range	Level Name	Level	Description
2	Object Corresponder	1	At this early level, a student puts objects into one-to-one correspondence, but with only intuitive understanding of resulting equivalence. For example, a student may know that each carton has a straw, but does not necessarily know there are the same numbers of straws and cartons.
2	Perceptual Comparer	2	At this level, a student can compare collections that are quite different in size (for example, one is at least twice the other) and know that one has more than the other. If the collections are similar, the student can compare very small collections.
3	Nonverbal Comparer of Similar Items	3	At this level, a student can identify that different organizations of the same number of small groups are equal and different from other sets (1–4 items). For example, a student can identify ••• and •••• as equal and different from •• or ••.
3	Nonverbal Comparer of Dissimilar Items	4	At this level, a student can match small, equal collections of dissimilar items, such as shells and dots, and show that they are the same number.
4	Matching Comparer	5	As students progress, they begin to compare groups of 1–6 by matching. For example, a student gives one toy bone to every dog and says there are the same number of dogs and bones.
4	Knows-to-Count Comparer	6	A significant step occurs when the student begins to count collections to compare. At the early levels, students are not always accurate when a larger collection's objects are smaller in size than the objects in the smaller collection. For example, a student at this level may accurately count two equal collections, but when asked, says the collection of larger blocks has more.
4	Counting Comparer (Same Size)	7	At this level, students make accurate comparisons via counting, but only when objects are about the same size and groups are small (about 1–5 items).
5	Counting Comparer (5)	8	As students develop their ability to compare sets, they compare accurately by counting, even when a larger collection's objects are smaller. A student at this level can figure out how many more or less.
5	Ordinal Counter	9	At this level, a student identifies and uses ordinal numbers from "first" to "tenth." For example, the student can identify who is "third in line."
5	Serial Orderer to 6+	10	Students demonstrate development in comparing when they begin to order lengths marked into units (1–6, then beyond). For example, given towers of cubes, this student can put them in order, 1 to 6. Later the student begins to order collections. For example, given cards with one to six dots on them, the student can put them in order.
6	Counting Comparer (10)	11	This level can be observed when the student compares sets by counting, even when a larger collection's objects are smaller, up to 10. A student at this level can accurately count two collections of 9 items each, and says they have the same number, even if one collection has larger blocks.
6	Mental Number Line to 10	12	As students move into this level, they begin to use mental rather than physical images and knowledge of number relationships to determine relative size and position. For example, a student at this level can answer which number is closer to 6, 4, or 9 without counting physical objects.
7	Place Value Comparer	13	Further development is made when a student begins to compare numbers with place value understanding. For example, a student at this level can explain that "63 is more than 59 because six tens is more than five tens, even if there are more than three ones."
7	Mental Number Line to 100	14	Students demonstrate the next level in comparing and ordering when they can use mental images and knowledge of number relationships, including ones embedded in tens, to determine relative size and position. For example, when asked, "Which is closer to 45, 30 or 50?" a student at this level may say "45 is right next to 50, but 30 isn't."
8+	Mental Number Line to 1,000s	15	At about age 8, students may begin to use mental images of numbers up to 1,000 and knowledge of number relationships, including place value, to determine relative size and position. For example, when asked, "Which is closer to 3,500—2,000 or 7,000?" a student at this level may say "70 is double 35, but 20 is only fifteen from 35, so twenty hundreds, 2,000, is closer."

Learning Trajectories

Developmental Levels for Recognizing Number and Subitizing (Instantly Recognizing)

The ability to recognize number values develops over the course of several years and is a foundational part of number sense. Beginning at about age 2, students begin to name groups of objects. The ability to instantly know how many are in a group, called *subitizing,* begins at about age 3. By age 8, with instruction and number experience, most students can identify groups of items and use place values and multiplication skills to count them. Most students follow a natural developmental progression in learning to count with recognizable stages or levels. This developmental path can be described as part of a learning trajectory.

Age Range	Level Name	Level	Description
2	Small Collection Namer	1	The first sign occurs when the student can name groups of 1 to 2, sometimes 3. For example, when shown a pair of shoes, this young student says, "two shoes."
3	Nonverbal Subitizer	2	This level occurs when, shown a small collection (1 to 4), the student can put out a matching group nonverbally, but cannot necessarily give the number telling how many. For example, when 4 objects are shown, the student makes a set of 4 objects to "match."
3	Maker of Small Collections	3	At this level, a student can nonverbally make a small collection (no more than 5, usually 1 to 3) with the same number as another collection. For example, when shown a collection of 3, the student makes another collection of 3.
4	Perceptual Subitizer to 4	4	Progress is made when a student instantly recognizes collections up to 4 and verbally names the number of items. For example, when shown 4 objects briefly, the student says "4."
5	Perceptual Subitizer to 5	5	This level is the ability to instantly recognize collections up to 5 and verbally name the number of items. For example, when shown 5 objects, the student says "5."

Age Range	Level Name	Level	Description
5	Conceptual Subitizer to 5	6	At this level, the student can verbally label all arrangements to 5, using groups. For example, a student at this level might say, "I saw 2 and 2, and so I saw 4."
5	Conceptual Subitizer to 10	7	This step is when the student can verbally label most arrangements to 6, then up to 10, using groups. For example, a student at this level might say, "In my mind, I made 2 groups of 3 and 1 more, so 7."
6	Conceptual Subitizer to 20	8	Next, a student can verbally label structured arrangements up to 20, using groups. For example, the student may say, "I saw 3 fives, so 5, 10, 15."
7	Conceptual Subitizer with Place Value and Skip-Counting	9	At this level, a student is able to use skip-counting and place value to verbally label structured arrangements. For example, the student may say, "I saw groups of tens and twos, so 10, 20, 30, 40, 42, 44, 46...46!"
8+	Conceptual Subitizer with Place Value and Multiplication	10	As students develop their ability to subitize, they use groups, multiplication, and place value to verbally label structured arrangements. At this level, a student may say, "I saw groups of tens and threes, so I thought, 5 tens is 50 and 4 threes is 12, so 62 in all."

Developmental Levels for Composing (Knowing Combinations of Numbers)

Composing and decomposing are combining and separating operations that allow students to build concepts of "parts" and "wholes." Most prekindergartners can "see" that two items and one item make three items. Later, students learn to separate a group into parts in various ways and then to count to produce all of the number "partners" of a given number. Eventually students think of a number and know the different addition facts that make that number. Most students follow a natural developmental progression in learning to compose and decompose numbers with recognizable stages or levels. This developmental path can be described as part of a learning trajectory.

Age Range	Level Name	Level	Description
4	Pre-Part-Whole Recognizer	1	At the earliest levels of composing, a student only nonverbally recognizes parts and wholes. For example, when shown 4 red blocks and 2 blue blocks, a young student may intuitively appreciate that "all the blocks" includes the red and blue blocks, but when asked how many there are in all, the student may name a small number, such as 1.
5	Inexact Part-Whole Recognizer	2	A sign of development is that the student knows a whole is bigger than parts, but does not accurately quantify. For example, when shown 4 red blocks and 2 blue blocks and asked how many there are in all, the student may name a "large number," such as 5 or 10.
5	Composer to 4, then 5	3	At this level, a student begins to know number combinations. A student at this level quickly names parts of any whole, or the whole given the parts. For example, when shown 4, then 1 is secretly hidden, and then shown the 3 remaining, the student may quickly say "1" is hidden.

Age Range	Level Name	Level	Description
6	Composer to 7	4	The next sign of development is when a student knows number combinations to totals of 7. A student at this level quickly names parts of any whole, or the whole when given parts, and can double numbers to 10. For example, when shown 6, then 4 are secretly hidden, and then shown the 2 remaining, the student may quickly say "4" are hidden.
6	Composer to 10	5	This level is when a student knows number combinations to totals of 10. A student at this level may quickly name parts of any whole, or the whole when given parts, and can double numbers to 20. For example, this student would be able to say "9 and 9 is 18."
7	Composer with Tens and Ones	6	At this level, the student understands two-digit numbers as tens and ones, can count with dimes and pennies, and can perform two-digit addition with regrouping. For example, a student at this level may explain, "17 and 36 is like 17 and 3, which is 20, and 33, which is 53."

Learning Trajectories

Developmental Levels for Adding and Subtracting

Single-digit addition and subtraction is generally characterized as "math facts." It is assumed students must memorize these facts, yet research has shown that addition and subtraction have their roots in counting, counting on, number sense, the ability to compose and decompose numbers, and place value. Research has also shown that learning methods for addition and subtraction with understanding is much more effective than rote memorization of seemingly isolated facts. Most students follow an observable developmental progression in learning to add and subtract numbers with recognizable stages or levels. This developmental path can be described as part of a learning trajectory.

Age Range	Level Name	Level	Description
1	Pre +/−	1	At the earliest level, a student shows no sign of being able to add or subtract.
3	Nonverbal +/−	2	The first sign is when a student can add and subtract very small collections nonverbally. For example, when shown 2 objects, then 1 object being hidden under a napkin, the student identifies or makes a set of 3 objects to "match."
4	Small Number +/−	3	This level is when a student can find sums for joining problems up to $3 + 2$ by counting with objects. For example, when asked, "You have 2 balls and get 1 more. How many in all?" the student may count out 2, then count out 1 more, then count all 3: "1, 2, 3, 3!"
5	Find Result +/−	4	**Addition** Evidence of this level in addition is when a student can find sums for joining (you had 3 apples and get 3 more; how many do you have in all?) and part-part-whole (there are 6 girls and 5 boys on the playground; how many students were there in all?) problems by direct modeling, counting all, with objects. For example, when asked, "You have 2 red balls and 3 blue balls. How many in all?" the student may count out 2 red, then count out 3 blue, then count all 5. **Subtraction** In subtraction, a student can also solve take-away problems by separating with objects. For example, when asked, "You have 5 balls and give 2 to Tom. How many do you have left?" the student may count out 5 balls, then take away 2, and then count the remaining 3.
5	Find Change +/−	5	**Addition** At this level, a student can find the missing addend ($5 + \_ = 7$) by adding on objects. For example, when asked, "You have 5 balls and then get some more. Now you have 7 in all. How many did you get?" The student may count out 5, then count those 5 again starting at 1, then add more, counting "6, 7," then count the balls added to find the answer, 2. **Subtraction** A child can compare by matching in simple situations. For example, when asked, "Here are 6 dogs and 4 balls. If we give a ball to each dog, how many dogs will not get a ball?" a student at this level may count out 6 dogs, match 4 balls to 4 of them, then count the 2 dogs that have no ball.
5	Change To n +/−	6	A significant advancement occurs when a student is able to count on. This student can add on objects to make one number into another without counting from 1. For example, when told, "This puppet has 4 balls, but she should have 6. Make it 6," the student may put up 4 fingers on one hand, immediately count up from 4 while putting up 2 fingers on the other hand, saying, "5, 6," and then count or recognize the 2 fingers.

Age Range	Level Name	Level	Description
6	Counting Strategies +/−	7	This level occurs when a student can find sums for joining (you had 8 apples and get 3 more...) and part-part-whole (6 girls and 5 boys...) problems with finger patterns or by adding on objects or counting on. For example, when asked "How much is 4 and 3 more?" the student may answer "4...5, 6, 7. 7!" Students at this level can also solve missing addend ($3 + \_ = 7$) or compare problems by counting on. When asked, for example, "You have 6 balls. How many more would you need to have 8?" the student may say, "6, 7 [puts up first finger], 8 [puts up second finger]. 2!"
6	Part-Whole +/−	8	Further development has occurred when the student has part-whole understanding. This student can solve problems using flexible strategies and some derived facts (for example, "$5 + 5$ is 10, so $5 + 6$ is 11"), can sometimes do start-unknown problems ($\_ + 6 = 11$), but only by trial and error. When asked, "You had some balls. Then you get 6 more. Now you have 11 balls. How many did you start with?" this student may lay out 6, then 3, count, and get 9. The child may put 1 more, say 10, then put 1 more. The child may count up from 6 to 11, then recounts the group added, and say, "5!"
6	Numbers-in-Numbers +/−	9	Evidence of this level is when a student recognizes that a number is part of a whole and can solve problems when the start is unknown ($\_ + 4 = 9$) with counting strategies. For example, when asked, "You have some balls, then you get 4 more balls, now you have 9. How many did you have to start with?" this student may count, putting up fingers, "5, 6, 7, 8, 9." The child may look at his or her fingers, and say, "5!"
7	Deriver +/−	10	At this level, a student can use flexible strategies and derived combinations (for example, "$7 + 7$ is 14, so $7 + 8$ is 15") to solve all types of problems. For example, when asked, "What's 7 plus 8?" this student thinks: $7 + 8 = 7 + [7 + 1] = [7 + 7] + 1 = 14 + 1 = 15$. The student can also solve multidigit problems by incrementing or combining 10s and 1s. For example, when asked "What's $28 + 35$?" this student may think: $20 + 30 = 50; + 8 = 58$; 2 more is 60, and 3 more is 63. Combining 10s and 1s: $20 + 30 = 50$. $8 + 5$ is like 8 plus 2 and 3 more, so, it is 13–50 and 13 is 63.
8+	Problem Solver +/−	11	As students develop their addition and subtraction abilities, they can solve by using flexible strategies and many known combinations. For example, when asked, "If I have 13 and you have 9, how could we have the same number?" this student may say, "9 and 1 is 10, then 3 more makes 13. 1 and 3 is 4. I need 4 more!"
8+	Multidigit +/−	12	Further development is shown when students can use composition of 10s and all previous strategies to solve multidigit +/− problems. For example, when asked, "What's $37 − 18$?" this student may say, "Take 1 ten off the 3 tens; that's 2 tens. Take 7 off the 7. That's 2 tens and 0...20. I have one more to take off. That's 19." Or, when asked, "What's $28 + 35$?" this child may think, $30 + 35$ would be 65. But it's 28, so it's 2 less...63.

Developmental Levels for Multiplying and Dividing

Multiplication and division builds on addition and subtraction understanding and is dependent upon counting and place-value concepts. As students begin to learn to multiply, they make equal groups and count them all. They then learn skip-counting and derive related products from products they know. Finding and using patterns aids in learning multiplication and division facts with understanding. Students typically follow an observable developmental progression in learning to multiply and divide numbers with recognizable stages or levels. This developmental path can be described as part of a learning trajectory.

Age Range	Level Name	Level	Description
2	Nonquantitive Sharer "Dumper"	1	Multiplication and division concepts begin very early with the problem of sharing. Early evidence of these concepts can be observed when a student dumps out blocks and gives some (not an equal number) to each person.
3	Beginning Grouper and Distributive Sharer	2	Progression to this level can be observed when a student is able to make small groups (fewer than 5). This student can share by "dealing out," but often only between 2 people, although he or she may not appreciate the numerical result. For example, to share 4 blocks, this student may give each person a block, check that each person has one, and repeat this.
4	Grouper and Distributive Sharer	3	The next level occurs when a student makes small equal groups (fewer than 6). This student can deal out equally between 2 or more recipients, but may not understand that equal quantities are produced. For example, the student may share 6 blocks by dealing out blocks to herself and a friend one at a time.
5	Concrete Modeler ×/÷	4	As students develop, they are able to solve small-number multiplying problems by grouping—making each group and counting all. At this level, a student can solve division/sharing problems with concrete strategies, using concrete objects—up to 20 objects and 2 to 5 people—although the student may not understand equivalence of groups. For example, the student may distribute 20 objects by dealing out 2 blocks to each of 5 people, then 1 to each, until the blocks are gone.
6	Parts and Wholes ×/÷	5	A new level is evidenced when the student understands the inverse relation between divisor and quotient. For example, this student may understand "If you share with more people, each person gets fewer."

Age Range	Level Name	Level	Description
7	Skip-Counter ×/÷	6	As students develop understanding in multiplication and division, they begin to use skip-counting for multiplication and for measurement division (finding out how many groups). For example, given 20 blocks, 4 to each person, and asked how many people, the student may skip-count by 4, holding up 1 finger for each count of 4. A student at this level may also use trial and error for partitive division (finding out how many in each group). For example, given 20 blocks, 5 people, and asked how many each should get, this student may give 3 to each, then 1 more, then 1 more.
8+	Deriver ×/÷	7	At this level, students use strategies and derived combinations and solve multidigit problems by operating on tens and ones separately. For example, a student at this level may explain "7 × 6, five 7s is 35, so 7 more is 42."
8+	Array Quantifier	8	Further development can be observed when a student begins to work with arrays. For example, given 7 × 4 with most of 5 × 4 covered, a student at this level may say, "There's 8 in these 2 rows, and 5 rows of 4 is 20, so 28 in all."
8+	Partitive Divisor	9	This level can be observed when a student is able to figure out how many are in each group. For example, given 20 blocks, 5 people, and asked how many each should get, a student at this level may say, "4, because 5 groups of 4 is 20."
8+	Multidigit ×/÷	10	As students progress, they begin to use multiple strategies for multiplication and division, from compensating to paper-and-pencil procedures. For example, a student becoming fluent in multiplication might explain that "19 times 5 is 95, because 20 fives is 100, and one less five is 95."

Learning Trajectories

Developmental Levels for Measuring

Measurement is one of the main real-world applications of mathematics. Counting is a type of measurement which determines how many items are in a collection. Measurement also involves assigning a number to attributes of length, area, and weight. Prekindergarten students know that mass, weight, and length exist, but they do not know how to reason about these or to accurately measure them. As students develop their understanding of measurement, they begin to use tools to measure and understand the need for standard units of measure. Students typically follow an observable developmental progression in learning to measure with recognizable stages or levels. This developmental path can be described as part of a learning trajectory.

Age Range	Level Name	Level	Description
3	Length Quantity Recognizer	1	At the earliest level, students can identify length as an attribute. For example, they might say, "I'm tall, see?"
4	Length Direct Comparer	2	In this level, students can physically align 2 objects to determine which is longer or if they are the same length. For example, they can stand 2 sticks up next to each other on a table and say, "This one's bigger."
5	Serial Orderer to 6+	3	At this level, a student can order lengths, marked in 1 to 6 units. For example, given towers of cubes, a student at this level may put them in order, 1 to 6.
5	Indirect Length Comparer	4	A sign of further development is when a student can compare the length of 2 objects by representing them with a third object. For example, a student might compare the length of 2 objects with a piece of string. Additional evidence of this level is that when asked to measure, the student may assign a length by guessing or moving along a length while counting (without equal-length units). The student may also move a finger along a line segment, saying 10, 20, 30, 31, 32.
6	End-to-End Length Measurer	5	At this level, the student can lay units end-to-end, although he or she may not see the need for equal-length units. For example, a student might lay 9-inch cubes in a line beside a book to measure how long it is.

Age Range	Level Name	Level	Description
7	Length Unit Iterater	6	A significant change occurs when a student can use a ruler and see the need for identical units.
7	Length Unit Relater	7	At this level, a student can relate size and number of units. For example, the student may explain, "If you measure with centimeters instead of inches, you'll need more of them, because each one is smaller."
8	Length Measurer	8	As students develop measurement ability, they begin to measure, knowing the need for identical units, the relationships between different units, partitions of unit, and the zero point on rulers. At this level, the student also begins to estimate. The student may explain, "I used a meter-stick 3 times, then there was a little left over. So, I lined it up from 0 and found 14 centimeters. So, it's 3 meters, 14 centimeters in all."
8	Conceptual Ruler Measurer	9	Further development in measurement is evidenced when a student possesses an "internal" measurement tool. At this level, the student mentally moves along an object, segmenting it, and counting the segments. This student also uses arithmetic to measure and estimates with accuracy. For example, a student at this level may explain, "I imagine one meter-stick after another along the edge of the room. That's how I estimated the room's length to be 9 meters."

Developmental Levels for Recognizing Geometric Shapes

Geometric shapes can be used to represent and understand objects. Analyzing, comparing, and classifying shapes helps create new knowledge of shapes and their relationships. Shapes can be decomposed or composed into other shapes. Through their everyday activity, students build both intuitive and explicit knowledge of geometric figures. Most students can recognize and name basic two-dimensional shapes at 4 years of age. However, young students can learn richer concepts about shape if they have varied examples and nonexamples of shape, discussions about shapes and their characteristics, a wide variety of shape classes, and interesting tasks. Students typically follow an observable developmental progression in learning about shapes with recognizable stages or levels. This developmental path can be described as part of a learning trajectory.

Age Range	Level Name	Level	Description
2	Shape Matcher—Basic 1	1	The earliest sign of understanding shape is when a student can match basic shapes (circle, square, typical triangle) with the same size and orientation.
2	Basic 2a	2	A sign of development is when a student can match basic shapes with different sizes.
2	Basic 2b	3	This level of development is when a student can match basic shapes with different orientations.
3	Shape Prototype Recognizer and Identifier	4	A sign of development is when a student can recognize and name a prototypical circle, square, and, less often, a typical triangle. For example, the student names this a square. ☐ Some students may name different sizes, shapes, and orientations of rectangles, but also accept some shapes that look rectangular but are not rectangles. Students name these shapes "rectangles" (including the nonrectangular parallelogram).
3	Shape Matcher—3	5	As students develop understanding of shape, they can match a wider variety of shapes with the same size and orientation.
4	Shape Recognizer—Basic 1	6	This sign of development is when a student can recognize some nonprototypical squares and triangles and may recognize some rectangles, but usually not rhombi (diamonds). Often, the student does not differentiate sides/corners. The student at this level may name these as triangles.
4	Constructor of Shapes from Parts 1	7	A significant sign of development is when a student represents a shape by making a shape "look like" a goal shape. For example, when asked to make a triangle with sticks, the student may create the following: ☐ .

Age Range	Level Name	Level	Description
5	Shape Recognizer—Basic 2	8	As students develop understanding of shape, they recognize more rectangle sizes, shapes, and orientations of rectangles. For example, a student at this level may correctly name these shapes "rectangles."
5	Side Recognizer	9	A sign of development is when a student recognizes parts of shapes and identifies sides as distinct geometric objects. For example, when asked what this shape is, the student may say it is a quadrilateral (or has 4 sides) after counting and running a finger along the length of each side.
5	Angle Recognizer	10	At this level, a student can recognize angles as separate geometric objects. For example, when asked, "Why is this a triangle," the child may say, "It has three angles" and count them, pointing clearly to each vertex (point at the corner).
5	Shape Recognizer—3	11	As students develop, they are able to recognize most basic shapes and prototypical examples of other shapes, such as hexagon, rhombus (diamond), and trapezoid. For example, a student can correctly identify and name all the following shapes:
6	Shape Identifier	12	At this level, the student can name most common shapes, including rhombi, "ellipses-is-not-circle." A student at this level implicitly recognizes right angles, so distinguishes between a rectangle and a parallelogram without right angles. A student may correctly name all the following shapes:
6	Angle Matcher	13	A sign of development is when the student can match angles concretely. For example, given several triangles, the child may find 2 with the same angles by laying the angles on top of one another.

Learning Trajectories

Age Range	Level Name	Level	Description
7	Parts of Shapes Identifier	14	At this level, the student can identify shapes in terms of their components. For example, the student may say, "No matter how skinny it looks, that's a triangle because it has 3 sides and 3 angles."
7	Constructor of Shapes from Parts 2	15	A significant step is when the student can represent a shape with completely correct construction, based on knowledge of components and relationships. For example, when asked to make a triangle with sticks, the student may create the following:
8	Shape Class Identifier	16	As students develop, they begin to use class membership (for example, to sort) not explicitly based on properties. For example, a student at this level may say, "I put the triangles over here, and the quadrilaterals, including squares, rectangles, rhombi, and trapezoids, over there."
8	Shape Property Identifier	17	At this level, a student can use properties explicitly. For example, a student may say, "I put the shapes with opposite sides that are parallel over here, and those with 4 sides but not both pairs of sides parallel over there."

Age Range	Level Name	Level	Description
8	Angle Size Comparer	18	The next sign of development is when a student can separate and compare angle sizes. For example, the student may say, "I put all the shapes that have right angles here, and all the ones that have bigger or smaller angles over there."
8	Angle Measurer	19	A significant step in development is when a student can use a protractor to measure angles.
8	Property Class Identifier	20	The next sign of development is when a student can use class membership for shapes (for example, to sort or consider shapes "similar") explicitly based on properties, including angle measure. For example, the student may say, "I put the equilateral triangles over here, and the right triangles over here."
8	Angle Synthesizer	21	As students develop understanding of shape, they can combine various meanings of angle (turn, corner, slant). For example, a student at this level could explain, "This ramp is at a 45° angle to the ground."

Developmental Levels for Composing Geometric Shapes

Students move through levels in the composition and decomposition of two-dimensional figures. Very young students cannot compose shapes but then gain ability to combine shapes into pictures, synthesize combinations of shapes into new shapes, and eventually substitute and build different kinds of shapes. Students typically follow an observable developmental progression in learning to compose shapes with recognizable stages or levels. This developmental path can be described as part of a learning trajectory.

Age Range	Level Name	Level	Description
2	Pre-Composer	1	The earliest sign of development is when a student can manipulate shapes as individuals, but is unable to combine them to compose a larger shape.
3	Pre-Decomposer	2	At this level, a student can decompose shapes, but only by trial and error.
4	Piece Assembler	3	Around age 4, a student can begin to make pictures in which each shape represents a unique role (for example, one shape for each body part) and shapes touch. A student at this level can fill simple outline puzzles using trial and error.
5	Picture Maker	4	As students develop, they are able to put several shapes together to make one part of a picture (for example, 2 shapes for 1 arm). A student at this level uses trial and error and does not anticipate creation of the new geometric shape. The student can choose shapes using "general shape" or side length, and fill "easy" outline puzzles that suggest the placement of each shape (but note below that the student is trying to put a square in the puzzle where its right angles will not fit).
5	Simple Decomposer	5	A significant step occurs when the student is able to decompose ("take apart" into smaller shapes) simple shapes that have obvious clues as to their decomposition.
5	Shape Composer	6	A sign of development is when a student composes shapes with anticipation ("I know what will fit!"). A student at this level chooses shapes using angles as well as side lengths. Rotation and flipping are used intentionally to select and place shapes.
6	Substitution Composer	7	A sign of development is when a student is able to make new shapes out of smaller shapes and uses trial and error to substitute groups of shapes for other shapes in order to create new shapes in different ways. For example, the student can substitute shapes to fill outline puzzles in different ways.

Age Range	Level Name	Level	Description
6	Shape Decomposer (with Help)	8	As students develop, they can decompose shapes by using imagery that is suggested and supported by the task or environment.
7	Shape Composite Repeater	9	This level is demonstrated when the student can construct and duplicate units of units (shapes made from other shapes) intentionally, and understands each as being both multiple, small shapes and one larger shape. For example, the student may continue a pattern of shapes that leads to tiling.
7	Shape Decomposer with Imagery	10	A significant sign of development is when a student is able to decompose shapes flexibly by using independently generated imagery.
8	Shape Composer— Units of Units	11	Students demonstrate further understanding when they are able to build and apply units of units (shapes made from other shapes). For example, in constructing spatial patterns, the student can extend patterning activity to create a tiling with a new unit shape—a unit of unit shapes that he or she recognizes and consciously constructs. For example, the student may build *T*s out of 4 squares, use 4 *T*s to build squares, and use squares to tile a rectangle.
8	Shape Decomposer — Units of Units	12	As students develop understanding of shape, they can decompose shapes flexibly by using independently generated imagery and planned decompositions of shapes that themselves are decompositions.

Learning Trajectories

Developmental Levels for Comparing Geometric Shapes

As early as 4 years of age, students can create and use strategies, such as moving shapes to compare their parts or to place one on top of the other for judging whether two figures are the same shape. From Pre-K to Grade 2, they can develop sophisticated and accurate mathematical procedures for comparing geometric shapes. Students typically follow an observable developmental progression in learning about how shapes are the same and different with recognizable stages or levels. This developmental path can be described as part of a learning trajectory.

Age Range	Level Name	Level	Description
3	"Same Thing" Comparer	1	The first sign of understanding is when the student can compare real-world objects. For example, the student may say two pictures of houses are the same or different.
4	"Similar" Comparer	2	Thist sign of development occurs when the student judges two shapes to be the same if they are more visually similar than different. For example, the student may say, "These are the same. They are pointy at the top."
4	Part Comparer	3	At this level, a student can say that two shapes are the same after matching one side on each. For example, a student may say, "These are the same" (matching the two sides).
4	Some Attributes Comparer	4	As students develop, they look for differences in attributes, but may examine only part of a shape. For example, a student at this level may say, "These are the same" (indicating the top halves of the shapes are similar by laying them on top of each other).
5	Most Attributes Comparer	5	At this level, the student looks for differences in attributes, examining full shapes, but may ignore some spatial relationships. For example, a student may say, "These are the same."
7	Congruence Determiner	6	A sign of development is when a student determines congruence by comparing all attributes and all spatial relationships. For example, a student at this level may say that two shapes are the same shape and the same size after comparing every one of their sides and angles.
7	Congruence Superposer	7	As students develop understanding, they can move and place objects on top of each other to determine congruence. For example, a student at this level may say that two shapes are the same shape and the same size after laying them on top of each other.
8	Congruence Representer	8	Continued development is evidenced as students refer to geometric properties and explain transformations. For example, a student at this level may say, "These must be congruent, because they have equal sides, all square corners, and I can move them on top of each other exactly."

Developmental Levels for Spatial Sense and Motions

Infants and toddlers spend a great deal of time learning about the properties and relations of objects in space. Very young students know and use the shape of their environment in navigation activities. With guidance they can learn to "mathematize" this knowledge. They can learn about direction, perspective, distance, symbolization, location, and coordinates. Students typically follow an observable developmental progression in developing spatial sense with recognizable stages or levels. This developmental path can be described as part of a learning trajectory.

Age Range	Level Name	Level	Description
4	Simple Turner	1	An early sign of spatial sense is when a student mentally turns an object to perform easy tasks. For example, given a shape with the top marked with color, the student may correctly identify which of three shapes it would look like if it were turned "like this" (90 degree turn demonstrated), before physically moving the shape.
5	Beginning Slider, Flipper, Turner	2	This sign of development occurs when a student can use the correct motions, but is not always accurate in direction and amount. For example, a student at this level may know a shape has to be flipped to match another shape, but flips it in the wrong direction.
6	Slider, Flipper, Turner	3	As students develop spatial sense, they can perform slides and flips, often only horizontal and vertical, by using manipulatives. For example, a student at this level may perform turns of 45, 90, and 180 degrees and know a shape must be turned 90 degrees to the right to fit into a puzzle.
7	Diagonal Mover	4	A sign of development is when a student can perform diagonal slides and flips. For example, a student at this level may know a shape must be turned or flipped over an oblique line (45 degree orientation) to fit into a puzzle.
8	Mental Mover	5	Further signs of development occur when a student can predict results of moving shapes using mental images. A student at this level may say, "If you turned this 120 degrees, it would be just like this one."

Developmental Levels for Patterning and Early Algebra

Algebra begins with a search for patterns. Identifying patterns helps bring order, cohesion, and predictability to seemingly unorganized situations and allows one to make generalizations beyond the information directly available. The recognition and analysis of patterns are important components of the young student's intellectual development because they provide a foundation for the development of algebraic thinking. Although prekindergarten students engage in pattern-related activities and recognize patterns in their everyday environment, research has revealed that an abstract understanding of patterns develops gradually during the early childhood years. Students typically follow an observable developmental progression in learning about patterns with recognizable stages or levels. This developmental path can be described as part of a learning trajectory.

Age Range	Level Name	Level	Description
2	Prepatterner	1	A student at the earliest level does not recognize patterns. For example, a student may name a striped shirt with no repeating unit a "pattern."
3	Pattern Recognizer	2	At this level, the student can recognize a simple pattern. For example, a student at this level may say, "I'm wearing a pattern" about a shirt with black and white stripes.
4	Pattern Duplicator AB	3	A sign of development is when the student can duplicate an ABABAB pattern, although the student may have to work alongside the model pattern. For example, given objects in a row, ABABAB, the student may make his or her own ABABAB row in a different location.
4	Pattern Duplicator	4	At this level, the student is able to duplicate simple patterns (not just alongside the model pattern). For example, given objects in a row, ABBABBABB, the student may make his or her own ABBABBABB row in a different location.
5	Pattern Extender	5	A sign of development is when the student can extend simple patterns. For example, given objects in a row, ABBABBABB, he or she may add ABBABB to the end of the row.
6	Pattern Maker from n	6	As a student develops patterning, he or she is able to fill in a missing element of a pattern. For example, given objects in a row with one missing, ABBAB_ABB, he or she may identify and fill in the missing element.
7	Pattern Unit Recognizer	7	At this level, a student can identify the smallest unit of a pattern. For example, given objects in a row with one missing, ABBAB_ABB, he or she may identify and fill in the missing element.

Developmental Levels for Classifying and Analyzing Data

Data analysis contains one big idea: classifying, organizing, representing, and using information to ask and answer questions. The developmental continuum for data analysis includes growth in classifying and counting to sort objects and quantify their groups. Children typically follow an observable developmental progression, with recognizable stages or levels, in learning about patterns.

Age Range	Level Name	Level	Description
2	Similarity Recognizer	1	The first sign that a child can classify is when he or she recognizes, intuitively, two or more objects as "similar" in some way. For example, "that's another doggie."
2	Informal Sorter	2	A sign of development is when a child places objects that are alike in some attribute together, but switches criteria and may use functional relationships as the basis for sorting. A child at this level might stack blocks of the same shape or put a cup with its saucer.
3	Attribute Identifier	3	The next level is when the child names attributes of objects and places objects together with a given attribute, but cannot then move to sorting by a new rule.
4	Attribute Sorter	4	At the next level the child sorts objects according to given attributes, forming categories, but may switch attributes during the sorting. A child at this stage can switch rules for sorting if guided.
5	Consistent Sorter	5	A sign of development is when the child can sort consistently by a given attribute. For example, the child might put several identical blocks together.
6	Exhaustive Sorter	6	At the next level, the child can sort consistently and exhaustively by an attribute, given or created. This child can use the terms "some" and "all" meaningfully.
6	Multiple Attribute Sorter	7	A sign of development is when the child can sort consistently and exhaustively by more than one attribute, sequentially. For example, a child at this level can put all the attribute blocks together by color, then by shape.
7	Classifier and Counter	8	At the next level, the child is capable of simultaneously classifying and counting. For example, the child counts the number of colors in a group of objects.
7	List Grapher	9	In the early stage of graphing, the child graphs by simply listing all cases. For example, the child may list each child in the class and each child's response to a question.
8	Multiple Attribute Classifier	10	A sign of development is when the child can intentionally sort according to multiple attributes, naming and relating the attributes. This child understands that objects could belong to more than one group.
8+	Classifying Grapher	11	At the next level the child can graph by classifying data (e.g., responses) and represent it according to categories. For example, the child can take a survey, classify the responses, and graph the result.
8+	Classifier	12	A sign of development is when the child creates complete, conscious classifications logically connected to a specific property.
8+	Hierarchical Classifier	13	At the next level, the child can perform hierarchical classifications. For example, the child recognizes that all squares are rectangles, but not all rectangles are squares.
8+	Data Representer	14	At this level the child creates graphs and tables, compares parts of the data, makes statements about the data as a whole, and determines whether the graphs answer the questions posed initially.

Glossary

A

absolute value The distance of a number from 0. For example, the absolute value of 7, written as |7|, is 7. The absolute value of −4, written as |−4|, is 4.

acute angle An angle with a measure greater than 0 degrees and less than 90 degrees.

addend One of the numbers being added in an addition sentence. In the sentence 41 + 27 = 68, the numbers 41 and 27 are addends.

addition A mathematical operation used for "putting things together." Numbers being added are called *addends*. The result of addition is called a *sum*. In the number sentence 15 + 63 = 78, the numbers 15 and 63 are addends.

additive inverses Two numbers whose sum is 0. For example, 9 + −9 = 0. The additive inverse of 9 is −9, and the additive inverse of −9 is 9.

adjacent angles Two angles with a common side that do not otherwise overlap. In the diagram, angles 1 and 2 are adjacent angles. So are angles 2 and 3, angles 3 and 4, and angles 4 and 1.

algorithm A step-by-step procedure for carrying out a computation or solving a problem.

angle Two rays with a common endpoint. The common endpoint is called the vertex of the angle.

area A measure of the surface inside a closed boundary. The formula for the area of a rectangle or parallelogram is $A = b \times h$, where A represents the area, b represents the length of the base, and h the height of the figure.

array A rectangular arrangement of objects in rows and columns in which each row has the same number of elements and each column has the same number of elements.

attribute A feature such as size, shape, or color.

average See **mean**. The **median** and **mode** are also sometimes called the average.

axis (plural **axes**) A number line used in a coordinate grid.

B

bar graph A graph in which the lengths of horizontal or vertical bars represent the magnitude of the data represented.

base See **exponential notation.**

base (of a parallelogram) One of the sides of a parallelogram; also, the length of this side. The length of a perpendicular line segment between the base and the side opposite the base is the height of the parallelogram.

base (of a polyhedron) The "bottom" face of a polyhedron; the face whose shape determines the type of prism or pyramid.

base (of a rectangle) One of the sides of a rectangle; also, the length of this side. The length of the side perpendicular to the base is the height of the rectangle.

base (of a triangle) One of the sides of a triangle; also, the length of this side. The shortest distance between the base and the vertex opposite the base is the height of the triangle.

base ten The commonly used numeration system, in which the ten digits 0, 1, 2,…, 9 have values that depend on the place in which they appear in a numeral (ones, tens, hundreds, and so on, to the left of the decimal point; tenths, hundredths, and so on, to the right of the decimal point).

benchmark A number or measure used as a standard of comparison for other numbers or measures.

bisect To divide a segment, angle, or figure into two parts of equal measure.

C

capacity A measure of how much liquid or substance a container can hold. See also **volume.**

centi- A prefix for units in the metric system meaning one hundredth.

centimeter (cm) In the metric system, a unit of length defined as $\frac{1}{100}$ of a meter; equal to 10 millimeters or $\frac{1}{10}$ of a decimeter.

circle The set of all points in a plane that are a given distance (the radius) from a given point (the center of the circle).

circle graph A graph in which a circular region is divided into sectors to represent the categories in a set of data. The circle represents the whole set of data.

circumference The distance around a circle or sphere.

clipped range In a set of numbers, the range calculated without the greatest and least value, or with the two or three greatest and least values removed.

closed figure A figure that divides the plane into two regions, inside and outside the figure. A closed space figure divides space into two regions in the same way.

common denominator Any nonzero number that is a multiple of the denominators of two or more fractions.

common factor Any number that is a factor of two or more numbers.

complementary angles Two angles whose measures total 90 degrees.

composite function A function with two or more operations. For example, this function multiplies the input number by 5 then adds 3.

composite number A whole number that has more than two whole number factors. For example, 14 is a composite number because it has more than two whole number factors.

concave (nonconvex) **polygon** A polygon in which a line segment between two of the points on the boundary lies outside the polygon.

cone A space figure having a circular base, curved surface, and one vertex.

congruent Having identical sizes and shapes. Congruent figures are said to be congruent to each other.

convex polygon A polygon in which line segments between any two points on the boundary lie inside or on the polygon.

coordinate One or more numbers used to fix the position of a point (on a line, in a plane, in space, and so on).

coordinate grid A device for locating points in a plane by means of ordered pairs or coordinates. A coordinate grid is formed by two number lines that intersect at their 0-points.

corresponding angles Two angles in the same relative position in two figures, or in similar locations in relation to a transversal intersecting two lines. In the diagram below, angles 1 and 5, 3 and 7, 2 and 6, and 4 and 8 are corresponding angles. If the lines are parallel, then the corresponding angles are congruent.

corresponding sides Two sides in the same relative position in two figures. In the diagram, AB and A'B', BC and B'C', and AC and A'C' are corresponding sides.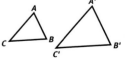

cube A space figure whose six faces are congruent squares that meet at right angles.

cubic centimeter (cm³) A metric unit of volume; the volume of a cube 1 centimeter on an edge. 1 cubic centimeter is equal to 1 milliliter.

cubic unit A unit used in a volume and capacity measurement.

customary system of measurement The measuring system used most often in the United States. Units for linear measure (length, distance) include inch, foot, yard, and mile; units for weight include ounce and pound; units for capacity (amount of liquid or other substance a container can hold) include fluid ounce, cup, pint, quart, and gallon.

cylinder A space figure having a curved surface and parallel circular or elliptical bases that are congruent.

D

decimal A number written in standard notation, usually one containing a decimal point, as in 3.78.

decimal approximation A decimal that is close to the value of a rational number. By extending the decimal approximation to additional digits, it is possible to come as close as desired to the value of the rational number. For example, decimal approximations of $\frac{1}{12}$ are 0.083, 0.0833, 0.08333, and so on.

decimal equivalent A decimal that names the same number as a fraction. For example, the decimal equivalent of $\frac{3}{4}$ is 0.75. The only rational numbers with decimal equivalents are those that can be written as fractions whose denominators have prime factors only of 2 and 5. For example, $\frac{1}{2}$, $\frac{1}{4}$, and $\frac{1}{20}$ have decimal equivalents, but $\frac{1}{6}$, $\frac{1}{7}$, and $\frac{1}{9}$ have only decimal approximations.

degree (°) A unit of measure for angles; based on dividing a circle into 360 equal parts. Also, a unit of measure for temperature.

degree Celsius (°C) In the metric system, the unit for measuring temperature. Water freezes at 0°C and boils at 100°C.

degree Fahrenheit (°F) In the U.S. customary system, the unit for measuring temperature. Water freezes at 32°F and boils at 212°F.

deltahedron A polyhedron whose faces are congruent equilateral triangles.

denominator The number of equal parts into which a whole is divided. In the fraction $\frac{a}{b}$, b is the denominator. See also **numerator.**

diameter A line segment, going through the center of a circle, that starts at one point on the circle and ends at the opposite point on the circle; also, the length of such a line segment. The diameter of a circle is twice its radius. AB is a diameter of this circle.

See also **circle.**

difference The result of subtraction. In the subtraction sentence 40 − 10 = 30, the difference is 30.

digit In the base-ten numeration system, one of the symbols 0, 1, 2, 3, 4, 5, 6, 7, 8, 9. Digits can be used to write a numeral for any whole number in the base-ten numbering system. For example, the numeral 145 is made up of the digits 1, 4, and 5.

distributive law A law that relates two operations on numbers, usually multiplication and addition, or multiplication and subtraction. Distributive law of multiplication over addition: $a \times (b + c) = (a \times b) + (a \times c)$

dividend See **division.**

divisibility rule A rule that indicates whether a whole number is divisible by another whole number. For example, to tell whether a number is divisible by 3, check whether the sum of its digits is divisible by 3. The number 48 is divisible by 3 since 4 + 8 = 12, and 12 is divisible by 3.

divisible by One whole number is divisible by another whole number if the result of the division is a whole number (with a remainder of 0). For example, 35 is divisible by 5, because 35 divided by 5 is 7 with a remainder of 0. If a number n is divisible by a number x, then x is a factor of n. See also **factor of a whole number n.**

division A mathematical operation used for "equal sharing" or "separating into equal parts." Division is the inverse operation of multiplication. The *dividend* is the total before sharing. The *divisor* is the number of equal parts or the number in each equal part. The *quotient* is the result of division. For example, in 35 ÷ 5 = 7, 35 is the dividend, 5 is the divisor, and 7 is the quotient. If 35 objects are separated into 5 equal parts, there are 7 objects in each part. If 35 objects are separated into parts with 5 in each part, there are 7 equal parts. The number left over when a set of objects is shared equally or separated into equal groups is called the *remainder*. For 35 ÷ 5, the quotient is 7 and the remainder is 0. For 36 ÷ 5, the quotient is 7 and the remainder is 1.

divisor See **division.**

dodecahedron A space figure with twelve faces. In a regular dodecahedron, each face is formed by a pentagon.

E

edge The line segment where two faces of a polyhedron meet.

endpoint The point at either end of a line segment; also, the point at the end of a ray. Line segments are named after their endpoints; a line segment between and including points A and B is usually called segment AB or segment BA.

equation A mathematical sentence that states the equality of two expressions. For example, 3 + 7 = 10, y = x + 7, and 4 + 7 = 8 + 3 are equations.

equilateral polygon A polygon in which all sides are the same length.

equivalent Equal in value, but in a different form. For example, $\frac{1}{2}$, $\frac{2}{4}$, 0.5, and 50% are equivalent forms of the same number.

equivalent fractions Fractions that have different numerators and denominators but name the same number. For example, $\frac{2}{3}$ and $\frac{6}{9}$ are equivalent fractions.

estimate A judgment of a time, measurement, number, or other quantity that may not be exactly right.

evaluate an algebraic expression To replace each variable in an algebraic expression with a particular number and then calculate the value of the expression.

evaluate a numerical expression To carry out the operations in a numerical expression to find the value of the expression.

even number A whole number such as 0, 2, 4, 6, and so on, that can be divided by 2 with no remainder. See also **odd number.**

event A happening or occurrence. The tossing of a coin is an event.

exponent See **exponential notation.**

exponential notation A shorthand way of representing repeated multiplication of the same factor. For example, 4^3 is exponential notation for $4 \times 4 \times 4$. The small raised 3, called the *exponent*, indicates how many times the number 4, called the *base*, is used as a factor.

expression A group of mathematical symbols (numbers, operation signs, variables, grouping symbols) that represents a number (or can represent a number if values are assigned to any variables it contains).

F

face A flat surface on a space figure.

fact family A group of addition or multiplication facts grouped together with the related subtraction or division facts. For example, 4 + 8 = 12, 8 + 4 = 12, 12 − 4 = 8, and 12 − 8 = 4 form an addition fact family. The facts $4 \times 3 = 12$, $3 \times 4 = 12$, 12 ÷ 3 = 4, and 12 ÷ 4 = 3 form a multiplication fact family.

Glossary

factor (noun) One of the numbers that is multiplied in a multiplication expression. For example, in $4 \times 1.5 = 6$, the factors are 4 and 1.5. See also **multiplication.**

factor (verb) To represent a quantity as a product of factors. For example, 20 factors to 4×5, 2×10, or $2 \times 2 \times 5$.

factor of a whole number n A whole number, which, when multiplied by another whole number, results in the number n. The whole number n is divisible by its factors. For example, 3 and 5 are factors of 15 because $3 \times 5 = 15$, and 15 is divisible by 3 and 5.

factor tree A method used to obtain the prime factorization of a number. The original number is represented as a product of factors, and each of those factors is represented as a product of factors, and so on, until the factor string consists of prime numbers.

fair A coin, spinner, number cube, and so on is said to be fair if, over a large number of tosses, the results are consistent with the predictions of probability. On a fair coin, heads and tails should come up about equally often; the six sides of a fair number cube should come up about equally often.

fair game A game in which each player has the same chance of winning. If any player has an advantage or disadvantage (for example, by playing first), then the game is not fair.

finger sets An organized way taught in *Real Math* of showing numbers using fingers.

formula A general rule for finding the value of something. A formula is usually written as an equation with variables representing unknown quantities. For example, a formula for distance traveled at a constant rate of speed is $d = r \times t$, where d stands for distance, r for rate, and t for time.

fraction A number in the form $\frac{a}{b}$, where a and b are integers and b is greater than 0. Fractions are used to name part of a whole object or part of a whole collection of objects, or to compare two quantities. A fraction can represent division; for example, $\frac{2}{5}$ can be thought of as 2 divided by 5.

frequency The number of times an event or value occurs in a set of data.

function machine An imaginary machine that processes numbers according to a certain rule. A number (input) is put into the machine and is transformed into a second number (output) by application of the rule.

G

greatest common factor The largest factor that two or more numbers have in common. For example, the common factors of 24 and 30 are 1, 2, 3, and 6. The greatest common factor of 24 and 30 is 6.

H

height (of a polygon) The length of the line segment perpendicular to the base of the polygon (or an extension of the base) from the opposite side or vertex.

height (of a polyhedron) The perpendicular distance between the bases of the polyhedron or between a base and the opposite vertex.

heptagon A polygon with seven sides.

hexagon A polygon with six sides.

histogram A bar graph in which the labels for the bars are numerical intervals.

hypotenuse In a right triangle, the side opposite the right angle.

I

icosahedron A space figure with twenty triangular faces.

improper fraction A fraction that names a number greater than or equal to 1; a fraction whose numerator is equal to or greater than its denominator. Examples of improper fractions are $\frac{4}{3}$, $\frac{10}{8}$, and $\frac{4}{4}$.

inch (in.) In the U. S. customary system, a unit of length equal to $\frac{1}{12}$ of a foot.

independent events Events A and B for which knowing that event A has occurred does not influence the probability that event B will occur.

indirect measurement Methods for determining heights, distances, and other quantities that cannot be measured or are not measured directly.

inequality A number sentence stating that two quantities are not equal. Relation symbols for inequalities include < (is less than), > (is greater than), and ≠ (is not equal to).

integers The set of integers is $\{..., -4, -3, -2, -1, 0, 1, 2, 3, 4, ...\}$. The set of integers consists of whole numbers and their opposites.

intersect To meet (at a point, a line, and so on), sharing a common point or points.

interior The set of all points in a plane "inside" a closed plane figure, such as a polygon or circle. Also, the set of all points in space "inside" a closed space figure, such as a polyhedron or sphere.

K

kilo- A prefix for units in the metric system meaning one thousand.

L

least common denominator The least common multiple of the denominators of every fraction in a given set of fractions. For example, 12 is the least common denominator of $\frac{2}{3}$, $\frac{1}{4}$, and $\frac{5}{6}$. See also **least common multiple.**

least common multiple The smallest number that is a multiple of two or more numbers. For example, some common multiples of 6 and 8 are 24, 48, and 72. 24 is the least common multiple of 6 and 8.

leg of a right triangle A side of a right triangle that is not the hypotenuse.

line A straight path that extends infinitely in opposite directions.

line graph (broken-line graph) A graph in which points are connected by line segments to represent data.

line of symmetry A line that separates a figure into halves. The figure can be folded along this line into two parts which exactly fit on top of each other.

line segment A straight path joining two points, called *endpoints* of the line segment. A straight path can be described as the shortest distance between two points.

line symmetry A figure has line symmetry (also called *bilateral symmetry*) if a line of symmetry can be drawn through the figure.

liter (L) A metric unit of capacity, equal to the volume of a cube 10 centimeters on an edge. $1 \text{ L} = 1,000 \text{ mL} = 1,000 \text{ cm}^3$. A liter is slightly larger than a quart. See also **milliliter (mL).**

M

map scale A ratio that compares the distance between two locations shown on a map with the actual distance between them.

mean A typical or central value that may be used to describe a set of numbers. It can be found by adding the numbers in the set and dividing the sum by the number of numbers. The mean is often referred to as the *average*.

median The middle value in a set of data when the data are listed in order from least to greatest (or greatest to least). If the number of values in the set is even (so that there is no "middle" value), the median is the mean of the two middle values.

isosceles Having two sides of the same length; commonly used to refer to triangles and trapezoids.

meter (m) The basic unit of length in the metric system, equal to 10 decimeters, 100 centimeters, and 1,000 millimeters.

metric system of measurement A measurement system based on the base-ten numeration system and used in most countries in the world. Units for linear measure (length, distance) include millimeter, centimeter, meter, kilometer; units for mass (weight) include gram and kilogram; units for capacity (amount of liquid or other substance a container can hold) include milliliter and liter.

midpoint A point halfway between two points.

milli- A prefix for units in the metric system meaning one thousandth.

milliliter (mL) A metric unit of capacity, equal to 1/1,000 of a liter and 1 cubic centimeter.

millimeter (mm) In the metric system, a unit of length equal to 1/10 of a centimeter and 1/1,000 of a meter.

minuend See **subtraction.**

mixed number A number greater than 1, written as a whole number and a fraction less than 1. For example, $5\frac{1}{2}$ is equal to $5 + \frac{1}{2}$.

mode The value or values that occur most often in a set of data.

multiple of a number _n_ The product of a whole number and the number _n_. For example, the numbers 0, 4, 8, 12, and 16 are all multiples of 4 because $4 \times 0 = 0$, $4 \times 1 = 4$, $4 \times 2 = 8$, $4 \times 3 = 12$, and $4 \times 4 = 16$.

multiplication A mathematical operation used to find the total number of things in several equal groups, or to find a quantity that is a certain number of times as much or as many as another number. Numbers being multiplied are called _factors_. The result of multiplication is called the _product_. In $8 \times 12 = 96$, 8 and 12 are the factors and 96 is the product.

multiplicative inverses Two numbers whose product is 1. For example, the multiplicative inverse of $\frac{2}{5}$ is $\frac{5}{2}$, and the multiplicative inverse of 8 is $\frac{1}{8}$. Multiplicative inverses are also called _reciprocals_ of each other.

N

negative number A number less than 0; a number to the left of 0 on a horizontal number line.

number line A line on which equidistant points correspond to integers in order.

number sentence A sentence that is made up of numerals and a relation symbol ($<$, $>$, or $=$). Most number sentences also contain at least one operation symbol. Number sentences may also have grouping symbols, such as parentheses.

numeral The written name of a number.

numerator In a whole divided into a number of equal parts, the number of equal parts being considered. In the fraction $\frac{a}{b}$, a is the numerator.

O

obtuse angle An angle with a measure greater than 90 degrees and less than 180 degrees.

octagon An eight-sided polygon.

octahedron A space figure with eight faces.

odd number A whole number that is not divisible by 2, such as 1, 3, 5, and so on. When an odd number is divided by 2, the remainder is 1. A whole number is either an odd number or an even number.

opposite of a number A number that is the same distance from 0 on the number line as the given number, but on the opposite side of 0. If a is a negative number, the opposite of a will be a positive number. For example, if $a = -5$, then $-a$ is 5. See also **additive inverses.**

ordered pair Two numbers or objects for which order is important. Often, two numbers in a specific order used to locate a point on a coordinate grid. They are usually written inside parentheses; for example, (2, 3). See also **coordinate.**

ordinal number A number used to express position or order in a series, such as first, third, tenth. People generally use ordinal numbers to name dates; for example, "May fifth" rather than "May five."

origin The point where the x- and y-axes intersect on a coordinate grid. The coordinates of the origin are (0, 0).

outcome The result of an event. Heads and tails are the two outcomes of the event of tossing a coin.

P

parallel lines (segments, rays) Lines (segments, rays) going in the same direction that are the same distance apart and never meet.

parallelogram A quadrilateral that has two pairs of parallel sides. Pairs of opposite sides and opposite angles of a parallelogram are congruent.

parentheses A pair of symbols, (and), used to show in which order operations should be done. For example, the expression $(3 \times 5) + 7$ says to multiply 5 by 3 then add 7. The expression $3 \times (5 + 7)$ says to add 5 and 7 and then multiply by 3.

pattern A model, plan, or rule that uses words or variables to describe a set of shapes or numbers that repeat in a predictable way.

pentagon A polygon with five sides.

percent A rational number that can be written as a fraction with a denominator of 100. The symbol % is used to represent percent. 1% means 1/100 or 0.01. For example, "53% of the students in the school are girls" means that out of every 100 students in the school, 53 are girls.

perimeter The distance along a path around a plane figure. A formula for the perimeter of a rectangle is $P = 2 \times (B + H)$, where B represents the base and H is the height of the rectangle. Perimeter may also refer to the path itself.

perpendicular Two rays, lines, line segments, or other figures that form right angles are said to be perpendicular to each other.

pi The ratio of the circumference of a circle to its diameter. Pi is the same for every circle, approximately 3.14 or $\frac{22}{7}$. Also written as the Greek letter π.

pictograph A graph constructed with pictures or icons, in which each picture stands for a certain number. Pictographs make it easier to visually compare quantities.

place value A way of determining the value of a digit in a numeral, written in standard notation, according to its position, or place, in the numeral. In base-ten numbers, each place has a value ten times that of the place to its right and one-tenth the value of the place to its left.

plane A flat surface that extends forever.

plane figure A figure that can be contained in a plane (that is, having length and width but no height).

point A basic concept of geometry; usually thought of as a location in space, without size.

polygon A closed plane figure consisting of line segments (sides) connected endpoint to endpoint. The interior of a polygon consists of all the points of the plane "inside" the polygon. An n-gon is a polygon with n sides; for example, an 8-gon has 8 sides.

polyhedron A closed space figure, all of whose surfaces (faces) are flat. Each face consists of a polygon and the interior of the polygon.

power A product of factors that are all the same. For example, $6 \times 6 \times 6$ (or 216) is called 6 to the third power, or the third power of 6, because 6 is a factor three times. The expression $6 \times 6 \times 6$ can also be written as 6^3.

power of 10 A whole number that can be written as a product using only 10 as a factor. For example, 100 is equal to 10×10 or 10^2, so 100 is called 10 squared, the second power of 10, or 10 to the second power. Other powers of 10 include 10^1, or 10, and 10^3, or 1,000.

precision (of a count or measurement) An indicator of how close a count or measure is believed to be to the actual count or measure. The precision of a measurement may be improved by using measuring instruments with smaller units.

prime factorization A whole number expressed as a product of prime factors. For example, the prime factorization of 18 is $2 \times 3 \times 3$. A number has only one prime factorization (except for the order in which the factors are written).

prime number A whole number greater than 1 that has exactly two whole number factors, 1 and itself. For example, 13 is a prime number because its only factors are 1 and 13. A prime number is divisible only by 1 and itself. The first five prime numbers are 2, 3, 5, 7, and 11. See also **composite number.**

prism A polyhedron with two parallel faces (bases) that are the same size and shape. Prisms are classified according to the shape of the two parallel bases. The bases of a prism are connected by parallelograms that are often rectangular.

probability A number between 0 and 1 that indicates the likelihood that something (an event) will happen. The closer a probability is to 1, the more likely it is that an event will happen.

product See **multiplication.**

protractor A tool for measuring or drawing angles. When measuring an angle, the vertex of the angle should be at the center of the protractor and one side should be aligned with the 0 mark.

pyramid A polyhedron in which one face (the base) is a polygon and the other faces are formed by triangles with a common vertex (the apex). A pyramid is classified according to the shape of its base, as a triangular pyramid, square pyramid, pentagonal pyramid, and so on.

Pythagorean Theorem A mathematical theorem, proven by the Greek mathematician Pythagoras and known to many others before and since, that states that if the legs of a right triangle have lengths a and b, and the hypotenuse has length c, then $a^2 + b^2 = c^2$.

Q

quadrilateral A polygon with four sides.

quotient See **division.**

R

radius A line segment that goes from the center of a circle to any point on the circle; also, the length of such a line segment.

random sample A sample taken from a population in a way that gives all members of the population the same chance of being selected.

range The difference between the maximum and minimum values in a set of data.

rate A ratio comparing two quantities with unlike units. For example, a measure such as 23 miles per gallon of gas compares mileage with gas usage.

ratio A comparison of two quantities using division. Ratios can be expressed with fractions, decimals, percents, or words. For example, if a team wins 4 games out of 5 games played, the ratio of wins to total games is $\frac{4}{5}$, 0.8, or 80%.

rational number Any number that can be represented in the form $a \div b$ or $\frac{a}{b}$, where a and b are integers and b is positive. Some, but not all, rational numbers have exact decimal equivalents.

ray A straight path that extends infinitely in one direction from a point, which is called its *endpoint.*

reciprocal See **multiplicative inverses.**

rectangle A parallelogram with four right angles.

reduced form A fraction in which the numerator and denominator have no common factors except 1.

reflection A transformation in which a figure "flips" so that its image is the reverse of the original.

regular polygon A convex polygon in which all the sides are the same length and all the angles have the same measure.

regular polyhedron (plural **polyhedra**) A polyhedron with faces that are all congruent regular polygons with their interiors. The same number of faces meet at each vertex. There are five regular polyhedra:

tetrahedron four faces, each formed by an equilateral triangle

cube six faces, each formed by a square

octahedron eight faces, each formed by an equilateral triangle

dodecahedron twelve faces, each formed by a regular pentagon

icosahedron twenty faces, each formed by an equilateral triangle

relation symbol A symbol used to express the relationship between two numbers or expressions. Among the symbols used in number sentences are $=$ for "is equal to," $<$ for "is less than," $>$ for "is greater than," and $\neq$ for "is not equal to."

remainder See **division.**

rhombus A parallelogram whose sides are all the same length.

right angle An angle with a measure of 90 degrees, representing a quarter of a full turn.

right triangle A triangle that has a right angle.

rotation A transformation in which a figure "turns" around a center point or axis.

rotational symmetry Property of a figure that can be rotated around a point (less than a full, 360-degree turn) in such a way that the resulting figure exactly matches the original figure. If a figure has rotational symmetry, its order of rotational symmetry is the number of different ways it can be rotated to match itself exactly. "No rotation" is counted as one of the ways.

rounding Changing a number to another number that is easier to work with and is close enough for the purpose. For example, 12,924 rounded to the nearest thousand is 13,000 and rounded to the nearest hundred is 12,900.

S

sample A subset of a group used to represent the whole group.

scale The ratio of the distance on a map or drawing to the actual distance.

scalene triangle A triangle in which all three sides have different lengths.

scale drawing An accurate picture of an object in which all parts are drawn to the same scale. If an actual object measures 32 by 48 meters, a scale drawing of it might measure 32 by 48 millimeters.

scale model A model that represents an object or display in proportions based on a determined scale.

scientific notation A method of expressing a number as the product of two factors, one of which is a number greater than or equal to 1 but less than 10, and the other of which is a power of 10. The notation is used to describe very great (or very small) numbers. For example, 4,000,000 in scientific notation is 4×10^6.

similar figures Figures that are exactly the same shape but not necessarily the same size.

space figure A figure which cannot be contained in a plane. Common space figures include the rectangular prism, square pyramid, cylinder, cone, and sphere.

sphere The set of all points in space that are a given distance (the radius) from a given point (the center). A ball is shaped like a sphere.

square number A number that is the product of a whole number and itself. The number 36 is a square number, because $36 = 6 \times 6$.

square of a number The product of a number multiplied by itself. For example, 2.5 squared is $(2.5)^2$.

square root The square root of a number n is a number which, when multiplied by itself, results in the number n. For example, 8 is a square root of 64, because $8 \times 8 = 64$.

square unit A unit used to measure area—usually a square that is 1 inch, 1 centimeter, 1 yard, or other standard unit of length on each side.

standard notation The most familiar way of representing whole numbers, integers, and decimals by writing digits in specified places; the way numbers are usually written in everyday situations.

statistics The science of collecting, classifying, and interpreting numerical data as it is related to a particular subject.

stem-and-leaf plot A display of data in which digits with larger place values are named as stems, and digits with smaller place values are named as leaves.

straight angle An angle of 180 degrees; a line with one point identified as the vertex of the angle.

subtraction A mathematical operation used for "taking away" or comparing ("How much more?"). Subtraction is the inverse operation of addition. The number being subtracted is called the *subtrahend*; the number it is subtracted from is called the *minuend*; the result of subtraction is called the *difference*. In the number sentence $63 - 45 = 18$, 63 is the minuend, 45 is the subtrahend, and 18 is the difference.

subtrahend See **subtraction.**

supplementary angles Two angles whose measures total 180 degrees.

surface area The sum of the areas of the faces or surfaces of a space figure.

symmetrical Having the same size and shape across a dividing line or around a point.

T

tessellation An arrangement of closed shapes that covers a surface completely without overlaps or gaps.

tetrahedron A space figure with four faces, each formed by an equilateral triangle.

theorem A mathematical statement that can be proved to be true (or, sometimes, a statement that is proposed and needs to be proved). For example, the Pythagorean Theorem states that if the legs of a right triangle have lengths a and b, and the hypotenuse has length c, then $a^2 + b^2 = c^2$.

transformation An operation that moves or changes a geometric figure in a specified way. Rotations, reflections, and translations are types of transformations.

translation A transformation in which a figure "slides" along a line.

transversal A line which intersects two or more other lines.

trapezoid A quadrilateral with exactly one pair of parallel sides.

tree diagram A tool used to solve probability problems in which there is a series of events. This tree diagram represents a situation where the first event has three possible outcomes and the second event has two possible outcomes.

triangle A polygon with three sides. An *equilateral* triangle has three sides of the same length. An *isosceles* triangle has two sides of the same length. A *scalene* triangle has no sides of the same length.

U

unit (of measure) An agreed-upon standard with which measurements are compared.

unit fraction A fraction whose numerator is 1. For example, $\frac{1}{2}$, $\frac{1}{3}$, and $\frac{1}{10}$ are unit fractions.

unit cost The cost of one item or one specified amount of an item. If 20 pencils cost 60¢, then the unit cost is 3¢ per pencil.

unlike denominators Unequal denominators, as in $\frac{3}{4}$ and $\frac{5}{6}$.

V

variable A letter or other symbol that represents a number, one specific number, or many different values.

Venn diagram A picture that uses circles to show relationships between sets. Elements that belong to more than one set are placed in the overlap between the circles.

vertex The point at which the rays of an angle, two sides of a polygon, or the edges of a polyhedron meet.

vertical angles Two intersecting lines form four adjacent angles. In the diagram, angles 2 and 4 are vertical angles. They have no sides in common. Their measures are equal. Similarly, angles 1 and 3 are vertical angles.

volume A measure of the amount of space occupied by a space figure.

W

whole number Any of the numbers 0, 1, 2, 3, 4, and so on. Whole numbers are the numbers used for counting and zero.

Addition (Whole Numbers)

	PreK	K	1	2	3	4	5	6
Meaning of addition	•	•	•	•				
Basic facts			•	•	•	•	•	•
Missing addend problems			•	•	•	•	•	•
Three or more addends			•	•	•	•	•	•
Two-digit numbers			•	•	•	•	•	•
Three-digit numbers				•	•	•	•	•
Greater numbers					•	•	•	•
Adding money			•	•	•	•	•	•
Estimating sums			•	•	•	•	•	•

Algebra

	PreK	K	1	2	3	4	5	6
Properties of whole numbers				•		•	•	•
Integers (negative numbers)					•	•	•	•
Operations with integers						•	•	•
Missing-term problems	•			•	•	•	•	•
Making and solving number sentences and equations				•	•	•	•	•
Variables					•	•	•	•
Parentheses and order of operations						•	•	•
Inverse operations			•	•	•	•	•	•
Function machines/tables		•	•	•	•	•	•	•
Function rules		•	•	•	•	•	•	•
Inverse functions			•	•	•	•	•	•
Composite functions				•	•	•	•	•
Coordinate graphing								
One quadrant					•	•	•	•
Four quadrants						•	•	•
Graphing linear functions					•	•	•	•
Graphing nonlinear functions								•
Using formulas						•	•	•
Square numbers					•	•	•	•
Square roots						•	•	•

Decimals and Money

	PreK	K	1	2	3	4	5	6
Place value				•	•	•	•	•
Comparing and ordering				•	•	•	•	•
Rounding						•	•	•
Relating decimals and fractions				•	•	•	•	•
Relating decimals and percents						•	•	•
Adding				•	•	•	•	•
Estimating sums				•	•	•	•	
Subtracting				•	•	•	•	•
Estimating differences				•	•	•	•	•
Multiplying by powers of 10						•	•	•
Multiplying by a whole number						•	•	•
Multiplying by a decimal							•	•
Estimating products						•	•	•
Dividing by powers of 10						•	•	•
Dividing by a whole number					•	•	•	•
Dividing by a decimal								•
Estimating quotients								•

	PreK	K	1	2	3	4	5	6
Identifying and counting currency		•	•	•	•	•		
Exchanging money		•	•	•	•			
Making change			•	•	•			
Computing with money		•	•	•	•	•	•	•

Division (Whole Numbers)

	PreK	K	1	2	3	4	5	6
Meaning of division	•	•	•	•	•	•		
Basic facts				•	•	•	•	•
Remainders					•	•	•	•
Missing-term problems				•	•	•	•	•
One-digit divisors					•	•	•	•
Two-digit divisors						•	•	•
Greater divisors							•	•
Dividing by multiples of 10							•	•
Dividing money					•	•	•	•
Estimating quotients					•	•	•	•

Fractions

	PreK	K	1	2	3	4	5	6
Fractions of a whole		•	•	•	•	•	•	•
Fractions of a set			•	•	•	•	•	•
Fractions of a number			•	•	•	•	•	•
Comparing/ordering			•	•	•	•	•	•
Equivalent fractions			•	•	•	•	•	•
Reduced form						•	•	•
Mixed numbers and improper fractions					•	•	•	•
Adding—like denominators					•	•	•	•
Adding—unlike denominators						•	•	•
Adding mixed numbers						•	•	•
Subtracting—like denominators					•	•	•	•
Subtracting—unlike denominators						•	•	•
Subtracting mixed numbers						•	•	•
Multiplying by a whole number						•	•	•
Multiplying by a fraction or mixed number						•	•	•
Reciprocals							•	•
Dividing a fraction by a whole number							•	•
Dividing by a fraction or mixed number							•	•

Geometry

	PreK	K	1	2	3	4	5	6
Identifying/drawing figures	•	•	•	•	•	•	•	•
Classifying figures	•	•	•	•	•	•	•	•
Classifying triangles				•	•	•	•	•
Classifying quadrilaterals				•	•	•	•	•
Solid figures		•	•	•	•	•	•	•
Congruence	•	•	•	•	•	•	•	•
Similarity					•	•	•	•
Line symmetry		•	•	•	•	•	•	•
Rotational symmetry						•	•	•
Translation/reflection/rotation	•			•	•	•	•	•
Measuring and classifying angles				•	•	•	•	•
Parallel and perpendicular lines				•	•	•	•	•
Relationships with parallel lines				•	•	•	•	•
Perimeter				•	•	•	•	•

	PreK	K	1	2	3	4	5	6
Radius and diameter					•	•	•	•
Circumference					•	•	•	•
Areas of triangles					•	•	•	•
Areas of quadrilaterals				•	•	•	•	•
Surface area					•	•	•	•
Volume				•	•	•	•	•
Pythagorean Theorem						•		•
Points, lines, and planes (new category)						•	•	•
Open and closed figures (new category)			•					
Spatial visualization	•					•	•	•

Manipulatives

	PreK	K	1	2	3	4	5	6
Used in concept development	•	•	•	•	•	•	•	•
Used in reteaching and individualized instruction	•	•	•	•	•	•	•	•

Measurement

	PreK	K	1	2	3	4	5	6
Converting within customary system					•	•	•	•
Converting within metric system					•	•	•	•
Length								
Estimate	•	•	•	•	•	•	•	•
Compare	•	•	•	•	•	•	•	•
Use nonstandard units	•	•	•	•	•			
Use customary units				•	•	•		•
Use metric units				•	•	•	•	•
Mass/Weight								
Estimate	•	•	•	•	•			
Compare	•	•	•	•				
Use nonstandard units		•	•	•				
Use customary units				•	•	•	•	•
Use metric units				•	•	•	•	•
Capacity								
Estimate	•	•	•	•				
Compare	•	•	•					
Use nonstandard units			•	•	•			
Use customary units				•	•	•	•	•
Use metric units				•	•	•	•	•
Temperature								
Estimate		•						•
Use degrees Fahrenheit				•	•	•	•	•
Use degrees Celsius				•	•	•	•	•
Telling time								
To the hour		•	•	•	•			
To the half hour			•	•	•			
To the quarter hour				•	•			
To the minute				•	•			
Adding and subtracting time					•	•	•	
A.M. and P.M.				•	•			
Estimating time		•	•					
Calculating elapsed time			•	•	•	•	•	
Reading a calendar		•	•	•	•		•	
Reading maps		•	•	•	•	•	•	•

Mental Arithmetic

	PreK	K	1	2	3	4	5	6
Basic fact strategies—addition and subtraction								
Use patterns			•	•				
Count on			•	•				
Count on or back	•	•	•	•		,		
Use doubles			•	•				
Use doubles plus 1			•	•				
Multiples of 10/Base-ten		•	•	•	•	•		
Use properties			•	•	•			
Use related facts			•	•				
Basic fact strategies—multiplication and division								
Use patterns				•	•	•		
Use skip counting				•	•			
Use properties					•	•		
Use related facts					•	•		
Chain calculations				•		•	•	•
Multidigit addition and subtraction				•		•	•	•
Multidigit multiplication and division					•	•	•	•
Multiples and powers of 10			•	•		•	•	•
Using computational patterns				•	•	•	•	•
Approximation					•	•	•	•
Find a fraction of a number						•	•	•
Find a percent of a number						•	•	•
Use divisibility rules							•	•
Find equivalent fractions, decimals, and percents						•	•	•

Multiplication (Whole Numbers)

	PreK	K	1	2	3	4	5	6
Meaning of multiplication			•	•	•	•	•	•
Basic facts				•	•	•	•	•
Missing-factor problems				•	•	•	•	•
One-digit multipliers					•	•	•	•
Two-digit multipliers						•	•	•
Greater multipliers						•	•	•
Multiplying by multiples of 10					•	•	•	•
Multiplying money					•	•	•	•
Estimating products						•	•	•

Number and Numeration

	PreK	K	1	2	3	4	5	6
Reading and writing numbers	•	•	•	•	•	•	•	•
Number lines	•	•	•	•	•	•	•	•
Counting	•	•	•	•	•	•		
Skip counting			•	•	•	•		
Ordinal numbers	•	•	•	•				
Place value				•	•	•	•	•
Comparing and ordering numbers	•	•	•	•	•	•	•	•
Rounding				•	•	•	•	•
Estimation/Approximation			•	•	•	•	•	•
Integers (negative numbers)								•
Even/odd numbers			•	•	•	•		
Prime and composite numbers						•	•	•
Factors and prime factorization						•	•	•

	PreK	K	1	2	3	4	5	6
Common factors						•	•	•
Common multiples						•	•	•
Checking divisibility						•	•	•
Exponents						•	•	•
Exponential notation and scientific notation							•	•
Square roots						•		•

Patterns, Relations, and Functions

	PreK	K	1	2	3	4	5	6
Classifying objects	•	•	•	•				
Number patterns	•	•	•	•	•	•	•	•
Picture patterns	•	•	•	•				
Geometric patterns	•	•	•	•		•		•
Ordered pairs					•	•	•	•
Graphing ordered pairs					•	•	•	•
Inequalities			•	•		•	•	•
Function machines/tables		•	•	•	•	•	•	•
Function rules		•	•	•	•	•	•	•
Graphing functions					•	•	•	•

Probability

	PreK	K	1	2	3	4	5	6
Determining possible outcomes		•	•	•	•	•	•	•
Predicting outcomes		•	•	•	•	•	•	•
Conducting experiments		•	•	•	•	•	•	•
Experimental probability		•	•	•	•	•	•	•
Theoretical probability						•	•	•
Using probability to plan strategies				•	•	•	•	•

Problem Solving

	PreK	K	1	2	3	4	5	6
Multistep problems			•	•	•	•	•	•
Multiple solutions			•	•	•	•	•	•
No solutions			•	•	•	•	•	•
Interpreting data		•	•	•	•	•	•	•
Checking reasonableness		•	•	•	•	•	•	•
Solving problems with too much information			•	•	•	•	•	•
Interpreting the quotient and remainder					•	•	•	•
Choosing the appropriate operation		•	•	•	•	•	•	•
Using estimation		•	•	•	•	•	•	•
Using guess, check, and adjust		•	•	•	•	•	•	•
Solving a simpler problem					•	•	•	•
Eliminating possibilities						•	•	•
Acting it out	•	•	•	•	•	•	•	•
Using/finding a pattern		•	•	•	•	•	•	•
Using/making a table			•	•	•	•	•	•
Using/drawing a picture or diagram	•	•	•	•	•	•	•	•
Using manipulatives	•	•	•	•	•	•	•	•

Ratio and Proportion

	PreK	K	1	2	3	4	5	6
Meaning/use of ratio and proportion						•	•	•
Rates						•	•	•
Similar figures						•	•	•
Map scales							•	•
Meaning of percent						•	•	•
Percent of a number						•	•	•

	PreK	K	1	2	3	4	5	6
Percent discounts							●	●
Sales tax							●	●
Simple/compound interest							●	●

Statistics and Graphing

	PreK	K	1	2	3	4	5	6
Surveying			●	●	●	●	●	●
Tallying			●	●	●	●	●	●
Making tables with data			●	●	●	●	●	●
Real and picture graphs		●	●	●	●	●		
Bar graphs		●	●	●	●	●	●	●
Line graphs				●	●	●	●	●
Circle graphs					●	●	●	●
Analyzing graphs		●	●	●	●	●	●	●
Finding the mean					●	●	●	●
Finding the median					●	●	●	●
Finding the mode					●	●	●	●

Subtraction (Whole Numbers)

	PreK	K	1	2	3	4	5	6
Meaning of subtraction	●	●	●	●				
Basic facts			●	●	●	●	●	●
Missing-term problems			●	●	●	●	●	●
Two-digit numbers			●	●	●	●	●	●
Three-digit numbers				●	●	●	●	●
Greater numbers					●	●	●	●
Subtracting money			●	●	●	●	●	●
Estimating differences				●	●	●	●	●

Technology

Calculators

	PreK	K	1	2	3	4	5	6
Computation with whole numbers						●	●	●
Computation with decimals						●	●	●
Computation with fractions							●	●
Computation with integers (negative numbers)							●	●
Using function rules						●	●	●
Order of operations							●	●
Function keys							●	●

Computers

	PreK	K	1	2	3	4	5	6
Spreadsheets					●	●	●	●
Functions		●	●	●	●	●	●	●
Graphs			●	●	●	●	●	●
Geometry	●	●	●	●	●	●	●	●
Charts and tables				●	●	●	●	●

Game Directory

Game	Principle Skills	Begin Using* Student Edition	Begin Using* Teacher's Edition
Tracing and Writing Numbers	Tracing, writing, ordering, and finding numbers 0–10	Page 4	Lesson 1.1
Odds-Evens Game	Identifying odd and even numbers through ten	Page 6	Lesson 1.2
Counting and Writing Numbers	Counting and writing numbers 0–100	Page 8	Lesson 1.3
Yard Sale Game**	Changing money ($1 bills for $10 bills, $10 bills for $100 bills)		Lesson 1.5
Calendar Game ⓔ Games	Using a monthly calendar		Lesson 1.6
Addition Table Game	Using an addition table with two addends of 5 or less		Lesson 2.1
Harder Addition Table Game	Using an addition table with two addends of 10 or less		Lesson 2.1
Addition Crossing Game	Practicing basic facts; using addends up to 10; using mathematical reasoning		Lesson 2.3
Doubles Game	Adding doubles	Page 50	Lesson 2.4
Frog Pond Game	Adding with two addends of 10 or less		Lesson 2.5
Harder Frog Pond Game	Adding with two addends of ten or less		Lesson 2.5
Roll a 15 ⓔ Games	Adding two, three, or four numbers (0–10); using intuitive notions of probability	Page 60	Lesson 2.7
Space Game	Solving addition and missing-addend problems with sums of 10 or less		Lesson 3.2
Harder Space Game	Solving addition, subtraction, missing-addend, missing-minuend, and missing-subtrahend problems with numbers 10 or less		Lesson 3.2
Roll 20 to 5 ⓔ Games	Subtracting 10 or less from numbers through 20	Page 84	Lesson 3.3
Find the Distance 1 Game	Estimating straight distances to the nearest centimeter; comparing line lengths		Lesson 4.2
Find the Distance 2 Game	Estimating straight distances to the nearest centimeter; comparing line lengths		Lesson 4.2
Get to 100 by Tens or Ones ⓔ Games	Adding mentally with numbers through 100	Page 162	Lesson 5.1
Roll a Problem	Adding multidigit numbers; place value; using intuitive notions of probability	Page 179	Lesson 5.8

Game	Principle Skills	Begin Using* Student Edition	Begin Using* Teacher's Edition
Roll a Problem (Subtraction)	Subtracting multidigit numbers; place value; using intuitive notions of probability	Page 216	Lesson 6.6
Fraction Game **ⓔGames**	Recognizing fractional areas of a circle; recognizing which fractional areas when combined are more than half the area of a circle		Lesson 7.6
Harder Counting and Writing Numbers	Counting in the 0–1,000 range; writing numbers in the 0–1,000 range	Page 334	Lesson 9.1
Rummage Sale Game	Changing money ($1, $10, and $100 bills for those of larger denominations); regrouping in preparation for multidigit addition		Lesson 9.4
Checkbook Game	Adding and subtracting two-digit and three-digit numbers; maintaining a record of money transactions		Lesson 9.7
Make 1,000 **ⓔGames**	Approximating answers to multidigit addition and subtraction problems; solving multidigit addition and subtraction problems	Page 354	Lesson 9.10
Map Game **ⓔGames**	Using numbers to represent magnitude and direction; using compass directions		Lesson 10.2
Harder Time Game	Telling time to the hour, half hour, and quarter hour		Lesson 10.9
Multiplication Table Game **ⓔGames**	Using a multiplication table; multiplying with two factors of 5 or less		Lesson 11.5
Harder Multiplication Table Game	Using a multiplication table; multiplying with two factors of 10 or less		Lesson 11.5
Harder What's the Problem?	Using addition, subtraction, multiplication, and division to make different number sentences with the same answers		Lesson 12.6

* These games and their variations should be used many times throughout the year. Feel free to use them again anytime after they are introduced.
** Games in red are from the Game Mat Kit.
ⓔGames These games are available as *eGames.*

ADDITION CROSSING

+	0	1	2	3	4	5	6	7	8	9	10
0	0	1	2	3	4	5	6	7	8	9	10
1	1	2	3	4	5	6	7	8	9	10	11
2	2	3	4	5	6	7	8	9	10	11	12
3	3	4	5	6	7	8	9	10	11	12	13
4	4	5	6	7	8	9	10	11	12	13	14
5	5	6	7	8	9	10	11	12	13	14	15
6	6	7	8	9	10	11	12	13	14	15	16
7	7	8	9	10	11	12	13	14	15	16	17
8	8	9	10	11	12	13	14	15	16	17	18
9	9	10	11	12	13	14	15	16	17	18	19
10	10	11	12	13	14	15	16	17	18	19	20

Math Focus:
- Practicing basic facts – using addends up to 10
- Using an addition table

Object of the Game: To be the first to complete a continuous path across the board

Players: Two

MATERIALS

Two cubes

25 counters of the same color for each player

SET UP

▲ Choose a direction. One of you will move horizontally (left to right) and the other will move vertically (up and down).

▲ Players roll the 0–5 **Number Cube.** The person who rolls the greater number chooses his or her counters and is followed by the second player.

HOW TO PLAY

① Take turns rolling any two cubes. Put a counter on any square that shows the sum of the addition fact you rolled. (For example, if you roll 3 and 8, you can put a counter on 3 + 8 or 8 + 3).

② The first player to make a continuous path from one side to the opposite side is the winner. Your path can go up, down, forward, backward, or diagonally, as long as all the squares are touching each other.

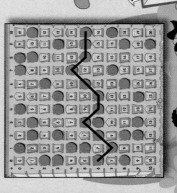

ADDITION TABLE GAME

Math Focus:
- Practicing basic facts—using two addends of 5 or less
- Using an addition table

Object of the Game: To have more counters at the end of the game

Players: Two

MATERIALS

Two cubes

36 counters or pennies

SET UP

▲ Every circle on the mat must be covered with a counter.

▲ Players roll the 0–5 *Number Cube.* The person who rolls the higher number goes first.

HOW TO PLAY

1. Players take turns rolling both cubes and making addition sentences out of the numbers. For example, if a 4 and a 2 are rolled, the player could say either "4 plus 2 equals 6" or "2 plus 4 equals 6."

2. After giving the addition sentence, players check their answers by looking under the appropriate counter. If correct, the player keeps the counter; if incorrect, the player replaces the counter.

3. Once the counter on a circle has been won, the circle remains empty. A player who cannot make an addition sentence that applies to a *covered circle* cannot win a counter that turn.

4. The player with more counters at the end of the game wins.

+	0	1	2	3	4	5
0	0	1	2	3	4	5
1	1	2	3	4	5	6
2	2	3	4	5	6	7
3	3	4	5	6	7	8
4	4	5	6	7	8	9
5	5	6	7	8	9	10

HARDER ADDITION TABLE GAME

Addition Table Game

+	5	6	7	8	9	10
5	10	11	12	13	14	15
6	11	12	13	14	15	16
7	12	13	14	15	16	17
8	13	14	15	16	17	18
9	14	15	16	17	18	19
10	15	16	17	18	19	20

HOW TO PLAY

1. There are actually two harder versions of this game. One game is played rolling one 0–5 and one 5–10 *Number Cube.* The second game is played with two 5–10 *Number Cubes.* Players decide which game to play and choose the appropriate cubes.

2. Players take turns rolling both cubes and making addition sentences out of the numbers. For example, if a 4 and a 9 are rolled, the player could say either "4 plus 9 equals 13" or "9 plus 4 equals 13."

3. After giving the addition sentence, players check their answers by looking under the appropriate counter. If correct, the player keeps the counter; if incorrect, the player replaces the counter.

4. Once the counter on a circle has been won, the circle remains empty. A player who cannot make an addition sentence that applies to a covered *circle* cannot win a counter that turn.

5. The player with more counters at the end of the game wins.

HARDER ADDITION TABLE GAME

+	5	6	7	8	9	10
0	5	6	7	8	9	10
1	6	7	8	9	10	11
2	7	8	9	10	11	12
3	8	9	10	11	12	13
4	9	10	11	12	13	14
5	10	11	12	13	14	15

Math Focus:
- Practicing basic facts—using two addends of 10 or less
- Using an addition table

Object of the Game: To have more counters at the end of the game

Players: Two

MATERIALS

Cube

Two cubes

36 counters or pennies

SET UP

▶ Every circle on the mat must be covered with a counter.

▶ Players roll the 0–5 *Number Cube.* The person who rolls the higher number goes first.

CALENDAR GAME

SUNDAY	MONDAY	TUESDAY	WEDNESDAY	THURSDAY	FRIDAY	SATURDAY

START ➡

				1	2	3
4	5	6	7	8	9	10
11	12	13	14	15	16	17
18	19	20	21	22	23	24
25	26	27	28	29	30	31

FINISH

Math Focus: Using a monthly calendar

Object of the Game: To be the first to reach FINISH

Players: Two or three

MATERIALS

Cube

Place marker and counter of the same color per player

SET UP

▶ Players place their counters on one of the days of the week. Players must choose different days.

▶ The players then put their place markers on START.

▶ Players roll the 0–5 **Number Cube.** The person who rolls the highest number goes first.

HOW TO PLAY

1. Players take turns rolling the cube and advancing through the 31 days of the month. Players must say aloud the day of the week where they land.

2. A player who lands on an opponent's chosen day must either return to START if still within the first seven days of the month or go back seven days. The player remains on this space until the next roll.

3. If a player is already on an opponent's chosen day and rolls a 0, he or she must move back another seven days.

4. The first player to reach FINISH wins.

Sunday	Monday	Tuesday	Wednesday	Thursday	Friday	Saturday
Start Your Balance is $1000	**1** Supermarket — Pay $35	**2** Dentist Bill — Pay $50	**3** Electric Bill — Pay $26	**4** STOCK DIVIDEND — Earn $50	**5** Insurance Bill — Pay $38	**6** THEATER TICKETS — Pay $20
7 Eat in Restaurant — Pay $20	**8** WORK OVERTIME — Earn $23	**9** Supermarket — Pay $51	**10** United Fund — Pay $100	**11** Go Back 7 Spaces	**12** Income TAX — Pay $212	**13** Go to Movies — Pay $5
14 Visit Museum — FREE	**15** RENT — Pay $150	**16** Holiday! — No bills today	**17** Supermarket — Pay $47	**18** BUY BOOKS — Pay $14	**19** Telephone Bill — Pay $17	**20** Receive Rebate Check — Earn $15
21 VISIT ZOO — FREE	**22** Supermarket — Pay $35	**23** Go Back 7 Spaces	**24** Parking Ticket — Pay $5	**25** Go Ahead 2 Spaces	**26** Automobile Repairs — Pay $285	**27** WORK OVERTIME — Earn $48
28 Eat in Restaurant — Pay $22	**29** NEW SHOES — Pay $15	**30** Supermarket — Pay $51	**31** Go Back 7 Spaces	**Finish** Wait until all players finish		

Copyright © SRA/McGraw-Hill. R37819.06

CHECKBOOK GAME

Math Focus:
- Adding and subtracting two-digit and three-digit numbers
- Maintaining a record of money transactions

Object of the Game: To have the largest balance at the end of the month

Players: Two or three

MATERIALS

Place markers

Cube

One balance sheet per player

SET UP

▶ Photocopies of the sample balance sheet can be handed out to students.

▶ Players prepare their balance sheets by writing "Start" on the first line under DATE and "$1000" on the first line under BALANCE.

▶ Players put their place markers on START.

▶ Players roll the 0–5 **Number Cube**. The person who rolls the highest number goes first.

HOW TO PLAY

❶ Players take turns rolling the cube and moving their markers the number of spaces indicated.

❷ Players follow the directions on the spaces where they land, entering the date and all payments or earnings on their balance sheets and recalculating their balances.

❸ Play continues until all the players have either reached FINISH or run out of money.

❹ The player with the largest balance at the end of the game is declared the winner. The other players then check the addition and subtraction in the winner's balance sheet. If the balance does not check, the player with the highest correct balance becomes the winner.

SAMPLE BALANCE SHEET

Date	Earn	Pay	Balance

CHECKBOOK GAME

Sunday	Monday	Tuesday	Wednesday	Thursday	Friday	Saturday
Start Your Balance is $1000.00	**1** Supermarket — Pay $35.22	**2** Dentist Bill — Pay $50.00	**3** Electric Bill — Pay $26.14	**4** STOCK DIVIDEND — Earn $50.00	**5** Insurance Bill — Pay $38.17	**6** THEATER TICKETS — Pay $20.00
7 Eat in Restaurant — Pay $20.82	**8** WORK OVERTIME — Earn $23.50	**9** Supermarket — Pay $51.62	**10** United Fund — Pay $100.00	**11** Go Back 7 Spaces	**12** Income TAX — Pay $212.00	**13** Go to Movies — Pay $5.00
14 Visit Museum — FREE	**15** RENT — Pay $150.00	**16** Holiday! — No bills today	**17** Supermarket — Pay $47.94	**18** BUY BOOKS — Pay $14.50	**19** Telephone Bill — Pay $17.36	**20** WORK OVERTIME — Earn $43.71
21 VISIT ZOO — FREE	**22** Supermarket — Pay $35.61	**23** Go Back 7 Spaces	**24** Parking Ticket — Pay $5.00	**25** Go Ahead 2 Spaces	**26** Automobile Repairs — Pay $285.00	**27** JOB BONUS — Earn $250.00
28 Eat in Restaurant — Pay $22.16	**29** NEW SHOES — Pay $15.45	**30** Supermarket — Pay $51.62	**31** Go Back 7 Spaces	**Finish** Wait until all players finish		

HARDER CHECKBOOK GAME

Math Focus:
- Adding and subtracting two-digit, three-digit, and four-digit numbers
- Maintaining a record of money transactions

Object of the Game: To have the largest balance at the end of the month

Players: Two or three

MATERIALS

Place markers

Cube

One balance sheet per player

SET UP

► Photocopies of the balance sheet for the **Harder Checkbook Game** can be handed out to students.

► Players prepare their balance sheets by writing "Start" on the first line under DATE and "$1000" on the first line under BALANCE.

► Players put their place markers on START.

► Players roll the 0–5 **Number Cube.** The person who rolls the highest number goes first.

HOW TO PLAY

❶ Players take turns rolling the cube and moving their markers the number of spaces indicated.

❷ Players follow the directions on the spaces where they land, entering the date and all payments or earnings on their balance sheets and recalculating their balances.

❸ Play continues until all the players have either reached FINISH or run out of money.

❹ The player with the largest balance at the end of the game is declared the winner. The other players then check the addition and subtraction in the winner's balance sheet. If the balance does not check, the player with the highest correct balance becomes the winner.

SAMPLE BALANCE SHEET

Date	Earn	Pay	Balance

HARDER CHECKBOOK GAME

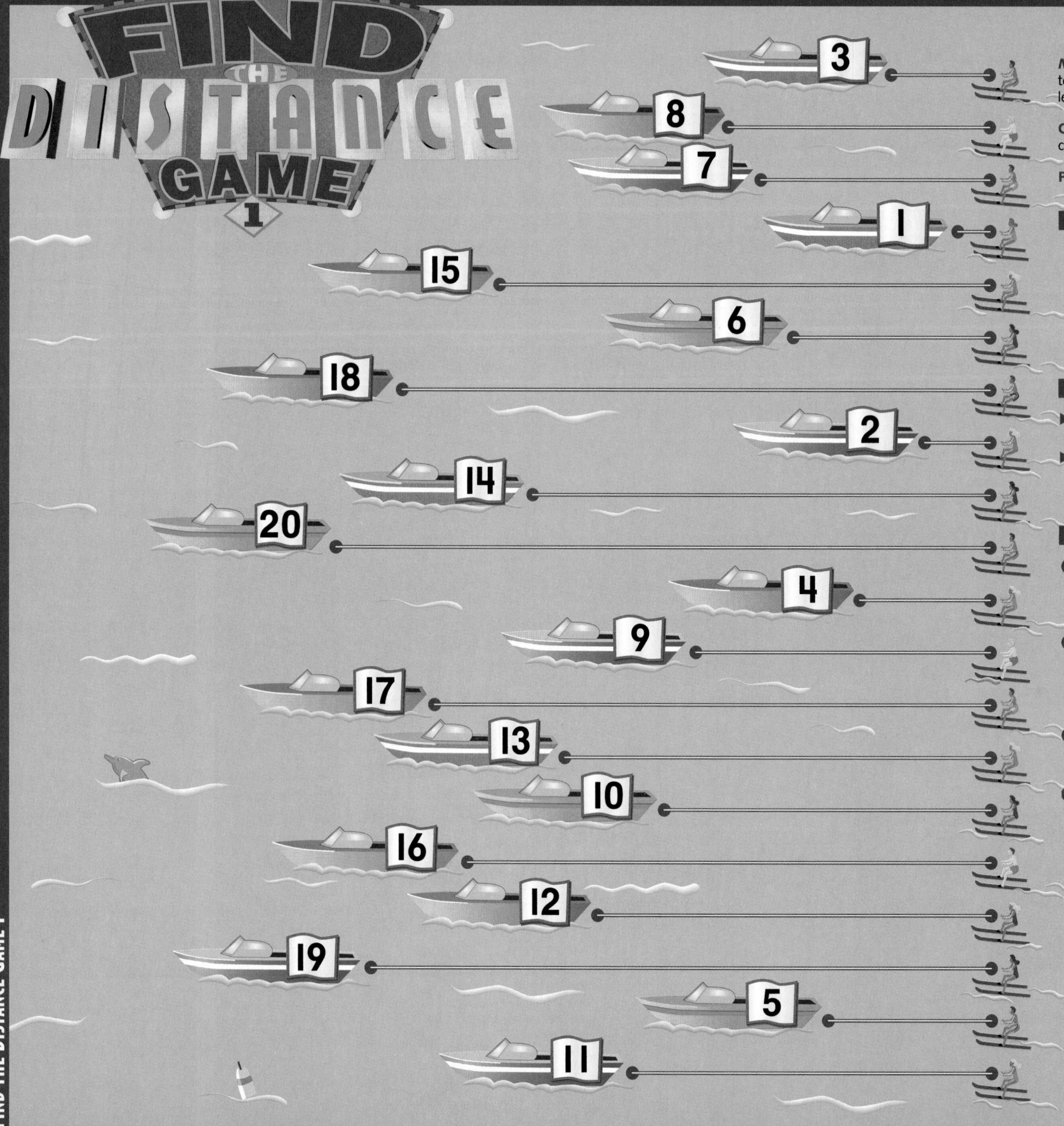

Math Focus: Estimating straight distances to the nearest centimeter; Comparing line lengths; Practicing basic addition facts

Object of the Game: To have the most counters at the end of the game

Players: Two or three

MATERIALS

Two cubes

Two cubes

Ten counters or pennies

SET UP

▲ Every number must be covered with a counter.

▲ Players roll the 0–5 *Number Cube*. The person who rolls the highest number goes first.

HOW TO PLAY

1. Players take turns choosing two cubes to roll and finding their sum. The player then identifies the line on the mat which is that many centimeters long.

2. Players check their answers by looking under the counter. If correct, the player keeps the counter. If incorrect, the player replaces the counter and must wait until the next turn to roll again.

3. Players who roll a 0 or a sum that has already been won must wait until the next turn to roll again.

4. The player with the most counters at the end of the game wins.

Measurement Key

= 2 centimeters

0 1 2

Copyright © SRA/McGraw-Hill. R37800.13

FIND THE DISTANCE GAME 1

Math Focus: Estimating straight distances to the nearest centimeter; Comparing line lengths; Practicing basic addition facts

Object of the Game: To have the most counters at the end of the game

Players: Two or three

MATERIALS

Two cubes

Two cubes

Twenty counters or pennies

SET UP

► Every number must be covered with a counter.

► Players roll the 0–5 **Number Cube.** The person who rolls the highest number goes first.

HOW TO PLAY

1. Players take turns choosing two cubes to roll and finding their sum. The player then identifies the line on the mat which is that many centimeters long.

2. Players check their answers by looking under the counter. If correct, the player keeps the counter. If incorrect, the player replaces the counter and must wait until the next turn to roll again.

3. Players who roll a 0 or a sum that has already been won must wait until the next turn to roll again.

4. The player with the most counters at the end of the game wins.

BALLOONS

Measurement Key

6
5
4
3   = **6** centimeters
2
1
0

FIND THE DISTANCE
GAME 2

FRACTION GAME

The circles shown contain the following fractions:

1/1

1/2 | 1/2

1/2 | 1/2

1/2 (top) / 1/2 (bottom)

1/2 (left) / 1/2 (right)

1/3 | 1/3 | 1/3

1/3 1/3 / 1/3

1/3 1/3 / 1/3 1/3

1/3 1/3 / 1/3

1/4 1/4 / 1/4 1/4

1/4 1/4 / 1/4 1/4

1/4 1/4 / 1/4 1/4

1/4 1/4 / 1/4 1/4

1/5 1/5 / 1/5 1/5 1/5

1/5 1/5 / 1/5 1/5 1/5

1/5 1/5 / 1/5 1/5 1/5

1/5 1/5 / 1/5 1/5 1/5

Math Focus:
- Recognizing fractional areas of a circle up to fifths
- Recognizing which common fractions sum to more than one half when added together

Object of the Game: To own more circles at the end of the game

Players: Two

MATERIALS

Two cubes

25 counters of the same color for each player, or 25 pennies and 25 nickels

SET UP

▶ Players roll the 0–5 **Number Cube.** The person who rolls the higher number goes first.

▶ The first player chooses his or her counters. The second player uses the remaining pieces.

HOW TO PLAY

1. Players take turns rolling the cubes and making fractions equal to or less than 1.

2. Players may divide their roll between more than one circle. For example, a player who rolls a 4 and a 5 may cover 1/5 of one circle and 3/5 of another.

3. Players who roll one 0 cannot place a counter. Players who roll double 0s may roll both cubes again.

4. A circle is awarded to a player who has covered more than half of it. That player puts a counter in the center of the circle and returns any of the opponent's counters. If half of a circle is covered by one player and half by the other player, neither player may own the circle.

5. Play continues until all the circles are either owned or completely covered. The player with more circles is the winner.

FRACTION GAME

FROG POND GAME

Go

0 + 9 = 9

4 + 4 = 8

9 + 3 = 12

10 + 10 = 20

5 + 6 = 11

8 + 8 = 16

1 + 8 = 9

8 + 7 = 15

10 + 4 = 14

7 + 2 = 9

6 + 9 = 15

3 + 6 = 9

2 + 9 = 11

7 + 6 = 13

5 + 1 = 6

3 + 2 = 5

bank

Math Focus: Practicing basic math–using two addends of 10 or less

Object of the Game: To have the most counters at the end of the game

Players: Two or three

MATERIALS

Place markers

Cube

20 counters or pennies per player

SET UP

▶ Every circle on the mat must be covered with a counter.

▶ Extra counters are placed on the space marked BANK.

▶ Players put their place markers on GO.

▶ Players roll the 0–5 *Number Cube.* The person who rolls the highest number goes first.

HOW TO PLAY

1. Players take turns rolling the cube and moving their markers the number of spaces indicated.

2. After landing on a space, a player may win the counter there by correctly completing the addition sentence.

3. Players check their answers by lifting the counters. If correct, the player keeps the counter. If incorrect, the player replaces the counter and remains on that space.

4. A player cannot win a counter if there is none in a space. A player who gives an incorrect answer and rolls a 0 on the next turn can try again to win the counter.

5. Players collect two counters from the bank each time they pass or land on GO.

6. The player with the most counters at the end of the game wins.

MAP GAME

Math Focus: Using compass directions and mathematical reasoning

Object of the Game: To be the first to cover six pictures

Players: Two or three

MATERIALS

Place markers

Cube

Ten counters of the same color for each player, or ten pennies, nickels, and dimes

SET UP

▲ Players roll the 0–5 *Number Cube.* The person who rolls the highest number chooses which counters to use and is followed by the other players.

▲ Players put their place markers on START.

▲ The person who rolled the highest number also goes first.

HOW TO PLAY

1. Before rolling, players must announce in which direction they intend to move that turn. Players who forget to announce their direction before rolling cannot move that turn.

2. Players roll the cube and move their markers the number of spaces indicated. If they land on a picture, they cover it with a counter.

3. Players cannot move if they roll a number that would land them on a picture that is already covered. Also, players who roll a number that would take them off the board cannot move that turn.

4. During the game, players can move freely back and forth across the START square.

5. The first player to cover six pictures wins the game.

EAST

NORTH

START

SOUTH

WEST

Multiplication Table Game

×	0	1	2	3	4	5
0	0	0	0	0	0	0
1	0	1	2	3	4	5
2	0	2	4	6	8	10
3	0	3	6	9	12	15
4	0	4	8	12	16	20
5	0	5	10	15	20	25

Math Focus:
- Practicing basic facts–multiplying two factors of 5 or less
- Using a multiplication table

Object of the Game: To have more counters at the end of the game

Players: Two

MATERIALS

Two cubes

36 counters or pennies

SET UP

▲ Every circle on the mat must be covered with a counter.

▲ Players roll the 0–5 *Number Cube*. The person who rolls the higher number goes first.

HOW TO PLAY

1. Players take turns rolling both cubes and making multiplication sentences out of the numbers. For example, if a 4 and a 2 are rolled, the player could say either "4 times 2 equals 8" or "2 times 4 equals 8."

2. After giving the multiplication sentence, players check their answers by looking under the appropriate counter. If correct, the player keeps the counter; if incorrect, the player replaces the counter.

3. Once the counter on a circle has been won, the circle remains empty. A player who cannot make a multiplication sentence that applies to a covered circle cannot win a counter that turn.

4. The player with more counters at the end of the game wins.

HARDER Multiplication Table Game

Math Focus:
- Practicing basic facts–multiplying two factors of 10 or less
- Using a multiplication table

Object of the Game: To have more counters at the end of the game

Players: Two

SET UP

▶ Every circle on the mat must be covered with a counter.

▶ Players roll the 0–5 **Number Cube.** The person who rolls the higher number goes first.

MATERIALS

Cube

Two cubes

36 counters or pennies

HOW TO PLAY

1. There are actually two harder versions of this game. One game is played rolling one 0–5 and one 5–10 **Number Cube.** The second game is played with two 5–10 **Number Cubes.** Players take turns rolling both cubes and making multiplication sentences out of the numbers. For example, if a 4 and a 9 are rolled, the player could say either "4 times 9 equals 36" or "9 times 4 equals 36."

2. After giving the multiplication sentence, players check their answers by looking under the appropriate counter.

3. If correct, the player keeps the counter; if incorrect, the player replaces the counter.

4. Once the counter on a circle has been won, the circle remains empty. A player who cannot make a multiplication sentence that applies to a covered circle cannot win a counter that turn.

5. The player with more counters at the end of the game wins.

Table (top right)

✗	5	6	7	8	9	10
5	25	30	35	40	45	50
6	30	36	42	48	54	60
7	35	42	49	56	63	70
8	40	48	56	64	72	80
9	45	54	63	72	81	90
10	50	60	70	80	90	100

Table (bottom right)

✗	5	6	7	8	9	10
0	0	0	0	0	0	0
1	5	6	7	8	9	10
2	10	12	14	16	18	20
3	15	18	21	24	27	30
4	20	24	28	32	36	40
5	25	30	35	40	45	50

HARDER MULTIPLICATION TABLE GAME

RUMMAGE SALE GAME

$100

$22

$10

$23

$201

$110

$47

$63

$114

$101

$3

$35

$14

$81

$25

$5

GO!

RUMMAGE SALE GAME

SET UP

▲ Players sort the money into piles next to the game mat.

▲ Players put their place markers on GO.

▲ Players roll the 0–5 *Number Cube.* The person who rolls the highest number goes first.

HOW TO PLAY

1. Players take turns rolling the cube and moving their place markers the number of spaces indicated.

2. After landing on a space, the player says the price of the object pictured there and collects that amount from the money next to the game mat. Players must count the bills aloud.

3. Players do not collect money for passing or landing on GO.

4. Players should keep their $1, $10, and $100 bills in separate piles. They must trade up whenever possible: ones for tens, tens for hundreds, and hundreds for a thousand. The first player to collect a $1,000 bill wins the game.

Math Focus:
- Changing money ($1, $10, $100)
- Practicing regrouping in preparation for multidigit addition

Object of the Game: To be the first player to collect a $1,000 bill

Players: Two or three

MATERIALS

Cube

Per player:
ten $1 bills
ten $10 bills
ten $100 bills
one $1,000 bill

Place markers

Copyright © SRA/McGraw-Hill. All photos: © PhotoDisc R37819.09

HARDER RUMMAGE SALE GAME

RUMMAGE SALE GAME

GO!

Math Focus:
• Changing money (various bills and coins)
• Practicing regrouping in preparation for multidigit addition

Object of the Game: To be the first player to collect a $1,000 bill

Players: Two or three

SET UP

▲ Players sort the money into piles next to the game mat.

▲ Players put their place markers on GO.

▲ Players roll the 0–5 *Number Cube.* The person who rolls the highest number goes first.

HOW TO PLAY

1. Players take turns rolling the cube and moving their place markers the number of spaces indicated.

2. After landing on a space, the player says the price of the object pictured there and collects that amount from the money next to the game mat. Players must use the fewest possible bills and coins as they count the money aloud, largest bills first. Players who make errors in counting or use too many bills or coins must return the money to the bank and collect nothing for that turn.

3. Players do not collect money for passing or landing on GO.

4. Players should keep their bills and coins in separate piles. They must trade up whenever possible: ones for tens, tens for hundreds, and so on. The first player to collect a $1,000 bill wins the game.

MATERIALS

Place markers

Cube

Per player:
ten $1 bills
two $5 bills
five $10 bills
two $20 bills
two $50 bills
ten $100 bills
one $1,000 bill

five pennies
two nickels
five dimes
two quarters
two half dollars

$1.23

$101.20

$86.45

$274.79

$12.01

$40.00

$12.73

$18.47

$10.00

$76.00

$343.18

$50.00

$2.46

$197.00

$62.35

$4.37

Game Mats **D17**

SPACE GAME

$4 + 4 = 8$

$6 + 3 = 9$

$5 + 5 = 10$

$0 + 7 = 7$

$6 + 4 = 10$

$7 + 3 = 10$

$0 + 3 = 3$

$1 + 1 = 2$

$3 + 4 = 7$

$4 + 6 = 10$

$0 + 0 = 0$

$7 + 3 = 10$

$3 + 3 = 6$

$0 + 5 = 5$

$8 + 2 = 10$

$9 + 0 = 9$

$2 + 2 = 4$

$9 + 1 = 10$

Math Focus: Solving mixed addition and missing-addend problems with sums of 10 or less

Object of the Game: To have the most counters at the end of the game

Players: Two or three

MATERIALS

Cube

Cube

18 counters or pennies

SET UP

▶ Players cover any one number in each equation.

▶ Players roll the 0–5 **Number Cube.** The person who rolls the highest number goes first.

HOW TO PLAY

❶ Players take turns rolling either cube and using the number rolled to complete one of the equations on the mat. The player must correctly say the entire equation.

❷ Players check their answers by looking under the counters. If correct, the player keeps the counter. If incorrect, the player replaces the counter.

❸ The player with the most counters at the end of the game wins.

SPACE GAME

HARDER SPACE GAME

$10 - 7 = 3$

$7 - 2 = 5$

$0 + 0 = 0$

$3 + 6 = 9$

$6 - 1 = 5$

$6 - 5 = 1$

$1 + 9 = 10$

$3 + 6 = 9$

$3 + 6 = 9$

$5 + 5 = 10$

$1 - 0 = 1$

$5 - 3 = 2$

$1 + 8 = 9$

$8 - 4 = 4$

$6 + 4 = 10$

$2 + 1 = 3$

$4 + 2 = 6$

$8 - 3 = 5$

Math Focus: Solving mixed addition, subtraction, missing-addend, -minuend, and -subtrahend problems with numbers of 10 or less

Object of the Game: To have the most counters at the end of the game

Players: Two or three

MATERIALS

Cube

Cube

●
18 counters or pennies

SET UP

► Players cover any one number in each equation.

► Players roll the 0–5 **Number Cube.** The person who rolls the highest number goes first.

HOW TO PLAY

❶ Players take turns rolling either cube and using the number rolled to complete one of the equations on the mat. The player must correctly say the entire equation.

❷ Players check their answers by looking under the counters. If correct, the player keeps the counter. If incorrect, the player replaces the counter.

❸ The player with the most counters at the end of the game wins.

Go

Time Game

9:15

2:40

8:40

12:10

1:25

3:35

2:05

11:05

9:25

6:50

12:50

4:45

4:10

5:55

10:20

7:05

Math Focus: Telling time to five-minute intervals

Object of the Game: To have the most counters at the end of the game

Players: Two or three

MATERIALS

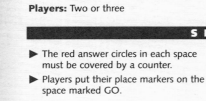

Place markers   Cube   16 counters or pennies

SET UP

▶ The red answer circles in each space must be covered by a counter.

▶ Players put their place markers on the space marked GO.

▶ Players roll the 0–5 *Number Cube.* The person who rolls the highest number goes first.

HOW TO PLAY

❶ Players take turns rolling the cube and moving their place markers the number of spaces indicated. Players must correctly state the time indicated on the clock in each space where they land.

❷ Players check their answers by looking under the counter. If correct, the player keeps the counter; if incorrect, the player replaces the counter.

❸ A player who gives an incorrect answer and then rolls a 0 on the next turn may try again to win the counter.

❹ Players who land on empty circles cannot win a counter and must wait until the next turn to roll again.

❺ Players who land on the space marked PENALTY must, if possible, place one of their own counters on an empty circle.

❻ The player with the most counters at the end of the game wins.

Penalty
COVER AN ANSWER

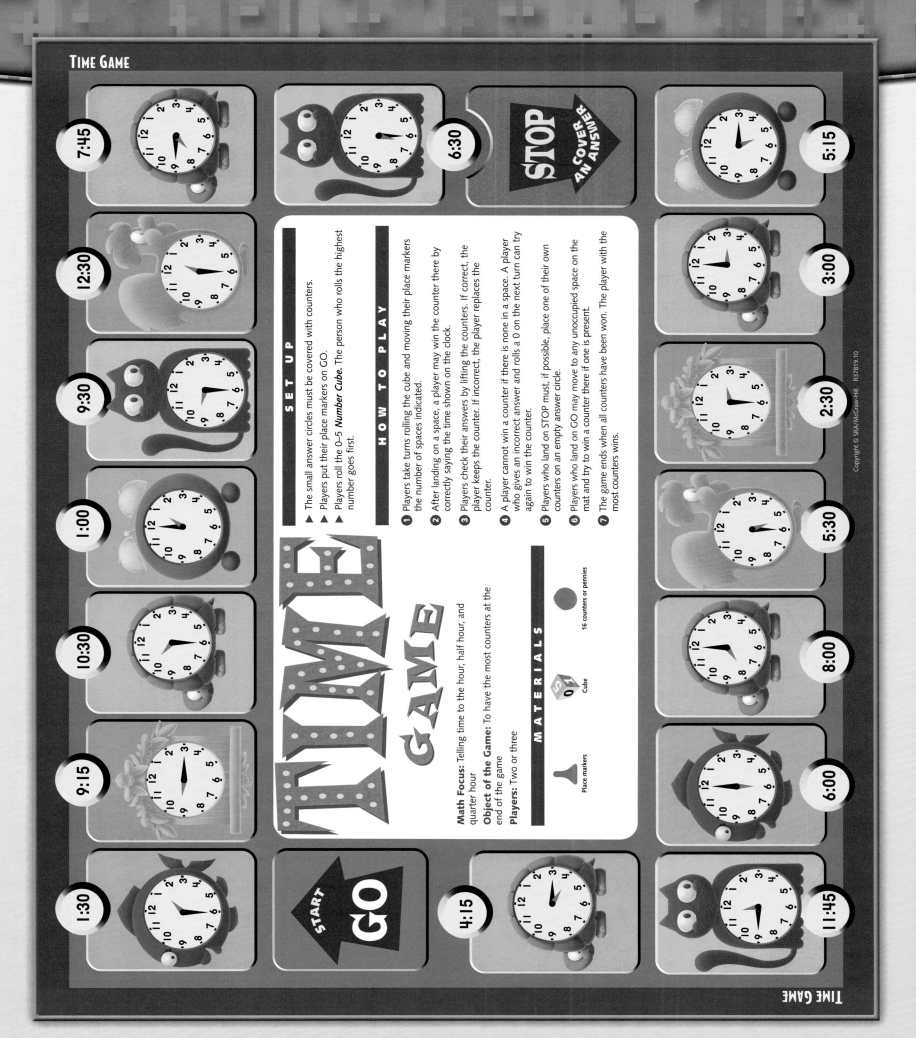

TIME GAME

Math Focus: Telling time to the hour, half hour, and quarter hour

Object of the Game: To have the most counters at the end of the game

Players: Two or three

MATERIALS

Place markers

Cube

16 counters or pennies

SET UP

▲ The small answer circles must be covered with counters.

▲ Players put their place markers on GO.

▲ Players roll the 0–5 *Number Cube.* The person who rolls the highest number goes first.

HOW TO PLAY

1 Players take turns rolling the cube and moving their place markers the number of spaces indicated.

2 After landing on a space, a player may win the counter there by correctly saying the time shown on the clock.

3 Players check their answers by lifting the counters. If correct, the player keeps the counter. If incorrect, the player replaces the counter.

4 A player cannot win a counter if there is none in a space. A player who gives an incorrect answer and rolls a 0 on the next turn can try again to win the counter.

5 Players who land on STOP must, if possible, place one of their own counters on an empty answer circle.

6 Players who land on GO may move to any unoccupied space on the mat and try to win a counter there if one is present.

7 The game ends when all counters have been won. The player with the most counters wins.

7:45

6:30

STOP
AN COVER AN ANSWER

5:15

12:30

3:00

9:30

2:30

1:00

5:30

10:30

8:00

9:15

6:00

1:30

GO
START

4:15

11:45

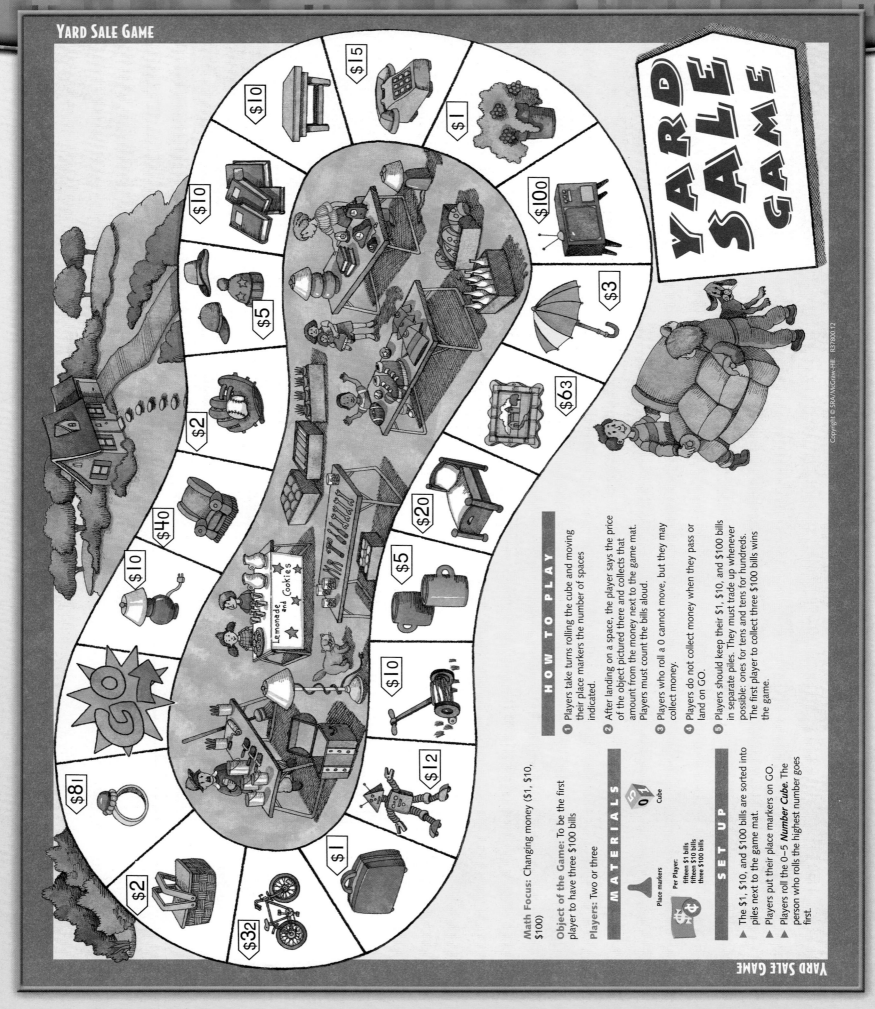

Math Focus: Changing money ($1, $10, $100)

Object of the Game: To be the first player to have three $100 bills

Players: Two or three

MATERIALS

Place markers   Cube

Per Player:
fifteen **$1** bills
fifteen **$10** bills
three **$100** bills

SET UP

▲ The $1, $10, and $100 bills are sorted into piles next to the game mat.

▲ Players put their place markers on GO.

▲ Players roll the 0–5 *Number Cube.* The person who rolls the highest number goes first.

HOW TO PLAY

❶ Players take turns rolling the cube and moving their place markers the number of spaces indicated.

❷ After landing on a space, the player says the price of the object pictured there and collects that amount from the money next to the game mat. Players must count the bills aloud.

❸ Players who roll a 0 cannot move, but they may collect money.

❹ Players do not collect money when they pass or land on GO.

❺ Players should keep their $1, $10, and $100 bills in separate piles. They must trade up whenever possible: ones for tens and tens for hundreds. The first player to collect three $100 bills wins the game.

YARD SALE GAME

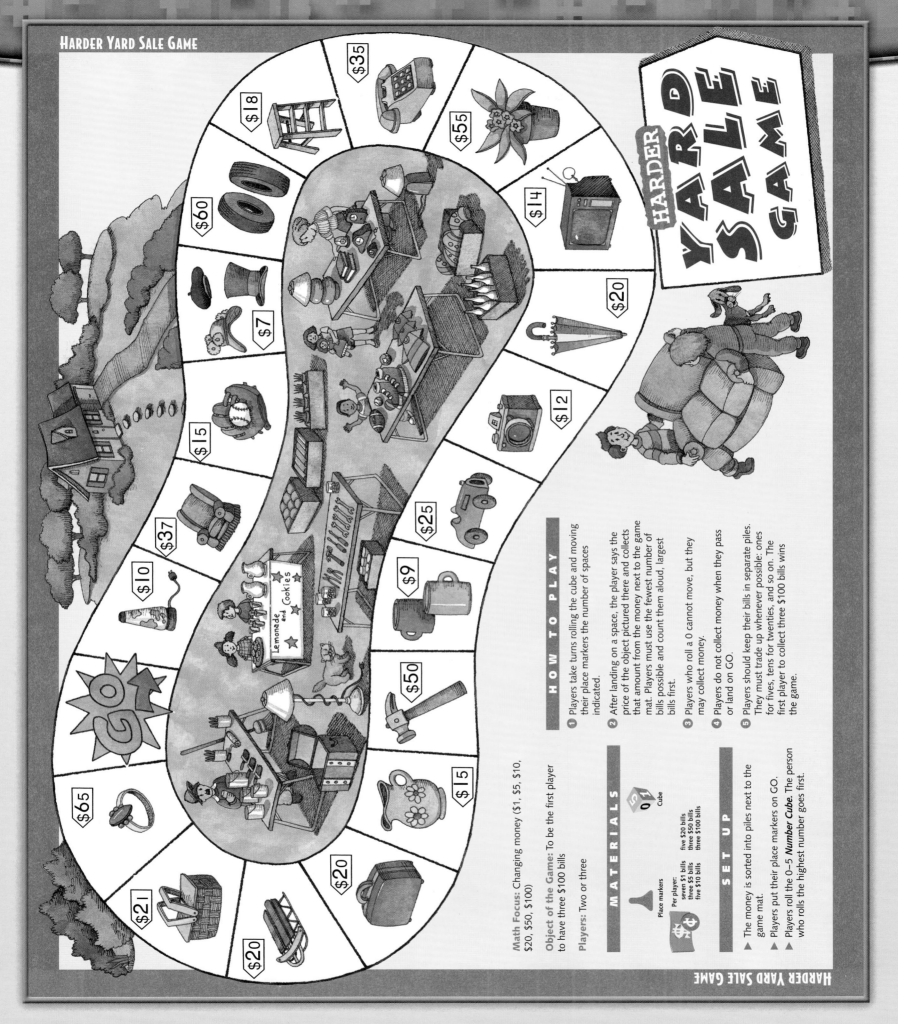

HARDER YARD SALE GAME

YARD SALE GAME

$35 — $18 — $60 — $7 — $15 — $37 — $10 — $65 — $21 — $20 — $20 — $15 — $50 — $9 — $25 — $12 — $20 — $14 — $55

Lemonade and Cookies

GO

Math Focus: Changing money ($1, $5, $10, $20, $50, $100)

Object of the Game: To be the first player to have three $100 bills

Players: Two or three

MATERIALS

Place markers

Cube

Per player:
seven $1 bills
three $5 bills
five $10 bills

five $20 bills
three $50 bills
three $100 bills

SET UP

▲ The money is sorted into piles next to the game mat.

▲ Players put their place markers on GO.

▲ Players roll the 0–5 *Number Cube.* The person who rolls the highest number goes first.

HOW TO PLAY

1 Players take turns rolling the cube and moving their place markers the number of spaces indicated.

2 After landing on a space, the player says the price of the object pictured there and collects that amount from the money next to the game mat. Players must use the fewest number of bills possible and count them aloud, largest bills first.

3 Players who roll a 0 cannot move, but they may collect money.

4 Players do not collect money when they pass or land on GO.

5 Players should keep their bills in separate piles. They must trade up whenever possible: ones for fives, tens for twenties, and so on. The first player to collect three $100 bills wins the game.

Index

Index

Index

Index

Index

TEXAS

Texas Mathematics Essential Knowledge and Skills

The following pages contain an in-depth grade-specific correlation to the Texas Essential Knowledge and Skills for mathematics. The correlation can be used to determine where each of the TEKS is taught, practiced, and assessed in *Real Math*. The correlation provides a thorough correlation of the TEKS to all print and technology resources.

- Student Edition
- Teacher Edition
- Reteach

- Texas Practice
- Enrichment
- Texas Assessment

- TEKS/TAKS Practice
- Games
- Game Mats

- eGames
- eMathTools
- Building Blocks

TEKS are also referenced in the Chapter Planners, Lesson Planners, and on the Teacher and Student Edition lesson pages.

Core and Integrated Standards

Real Math provides systematic and explicit standards coverage. The program also integrates standards to show the connections among the strands of mathematics. The page references in the correlation include standards that have been sorted into one of two categories: Core and Integrated.

Core standards are those standards that are the focus of the lesson. These standards are listed in the Texas Chapter. Planner in the front of each chapter, the Lesson Planner located on the first page of each lesson, and the header of the second page of each lesson. One Core Standard is identified as the Key Standard for the lesson and appears on the student page, as well as in the Vertical Alignment at the beginning of each lesson in the Teacher's Edition.

Integrated standards are standards woven into a lesson to reflect the interconnectedness of the TEKS and mathematical strands. These standards also provide students with a thorough review of previously taught Core standards. A list of Integrated standards can also be found in a blue box in each Lesson Planner. Integrated standards that do not apply to the entire lesson are also identified in the Teacher's Edition in every Mental Math section, as well as other locations, as indicated by a blue box.

Using the Correlation

Overview   Set below each of the specific TEKS is a brief overview as to how the standard is met, a general location as to where the standard is taught, and any additional tools that may be of use in developing mastery of the standard.

Taught   The pages set in the row labeled *Taught* are those pages in which the skill, concept, or mathematical strand is introduced at that grade. These pages indicate where teachers should reference activities or questions to introduce a specific standard.

Practiced/Reinforced   The page references in the row labeled *Practiced/Reinforced* are pages that contain activities, questions, games, or technology with which students can reinforce skills or concepts related to the standard mentioned. In some cases an eMathTool is listed under the *Practiced/Reinforced* row, meaning that the tool can be used in practicing fluency of the standard.

Mastered/Assessed   The last row, labeled *Mastered/Assessed*, contains page references that are to be used for assessment purposes. These include pages found in **Texas Assessment, TEKS/TAKS Practice,** as well as pages from practice tests in the Student and Teacher's Editions. In addition to the citations listed for the *Mastered/Assessed* row, *Real Math's* eAssess software offers teachers the capability to create many additional tests that are based on standards. These tests can be taken using a computer or printed and taken as a paper-and-pencil test.

TAKS Objectives

Each TAKS Objective has been correlated to the corresponding mathematics strand that is expressed in the TEKS for mathematics. Knowing this information will allow teachers the opportunity to assess students' knowledge of the TAKS objectives using the TAKS Preparation book. This book has been created so that teachers can determine how well students retained information from the standards that relate to specific TAKS Objectives.

Vertical Alignment

To see how standards connect across grade levels, *Real Math* includes a Vertical Alignment of standards prior to and after the grade level being studied. This Vertical Alignment can be found in the Teacher's Edition at the top of the first page of each lesson. The standard listed for the grade being examined is what is considered the Key Standard. The Key Standard is the focal point of the lesson being studied. This Key Standard is also printed on the first page of each lesson in the Student Edition. To see the big picture, a K-6 vertical alignment has been placed on the *Real Math* website, www.realmath.com. This vertical alignment allows teachers to view prerequisite skills for specific grade levels and identify the foundations for subsequent years, as determined by the TEA.

TEKS Correlations

(2.1) Knowledge and Skill Number, operation, and quantitative reasoning. The student understands how place value is used to represent whole numbers.

Standard: (2.1.A) The student is expected to use concrete models of hundreds, tens, and ones to represent a given number (up to 999) in various ways.

TAKS Objective 1: The student will demonstrate an understanding of numbers, operations, and quantitative reasoning.

Grade 2 *Real Math* dedicates several comprehensive lessons to the topic of Place Value and comparing numbers in groups of hundreds, tens, and ones. To increase skills with representing whole numbers, students can use the eMathTools: Base Ten tool, with which they can create sets representing three-digit numbers and then add the two sets together. A myriad of resources are available, such as Game Mats and interactive tools, to augment the lesson content.

	Student Edition	Teacher Edition	Other Components
Taught	5, 11, 160, 161, 205, 331, 337	5B, 7B, 11B, 159-160, 161B, 165B, 167B, 205B, 331B, 337B, 339B	**Reteach** pages 1, 6
Practiced/ Reinforced	12, 206, 332, 339, 341, 343, 17, 318, 350	5-6, 7-8, 11-12, 161-162, 165-166, 167-168, 205-206, 331-332, 337-338, 339, 341B, 341-342, 343B, 343-344, 17-18, 317-318, 349-350	**Enrichment** pages 2, 5, 40 **Texas Practice** pages 2, 40, 43, 52, 86, 87, 88, 89 **Get to 100 by Tens or Ones Game, Make 1,000 Game, Harder Counting and Writing Numbers Game, and Yard Sale Game Mat** **eMathTools Base Ten Tools**
Mastered/ Assessed	35, 36, 198, 199, 239, 318	18A, 35-36, 197-198, 350A, 197-198, 199-200, 239-240, 317-318	**Texas Assessment** pages 110, 119, 120, 126, 212, 213, 230, 244 **TEKS/TAKS Practice** pages 1, 2, 3, 4

Standard: (2.1.B) The student is expected to use place value to read, write, and describe the value of whole numbers to 999.

TAKS Objective 1: The student will demonstrate an understanding of numbers, operations, and quantitative reasoning.

Students learn to read, write, and describe three-digit numerals throughout Grade 2. In the lessons, students relate the numeral to a set of craft sticks, in function machines, and through regrouping exercises. Students reinforce the concepts through games such as Rummage Sale game, and electronic tools, such as the eMathTools: Base Ten Tool.

	Student Edition	Teacher Edition	Other Components
Taught	3, 13, 161, 175, 177, 331, 333, 339	3B, 13B, 161B, 175B, 177B, 331B, 333B, 339B	**Reteach** pages 6, 7
Practiced/ Reinforced	14, 18, 34, 56, 89, 176, 178, 232, 332, 337, 340, 365	13-14, 16A, 17-18, 33-34, 55-56, 89-90, 175-176, 177-178, 211B, 231-232, 331-332, 333-334, 337-338, 339-340, 365-366	**Enrichment** pages 1, 5, 6, 40, 83, 84 **Texas Practice** pages 1, 5, 6, 40, 42, 43, 83, 84 **Harder Counting and Writing Numbers Game**
Mastered/ Assessed	37, 38, 198, 199, 367, 368, 369	18A, 35-36, 37-38, 197-198, 199-200	**Texas Assessment** pages 74, 75, 111, 119, 127, 214, 215, 230, 231 **TEKS/TAKS Practice** pages 5, 6, 7, 8

Standard: (2.1.C) The student is expected to use place value to compare and order whole numbers to 999 and record the comparisons using numbers and symbols ($<$, $=$, $>$).

TAKS Objective 1: The student will demonstrate an understanding of numbers, operations, and quantitative reasoning.

In Chapter 1, students review counting and writing numbers, including working with placement on a number line to reinforce understanding of concepts of "greater than," "less than," and "equal to." Practice exercises challenge students to write number sentences that reflect simple real-world comparisons of objects. Students review equalities and inequalities as they compare numbers in story problems presented on review pages and on mastery pages. Hands-on practice with the eMathTools Number Line affords another opportunity for students to set up their own experiments in comparing numbers.

	Student Edition	Teacher Edition	Other Components
Taught	23, 225, 335	23B, 225B, 335B, 357B	Reteach page 10, 14
Practiced/ Reinforced	24, 30, 34, 67, 225, 226, 336, 366	23-24, 29-30, 33-34, 67-68, 225-226, 267B, 269B, 335B, 343B, 345B, 365-366, 453B	Enrichment pages 9, 60, 85 Texas Practice pages 9, 85 Building Blocks Number Compare 4 and Double Compare 1-10
Mastered/ Assessed	67, 74, 237, 369	18A, 73-74, 237-238, 369-370	Texas Assessment pages 83, 111, 120, 127, 246, 214, 232 TEKS/TAKS Practice pages 9,10, 11, 12

(2.2) Knowledge and Skill

Number, operation, and quantitative reasoning. The student describes how fractions are used to name parts of whole objects or sets of objects.

Standard: (2.2.A) The student is expected to use concrete models to represent and name fractional parts of a whole object (with denominators of 12 or less).

TAKS Objective 1: The student will demonstrate an understanding of numbers, operations, and quantitative reasoning.

Grade 2, Chapter 7 presents the concept of using concrete models to represent and name fractional parts of a whole object. Students use area models to explore halves, fourths, and thirds. Students work with paper folding and with coloring sections or shapes, and also can use the eMathTools: Fractions Tool to expand their familiarity. The introductory Exploring Problem Solving lesson for Chapter 7 presents a real-world scenario, which will generate discussion of parts of a whole, and invite creative strategies for solving the problems.

	Student Edition	Teacher Edition	Other Components
Taught	249, 250, 289, 290	249-250, 289B, 289-290	Reteach pages 11, 12
Practiced/ Reinforced	244, 245, 246, 247, 248, 251, 252, 253, 254, 255, 256, 257, 258, 261, 262, 263, 264, 265, 266, 267, 268, 269, 270, 271, 272, 283, 284	243I, 243-244, 244A, 245B, 245-246, 247B, 247-248, 249B, 251B, 251-252, 253B, 253-254, 255B, 255-256, 257-258, 258A, 261B, 261-262, 263B, 263-264, 265B, 265-266, 267B, 267-268, 269B, 269-270, 271-272, 272A, 283A, 283B, 283C, 283D, 283E, 283-284, D10	Enrichment pages 62, 63, 64, 65, 66, 67, 68, 69, 72 Texas Practice pages 62, 63, 64, 65, 66, 67, 68, 69, 72 Fraction Game Mat Building Blocks: Super shape 2 *Real Math* Manipulative Kit: Fraction Tiles eGames: Fractions Games eMathTools: Shape Creator, Sketch Tool, and Fraction Tool
Mastered/ Assessed	279, 280, 282, 323, 325	260A, 279-280, 281-282, 298A, 323-324, 325-326	Texas Assessment pages 122, 123, 236, 238 TEKS/TAKS Practice pages 13, 14

TEKS Correlations

Standard: (2.2.B) The student is expected to use concrete models to represent and name fractional parts of a set of objects (with denominators of 12 or less).

TAKS Objective 1: The student will demonstrate an understanding of numbers, operations, and quantitative reasoning.

Real Math students began the study of fractions in Grade 1. Grade 2 Chapter 7 reintroduces the concepts of halves and fourths using linear and measurement models. The concept is developed using a variety of models: fractions are considered in terms of parts of a shape or parts of a set, then they are considered as a part of numbers, such as money and bundles of 10 craft sticks. The Chapter 7 Exploring Problem Solving lessons enhance the learning by challenging students with engaging scenarios related to the lesson concepts. *Real Math* offers a wealth of opportunity, described below, to reinforce the concepts of parts of a whole.

	Student Edition	Teacher Edition	Other Components
Taught	253, 262, 263	253B, 261B, 263B	**Reteach** pages 11, 12
Practiced/ Reinforced	254, 255, 264, 274, 278, 349, 361	253-254, 263-264, 273-274, 277-278, 293B, 349-350, 361-362	**Enrichment** pages 66, 67, 68, 69 **Texas Practice** pages 66, 67, 68 **Fraction Game Mat** **Building Blocks: Super shape 2** *Real Math* **Manipulative Kit: Fraction Tiles** **eGames: Fractions Games** **eMathTools: Shape Creator, Sketch Tool, and Fraction Tool**
Mastered/ Assessed	279	279-280, 281-282, 298A	**Texas Assessment** pages 122, 123, 236, 237 **TEKS/TAKS Practice** pages 15, 16

Standard: (2.2.C) The student is expected to use concrete models to determine if a fractional part of a whole is closer to 0, ½, or 1.

TAKS Objective 1: The student will demonstrate an understanding of numbers, operations, and quantitative reasoning.

Chapter 7 of *Real Math* expands students' knowledge of fractions. Students routinely consider the magnitude of fractional quantities by expressing fractions as being closer to 0, 1/2, or 1. Students also can refer to the Fraction Game Mat in which students must fill more than half of a circle to claim it as theirs and the person with the most circles wins.

	Student Edition	Teacher Edition	Other Components
Taught	247, 255, 269, 270	9B, 245B, 247B, 255B, 269B	Reteach pages 11, 12
Practiced/ Reinforced	248, 256, 270,	247-248, 255-256, 269-270	**Enrichment** pages 62, 63, 64, 65, 66, 67, 68 **Texas Practice** pages 72 **Fraction Game Mat** **Building Blocks: Super shape 2** *Real Math* **Manipulative Kit: Fraction Tiles** **eGames: Fractions Games** **eMathTools: Shape Creator, Sketch Tool, and Fraction Tool**
Mastered/ Assessed	282	260A, 281-282	**Texas Assessment** pages 122, 123, 185, 236, 237, 238, 239 **TEKS/TAKS Practice** pages 17, 18

(2.3) Knowledge and Skill
Number, operation, and quantitative reasoning. The student adds and subtracts whole numbers to solve problems.

Standard: (2.3.A) The student is expected to recall and apply basic addition and subtraction facts (to 18).

TAKS Objective 1: The student will demonstrate an understanding of numbers, operations, and quantitative reasoning.

Real Math, in Grade 2, covers computation comprehensively, in a variety of ways. Each lesson begins with Mental Math which, in the numerous places in Grade 2 that computation is occurring, offers a considerable aggregate amount of practice with computation. Teachers also have the option of offering the students fun games to enrich their learning, along with the *Real Math* suite of interactive math tools and activities.

	Student Edition	Teacher Edition	Other Components
Taught	43, 47, 49, 51, 53, 57, 59, 61, 63, 65, 83, 85, 87, 91, 93, 95, 97, 99, 163, 165, 169, 181, 207	43B, 45B, 47B, 49B, 51B, 53-54, 54A, 57B, 59B, 63, 65-66, 83B, 85B, 87-88, 91B, 93B, 95B, 97B, 99-100, 163B, 165B, 169B, 181B, 207B	**Reteach** pages 2, 3, 6, 7, 8, 9
Practiced/ Reinforced	44, 45, 48, 50, 52, 54, 58, 59, 60, 61, 62, 64, 66, 68, 71, 72, 84, 86, 87, 90, 92, 94, 96, 98, 100, 101, 105, 106, 164, 166, 170, 181, 191, 192, 197, 208, 220, 259, 298, 317,	39A-39E, 43-44, 45-46, 47-48, 49-50, 51-52, 57-58, 59-60, 61-62, 63-64, 66A, 67-68, 71-72, 77A-77E, 83-84, 85-86, 88A, 89-90, 91-92, 93-94, 95-96, 97-98, 100A, 101-102, 105-106, 115B, 117B, 119B, 121B, 123B, 141B, 161B, 163B, 163-164, 165-166, 169-170, 181-182, 183B, 185B, 191-192, 197-198, 207-208, 219-220, 259-260, 297-298, 317-318, 331-332, 419B, 421B, 455B, 457B	**Enrichment** pages 11, 12, 13, 14, 15, 16, 17, 19, 21, 22, 23, 24, 26, 48 **Texas Practice** pages 11, 12, 13, 14, 15, 16, 17, 19, 20, 21, 22, 23, 24, 41 **Frog Pond Game, Get to 10 by Tens or Ones Game, Roll a Problem (Addition) Game,** **Roll a Problem (Subtraction) Game, Make 1,000 Game,** **Checkbook Game, Checkbook Game Mat, and Rummage Sale Game Mat** **eMathTools: Addition Table and Set Tool** **Building Blocks: Eggcellent**
Mastered/ Assessed	73, 74, 75, 76, 107, 108	56A, 73-74, 75-76, 107-108	**Texas Assessment** pages 76, 77, 78, 79, 114, 220 **TEKS/TAKS Practice** pages 19, 20

TEKS Correlations

Standard: (2.3.B) The student is expected to model addition and subtraction of two-digit numbers with objects, pictures, words, and numbers.

TAKS Objective 1: The student will demonstrate an understanding of numbers, operations, and quantitative reasoning.

In Grade 2, Chapter 5, *Real Math* uses modeling extensively to help students acquire strong number sense of two-digit addition. Students prepare for double-digit addition by learning to regroup two-digit numbers into tens and ones through the use of sticks (or the eMathTools: Base Ten Tool) and student Number Cubes. In a subsequent lesson, students model the actual process of two-digit addition through a demonstration involving the counting of many student fingers in front of the class. Through this process, students learn the value of grouping items according to place value. Subtraction is taught in a similar fashion, with multiple activities involving models.

	Student Edition	Teacher Edition	Other Components
Taught	19, 21, 25, 163, 165, 167, 169, 171, 175, 177, 179, 181, 183, 185, 187, 189, 204, 207, 209, 211, 213, 215, 217, 221, 223, 225, 227, 229, 379	19B, 21B, 25B, 163B, 165B, 167B, 169B, 171-172, 175B, 177B, 179B, 181B, 183B, 185B, 187B, 189-190, 203I-203-204, 207B, 209B, 211B, 213B, 215B, 217-218, 221B, 223B, 225B, 227B, 229-230, 379B	**Reteach** pages 6, 7, 8, 9
Practiced/ Reinforced	20, 22, 26, 128, 164, 166, 168, 170, 172, 173, 176, 178, 180, 182, 184, 186, 188, 190, 191, 192, 195, 196, 208, 210, 212, 214, 216, 218, 219, 220, 222, 224, 226, 228, 230, 231, 235, 236, 259, 260, 297, 318, 340, 350, 362, 380, 429, 464	19-20, 21-22, 25-26, 127-128, 163-164, 165-166, 167-168, 169-170, 172A, 173-174, 175-176, 177-178, 179-180, 181-182, 183-184, 185-186, 187-188, 190A, 191-192, 195-196, 204A, 205B, 207-208, 209-210, 211-212, 213-214, 215-216, 218A, 219-220, 221-222, 223-224, 225-226, 227-228, 230A, 231-232, 235-236, 245B, 247B, 249B, 251B, 253B, 255B, 259-260, 261B, 263B, 287B, 289B, 297-298, 299B, 301B, 303B, 305B, 307B, 311B, 317-318, 331B, 333B, 339-340, 341B, 349-350, 355B, 361-362, 379-380, 429-430, 463-464	**Enrichment** pages 8, 41, 42, 43, 44, 45, 46, 47, 49, 50, 51, 53, 54, 55, 56, 57, 58, 59, 60, 61 **Texas Practice** pages 41, 42, 43, 44, 45, 46, 47, 48, 49, 50, 51, 53, 54, 55, 56, 57, 58, 59, 60, 61, 86, 88 **Addition Table Game Mat, Harder Addition Table Game Mat, Get to 100 by Tens or Ones Game, Roll a Problem (Addition) Game, Roll a Problem (Subtraction) Game,** **Rummage Sale Game Mat, Harder Rummage Sale Game Mat, Checkbook Game Mat, Harder Checkbook Game Mat, Make 1,000 Game,** **Yard Sale Game Mat, and** **Harder Yard Sale Game Mat**
Mastered/ Assessed	197, 198, 200, 237, 238, 239, 240	174A, 197-198, 199-200, 220A, 237-238, 239-234,	**Texas Assessment** pages 81, 82, 84, 118, 119, 120, 121, 228, 229, 231, 232, 233, 234, 235 **TEKS/TAKS Practice** pages 21, 22, 23, 24

Standard: (2.3.C) The student is expected to select addition and subtraction to solve problems using two-digit numbers, whether or not regrouping is necessary.

TAKS Objective 1: The student will demonstrate an understanding of numbers, operations, and quantitative reasoning.

In *Real Math*, Grade 2, students gain familiarity with number sentences and learn to use them in problem-solving situations. In Chapter 5, students learn the algorithm for two-digit addition and have many opportunities to solve problems involving addition. Chapter 6 first introduces regrouping tens as ones in preparation for two-digit subtraction and then focuses on learning and practicing subtraction. In numerous Exploring Problem Solving lessons, students can choose to employ number sentences as part of their problem-solving strategy. For instance, in one Exploring Problem Solving lesson in Chapter 5, students may choose to write a number sentence to determine if there are enough juice boxes for every student at a picnic.

	Student Edition	Teacher Edition	Other Components
Taught	160, 179, 204, 207, 217, 223, 227	159-160, 179B, 203-204, 207B, 217-218, 223B, 227B	**Reteach** pages 6, 7, 8, 9
Practiced/ Reinforced	163, 164, 170, 171, 172, 176, 178, 180, 182, 184, 186, 206, 208, 210, 212, 214, 215, 218, 222, 224, 226, 228, 236	163-164, 169-170, 171-172, 175-176, 177-178, 179-180, 181-182, 183-184, 185-186, 205-206, 207-208, 209-210, 211-212, 213-214, 215-216, 218A, 221-222, 223-224, 225-226, 227-228, 235-236, 483A-483E	**Enrichment** pages 41, 42, 43, 45, 46, 47, 49, 53, 54, 55, 56, 57, 58, 59, 60, 61 **Texas Practice** pages 25, 26, 43, 44, 45, 46, 47, 49, 50, 51, 52, 53, 55, 56, 57, 58, 59, 61, 88 **Addition Table Game Mat, Harder Addition Table Game Mat, Addition Crossing Game Mat, Doubles Game, Frog Pond Game Mat, Harder Frog Pond Game Mat, Roll a 15 Game, Space Game Mat, Harder Space Game Mat, Get to 100 by Tens or Ones Game, Roll a Problem (Addition) Game, Roll a Problem (Subtraction) Game, Checkbook Game Mat, and Harder Checkbook Game Mat**
Mastered/ Assessed	198, 200	197-198, 199-200	**Texas Assessment** pages 84, 85, 118, 119, 120, 121, 229, 231, 233, 235 **TEKS/TAKS Practice** pages 25, 26, 27, 28

Standard: (2.3.D) The student is expected to determine the value of a collection of coins up to one dollar.

TAKS Objective 1: The student will demonstrate an understanding of numbers, operations, and quantitative reasoning.

Money is used on equal terms with important mathematical concepts such as composing numbers, factors, multiples, as well as place value and adding and subtracting. Students use these concepts in numeral form as well as handling monetary amounts. By using these measurement tools and techniques side by side, students will be able to determine separate values of a set of coins, and find combinations of various coins and bills. Dealing with monetary amounts is also a useful application for computation with decimals. Students can also refer to the eMathTools Coins and Money Tool to enhance learning.

	Student Edition	Teacher Edition	Other Components
Taught	12, 161, 168, 241, 263, 351	11B, 161B, 167B, 351B,	
Practiced/ Reinforced	29, 67, 71, 105, 170, 195, 242, 264, 352	11-12, 23-24, 25-26, 29-30, 67-68, 71-72, 105-106, 139-140, 163B, 161-162, 167-168, 169-170, 195-196, 241A-241E, 263B, 343B, 351-352	**Enrichment** pages 5, 69, 91 **Texas Practice** pages 5, 40 **Yard Sale Game, Rummage Sale Game, and Checkbook Game** **eMathTools: Coins and Money**
Mastered/ Assessed	195, 200	195-196, 199-200	**Texas Assessment** pages 94, 119, 231, 233, 247 **TEKS/TAKS Practice** pages 29, 30, 31, 32, 33, 34

TEKS Correlations

Standard: (2.3.E) The student is expected to describe how the cent symbol, dollar symbol, and the decimal point are used to name the value of a collection of coins.

TAKS Objective 1: The student will demonstrate an understanding of numbers, operations, and quantitative reasoning.

Grade 2 *Real Math* reviews the names and values of coins and bills in the Cumulative Reviews. In Grade 2, money is also used as a manner in which to understand place value. Students may also use the eMath Tools, especially the Coins and Money Tool, to gain knowledge over monetary values. By using this tool, students will be able to identify and name the value of various coins and will also be able to count various coin and dollar combinations.

	Student Edition	Teacher Edition	Other Components
Taught	12, 351	11B, 263B, 351B,	**Reteach** pages 16
Practiced/ Reinforced	29, 33, 67, 71, 105, 147, 148, 195, 263, 241, 242, 264, 350, 352, 366	11-12,29-30, 33-34, 67-68, 71-72, 105-106, 147-148, 195-196, 235-236, 241-242, 263-264, 349-350, 351-352, 365-366	**Enrichment** pages 5, 40, 69, 70, 79 **Texas Practice** pages 5, 40 **Yard Sale Game, Rummage Sale Game, and Checkbook Game** **eMathTools: Coins and Money**
Mastered/ Assessed	35, 37, 73, 107, 109, 370	35-36, 73-74, 75-76, 107-108, 109-110, 369-370	**Texas Assessment** pages 84, 86, 94, 110, 112, 115, 212, 214, 231, 233, 235, 247 **TEKS/TAKS Practice** pages 31, 32, 33, 34

(2.4) Knowledge and Skill
Number, operation, and quantitative reasoning. The student models multiplication and division.

Standard: (2.4.A) The student is expected to model, create, and describe multiplication situations in which equivalent sets of concrete objects are joined.

TAKS Objective 1: The student will demonstrate an understanding of numbers, operations, and quantitative reasoning.

Real Math, Grade 2 students demonstrate the joining and separating of sets with objects through the use of eMathTools or physical counters. In Chapter 11, the students are introduced to multiplication and division of whole numbers. The teacher has the choice of using either counters or the eMathTools: Array Tool, Multiplication Table, Sets Former and Function Machine to help the students gain an understanding of the inverse relationship of multiplication and division. The teacher writes a multiplication problem on the board, and uses a manipulative (virtual or real) to demonstrate. To demonstrate the inverse, the teacher would write the inverse division problem and demonstrate the results in a similar fashion. *Real Math* supplements this type of Whole Group instruction with eGame: Multiplication Table Game to solidify student understanding of mathematical operations.

	Student Edition	Teacher Edition	Other Components
Taught	415, 416, 417, 418, 419, 423, 425, 427, 437	415B, 417B, 419B, 423B, 425B, 427-428, 437-438	**Reteach** pages 19, 20
Practiced/ Reinforced	416, 418, 420, 421, 422, 424, 426, 428, 430, 434, 438, 440, 443, 444, 449, 450, 463	414A, 415-416, 417-418, 419-420, 421-422, 423-424, 425-426, 428A, 429-430, 433B, 433-434, 438A, 439-440, 443-444,449-450, 459B, 463-464, 467B,	**Enrichment** pages 105, 106, 107, 108, 109, 110 **Texas Practice** pages 105, 106, 107, 108, 109, 110, 111, 112 **eMathTools: Number Line,** **Array Tool, Multiplication Table, Sets Former, and** **Function Machine** **eGames: Multiplication Table Game** **Building Blocks: Clean the Plates, Comic Book Shop, and Arrays in Area**
Mastered/ Assessed	445, 446, 447, 448	430A, 445-446, 447-448	**Texas Assessment** pages 96, 97, 130, 131, 252, 253, 254, 255, 256 **TEKS/TAKS Practice** pages 35, 36

Standard: (2.4.B) The student is expected to model, create, and describe division situations in which a set of concrete objects in separated into equivalent sets.

TAKS Objective 1: The student will demonstrate an understanding of numbers, operations, and quantitative reasoning.

From the beginning of *Real Math*, Grade 2, students gain number sense through the use of manipulatives. In Chapter 1, students learn the concept of "even" by splitting a set of Dinosaur Counters into two equal sets (as an alternative, this concept can also be modeled through the use of the eMathTools:Sets Former). Later, in Chapter 11, students are introduced to the concept of division by splitting 30 counters equally among five students. In Chapter 11, the students are introduced to multiplication and division of whole numbers. The teacher has the choice of using either counters or the eMathTools: Array Tool, Multiplication Table, Sets Former and Function Machine to help the students gain an understanding of the inverse relationship of multiplication and division.

	Student Edition	Teacher Edition	Other Components
Taught	431, 433, 435, 437	431B, 433B, 435B, 437-438,	**Reteach** page 19, 20
Practiced/ Reinforced	432, 434, 436, 438, 440, 443, 444	7B, 431-432, 433-434, 435-436, 438A, 439-440, 443-444	**Enrichment** pages 111, 112, 113 **Texas Practice** pages 111, 112, 113 **eMathTools: Number Line, Array Tool, Multiplication Table, Sets Former, and Function Machine** **eGames: Multiplication Table Game** **Building Blocks: Clean the Plates, Comic Book Shop, and Arrays in Area**
Mastered/ Assessed	445, 446, 447, 448	430A, 445-446, 447-448	**Texas Assessment** pages 130, 131, 252, 254, 255 **TEKS/TAKS Practice** pages 37, 38

TEKS Correlations

(2.5) Knowledge and Skill Patterns, relationships, and algebraic thinking. The student uses patterns, in numbers and operations.

Standard: (2.5.A) The student is expected to find patterns in numbers such as in the 100s chart.

TAKS Objective 2: The student will demonstrate an understanding of patterns, relationships, and algebraic thinking.

Grade 1 of *Real Math* introduces and thoroughly reinforces skip counting by twos, threes, fives, and tens. This concept is reviewed in Grade 2 in two detailed lessons, 11.1 and 11.2, which focus on reintroducing skip counting and repeated addition using models and illustrations. A firm foundational understanding of skip counting and repeated addition allows students to transition more smoothly into learning multiplication in the following lessons. Teachers can also engage students in skip counting by utilizing the interactive technology component, eMathTools: Number Line. In Chapter 12, students explore patterns and use numbers in different ways.

	Student Edition	Teacher Edition	Other Components
Taught	23, 43, 47, 49, 51, 423, 453,	23B, 43B, 47B, 49B, 51B, 423B, 453B,	**Reteach** pages 21
Practiced/ Reinforced	24, 44, 48, 50, 52, 56, 72, 163, 164, 181, 182, 424, 454, 464, 477	23-24, 43-44, 47-48, 49-50, 51-52, 55-56, 71-72, 163B, 181B, 423-424, 453-454, 463-464, 477-478	**Enrichment** pages 11, 13, 14, 15 **Texas Practice** pages 114 **Get to 100 by Tens or Ones Game** **eMathTools: Number Line and Function Machine** **Building Blocks: Function Machine 1, 2, 3 and Marching Patterns 3**
Mastered/ Assessed	35, 36, 37, 38, 481,	18A, 35-36, 37-38, 481-482	**Texas Assessment** pages 110, 111, 212, 213, 214, 215, 258, 259 **TEKS/TAKS Practice** pages 39, 40, 41, 42

Standard: (2.5.B) The student is expected to use patterns in place value to compare and order whole numbers though 999.

TAKS Objective 2: The student will demonstrate an understanding of patterns, relationships, and algebraic thinking.

In Chapter 1 of Grade 2, students count on and count back with whole numbers up to 99. They work with simple number strips that have blanks, and move onto everyday applications such as counting how many students are in the classroom, how many teachers are in the school, and so forth. The concept is enhanced in Chapter 9, where students equate ordering numbers with the concept of equalities and relation signs. Plentiful resources are available for practice and reinforcement, including the daily Mental Math activities, and various games and Enrichment activities, as listed below.

	Student Edition	Teacher Edition	Other Components
Taught	11, 331, 335, 453,	11B, 331B, 333B, 335B, 453B,	**Reteach** pages 13, 14, 21, 22
Practiced/ Reinforced	12, 332, 333, 334, 350, 365, 366, 454, 477	11-12, 331-332, 333-334, 335-336, 349-350, 365-366, 453-454, 477-478	**Texas Enrichment** pages 5, 83, 84, 85, 114 **Texas Practice** pages 83, 85, 114, 116 **eGame: Make 1,000 Game and Numbers Game** **eMathTools: Number Line and Function Machine** **Building Blocks: Function Machine 1, 2, 3 and Marching Patterns 3**
Mastered/ Assessed	369, 481	83, 369-370, 481-482	**Texas Assessment** pages 127, 133, 244, 245, 246, 258 **TEKS/TAKS Practice** pages 43, 44, 45, 46

TEXAS

Standard: (2.5.C) The student is expected to use patterns and relationships to develop strategies to remember basic addition and subtraction facts. Determine patterns in related addition and subtraction number sentences (including fact families) such as $8 + 9 = 17$, $9 + 8 = 17$, $17 - 8 = 9$, and $17 - 9 = 8$.

TAKS Objective 2: The student will demonstrate an understanding of patterns, relationships, and algebraic thinking.

Grade 2 *Real Math* picks up on relationships among whole numbers where Grade 1 left off. In Chapter 1, students review counting and writing numbers, including working with placement on a number line. Students review equalities and inequalities as they compare numbers. In Chapter 5, student practice two-digit addition algorithms using multiples of 10s. Chapter 6 begins with content covering expanded form of two-digit numbers, and students learning to exchange tens for ones. The daily Mental Math exercises offer plentiful opportunities for students to practice and grow more familiar with relationships among base-ten whole numbers.

	Student Edition	Teacher Edition	Other Components
Taught	25, 43, 45, 47, 51, 57, 81, 83, 85, 91, 97,	25B, 43B, 45B, 47B, 51B, 57B, 81B, 83B, 85B, 91B, 97B,	**Reteach** pages 2, 3, 6
Practiced/ Reinforced	26, 30, 44, 46, 48, 52, 55, 58, 68, 71, 72, 82, 84, 86, 90, 92, 98, 128, 147, 148, 191, 192,	25-26, 29-30, 43-44, 45-46, 47-48, 51-52, 55-56, 57-58, 63-64, 67-68, 71-72, 81-82, 83-84, 85-86, 89-90, 91-92, 97-98, 127-128, 147-148, 191-192, 455B	**Enrichment** pages 10, 11, 12, 13, 15, 16, 20, 21, 23, 26 **Texas Practice** pages 8, 10, 11, 12, 13, 14, 15, 16, 19, 20, 21, 23, 24 **Tracing and Writing Numbers Game, Addition Table Game Mat, and Harder Addition Table Game Mat**
Mastered/ Assessed	73, 74, 75, 76, 107, 108, 109, 110, 197	73-74, 75-76, 107-108, 109-110, 197-198	**Texas Assessment** pages 76, 77, 78, 79, 102, 112, 113, 213, 214, 216, 217, 218, 219 **TEKS/TAKS Practice** pages 47, 48

(2.6) Knowledge and Skill
Patterns, relationships, and algebraic thinking. The student uses patterns to describe relationships and make predictions.

TEXAS

Standard: (2.6.A) The student is expected to generate a list of paired numbers based on a real-life situation such as number of tricycles related to number of wheels.

TAKS Objective 2: The student will demonstrate an understanding of patterns, relationships, and algebraic thinking.

In *Real Math* Grade 2, Chapters 1 and 12 present opportunities for students to think of paired numbers in real-life situations and explore patterns and use numbers in various ways. In addition to the practice offered within the standard numbered lessons, teachers can also engage students in eMathTool: Function Machine and Building Blocks: Function Machine 1, 2, and 3, and Word Problems with Tools 7 and 9. Instructors can also refer to the Practice or Enrichment books, if further reinforcement of the subject matter is necessary.

	Student Edition	Teacher Edition	Other Components
Taught	7, 457	7B, 457B	**Reteach** pages 21
Practiced/ Reinforced	8, 457, 477, 478	7-8, 457-458, 477-478	**Enrichment** pages 3, 116 **Texas Practice** pages 114, 115, 116 **eMathTool: Function Machine** **Building Blocks: Function Machine 1, 2, 3, Marching Patterns, and Word Problems with Tools 7 and 9**
Mastered/ Assessed	479, 480, 481, 482	479-480, 481-482	**Texas Assessment** pages 132, 256, 258, 259 **TEKS/TAKS Practice** pages 49, 50

TEKS Correlations

Standard: (2.6.B) The student is expected to identify patterns in a list of related number pairs based on real-life situation and extend the list.

TAKS Objective 2: The student will demonstrate an understanding of patterns, relationships, and algebraic thinking.

Chapter 12 of Grade 2 *Real Math* offers comprehensive lessons, where students identify and extend patterns using numbers. Appearing at the beginning, middle, and end of every Chapter, Exploring Problem Solving lessons present real-world problems that students can solve by analyzing how number pairs are used. Finally, students can explore patterns further with Building Blocks: Marching Patterns 3.

	Student Edition	Teacher Edition	Other Components
Taught	399, 431, 433	399-400, 431B, 433B	**Reteach** pages 21
Practiced/ Reinforced	400, 432, 434, 443, 444, 457, 458	400A, 431-432, 433-434, 443-444, 457-458	**Enrichment** pages 111, 112, 116 **eMathTool:** Function Machine **Building Blocks:** Function Machine 1, 2, and 3, Marching Patterns, and Word Problems with Tools 7 and 9
Mastered/ Assessed	479, 480, 481, 482	479-480, 481-482	**Texas Assessment** pages 132, 256, 258, 259 **TEKS/TAKS Practice** pages 49, 50

Standard: (2.6.C) The student is expected to identify, describe, and extend repeating and additive patterns to make predictions and solve problems.

TAKS Objective 2: The student will demonstrate an understanding of patterns, relationships, and algebraic thinking.

In *Real Math*, real-world problem solving appears primarily in integrated coverage of the Exploring Problem Solving lessons. In these lessons, students have plenty of opportunity to identify repeating and growing patterns in the environment, and they even use this knowledge to solve true-to-life problems. For example, in one lesson students apply what they have been learning about function rules and patterns to actual textile patterns. They create their own rugs, describe their design so others can make it, and figure out which designs go with which descriptions.

	Student Edition	Teacher Edition	Other Components
Taught	57, 415, 417, 455, 461, 471	57B, 415B, 417B, 455B, 461-462, 471-472	**Reteach** pages 21, 22
Practiced/ Reinforced	58, 416, 418, 440, 443, 456, 459, 460, 462, 464, 472, 477, 478	57-58, 415-416, 417-418, 439-440, 443-444, 455-456, 459-460, 462A, 463-464, 472A, 477-478	**Enrichment** pages 16, 105, 106, 115, 117 **Texas Practice** pages 111, 114, 115, 116 **eMathTool:** Function Machine **Building Blocks:** Function Machine 1, 2, and 3, Marching Patterns, and Word Problems with Tools 7 and 9
Mastered/ Assessed	447, 448, 479, 481, 482	447-448, 479-480, 481-482	**Texas Assessment** pages 130, 131, 132, 133, 252, 253, 254, 255 **TEKS/TAKS Practice** pages 55, 56, 57, 58

(2.7) Knowledge and Skill Geometry and spatial reasoning. The student uses attributes to identify two- and three-dimensional geometric figures. The student compares and contrasts two- and three-dimensional geometric figures or both.

Standard (2.7.A): The student is expected to describe attributes (the number of vertices, faces, edges, sides) of two- and three-dimensional geometric figures such as circles, polygons, spheres, cones, cylinders, prisms, and pyramids, etc.

TAKS Objective 3: The student will demonstrate an understanding of geometry and spatial reasoning.

In *Real Math* Grade 2, Chapter 8 presents a wealth of opportunities for students to sort, classify, and label objects by attributes. In addition to the practice offered within the standard numbered lessons, teachers can also engage students in classifying objects with eMathTools: Shape Tool or eMathTools: Venn Diagram. Instructors can also refer to the Practice or Enrichment books, if further reinforcement of the subject matter is necessary.

	Student Editio	Teacher Edition	Other Components
Taught	293, 294, 305, 306, 307	287B, 293B, 293-294, 307B, 310A	
Practiced/ Reinforced	61, 72, 128, 300, 308, 309, 310, 311, 312, 313, 314, 319, 320, 321, 322, 350	61B, 71-72, 115-116, 127-128, 266C, 299B, 303B, 303-304, 305B, 305-306, 307-308, 309-310, 311B, 311-312, 313-314, 314A, 319A, 319-320, 321A, 321-322, 337-338, 349-350, 379B	**Enrichment** pages 76, 80, 81, 82 **Texas Practice** pages 76, 77, 80, 81, 82 **eMathTools: Shape Tool, Geometry Sketch Tool, and Net Tool** **Building Blocks Shape Shop 1-3, Shape Parts 1-7, and Legend of the Lost Shape**
Mastered/ Assessed	76, 323, 324, 325, 326	75-76, 298A, 323-324, 325-326	**Texas Assessment** pages 91, 92, 124, 142, 186, 187, 189, 190, 240, 242, 243 **TEKS/TAKS Practice** pages 59, 60, 61, 62

Standard (2.7.B): The student is expected to use attributes to describe how 2 two-dimensional figures or 2 three-dimensional geometric figures are alike or different.

TAKS Objective 3: The student will demonstrate an understanding of geometry and spatial reasoning.

Throughout Chapter 8 of Grade 2, students will review and become familiarized with the names and some of the properties of common shapes such as triangles, circles, squares, trapezoids, and parallelograms. Students should be expected to identify, compare, and name these shapes, as well as distinguishing one shape from another, including a description of why one shape is sorted in a different category from another shape. In this Chapter, students will also be able to learn the formal definitions for four-sided plane figures (quadrilaterals) and be able to identify the unique characteristics of quadrilaterals.

	Student Edition	Teacher Edition	Other Components
Taught	132, 301, 302, 311, 312	131B, 293B, 301B, 311B, 314A	
Practiced/ Reinforced	131, 286, 288, 293, 294, 303, 304, 313, 314, 319, 320	131-132, 285I, 285-286, 286A, 287B, 293-294, 301-302, 303B, 303-304, 311-312, 313-314, 319-320, 321A	**Enrichment** pages 78, 79, 82 **Texas Practice** pages 76, 78, 79, 82
Mastered/ Assessed	323, 325, 326	298A, 323-324, 325-326	**Texas Assessment** pages 124, 142, 188, 189, 240, 242, 243 **TEKS/TAKS Practice** pages 63, 64

TEKS Correlations

Standard (2.7.C): The student is expected to cut two-dimensional geometric figures apart and identify the new geometric figures formed.

TAKS Objective 3: The student will demonstrate an understanding of geometry and spatial reasoning.

Students will be able to identify shapes in various ways by composing and decomposing other two-dimensional figures. Students will gain knowledge of various orientations by creating mental images of geometric shapes using spatial memory and spatial visualization. Mastering these skills will allow the student to recognize and represent shapes from different perspectives.

	Student Edition	Teacher Edition	Other Components
Taught	287, 288, 291, 292	287B, 287-288, 291B	
Practiced/ Reinforced	289, 290, 293, 294, 298, 321, 322, 429	289B, 289-290, 291-292, 293B, 293-294, 297-298, 321-322, 429-430	**Enrichment** page 73, 74, 75, 76 **Texas Practice** pages 73, 74, 75, 76 eMathTools Tessellations and Shape Tool
Mastered/ Assessed	325, 326	298A, 325-326	**Texas Assessment** pages 125, 142, 186, 187, 241, 242, 243 **TEKS/TAKS Practice** pages 65, 66

(2.8) Knowledge and Skill
Geometry and spatial reasoning. The student recognizes that a line can be used to represent a set of numbers and its properties.

Standard (2.8): The student is expected to use whole numbers to locate and name points on a number line.

TAKS Objective 3: The student will demonstrate an understanding of geometry and spatial reasoning.

In *Real Math*, Grade 2 students are exposed to number lines in a multitude of applications. In Chapter 1 they learn to use a number line to count on and count back. Students then use number lines to demonstrate inverse operations, fact families, and skip counting.

	Student Editio	Teacher Edition	Other Components
Taught	19, 21, 415	19B, 21B, 331B, 355B, 415B	
Practiced/ Reinforced	20, 25, 30, 33, 68, 127, 173, 332, 349, 375, 376, 401	19-20, 21-22, 25B, 29-30, 33-34, 67-68, 71A, 127-128, 141B, 173-174, 349-350, 375B, 375-376, 401-402	**Enrichment** pages 7, 95, 105 **Texas Practice** pages 7, 10, 83, 95, 105 eMathTools Number line **Building Blocks Rocket Blast 1-3 and Clean the Plates**
Mastered/ Assessed	38, 410	37-38, 409-410	**Texas Assessment** pages 129, 151, 250 **TEKS/TAKS Practice** pages 67, 68, 69, 70

(2.9) Knowledge and Skill Measurement. The student directly compares the attributes of length, area, weight/mass, and capacity, and uses comparative language to solve problems and answer questions. The student selects and uses nonstandard units to describe length, area, capacity, and weight/mass. The student recognizes and uses models that approximate standard units (from both SI, also known as metric, and customary systems) of length, weight/mass, capacity, and time.

Standard (2.9.A): The student is expected to identify concrete models that approximate standard units of length and use them to measure length.

TAKS Objective 4: The student will demonstrate an understanding of the concepts and uses of measurement.

Continuing the importance of measurement concepts, students will take the knowledge they have gained from exploring and learning measurement systems and calculations, and apply it to the actual hands-on work of measuring length. Students will learn and use standard and non-standard units. By exploring and using the necessary tools, students should master and be able to measure successfully.

	Student Editio	Teacher Edition	Other Components
Taught	9, 10, 115, 116	9B, 9-10, 115B, 115-116	
Practiced/ Reinforced	34, 102, 117, 118, 123, 124, 125, 126, 127, 147, 148, 149, 150, 151, 191, 349, 361, 411, 412	33-34, 101-102, 113I, 113-114, 114A, 114C, 117B, 117-118, 123B, 123-124, 125-126, 126A, 127-128, 147-148, 149A, 149-150, 151-152, 191-192, 349-350, 361-362, 411A, 411B, 411C, 411D, 411E, 411-412	**Enrichment** pages 27, 28 **Texas Practice** pages 27, 28, 29, 30, 31 **Building Blocks Workin' on the Railroad**
Mastered/ Assessed	153, 155, 156, 409	128A, 153-154, 155-156, 388A, 409-410	**Texas Assessment** pages 80, 117, 129, 138, 144, 162, 224, 225, 226, 227, 249 **TEKS/TAKS Practice** pages 71, 72

Standard (2.9.B): The student is expected to select a non-standard unit of measure such as square tiles to determine the area of a two-dimensional surface.

TAKS Objective 4: The student will demonstrate an understanding of the concepts and uses of measurement.

In Grade 2 of the *Real Math* series, students learn about area as a tool in determining multiplication facts. Students also informally study area through an Exploring Problem Solving lesson in the middle of Chapter 10.

	Student Edition	Teacher Edition	Other Components
Taught	421, 422	421B, 421-422	
Practiced/ Reinforced	385, 386, 441, 442, 444	385-386, 386A, 441-442, 443-444	**Enrichment** pages 108 **Texas Practice** pages 108 **Building Blocks Arrays in Area**
Mastered/ Assessed	447, 448	447-448	**Texas Assessment** pages 131, 203, 254, 255 **TEKS/TAKS Practice** pages 73, 74

Standard (2.9.C): The student is expected to select a non-standard unit of measure such as a bathroom cup or a jar to determine the capacity of a given container.

TAKS Objective 4: The student will demonstrate an understanding of the concepts and uses of measurement.

Measurement is an important strand in mathematics, and Grade 2 provides a heavy exploration and teaching of core measurement concepts. Students will learn and use units for capacity and are given many opportunities to apply their knowledge. Estimation is a key to measuring. In *Real Math*, students are guided and encouraged always to estimate first, and then to measure to check their estimate.

	Student Edition	Teacher Edition	Other Components
Taught	389, 391	389B, 391B	
Practiced/ Reinforced	390, 392, 403, 404, 405, 406	389-390, 391-392, 403-404, 405-406	**Enrichment** pages 100, 101 **Texas Practice** pages 100, 101
Mastered/ Assessed	407	388A, 407-408	**Texas Assessment** pages 58, 68, 128, 144, 199, 200, 248 **TEKS/TAKS Practice** pages 75, 76

Standard (2.9.D): The student is expected to select a non-standard unit of measure such as beans or marbles to determine the weight/mass of a given object.

TAKS Objective 4: The student will demonstrate an understanding of the concepts and uses of measurement.

Grade 2 provides a heavy exploration and teaching of core measurement concepts. Students will learn and use units for weight/mass and apply their knowledge. Chapter 10 includes numerous lessons on measurement and two specifically devoted to weight/mass.

	Student Edition	Teacher Edition	Other Components
Taught	382, 384	381B, 383B	
Practiced/ Reinforced	381, 383, 387, 403, 405	381-382, 383-384, 387-388, 403-404, 405-406	**Enrichment** pages 98, 99 **Texas Practice** pages 98, 99
Mastered/ Assessed	408	388A, 407-408	**Texas Assessment** pages 58, 68, 128, 144, 198, 199, 248 **TEKS/TAKS Practice** pages 77, 78

(2.10) Knowledge and Skill

Measurement. The student uses standard tools to estimate and measure time and temperature (in degrees Fahrenheit).

Standard (2.10.A): The student is expected to read a thermometer to gather data.

TAKS Objective 4: The student will demonstrate an understanding of the concepts and uses of measurement.

The Fahrenheit scale is introduced in *Real Math* in Grade 2. Students demonstrate how to read a Fahrenheit thermometer. Students learn benchmark temperatures.

	Student Editio	Teacher Edition	Other Components
Taught	375, 376	375B, 375-376	
Practiced/ Reinforced	139, 140, 404	139B, 139-140, 374C, 403A, 403-404	**Enrichment** pages 95 **Texas Practice** pages 95
Mastered/ Assessed	410	388A, 409-410	**Texas Assessment** pages 129, 144, 197, 250 **TEKS/TAKS Practice** pages 79, 80

Standard (2.10.B): The student is expected to read and write times shown on analog and digital clocks using five-minute increments.

TAKS Objective 4: The student will demonstrate an understanding of the concepts and uses of measurement.

Grade 2 focuses on different aspects of time and the application of time to other mathematical concepts such as angles, fractions, and measurement. But the most important skill is being able to read, tell and write the time to the nearest five-minute increment. Chapter 7 builds on students' work with models to introduce telling time, and relates an understanding of fractions using clock models. In Chapter 10, students will progress from writing time to the hour and half-hour to writing time to the nearest minute.

	Student Edition	Teacher Edition	Other Components
Taught	265, 266, 299, 395, 396	265B, 265-266, 395B, 395-396	
Practiced/ Reinforced	17, 267, 268, 274, 300, 318, 393, 394, 395, 396, 397, 398, 402, 404, 405, 464	17-18, 244C, 267B, 267-268, 273-274, 275A, 299B, 299-300, 317-318, 393B, 393-394, 397B, 397-398, 403-404, 405-406, 463-464	**Enrichment** pages 70, 71, 102, 103, 104 **Texas Practice** pages 70, 71, 77, 103, 104 **Time Game Mat** **Harder Time Game Mat**
Mastered/ Assessed	279, 280, 324, 368, 409, 410	279-280, 323-324, 367-368, 388A, 409-410	**Texas Assessment** pages 59, 69, 89, 90, 122, 125, 127, 129, 144, 184, 201, 236, 237, 241, 245, 250, 253 **TEKS/TAKS Practice** pages 81, 82

Standard (2.10.C): The student is expected to describe activities that take approximately one second, one minute, and one hour.

TAKS Objective 4: The student will demonstrate an understanding of the concepts and uses of measurement.

Measurement is an important strand in mathematics, and Grade 2 provides a heavy exploration and teaching of core measurement concepts. Estimation is a key to measuring. Students estimate times by describing activities that can be done in a specific amount of time.

	Student Edition	Teacher Edition	Other Components
Taught	398	393B,	
Practiced/ Reinforced	223, 397, 399, 402	395-396, 397B, 399-400, 401-402	eMathTools Stopwatch
Mastered/ Assessed	408, 409	407-408, 409-410	**Texas Assessment** pages 128, 129, 201, 248, 249 **TEKS/TAKS Practice** page 83, 84

(2.11) Knowledge and Skill

Probability and statistics. The student organizes data to make it useful for interpreting information.

Standard (2.11.A): The student is expected to construct picture graphs and bar-type graphs.

TAKS Objective 5: The student will demonstrate an understanding of probability and statistics.

Not only is gathering information important, but displaying it is equally important. In *Real Math* Grade 2, students use a variety of opportunities to display information. Students are given the opportunity to solve a problem with many solutions based on proportional reasoning, and can use the information to draw a reasonable conclusion.

	Student Editio	Teacher Edition	Other Components
Taught	135, 137	135B, 137B	
Practiced/ Reinforced	136, 138, 141, 142, 145, 146, 150, 297, 387, 439	135-136, 137-138, 141B, 141-142, 143-144, 145-146, 146A, 149-150, 297-298, 387-388, 439-440	**Enrichment** pages 35, 36, 38 **Texas Practice** pages 35, 36, 38 eMathTools Graphing Tool
Mastered/ Assessed	154	153-154	**Texas Assessment** pages 162, 163, 164, 166, 167, 226 **TEKS/TAKS Practice** pages 85, 86, 87, 88

TEXAS

Standard (2.11.B): The student is expected to draw conclusions and answer questions based on picture graphs and bar-type graphs.

TAKS Objective 5: The student will demonstrate an understanding of probability and statistics.

In Chapter 4, students are given an in-depth look at data analysis, probability, and how to represent information. Students will conduct probability experiments, where they will determine the results of the findings, as well as defining the best methods to represent their data. Students can use the **Across the Curriculum** projects located in each Chapter to provide a real-life application of the skills students learn.

	Student Edition	Teacher Edition	Other Components
Taught	139, 140	135B, 137B, 139B	
Practiced/ Reinforced	135, 136, 137, 138, 141, 142, 151, 174, 473	135-136, 137-138, 139-140, 141B, 141-142, 151-152, 173-174, 473-474	**Enrichment** pages 35, 36, 37, 38 **Texas Practice** pages 35, 36, 37, 38 **eMathTools Graphing Tool**
Mastered/ Assessed	154	153-154	**Texas Assessment** pages 65, 167, 226 **TEKS/TAKS Practice** pages 89, 90, 91, 92

TEXAS

Standard (2.11.C): The student is expected to use data to describe events as more likely or less likely such as drawing a certain color crayon from a bag of seven red crayons and three green crayons.

TAKS Objective 5: The student will demonstrate an understanding of probability and statistics.

In *Real Math*, students are given many probability experiments, the most common of which is predicting the outcome, whether there are two, three, or more outcomes. Students should be able to identify and recognize possibilities and patterns, and present their findings to their peers. They then should be able to communicate their mathematical thinking clearly and coherently.

	Student Edition	Teacher Edition	Other Components
Taught	129, 134, 144	129B, 133B, 143B,	**Reteach** pages 4
Practiced/ Reinforced	130, 133, 137, 143, 157, 158	129-130, 133-134, 137B, 137-138, 143-144, 157A, 157B, 157C, 157D, 157E, 157-158	**Enrichment** pages 32, 34, 39 **Texas Practice** pages 32, 34, 38, 39 **eMathTools Probability Tool**
Mastered/ Assessed	155	155-156	**Texas Assessment** pages 165, 168, 227 **TEKS/TAKS Practice** pages 93, 94, 95, 96

TEKS Correlations

(2.12) Knowledge and Skill

Underlying processes and mathematical tools. The student applies Grade 2 mathematics to solve problems connected to everyday experiences and activities in and outside of school.

Standard (2.12.A): The student is expected to identify the mathematics in everyday situations.

TAKS Objective 6: The student will demonstrate an understanding of the mathematical processes and tools used in problem solving.

One of the goals laid out in the *Real Math* curriculum is for students to see math as an enjoyable content area that is useful and helpful in understanding their environment. Therefore, *Real Math* has gone to great lengths to create lessons which focus on mathematics found in everyday situations. All of the Exploring Problem Solving lessons and Chapter Projects reflect the use of mathematics in everyday situations.

	Student Edition	Teacher Edition	Other Components
Taught	13, 114, 345, 359, 469, 470	13B, 113I, 345B, 359-360, 469B, 469-470	
Practiced/ Reinforced	2, 14, 39, 40, 229, 230, 231, 267, 268, 283, 284, 346, 360, 362, 371, 372, 377, 378, 414,	13-14, 39A, 39B, 39C, 39D, 39E, 39-40, 45B, 93-94, 113-114, 114A, 175-176, 213-214, 221B, 223B, 227B, 229-230, 230A, 231-232, 267B, 267-268, 283A, 283B, 283C, 283D, 283E, 283-284, 339-340, 343-344, 345-346, 351-352, 353-354, 355-356, 357-358, 360A, 361-362, 371A, 371B, 371C, 371D, 371E, 371-372, 377B, 377-378, 383B, 389-390, 395-396, 397B, 413I, 413-414, 414A, 424-425, 431-432, 433-434, 435B, 453-454	**Enrichment** pages 90, 120, 96 **Texas Practice** pages 90, 120 **Calendar Game, Map Game, and Yard Sale Game** **eGame Calendar Game and Map Game** **Building Blocks Word Problems with Tools**
Mastered/ Assessed	107, 108, 109, 110, 153, 154, 155, 156, 280, 368, 369, 370, 408, 409, 410, 479, 480, 481, 482	107-108, 109-110, 153-154, 155-156, 279-280, 367-368, 369-370, 407-408, 409-410, 479-480, 481-482	**Texas Assessment** pages 116, 117, 122, 123, 126, 127, 132, 194, 204, 210, 220, 221, 222, 223, 224, 225, 226, 227, 236, 237, 244, 245, 246, 247, 248, 249, 250, 251, 256, 257, 258, 259 **TEKS/TAKS Practice** pages 97, 98

Standard (2.12.B): The student is expected to solve problems with guidance that incorporates the processes of understanding the problem, making a plan, carrying out the plan, and evaluating the solution for reasonableness.

TAKS Objective 6: The student will demonstrate an understanding of the mathematical processes and tools used in problem solving.

Grade 2 of *Real Math* develops students' abilities in problem solving through numerous Exploring Problem Solving lessons found in each Chapter. Also, students invest time in learning how to solve problems by applying a problem solving strategy within the context of various lessons found in the curriculum.

	Student Edition	Teacher Edition	Other Components
Taught	95, 96, 227, 229	95B, 95-96, 227B, 229-230, 230A	
Practiced/ Reinforced	125, 126, 145, 146, 171, 172, 228, 230, 241, 242, 271, 272, 315, 316, 330, 359, 360, 437, 438, 449, 450, 463	47B, 51B, 59B, 125-126, 126A, 145-146, 146A, 171-172, 172A, 227-228, 241A, 241B, 241C, 241D, 241E, 241-242, 271-272, 272A, 315-316, 316A, 329I, 329-330, 330A, 359-360, 360A, 371A, 371B, 371C, 371D, 371E, 371-372, 413I, 413-414, 414A, 437-438, 438A, 449A, 449B, 449C, 449D, 449E, 449-450, 463-464	**Enrichment** pages 25, 61 **Texas Practice** pages 61 **Addition Crossing Game, Frog Pond Game, and Roll a 15 Game** **eGame Roll a 15**
Mastered/ Assessed	107, 108, 109, 110, 238, 240, 408, 409, 410	107-108, 109-110, 237-238, 239-240, 407-408, 409-410	**Texas Assessment** pages 84, 85, 86, 204, 220, 221, 222, 223 **TEKS/TAKS Practice** pages 99, 100

Standard (2.12.C): The student is expected to select or develop an appropriate problem-solving plan or strategy including drawing a picture, looking for a pattern, systematic guessing and checking, or acting it out in order to solve a problem.

TAKS Objective 6: The student will demonstrate an understanding of the mathematical processes and tools used in problem solving.

The Exploring Problem Solving lessons in each Chapter examine in depth various strategies used in solving problems. In all of the Problem Solving lessons found in the middle of each Chapter students study how different strategies can be applied and lead to the same solution as another strategy. Also, *Real Math* highly encourages teachers to have an intelligent dialogue with students to better understand what strategies students excel or lack knowledge in.

	Student Edition	Teacher Edition	Other Components
Taught	15, 16, 87, 88, 257, 258	15-16, 16A, 87-88, 88A, 257-258, 258A	
Practiced/ Reinforced	2, 27, 28, 65, 66, 99, 100, 171, 172, 189, 190, 204, 217, 218, 229, 230, 271, 272, 295, 296, 315, 316, 347, 348, 373, 374. 385, 386, 399, 400, 427, 428, 451, 452, 461, 462	1I, 1-2, 2A, 27-28, 28A, 65-66, 66A, 99-100, 100A, 171-172, 172A, 189-190, 190A, 203I, 203-204, 204A, 217-218, 218A, 229-230, 230A, 271-272, 272A, 295-296, 296A, 315-316, 316A, 347-348, 348A, 373I, 373-374, 374A, 385-386, 386A, 399-400, 400A, 427-428, 428A, 451I, 451-452, 452A, 461-462, 462A, 483A, 483B, 483C, 483D, 483E, 483-484	**Building Blocks Word Problems with Tools**
Mastered/ Assessed	408, 409, 410, 446, 447, 448	407-408, 409-410, 445-446, 447-448	**Texas Assessment** pages 84, 85, 86, 129, 204, 248, 249, 250, 251 **TEKS/TAKS Practice** pages 101, 102, 103, 104

Standard (2.12.D): The student is expected to use tools such as real objects, manipulatives, and technology to solve problems.

TAKS Objective 6: The student will demonstrate an understanding of the mathematical processes and tools used in problem solving.

The use of manipulatives, objects, and technology is consistent throughout Grade 2 of *Real Math*. Students use a variety of manipulatives to measure and expand their knowledge of number sense, measurement, and geometry. Also, the teacher can use the eMathTools to have students demonstrate content fluency.

	Student Edition	Teacher Edition	Other Components
Taught	63, 64, 125, 126, 185	63B, 63-64, 125-126, 126A, 185B, 185-186, 457B	
Practiced/ Reinforced	15, 16, 55, 127, 128, 131, 132, 159, 160, 174, 186, 187, 188, 191, 298, 349, 361, 379, 380, 430	15-16, 16A, 43B, 55-56, 57B, 71A, 127-128, 131B, 131-132, 159I, 159-160, 160A, 169B, 173-174, 187B, 187-188, 191-192, 297-298, 349-350, 361-362, 379B, 379-380, 429-430	**Enrichment** pages 19, 33, 50, 51 **Texas Practice** pages 7, 10, 19, 21, 27, 28, 30, 31, 40, 43, 50, 51, 75, 105, 109 **eMathTools: Graphing tool, Venn Diagram, 100 table, Sets Former, Base Ten, Coins and Money, Tessellations, Shape Tool, and Calendar**
Mastered/ Assessed	35, 36, 198, 199, 200, 326	35-36, 56A, 90A, 128A, 174A, 197-198, 199-200, 220A, 260A, 298A, 325-326, 388A	**Texas Assessment** pages 57, 62, 67, 80, 94, 110, 113, 119, 136, 137, 138, 139, 140, 141, 142, 144, 146, 150, 151, 162, 163, 169, 170, 171, 174, 175, 176, 183, 186, 187, 203, 212, 213, 225, 230, 243, 250, 251 **TEKS/TAKS Practice** pages 105, 106

TEKS Correlations

(2.13) Knowledge and Skill

Underlying processes and mathematical tools. The student communicates about Grade 2 mathematics using informal language.

TEXAS

Standard (2.13.A): The student is expected to explain and record observations using objects, words, pictures, numbers, and technology.

TAKS Objective 6: The student will demonstrate an understanding of the mathematical processes and tools used in problem solving.

Grade 2 offers extensive coverage on the communication of math concepts using words, objects, pictures, numbers or technology in a meaningful way. Students are asked to communicate using written and verbal prompts through Journal entries, Extended Response questions, Guided Discussions, Exploring Problem Solving lessons, and Thinking Stories.

	Student Edition	Teacher Edition	Other Components
Taught	5, 6, 53, 54, 377, 378	5B, 5-6, 53-54, 54A, 377B, 377-378	**Reteach** pages 1, 4, 5
Practiced/ Reinforced	9, 10, 19, 20, 33, 34, 67, 68, 77, 78, 80, 102, 115, 116, 125, 126, 129, 130, 133, 134, 139, 140, 143, 144, 173, 245, 246, 247, 248, 260, 273, 286, 298, 321, 322, 362, 388, 399, 400, 414, 439, 452, 467, 468, 474, 478	3B, 7B, 9B, 9-10, 11B, 13B, 19B, 19-20, 33-34, 45-46, 49-50, 51-52, 61-62, 63B, 67-68, 71-72, 77A, 77B, 77C, 77D, 77E, 77-78, 79I, 79-80, 80A, 83B, 91B, 101-102, 115B, 115-116, 119B, 119-120, 121B, 121-122, 123B, 123-124, 125-126, 126A, 129B, 129-130, 133B, 133-134, 139B, 139-140, 143B, 143-144, 167-168, 173-174, 179B, 183B, 205B, 209-210, 211-212, 215-216, 245B, 245-246, 247B, 247-248, 259-260, 273-274, 285I, 285-286, 286A, 297-298, 321-322, 361-362, 387-388, 399-400, 400A, 413I, 413-414, 414A, 439-440, 451I, 451-452, 452A, 459-460, 467B, 467-468, 473-474, 477-478	**Enrichment** pages 2, 4, 7, 27, 30, 31, 32, 34, 37, 39, 62, 119 **Texas Practice** pages 27, 30, 32, 34, 37, 39, 96, 119 **eMathTools: Graphing tool, Venn Diagram, 100 table, Sets Former, Base Ten, Coins and Money, Tessellations, Shape Tool, and Calendar**
Mastered/ Assessed	37, 38, 75, 76, 199, 200, 281, 282, 325, 326, 369, 370, 447, 448, 481, 482	37-38, 75-76, 90A, 199-200, 220A, 281-282, 298A, 325-326, 369-370, 447-448, 481-482	**Texas Assessment** pages 117, 122, 123, 132, 137, 140, 142, 164, 197, 209, 226, 227, 236, 237, 238, 239, 258, 259 **TEKS/TAKS Practice** pages 107, 108

TEXAS

Standard (2.13.B): The student is expected to relate informal language to mathematical language and symbols.

TAKS Objective 6: The student will demonstrate an understanding of the mathematical processes and tools used in problem solving.

Real Math has been designed so that students informally examine, discuss, and represent mathematical content. Then as students progress through the program they begin to learn and develop an awareness of the more formal language and symbols.

	Student Edition	Teacher Edition	Other Components
Taught	23	23B, 299B	
Practiced/ Reinforced	24, 30, 67, 260, 273, 299, 300, 349, 350, 401, 419, 420, 430, 451, 464, 471, 472	19B, 23-24, 29-30, 67-68, 259-260, 273-274, 299-300, 349-350, 401-402, 417-418, 419B, 419-420, 429-430, 451I, 451-452, 452A, 463-464, 467B, 469B, 471-472, 472A	**Enrichment** pages 9, 77, 107 **Texas Practice** pages 9, 77, 107
Mastered/ Assessed	36, 37, 74, 155, 237, 323, 369, 445, 447, 448	35-36, 37-38, 73-74, 155-156, 237-238, 323-324, 350A, 369-370, 430A, 445-446, 447-448	**Texas Assessment** pages 67, 69, 83, 88, 91, 110, 111, 131, 143, 145, 212, 213, 214, 253, 254, 255 **TEKS/TAKS Practice** pages 109, 110

Underlying processes and mathematical tools. The student uses logical reasoning.

Standard (2.14): The student is expected to justify his or her thinking using objects, words, pictures, numbers, and technology.

TAKS Objective 6: The student will demonstrate an understanding of the mathematical processes and tools used in problem solving.

Grade 2 offers extensive coverage on the justification of math concepts using words, objects, pictures, numbers and technology in a meaningful way. Students are asked to communicate using written and verbal prompts through Guided Discussions and Exploring Problem Solving lessons. Teachers also have the freedom of using many of the eMathTools as a way for students to explain answers.

	Student Edition	Teacher Edition	Other Components
Taught	42, 139, 144, 244, 330	41I, 41-42, 59B, 59-60, 117B, 117-118, 139B, 139-140, 143B, 243I, 329I, 329-330	
Practiced/ Reinforced	53, 54, 72, 80, 102, 105, 111, 112, 126, 134, 141, 142, 148, 171, 172, 189, 190, 232, 236, 260, 362, 374, 385, 386, 414, 428, 437, 438	3B, 3-4, 4A, 9-10, 11-12, 53-54, 54A, 71-72, 79I, 79-80, 80A, 83B, 91B, 95B, 97-98, 111A, 111B, 111C, 111D, 111E, 111-112, 121B, 125-126, 126A, 133B, 133-134, 135B, 135-136, 137-138, 141B, 141-142, 143-144, 161-162, 171-172, 172A, 175-176, 177-178, 187-188, 189-190, 190A, 201A, 201B, 201C, 201D, 201E, 201-202, 207-208, 209B, 215B, 221B, 223B, 243-244, 244A, 245B, 247B, 249B, 249-250, 265B, 265-266, 267B, 267-268, 301-302, 327A, 327B, 327C, 327D, 327E, 327-328, 330A, 373I, 373-374, 374A, 375B, 379-380, 381B, 385-386, 386A, 413I, 413-414, 414A, 427-428, 428A, 437-438, 438A	**Enrichment** pages 39 **Texas Practice** pages 38, 39 **eMathTools:** Graphing tool, Venn Diagram, 100 table, Sets Former, Base Ten, Coins and Money, Tessellations, Shape Tool, and Calendar
Mastered/ Assessed	76, 109, 110, 155, 156, 200, 240, 282, 370, 448	75-76, 109-110, 155-156, 199-200, 239-240, 281-282, 369-370, 447-448	**Texas Assessment** pages 113, 115, 117, 222, 223, 226, 227, 238, 239 **TEKS/TAKS Practice** pages 111, 112, 113, 114